THE
GARDENER'S GUIDE

THE
GARDENER'S GUIDE

CAXTON

© Macdonald & Co. (Publishers) Ltd 1988, 1989
© Orbis Publishing Ltd 1979, 1982, 1985

Some of the material in this book previously appeared in
Greenfingers

This edition specially produced for CEEPI Ltd/Dealerfield Ltd in 1989

ISBN 0 907 305 26 1

Printed and bound in Yugoslavia by Mladinska Knjiga.

CONTENTS

FLOWERING TREES AND SHRUBS *179*

PART 1

PLANNING A GARDEN

INTRODUCTION

The number of books and publications on gardening and horticulture are legion. They deal with crops and cultivation, annuals, biennials and herbaceous plants, shrubs, trees and lawns, as well as equipment, garden buildings and patios.

There is in fact so much material to read and assimilate that one can become not only bogged down but completely disheartened, and it is easy to see why so many gardens reflect this muddled thinking.

Although the individual subjects within the boundaries are covered in great detail there are very few books that really tell you how to either create a garden from scratch or how to sensibly modify an existing layout to suit very personal requirements.

The whole subject of design and 'designers' is a little taboo to most people; it smacks of fanciful ideas in glossy magazines. But really design is the basis of any layout, inside or outside the home, and can be summed up as the most practical solution to the problem in hand.

Although most people feel relatively happy when planning a kitchen or living-room, their ideas tend to dry up when they move outside. This is partly due to the fact that we tend to think of house and garden as two separate entities, one for living in, the other for everything else. If we think of the garden as an outside room, an extension of the home where each activity can fit into an overall pattern, things would not only work better but they would be more attractive and easier to maintain.

It is fair to say that as homes and gardens increase in number the latter, on average, become smaller. Subsequent demand on use of that space is therefore greater and the need to design it properly even more important. The most difficult thing is knowing where to begin.

We have already seen that danger lies in overcomplication; the golden rule is not to rush out and start right away. Whatever the problems, give them time to get into perspective and as an initial exercise try jotting your ideas down on paper, not as a plan at this stage but rather in the form of check-lists that indicate both what you want and what you have got.

As a general guide, you might include a terrace or patio, lawn, vegetables, shed, greenhouse, fruit, planting, room for swing and slide, room for ball games, a path for easy access and wheeled toys, sandpit, trees, pool, rockery, room for washing-line or rotary drier, dustbin store, solid fuel bunkers or oil tank, incinerator, compost and even hutches for pets. When your ideas dry up you'll probably find you have catered for most eventualities.

Once you know what you want, the next job is to try and incorporate all these ideas into some sort of logical order; but before you start on the design, you need to know something else – what you have in terms of existing features.

Many people, moving into a new house with a virgin plot of ground, would think they have very little, but in every case it will be worth making a scale-drawing of the garden and marking in everything that might affect the future layout. It is worth doing this on a piece of squared or graph paper, using a simple scale of a small square to each foot. Mark in the house and garage in relation to the boundaries, the position of doors and windows, the length of the boundaries themselves, any changes in level, existing shrubs, trees and other features, good views or bad, prevailing winds and, most important of all, the north point, or where the sun is in relation to the house.

Once all this information is to hand you can see not only what you want to put into the garden, you also see that the components themselves fall into two broad categories: the plants, lawn, hedges and trees, which can loosely be termed 'soft landscape', and the paths, paving, fences, walling, steps and other items that form the 'hard landscape'.

As with all living things, the bones or framework come first. These are the basis of the composition and in gardening terms, the designer must start with the hard landscape 'skeleton' and follow on with the softer filling-in of plant material.

It is fair to say that no two gardens are alike, for even if they might be of similar proportions they would have different aspects and be subject to different climatic conditions. Most important of all, they would belong to different people. Neither should a garden be 'copied' from this or any other book. By all means get ideas and see how materials can be used in unusual and interesting ways, but adapt these to your personal requirements and by so doing create something original and unique.

In this section we've taken as a basis the principle of hard and soft landscape. First we consider specific gardens and the materials from which they are built. Our patio garden relies heavily on hard surfacing and we look at its construction step by step. From here we move on to other surfaces, some unusual and some common, but all used sensibly so that both the material and the situation in which it is used is shown off to its best advantage.

Front gardens can be a headache; after all, first impressions count, but we do offer practical guidance. Town gardens, courtyard gardens, odd plots and problem plots, a garden for the disabled, and even roof gardens are covered in detail. And individual components such as gates, walls, fences, paths and screens are described, as is that most difficult but rewarding problem, the sloping site.

Here there is ample room for design. Have you considered, for instance, using railway sleepers or logs bedded into a bank for steps? We have, together with a great deal of other stimulating ideas.

From individual gardens we turn our attention to plants and planting – the soft landscape.

The planning of borders and island beds, together with the correct use of specific plant material is explained so that it can be used in a controlled rather than a haphazard manner, while the basic soil types are outlined, together with the species that thrive upon them. Just as there are rules governing the design and construction of a garden, so too are there guidelines to planting. Not only should plants provide colour and interest throughout the

year but they must also act as screens to block bad views, give shelter from prevailing winds and form divisions within the garden itself. The mechanics of planting design are explained so that you can build up a framework of background plants that give stability to the composition and allow a second stage of filling-in with lighter, more colourful material.

Throughout this section, both in the chapter dealing with design and construction and those on planting, you can see that certain basic rules are underlined again and again. This does not mean that all gardens are similar. As we shall see, they are far from that, but it does mean that a successful garden is based on a well-tried formula that takes every relevant factor into account and moulds them to fit a particular requirement.

It is sensible to use an architectural theme close to the building, so that a brick terrace matches the materials used in the house. Exterior woodwork such as a pergola or overhead beams are painted to link with the colour of existing doors and windows. The layout of a terrace should match the house too and rectangles here, used in interesting interlocking patterns, will be far more successful than at a point farther down the garden. In fact the farther away from the house we get, the softer and looser the composition should become, thus providing a feeling of space and movement that diverts attention from rectangular boundaries and makes the garden appear larger than it really is.

Planting too can reflect this theme and strongly formed shapes such as yuccas, acanthus, euphorbias and phormium will reinforce a crisp architectural setting while softer, looser species create a feeling of depth and tranquility. Certain plants, such as conifers on a small scale and Lombardy poplars in the larger landscape, may act as punctuation marks and should be used carefully to highlight a carefully chosen position. Colour too, both in planting and individual features such as pots or seats, is important. A barrel full of brilliant flowers is fine close to the house but when placed at the bottom of the garden will draw the eye and foreshorten the space.

Not only should colour schemes be intelligently deployed but you also have to remember that flowering times vary. Soil types and the availability of sun and shade will determine what species can be grown.

This section is not a guide to a single subject or situation, but an introduction to the whole art of using the garden as an extension of the home. A garden can offer as much hard work and maintenance as you are prepared to put into it. It can be a full-time concern for the keen gardener or a place for recreation that all the family can use, with minimum upkeep. It can be a dining-room and playground, allotment and flower garden.

Most importantly the garden should serve you and not the reverse. This book helps you to do just that: once the rules are understood and the problem assessed, a most exciting project can be embarked upon.

DESIGN AND CONSTRUCTION

THE PATIO GARDEN

How would you like to transform an old back yard into a decorative patio garden? This scheme has been devised for those of you who feel the urge to 'do it yourself'. By following our instructions you will soon be able to enjoy your own handiwork.

Moving into a new home, especially in towns or cities, many people find themselves in possession of only a tiny garden, hardly big enough to encompass a patch of lawn or a flower bed, let alone a greenhouse, vegetable garden, or swimming pool. Such a garden is often called a patio. The word comes from Spain, where it means an inner courtyard, open to the sky, and conjures up visions of pools, fountains, and cool green ferns giving relief from the heat of the day.

In reality you are more likely to have inherited a grey concrete desert without even a flower tub in sight.

As awareness of the importance of outdoor living has increased, so has the potential of 'back yards', and the art of patio gardening has developed these concrete deserts into an extension of the home. We believe that no plot is too small, dark or dingy to be declared a hopeless case. With careful planning the most unpromising site can be turned into anything from a miniature jungle to a spacious outdoor room for all the family.

Our first patio design introduces you to some of the basic principles of successful patio gardening. We have taken an area measuring some 7 metres (23 feet) square and built a patio on two levels which not only adds visual interest but also provides built-in seating, and allows plenty of room for sunbathing and outdoor eating as well. We have introduced an interesting combination of textures and a wide variety of plants. The flooring, a mixture of bricks, wooden deck planks and paving stones, is hard-wearing and easy to clean, while most of the plants are conveniently planned for decorative containers.

The idea behind using containers is that they need not be permanently positioned, but can be moved around according to the season and which plants are looking their best. You can have shrubs, annuals alternating with seasonal bulbs, and anything else that happens to take your fancy.

We have added height to the whole design by means of a pergola. Covered with a quick-growing creeper, it provides privacy with its rooftop greenery, and underneath it there is a mini-woodland of shade-loving plants. The pergola itself is strong enough to support a child's swing. A weatherproof blackboard fixed to the wall also helps to keep the children entertained, while a chequerboard painted onto the paving will keep games-lovers amused.

Creating a feeling of light and spaciousness makes the patio seem much larger than its actual size. Clever use of mirrors, combined with a light-coloured paint on two or more walls, and 'false perspective' trellis work all help to achieve this effect.

As with any major undertaking, to create this patio requires careful initial planning and some hard work, but thereafter it is easy to care for and provides a welcoming environment for all members of the family. It is also a very flexible design, easy to adapt to suit your own particular needs.

To give you an idea of the correct sequence of work involved we have broken down the schedule into seven stages, but within this order you will, of course, undertake the work in your own time and at your own pace. It is not a rushed job to get behind you in a few weekends but a professionally-designed patio of which you and your family will be proud for years to come.

PATIO GROUND PLAN

1 brick-paving	6 blackboard
2 timber-decking	7 planted area
3 pergola	8 two steps down
4 mirrors	9 French windows
5 raised stone-paving	10 trellised wall

7 metres (23 feet) square

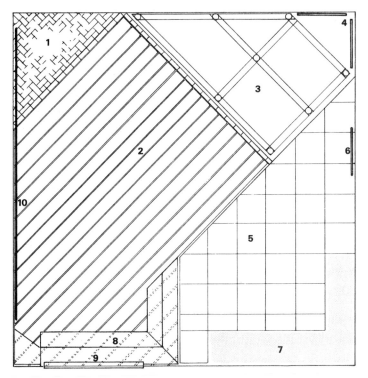

SCHEDULE OF WORK

Stage 1 SITE clearing of; topsoil to pergola area; repointing/repainting ext. walls; establishing datum level with pegs. MAIN RETAINING WALL marking out, excavating and laying foundations.

Stage 2 MAIN RETAINING WALL mixing mortar; bricklaying; building and pointing; drainage weep-holes.

Stage 3 SITE further levelling; TIMBER-DECKED AREA concrete raft: erecting timber shuttering; drainage holes, laying concrete; building retaining wall for decking.

Stage 4 SITE final levelling; backfilling planted area.
BRICK-PAVED AREA levelling site.
PERGOLA AREA sinking upright sockets; site preparation.
STONE-PAVED AREA site preparation; laying and cutting stones; pointing.

Stage 5 BRICK-PAVED AREA laying bricks. TIMBER-DECKED AREA measuring; damp proof course; building sleeper wall.

Stage 6 TIMBER-DECKED AREA laying DPC, joists and decking; timber steps.
PERGOLA AREA erecting timbers.

Stage 7 Make PERSPECTIVE TRELLIS.
Fix MIRRORS, BLACKBOARD
Paint CHEQUERBOARD.

Planning

Although the constructional details we will be giving apply to this specific patio, the techniques involved can easily be adapted to suit different circumstances and a whole range of sites.

Our Patio Garden is designed around a natural slope in the ground, and the differing levels are arranged so as to minimize excavation work and avoid having to carry the excavated soil through the house. One important point to bear in mind early in the planning stage is the level of the house damp proof course (DPC). It is vital that any paved or planted areas are kept at least 15cm (6 in) below the DPC level.

Costing

Before starting, work out the quantities of materials you need so that you can estimate the total cost.

At this stage it is also as well to make a list of the various tools you will need to carry out all of the construction work so that everything is to hand and you aren't held up for a vital piece of equipment. A complete set of tools is essential if the work is to flow smoothly; you can rent some of the specialist ones from your local tool hire firm.

Main materials

(approximate quantities)
4 cu m (5 cu yd) of 20mm (¾ in) all-in ballast, *for all foundation concrete and base for paving stones.*
1·5 cu m (2 cu yd) building sand, *for brickwork and brick-paved area base.*
twenty-four 50kg (1 cwt) bags cement, *for concrete mortar mix.*
37 paving stones, 600mm sq (2 ft sq).
1400 bricks, *for general brick-work and brick-paved area.*
5 circular slabs *for pergola area.*
100m (110 yd) planed timber (preferably in 3m (10 ft) lengths, 250 × 25mm (10 × 1 in), *for decking and steps.*
55m (60 yd) sawn timber, 75 × 50mm (3 × 2 in), *for joists.*
8 lengths salt-glazed pipe, 600mm × 100mm dia (2 ft × 4 in dia), *for pergola sockets.*

Additional items

plasticizer *for mortar mix.*
hard core.
50mm (2 in) × No. 10 brass counter-sunk wood screws, *for decking and steps.*
150mm (6 in) nails, *for pergola.*
8 rustic poles, 2·8m × approx. 100mm dia (9 ft × 4 in dia), *for pergola uprights.*

6 pergola horizontal members, approx. 100mm (4 in dia), as: one 1·8m (6 ft); two 2·6 m (8 ft 6 in); one 2·8m (9 ft); one 3·4m (11 ft); one 4m (13 ft) one 2100 × 900mm (7 × 3 ft) sheet of 12mm (½ in) marine plywood, *for perspective trellis.*
8 sq m (9½ sq yd) trellis.
paint and/or wood preservative, *for trellis work.*
2 mirrors, 1m sq (3 ft sq)
blackboard, 1m sq (3 ft sq)
wall fixing screws, wall plugs and washers, *for mirrors and blackboard.*

General tools

spade; fork; shovel; pick-axe; heavy rake; wheelbarrow; thumper; club hammer; brick chisel; spirit level; two saw-horses; timber staight-edge; twenty 50mm (2 in) square timber pegs; shuttering timber (scaffold boards).

For bricklaying

trowel; brick line and pegs; pointing tool; plywood (or chipboard) spot board 600mm sq (24 in sq); soft brush.

For woodworking

saw; hammer; chisel; screw-driver; plane; drill and jig saw.

Material quantities

Calculating quantities and ordering of most materials, such as timber, paving stones and slabs and similar items, is quite straightforward, the measurements being taken direct from a scale drawing. Estimating quantities of ballast, sand, cement and bricks, however, can prove a little difficult for anyone unfamiliar with the measures and methods of calculation used in the trade. Estimates, in any case, are only approximate, and it is best to err on the generous side in order to avoid running out.

Ballast and sand are normally supplied by the cubic metre or yard so here you must estimate the total volume required for the different jobs involved. Take your measurements direct from the scale drawing.

Cement is supplied in 50kg (1 cwt) bags and you need approximately six bags per cubic metre of ballast for a foundation concrete mix, and about 12 bags per cubic metre of sand for mortar mixes.

Bricks are normally supplied in multiples of 100, with approximately 120 required per square metre of double skin brickwork, and 60 for single skin work.

Ordering and delivery of materials must tie in with the progress of the work.

BACKDROP TO THE PATIO

If the patio is very much an extension of the home, then the house can also be viewed as an extension of the patio. So it is worth making the house wall look as attractive as possible. Slapping on a cover-up coat of paint is not the answer, however, and this is where our do-it-yourself project starts: giving you the necessary detailed information to make a really good job of your exterior walls. Here and on page 20 we tell you how to complete Stage 1 of the work.

Before you start painting an exterior wall, make sure that it is clean and in good condition, or the new paint will flake off. It makes sense, in any case, to keep your house wall in good repair and weatherproof, because small cracks rapidly become large holes and damp will then find its way indoors with disastrous results.

The following list outlines items that should be attended to before you paint.

View of the patio house wall, showing the planted area in the raised paving

Efflorescence

This shows as powdery white patches on brickwork or plastered walls. It forms when water-soluble salts in the bricks permeate through to the surface and crystallize, and mostly occurs in new buildings that are still drying out. It may also be a sign of dampness, so check for possible causes before treating your wall.

Efflorescence should be removed before painting the wall. You can brush the patches with a stiff (not wire) brush, but for a more effective treatment paint on a fluid such as Efforless, that penetrates the bricks and neutralizes the salts.

Lime-leaching

Lime which has leached into the bricks from the mortar can look very similar to efflorescence. Remove these white stains with a proprietary solution such as Gostan.

Fungus and lichens

Green stains on the brickwork may be a sign of dampness and you should investigate the cause before treating the symptoms. Then clean the wall with a stiff-bristled brush, and apply a proprietary fungicide. If possible, treat the entire wall, as fungus spores could easily be concealed all over it.

Repointing

'Pointing' refers to the mortar between the bricks. If it is crumbling you must replace it or rain will penetrate the brickwork. Chip away the damaged mortar thoroughly, brush the wall to remove dust and loose particles and then apply the new mortar. On the next page you will find full details of how to go about this important job.

If only a small area is to be repaired, you may find it more convenient to buy a bag of ready-mixed mortar.

Broken or chipped bricks

Bricks may be damaged by external causes or may crumble from within. This can happen when water that has been absorbed by the porous brickwork freezes and then expands, causing the bricks to crack.

Remove the broken bricks and insert the replacements with fresh mortar. If

possible, match the new bricks to the existing brickwork. You can sometimes obtain old, weathered bricks from builders' merchants.

You can waterproof brick walls by treating them with a water-repellent to prevent the bricks freezing and cracking.

Damaged rendering

Rendered walls are coated with cement plaster. 'Roughcast' is a rendering in which small stones are mixed into the mortar. Rendering which has cracked or crumbled away to expose the brickwork can allow dampness to set in. Cover hairline cracks with a special masonry paint; open out larger cracks with a hammer and chisel so that you can spread new mortar in under the old rendering, and chip away crumbling edges of larger damaged patches. Bricks made visible by the damage may prove to have broken pointing, in which case you must repoint before repairing the rendering.

If the brickwork is very smooth, brush on a PVA bonding agent before applying new rendering. Mix your mortar as 1 part (by volume) cement, 3 parts sharp sand and 3 parts soft sand, 1 part hydrated lime or proprietary plasticizer. Apply this to the wall with a steel float in a layer about 13mm ($\frac{1}{2}$ in) thick. If the surface

lies below that of the surrounding rendering, score the new mortar deeply with a nail to provide a 'grip' for a second layer, and leave to dry for 24 hours. Once the second layer has been applied, the new patch should be slightly thicker than the old rendering. To achieve a smooth, flush finish draw a flat piece of wood across the patch to scrape off excess mortar.

Patching pebble-dash

This is a finish achieved by embedding small stones in rendering when it is still wet. To repair a 'bald' patch, renew the rendering and then throw pebbles against the fresh mortar with a small trowel. Place a piece of sacking under the working area to catch the pebbles that fall. Press the pebbles firmly into place with a length of flat board or a wooden float. If you are able to mix in some old pebbles that have fallen off the wall, they will help to disguise the repair.

Settlement and shrinkage cracks

Long, wide cracks in the walls are usually caused by movement of the ground beneath the house. You should obtain an expert opinion as to the extent of the problem before attempting any repairs. Only after that should you replace and

repair any damaged bricks and pointing, before embarking on other constructional work. Most new buildings are liable to some shrinkage, and zig-zag cracks may appear in a year or so, when they should be repaired.

Safety precautions

If using a lean-to ladder, tie the base firmly to a long peg hammered into the ground. If the ladder is resting on concrete, place something really heavy in front of the legs to prevent it slipping. The upper end must also be made secure by tying firmly to a good anchor point. If there is no safe point of attachment, then a screw-eye should be fixed to the wall, and the ladder attached to that. The eye can be left in position for future occasions. Be careful not to lean the ladder against a window or plastic guttering.

If much work is to be done above standing height, then a platform composed of a plank laid between a step-ladder and a hop-up is the safest and most time-saving way to work. For very tall jobs, two step-ladders with a plank between them may be needed.

Protect your eyes from flying chips of mortar by wearing goggles, and be sure that both your eyes and your skin are well protected when applying fungicides.

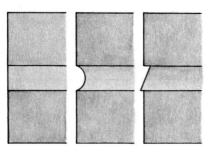

1 *Choose the type of pointing to give the best effect to your brickwork. Left: for flush pointing, surfaces of the joints are level with the bricks. Centre: for keyed pointing, surfaces of the joints are pressed in to give a slightly concave finish. Right: for weathered pointing, sloped surface allows rainwater to run off*

2 *Rake out damaged mortar with chisel and hammer. Brush away loose mortar and dust. Dampen bricks*

3 *Fill vertical joints with mortar, then press it well in with trowel. Catch excess mortar on your hawk (board)*

4 *For keyed pointing, run curved side of bent pipe along joint for indented finish. Trim off excess mortar. Smooth with piece of wood to make watertight*

5 *Weathered pointing: for vertical joint press in 3mm ($\frac{1}{8}$ in) at left side of joint, slope mortar up to right, finishing flush with right-hand brick. For horizontal joint press mortar in 3mm ($\frac{1}{8}$ in) at top edge and slope out till flush with lower brick. Hold straight-edge parallel to joint and trim mortar neatly with a frenchman*

6 *Flush pointing: when the mortar is nearly dry, rub joints with a piece of clean sacking until almost smooth*

7 *Flush pointing: when mortar is completely dry, scrape over surface of joints with piece of wood until smooth*

8 *After repointing is completed, brush over all joints with soft hand brush when mortar has hardened, to give a clean-looking surface*

REPOINTING

If your exterior walls have gaps between the bricks where mortar used to be, then it is time you repointed them. Dampness and worse, such as bugs, soon find their way into damaged brickwork.

General points

Start each stage of the job at the top of the wall and work downwards.

Chip away all damaged pointing to a depth of about 13mm ($\frac{1}{2}$ in) and brush the wall free of dust and chippings.

If repointing a large area, complete about 1 sq m (1 sq yd) at a time.

Do the vertical joints first and then the horizontal ones.

Be sure to match the new pointing to the style of the original joints.

The life of mortar is only about two hours, so mix in small quantities.

Always dampen any surface to which mortar is to be applied.

To avoid splashes of mortar, cover as much of the ground and wall as possible with polythene sheeting propped against the wall with wooden battens. When dry, scrape off any mortar splashes on bricks with a clean trowel.

Making the mortar

The mortar used consists of 1 part cement, 6 parts soft sand and 1 part hydrated lime or plasticizer. For mending small patches, use cup measure rather than buckets. The lime or plasticizer helps to make the mortar more workable and minimizes shrinking or cracking.

Mix the dry ingredients thoroughly on a piece of board. Add water, a very little at a time, turning the mix constantly.

Tools for repointing

You will need a pointed cold chisel and a club hammer; a pointing trowel and a hawk; a stiff-bristled brush for pre-cleaning and a soft brush for finishing; and a frenchman and a straight-edge for trimming off surplus mortar.

The straight-edge is a piece of wood with a square of wood or hardboard attached to each end to hold it slightly away from the wall and allow excess mortar to fall cleanly. You can make up a frenchman from an old table knife by bending about 2·5cm (1 in) of the tip of the blade at right-angles to the main blade.

To give flush pointing a good finish, you will need an old piece of sacking and a small, flat piece of wood. For keyed pointing you will also need a curved piece of metal such as a bent strip of narrow piping (see far left).

PAINTING

Painting, or repainting, outside walls is often thought of as a job for experts. But by making careful preparations, choosing the right tools and buying paint suitable for exterior work, the job can be straightforward and the results rewarding.

General points

Paint will not stay on loose, dusty or dirty surfaces, so you must first give the wall a thorough brushing to ensure a solid, clean surface.

Where the surface is generally crumbly you should apply a purpose-made primer/sealer as an undercoat.

If lichen, moss or other plant growth is present then the area must be treated with a suitable fungicide before painting. So paint when the air (and the wall) is warm and dry, and, ideally, when rain is not expected for a few days.

Always start painting at the top of the wall and work downwards.

When working from a ladder, have the paint in a paint-kettle, which can then be hung safely from the ladder by an S-hook. Never put a paint pot or a roller tray on a gutter or windowsill. Secure the top of the ladder to the wall with a strong hook and tie.

Protect the ground and all projecting surfaces with polythene sheeting.

Tools for painting

It pays to buy good quality brushes as they last longer, hold more paint and shed fewer bristles. New brushes always shed some bristles, so break them in on undercoats. You will need a fairly large brush: a good size is 100mm (4 in). Also useful are a cutting-in brush (for straight-edge work) and a crevice brush with a flexible metal handle (for painting behind pipes). Where a rendered or reasonably flat wall surface is to be painted then you can use a roller; a sheepskin one is best.

Cleaning painting tools

First lay the brushes on several layers of newspaper, and with the back of a knife scrape off as much paint as possible from all four sides.

Oil-based paints should be cleaned off with white spirit and brushes washed in warm, soapy water and rinsed. For storing overnight, suspend brushes in water and then dry with paper or rags before using again.

Emulsion paint should be washed off in cold water before it hardens.

Rollers and roller trays should be cleaned with white spirit or warm soapy water, according to paint type.

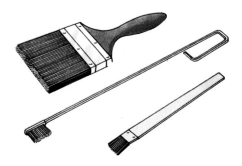
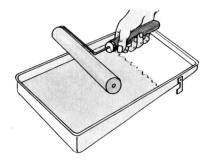

1 *Paint rollers should be well soaked in paint but not dripping with it*
2 *Hang your paint-kettle from an S-hook*
3 *General-purpose 100mm (4 in) brush, cutting-in, and crevice, brushes*
4 *Scrape paint off before washing brush*

5 *Anchor ladder safely at base, using a reef knot on rope ties*
6 *Pad ladder tops with rags to stop them marking new paintwork, and tie to a hook below the guttering if possible*
7 *To store oil-based paint brushes overnight, push a nail or stick through a hole drilled in the brush handle and suspend in a jar of water. Brush must not touch bottom of jar*
8 *A simple platform for working just above head-height is made by laying a plank between step-ladder and hop-up*

LAYING PATIO FOUNDATIONS: MIXING MORTAR AND BRICKLAYING

After getting the house brickwork and boundary walls in good shape it is time to start preparing the foundations for the raised, paved area.

Although the instructions apply specifically to our patio design, you can easily adapt them to suit your own circumstances. In this Patio Garden we will repeat the essential diagrams so that you can work at your own pace from the seven stages as set out in our Schedule of Work on page 15 without having to turn back for reference.

If you don't feel able to tackle all the work involved yourself, ask a more experienced friend to come and help you with the job.

Farther on we continue with Stages 3 and 4 of the Schedule of Work—preparing for the timber decking and laying the paving stones.

When carrying out work of this type it is essential to undertake the various jobs involved in an organized way so as to avoid unnecessary shifting of materials and to allow the work to proceed smoothly.

SCHEDULE OF WORK Stage 1

After you have completed any necessary repointing of the brickwork and painting of the exterior walls, you must clear the site of all unwanted vegetation and roughly level it. Remove the topsoil from the areas to be excavated and deposit it in the pergola area, for re-use in the plantings there. This not only saves having to import topsoil at a later date and carry it through the house, but also uses up the unwanted soil from the other areas.

Before any excavation work is started you must establish a 'datum' to which all other levels can be quickly related. Normally for this type of work the datum should be located at the highest level and in the case of our Patio Garden this would be at the finished level of the paved area adjacent to the house. Any paved or planted areas must be kept at least 15cm (6 in) below the house damp proof course (DPC) level.

To establish the datum, first excavate a small area adjacent to the house wall and with a base about 40cm (15 in) below the house DPC level. Now hammer a wooden peg into the ground so that the top is 15cm (6 in) lower than the DPC (see raised area diagram).

Main retaining wall

Using timber pegs and the brick line of the house wall, mark the boundary of the raised, paved area. A brick retaining wall must be built at this line in order to support the paving slabs and to retain safely the trapped earth (see the section plan diagram). A wall of this type is normally reckoned to retain a height of roughly three times its thickness. So for the wall specified, a 22·5cm (9 in) thickness, i.e. two bricks, is necessary. To be stable the wall must sit on a firm concrete foundation as illustrated in the section plan and raised area diagrams.

Retaining wall foundation

To establish the depth of the foundation trench, dig away some earth immediately below the marked border line. Using the original datum peg as a reference for the level, hammer a second peg about 60cm

Ground plan, drawn to scale, is an essential reference while you work on the patio site

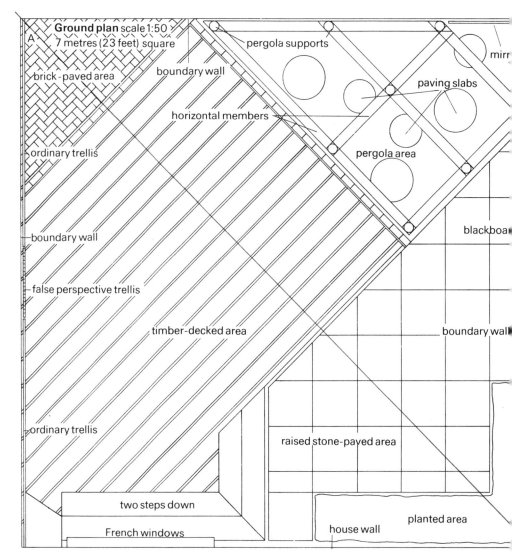

Ground plan scale 1:50
7 metres (23 feet) square
brick-paved area
boundary wall
ordinary trellis
boundary wall
false perspective trellis
timber-decked area
ordinary trellis
two steps down
French windows
pergola supports
horizontal members
paving slabs
pergola area
blackboa
boundary wall
raised stone-paved area
house wall
planted area
mirr

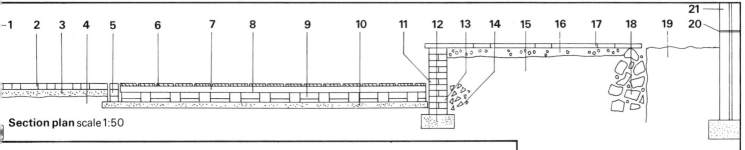

Section plan scale 1:50

(24 in) inside the paved area confine and level off, using the timber straight-edge and spirit level (as shown in the raised area diagram).

With the straight-edge laid on top of the two pegs, some measure can be gained of the excavation necessary to complete the wall foundation trench.

Next dig the trench and hammer in pegs to the finished concrete level (raised area diagram). Pile up the subsoil as you remove it ready for back-filling after the wall has been completed. With the trench neatly finished pour in concrete and level it to the tops of the wooden pegs.

Concrete mix
A suitable mix for this purpose is 1 part cement to 4·5 parts 20mm ($\frac{3}{4}$ in) all-in ballast. Mix dry ingredients first on a clean surface and then add sufficient water to produce a stiff mix. This must be poured into the foundation trench and carefully tamped level with the peg tops. Take care at this stage to produce a neat, flat surface as this will do much to simplify subsequent bricklaying.

SCHEDULE OF WORK Stage 2
For a wall that is subject to virtually constant dampness from the retained earth, a hard type of brick will prove more durable than a soft or 'common' type. Similarly, hard bricks will also be

required for the brick-paved corner in the patio. It is worth spending some time finding the best type of brick available.

Mortar for bricklaying
Bricks are laid using a mortar mix of 3 parts soft sand to 1 part cement. Adding a plasticizer will make the mix more workable as well as minimizing subsequent shrinkage or cracking.

Mix the dry ingredients first on a clean surface and then add the water and plasticizer to produce a fairly stiff, but workable, mix. Transfer 2–3 shovels of mortar to your spot board which should be positioned near the work.

Building the main retaining wall
The art of bricklaying is something that can only be acquired with practice, but a relatively low wall of this type should be within the scope of most people provided the work is tackled in the order shown. Be sure to use the spirit level constantly to check that you are building the wall absolutely vertical.

Using the timber straight-edge as a guide, lay a line of bricks along the complete length of the wall. Next build up the ends and then the angled corner. Use a length of timber, marked with the brick courses and mortar joints, as a gauge to ensure that the building of the three columns proceeds accurately.

Key
1 boundary wall 2 brick paving
3 sand/cement base 4 subsoil/hardcore
5 retaining wall 6 timber decking
7 75mm x 50mm (3in x 2in) joist
8 DPC between bricks and timber
9 brick sleeper wall 10 concrete raft
11 main retaining wall
12 concrete foundation
13 drainage weep-holes 14 hardcore infill
15 subsoil/hardcore 16 ballast infill
17 paving stones 18 loose-laid rubble wall
19 topsoil (planted area) 20 DPC 21 house wall

Once this part of the work has been completed, 'filling in' is simply a matter of stretching the brick line to the courses of bricks and progressively building upward, one course at a time. The mortar joints, or pointing, should be finished as described on page 14.

Drainage weep-holes
To prevent a possible build-up of water behind the retaining wall, leave weep-holes in the course of bricks immediately above the concrete raft level for the timber decking (see section plan). To do this, simply omit the vertical mortar joint at about 70cm (27 in) intervals as the bricks are laid.

Raised area diagram reference for Stage 1

HARDCORE AND BALLAST
Hardcore consists of broken-up pieces of brick and other building materials. Quality and size of particles varies, but it is essential to get hardcore that is composed mainly of solid material, otherwise it will gradually break down and be detrimental to the foundations.

Ideally you should obtain brick hardcore that is free from foreign matter. You can buy it from builders or break up bricks yourself.

Ballast (or aggregate) adds bulk and strength to concrete. It consists of fine and coarse sand and small pebbles in different sizes, according to the job requirement.

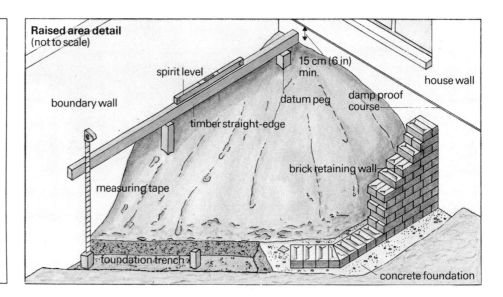

Raised area detail (not to scale)

spirit level

boundary wall

measuring tape

foundation trench

15 cm (6 in) min.

datum peg

timber straight-edge

house wall

damp proof course

brick retaining wall

concrete foundation

MIXING MORTAR

To mix by hand: if necessary, measure out cement in a bucket, shaking it well down and scraping it off level. Thoroughly mix cement with sand, make a well in the middle of the heap and pour in water (and plasticizer if used), until the mix is fairly stiff but still workable (right).

Shovel the dry ingredients into the centre to absorb the water and turn the heap to obtain an even, moist mixture. Add more water if required, but don't over-do it and take care not to let the walls fall in.

Then test by ridging with a shovel to leave clear cut marks (far right, above). Too much, or too little, water will not leave distinct ridges, so correct the water quantity now.

Cut off a slice of mortar with your trowel, and shape the back to a curve, using a sawing action (right), before picking it up. To lift a full load of mortar at a time, sweep your trowel underneath the slice, from the back, to give a good, sausage-like portion (far right).

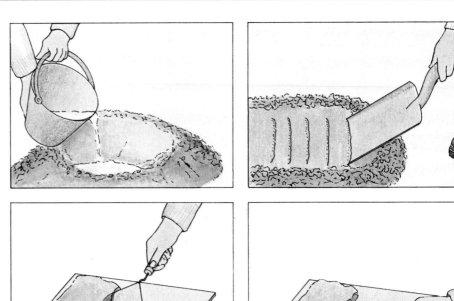

BRICKLAYING

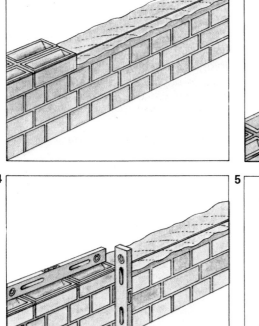

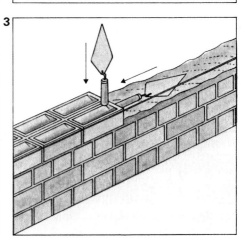

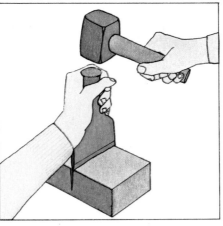

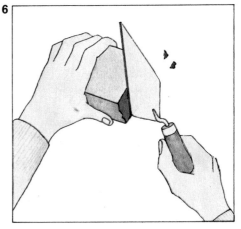

Transfer a few shovels of mortar to a spot board. Roll off a sausage of mortar mix onto the row of bricks in one smooth action by pulling the trowel back towards you. **1** Then smooth this mortar layer with the point of the trowel to form a bed of about 10mm ($\frac{3}{8}$ in) deep.

2 Before laying a brick 'butter' the end forming an upright joint with a sausage of mortar.

3 Tap brick into position horizontally and vertically with the trowel handle.

4 Check horizontal and vertical levels with a spirit level.

5 Cut bricks by marking a line then, on a firm surface, hold a chisel in position and strike a hard blow with a club hammer.

6 Clean rough edges with edge of trowel.

DECKING AND PAVING THE PATIO

You are now in the thick of making your own patio and for Stages 3 and 4 of the Schedule of Work you must check with the ground plan illustrated to scale on page 20.

SCHEDULE OF WORK Stage 3

With the main wall completed, you can proceed with further levelling and re-shaping of the site by piling the surplus subsoil from the lower level into the higher level. Take care to see that no pressure is applied to this main retaining wall until the mortar has set solidly. Now you should be ready to prepare the timber-decked area.

The ground plan and general detail diagram illustrate the layout of the timber decking. For this you must make a concrete raft foundation to which the timber structure will be laid.

Preparing for the raft foundation

The first stage of the work involves re-moving the topsoil to the pergola area. Once this has been accomplished, and fairly firm subsoil exposed, you can begin work adjusting the whole area to the necessary level. Lay straight-edge across the two previously positioned high-level datum pegs so that it overhangs the re-taining wall. Now measure vertically down to the lower level, using the spirit level as a guide, as shown in the raised area diagram (see page 21). Hammer in the supplementary datum peg to the finished top level of the concrete raft. You can then carry out further levelling using the straight-edge and spirit level for a regular surface over all the raft site.

Where the excavation work has ex-posed reasonably firm subsoil, then the concrete may be laid directly onto this. However, where topsoil removal has re-duced the level below that required, the difference must be made up with clean, broken brick, stones or similar 'hard-core' material.

The concrete raft must be approxi-mately 30cm (12 in) oversize to the timber decking along the pergola and brick-paved edges. This is to provide a foundation for the retaining walls that are necessary to cope with the difference

Use a scaffolding board, first across, then along the raft concrete, on the top surface of the shuttering timbers

in levels at these junctions (see general detail diagram).

Laying the shuttering

Concrete shuttering, or formwork, con-sists of planks of timber laid to the edges of the area to be concreted. This forms an edge to which the top of the concrete can easily be levelled and also contains, and provides, a clean edge to the work in hand.

Timber for shuttering must be solid: scaffolding boards are ideal. With the aid of the spirit level and straight-edge, lay the top edge of the boards flush to the top of the supplementary datum peg. Hammer supporting timber pegs into the outside edge of the shuttering so that it does not move under the pressure of the poured concrete.

Drainage holes

The raft foundation will be surrounded by walls when the work is completed and for this reason drainage holes must be left through the concrete at about 1m (3 ft 3 in) centres. To do this, lay blocks of wood in the area prior to pouring the concrete, and then remove them before the concrete finally sets.

Where the subsoil consists of heavy clay and is not self-draining, it may be necessary to excavate a soakaway pit to ensure adequate drainage.

This would normally mean digging a 60cm (24 in) cube-shaped hole and filling it with hardcore under one main drain-age hole. It would also be necessary to slope the concrete surface slightly to-wards the drainage point.

Pouring the raft concrete

A suitable mix for the raft concrete is 1 part cement to 4·5 parts 20mm ($\frac{3}{4}$ in) all-in ballast. Mix the dry ingredients first on a clean surface and then add sufficient water to produce a stiff mix. After pour-ing, tamp and level the concrete ready for the next stage of the work. Tamping and levelling can be carried out with a scaffolding board used on edge along the top surface of the shuttering (see below).

Decked area retaining walls

Next build brick retaining walls to the edge of the concrete raft (see the section plan and general detail diagram). As the height of this wall is only 22·5cm (9 in), a single skin wall will prove adequate.

Do the bricklaying by the same method described for the main retaining wall for the raised area on page 17, the only difference being in the bond used, which you can see illustrated in the general detail diagram.

SCHEDULE OF WORK Stage 4

With all the retaining walls built and dry, you can proceed with the final back-filling and levelling work. Some broken brick or other hardcore must be laid at the inside base of the main retaining wall (see section plan), to allow free drainage through the weep-holes. Then use well-compacted hardcore and excavated sub-soil to fill the main raised area. The division between paved and planted area is built up as necessary, using loosely-laid brick or stone as back-filling proceeds. The planted area should also be back-filled with topsoil.

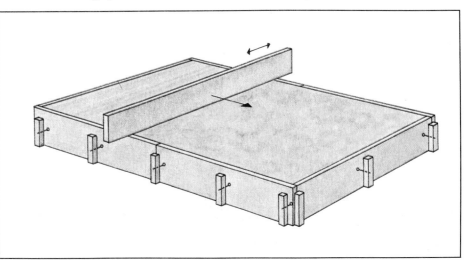

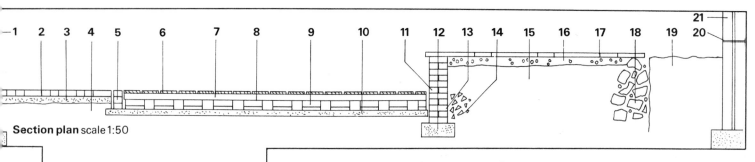

Section plan scale 1:50

Key
1 boundary wall 2 brick paving
3 sand/cement base 4 subsoil/hardcore
5 retaining wall 6 timber decking
7 75mm x 50mm (3in x 2in) joist
8 DPC between bricks and timber
9 brick sleeper wall 10 concrete raft
11 main retaining wall
12 concrete foundation
13 drainage weep-holes 14 hardcore infill
15 subsoil/hardcore 16 ballast infill
17 paving stones 18 loose-laid rubble wall
19 topsoil (planted area) 20 DPC 21 house wall

Levelling the brick-paved area

This area must be levelled in a similar way, with hardcore and subsoil being well compacted as a foundation for paving. Be sure to include pockets of subsoil as work proceeds, ready for subsequent planting of trees and shrubs. We have allowed for a *Magnolia grandiflora* to grow out of such a pocket against the trellised wall. Otherwise you must confine your plantings to tubs.

Preparing for the pergola

The first task here is to provide sockets for the rustic timber uprights. For this you should use 600mm (24 in) lengths of 100mm (4 in) diameter salt-glazed soil pipe. Position these in the ground (as shown in the general detail diagram); set them upright, using a post and the spirit level as a guide.

The main pergola area consists of topsoil that will support the woodland and other shade-loving plants to be planted here. Circular paving slabs give easy access, and to make a foundation for these, lay subsoil and ballast in the appropriate spots as you carry out the back-filling with topsoil.

Laying the raised area paving

As with bricklaying, the skill of laying paving stones can only be finally achieved through practice. However, by taking extra care and frequently using the spirit level and string guide, the beginner can produce a neat job.

Prepare the ground (see next page),

noting that the finished level of the ballast must be flush with the top of the main retaining wall (see general detail diagram).

Before starting to lay the paving stones, carefully set out the pattern to which the stones will be laid so as to avoid the use of small pieces of cut stone. The ground plan illustrates this point, where the cut stones along the retaining wall edge are all kept to a reasonable size.

Using the brick line and pegs, establish a line at right-angles to the planted area edge and as parallel as possible to the adjoining boundary wall. The line must be one paving stone width plus 2·5cm (1 in) maximum from the wall and positioned to represent the finished paving level, which should of course be flush with the top of the original datum peg.

Lay the first line of stones to the string line and then work backwards over the whole area until all the whole stones have been laid checking levels as you go.

Refer to the general detail diagram (below) and section plan (above) at all stages

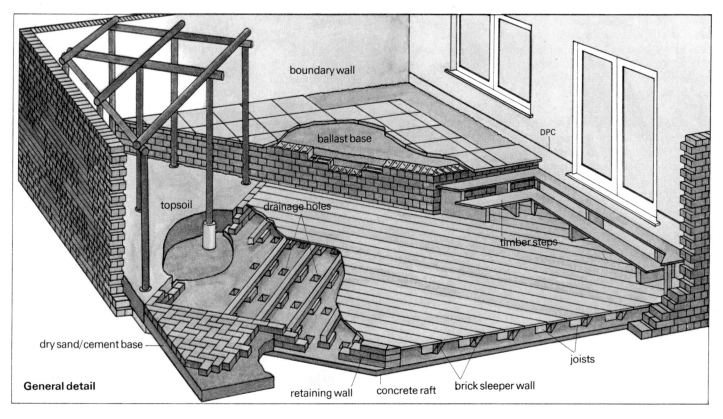

General detail

LAYING PAVING STONES

Having chosen your type of paving, estimated the quantity of stones needed and arranged for them to be delivered, it is time to prepare the ground.

If necessary, remove soil to a depth of 7–10cm (3–4 in) below the final required level. Then roll or tamp in a 5cm (2 in) layer of ballast. On springy or spongy soil use a 5cm layer of hardcore topped with sand. Check with a spirit level to ensure that the finished surface of your foundation is flat and accurate in all directions. Extra care taken at this stage will do much to simplify subsequent paving work.

You will need to mark out the area for paving with string, and then set out the pattern of your stones in such a way as to avoid having to use small, cut pieces. The stone supplier may be able to supply stones according to your specifications. Sizes and shapes for the cut stones should be taken direct from the plan of your paved area. To cut the stones yourself, follow the instructions below and practise on a spare bit of paving.

1 Mark out the edge of the first row with a string line. Each paving stone is then set on five blobs of a stiff 3 to 1 sand/cement mortar mix (that is, four blobs set just in from each corner and one in the centre).

2 To allow 9mm ($\frac{3}{8}$ in) gap between

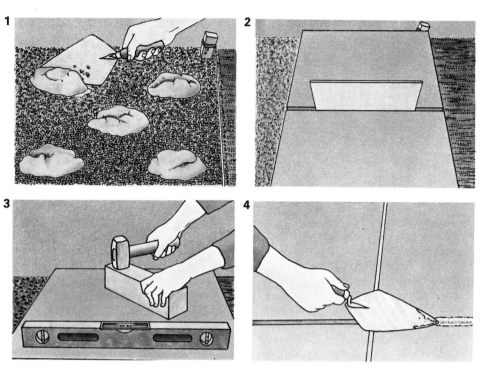

stones for final pointing, you need to use pieces of chipboard or plywood as temporary spacers.

3 Then tap each stone level, using a club hammer over a block of wood, until it lies level with its neighbours and no longer rocks on the foundation. With a trowel, cut away any surplus cement that may be squeezed out.

Always work backwards from your

first row of paving, and refer frequently to your spirit level and string guide during laying so as to maintain a flat and even surface.

4 About a week after laying the paving you will need to point the spaces between the stones. For this, use the same 3 to 1 part sand/cement mortar mix and pack it into the joints, smoothing it with a trowel to slightly below level of stones.

CUTTING PAVING STONES

While it is possible to cut the stones by using a club hammer and bolster (or brick chisel), a far more satisfactory method is to hire a purpose-made power cutter from a tool hire firm. However, if you decide to do-it-yourself, it is worth taking your time to achieve a neat job.

1 Mark your cutting line, with a chalk or even a soft pencil, across both faces and edges of the stone.

Place the stone to be cut on a bed of soft soil and press it firmly down so that it will remain steady while you are chiselling.

2 Using a club hammer and bolster, cut a shallow scratch, about 2mm ($\frac{1}{16}$ in) deep, as evenly and straight as possible. At the end of your cutting line, chisel across the thickness of the stone. Then turn the stone over carefully and chisel across the second face.

3 Place a block of wood at one end of the scratch and strike it firmly with the club hammer. Repeat the process along the length of the scratch. You should hear the ringing tone turn to a dull thud.

4 Clean off any uneven edges with the bolster to obtain a neat join.

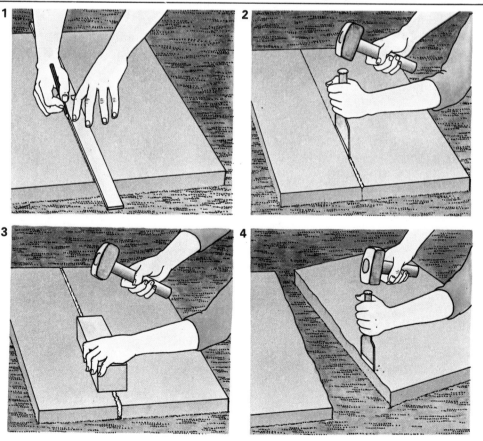

FINAL STAGES IN THE PATIO GARDEN

Following our Patio Garden design you will have learned how to do many things yourself – from preparing foundations, laying a damp proof course and building brick walls, to the surface work of laying stone or brick paving and timber decking, as well as repointing and painting old brickwork.

After the building work comes the pleasure of choosing what plants to grow where, the right containers for them, and how to plant the deep bed in the raised, paved area. These details are given along with other garden designs later in the book.

SCHEDULE OF WORK Stage 5

When you have successfully completed the first four stages of work you will be ready to lay the decorative brick paving in the far left corner, opposite the French windows.

Laying the brick-paved area

For this brick paving a slightly different laying technique is employed from that for the stone-paved area we described earlier.

Here you should lay a 5cm (2 in) thick bed of a very stiff 5 to 1 sand/cement mix and carefully level it so that when the bricks are laid in position and gently tapped, the surface will become flush to the adjacent 11–12cm (4½ in) thick retaining wall.

You can obtain the right stiff mix by adding just sufficient water to produce a crumbly texture. Use a string line in conjunction with the spirit level to help you make a neat job of it. The dry sand/cement bed should be lightly dampened as work proceeds, using a watering can with a sprinkler rose.

Leave a 9mm (⅜ in) pointing gap between all the bricks and fill this with a 3 to 1 mortar mix after you have completed all the paving. Lay all the full-sized bricks first, before you insert any necessary cut pieces. You can cut the bricks to the required size with a club hammer and brick chisel. (You can follow the same laying technique if you wish to use a broken stone paving.)

Timber for decking and joists

An ideal timber for this purpose is Western red cedar, but if this type is too costly or not readily available, you should consult your local timber merchant as to the best alternative available. With some types of timber the supplier may suggest pre-impregnation with a preservative.

The 250 × 25mm (10 × 1 in) decking is fitted to 75 × 50mm (3 × 2 in) joists, which

Fix trellis either side of your false perspective arched pathway, and paint to choice, or protect with preservative

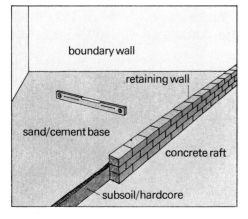

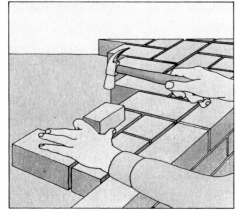

For brick paving: (top) level the sand/cement base; (top right) keep the bed lightly dampened as you lay the bricks;

(above left) if gently tapped, the laid bricks become flush to retaining wall; (above) point the gaps between bricks

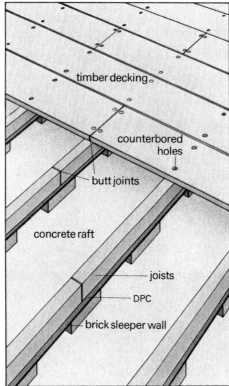

For timber decking: fit timber to joists supported on brick sleeper wall, with DPC between timber and bricks. Fill counter-sunk screw-holes with plugs

in turn are supported on a brick 'sleeper' wall with a damp proof course between brick and timber. The joists must be set at 40cm (16 in) centres and the planks of the decking laid with 9mm ($\frac{3}{8}$ in) gaps between each to allow surface water to run through (see ground and section plans and general detail diagram). Take care with all the timber work to ensure that the timber never comes into direct contact with any concrete or masonry.

Building the sleeper wall

Set one brick in a corner accurately to the sleeper wall height and then use this as a datum to transfer the levels, through the straight-edge and spirit level, to a second brick positioned at the far end of this first sleeper wall. You can then stretch a string line to the bricks to lay the remainder of the wall accurately. The space between bricks should be about 15cm (6 in); see section plan. Build the balance of sleeper walls the same way.
Note For Patio ground plan, see page 20, for section plan, pages 21 and 24, and general detail diagram, page 24.

SCHEDULE OF WORK Stage 6

Having fitted the decking to the joists, now follow the correct sequence of work.

Laying the decking

After the mortar has set, lay a strip of DPC material on top of the wall before laying the joists in position. Then fix the decking to the joists, using rust-proofed screws (ideally brass ones), countersunk below the surface. Fill the holes with a matching timber plug.

Timber for steps

To give access from the house down to the timber decking and also up to the raised paved area, you will need steps. Build these up from timber left over from decking (see general detail diagram).

Erecting the pergola

Cut the vertical rustic poles, all about 100mm (4 in) in diameter, to a 2·8m length (9 ft) and then drop them into the previously prepared sockets (see Stage 4 on page 24). Cut the three horizontal under members to length and fit them to the tops of the vertical members by nailing through. Then fix the second horizontal layer (see general detail diagram).

SCHEDULE OF WORK Stage 7

No matter how small a patio, a trellis like this one, designed to give the illusion of depth, looks effective. We fitted ours to the left-hand boundary wall.

False perspective trellis work

This is quite simple to carry out if you follow our grid pattern. First of all, lightly pencil 10cm (4 in) squares onto a sheet of 12mm (½ in) thick marine plywood. You can then 'transfer' the design to the plywood panel by reference to the grid pattern. Cutting is best carried out using either a self-powered or drill jig saw attachment. After cutting, smooth all edges by sanding before painting with one coat of primer, two undercoats and one top coat of oil paint.

This false perspective trellis is flanked on both sides by the more conventional rectangular trellis which you buy ready-made. You can paint this any colour to suit your scheme, or leave it natural and protect it with wood preservative.

To fix all the trellis work to the brick walls, use conventional plastic wall plugs and screws. In order to prevent contact between the trellis timber and wall brickwork (as this provides a point where early rotting and staining may occur) use 100mm (4 in) long fixing screws with 35mm (1½ in) long plastic tube spacers fitted over the screw shank between the trellis and wall.

Fixing the mirrors and blackboard

Reflections from the two square mirrors fitted to the boundary walls under the pergola (see ground plan) add an air of mystery to the patio. Be sure to get the waterproof-backed type and fit them to the walls with standard-type plastic wall fixing plugs and brass screws through holes pre-drilled in the mirrors. The holes for the screws must be loosely-sized and a thick rubber washer fitted to the screw shank between mirror and wall to allow for expansion and contraction of the glass during extremes of temperature.

For the children's benefit it is well worth making an outdoor blackboard. Cut this yourself from a sheet of water-proof plywood and treat it with a special blackboard paint (and renew this as necessary). Fix it to the wall near to the main paved area (see ground plan) in the same way as the mirrors.

Painting the chequerboard

You can paint any pattern you like on the raised paving, but we thought a simple chequerboard was useful for the games enthusiasts and decorative in its own right. The area must be completely dust-free and lightly dampened before you start applying an emulsion paint.

Use grid to transfer your perspective pattern to marine plywood. You can add mirror glass panels here to good effect

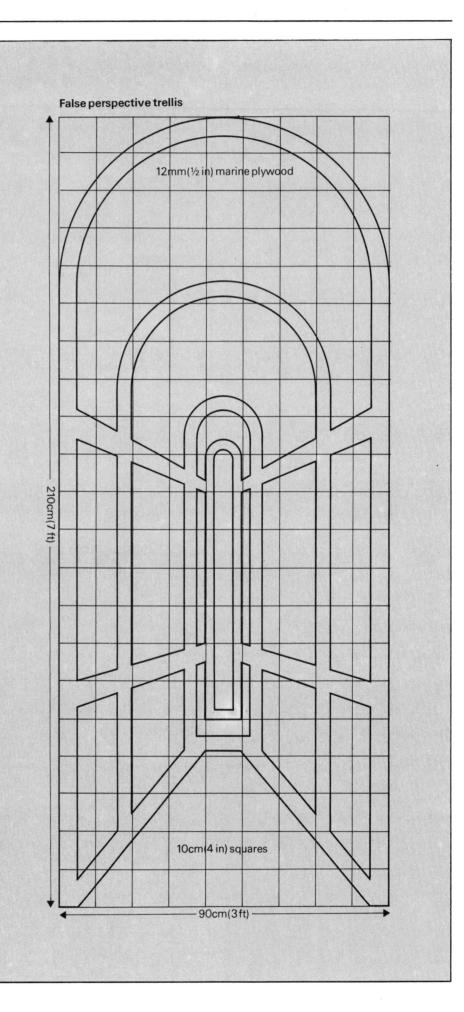

False perspective trellis

12mm (½ in) marine plywood

210cm (7 ft)

10cm (4 in) squares

90cm (3 ft)

GRAVEL SURFACING

Gravel can be used anywhere, but looks best when close to buildings; less formal than paving, though more severe than grass, it acts as a visual link between the two. It is useful around plantings and the base of trees as it allows the roots to breathe and absorb water.

When laying gravel, the various stages of preparation are very important, especially in driveways where heavy traffic can quickly cause havoc with a badly-executed job.

Preparation and laying
For the best results, really thorough consolidation is necessary at each juncture and, where space permits, you can hire a mechanical 'vibrating' roller and this will give ideal results in the minimum time. In cramped areas, or paths, a 500–750kg (10–15 cwt) hand roller may be all that is practical. Therefore it makes sense to facilitate rolling by keeping the shapes of gravel areas simple.

If you are thinking of using gravel for a drive, you will find that a 'sub base' is normally needed. This will have been carried out by a combination of the builders and traffic over the years on a developed site. When you are operating on virgin ground, it would be wise to call in a contractor to do at least the basic soil-shifting and levelling.

Assuming that the sub base is sound, continue with the main stages of construction. First of all, clean the surface thoroughly, grubbing out all vegetation, moss and weeds, and filling any pot-holes with rammed hardcore.

Lay a base of hardcore, crushed stone

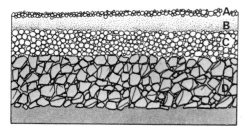

Cross-section of gravel A, laid on 2·5cm (1 in) layer of hoggin B, and 5cm (2 in) layer of coarse gravel C, over hardcore D

or clinker, and roll it to a finished thickness of 10cm (4 in). Then put down a layer of coarse gravel, small enough to pass through a 5cm (2 in) screen, and roll it to a finished thickness of 5cm (2 in). Roll on a 2·5cm (1 in) covering of fine gravel mixed with hoggin as a binder. 'Hoggin' is a technical term used by contractors and is simply a clay, usually from the same pit as the gravel, that seals

and binds the surface together. Wet it just enough to achieve an even spread; if too wet, it will clog rollers and tools, sticking to everything except the surface of the drive itself.

On top, to finish with, spread and roll 13mm ($\frac{1}{2}$ in) washed 'pea' shingle. The surface should now be firm; there is nothing worse than a treadmill effect on your way to the front door.

Drainage
It is especially important to provide drainage with gravel and if, after digging a trial hole, you find the water-table to be within 60cm (2 ft) of the surface, lay a simple drain on one or both sides of the drive. (See bottom diagram).

Retaining edges
The gravel may well be retained by a building or some kind of paving but, where it meets a soft surface such as plantings or grass, you may need a definite edge. You can obtain a neat and

attractive finish by laying bricks on edge, but make sure that these are a hard, well-fired variety that will resist frost. Set the bricks in concrete and bring the gravel within 13mm ($\frac{1}{2}$ in) of the top. If the area abuts a lawn, the grass should, in turn, be 13mm ($\frac{1}{2}$ in) above the brick, allowing the mower to run easily along the top.

Plants for use with gravel
Architectural foliage blends well with gravel and enhances the composition by highlighting and ornamenting its edge. The large strongly-veined leaves of *Hosta sieboldiana*, a blue-leaved plantain lily, contrast effectively with the tall spiky uprights of *Yucca flaccida* (Adam's needle). *Fatsia japonica* (Japanese aralia or figleaf palm), hellebores, bergenia (pig squeak) and sinarundinaria – better known as bamboo – can also be included. These will mature to form a dramatic and virtually maintenance-free composition. Avoid 'spotty' effects of single specimens by planting in small groups.

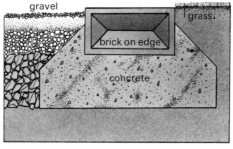

Above: cross-section showing edging brick set in concrete with gravel below on one side and grass above on the other

Above: cross-section of gravel abutting a lawn and laid against a building that acts as a retaining edge

Below: cross-section of a 10cm (4in) land drain installed on one side of the gravel area; graded porous fill allows seepage, making a new water-table

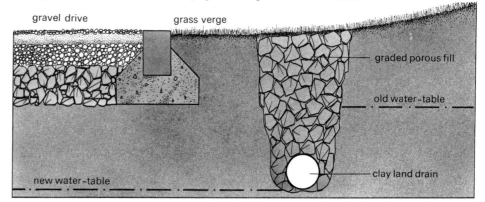

COBBLES

Smooth surfaces, such as concrete, paving slabs and tarmac, invite pedestrian traffic. A surface area of small, uneven 'modules', such as a pebble path, has the opposite effect, while cobbles are a positive deterrent.

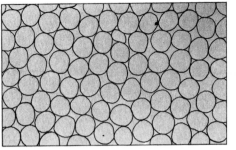 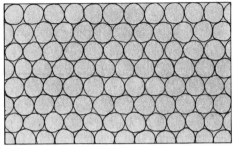

Above: plans of how to lay cobbles in a random pattern (left), and in courses (right)
Below: a more ambitious design, showing how to lay cobbles in a radius pattern

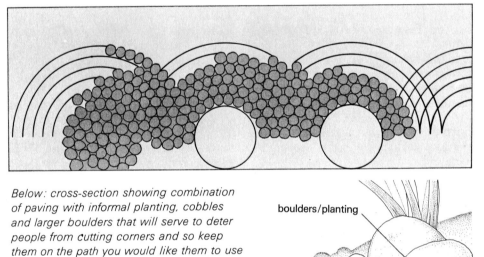

Cobbles are useful as they prevent people from cutting corners, protect beds by the front door from the delivery men, and generally direct the necessary tread of feet along the right paths.

They are round or oval stones, often flint, and similar to those found on the beach. Cobbles come in graded sizes up to 10cm (4 in) in diameter and can be laid in a variety of patterns, ranging from sophisticated formal designs, utilizing stones of different size, to loosely-arranged piles.

It is important to lay cobbles (or any small module) correctly, remembering that it's the material itself that counts, and not the background. The 'currant

*Cross section of cobbles **A**, laid on 5cm (2 in) layer of concrete **B**, and 5cm (2 in) layer of sand **C**, over a hardcore base **D**

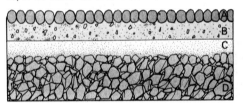

Below: cross-section showing combination of paving with informal planting, cobbles and larger boulders that will serve to deter people from cutting corners and so keep them on the path you would like them to use

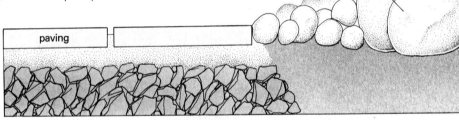

bun' effect, where a few cobbles are dotted at random in a sea of concrete, is to be avoided. The overall impression should be one of 'eggs in a crate', with little or no mortar showing between tightly-packed stones.

Where you intend cobbles to withstand cars (as an oil-drip), or pedestrians, a well-consolidated base of hardcore or crushed stone will be necessary. Put a layer of sand on top of this and roll it to a finished thickness of 5cm (2 in). Next, spread concrete (2 parts cement to 6 parts sand and gravel mixture) 5cm (2 in) thick and press the cobbles into this by hand. Use a straight-edge to ensure that the finished surface is flat and tamp any high stones down to the level of the rest.

An alternative, often used in Europe, is to lay the cobbles on a dry mortar or a concrete mix and then wet the mix from a watering can (with the rose on), thus preventing any of the cobbles becoming marked with cement which would be virtually impossible to remove.

Below: use of paving, loose cobbles and brick edging as part of overall design scheme

LAYING BRICK PATHS

Brick paving is like a good wine – it needs to be carefully laid down, is rich in flavour and improves with age.

As with all surfacing materials, brick has a character of its own, and because of its size, tends to be used where detail and intimacy are important. The incongruity of having vast areas of brick paving around some of the newer public buildings is immediately apparent because, besides being prohibitively expensive, it can be desperately monotonous.

It is, then, a surface to be used carefully, taking into consideration the immediate surroundings and any other relevant parts of the design.

Although bricks are available in a standard size of $225 \times 113 \times 75$mm ($9 \times 4\frac{1}{2} \times 3$ in), the range of textures and finishes is enormous. The density or hardness can also vary from a virtually indestructible 'engineering' brick to a much softer stock.

Taking these differences into account, it is quite obvious that while a perfectly uniform engineering brick could look superb in an austere modern composition, it would look out of place in a cottage garden.

The method of laying bricks also alters their character; open joints emphasize each module, while flush pointing provides a more uniform surface.

Remember, too, that bricks can be laid either flat or on edge and that this, as well as the type and direction of the bond, will affect the finished composition.

Assuming these factors have been taken into account during the design stage we can now start to look at the various methods of laying brick paving.

Laying a path
Ideally, the foundation for a path should consist of 8cm (3 in) of well-consolidated hardcore. If surface drainage is likely to

Above: Alchemilla mollis *spilling onto brick path laid in a stretcher bond*
Below: warm clay texture of this path leads eye and foot gently to conservatory

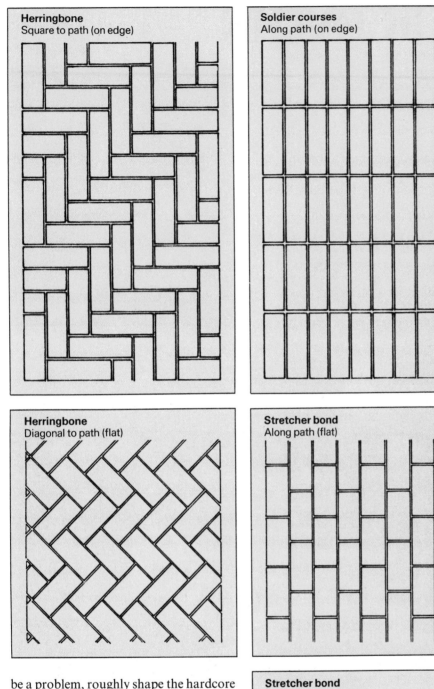

Herringbone
Square to path (on edge)

Soldier courses
Along path (on edge)

weave – although there are modifications to these that will extend the range.

Stretcher bond This is exactly what it says, with the bricks laid end to end, as in a wall. The pattern can either be across or down the length of the path. This obviously has an effect on the overall design of the garden. If the line is down the path, the length and direction of the feature will be emphasized; bricks laid across a path give it a feeling of greater width. Stretcher bond also allows a camber to be easily incorporated and so will drain quickly after rain.

Herringbone You can see fine examples of this traditional paving pattern in its original form at many historic buildings. As with stretcher bond, the bricks can be laid flat or on edge, and either parallel or diagonally across the line of the path.

This is an intrinsically complicated design, and looks it. It is therefore better to use it in an intricate, detailed situation – too much of it could become fussy and oppressive to the eye. A camber is difficult to lay and the pattern should be worked to a straight cross fall.

Herringbone
Diagonal to path (flat)

Stretcher bond
Along path (flat)

Basketweave (flat)

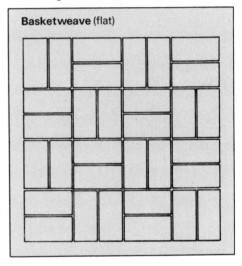

be a problem, roughly shape the hardcore to a slight camber or cross fall.

The usual method of laying brick paving on the prepared hardcore foundation is as follows: bed the bricks on a 5cm (2 in) thick, dry layer of sand and cement (using – by volume – 1 part sand to 4 parts cement). When you have finished the path, or section of path, wet the surface with water from a can (keeping the rose on) and then brush the same mix into the open joints. When the joints have almost set you can rub them back to accentuate individual bricks and emphasize the pattern as a whole.

A choice of patterns
Bricks can be laid in three basic patterns – stretcher bond, herringbone and basket-

Stretcher bond
Across path (on edge)

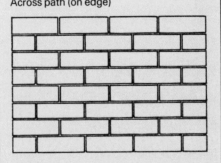

Above: illustrations of brick paving laid in three different patterns – herringbone, stretcher bond (soldier coursing is a variant of this, without the staggering) and basketweave

Basketweave Again, this pattern is a traditional one. Bricks can be laid flat in pairs, or on edge in threes. The effect is more static, as bolder squares give stability to the overall design

If the path is on a slope and you don't need steps, it is possible to 'haunch', or lay the bricks at a slight angle, to obtain a better foothold. This is really only practical with a simple pattern, as in the stretcher bond, laid across the path.

Finally, it is essential to be neat in your work. Bricks are a small module and there are a lot of joints in relation to the total surface area. The beauty of a brick path lies in its precise pattern and texture; to spoil this with unsightly splashes of mortar or loose jointing is a sure sign of poor workmanship.

PRE-CAST CONCRETE PATHS

Paths are not only an essential part of any garden but also an important design element, leading the eye as well as the feet. In this section we show how the various materials differ in character.

Pre-cast concrete slabs are probably the most widely-used material for paving. They come in many different shapes, sizes and colours from a standard grey laid in conventional pattern to interesting hexagonal and interlocking designs. Their relatively low price makes them more competitive than natural stone. As well as being durable, various textures are available, the non-slip varieties being particularly useful in the garden.

For medium-to-heavy traffic Lay a base of rammed hardcore 15cm (6 in) thick. Bed slabs on a 5cm (2 in) layer of mortar, leaving 6mm (¼ in) gaps for pointing.

For light traffic Lay each slab on five spots of mortar, in centre and at corners.

For stepping stones in a lawn Remove a section of turf and simply place slab in position, making sure that the hard surface is 13mm (½ in) below the lawn, to avoid damaging a mower.

For aggregate slabs With a surface of small stones or pebbles (exposed by brushing before concrete finally hardens)

these non-slip slabs should be laid to a slight 'fall' to avoid water standing in the rougher texture and freezing in winter.

FOR CURVED PATHS

Straight paths, using rectangular or square slabs, are relatively simple to lay but curves are more involved. Here you must peg out the line in advance, marking this with a sharpened stick or 'scribe' that is swung on the end of a cord secured to the appropriate radius. When the slabs are laid to this line a wedge-shaped joint ensues (see diagram). This can either be left open and planted with low-growing aromatic herbs or, if traffic is heavy, be carefully filled with small cobbles bedded in mortar.

HEXAGONAL OR INTERLOCKING

Six-sided slabs form attractive paths but the key to success here is to lay a random pattern that echoes the irregular shape of the module itself. This is particularly effective crossing a planted area, the hard and soft materials overlapping so that it is difficult to define a precise boundary between the two.

Interlocking concrete shapes, rather like pieces of jig-saw puzzle, should be treated in the same way as hexagonal paths, as a rigid edge looks clumsy.

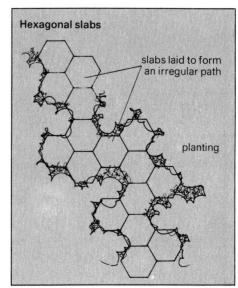

Hexagonal slabs

slabs laid to form an irregular path

planting

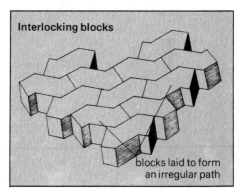

Interlocking blocks

blocks laid to form an irregular path

Hexagonal slabs or interlocking blocks both look better in irregular patterns, while with a curved path (left) you must work out your line in advance from radius points

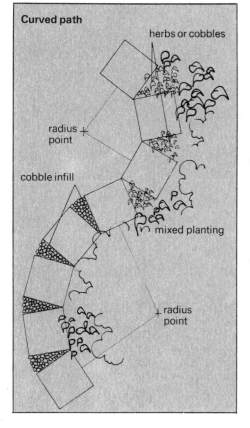

Curved path

herbs or cobbles

radius point

cobble infill

mixed planting

radius point

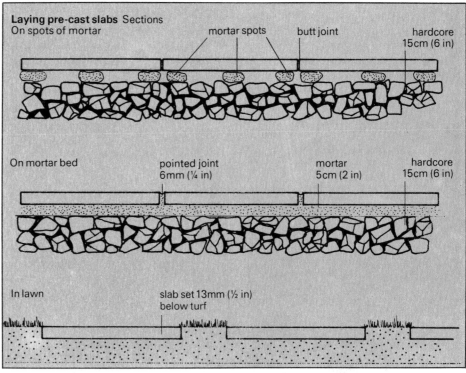

Laying pre-cast slabs Sections
On spots of mortar — mortar spots — butt joint — hardcore 15cm (6 in)

On mortar bed — pointed joint 6mm (¼ in) — mortar 5cm (2 in) — hardcore 15cm (6 in)

In lawn — slab set 13mm (½ in) below turf

33

BUILDING A RAMP

On previous pages we have described the different forms of surfacing a garden. Here we look at a further alternative – ramps – and give practical advice on how to build them.

Steps, circular or otherwise, are not always practical on a slope requiring wheeled access. Here a different solution is needed to cater for bicycles, wheelbarrows, prams or wheelchairs. A ramp is the obvious answer and the ways in which this can be constructed are as numerous as steps.

As a general rule the gradient should remain constant, both from a visual and a practical point of view. Steep ramps are tiring and if the slope is too great to tackle in one run, you should incorporate a 'hairpin' so that you go up in two evenly-graded sections.

Concrete for ramps

Concrete is the obvious material for this purpose. Laid on a suitably-compacted layer of hardcore, a final level is achieved by using wooden shutters, held in place by pegs. The finish with concrete can be varied, the easiest way being simply to tamp the top, between the shutters, with a long straight-edge. This will produce a ribbed effect, giving better traction for wheels and feet alike.

Brushed concrete (see page 90) can look effective and there is a wheeled tool available with an embossed face that you run over the concrete when partially dry to achieve the dimpled effect often seen in driveways and pavement edges laid by the local authorities. An important point to remember is to keep the concrete mix fairly 'dry'. As work progresses you will find that the tamping and trowelling will bring ample moisture to the surface. Too much moisture weakens the mix.

Brick, stone, cobbles or setts

Ramps can be made from brick, stone, or cobbles. Granite setts are also suitable and you can sometimes obtain old ones from city streets being demolished.

Setts are either full-sized (about the size of a thick brick), or half-sized (virtually square). The advantage this type of module has over concrete or tarmac is that it can be 'haunched' up at an angle, each course being tilted to obtain a better foothold on the slope.

When laying any small-scale material make sure you keep the surface clear from mortar; there is nothing worse than seeing the finished job spoilt in this way – it is also the trademark of a poor workman.

A ramp, with steps alongside to provide extra safety for pedestrians

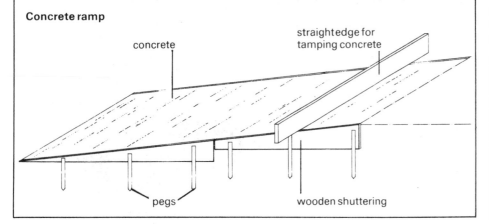

Left: tamp concrete for a non-slip surface
Below: angled granite setts make a good alternative to a ramp-type driveway

Concrete ramp

concrete

straight edge for tamping concrete

pegs

wooden shuttering

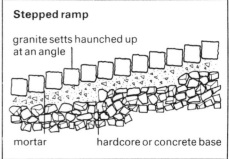

Stepped ramp

granite setts haunched up at an angle

mortar   hardcore or concrete base

FENCES AND SCREENS

Screening around or within the garden can be natural – in the form of a hedge or other planting – or prefabricated. While the former takes time to establish and needs a certain amount of maintenance, the latter is visually 'stiffer' and requires less upkeep – although it does involve a greater outlay of capital.
Here we describe and illustrate a varied selection of fences and screens, including the ubiquitous ranch fence, and the pastoral ha-ha – in effect, a dry moat, conceived to prevent stray cattle wandering into the garden.

Most people look at a fence, *call* it a fence, and leave it at that, when in fact the possibilities are endless. Fences are generally considered as a background, the usual approach being to hide them as soon as possible. While this is logical up to a point, might it not also be feasible to use at least part of this expensive item as a positive feature?

With the passing of hand craftwork and the inevitable change to mass production, a great deal of individuality has been sacrificed. Fences are no exception: time was when you could cross Britain and see a wide range of local designs, but this is virtually impossible today.

Fence of battened slats complements the angle of the terrace design

Battened slats
A number of interesting vertical screens can be made with 150 × 19mm (6 × ¾ in) slats, these being battened from behind so that the fixings are virtually invisible. Stain the wood with brown Cuprinol (not creosote, as this is toxic to plants), and use the composition in an architectural setting, close to the house and perhaps as a foil to the horizontal lines of white overhead beams. Slats could alternatively be set at an angle of 45 degrees (see illustration below).

Ranch fence
This type often fails to fulfill its real potential. It is an architectural feature, and can be used to great advantage on a sloping site, emphasizing a pattern of steps or terraced lawns. Use colour sensibly – why should such a fence, if painted, inevitably be white? Congo brown (BS 3–038) is a splendid landscape colour, and if your house is a certain colour don't be afraid to continue this for a distance in the garden.

Interwoven panels
Most people will be familiar with interwoven-panel fencing, and it is invariably erected with the weave running horizontally. Try turning the panels to a vertical position, either the whole run or in groups of two or three. The complete character of the fence is altered and it becomes far more attractive. Link the

ensuing pattern with boldly-planted beds for optimum effect.

Timber in all its guises has infinite permutations, but as the cost continues to rise and rise it is best to try to save money wherever possible. Rough-sawn timber is markedly cheaper than boards that are planed all round (PAR).

Scaffold poles
Everyone has seen scaffold poles but how many people have considered using them as a screen? Get them cut to the length you want (adding 45cm/18 in for the distance below ground), and concrete them into prepared holes, varying the distance between each pole for greater or lesser visibility. They are particularly effective for dividing areas of the garden, a partial view through the fence adding to the attraction. Climbing plants will quickly ramble up the poles, and remember that painting it white makes an open screen harder to see past than if you use darker colours.

Wattle hurdles
There are still one or two attractive local fencing materials available, the best and probably most widespread being wattle hurdles. These are woven by craftsmen from hazel branches and were originally used for penning sheep, each shepherd carrying four hurdles on his back and erecting a screen wherever necessary. Today they are becoming increasingly

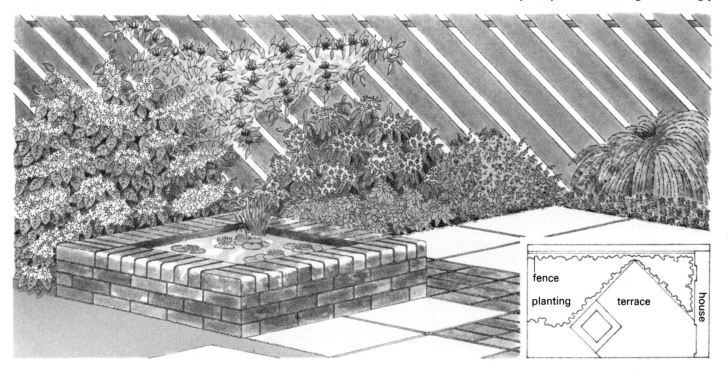

fence
planting   terrace
house

popular for garden use. They are cheaper than most mass-produced fencing, and although they have a life of only about 6–8 years, they blend well with virtually any background and make a superb foil for plants.

Ha-ha or post-and-rail?
In a rural situation, if you want a fence at all, you will probably want it to be inconspicuous. The traditional method of merging a garden and landscape was the ha-ha, a ditch stone-faced on one side, that allowed the view to run out without letting the cattle in. Today few people have the money or space to build this sort of feature, and a simple post-and-rail often looks the best. If you worry about dogs or small children, attach a section of sheep netting from ground level up to the first rail: this will be virtually invisible

Interwoven fencing (top right) with alternately-arranged panels
Wattle hurdles (above right) blend well with almost any background planting
Ranch fences (right and bottom) are particularly suited to sloping sites
Below: use scaffold poles for climbers

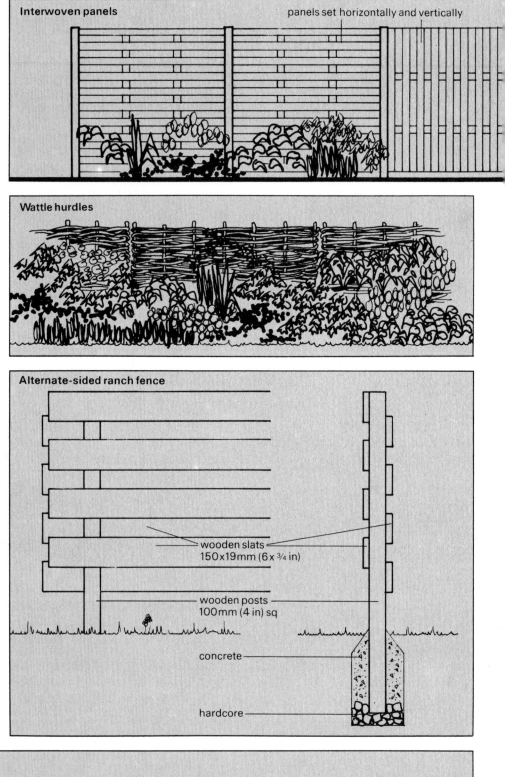

Interwoven panels — panels set horizontally and vertically

Wattle hurdles

Alternate-sided ranch fence — wooden slats 150x19mm (6 x ¾ in) — wooden posts 100mm (4 in) sq — concrete — hardcore

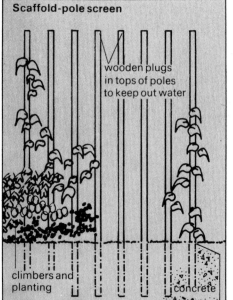

Scaffold-pole screen — wooden plugs in tops of poles to keep out water — climbers and planting — concrete

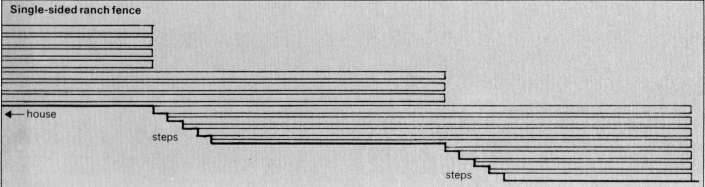

Single-sided ranch fence — house — steps — steps

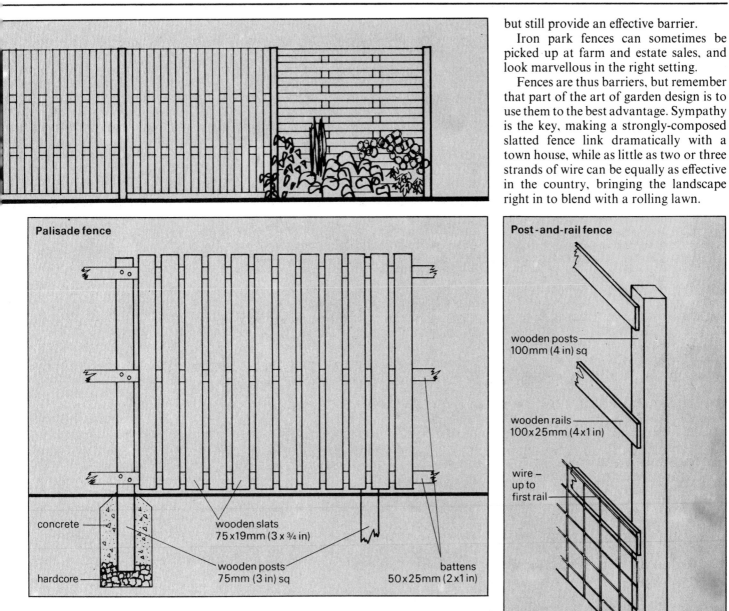

but still provide an effective barrier.

Iron park fences can sometimes be picked up at farm and estate sales, and look marvellous in the right setting.

Fences are thus barriers, but remember that part of the art of garden design is to use them to the best advantage. Sympathy is the key, making a strongly-composed slatted fence link dramatically with a town house, while as little as two or three strands of wire can be equally as effective in the country, bringing the landscape right in to blend with a rolling lawn.

Palisade fence

concrete

hardcore

wooden slats
75 x 19mm (3 x ¾ in)

wooden posts
75mm (3 in) sq

battens
50 x 25mm (2 x 1 in)

Post-and-rail fence

wooden posts
100mm (4 in) sq

wooden rails
100 x 25mm (4 x 1 in)

wire –
up to
first rail

Palisade fence (above) has slats nailed or screwed to horizontal battens
Post-and-rail (right) includes section of sheep netting between ground and first rail to keep small children and pets within the garden
Rural ha-ha (below) allows clear view of surrounding countryside

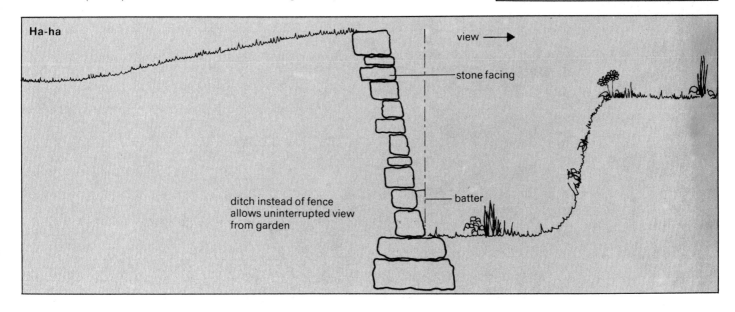

Ha-ha

view ➡

stone facing

batter

ditch instead of fence
allows uninterrupted view
from garden

MAKING FEDGES

Another device useful for dividing a garden merits close attention.

A fedge is exactly what it sounds – a cross between a fence and a hedge. This is not as extraordinary as it seems, for a fedge is a useful device with a positive role to play in the garden.

Basically, a fedge consists of climbing plants covering a prefabricated framework; this might be an old wall, fence or purpose-built wire screen. Once the plants are established, the framework becomes incidental and completely obscured.

Such a feature opens up interesting design possibilities and combines an architectural form with the softer, sprawling nature of the climbers used, providing a useful link between house and garden.

By its nature a fedge is most effective up to a maximum height of 2m (6½ ft). Beyond this many climbers tend to get a little straggly and the bottom growth becomes sparse and untidy. For this reason fedges are not really suited for use on a boundary where screening is important but are better adapted to the garden's own internal divisions – perhaps between a lawn and a vegetable plot, or for marking off a play area.

Constructing a fedge

The traditional method of constructing a fedge is to use chestnut fencing, allowing the climber simply to ramble up and over it. Although cheap and flexible, it is likely to decay fairly quickly. A sturdier method, and one that can give rise to a wide range of architectural patterns, involves using a combination of 10mm (⅜ in) mild steel rods of the type used in reinforced concrete, in combination with a plastic mesh such as Netlon.

First, decide on the height and length of the fedge, remembering that it need not be a straight or a necessarily continuous run; if you are in doubt about the final result in relation to the rest of the garden, work out the pattern to scale on graph paper. Next, select the finished shape you want; this can be rectangular, hooped or wedge shaped. Each shape, being more or less formal, will have its own characteristic.

The reinforcing rods are then carefully bent in a vice to the shape of a simple template (a pattern used as a guide in cutting) made from plywood or hardboard, thus ensuring that each hoop matches the next.

The hoops in a fedge 1·5m (5 ft) high should be under a metre (or yard) apart.

An effective method of anchoring them is to slide each section into a length of scaffold pole set into the ground. The plastic mesh is then stretched over the finished line of hoops and neatly fixed by plastic-coated wire.

While this technique is suitable for fedges of considerable length and scale in the larger garden, another simple form of fedge can be made from railway sleepers set vertically into the ground 2m (6½ ft) apart. The netting in this case should be nailed to the outside of the sleepers, and climbers planted in the usual way.

Plants for fedges

Of all fedging plants, hedera (ivy) is undoubtedly the best – tough, evergreen, and relatively fast to cover a framework. The large-leaved varieties are the most suitable and *Hedera colchica*, with its bold, heart-shaped green leaves, is ideal. *H. c.* Variegata has the added bonus of really large leaves, the dark centres of which are in striking contrast to the soft, yellow, outer variegations. Hedera is also useful in that it tolerates shade – a point to remember when screening some of those awkward features such as compost heaps and bonfire areas.

Of the other climbers, aristolochia (Dutchman's pipe), lonicera (honeysuckle), passiflora (passion flower) and *Polygonum baldschuanicum* (Russian vine) can all be used, but be sure the lonicera you choose is an evergreen and remember that some climbers, the Russian vine in particular, will need continual pruning to keep them in check.

Maintaining a fedge

Fedge maintenance is normally confined to keeping it neat and tidy, removing dead leaves before they get clogged in the structure and pruning the more prominent climbers to keep them in hand. Pruning need not be too severe; if there is room, the climber can be allowed to run along the ground too, sweeping up and over the fedge in a continuous run.

Once established, the fedge will be a permanent and attractive feature, part of the basic framework forming a background for softer elements in the design.

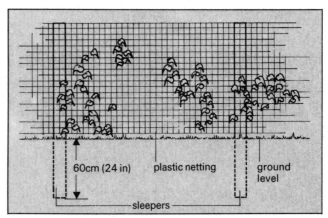

60cm (24 in)   plastic netting   ground level
— sleepers —

Left: fedge for the larger garden with climbers on plastic netting secured to the outside of railway sleepers
Below: climbers on wire frameworks bent to a variety of interesting shapes

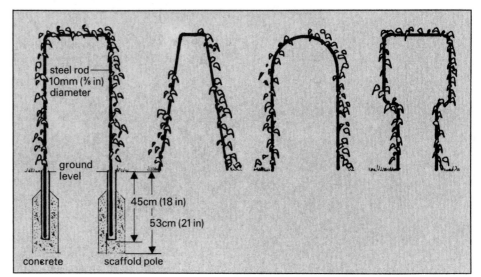

steel rod 10mm (⅜ in) diameter
ground level
45cm (18 in)
53cm (21 in)
concrete   scaffold pole

WALLS

Walls can be made from a variety of materials and take on several forms, suiting – where possible – the character of their surroundings. Here we outline some alternatives.

Walls are an integral part of many gardens, providing shelter and division, as well as an interest of their own.

We have already seen when laying the patio foundations (page 20) the constructional techniques involved in using a wide range of materials, but it is worth remembering that the initial choice of what type of wall to use can have an immediate and lasting effect on the design as a whole.

Walls can be broadly classified into functional and decorative, and to get the best out of either type it is wise to follow certain rules that are largely governed by the characteristic qualities of the material that you decide to use.

As with all design, try to be sympathetic to the immediate surroundings. If your house is brick, then use a similar brick in a wall running out from the building; if stone is predominant, follow suit. The incongruity of a Cotswold-stone wall in the middle of a brick-built suburban estate should be obvious!

First, then, you must consider what options are open to you, and how these can be used to the best advantage.

Brick walling
Brick is the most widely-available walling material, the range of finishes and constructional possibilities being vast. As a general rule, 11·5 and 23cm (4½ and 9 in) thicknesses are used for garden walling and, of course, the latter is stronger and more visually correct. An 11·5cm (4½ in) wall is obviously cheaper but will need buttressing every 1·8–3m (6–10 ft), depending on the height, and will look much too flimsy when close to a building. The top, or coping, of such a wall is also a problem. Bricks set on end tend to emphasize the visual instability, and the neatest finish probably consists of bricks cut in half (cut headers), or a neat pre-cast concrete strip.

Right, above: low, double stone wall separating patio from lawn and marking a change of level in the garden; the hollow on top of the wall has been earth-filled and planted with geraniums, forming its own miniature border
Right: see-through, honeycomb brick wall

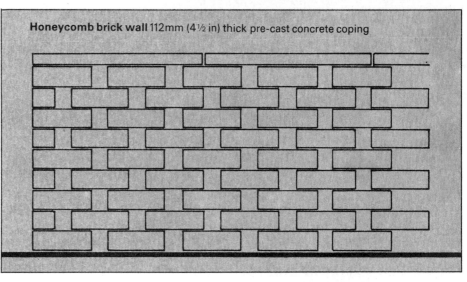

Honeycomb brick wall 112mm (4½ in) thick pre-cast concrete coping

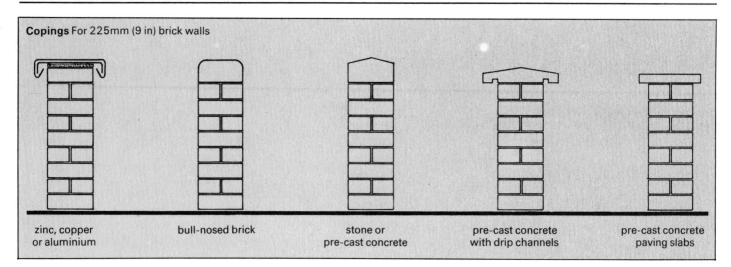

Copings For 225mm (9 in) brick walls

zinc, copper
or aluminium

bull-nosed brick

stone or
pre-cast concrete

pre-cast concrete
with drip channels

pre-cast concrete
paving slabs

Staggered wall

Top: alternative copings for brick walls
Above: staggering can be used to break
up a long, monotonous stretch of wall

A honeycomb, or pierced 11·5cm (4½ in) wall can be most attractive, combining the best of brick and screen blocks. It will still need buttresses, but farther apart as there is less wind resistance.

A 23cm (9 in) wall is best finished with a row of bricks on edge, although once again a wide variety of pre-cast concrete and stone copings are available. These might well be appropriate if you are matching existing walls in the garden or even a particular detail in the house itself.

If you want a particularly long wall, you may have to incorporate expansion joints at regular intervals. These are simply gaps of approximately 13mm (½ in) and will prevent cracks forming due to variations in temperature or possible slight subsidence. An attractive way to handle a long run of garden walling is to use a staggered pattern with sections overlapping one another, and then planting to add interest to the composition.

Stone walling
Stone is a superb walling material but as we have seen it must be carefully used, bearing in mind the overall design and locality. Here again, the thickness of a wall can vary and the coping usually matches traditional patterns. Working in stone is not easy and is a job best left to

craftsmen; don't let an odd-job man persuade you otherwise.

Walling with concrete blocks
Many people are shy of using concrete blocks for walling, feeling that they are too utilitarian. Such blocks, available in 115 and 235mm (4½ and 9 in) thicknesses, can be ideal, however, and the hollow pattern, measuring 235 × 235 × 450mm (9 × 9 × 18 in) is perfect for a boundary wall. The surface texture of blocks varies but some of the smooth finishes can look really crisp and architectural, if carefully pointed with a slightly-recessed joint. They readily accept paint and if you extend an interior colour along such a wall, the link between house and garden

Landscape bloc wall

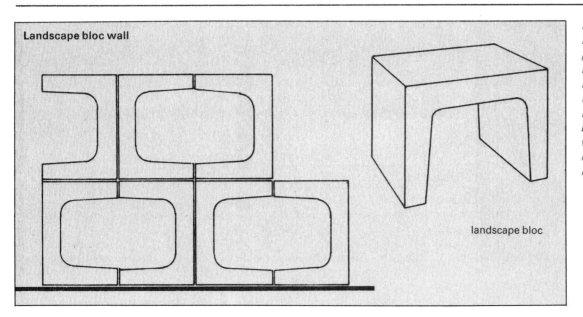

landscape bloc

*Left: the landscape bloc
is a new and versatile
pre-cast concrete unit
Below left: here the
landscape bloc doubles
up as a seat and a
retaining wall
Bottom: screen block
wall with fleur-de-lis
motif, a popular form
in town gardens*

Seat and retaining wall
Section

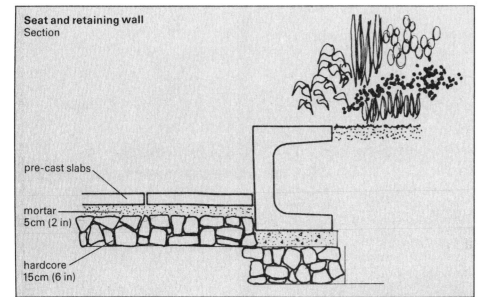

pre-cast slabs

mortar
5cm (2 in)

hardcore
15cm (6 in)

becomes particularly strong. Coping can be made either from brick on edge or a pre-cast concrete strip.

Walling with screen blocks

The ubiquitous screen block, measuring $300 \times 300 \times 115$mm ($12 \times 12 \times 4\frac{1}{2}$ in), is now one of the more popular materials as it is relatively cheap and decorative. Unfortunately, its very popularity has led to its abuse; it is used in every possible situation often without any real thought. In many cases, a honeycomb brick wall would be more appropriate close to a building, but when you are using screen blocks, try and be sympathetic, picking up any building lines and using lots of climbing plants to soften the outline. They can be painted, but do avoid prettying them; they look 'busy' enough already.

'Landscape bloc' walls

One of the most exciting walling designs in recent years is the 'landscape bloc'. Each bloc measures $560 \times 415 \times 415$mm ($22 \times 16 \times 16$ in), having a u-shaped section. These blocs can be put together to form endless permutations, not only for making screen walls, but retaining walls, steps and even tables and chairs. They are made of pre-cast concrete and the off-white finish is sufficiently unobtrusive to make them acceptable nearly everywhere. One word of caution though: don't get carried away with any good idea – a surfeit can be very boring.

The building of walls is not therefore an afterthought in the overall garden layout. Careful evaluation of your needs and existing features will be necessary to get the best out of the material you choose. In the final analysis, the old design criterion of 'simplicity is best' works every time.

Throughout the book we are trying to show how a garden can best reflect the needs of its owner. Much of the hard work involved in garden planning is taken for granted by a visitor and it is invariably the finishing touches that catch the eye, making or marring the composition.

Gates are just such details and it is worth considering which will be the most appropriate for your needs.

Front gates

The front gate is usually the most important of the property; first impressions count after all. A large garden may have two or more front gates, one for the drive and one for pedestrians. A smaller garden may only need one, while tiny spaces with just enough room for car-standing and the simplest design may well be more practical with no gate at all.

Pretension should be avoided at all costs – the incongruity of heavily-worked, wrought-iron gates in front of a suburban villa should be self evident! What is really needed is a link between house and garden, achieved by sympathetic use of materials.

Don't forget also that the gate should be in keeping with an adjoining fence, congruent with the latter's height and line as well as style.

Modern gates

If the house is relatively modern, with perhaps part of the exterior, garage and carport in white timber, it would be logical to have a boundary that follows suit. Here, a fence of horizontal slats would be ideal, with the gate or gates continuing in line in a similar construction; hinges and incidental details will be quite sufficient to indicate the entrance. Such a line will also increase the apparent width of the garden, while planting should be used to soften and emphasize the points of entry.

CHOOSING GATES

Front gates, back gates, side gates, farm gates, gates within the garden and gates without – all perform different functions and each should have a character of its own. A careful choice can enhance your garden composition.

Period gates

An older Edwardian or Victorian property has a different character and the gates should follow suit. Wrought iron could be correct here, but is expensive. A better solution would be to use a heavy timber construction, a solid five-bar gate being quite acceptable. If you are really keen on finding a 'period' gate it can be rewarding to keep your eyes open when you are out and about. Old properties undergoing conversion often yield un-expected treasures and the old gate, in need of some repair, is often dumped into a rubbish 'skip' outside the house.

A word about wrought iron here. It can be superb for gates in the right situation – no stately home should be without them for instance – but on a smaller scale you have to be careful. The 'off the peg' gates that are on sale at so many garden centres are at best scaled down versions of something grander, or, instead, poor examples of craftsmanship that really do

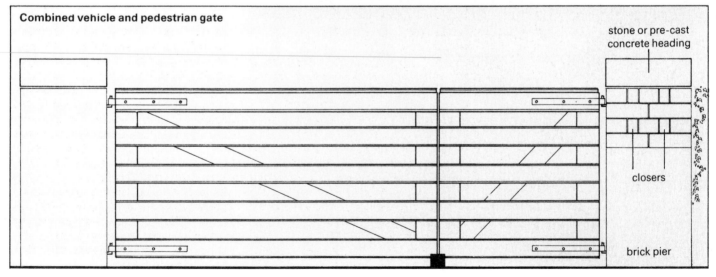

Combined vehicle and pedestrian gate

stone or pre-cast concrete heading

closers

brick pier

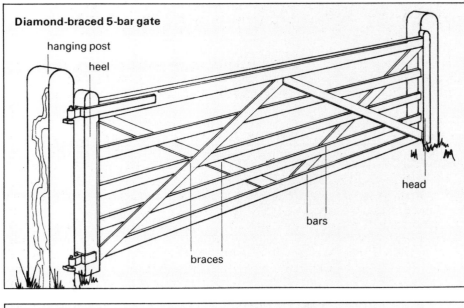

Diamond-braced 5-bar gate

hanging post
heel
head
bars
braces

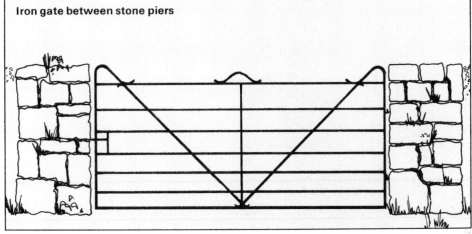

Iron gate between stone piers

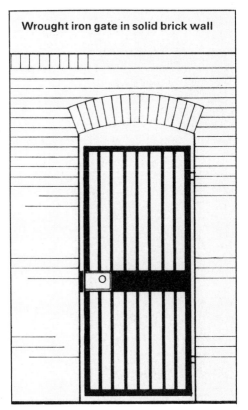

Wrought iron gate in solid brick wall

Many different styles of gate are available to satisfy the functional and aesthetic requirements of the owner. For a design to succeed, the style must be appropriate to the setting. Clockwise from bottom, far left: two-in-one, for pedestrians and vehicles; elaborate formality in wrought iron; traditional country-style 5-bar gate; simplicity in iron and stone; unfussy wrought iron for maximum contrast with brick

little credit to the makers or the garden they grace. As with all design, simplicity is the key; a plain wrought-iron railing and gate, for instance, is the perfect foil for a classical town house.

Gates in the country

Country houses, on the other hand, have completely different requirements. Here the locality is all-important and gates, as with all building materials, should respect both their surroundings and their neighbours.

Here, too, a front gate is often the only gate, serving cars, pedestrians and, if a farm, machinery as well. Sufficient width is therefore important and the usual opening for a gate of this type is 4·3m (14 ft). A private drive is smaller, 2·4 or 3m (8 or 10 ft) being ideal (the latter size allowing room for the ubiquitous oil tanker), while private footpaths should be 90cm (3 ft) wide.

In the country it can be most effective to contrast the gate with its posts, the solidity of massive piers acting as a superb foil to a simple iron gate. Remember though that the gate must always be visually 'lighter' than the adjoining boundary, a solid gate in a post-and-rail fence looking ludicrous.

Timber gates

Timber is by far the most common material in the country and gates should therefore be as light as possible whilst retaining maximum strength. It is standard practice to design the 'heel' (the upright timber that carries the hinges) and the load-bearing struts in thicker sections than the rest of the gate.

Weights of timber gates will also vary, depending on the wood used. Of the hardwoods, oak and Spanish chestnut are best, being the heaviest and most durable and weighing anything up to 56 kilos (125 lb) for a 3m (10 ft) opening. If wear is likely to be less, pine or spruce should be quite adequate, but remember that these need particularly regular applications of preservative and, of course, should be well seasoned in the first place.

All gates, whether in town or country, should open inwards, for obvious safety reasons.

In view of harmony

Having said so much about main gates, we should also look at others that are more utilitarian but nonetheless important. Back and side gates should blend with their surroundings. Gates in brick walls, where the wall carries over the gate, are usually best close-boarded, although this can be a situation for a well-designed pattern, in wrought iron, particularly if you want a view in or out of the garden.

Colour is also important and should form a positive link with the fence or the adjoining house. The fad for painting garden gates in a garish colour really has no merit. True, it draws the eye, but it detracts from all else and often foreshortens an interesting view.

In the final analysis, a gate should represent the way through a boundary, by using materials that are sympathetic and practical. Avoid anything flashy – this belongs elsewhere – and remember that simplicity is always best.

SLOPING SITE GARDENS

From a design standpoint, a completely flat garden raises problems, for it can so easily become dull and obvious. Slopes are helpful because they give variety and this can be exploited to great advantage. But sloping ground is harder to work than a level site and if terracing is introduced it can also be more costly to lay out. It is, however, extremely useful for breaking up the shape of the slope.

Here we confine ourselves to the methods of terracing. Then we go on to look at other ways of dealing with a sloping site, from paths, planted banks and rock gardening, to a variety of steps that can be adapted to sloping sites.

The first question you have to decide upon is whether to terrace and so convert the slope into a series of levels, or whether to accept it as it is. In a tiny garden it will have to be either one or the other, but where there is more space to play with it may be better to combine the two, contrasting the obvious artificiality of terraces with the more natural appearance of irregularly-contoured land. This can accord well with the common practice of allowing the garden to become progressively less formal the farther it is from the house.

One or two terraces close to the house may serve the dual purpose of providing comfortable outdoor 'rooms' in which chairs and tables can be placed when required, and at the same time providing a firm setting for the building. If a garden slopes uninterruptedly downward from a house, it will inevitably give it a slight appearance of instability, as if the building itself might one day begin to slip down the incline. An upward slope will give an opposite impression of the garden sliding down into the living rooms (and something of the kind does happen occasionally when freak rain storms

The gardens at Bodnant, looking from the croquet terrace to the rose terrace. Steps divide on either side of a fountain and pool, and the wall provides shelter for a wide variety of shrubs

Measuring with boning rods

← visual sighting

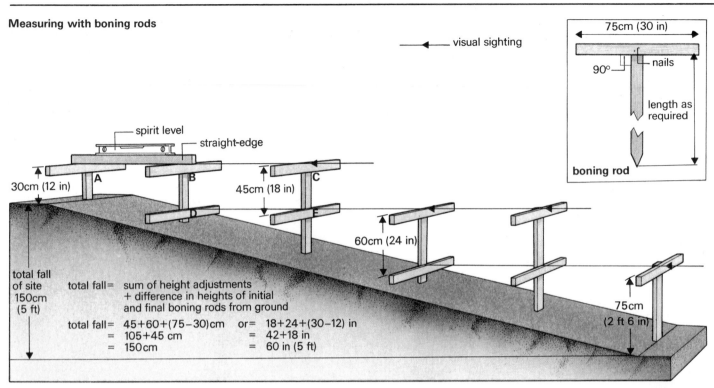

spirit level
straight-edge
A
B
C
D
E
30cm (12 in)
45cm (18 in)
60cm (24 in)
75cm (2 ft 6 in)

75cm (30 in)
90°
nails
length as required
boning rod

total fall of site 150cm (5 ft)

total fall = sum of height adjustments + difference in heights of initial and final boning rods from ground

total fall = 45+60+(75−30)cm or= 18+24+(30−12) in
= 105+45 cm = 42+18 in
= 150cm = 60 in (5 ft)

occur). Good wide terraces, solidly retained with masonry, can completely correct either impression.

In making good terraces, especially if there are several of them, it is essential that they should all differ in width, depth and treatment. The advantage of this diversity can be seen very clearly in some of Britain's famous gardens; for example, at Bodnant in north Wales, five magnificent terraces overlook the valley of the river Conway, and at Powis Castle, Welshpool, the slope is even steeper and the terraces more architectural. No one would suggest that in small gardens these grandeurs should be imitated, but they do forcefully illustrate the advantages of variety, and that is possible however modest the scale of the operation.

Terracing with boning rods

To begin with, draw a plan of your site to scale on graph paper. You will invariably find that slopes are steeper than they appear and it is absolutely essential to know what the differences in level are before embarking on any scheme of terracing. There is no need to use expensive equipment such as a theodolyte for this preliminary survey. On a small scale it can all be carried out with a straight-edged plank, a spirit level, and some stakes with a short piece of board nailed across the top of each in the form of a letter T. These are known as 'boning rods' and they are very useful for sighting across once a preliminary level, or for that matter any desired angle of slope, has been established (see diagram).

Armed with correct level distances, and the scale plan of the site, you can set about determining how wide each terrace should be, how deep its retaining wall or bank and how much, if any, of the land should be left with its natural slope. If the land falls across the site as well as along its length, it will be necessary for you to take levels in both directions, and then to make the required provisions for soil movement and retention.

To measure slopes for terracing First, drive in a short boning rod (**A**) at the highest point of the slope, and then place one end of the plank on the edge of this and drive in a longer boning rod (**B**) down the slope to support the other end of the plank. Lay the spirit level on the top of the plank and adjust the second stake until the bubble is at dead centre. This means that the tops of the two boning rods will now be level, and by taking a sighting across them you will then be able to drive in a third rod (**C**) farther down the slope, without needing to use the spirit level or plank again.

If the slope is steep, it will quickly become impractical to make boning rods tall enough to maintain the original level, so that instead you measure an identical distance down the last two rods, nail on additional cross pieces at this new lower level, and continue as before. The sum of the height adjustments made in this way, plus the difference in height from soil level to the top of the first boning rod and to the top of the last boning rod, is the difference in level from the top to the bottom of the slope.

Steep banks

Terraces can be retained by steep banks, but they may easily prove a nuisance to maintain. It is difficult to cut steeply sloping banks, and rocky banks take a lot of weeding. Ground cover can be fairly satisfactory, especially if some very soil-binding evergreen is used such as *Hypericum calycinum*, but then you must take care that it does not stray farther than it is required. Some small shrubs also grow well on steep banks, and in warm sunny places, cistus, available in considerable variety, can be very effective. There are also cotoneasters such as *Cotoneaster dammeri, C. microphylla, C. horizontalis* and *C. salicifolius repens* that thrive on sunny banks and, in the shade, both the

Right: natural approach to a gradient and formal effect (below right) at Dartington Hall in Devon. Below: an effective use of terracing and planting can transform a short, sharp slope into an attractive miniature garden

greater and lesser periwinkles (*Vinca major* and *V. minor*) will grow well.

Retaining walls

You will save labour in the long run by retaining terraces with walls and if they are cleverly designed and well built these also give the best effect. However, walls can be expensive, even when built at home, so it will be wise to check on the quantity of the stone or brick you would require and the probable cost before coming to any decision.

Whatever the material used, walls can be either mortared or unmortared (usually known as 'dry'). Mortared walls are strong and durable, excellent for climbing or trained plants, but useless as a home for plants. For that, dry walls are essential, with plenty of good soil packed between each course and uninterrupted access for roots to the main body of soil behind. In fact well-built dry walls, by simulating more closely the conditions rock plants are accustomed to growing in (often vertical crevices), are better for many of them than rock gardens.

Lewisias, ramondas and haberleas often prove difficult to manage on the flat, but are perfectly at home in the crevices of a good dry wall and this kind of gardening can become an interesting hobby in itself. Alternatively there are easy plants such as arabis, perennial alyssum, aubrietia and

Above: Cytisus × kewensis *on a dry wall*
*Left: sloping garden incorporating varying
styles, with artificial terraces at the
far end and a shrubbery in the foreground*

Stone and turf wall

Side section

Front elevation

180cm (6 ft)

turf

batter

rammed soil

30cm (12 in)

grass and plants
growing over wall

many trailing campanulas that grow profusely in walls either planted on the face or established on top and allowed to cascade downwards. A dry wall need never be dull.

Building a dry wall

These are built in much the same way as mortared walls with the important difference that soil takes the place of cement. They can be made with dressed or undressed stone, or any of the various building blocks available from merchants. Alternate rows of stone must be staggered to give the wall a bond, just as bricks are bonded in any constructional work. The first row of stones must be well

*Above: front elevation and side section
showing how to build a dry stone and turf
wall using squarish stones bonded with
turf that also acts as a planting medium*

bedded into the soil and if the wall is over 1 metre (3 ft) high it is usually best to build it with a slight inward slope, or 'batter', for greater stability. Soil should not only be spread fairly thickly between the blocks but also rammed in behind them so that there are no hollow places left. When mortared walls are made, leave holes every few feet to allow water to drain out of the retained soil; this is not necessary with unmortared walls since every crevice acts as a drainage channel.

Steps and balustrades

Terraces necessitate steps for access and again these permit considerable diversity in style, material and planting. There is no reason why steps should follow the most obvious straight line. Sometimes a change in direction can produce interesting shapes or contrasts of light and shade. Materials can be varied, too, possibly with panels or surrounds of paving brick to contrast with concrete or stone slabs. But steps should always be set in mortar for they are likely to get a lot of wear, and loose or irregular steps can be dangerous.

When steps require balustrades, these may provide additional scope for training plants, particularly soft-stemmed climbers such as vines or clematis that won't catch in clothing or harm anyone.

Terraces

Because terraces are so clearly artificial it is appropriate that their design and planting should be seen to be man-made. They are the wrong place for rock gardens and cascades and the right place for carefully-proportioned beds, fountains and ornamental plant containers. Garden roses look well on terraces as do other highly-developed flowers such as fuchsias, pelargoniums and many bedding plants. If your fancy runs to topiary, a terrace is as good a place as any on which to display it. Here, too, lavender can be used to form little hedges or the shapes of beds can be more sharply defined with clipped edges

*Above: 'stagger' steps for a soft effect
Right: logs with gravelled treads set
into the slope lend strength and charm
to a woodland garden*

of box, thyme or santolina (cotton lavender). In fact it is only when there are differences of level that the old-fashioned formal style of gardening can be fully appreciated, for you need to be able to look down on a pattern of beds or flowers from above to see it at its best.

Topsoil and subsoil
Terracing involves the movement of soil and it is important when doing this not to leave the relatively infertile subsoil on top and bury the good topsoil. To avoid this danger, remove the topsoil to a depth of at least 20cm (8 in) and stack it in some convenient place. Then make the necessary adjustment of level and when this is done replace the topsoil where it belongs, on top, but not under paving or other areas where there will be no plants.

Problems of subsidence
Soil that has been removed takes a considerable time to settle. This can be shortened by treading and ramming as the in-filling proceeds, but even then some subsidence is bound to occur over a period of weeks if not months. So it is unwise to be in too great a hurry to complete such tasks as permanent planting, lawn making and the laying of paths. It is better to make a temporary display with annuals and bedding plants and to cover paths and lawn sites with cheap, quick-growing rye grass, until the site is firm and no further subsidence feared.

Retaining levels around trees

When terracing a slope, the position of trees is an important factor. Most mature trees are very sensitive to any changes in level around the trunk or bulk of the root system.
To overcome this problem, make a shelf around the tree, using the existing level as its base. The size of this shelf should approximate to that of the canopy or spread of branches overhead and it will need to be retained by a wall where it drops down to meet the natural slope of the ground. The type of wall will depend on the
overall design of the area and it can be allowed to blend gradually into the slope on either side.
If you think the wall looks too severe, you can construct a platform using a steep earth bank to regain the lower level. You may need to stabilize this with planting; a rampant ground cover, such as Hypericum calycinum, Vinca minor *or* Hedera colchica *is ideal, as it knits together quickly and prevents long-term soil erosion.*
Young trees being far more adaptable, are less troublesome

PLANTING SLOPES

Having dealt with the methods and merits of terracing, it is time to look at planting schemes that do not involve so much labour in shifting soil and building retaining walls.

One method, similar to terracing, is to turn the slope into a series of banks separated by level paths. If the nature of the site permits it, both banks and paths can be curved to give the effect of an amphitheatre, although this may involve more soil-moving than would be necessary with straight banks and paths.

Grassed banks

It is unwise to put banks, straight or curved, down to grass without very careful consideration of the work this will involve. Grassed banks can look very effective, as many old formal gardens prove, but invariably they are difficult and tiring to mow. Since the introduction of light rotary hover mowers such as the Flymo Domestic, bank cutting is easier than it was, as these mowers can be moved freely in all directions, and be swung like a pendulum from the top of a bank. But it is still a fairly tricky job, for a rotary hover mower out of control can be a menace, since it will slide down any slope, cutting everything that comes into its path.

It is also sensible to make fairly shallow banks that you can tend from the adjacent paths with a minimum need to scramble on them. This applies equally, whether the banks are grassed or planted, for even the densest of ground cover will need some attention.

Planted banks

If you decide upon planting, the possibilities are almost endless, with the one proviso that the plants chosen must be able to withstand the sharp drainage and the occasional dryness of such places.

Small shrubs such as cistus and broom are ideal, as well as many creeping or sprawling rock plants such as helianthemum, aubrietia, arabis, alyssum and numerous campanula and dianthus (pinks).

Many grey or silver-leaved plants such as santolina, artemisia, anaphalis and helichrysum thrive on banks, but very rampant plants like cerastium enjoy the conditions so much that they become weeds.

Some sprawling roses such as Max Graf and *Rosa × paulii* grow well on banks, but their thorny stems make it rather difficult to move amongst them when they need pruning and weeding.

This is a case where shallow banks that can be tended from the level paths are almost a necessity.

Annuals and bedding plants usually thrive on sunny banks as many of them come from countries like South Africa and Australia, or areas of Central and South America that have warm, sunny climates. But most of these plants flower exclusively in summer and will leave the banks bare in winter, unless you include some evergreen shrubs as a permanent framework.

Bank gardening of this kind can produce effects just as formal and dignified as those characteristic of walled terraces, but at a much lower cost of construction, since no expensive walling stone is required. But many people do not like formal gardens or else they may wish for a gradual transition, from formality close to the house, to more natural styles farther away. This approach can offer numerous interesting variations, and sloping sites are just as suited to it as they are to terracing.

Plants for banks: helianthemum Brilliant (below) give a blaze of colour in summer and Artemisia arborescens *with* Senecio greyii *(bottom) give good contrast*

Woodland glade gardening

What is a little misleadingly called 'woodland', or 'woodland glade', gardening can be very satisfactory even on the steepest of slopes. There need be no forest trees in the woodland; indeed, unless the area to be planted is half an acre or more, there almost certainly should be none.

The woodland can be artificially created using small ornamental trees. However, avoid anything larger than a mountain ash or amelanchier (snowy mespilus) and mix in some of the smaller maples and birches, laburnums, ornamental crab apples, Japanese cherries (if the site is not so rural that every bud will be stripped by birds) and magnolias (which never seem to be attacked by anything).

If the soil is lime-free, rhododendrons, azaleas and camellias will thrive under the trees and, whatever its character, it will be possible to grow skimmias and hydrangeas. Below these again, you can grow herbaceous perennials, hostas (green, blue-grey and variegated), foxgloves,

Plants for woodland: Amelanchier canadensis *(left) has a height and spread of 3m (10 ft) when fully grown; woodland hosta (below) likes shade*

cyclamen, polygonatum (Solomon's seal), lilies of the valley, dog's tooth violets, snowdrops and daffodils. Woodland gardens do not produce a lot of weeds because of the tree canopy and so are easy to look after.

Rock gardens

Rock gardens, by contrast, can make a lot of work, for most of the weeding must be done by hand, but a naturally hilly site is ideal for them. It makes construction easy, too, since the rocks can be bedded into the slope to create the effect of a natural outcrop. Stone-chipping paths can be distributed in a natural way through the rocks, providing easy access to the plants. If you desire some more open spaces, they can be created with carpet-forming plants such as *Arenaria balearica*, various acaena and *Cotula squalida*, underplanted with small bulbs such as crocus and narcissus species, chionodoxas, muscari and scillas.

Small shrubs also fit well into the rock garden setting, not simply the dwarf conifers but flowering shrubs such as daphne, cistus, various small brooms, such as *Cytisus kewensis* and *C. beanii*, and shrubs such as *Cotoneaster adpressus* and *C. microphyllus thymifolia*.

AN INTRODUCTION TO STEPS

Most people think of steps situated in the garden as being regularly spaced, rectangular and straight. As a result, the majority of flights are built to a standard pattern, when often a different approach could provide interest and create an attractive feature that can become a permanent part of the 'hard' landscape.

You can construct steps from a wide variety of materials. Cobbles and stone, timber and gravel, concrete and brick are all available to form numerous permutations. The shape of the individual steps can be round or hexagonal and the flights can be staggered or straight. Whatever the composition, it can be softened by planting.

Steps for steep slopes

A steep slope normally requires a sensible, neat flight with a number of closely-spaced treads. You should vary your material to suit the situation: timber is less formal than brick which is not as formal as stone, pre-cast slabs and concrete. With stone or pre-cast slabs, make the tread overhang the riser by about 5cm (2 in). This will then cast an aesthetically pleasing shadow on the tread below.

Steps for gentle slopes

Gentle slopes give a wider range of choice, but remember that simplicity is the key to all design and in building steps, you are forming a pattern that should not become 'fussy'. If, for example, you are using a combination of brick and pre-cast slabs, be sure to arrange them in sensible proportions. Brick is dominant visually and is therefore particularly suitable at the top and bottom of the flight. Use a well-fired variety, and avoid soft bricks that may shatter in frosty weather. 'Bull-nosed' bricks, with a specially-rounded leading edge, are available for the front of the step.

Irregular steps

Steps that have free or irregular outlines present problems of their own. Slabs, stone and even brick are unsuitable as they have to be cut at the edges. This is a lengthy, laborious and expensive proposition, especially if you have to hire a contractor to carry it out. In this instance, materials such as concrete, tarmac and very small paving modules like cobbles, come into their own as they can all be adapted to a specific shape.

Big steps

Do not be put off by the idea of big steps; they give an impression of space and tranquillity. The infill is of brushed concrete and takes advantage of a technique used all too little in this country. It simply involves laying a normal concrete mix of 1:2:3 – one part cement, two parts sand, three parts aggregate – ensuring that the aggregate is made up from an attractive selection of small rounded pebbles. Once the job starts to harden, or 'go off', brush the surface carefully with a stiff broom. This will expose the aggregate and produce a striking marbled effect when dry. In very hot weather cover the surface with damp sacking to prevent damage. In frosty weather dry sacking will suffice.

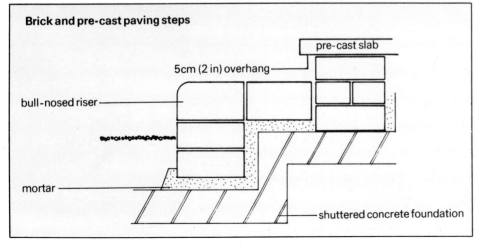

Brick and pre-cast paving steps

pre-cast slab

5cm (2 in) overhang

bull-nosed riser

mortar

shuttered concrete foundation

Above left: the charm of irregular steps of natural stone, seen at Wisley
Left: construction of overhanging treads, and bull-nosed riser for a bottom step

CANTILEVERED AND HEXAGONAL STEPS

A change of level in your garden gives you an excuse to build an imaginative flight of steps. Having given you ideas for steep and gentle slopes, and told you how to make steps from brick and pre-cast paving, here we suggest more ambitious designs to form focal points in your garden.

Cantilever steps

These are unusual steps and can be built to negotiate the face of a retaining wall. Concrete is best for this operation as you can bed reinforcing rods into the basic structure. You can easily adapt some types of lintel and these can be bought ready-made from a builder's merchant. Natural stone can be used in a similar way. Be sure that at least half the step is bedded into the wall and, as a general rule, try to match the materials so that the flight is compatible with its background.

Above right: set a graceful flight of cantilevered steps into a retaining wall Below: ground plan, showing how steps are set 50 per cent into the wall. Allow 5 cm (2 in) overlap between each step

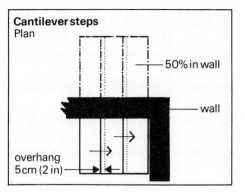

Hexagonal steps

In the ground plan drawing we show a series of interlocking hexagonal steps that would be ideal for linking two levels close to a building; the obvious geometry provides a strong visual link with the house. Each hexagon could be anything from up to 3m (10 ft) across with one step overlapping another to give a feeling of gentle progression. The low retaining walls forming the risers are approximately 15cm (6 in) high and built of brick. With big steps, 23cm (9 in) brickwork looks far better than 11cm (4½ in) and the extra effort is amply repaid by the end result.

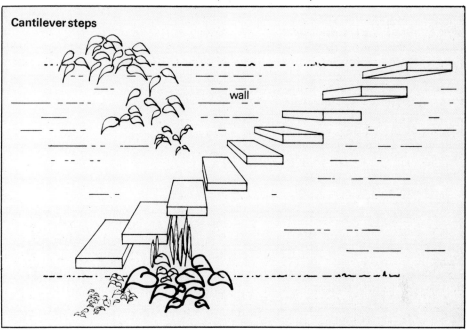

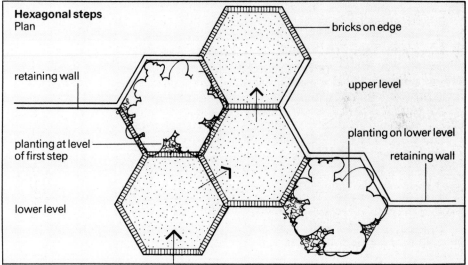

Above: ground plan showing successful use of hexagonal steps to link a relatively large area. Below: section showing foundation details of hexagonal steps

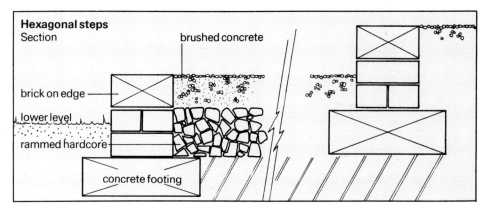

CIRCULAR STEPS

It is surprising how often you need steps in the garden. Now that we have described the art of making hexagonal or cantilevered ones, we look at circular steps and their construction.

As a general rule rectangular shapes link naturally with the house while circular patterns are more suitable for informal situations, woodland and the further reaches of the garden. Such basic rules also apply to individual features and circular steps can be particularly interesting in this context.

Circular steps
These may be of any size and can be built in a number of attractive ways. Where space is unlimited large circular brick retaining walls, up to 3m (10 ft) in diameter can overlap one another to form the risers of a slow, lazy flight. You can vary the sizes of the circle and fill them with a wide range of materials, including grass, concrete, cobbles and even tarmac, the choice depending on the underlying design of the area. The point to remember when dealing with 'free' shapes is that the infill material must be flexible, thus cobbles are fine, while pre-cast concrete slabs or stone would involve a great deal of cutting to conform to the pattern.

A 23cm (9 in) wall is structurally correct for the surround and this will need to stand on a concrete footing 45cm (18 in) wide, the depth being dependent on the conditions of the ground.

Concrete pipes for steps
Another simple and relatively cheap step is formed by using large-diameter concrete pipes. Sewer pipes are ideal, as they are available in a wide range of sizes from 1–3m (3–10 ft). Here you sink most of the pipe in the ground, leaving just enough of one end above the surface to form the riser of the step. Again you can vary sizes within the flight and a staggered pattern looks most attractive, with planting to soften the outline.

This technique need not be confined to dry land, stepping stones across a large pool being made in a similar way. In this case paint the outside of the pipe with a bituminous sealer (such as Synthaprufe) thus effectively disguising the depth of concrete below the surface. Fill the pipes with any of the materials already mentioned. It is, of course, essential to drain the pool while work is in progress.

Above: a dramatic effect achieved with the use of granite setts for risers, with half-setts for treads and cobbles as a top surface
Below: plan of another set of steps shows how circle sizes and surface materials can vary
Right: cross-section, with brick surround set below lawn level to facilitate mowing

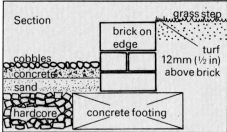

Section

brick on edge

grass step

cobbles

concrete

sand

turf 12mm (½ in) above brick

hardcore   concrete footing

Circular steps
Plan

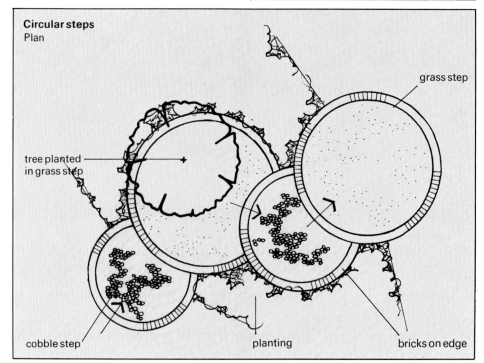

tree planted in grass step

grass step

cobble step

planting

bricks on edge

RAILWAY SLEEPERS FOR STEPS

Railway sleepers constitute a versatile material that will blend well into a natural setting. You can give a new lease of life to these solid timbers by using them as steps; they can also be adapted for paving or a retaining wall.

Timber is an essential part of garden design and is used in a wide range of applications from fencing to summerhouses and steps.

Railway sleepers, though often neglected, form an interesting and relatively cheap constructional material and are now becoming readily available as railways switch over to using concrete for track-laying.

Sources of supply vary; they can be obtained either from your local rail depot or from a middle man. In any event, enquire first at the rail depot, where you will normally be referred to the right person.

Sleepers are dark brown or black in colour, measure approximately 2·45m × 20cm × 13cm (8 ft × 8 in × 5 in), and need only two people to lift them with ease. This makes them ideal material for the rapid building of steps, retaining walls and raised beds.

As they have been weather-proofed with tar, you can expect sleepers to last indefinitely, and they can be maintained by a biennial treatment with a non-toxic wood preservative. Although creosote is in common use, remember that it is toxic and needs at least twelve months to become neutral and safe for any plants you want to put in.

Preparation and laying
In aesthetic terms, sleepers blend equally well with an architectural feature or a softly-planted bank, as their long, solid outline provides a feeling of stability and sympathy with the immediate surroundings. This is due largely to the fact that they are man-made from a natural material and so can adapt themselves equally well to fit into a natural or an artificial setting.

When you are considering how sleepers can be used in a particular situation, look at the overall design of the area.

If, for example, you need informal steps, use them in a staggered pattern and soften the outline with planting, adding one or two boulders for sculptural detail. In this instance, they can be laid 'dry' as the bank can be quite simply cut out to accept them and their weight alone will be sufficient to hold them in place.

You can create a more formal effect by building a straight or staggered flight of steps and filling the space between the sleepers with rolled gravel, hoggin (a binding mixture of clay and gravel) or crushed stone. This will give a long easy climb that would be perfect for linking a terrace with a less formal woodland or wild garden.

If the tops of sleepers are going to be exposed, as in the case of steps or paving, they should be laid upside down, to hide the bolt holes.

Below: a natural effect; front view of railway sleepers for steps and slopes, using a staggered pattern and softening the outline with plants and boulders
Below right: a side section of the same
Right: a formal effect; retaining wall, with sleepers and paving slabs in mortar

Paving slabs and retaining walls
You can achieve a really crisp architectural design by using sleepers in conjunction with pre-cast paving. The slab can either overhang the sleeper, possibly bedded in concrete, or sit flush behind it; the latter method allows the edge of the step to be clearly seen.

When you are building retaining walls and raised beds, work out the design in advance. Cutting sleepers can be hard work with a manual bow saw so try to borrow or hire a chain saw. The sleepers are stretcher-bonded in the same way as brickwork and either laid dry, or bedded on the soil, allowing plants to grow in between the joints.

You do not need complicated foundations for simple structures. Merely sink the first course into the ground so that the tops are flush with the surface. If the ground is heavy or unstable and high retaining walls of over a metre (or yard) are necessary, it may be advisable to bolt the sleepers onto steel angles in the ground before work starts. The wall can also be built to a slight angle, with several joints left open along its length to provide drainage.

A light or open-textured fill behind the wall will help drainage and lengthen the life of the timber.

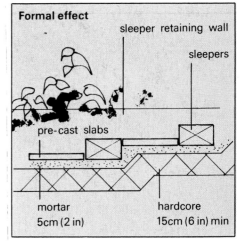

Formal effect
sleeper retaining wall
sleepers
pre-cast slabs
mortar 5cm (2 in)
hardcore 15cm (6 in) min

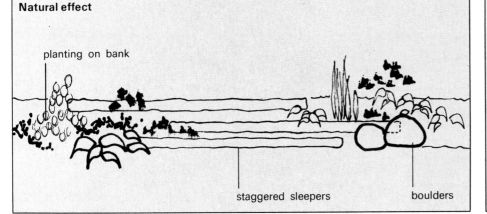

Natural effect
planting on bank
staggered sleepers
boulders

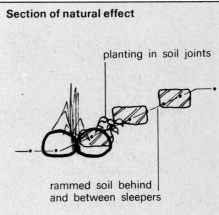

Section of natural effect
planting in soil joints
rammed soil behind and between sleepers

LOGS FOR STEPS

Log steps should be broad, easy and inviting, a natural material to lead you from lawn to wild garden. We also show logs used as paving, seats and stepping stones.

If you are lucky enough to live in an area where timber is readily available in the form of logs, you will find that you have the basic material for a number of interesting garden projects.

Logs have an informal character and are ideal in a softly-planted woodland or in the farthest reaches of a garden where different features need to blend with one another. They can also be used in more architectural patterns as a link between the obvious, regular geometry around a building and the natural setting of the open areas beyond.

You can use virtually any type of timber; the hardwoods include beech, oak and elm, and last the longest. If you are thinking of using elm, remember that it may have been affected by Dutch Elm disease and still be capable of harbouring infection. It is wise to strip the bark off any elm logs and burn it immediately.

Making steps
Steps can be formed in a number of ways, using long or short lengths. Don't worry if the longer logs are slightly bent or twisted, as this will add to the character of the flight of steps.

You can make wide steps using single tree trunks quite simply by bedding them into the slope and driving wedges into the ground in front of each log to prevent movement. The treads can then be filled with crushed stone, hoggin or rammed soil. The length between each step need not be constant as some variety adds interest to the flight. It's also a good idea to 'stagger' the logs and encourage plant growth at the sides to soften and hide the ends of the timber.

If you can only obtain short logs, say 50cm (20 in) long, you can still make steps out of them. In this instance, drive them vertically into the ground, close together, so that the complete row forms a riser of the desired length.

Retaining walls
You can extend this technique by using longer logs to hold back sections of a slope and create retaining walls. Once again, the pattern can be varied, allowing the height of each platform to be slightly different. If the bank is in an informal part of the garden, the spaces between the log walls can be filled with softly-spreading foliage. If, on the other hand, the area is more formal, it might be better to use loose cobbles in conjunction with boulders and architectural planting.

Paving and stepping stones
Offcuts can be particularly useful in a number of ways, either as paving or as stepping stones. As paving, sections can be bedded into mortar in the usual way, or laid dry, allowing the occasional low plant to grow in soil that has been brushed into the joints.

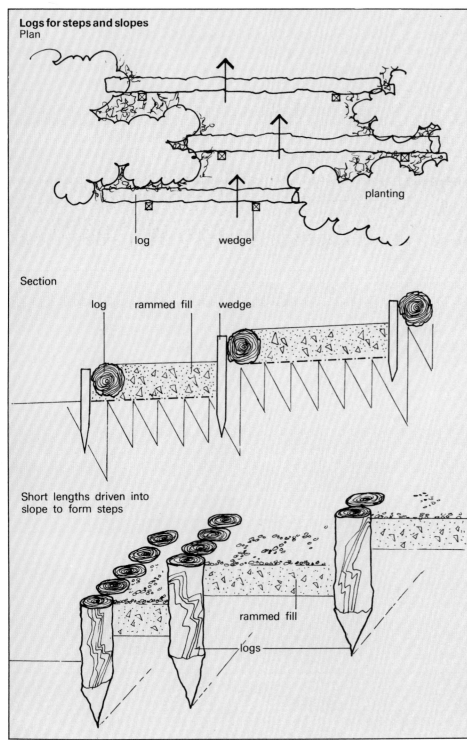

Logs for steps and slopes
Plan

planting

log   wedge

Section

log   rammed fill   wedge

Short lengths driven into slope to form steps

rammed fill

logs

Above left: ground plan (top) and section of single logs laid lengthwise to form shallow steps. The filling can be dispensed with if the ground is firm and the traffic light
Left: short logs, sharpened at one end and driven into the ground, also blend well into a country setting

Stepping stones can be laid dry, but if they are to cross a lawn, make sure that the logs are set just below the surface of the turf so that a mower can run smoothly over the top.

The 'stones' made of wood achieve just the right visual balance through planting and woodland, where real stone or pre-cast slabs might seem out of place.

Right: offcuts used as stepping stones make an effective pathway
Below: plan (top) and sections showing how to arrange logs as a retaining wall

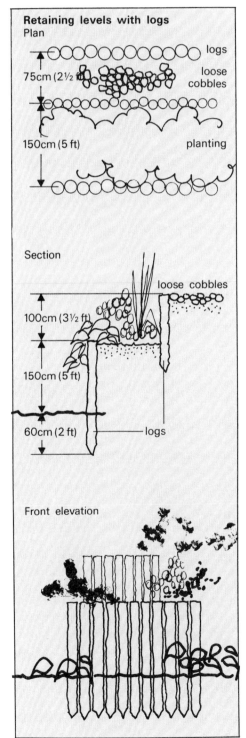

Retaining levels with logs
Plan

logs
loose cobbles
75cm (2½ ft)
150cm (5 ft)
planting

Section

loose cobbles
100cm (3½ ft)
150cm (5 ft)
60cm (2 ft) — logs

Front elevation

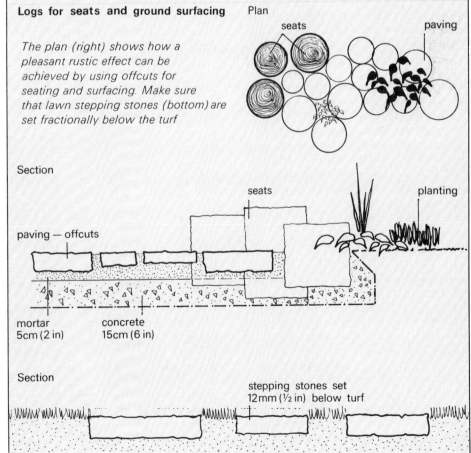

Logs for seats and ground surfacing
Plan

seats
paving

The plan (right) shows how a pleasant rustic effect can be achieved by using offcuts for seating and surfacing. Make sure that lawn stepping stones (bottom) are set fractionally below the turf

Section

seats
planting

paving — offcuts

mortar 5cm (2 in)
concrete 15cm (6 in)

Section

stepping stones set 12mm (½ in) below turf

THE FRONT APPROACH: improving your front garden

First impressions do count, as anyone who has approached a property with a view to buying it knows. And it is not only what the house looks like that is important but what its front garden looks like too. It need not be a riot of flowers, and since many frontages face north this is difficult anyway, but it must be welcoming. On page 61 we suggest how to decorate your front garden to good effect.

The standard front garden layout with separate garage and side entrance to the back door. The garden is split up into six strips of grass and paths, and fragmented with two circular beds in the grass. The effect flatters neither house nor garden.

Visitors to the home with a front garden area (and that, don't forget, includes the milkman and the dustman), want a hard, dry, easy access, with a minimum of steps or loose slabs, or eye-height hanging baskets. The driver wants room to park, with space for his passenger and himself to get out easily from his car without landing in a rose bed. If oil deliveries are expected, there must be easy access for the storage tank without the feed-pipe having to trail through areas of planting. The dustman wants his bins as close to his cart

as possible, as do you, to cut down on the inevitable trail of rubbish that is left. The postman, if he is allowed, will beat a path to the next house through your hedge unless he is deterred or directed another way. These are aspects of a front area as seen from the visitors' point of view – for them it is more of a place of arrival and departure than a true garden. With the visitors' needs in mind, now consider what are your own. You wish to present a pleasant face to the world and the materials you use to make up that face

should suit the style of house and location. For the front garden is often public and seen as one of many in a street or close, and while having a character of its own, it should not ruin its neighbours' outlook or strike a jarring note.

Types of enclosure
Consider the types available, and indeed whether you want them at all. Some enclosures will, of course, give you some privacy, will possibly keep your children and pets in and other peoples' out, and

Plan A (right): an improved front approach with carport extended to form a covered way, well-planned combination of paving, concrete and loose gravel surfacing and a shrub planting area for privacy

Plan B (below): an alternative, combining brick and stone or concrete paving, and allowing for an open grass frontage (this is sometimes a local regulation); shrubs provide a screened area to the left, with room for a favourite garden ornament

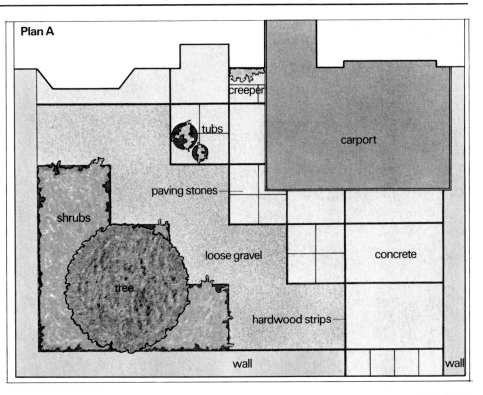

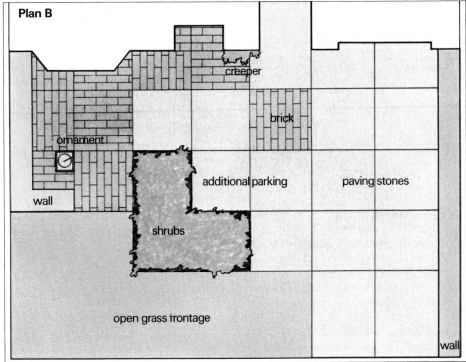

will also help to cut out noise if you are on a busy road.

Walling This is the most expensive form of enclosure, and if built in brick or stone to match your house it looks very smart. Concrete block, rendered, if you like, with a brick or slab coping, is a cheaper version.

Openwork concrete screening You can soften this form of screening with large-leaved climbers like vines rambling through it, but it is too heavy a material to use in conjunction with a small front area.

Fencing Coming down in scale, there are dozens of types of fencing available in timber. You can even try making your own over a small run. Consider, too, a combination low wall and timber fence, which has the advantage of preventing timber rotting along the bottom.

A more open fencing can be obtained by using picket fencing or railings. Fencing is also available in a glass-reinforced plastic such as Fibreglass, that needs little maintenance other than the occasional wash-down.

Hedging If you consider a hedge surround to your garden, think further than privet, which needs endless clipping, and *Cupressocyparis leylandii* (cypress), which will not magically stop growing at the height you want. They become trees 10m (40 ft) high in no time at all!

Other than the traditional type of hedge – beech, hornbeam, thorn or yew – consider holly, which grows slowly, needs little clipping and is a good deterrent for undesirable visiting pets. Or pyracantha, which with minimal clipping will flower and have berries. You could use the upright form of escallonia for a sunny position and even upright rosemary for a looser effect.

Planning out your front area

Within your selected enclosure, list the facilities you require on your site, whether you are starting from scratch or not – front access, side access, garage access and so on. If they can all work as one it means that the garden will not be cut up into masses of little areas with irritating spaces between interlocking paths that need to be filled with plants.

Do you require room to park a second car or a caravan or boat? Will these go in the area at the side of the house, if you have a space there, and if so can they be screened in any way? You may need a washdown area, a hard surface and a tap for this job and some form of drainage so that the surplus water does not flow into the garage. If there is an oil-storage tank at the side of the house, you must allow for access to this, and, of course, to the dustbin area as well.

Now make an accurate plan of the area, marking in the obvious locations for these functions, and join them together with hard surfacing. You should then at least have a practical layout. When moving into a house that the developer or previous owner has already planned, it is worth going through the same exercise even if you have to compromise with what you have inherited and what you really want. Even if this front area does not constitute a garden for relaxing in, your

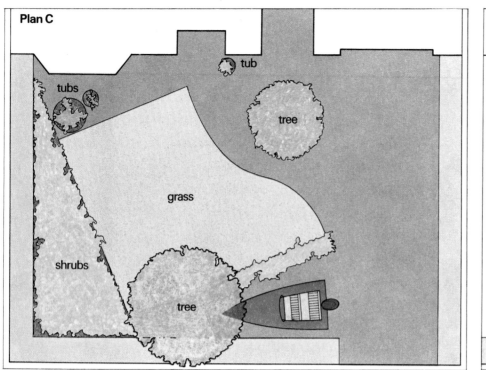

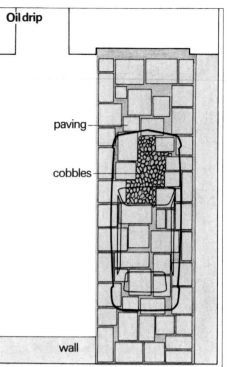

Plan C (above): a different free-form approach with small, manageable lawn and a tarmac or gravel surface, allowing for room to park a boat conveniently. Above right: a York stone drive-in with decorative cobbled oil-drip area for car

design should still divide off the more public area from the private.

Types of ground surfacing
Because the front area takes such heavy wear, the materials which you use to build it should be of the best (not necessarily the most expensive) and they should be well laid. Badly-jointed paving – crazy or not – can be lethal when grass comes through the joints, making the surface slippery in rain or with rotting autumn leaves on it. It cannot be over-emphasized that a good surface is the key to a serviceable front area. Stone in a country area and brick in a more sophisticated setting are very handsome as paving materials, particularly if you can use the same as the structure of the house.

Brick For paving, if you buy paviors, (which are slightly larger and thinner than a building brick laid flat and fairly expensive), you need fewer than if you paved with conventional building bricks. It is worth remembering, too, that while the cost of materials like brick, or granite setts, is moderately high, it is the time and labour of laying them that really puts up the price.

Old York stone Where it is available, York stone is ideal paving for a town garden, although it does become stained by oil. To prevent this happening you could insert a cobbled oil-drip area just under where the car usually stands.

Concrete paving stone This now comes in all shapes, sizes and textured finishes. If you are using the straightforward square or rectangular stones, stick to one colour, for it is only a front garden you are laying, not an Italian piazza! New paving stones come textured as granite setts, cobbled, or as stable tiles (rather like slabs of chocolate), and can be attractive in the right setting. The cheaper slabs tend to crack easily and are difficult to cut without breaking. Most of these stones should be laid on concrete if they are to bear the weight of vehicles.

Small interlocking paving stones are available that fit together not unlike a simple jigsaw. They are easy to lay, and being a small irregular element are ideal for a setting that is not totally flat. For a small-scale area, a small paving unit of brick or tile is more attractive than slabs of concrete.

Tarmac On larger areas of frontage you may consider using tarmac, or be talked into re-laying it on an existing drive by door-to-door representatives from small firms offering this service. While some are specialists in this work, many are not. Before parting with any money, obtain a detailed specification of the work they propose to do, ensuring that an adequate base and foundation are laid for the weight of car you put on it. Other possibilities here are coloured tarmac, or rolling a local stone into the surface for a gravelled effect, or just using areas of tarmac within paving. Do not, though, allow a firm to scatter at random the odd white chip in the surface which will end up looking like a piece of candy.

When surfacing with tarmac you will need a curbed edge of brick or concrete, or the surface will break away at the edges because of frost. As you will get a quicker water run-off after rain, you must look to your drainage as well.

Concrete A cheaper broad-scale treatment for the drive-in might well be concrete laid *in situ*, and brushed when nearly dry, or 'green' as it is called, to expose the gravel or aggregate in the concrete. It should be laid in squares to allow for expansion, and these can be broken up with brick or any other small element to make an attractive pattern.

Gravel The cheapest large-scale medium is probably gravel. The disadvantage here is that it is picked up easily and gets carried indoors, but if a foot-scraper is provided you should not suffer from this hazard. Be sure to lay the gravel on hardcore and 'binding' gravel. The latter is unwashed and the clay content hardens and binds it together. If you put the finishing gravel layer on too thickly it will bog you down; to consolidate the finished surface, roll and water it. Gravel comes either as a chipping from a local stone quarry (when it is sharp-edged and not too good for children to fall down on) or preferably rounded (washed by water).

After deciding on your ground surface, you can spend many happy hours considering what trees, shrubs and flowers to plant.

A view of the finished front approach incorporating improvements suggested in Plan A on page 59, with an extended carport, a combination of paving, concrete and loose gravel surfacing, and a shrubbery giving your home outlook and seclusion Overleaf: tubs to mark your front door: mahonia Charity (left) which flowers through winter to spring, and acanthus (right) with its characteristic leaves, which blooms in the summer

ADDING COLOUR TO THE FRONT GARDEN

We have just looked at types of enclosure and suggested varieties of ground surfacing to guide you in planning and structuring your front garden area. Now we give you a selection of suitable plants and shrubs to help you to determine its final appearance.

The plantings of the leftovers, the bits between the hard surfacing and against the house and garage should be fairly tough, with a good proportion of evergreen for an all-year-round effect. Evergreen conjures up ideas of laurel and privet (which incidentally are both effective when used well), but there are many other suitable plants, such as cotoneasters, certain viburnums, hebes, fatsia, senecio and choisya which are all attractive evergreens that flower, and some have berries too. These can also survive in an area with not too much sun. The ever-popular conifer, however, being by its shape a point-of-emphasis plant, is not suitable for most frontages.

In your layout, try to avoid little pieces of lawn which are tedious to cut, and consider instead areas of low ground cover. Here you will want something flat. Ivy is suitable in this situation, and hypericum (St John's wort or rose of Sharon), or low juniper would be admirable. Plant boldly and simply for the positive effect that is needed.

Before making your final selection of plants, do some homework on their ultimate size. A weeping willow in the middle of the front garden may look charming for a year or two, but very quickly grows to 10m (30 ft) across. And there is no point in planting shrubs on either side of a path if they need cutting back each year to allow you to walk there.

You could choose a particularly handsome sculptural plant adjacent to the front door, marking its importance. Tubs with bay trees have traditionally been used here, or, more recently, conifers again. But what about *Mahonia bealei*, or its near relation *M*. Charity? The leaves are an attractive, waxy evergreen, and the yellow flowers smell delicious in the early spring. Euphorbias (or spurges) make another good sculptural plant, or for a sunny situation try the upright-growing rosemary Miss Jessup. A good herbaceous plant in the sun is the beautiful-leafed acanthus.

Scent on entering a garden is always appreciated. Mahonia again is good, as is the evergreen *Daphne odora marginata*. *Choisya ternata*, the Mexican orange blossom, has scented white flowers and glossy foliage for cutting all year round.

If you are thinking of a climber up the front of the house or on the garage wall, consider a honeysuckle, for its scent. But, whichever climber you settle on, remember that it is the plant you have put there for display, not its means of support. Use simple wires running along the brick courses rather than complicated patterns of trellis that are liable to rot.

For points of coloured emphasis use window boxes, or pots filled with bulbs and annuals.

Highlighting your home

Lastly, if you provide a serviceable and welcoming frontage to your house, do help your visitors to find it. Put a name or number in a position not only visible to pedestrians but also to car drivers. It helps, too, if the lettering is legible and not too much in the mock Tudor rustic style. Let the name and number be illuminated at night, as well as any change of level at the entrance. With luck this may deter the night intruder, as well as guide the more welcome guest.

Top left: evergreen hebe Autumn Glory
Top right: the scented Choisya ternata
Above left: Fatsia japonica *in flower*
Above: Hedera canariensis *on tree stump*
Below: Mahonia bealei, *cultivated in Japan*

A SMALL TOWN GARDEN

Town gardens are often tiny, and here we look at their possibilities and their limitations. On page 66 we give details of construction and planting.

No two garden designs should look exactly the same, with their size, shape and situation all varying to determine an individual composition. Each site has its own difficulties and town gardens present their own quite distinct limitations.

First, space is likely to be limited, walls of surrounding buildings will cast heavy shade and the views will often be dull and oppressive. On the other side of the coin, shelter is excellent and the chances of severe frost are considerably less than in a garden that stands open to the elements.

Because the area is likely to be small, careful planning is obviously important, but it is also true to say that once completed, a town garden can be a real asset, acting as an extension of the house and demanding very little maintenance. However, in such a situation people often refuse to take up the challenge, feeling that the problems are either insurmountable or too small to bother about. They may be quite adept at designing the rooms inside the house, but the outside 'room' – probably much bigger – gets neglected.

When space is limited a simple approach is called for. Grass is often impossible in an urban area, with shade making growth difficult and concentrated activity quickly producing a quagmire. A hard surface, on the other hand, will provide a solid base for a table and chairs, children's bicycles and even an ironing board for those who like to do their household chores outdoors. Hard surfaces also dry quickly after rain and consequently get maximum use throughout the year.

Planting is important to soften the walls and take the edges off the inevitably rectangular boundaries. Some of the beds will be in shade, meaning that the choice of plant species is important. It is also very helpful to raise the planted areas – this not only gives the young shrubs and herbaceous material initial height, but it makes any maintenance considerably easier.

If views of surrounding buildings are gloomy, rather than increase the height of walls and fences in an attempt to blot them out, it is far better to work on the principle of creating a partial screen, utilizing a possible combination of trellis, planting and perhaps a carefully-chosen small tree. Overhead beams, running out from the house, are useful in this respect as well, giving support for climbing plants and giving a feeling of enclosure without being too dominant. As a general rule it is probably best to leave the beams as an open framework – a canopy of perspex or PVC tends to gather leaves and general debris and dirt.

Water is a definite asset in a town garden where hot summer weather can become oppressive. However, a conventional pool takes up valuable space as well as being a hazard for young children so a small raised pool, tucked into a corner, with a lion's head or other decorative spout, is a traditional solution. But several other interesting permutations revolve around the use of boulders, cobbles and even old millstones, water being pumped through and over them to form a delightful feature. By using these techniques you can emphasize an important fact – it is the sound of running water that really counts in providing a cooling influence on the immediate surroundings.

Perhaps the most important factor of all is the planting. It not only has to undergo close scrutiny throughout the year but also withstand the restrictions of shade and a partially-polluted atmosphere. Plants are easily affected by dust and dirt in the air and this can have the effect of blocking the tiny pores or 'stomata' through which they breathe. Some of the felty, grey-leaved species are particularly susceptible, the hairs on the leaves trapping and holding a thick layer of dirt that is difficult to remove.

These, then, are some of the factors and restrictions that govern the creation of a town garden; but they are by no means insuperable. With careful planning it need not be difficult to create a charming composition.

Planning our town garden

The garden shown here is typical of the 'yard' at the back of many older terraced houses, the main area measuring 3.5 × 5m (12 × 16 ft), while a side passage leads to a door out of the dining room. As with all garden design, we first drew up both a list of priorities and a plan of the existing area, marking in the north point, good or bad views, the heights of walls and fences, the position of drains, pipes, manholes, changes of level, doors and windows, as well as any existing vegetation.

If you have just moved in, look out for any seedling trees, particularly sycamore: if they grow to more than, say, 7.5m (25 ft), have them out. There are occasional exceptions when you come across the odd huge tree that, although completely dominant, is the making of a small garden.

The choice of surfacing

Many terraces have no rear or side access, meaning that all materials have to come in and out through the house. This makes careful planning absolutely essential. In our garden the existing surface was an uneven mass of poorly-laid concrete, and under normal circumstances you would think nothing of digging it up and loading it onto a waiting skip or lorry. In a confined space, however, this is a nightmare as every shovel load has to be bagged up and carried through the house. This is where a little forethought is invaluable: raised beds, as we have already mentioned, save maintenance and as the plants will thrive in 45cm (18 in) of topsoil this leaves a considerable height to be made up. Broken concrete makes good hardcore, is sharp-draining and will be an ideal filler for the bottom of those beds.

The raised areas in our design wrap themselves around two sides of the garden, just enough to look after the unwanted material and leave the ground clean. The main part of the 'floor' is given over to paving and measures approximately 3 × 2.5m (10 × 8 ft), the size of a reasonable room inside the house. As the house and the surrounding boundary walls were built of brick it seemed reasonable to incorporate at least some of this material in the 'floor'. A good, well-fired, second-hand stock brick is fine for paving, despite the advice of some architects and surveyors. It has the added advantage of an immediate mellow look. Our pattern of brick was based on the main lines of the building and this allowed for a second 'infill' material.

Light, or lack of it, is often a problem in an urban situation and if you can use a pale, reflective material, so much the better. White paving is probably best avoided as it tends to pick up dirt easily. We chose a pale sandstone-coloured precast slab. This mixture of materials ties the composition together while the water feature is emphasized as a focal point.

Devising a water feature

The uses of water in a small garden are legion and as our ground space was limited we decided to try a somewhat different approach. We placed a polythene water tank in the existing raised bed and neatly fitted into this a drilled slate slab. A length of copper pipe was pushed through the hole in the slab and a submersible pump was fitted and the tank filled loosely with large cobbles. When the tank was filled with water and the pump turned on, a steady flow rose through and over the slab, the pressure being just enough to lift the jet clear of the surface. This looked attractive, was pleasing to the ear and was entirely safe with young children.

Improving the side passage

The side passage was only 1.5m (5 ft) wide, a long narrow space that was difficult to handle. The kitchen window not only looked onto it but was in turn overlooked by the upstairs windows of the house next door. To raise the wall would have cut virtually all the light out and involved considerable cost. An attractive solution was to fit timber beams above the passage; we painted these white to reflect the light and they made an ideal host for climbing plants. The direct view from the neighbouring windows was broken and so was the expanse of

brickwork that formed the house itself. The floor of the passage was shady and as the door from the dining room was only used occasionally, we laid a simple stepping-stone path with pre-cast slabs. The gaps between and around the slabs were planted with two tough ground-covering plants, *Epimedium × warleyense* (barrenwort) and *Vinca minor* (lesser periwinkle).

Built-in cupboard for storage

Storage in a small garden is a problem and there are always things to put away, often in a hurry when unexpected guests

The successful combination of different ingredients is the secret of this pleasant town garden. Brick and pre-cast paving provides an attractive hard surface, while ground cover such as Vinca minor *Caeruleo-plena (above right) fills the planting gaps between paving slabs*

Small Town Garden
Plan

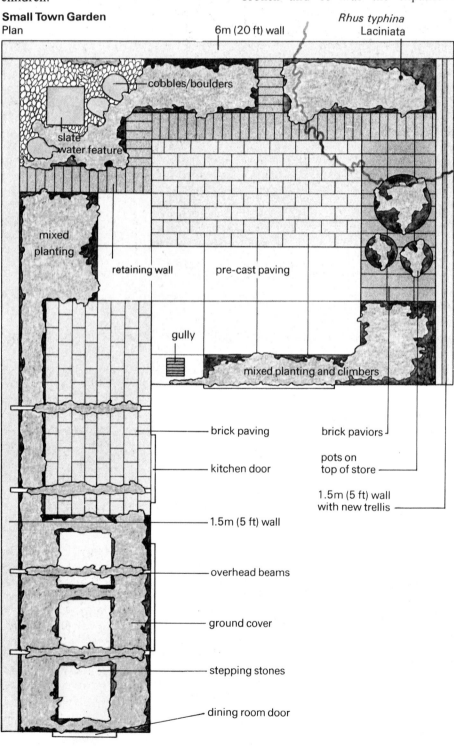

6m (20 ft) wall

Rhus typhina
Laciniata

cobbles/boulders

slate water feature

mixed planting

retaining wall

pre-cast paving

gully

mixed planting and climbers

brick paving

kitchen door

brick paviors

pots on top of store

1.5m (5 ft) wall with new trellis

1.5m (5 ft) wall

overhead beams

ground cover

stepping stones

dining room door

arrive. Instead of the usual motley shed we decided to build in a double cupboard of ample capacity. This fitted neatly with the raised beds and the top acted as both a worktop and a stand for potted plants. Remember that any storage outside, although dry, is likely to be damp in the long term. Lightly oil all tools and keep your cushions indoors; they quickly grow mould if left out, even in a cupboard.

Furnishing with plants
The planting of the garden finished the picture. Climbers are of paramount importance in a town garden, helping to cover and disguise the walls. Wires for support are neater and need less maintenance than a trellis and should be secured by masonry nails driven into the joints of the brickwork.

Make your selection of shrubs and herbaceous plants with the position of sun and shade in mind. Variations of leaf tones and texture are more effective in a small town garden than brash colour, evergreens being particularly important for winter interest. The whole plant composition should thus act as a backdrop to the completed garden, giving a balanced and welcoming display

CONSTRUCTING A SMALL TOWN GARDEN

We have now outlined the methods of planning and the limitations imposed by a small town garden. Here we take a more detailed look at the construction of the various features together with planting.

The various methods of laying paving have already been covered on pages 25, and 60 but it is worth repeating that all paved areas should be given a 'fall' or slight slope away from the house and towards any available gullies. This is particularly important where the whole outdoor area is given over to hard surfacing as puddles and slippery areas are a nuisance as well as being potentially dangerous.

Raising the levels
In order to reduce maintenance and soften the dominating surrounding walls we raised the main areas of planting at the back of the garden. The bricks used for the paving were matched in the raised beds and 230mm (9 in) brick walls. Although this was not essential from a practical point of view, it gives the composition visual stability, linking with the thickness of existing walls and being neatly finished with a brick-on-edge coping. We filled the bottom of the raised beds with broken concrete from the original yard surface and this provided good drainage for the subsequent planting. It is a good idea to leave an occasional open joint in the brickwork that supports raised beds, thus allowing drainage and preventing the soil from becoming sour.

Constructing the water feature
The main focal point is the water feature situated in the corner of the garden at the end of the raised bed. We housed this within a standard polythene water tank, carefully positioned so that its top is 4cm (1½ in) above the eventual soil level. We built two 230 × 230mm (9 × 9 in) brick piers inside the tank, using a 'hard' engineering brick that would not be affected by long immersion in water. The piers stopped short of the top of the tank so that the slate that formed the feature itself stands clear of the rim and the surrounding soil. As already mentioned, the slate was a fortunate find from a demolition site, but similar materials can

usually be picked up reasonably from a local monumental mason.

Offcuts of granite, slate or marble can be put to good use in the garden and the mason will usually be able to cut or drill any piece to your specification. Our slate was drilled centrally to accept a length of 12mm (½ in) copper pipe. This was pushed through the hole so that it was flush with the top, but projected about 5cm (2 in) on the underside, ready to accept the length of hose from the submersible pump. The latter was housed in the bottom of the tank and connected back to the house with the correct combination of exterior cable and sockets.

When laying a paved area it is often possible to incorporate an armoured cable underneath the slabs, thus avoiding a long run of wire above ground. Should you have any doubts concerning electrical work it is wise to seek the advice of a professional, particularly in the garden, where the hazards of moisture and accidental damage are obvious.

We left the final positioning of the slate, boulders and cobbles until the adjoining bed was filled with soil and the other features within the garden were finished, thus allowing any debris to be easily removed from the tank.

Building a worktop store
The next feature to tackle was the store cupboard that doubled as a worktop and stand for pot plants. We built the main framework with 115mm (4½ in) brick walls, each wall dividing the store into sections and acting as support for the lintels. The latter were of the 'prestressed' kind that are available from most large builders' merchants in various widths and lengths. The great advantage of this particular type lies in the thickness – approximately 5cm (2 in), as opposed to a cast lintel that takes anything up to 15cm (6 in) to achieve the same strength. We used three 23cm (9 in) wide lintels, (firmly bedded side by side in mortar) on top of the walls. We then laid glazed paving bricks 25mm (1 in) thick to form the top of the cupboard, the first course overhanging the front by 25mm (1 in).

The doors were constructed with tongue-and-groove boards, and then painted with a primer, undercoat and white topcoat. The hinges, catches and screws are brass, to resist rust.

The water feature, set amongst planting in the raised bed, makes a delightful focal point and, in the summer, has a cooling effect on the whole garden

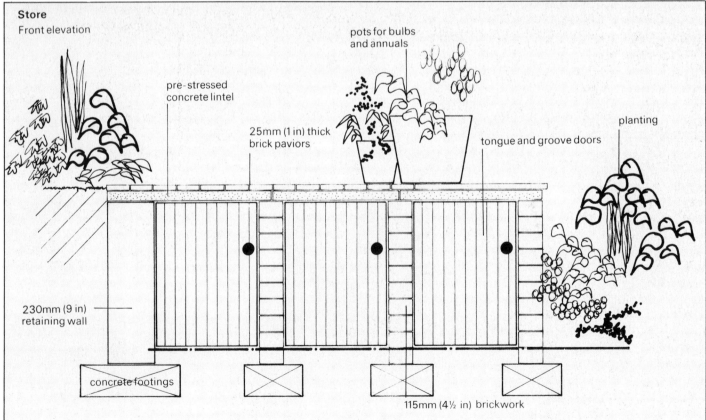

Store
Front elevation

pre-stressed
concrete lintel

pots for bulbs
and annuals

25mm (1 in) thick
brick paviors

tongue and groove doors

planting

230mm (9 in)
retaining wall

concrete footings

115mm (4½ in) brickwork

Decorating the passageway

The white beams that run over the passage to the dining room were hung next. These are constructed from 230 × 50mm (9 × 2 in) timbers and supported on the house side by joist hangers while scaffold poles form the uprights into the top of the wall.

The exact details are similar to those given for our Barbecue Garden on page 70. In order to help climbing plants onto the beams, we screwed metal eyes into the undersides and passed a wire through them. Once a plant has reached the required height it is simple enough to tuck the stems under the wire and eventually form an attractive canopy of vegetation. The wires also help maintenance as the eyes can be removed and the whole plant lowered when the beams need painting.

Filling the water tank

Before tackling the planting we finished the water feature by loosely filling the tank with large stones and cobbles. The hose from the pump we connected to the pipe inserted in the slab with a jubilee clip, and then the slate was carefully positioned on top of the brick piers. More loose cobbles and several boulders disguised the lip of the tank, the latter being filled with water to within 8cm (3 in) of the top. When the pump was switched on, water bubbled up through the slate and slid smoothly over the surface to descend into the tank in a continuing cycle.

The choice of planting

The last major operation involved planting and the preparation of the beds themselves. New soil was absolutely essential as what little there was from the original yard was of poor quality and extremely 'tired'. It is at this point that town gardeners score over their country cousins as they can virtually select the

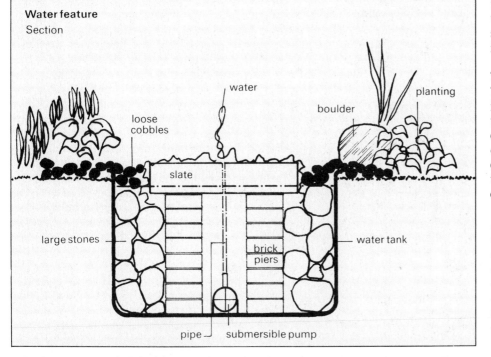

Water feature
Section

water

planting

boulder

loose cobbles

slate

large stones

brick piers

water tank

pipe

submersible pump

Far left, above: Fatsia japonica *is decorative in a shady situation*
Far left, below: the store cupboard acts as a work bench and a pot plant stand
Left: internal structure of the water feature is not completed until other construction work is finished
Below: Hydrangea macrophylla *Blue Wave*

type of soil they need. If you are a lover of rhododendrons, camellias or other acid-loving plants it is easy enough to prepare a soil of the correct pH value.

In town gardens shade is often a limiting factor but it should be remembered that the range of plants that enjoy these conditions is by no means small. In our garden, as you can see from the suggested planting plan, we have used many shade-lovers, some of which are described here. *Fatsia japonica* (fig-leaf palm of Japanese aralia) with its fine sculptural evergreen foliage is a good choice, together with *Hosta sieboldiana* (plantain lily) that contrasts with the upright form of *Iris foetidissima* Lutea.

Hydrangeas are invaluable and we have chosen one of the prettiest 'lacecap' varieties, *Hydrangea macrophylla* Blue Wave. *Viburnum davidii*, that grows into a compact rounded shrub, is another evergreen with attractive purple berries.

For vertical emphasis we have included *Rhus typhina* Laciniata, a small sumach tree of sculptural habit that can be carefully shaped to enhance its dramatic branch formations.

Climbers too are of paramount importance. *Jasminum nudiflorum* (winter jasmine), or the climbing *Hydrangea petiolaris* are particularly useful on a shady wall as is Virginia creeper, a good variety of which is *Parthenocissus tricuspidata* Veitchii. An unusual climber is featured on one of the beams, *Aristolochia durior* or *macrophylla* (Dutchman's pipe), taking its common name from the oddly-formed flowers. This, too, is happy in sun or semi-shade. Actinidia (Chinese gooseberry) is ideal for a sunny position while the many varieties of lonicera (honeysuckle) are invaluable for their fragrant blooms.

As planting is inevitably small when first introduced to its new home, it is a good idea to fill the initial gaps with bulky annuals and of course, bulbs. Nicotiana (tobacco plant) and matthiola (stocks) give the bonus of scent while helianthus (sunflowers) have more dramatic qualities to add in these early stages.

Imaginative planting clothes the composition, softening the hard line of walls and providing a backdrop to your outside room throughout the year.

Small Town Garden
Planting plan

Our planting plan shows one way to 'furnish' your garden with a variety of plants from bulbs to climbers. The ground plan, with details of other features, is given on page 64

Key to planting plan

Numerals after names denote quantities of plants

1 *Parthenocissus tricuspidata* Veitchii (Virginia creeper) ×1
2 *Iris foetidissima* Lutea ×4
3 *Hydrangea macrophylla* Blue Wave ×1
4 *Viburnum davidii* ×3
5 *Rhus typhina* Laciniata (sumach) ×1
6 *Vinca minor* (lesser periwinkle) ×9
7 Bulbs and annuals in plots
8 *Rosmarinus officinalis* Miss Jessop's Variety (rosemary) ×1
9 *Salvia officinalis* Purpurascens (common sage) ×1
10 *Festuca ovina* Glauca (blue fescue grass) ×7
11 *Hebe pinguifolia* Pagei (veronica) ×3
12 *Actinidia chinensis* (Chinese gooseberry) ×1
13 *Hypericum calycinum* (rose of Sharon) ×24
14 *Hedera canariensis* Gloire de Marengo (Canary Island ivy) ×1
15 *Lonicera japonica halliana* (honeysuckle) ×1
16 *Lonicera japonica* Aureoreticulata (honeysuckle) ×1
17 *Pachysandra terminalis* ×24
18 *Aristolochia (durior) macrophylla* (Dutchman's pipe) ×1
19 *Jasminum nudiflorum* (winter jasmine) ×1
20 *Hedera helix* Glacier (common ivy), as ground cover ×3
21 *Fatsia japonica* (Japanese aralia or fig-leaf palm) ×1
22 *Bergenia cordifolia* (pig squeak) ×5
23 *Hosta sieboldiana* (plantain lily) ×3

PLANNING A GARDEN AROUND A BARBECUE

A tempting design for outdoor living Overleaf: ground plans showing the terrace before and after redesigning. New features include the barbecue itself, a storage space and an L-shaped seat; an extended concrete and brick-paved area that will accomodate guests and garden furniture; and two extra walls, to provide shelter

Weather permitting, there's nothing so relaxing as eating out of doors whether it be a simple 'al fresco' meal or an elaborate barbecue party. Here we tell you how to plan a barbecue garden, and then we give instructions on how to build the brick barbecue.

Barbecue Garden

Original terrace
Ground plan

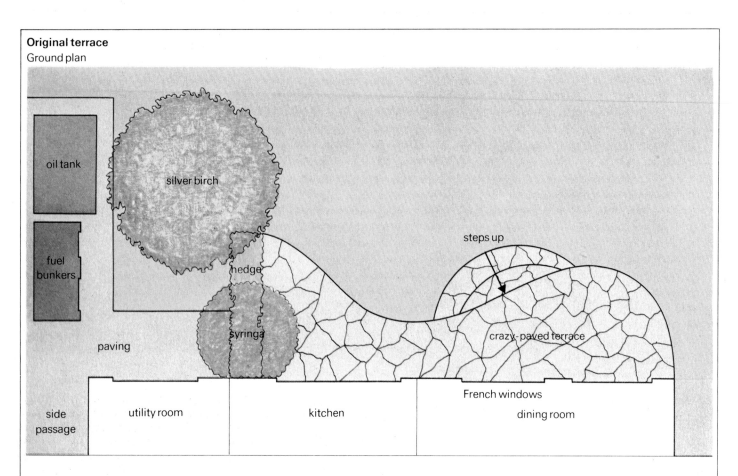

oil tank

fuel bunkers

silver birch

hedge

syringa

paving

steps up

crazy-paved terrace

French windows

side passage

utility room

kitchen

dining room

Redesigned terrace
Ground plan

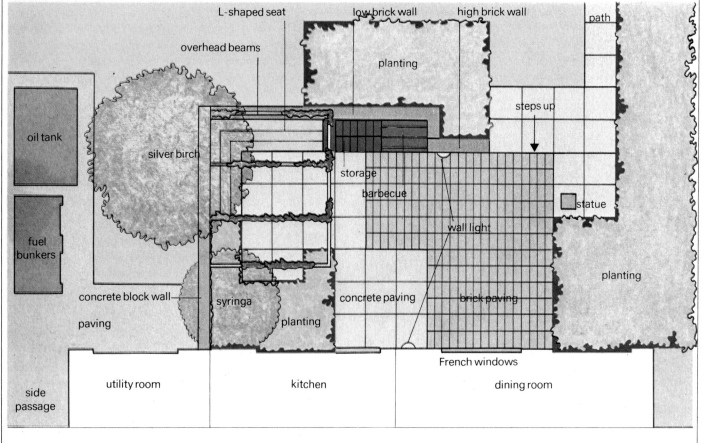

L-shaped seat

low brick wall

high brick wall

path

overhead beams

planting

steps up

oil tank

silver birch

storage

barbecue

statue

wall light

fuel bunkers

concrete block wall

syringa

planting

concrete paving

brick paving

planting

paving

French windows

side passage

utility room

kitchen

dining room

Living in the garden is not a new concept; both the Romans and the Persians built their houses around a central courtyard to benefit from shade and seclusion.

In Britain, however, it is really only during the last few decades that we have developed the 'outside room', allowing a whole range of activities, from household chores to full-scale meals, to take place in the garden.

As an occupation, barbecuing is relatively recent. The idea has been largely borrowed from the Americans who are expert at exploiting the backyard for every conceivable purpose. Barbecues do not appeal to everybody; for example, many people have been put off for life by a poorly-built model that coats both food and guests with charcoal powder.

Planning your barbecue

If you want to build your own barbecue, it is best to consider not only the barbecue grill itself, but the whole area that surrounds it. This space may be used for many different purposes, from children on bikes to family sun-bathing.

It is sometimes thought that a barbecue needs to face a prevailing wind. It is true that a good draught does help, but most small gardens are likely to be overshadowed by buildings and trees, and the subsequent turbulence means that winds may come from any direction. As a general rule, it is best to choose a site that is reasonably close to the house, but not directly under a window.

Barbecuing invariably involves groups of people, so a hard surface underfoot is essential, and the size of your paved area should not be less than 3.5×3.5m $(12 \times 12$ ft). This will allow room for a table and chairs for at least four people to sit around in comfort. Ideally, it should be 4.5×6m $(15 \times 20$ ft), the size of a large room inside a house.

Changing existing features

Before starting any work in the garden, have a careful look at the existing features and see how these could improve or detract from the finished design. In the garden we show, this was especially important, as the site had a marked fall away from the house, a scrubby hedge running up to the kitchen window and a view of an unsightly oil tank.

The first task was to create a level area outside the French doors that led from the dining room. As we wanted a large terrace we decided to use two paving materials: pre-cast slabs and brick. The latter material will provide contrast, in addition to visual link with the brickwork of the house.

Jasminum officinale, *common white jasmine, for softening overhead beams*

It is worth noting that the composition is built up from a series of interlocking rectangles; this design tends to extend the link visually between the house and the garden. When laying out the paving design, you should start from an obvious corner of the building and continue this pattern so that features are tied together. In our design you can see how the barbecue is strongly aligned with the French windows by the bold panel of brick. A seat in turn is held in place by the wall, while the beams bring a third dimension into play, forming the 'ceiling' of this outside room.

The area now began to take shape, but it still seemed exposed, particularly as the garden slopes away from the new side steps down from the terrace. To overcome this problem, we built another wall, at right-angles to the first one, but lower. This gave shelter on three sides and still allowed an attractive view across the lawn. The building of this second wall also gave ample room to incorporate the white seat and the barbecue itself, both becoming intentionally solid features within the overall design.

Brick for the barbecue

We built the barbecue from brick, and although this entails a reasonable amount of work, it is durable as well as being easily adapted to fit any situation. Nor need it be confined to its main function of cooking; it is large enough to have a paved worktop, set over a storage space for tools, charcoal and accessories.

It is best to use a glazed brick or quarry tile for the top, as these materials sponge down more easily than conventional bricks. However, beware of using *glazed* tiles; these look fine inside the home but frosty winters can soon shatter their surface. During the winter the grill and its supporting steel rods are best removed. This leaves a sunken rectangular space that you can then use as a tailor-made window box, filling it with bulbs or trailing plants that will provide a winter and spring display.

Plants for your terrace

Generally, planting should soften and surround the whole background area. In our garden we were lucky enough to have the lilac and, behind the new wall, a silver birch whose foliage came drooping down between the white, overhead beams. The walls themselves needed clothing and we have created new beds that would not interfere with access between indoor kitchen and outdoor barbecue grill.

Climbers are particularly useful, while the beds to either side of the steps contain a selection of flowering and evergreen plants that will provide colour and interest throughout the year. Fast and slower-growing plants are mixed and the initial gaps are filled with bulbs and annuals for colour. In this case, annuals can be quite simply hand-sown *in situ*, the drifts being thinned as they develop, a cheaper and quicker method than bedding out individual plants. Hand-sowing also results in more informal groupings that associate well with paved areas, avoiding the desperate regularity of most traditional bedding schemes.

BUILDING A BRICK BARBECUE
in your garden

The overall design of this barbecue garden was illustrated on page 71. Here we show the siting of the barbecue grill itself and give constructional details for building the major features.

For the 'floor' of this barbecue garden we chose brick or pre-cast paving and methods for laying these were given on pages 25 and 27.

Concrete block wall

The high wall running out from the house is a different matter, however, being built from hollow concrete blocks, a versatile material that could be used in the garden far more than it is. Concrete blocks come in a number of different sizes, the two most common being $115 \times 455 \times 230$mm ($4\frac{1}{2} \times 18 \times 9$ in), or $230 \times 455 \times 230$mm ($9 \times 18 \times 9$ in). They are constructed to withstand great pressure and are available in a rough or smooth finish, either of which can be given a finishing coat of stone paint.

Their size allows work to take shape quickly but it does mean that they are heavy, particularly in the larger size that you will need to use for a wall of anything over $1 \cdot 2$m (4 ft) high. Walls 230mm (9 in) thick, made either of block or brick, are visually and structurally most sound for garden work. Thinner walls of 115mm ($4\frac{1}{2}$ in) inevitably need buttresses and these detract from the appearance of the whole.

The wall here is $2 \cdot 3$m ($7\frac{1}{2}$ ft) high and for this you will need a good concrete 'footing' or foundation that will be twice as wide as the wall itself. The depth of the concrete will depend on the nature of the ground. If you are building on solid rock, virtually no footing is needed, but if the ground is marshy you will need an ample depth. On reasonable ground, as a general rule, a 75cm ($2\frac{1}{2}$ ft) trench, 45cm (18 in) wide is quite enough. This can be filled with 60cm (24 in) of concrete and allows the first course of blocks to be laid just below ground level.

You should use a simple stretcher bond, that is, lay all the blocks lengthways and stagger the joints, checking the levels as work progresses. Once five or six courses have been built, you will need a

simple scaffold or stage from which to work. Two people make the job a lot easier, with one laying blocks and the other mixing mortar and passing up the blocks as they are needed.

Joist hangers for overhead beams

As the wall nears completion you have to consider the insertion of 'joist hangers' that will hold the white overhead beams in place. These are triangular-shaped 'shoes', open at one end and with a strap that can be bedded between the top row of blocks and the brick on edge that acts as a coping. On some walls you will notice a double row of tiles just below the coping; this is known as 'creasing' and acts as a damp course that prevents water from penetrating into the top of the wall.

Low brick wall

The second, lower 1m ($3\frac{1}{2}$ ft) high wall is built of brick and will act as a host for the seat and barbecue.

On page 23 we showed a brick retaining wall built with English bond using alternate courses of headers and stretchers, or one course of bricks end on and the next one of bricks lengthways. For this wall you might try Flemish bond, where two stretchers and then a header are laid (see diagram) in the same course; this shows a pleasing finish without being difficult to build. It is essential to check your levels while working and make sure you point the joints (see page 18) at the end of each bricklaying session. With this wall you have to turn through 90 degrees behind the barbecue and, in order to marry the two angles together, you will need to cut a 'closer' brick to ensure the bond is correct (see diagram). The coping here will be brick, on edge again, but it is normal to omit the tile creasing from walls of this height.

Above right: section of joist hanger embedded in concrete block wall between top block and coping
Right: section of barbecue wall with brick laid in Flemish bond and with a 'closer' cut to accommodate the 90° turn
Far right: section of brick barbecue area showing store cupboard, adjustable cooking grill and high, sheltering wall

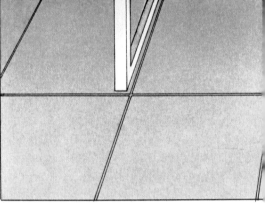

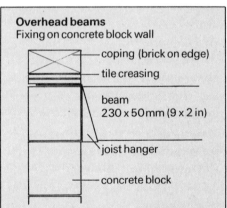

Overhead beams
Fixing on concrete block wall

- coping (brick on edge)
- tile creasing
- beam 230 x 50mm (9 x 2 in)
- joist hanger
- concrete block

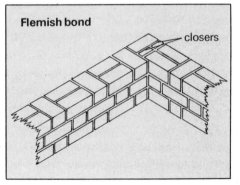

Flemish bond

- closers

Barbecue
Front elevation

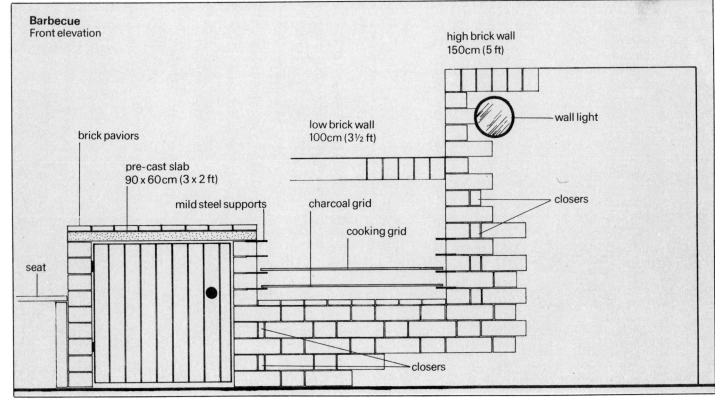

brick paviors

pre-cast slab
90 x 60 cm (3 x 2 ft)

mild steel supports

seat

low brick wall
100cm (3½ ft)

charcoal grid

cooking grid

high brick wall
150cm (5 ft)

wall light

closers

closers

Brick barbecue and high wall

The barbecue and the final 1·5m (5 ft) wall are built together. The barbecue is made up of two units: the store and the actual cooker. Construct the store with a single shelf and top it with a working surface. A simple 900 × 600mm (3 × 2 ft) pre-cast concrete paving slab can act as a bed for the final finish of glazed paving bricks, or 'paviors'. Make the door from tongue and groove boards, but remember that the hinges, screws and catch should be of brass or a non-ferrous metal, to stop rust.

Below grill level, the barbecue is a solid structure and the cavity formed by the four surrounding walls should be filled with rubble and hardcore, and surfaced with glazed paving bricks. As the walls rise on either side, remember that at the sixth and subsequent courses you have to allow for the supports to hold the adjustable cooking grid. If you want a higher cooking level you must take this

into consideration. Continue building the 1·5m (5 ft) wall in a Flemish bond with 'closers' as illustrated in diagram 2.

Barbecue grid

Modern foot-scrapers make remarkably effective grids and these can be held easily on several levels by 6mm ($\frac{1}{4}$ in) mild steel strips bedded into the joints of the brickwork. Alternatively, a garage or local engineer will often make up a grid of any size or specification for a reasonable charge. If you are burning charcoal, a second grid or tray can be used on the lowest position, but the beauty of a brick-built barbecue is that it will accept logs that can be burned directly on the brick top; they also give the cooked food a delicious flavour.

Garden seat

Once the barbecue is finished you are ready to build the seat to the left of the store. This can have an open or closed front, the latter being a little more complicated and expensive. The top consists of six lengths of 200 × 20mm ($7\frac{3}{4} \times \frac{7}{8}$ in) boards which you screw into 50 × 50mm (2 × 2 in) frames (see seat diagrams). In turn, the frames are plugged and screwed into the brick and concrete walls and paving. A neatly-

Left: down support married into beam
Below and below right: L-shaped garden seat of six boards screwed into frames, secured, in turn, to walls and paving

mitred butt joint will be necessary where the boards meet in the corner formed by the high concrete wall and the low brick one. Remember to chamfer the edges of all exposed wood surfaces, that is, round them off using a plane, and then finish them with a fine grade of sandpaper. The seat can either be painted white (primer, undercoat and top coat), or stained with a wood preservative, such as Cuprinol.

Overhead beams and down supports

The final feature is the white overhead beam structure that will fit into the joist hangers already inserted into the high concrete block wall. The timbers should be lengths of 230 × 50mm (9 × 2 in) and planed all round. Do not be tempted to use smaller beams as they will only look flimsy. Climbers will soften their outline.

There is a choice of down supports: either a 50mm (2 in) square steel section, or a simple scaffold pole, dowelled at the top to accept the beams. The supports are of different lengths, the longest being bedded into a secure concrete foundation that will be surrounded by planting. Use the same method as given for erecting the pergola poles on page 27. The shorter pole is fixed into the top of the lower brick wall and can be neatly married in with the coping. This is achieved by cementing it into a 5cm (2 in) hole in the middle of the brick. Paint the supports black and maintain them, along with the beams, by giving them a rub down and a fresh coat of paint every two years.

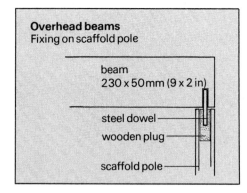

Overhead beams
Fixing on scaffold pole

beam
230 x 50mm (9 x 2 in)

steel dowel
wooden plug
scaffold pole

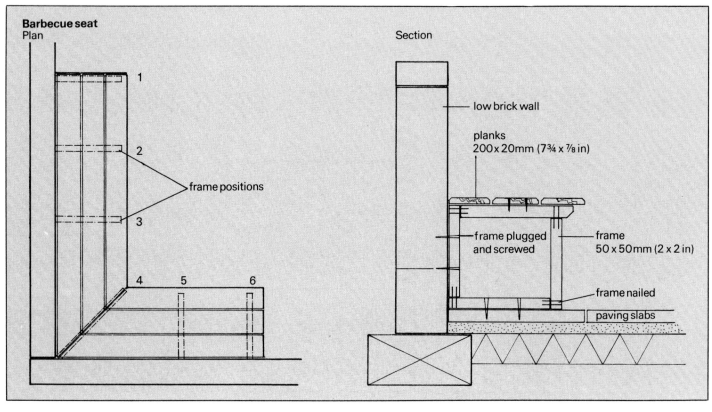

Barbecue seat
Plan

1
2
3
frame positions
4 5 6

Section

low brick wall

planks
200 x 20mm (7¾ x ⅞ in)

frame plugged and screwed

frame
50 x 50mm (2 x 2 in)

frame nailed

paving slabs

PLANNING A COURTYARD GARDEN

Our design for a Courtyard Garden shows how you can transform a central
area and make it into an extra 'room' clothed in vegetation, that
not only complements the house itself but facilitates indoor-outdoor living.

The success of any garden, ancient or modern, lies in its compatability with the building it adjoins. In this way the house merges with the outside room and plants and materials overlap so that it is difficult to define a precise boundary between the two elements.

A courtyard is a particularly architectural feature and it is worth remembering that the charm of such gardens was due to the ability of the designer to conceive the composition as a whole. Today, in all but a handful of situations, the opposite applies. The property may well be built as a carefully-designed unit, but the surrounding land is usually neglected.

The house and garden that we show is fortunate enough to be unashamedly urban. The low, two-storey building forms two sides of the sunny quadrangle while walls of surrounding properties close the gaps. The ensuing space is sheltered and secluded, a perfect retreat and the ideal outdoor room. Access from the house is available from the sitting room and dining room and both have large sliding glass doors, heightening the link between inside and out. In addition, the house has many windows and is in fact designed to overlook the courtyard. The brief for the garden called for an area with ample hard-surfacing, water as a central focus and enough planting to soften the harsh outlines without being a maintenance problem.

The obvious geometry of the surroundings established the theme for the design, based on a series of overlapping rectangles that extended the lines of the building. The hard surfaces are carefully chosen and help to define individual areas within the composition. Moving away from the house, we chose brick for the outdoor sitting and dining areas. The facing brick used in the building was a hard, well-fired variety and we were able to lay these, 'frog' (dent-side) down, in a stretcher bond, the bricks simply being bedded end to end, as shown in the plan.

The garden is, in fact, subtly divided in two, the pool and bed of annuals forming the link. Stepping stones cross both features and in this way you are compelled to walk over a particular route, avoiding short cuts and utilizing more of the garden as a result.

A pool as focal point

The pool is an essential part of the design, and being clearly visible from all points, acts as a pivot. Thus situated, a simple sheet of water is far more effective than a complicated series of falls and fountains. The sound of a 'bubble-jet' just breaking the water's surface is delightful and quite

Above: Eurphorbia griffithii *Fireglow adds a welcome splash of colour*
Previous page: our courtyard makes imaginative use of water and planting

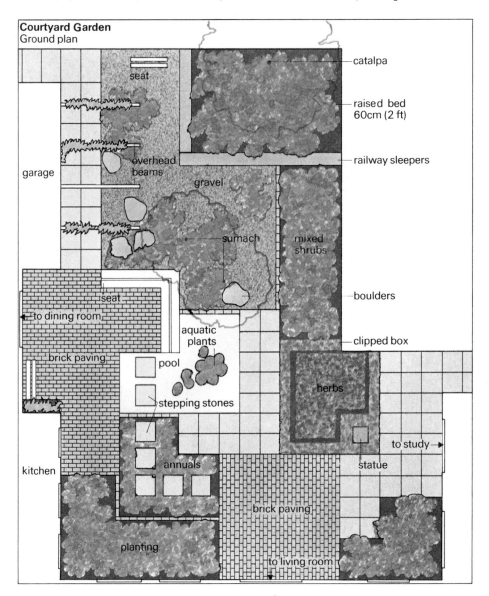

Courtyard Garden
Ground plan

catalpa

raised bed 60cm (2 ft)

railway sleepers

seat

overhead beams

garage

gravel

sumach

mixed shrubs

boulders

seat

to dining room

aquatic plants

clipped box

brick paving

pool

herbs

stepping stones

to study

kitchen

annuals

statue

brick paving

planting

to living room

adequate. In a similar way, straightforward detailing of the pool edge will produce a superb play of light and shadow, and you can enhance this by the careful positioning of aquatic plants.

As with the construction of steps and risers, slabs around a pool should overhang the water by 5cm (2 in). This is particularly important with the stepping stones that have brick supporting piers built to accommodate a similar overhang. In this way the slabs will appear to 'float' just clear of the surface.

Gravel with boulders and planting
As we considered grass to be impractical for maintenance reasons, we floored the area beyond the pool and built-in seat with gravel and highlighted it with a combination of boulders and planting, with two *Rhus typhina* (stag's horn sumach) providing vertical emphasis.

The back of the garage is perhaps the least interesting feature of the entire garden and this has become a support for a number of overhead beams forming a pergola. The beams are smothered with climbing plants and form an attractive walk that leads to the side passage and front of the house. The strong, horizontal lines of the beams are echoed closer to the ground by the raised bed built from railway sleepers. This gives initial height to young planting and has the effect of drawing attention to the *Catalpa bignonioides* (Indian bean tree) that acts as a secondary focal point.

The choice in planting
Planting is especially critical in a courtyard and not only softens the edges but adds to the feeling of form and space as well. Certain plants have definite sculptural qualities and these should be used in bold patterns to reinforce the underlying design.

Acanthus mollis (bear's breeches), the leaves of which adorn the tops of Corinthian columns, is a fine plant to grow through the gravel.

Of the euphorbias, there are three particularly fine varieties: *E. wulfenii* forms a large, rounded hummock; *E. griffithii* Fireglow has striking orange bracts, and *E. polychroma* acts as a sprawling but architectural ground cover.

Two or three yuccas with their magnificent flower spikes are invaluable, and such strong, rounded shapes are complemented by rounded forms, the shrubs cytisus and hebe being ideal examples. Herbs are included for their fragrance and culinary value and climbers are, of course, essential for training over beams and walls.

The finished composition should be planned for colour and interest throughout the year. A courtyard allows outside living over a far longer period than other garden forms as the walls provide shelter and warmth that are of benefit to plants and people alike.

Key to planting plan
Numerals after names denote plant quantities.

1 *Lonicera japonica halliana* (honeysuckle) ×1
2 *Viburnum plicatum* Lanarth (Japanese snowball) ×1
3 *Vinca minor* (lesser periwinkle) ×16
4 *Deutzia × rosea* Carmina ×3
5 *Catalpa bignonioides* (Indian bean tree) ×1
6 *Arundinaria murielae* ×2
7 *Hydrangea petiolaris* ×1
8 *Fatsia japonica* (Japanese aralia or figleaf palm) ×2
9 *Hydrangea macrophylla* Blue Wave (common hydrangea) ×3
10 *Anemone japonica* (windflower) ×4
11 *Daphne mezereum* (mezereon) ×2
12 *Spiraea × bumalda* Anthony Waterer ×3
13 *Buxus sempervirens* Suffruticosa (box) ×57
14 *Potentilla fruticosa* Tangerine (cinquefoil) ×3
15 *Yucca flaccida* ×2
16 *Cytisus × praecox* Allgold (Warminster broom) ×2
17 *Wisteria sinensis* (Chinese wisteria) ×1
18 *Euphorbia polychroma* (cushion spurge) ×7
19 *Hebe pinguifolia* Pagei (hebe) ×2
20 *Cistus × purpureus* (rock rose) ×1
21 *Lavatera olbia* Rosea (tree mallow) ×2
22 *Verbascum bombyciferum* (mullein) ×3
23 *Jasminum officinale* (common jasmine) ×1
24 *Choisya ternata* (Mexican orange blossom) ×2
25 *Salvia officinalis* Purpurascens (common sage) ×3
26 *Papaver orientale* (Oriental poppy) ×4
27 *Actinidia chinensis* (Chinese gooseberry) ×1
28 *Bergenia cordifolia* (pig squeak) ×9
29 *Euphorbia wulfenii* (spurge) ×1
30 *Rhus typhina* Laciniata (stag's horn sumach) ×2
31 *Hosta sieboldiana* (plantain lily) ×5
32 *Acanthus mollis* (bear's breeches) ×3
33 *Campsis tagliabuana* Madame Galen (trumpet creeper) ×1
34 *Hedera helix* Glacier (common ivy) ×5
35 *Aristolochia durior* (birthwort) ×1
36 *Cistus × lusitanicus* Decumbens (rock rose) ×2
37 *Lonicera japonica* Aureoreticulata (honeysuckle) ×1
38 *Euphorbia griffithii* Fireglow (spurge) ×1

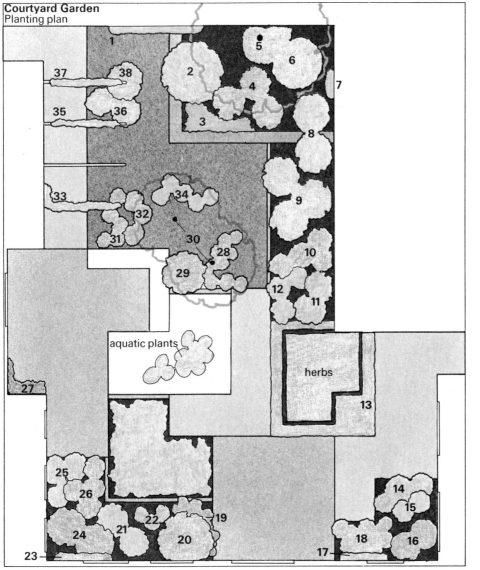

Courtyard Garden
Planting plan

aquatic plants

herbs

PLANNING A ROOF GARDEN

You don't need a ground-level site to experience the joys that gardening can bring: all that is necessary is a suitable roof and a little ingenuity.
The benefits that a roof garden can offer include a warm environment that will appeal to both plants and gardener alike; peace and privacy; and – if you are fortunate – an unhindered view.
Here we introduce our own design,
and later on we describe the formation of the basic features.

To create a garden on a roof means a departure from normal gardening techniques, and often involves an entirely new set of rules. As the height above ground increases so, too, do the difficulties – seemingly in direct ratio; access, shelter, irrigation and weight: all will assume quite new proportions.

Certain problems are peculiar to roof gardens. A common one is how to hide the rash of pipes that always seems to be in the most awkward position. Another frequently concerns weight: before undertaking any work you should be absolutely certain that the existing structure is sound and capable of supporting the proposed garden. If you are in any doubt, call in an architect or surveyor to make a professional assessment of the situation – it is better to be safe than sorry!

Apart from technical considerations though, the chief factor affecting your roof garden is likely to be the wind. In a built-up area calm is normally taken for granted. However, what may seem a gentle breeze in the street can be a biting wind three floors up. Providing adequate shelter is therefore of paramount importance, both from your plants' point of view, and your own.

Plan and design

As far as design is concerned, you should tackle the initial survey exactly as you would for a ground-level garden. Views, direction of prevailing wind, aspect, position of doors and windows, and the total dimensions must all be drawn on your basic plan, together with any other relevant information. If you do this on squared paper it will be easy to establish a scale and ensure that the features are correctly related to one another.

It would be wise to position heavy features around the perimeter, where the underlying framework will transfer the load onto the surrounding walls. As soil is usually the heaviest, your planting area will be strictly regulated.

Paving, in the conventional sense, will also present a weight problem. It is usual to find either asbestos tiles or some kind of specially-laid bituminous surface where access has been previously planned, but neither would be particularly attractive over large areas.

The limitations and possibilities should now be falling into some form of pattern, possibly similar to that shown on our detailed ground plan.

Roof gardens, in general, are small and ours is no exception, measuring approximately 10·5 × 6m (35 × 20 ft). It has a high wall on one side, and a lower wall topped by chimney pots on the other. The main view is from directly in front of the doorway leading to the house below. The floor was originally laid with asbestos tiles, and unsightly pipes were visible in a number of places. A television aerial hung from the higher wall, and the prevailing wind tended to sweep over the lower wall, making sitting outdoors impossible in all but the calmest weather.

Our first task, then, was to provide some form of shelter. To this end, we constructed a strong wooden canopy, and used clear corrugated rigid PVC to form the roof. We left the front open, but fitted the side facing the wind with open, horizontally-arranged slats to form a protective screen. The latter, while breaking the force of the wind, still allows some movement of air through the garden, so helping to keep the temperature reasonable on hot days. It also hides the pipes, and creates the small utility area that houses the tiny shed and the invaluable water butt for irrigation.

Raised beds and wooden seat form focal point of design, while a rigid PVC roof and slatted wall provide shelter

A timber handrail ran along the front of the roof. As children might use the garden we decided to close it in for safety, using plate glass with bevelled edges. This way we retain the view and reduce wind velocity within the garden even more.

Structurally, in addition to the supporting walls around the perimeter, we were lucky enough to have a wall running along the line of the horizontal slats. So we were able to plant along the edges of the roof, and also incorporate a planting feature in virtually the middle of the design. This led to the creation of an interesting composition involving planting on split levels, and a seat that gives definition to the main relaxation area.

Next we turned our attention to the floor. The asbestos tiles measured 23cm (9 in) square and covered the whole roof. After we had scrubbed them with a strong detergent their colour was a uniform grey that, although not unpleasant in moderation, was distinctly oppressive over the entire area.

As already mentioned, pre-cast paving is normally far too heavy for a roof, likewise the more traditional natural

Roof Garden plan

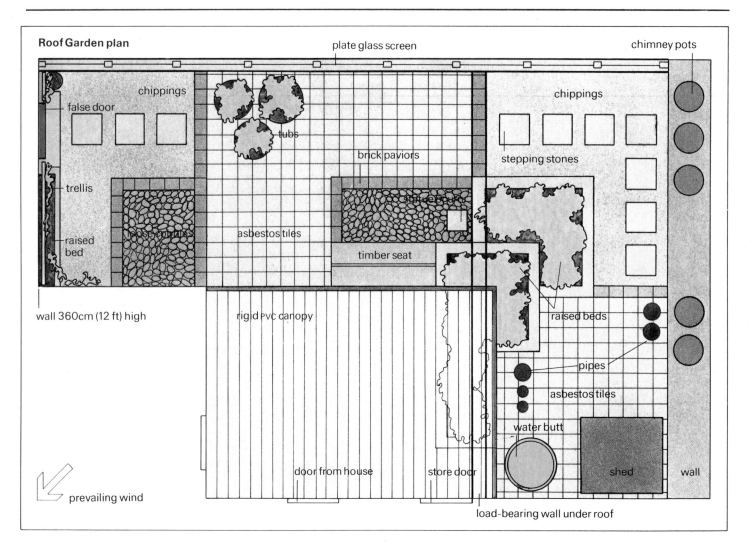

plate glass screen

chimney pots

chippings

false door

tubs

chippings

brick paviors

stepping stones

trellis

loose chippings

asbestos tiles

raised bed

timber seat

wall 360cm (12 ft) high

rigid PVC canopy

raised beds

pipes

asbestos tiles

water butt

prevailing wind

door from house

store door

shed

wall

load-bearing wall under roof

stone. Thinner paving bricks and quarry tiles are lighter, although where a large area is involved the weight would still be considerable.

In our design we divided the garden area into squares and worked out a simple geometric pattern. Some parts we left as the original surface, and others we edged with black paviors 25mm (1 in) thick. The resulting panels we filled with a thin covering of loose chippings – just enough to cover the tiles. As the stones were laid loose, drainage was unaffected, the occasional joint being left open in the brick surround to allow water to flow on its way to the main gutter. One word of warning: chippings come in a range of colours, but you should exercise particular care over your choice. It is advisable to steer clear of white as it can prove extremely dazzling in such an open situation; the same goes for painted surfaces. Buffs and browns are particularly restful and form a good background for plantings.

We had a bit of fun on the high wall. When the house was being converted a new front door was hung and its predecessor was due to be carted away with the rest of the rubbish. Instead, we rescued it and screwed it into position on the wall. We laid chippings over the area in front of the door and placed stepping stones to lead up to a small and quite obvious step. With a handle fitted, the door fooled numerous visitors, who either asked what was on the other side, or actually tried the handle. We fitted the wall on each side with squared trellis, and trained climbing plants over this.

After checking with a television engineer we discovered that the aerial could be removed and replaced with an indoor model.

Planting your roof garden

A special lightweight variety of soil is available that you can actually mix in your own home and we tell you more about this on page 85. If you are thinking of using pots or tubs make sure they are of ample size, for they will dry out far quicker on a roof than at ground level, with the combination of greater heat and drying wind in that situation.

It is essential that you water pots every single day in summer, which can lead to obvious problems at holiday time. Raised

Tackle initial survey as for ground-level garden, and draw basic plan on squared paper to establish scale and ensure features relate correctly to one another

beds on the other hand, will hold a greater depth of soil and thus retain moisture longer. You could use timber as a construction material, although it will be costly and require protection from damp on the inside by polythene or asbestos. A far easier method is to use lightweight concrete blocks such as Thermalite, from which you can build beds of any shape; simply bore holes through the blocks for drainage. To protect the blocks from the weather you can render them on the outside, or give them a coat of suitable stone paint, such as Sandtex.

Choose plants that will enjoy a hot sunny position. Cistus, potentilla, senecio, cytisus and yucca will all thrive in a roof setting, provided you erect shelter, while bulbs and annuals will also grow quickly. You can group your plants in the same way as you would in a ground-level garden, choosing species to provide colour and interest throughout the year.

CONSTRUCTING A ROOF GARDEN

We have not outlined the advantages of high-level gardens, introducing our own Roof Garden design as an easy-to-follow example. We go on to detail the basic features of the design, and give instructions for making the glass screen and creating split-level planting areas. The view towards the 'false door' is shown below.

The chief factor affecting your roof garden will probably be the wind. Here we look at the construction of the two features in our own design that break the force of the wind and provide shelter for both you and your plants.

Making the canopy

The canopy protects the relaxation area from the wind and is built in three stages (see diagram on next page). First you construct a framework of beams and supports; then you add the slatted screen that acts as the principal windbreak; finally you top the whole structure with a clear, rigid corrugated PVC roof.

Use 150×25mm (6×1 in) timbers, planed all round, to construct the main framework. Make it in the form of a box, and bolt it to the two load-bearing walls with special expanding masonry bolts. The beams should finish flush with the top of the wall, allowing the corrugated PVC

sheet to continue to the gutter beyond.

These PVC sheets, such as Novolux, are normally available in a standard width of 75cm (2½ ft), and can be bought with a tinted finish that is useful for cutting down glare. To ensure adequate fixing, you should space the 150mm (6 in) beams at 35cm (14 in) centres, but remember to drill through the high ribs of the corrugated sheets before screwing them into position. Standard fixing accessories – that is, screws, washers and caps – are usually sold along with the PVC sheets.

Use a 100mm (4 in) softwood post for the single down support, and fix it to the roof with either angle brackets or a single shoe.

An important point to remember when about to drill a hole in your roof is that you might cause dampness, or even leaks in the room below if you are not careful. Therefore, make as few holes as possible, and be sure always to use a sealer like mastic or bitumen. Should you have any doubts, call in professional help: it's best to play safe in such a situation.

For the horizontally-arranged wooden slats of the screen on the open side of the canopy, you can also use 150×25mm (6×1 in) timbers; screw them into the down support at one end, and to a simple 50×50mm (2×2 in) batten (screwed into the wall), at the other.

Erecting the glass screen
Erecting the glass screen at the front of the garden is a comparatively simple job. A handrail and hardwood posts were already in position on our roof-top area, so we simply had to fit brass lugs to accept the carefully-measured 6mm ($\frac{1}{4}$ in) plate glass panels. A glazier will be able to bevel the edges and drill the glass for you. Use brass nuts and bolts with fibre or plastic washers to protect both sides of the glass from abrasion.

Building the raised beds
Timber will not be the best material for building the raised beds, for it is expensive and involves complicated constructional techniques. Lightweight concrete blocks, such as Thermalite, are what you need.

Right: for detailed plan see page 82
Below: section of main canopy showing framework topped with rigid PVC sheet

Buy them measuring $80 \times 230 \times 450$mm ($3 \times 9 \times 18$ in), and lay them in a stretcher bond (lay blocks lengthways and stagger the joints). Where corners are involved a 'closer' cut to fit will be needed to adjust the bonding. An advantage of these blocks is that they can be sawn, producing neat joints.

The main feature in our garden comprises the seat and split-level beds, and is built up from blockwork two, three and four courses high respectively; the tops of the walls are neatly finished with glazed paving bricks, 25mm (1 in) thick. As lightweight blocks are porous you will have to render them with sand and

cement, and then apply a stone paint, such as Sandtex. You needn't render the inside of the bed as three coats of a bituminous paint will be satisfactory.

The highest bed is 90cm (3 ft), but it would be both unnecessary and unwise to fill with soil to this depth: 45cm (18 in) will be sufficient. Fit a false asbestos floor, which you can support with 6×50mm ($\frac{1}{4} \times 2$ in) steel strips bedded into the blockwork two courses from the top. Drill 25mm (1 in) holes, spaced at 23cm (9 in) centres, into the floor for drainage, and similar-sized holes through the blocks just above roof level, to allow water to drain into the main gutters.

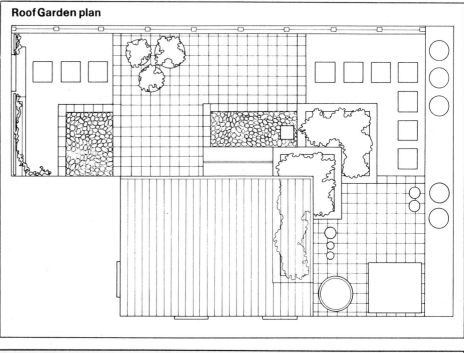

Roof Garden plan

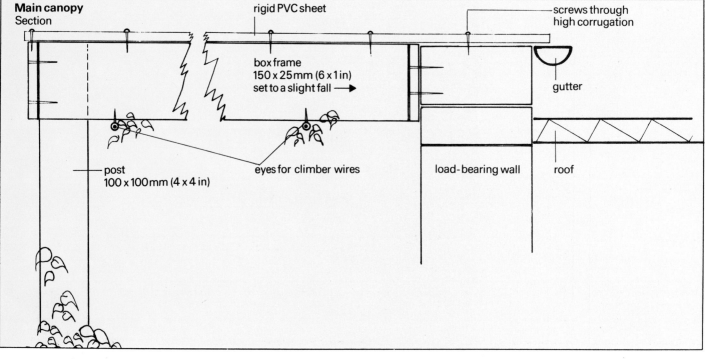

Main canopy Section

rigid PVC sheet

screws through high corrugation

box frame
150×25mm (6×1 in)
set to a slight fall →

gutter

post
100×100mm (4×4 in)

eyes for climber wires

load-bearing wall

roof

Insert plugs into the blockwork forming the bottom of the seat, and fit a 50 × 50mm (2 × 2 in) timber frame. Screw three 200 × 20mm (8 × ⅞ in) slats into this, and chamfer and carefully sand them, prior to painting.

Bedding the paving bricks

Glazed paving bricks, similar to those used on the top of the beds, are ideal for forming the retaining edges that define the areas of chippings. Bed the bricks in mortar, making sure that the joints are carefully pointed, and leaving an occasional gap to drain any trapped water. Stepping stones through the chippings

will need to be approximately 25mm (1 in) thick to match the bricks, and this rules out most pre-cast slabs that are normally in excess of 38mm (1½ in). Natural stone is often available in thinner gauges, however, and slate in particular will look very handsome against the paler surrounding surface. Bed the stones in mortar in the same way as the paving bricks.

In this design we have placed stepping stones to lead up to the old front door that we screwed to the wall on the left. With a handle fitted, the door to nowhere fools numerous visitors, who either ask what is on the other side, or actually try the handle. We fitted a squared trellis to the wall on each side of the door and trained climbing plants over this.

Soil mixture for raised beds

The soil to use in raised beds in a roof garden is a specially-prepared mix, lighter than that in an ordinary garden.

An ideal mix would be made up (by loose bulk) from 2 parts medium loam and 1 part each of peat, vermiculite granules and well-rotted manure. You

Left: section of plate glass screen attachment to post. Below: section of gravel area with chippings and stepping stone retained by glazed paving brick. Bottom: seat and split-level raised beds

could also add an additional 85g (3 oz) of superphosphate of lime per 50kg (1 cwt) of soilmix, although this is not essential. The vermiculite is a very light insulation material, giving the mixture bulk and reducing the overall weight of the soil.

Before adding the soil to the beds, spread a layer of broken crocks over the bottom, making sure that the holes are protected and won't become clogged with soil. Add the soil in layers, wetting each as work progresses; this will enable the roots of the plants to take up moisture evenly as soon as they are in position.

You can plant in exactly the same way as you would in a garden at ground level, but pay particular attention to the staking and tying of plants, remembering that the wind can easily uproot young specimens. Walls and beams can be neatly wired to take climbing plants, but the wire should be closer to the wall than normal to combat the force of the wind.

Maintenance of a roof garden is very important, water being the key to healthy plant development. Few people realize how quickly beds and pots dry out, and during hot weather it is prudent to use the watering can daily, little and often being a better rule rather than sporadic floods. Try also to water in the morning or evening, avoiding the extreme heat of the middle of the day.

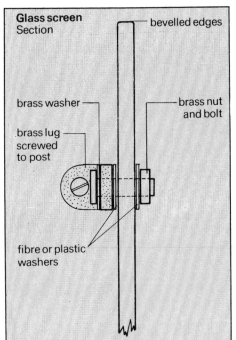

Glass screen
Section

bevelled edges

brass washer

brass nut and bolt

brass lug screwed to post

fibre or plastic washers

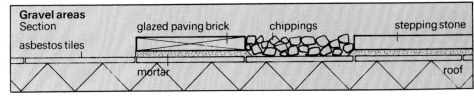

Gravel areas
Section

asbestos tiles

glazed paving brick

chippings

stepping stone

mortar

roof

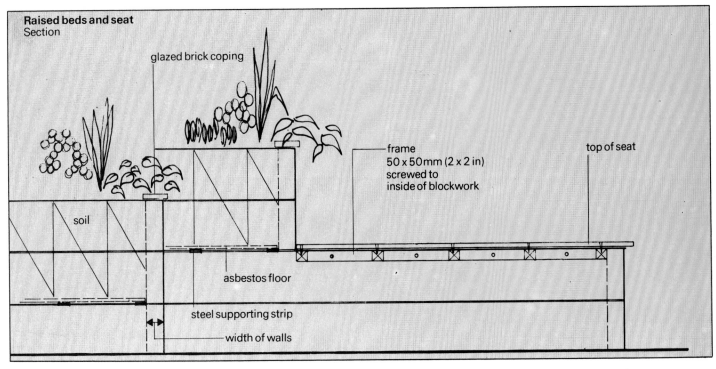

Raised beds and seat
Section

glazed brick coping

frame
50 x 50mm (2 x 2 in)
screwed to
inside of blockwork

top of seat

soil

asbestos floor

steel supporting strip

width of walls

DESIGNS FOR RECTANGULAR GARDENS

A regular-shaped plot with its formal straight lines can be just as much of a challenge as an odd-shaped plot. In the first of our designs for rectangular plots we look at ways of either turning straight boundaries into an asset or distracting the eye from them.

Although many people have odd-shaped gardens, still more possess one of standard rectangular proportions. Gardens on the whole are getting smaller – due to the demands on housing space – and the average size measures about 10m (35 ft) long by 7·5m (25 ft) wide.

With these proportions in mind, whether you start from scratch or inherit

an existing garden, the approach should be the same: setting out to create an environment that is not only right for you but at the same time attractive to family and visitors alike.

To many people the ability to 'design' implies a degree of professional skill, so it is often easier to think in terms of reorganization rather than a wholly

original scheme and, again, it is often the simplest solution where an established garden is in existence.

The initial planning can fall into two stages: what you want and what you've got. Your requirements can be tackled in exactly the same way as the family shopping list, but instead of the usual groceries you may list lawn, greenhouse, shed, vegetables, terrace, barbecue, pool, sandpit, swings, roses and so on. As far as existing features are concerned it is best to make a simple scale drawing, using graph paper, and note down the north point, good or bad views, existing planting, trees, positions of doors and windows,

Left: an imaginative use of pre-cast paving links house with garden. Below: a working design to scale is invaluable

changes in level, together with any other relevant information. Your plan might not look as neat as the one shown below but it should be sufficient to give you a good idea of how to use your own available space to the best advantage.

Nor need there be only one solution to the problem, for just as the furnishing and decoration of a room in the house can vary, so can its outdoor counterpart.

For some reason people tend to have a horror of rectangular gardens, probably because most designs involving straight lines fall into the trap of rigid formality. With a small space, however, it is often advantageous to accept the shape of the boundaries, softening them by all means, but using the outline to form a frame for a geometric composition, in much the same way as a contemporary artist might do.

Planning your priorities
An average family, with several children, various pets and busy parents, will have general requirements – from somewhere to sit and have the occasional meal, a vegetable area, shed or greenhouse, flowers for cutting, shrubs and herbaceous material for interest throughout the year, to room for bike riding, games and general children's activities. But above all easy maintenance must be the aim.

Choice of planting
Whether a design is based on rectangles or curves it is sound common sense to keep the areas close to the building reasonably architectural, creating a positive link between house and garden. There are a number of ways of doing this, the most obvious revolving around a paved area that will serve as a background for the many activities that call for an easily maintained, quick-drying surface.

Numerous types of paving are available, ranging from the more expensive natural stones and brick and granite setts, to pre-cast concrete slabs of various colours and textures. As a general rule crazy paving is not the best material to use close to a house, the conflicting shapes clashing with the cleaner lines of the building. It is also worth bearing in mind that although broken paving is cheap to buy, it is far from cheap or quick to lay. Be wary also of coloured pre-cast slabs: your terrace should be a background, not a gaudy feature in itself. If you are really set on using colours, keep them simple; use two at the most and make sure they don't clash.

DESIGN THEME - RECTANGLES
In our first design we have assumed that the house is built of brick and it is logical, therefore, to use this material on the terrace. A simple squared pattern of bricks laid flat was evolved, using the corners and projections of the building as starting points. The resulting squares were then filled in with a combination of rectangular pre-cast paving, planting and a raised bed, that might double as a sandpit or pool. As the entire garden is based on rectangles the lines of the terrace were extended on our plan and another series were drawn across the page at right-angles to form a grid. The approximate proportions of the various features we needed were then shaded in: vegetables, lawn, existing shed, swing and clothes drier. A pattern was starting to evolve and by the time we had screened the bad views, created a focal point and added

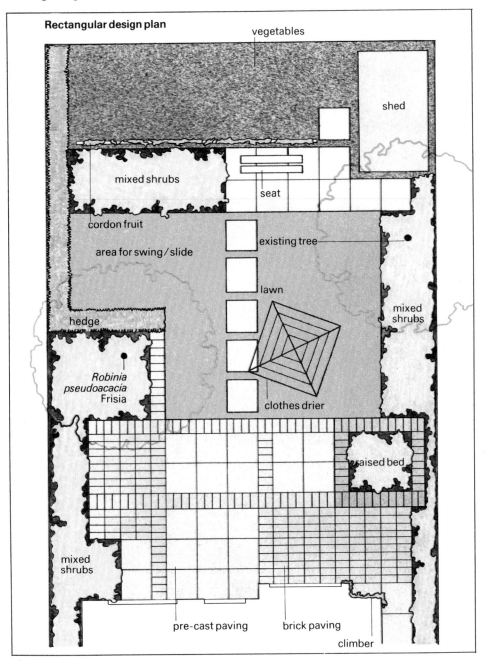

Rectangular design plan

vegetables

shed

mixed shrubs

seat

cordon fruit

area for swing/slide

existing tree

lawn

hedge

Robinia pseudoacacia Frisia

mixed shrubs

clothes drier

raised bed

mixed shrubs

pre-cast paving

brick paving

climber

trees for vertical emphasis the working design was virtually complete.

Planting within the design

Few people realize how quickly planting can soften a composition and it is therefore very important to have a strong ground plan initially, as a weak design very soon loses its line altogether. Planting also helps to reinforce the basic pattern and if you are working with rectangles, these can be linked together and enhanced by bold groupings. Whatever the size of a garden, individual specimens should be used sparingly and then only as a point of emphasis. Groups of three or four would be ideal in the size of garden shown here, while a large area could use drifts of 15 or 20 for a corresponding effect.

The treatment we have just suggested for the basic rectangular site was a plan based on straight lines which reinforced the basic pattern of the garden, with the fences acting as a positive framework. (A curved design would lead the eye away from the boundaries.)

We now put forward alternative plans, one based on diagonal lines, one based on a circle.

DESIGN THEME - DIAGONALS

However our second plan in this section turns the entire design diagonally across the garden. Diagonal lines are useful for creating a feeling of greater space as they not only direct you away from the main axis of the boundaries but also bring the longest dimensions into play, the distance between opposite corners of a rectangle

being the greatest single length available.

In this garden plan the back of the house faces due north, in which case only a minimal amount of paving is needed outside the French doors, just enough in fact to give access for the side passage and room for a single bench seat on which to enjoy the shade during particularly hot weather. A simple buff-coloured pre-cast slab was used, giving a visual link with the pale brown finish of the building.

Siting of focal point

Stepping stones cross the small lawn and draw the eye to the focal point provided by a carefully-chosen urn or statue. Statuary and the like can be delightful ornaments in a garden but remember that they are dominant features in their own right and should be used sparingly as

punctuation marks in the overall composition. As a general rule they should be softened and surrounded by planting, a glimpse of a bust or figure being far more subtle than glaring nudity!

Planting within the design

In our design the urn is backed by the soft foliage and flowers of climbing roses, these forming an effective screen to the small vegetable plot beyond. The path changes direction at the urn or statue, terminating at the main sitting area that is built up from an interlocking pattern of brick and pre-cast slabs. A tree behind the sitting area would be an important element in the design, giving both shade and vertical emphasis.

Few people realize that trees can be bought in a wide range of sizes, from semi-mature specimens that are far too big and heavy for the average householder to manage, right down to small saplings that will take many years to show any real potential. Different species obviously grow at different rates but when selecting a tree for an important position, such as ours, the size known as 'extra large nursery stock' can be ideal. These trees are most usually grown by specialist nurseries and although large, can be handled by one or two people. They will probably be about 4·2m (14 ft) high and have a girth of anything up to 25–30cm (10–12 in). They establish quickly in a suitably-prepared position and have a far better success rate than the 'semi matures' that can suddenly fail after two or three years in the ground. We chose one of the vast cherry family,

Our garden with a diagonal design was planned to give a feeling of extra space, while still incorporating most of the features required in the average suburban plot.
The seating area at the end of the path is shaded by a spreading wild cherry, Prunus avium *Grandiflora (above right)*

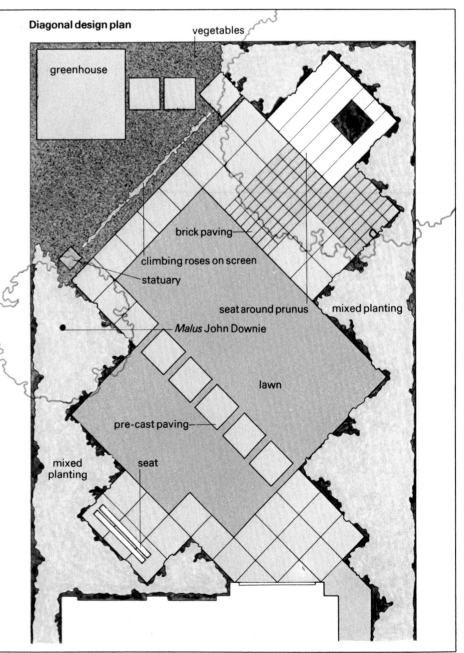

Diagonal design plan
vegetables
greenhouse
brick paving
climbing roses on screen
statuary
seat around prunus
mixed planting
Malus John Downie
lawn
pre-cast paving
mixed planting
seat

Prunus avium Grandiflora, a delightful wild cherry tree that bears double white blossoms in late spring to early summer (April to May). Because the tree was large when planted we felt that a seat around the base would not be out of place. This measured 1·8 × 1·8m (6 × 6 ft) and doubled as a table or even sun-lounger.

The vegetable area was big enough to incorporate a small greenhouse, while the strong pattern of lawn and borders was wrapped in planting designed to give variety of leaf and flower throughout the year.

DESIGN THEME – THE CIRCLE

This third alternative plan is a totally different concept; here we take the idea of using curves to create a completely circular pattern. A true circle is not the easiest design element to handle and where a major part of the garden is involved it is best to 'offset' the feature, thus giving the composition a feeling of emphasis in a particular direction. The resulting spaces between the circle and the surrounding fences are not, therefore, regular and become rather more interesting as a result.

Choice of paving

As in all our other gardens we needed a paved area at the rear of the house and here again the use of a circular design imposed certain restrictions. The shape of the paving was directly related to the geometry of the circle and became an extension of it, radii being extended until they reached and passed the line of the building. Each new circle represented a line of paving and where any circular pattern is involved small modules are the most adaptable. We had therefore a choice of brick, granite setts, stable paviors and cobbles. The last two we rejected on the grounds that they were too uneven for constant walking and the obvious use of tables and chairs. The setts were a possibility but looked a little 'hard' against the pebble dash of the building. Brick was ideal but in order to save expense and also a considerable amount of laying time we evolved a pattern of brick courses that could be filled in with brushed concrete.

For brushed concrete Lay a normal concrete mix of 1:2:3 – one part cement,

two parts sand, three parts aggregate – ensuring that the aggregate is made from an attractive selection of small rounded pebbles. Once the job has started to harden, or 'go off', brush with a stiff broom. This will expose the aggregate and produce a striking marbled effect when dry. To stop it drying too quickly in very hot weather cover the surface with damp sacking for a day or two; in frosty weather dry sacking will be sufficient.

The final planting

Climbers and planting soften the outline of the paving and house, and there is room for a small herb bed. As this garden was to be as maintenance-free as possible we decided against a conventional lawn and the main area of the circle was laid

Used with care, a circular design brings a refreshing look to a regular-shaped plot. A Japanese note is introduced with the siting of several boulders within the circle, which is surfaced with a layer of gravel on concrete and planted with two Rhus typhina Laciniata *(above right)*

with a weak mix of concrete, over which was spread 13mm ($\frac{1}{2}$ in) of washed gravel. Holes were left in the concrete to accept planting, including *Rhus typhina* Laciniata (stag's-horn sumach), while several groups of large boulders provide a sculptural and slightly Japanese feeling.

Stepping stones cross the gravel in a random pattern and lead to the shed that is neatly-screened by planting. A seat is carefully sited to one side of the sumachs, while the main border areas on the outside of the circle help to soften and hide the stiff rectangular line of the fences.

A high proportion of ground-covering plants help considerably in keeping the maintenance at a reasonable level and occasional raking ensures the gravel is free from leaves.

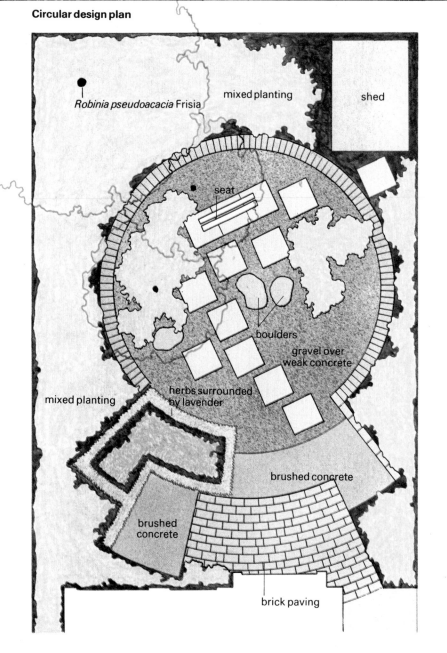

Circular design plan

Robinia pseudoacacia Frisia

mixed planting

shed

seat

boulders

gravel over weak concrete

mixed planting

herbs surrounded by lavender

brushed concrete

brushed concrete

brick paving

THE ODD PLOT
Plans for
difficult-shaped sites

Odd- or uneven-shaped sites provide plenty of problems, but none of
them is insoluble if care is taken in laying out the garden. To begin with,
an irregular shape often has much more character than a standard
square or rectangular site. Starting with a simple ground plan you
can design your garden, perhaps highlighting an unusual
boundary, and gradually incorporate all the features
that make up an outdoor living area.

*A corner site such as this can
provide a challenge, and the
plan shown (far right) is one
answer. The circular pattern of
the layout relates to the house and
ignores the outline of the site. The
space between house and fence is
planted out so that the shape of the
garden from the terrace is incidental.
Nevertheless, the basic ingredients of a
standard garden are all present*

For some reason a mystique has grown up and surrounds anything to do with design so that it has got itself the name of being an expensive luxury, and nowhere more so than in the garden. The down-to-earth horticulturist wants 'none of that fancy stuff'; but design should not be a fanciful, unsympathetic plan forced upon the unwilling host garden. If it is, it has missed its point, for today that valuable piece of ground surrounding your house, for which you paid so much and are probably still paying, has to do far more than grow a few flowers.

The garden is a place for all the family to use and the smaller the area the more difficult it is to fulfil this function. The average garden is often required to provide a play space, a sunbathing area and room for washing the car as well as housing the compost heap and garden shed; and all this besides beds for shrubs and colourful annuals, herb garden and vegetable patch, not forgetting paths for easy access in all weathers. Your design must permutate all these factors and make them work.

Principles of garden design

The garden should look well all the year round, not only as seen from indoors but also while wandering around different parts of the garden itself. Once this is

appreciated the shape of the plot is incidental. It is only another problem to be considered among so many and when it comes to the crunch the irregular shape often has considerably more character than the standard rectangular plot.

The main traffic of a family house usually leads directly into the garden from kitchen or living room. This is where any sort of terracing is normally laid. It makes sense that the line of any terracing, if not the texture and material of it, should relate visually to the remainder of the garden, and the resulting pattern should embrace all the desired elements of the garden. If the area is large enough it need have no relation to the odd shape of the site boundary at all as you arrange one pattern within another. The intervening area is then planted out, giving the garden a feeling of privacy and enclosure, for most families wish to create this feeling of being in their own little world, without being overlooked by the neighbours. But remember that the pattern you create

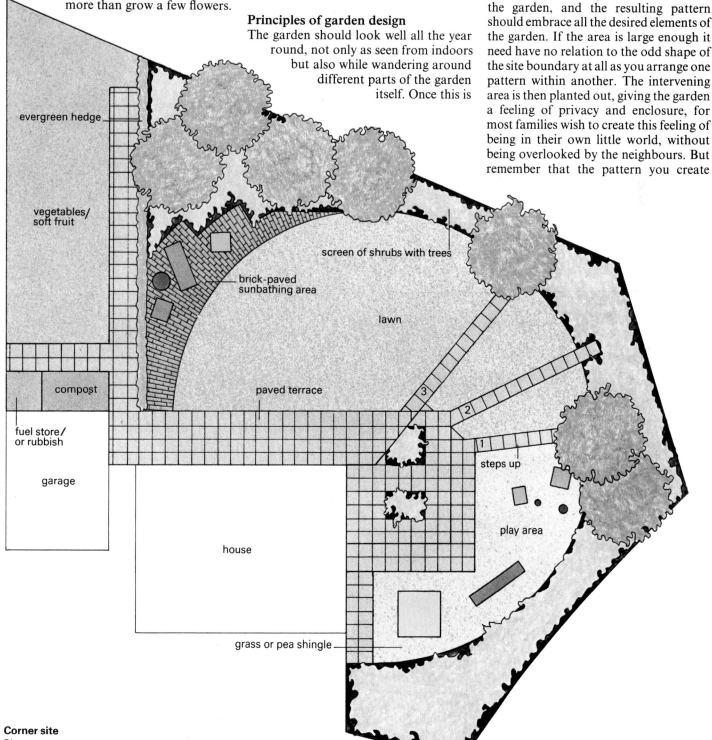

evergreen hedge

vegetables/
soft fruit

screen of shrubs with trees

brick-paved
sunbathing area

lawn

compost

paved terrace

3

2

fuel store/
or rubbish

1

steps up

garage

play area

house

grass or pea shingle

Corner site
Plan

93

should not be one of paths with bits left over in between, but of definite areas of different types of surfacing.

Create your ground plan pattern

Where there is not enough room to create a pattern ignoring the odd-shaped boundary line, you must accept the fact and perhaps make a feature of this limitation, relating the odd shape to the terrace in a meaningful way. Whatever the shape of the plot, the basic ground pattern should be clear and simple with no nasty little corners muffed over with the odd rock or pot. It is really a question of tailoring and the best-cut suit is the most comfortable and long-lasting because it fits the owner in every way. To a good tailor the shape of the body in front of him does not matter, the awkward one is only a little more challenging.

Your pattern, then, can run either from the house or from one aspect of the surrounding boundary: it can also be dictated by a special feature – a large existing tree, for instance, or a view to the church. More often than not you may find your feature consists of a collection of manhole covers slap in the middle of your site. Recognize your main feature, good or bad, and work with it to produce some sort of clear pattern.

To experiment with the design for your garden you will first have to measure up the site and accurately plot it, preferably to scale on graph paper. Onto this plan mark where it is convenient to have your terrace to get the sun and still see the baby

from the kitchen, or whatever else is relevant to your way of life. Then site a herb patch and vegetables, if possible near the kitchen, then the dustbin area convenient both for you and the man who has to collect, the compost heap, the washing line, a greenhouse, rose bed – whatever else you want.

Taking into account all these necessities, try to devise a pattern on the principles already outlined and keep it all very simple. The chances are that as the shape of the house is regular, and usually the boundary too, your pattern will be as well. If curves are not to look weak outdoors they have to be bold and generous, which demands space. Wiggly lines that are not generous tend to look like straight lines gone wrong!

At this planning stage of your garden firmly put from your mind anything to do with plants, along with decorative pots and seats; these are first 'infill' and secondly furnishing. Only when you have a practical working plan do you infill with taller shrubs at the rear to give you privacy and shelter, scaling down to the pretty ones which are seen against them. In the average small garden, trees should be seen either as part of the overall design or as a specimen to act like a piece of statuary. Scattered about at will they fracture your basic design. Finally, introduce into your layout pots and seats as foreground interest, to give the final touch of grace.

There is, of course, no standard solution for the many different-shaped

plots constituting a house and its garden, but by working to a few basic rules and getting your priorities right, you can make the best of your problem site.

Learn from interior design

You can learn quite a lot about how pattern and lines work from home decoration. You can correct your outdoor site deficiencies the same way that you would minimize an over-tall room. You would not want to emphasize the height by hanging vertically-striped wallpaper. A long, narrow site looks longer and narrower if a straight path runs down the middle whereas a pattern running from side to side will help correct this.

Where there is a pleasant view from the site, such as playing-fields at the end of the garden, concentrate on this, framing it with plantings as you would arrange the furnishings of your living room to enhance a picture or piece of furniture of which you were proud. Conversely, if your site has no view from it, turn the pattern in on itself and provide some sort of demanding feature as a full stop – a sundial, bird bath, or piece of statuary. Too many small features in a small garden fuss the arrangement, the eye is confused and the garden no longer peaceful. One of the qualities of a garden, and indeed its major function despite all the ancillary ones, should be to provide a place of tranquility for the owners – and that includes its visual appearance. Even if the garden is not used all 12 months of the year, it is still visible from indoors.

Design for a corner site

The site shown on the previous page is set in the middle of a corner plot. Outside its encircling solid timber fence, all of 1·5m (5 ft) high, there is a pedestrian path and roads that converge on the southern corner of the site. The curving pattern of the layout echoes the flow of movement around the area, although the planting inside the fence blocks out the unattractive view and, surprisingly, much of the noise as well.

The problem inside the garden was that the house faces east and the area farthest away from it gets the afternoon and evening sun, being the time when you are most likely to want to bask in the sun or just sit and have a drink. A terrace was therefore a priority in that area, away from the house but also connected to it so that the children could ride their bicycles on it and wander in and out of the house.

The next priorities were the siting of the dustbins, fuel store and rubbish, and the

small vegetable area convenient to both rear door and side service passage. These and the garage are all served with a hard-paved path for easy access. It is in the cold, wet days of winter when going out to cut a cabbage or pick some sprouts that you really appreciate this, and the straight run of path would also allow for a washing line. An evergreen hedge, composed of a mixture of yew, pyracantha and the odd holly, separates the vegetable area from the rest of the garden.

A further hazard in this garden was the fact that the site 'fell away' to a downward slope on the south corner of the house. The lawn pattern could have followed suit but it would have meant that the house terrace would have been at a higher level and the children shooting along on their bicycles might have gone over the end. By stepping the terrace and lawn (as shown in the aerial view), this hazard was avoided and the steps became a feature of

the layout. Where they converge they provide another little paved area on the south-east side of the house.

Below these steps the last flat area, although in fact an extension of the lawn, has been gravelled – or rather laid with rounded pea shingle. This is less sharp than gravel when fallen onto, and better than grass for a play area in bad weather. There is room for children's flowerbeds here and all the outdoor toys can be left out of sight of the main terrace. Since the area is not grassed it is easy to look after.

Between the defined outer lines of the garden and the boundary fence is a thick planting of mixed shrubs with the occasional tree sited into it. Plenty of evergreens are included here – like cotoneasters, large-leaved privets and pyracantha – to block out the noisy world outside. Colour planting, requiring seasonal attention, is confined to the sitting-out terraced area.

Design for a long, thin town garden

Typical of many town gardens behind the terraces of early Victorian houses, sometimes with a rear access, sometimes not, this site measures 30m long by 7·5m wide (100 × 25 ft). The problem is how not to make the layout seem even longer and thinner – which any sort of straight path down the middle would do – but to create a progression of small areas or 'rooms', staggered if possible, giving the ultimate view a lateral or side-to-side movement, and so apparently increase the width of the garden.

The first of these room areas behind the house is paved and used for many months of the year for eating out since it is so sheltered and surprisingly private with its old pear tree overhanging the area. It would be nice to pave such a setting in brick or old York stone. But if the expense prohibits it, you can use dark pre-cast concrete slabs instead.

The next area, down one small step, is gravelled and planted at random with perennials that seed themselves and look natural in such a setting; alchemilla (lady's mantle) and sisyrinchium (satin flower), for instance. The view is punctuated beyond this area by a piece of statuary (an old urn in fact) again to one side, and this is repeated on the other side of the garden beyond the next mown-grass room. A staggered path connects all these features and provides a dry, hard access to them.

The bottom room is allowed to be fairly wild with half-standard fruit trees planted in it and rough grass under them where spring and autumn bulbs and wild flowers can be encouraged. The borders on either side of the garden and against the old brick dividing walls are planted with a mixture of shrubs, including *Viburnum tinus* (laurustinus), syringa, philadelphus (mock orange) and choisya. When seen from the house the total effect is green and rather romantic, with the only colour being reserved for the tubs grouped on the eating terrace in the foreground. The view is a static one and planting and statuary are used to compose it. It is a garden for a middle-aged couple who enjoy pottering and the relaxed atmosphere of plants spilling out onto paving or gravel.

A strong lateral pattern progresses down this garden from one small 'room' to another. Near the house is a terrace with a gravel area beyond. A statue breaks up the pattern before the mown grass area and the last 'room' consists of rough grass with bulbs and fruit trees. The boundary fence is hidden by shrubs, and trees frame the general view

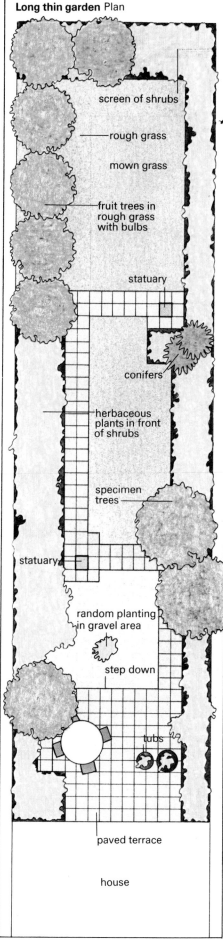

Long thin garden Plan

screen of shrubs

rough grass

mown grass

fruit trees in rough grass with bulbs

statuary

conifers

herbaceous plants in front of shrubs

specimen trees

statuary

random planting in gravel area

step down

tubs

paved terrace

house

Design for a country garden site

An irregular-shaped country garden can present just as many problems as the town gardens just described. Here we look at some possible solutions that would blend in with a less formal rural setting.

This site seemed to be the leftover bit between fields, surrounded by thorn hedges and very boggy at its farthest corner. The back of the period house was sited against the road, with the front door and main living room facing south onto the garden.

The plan shows clearly how the lines of the pattern should first start off with some regard to the shape of the house, usually with straight lines. These can then be continued on in curves to sweep about and encompass existing features and altogether be more gentle than a formal layout that in any case would not sit well within the boundary lines here.

The house is surrounded by a York stone paved terrace, so that the area outside the living room gets a long view down into the curving wild garden under a few old fruit trees. At the rear of the house the formal pattern has been broken down to form a small box-hedged herb garden conveniently near to the kitchen door. The existing hedge on this boundary has been replaced by a white picket fence along the roadside.

Where a house is set within a site the pattern of the garden should more or less follow, or at least compliment, the line of the house when surrounding it. As the pattern gets farther away it can become less regular. In our design the curves make a gentle, wild walk under old apple trees towards a summerhouse

Planting in the garden is mixed and colourful outside the front door, becoming wilder and more rampant as you progress down the length of the garden towards the pretty summerhouse.

At the side of the house facing west the grass is left rough, and bulbs are naturalized in it. The hedge has also been reduced in height so that the feeling of a neighbouring field rolling right in is encouraged and continues right up to the house. This rough grass motif is repeated in circular form to surround an old ash tree nearby. The internal pattern of this garden again pays little service to the existing boundary line, and thick intervening planting screens the discrepancy between the two.

In an old garden you tend to have old existing trees to work around. A feature has been made of the existing ash in this garden by surrounding it with a circle of rough grass containing massed spring and autumn bulbs.

The odd shape of this plot allows the summerhouse at the farthest end to be completely private from the house, approached by a winding, bordered path Below: plan, showing major features

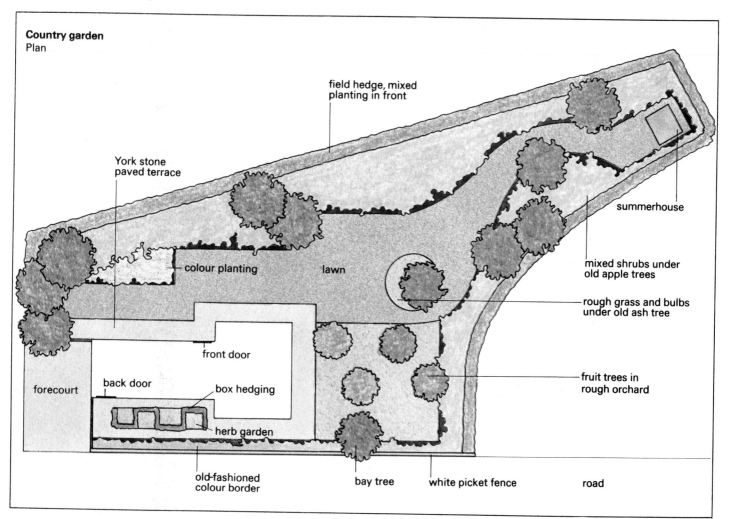

Country garden
Plan

field hedge, mixed planting in front

York stone paved terrace

summerhouse

colour planting

lawn

mixed shrubs under old apple trees

rough grass and bulbs under old ash tree

front door

back door

box hedging

forecourt

herb garden

fruit trees in rough orchard

old-fashioned colour border

bay tree

white picket fence

road

A GARDEN FOR THE ELDERLY OR DISABLED

Many people less able to cope with the normal exertions involved are still keen gardeners, and there is no need for them to be deprived of this pleasurable pastime. Here we show our ideas for an easily-worked garden and describe how to incorporate them into an existing one.

The average garden, however well planned, involves a considerable expenditure in physical energy. Mowing, digging, pruning, staking, fruit-picking, and weeding are jobs most people take for granted – time-consuming possibly, but none the less feasible.

Not everyone, however, is lucky enough to be completely fit and able to work on the construction and maintenance of a conventional garden. Some people have to spend a great deal of their time in a wheelchair, others have progressive diseases and most of us have to think of a time when we will be older and less able to cope with chores that seem easy today. Unfortunately, many people try to soldier on in a garden that becomes unattractive and completely unsuited to their particular needs; in consequence they are overwhelmed by the sheer impracticality of the situation and are never able to reap the reward of what should be a pleasant and relatively straightforward task.

Adapting the garden

The modifications needed to adapt a garden are in fact surprisingly few. Beds can be raised, steps made safer or changed to ramps for wheelchair access and paths made continuous and wide so that all parts of the garden can be easily reached. Common-sense also plays its part: paving should be completely 'true', with no poorly-laid stones that could tip or trip. Pools should be raised to minimize the possibility of accidents and to ease maintenance. Flowerbeds, if at ground level, should only be wide enough to be serviced conveniently from the adjoining path – and avoid using plants that need stakes, as these can be dangerous to an elderly gardener who may overbalance. Standard fruit trees may be too tall for easy cropping, while cordons or espaliers would be ideal in their place. Compost and rubbish should be in suitable bins of the correct height, while sheds and greenhouses can also be modified.

Hazards to avoid

Unless you can get additional help, a large garden is best avoided for obvious reasons, so we have chosen an average-sized plot measuring approximately 13.5×9m (45×30 ft). We have assumed that our garden has been inherited from a previous owner, and thus are able to show the pitfalls that a poorly-designed and badly-constructed composition might present.

Crazy paving, apart from clashing with the cleaner lines of the building, tends to have an uneven surface, and unless it is laid in mortar on a suitably-prepared base, soon becomes unsafe as the individual stones work loose. The steps are small and narrow while the meandering terrace lacks a wall, thus presenting an additional hazard. Once down the steps, the crazy paving continues, surrounding a small pool that should be raised to a height of 60cm (2 ft) to be made safe for children and adults alike.

The path is badly sited from a design aspect, chopping the garden into two unrelated sections. From the gardener's point of view it gives poor value, serving only the rose bed and failing to reach any other part of the garden. The main shrub border on the left is too wide for easy cultivation from a wheelchair – which also would be likely to bog down in the lawn after wet weather.

Giving a new look

In redesigning the garden we have tried to eliminate as many unsatisfactory features as possible. Constructional work of every type should be of the highest quality, for this will not only pay dividends in safety but also give greater pleasure in gardening terms and last a lifetime.

The terrace has been swept away and a new surface laid in a combination of brick paving and brushed concrete. Levels are particularly important in this situation

and you must always ensure that rainwater can drain away, either through pipes in the retaining walls, or to a suitable gully. Icy puddles could have unpleasant consequences.

The pool acts as a focal point from both the window and the large sliding doors. We raised it 60cm (2 ft) – which is also the ideal height for beds. A small store and worktop is sited to the right of the doors, while large tubs are ideal for bulbs, annuals and, of course, herbs.

A ramp gives access to the lower level, being safer and easier to negotiate than steps. The gradient should be no more than 1:15, as anything steeper will present difficulties for a wheelchair. The rough texture of the brushed aggregate will give the surface excellent grip. Once down the ramp, a path sweeps away round our garden, giving access to all parts of the scheme. Both paths and ramps should be at least 90cm (3 ft) wide and where the slabs are laid round the strong curve the open joints should be carefully pointed absolutely flush with the stones to make a really smooth surface.

Where both the raised beds on and below the terrace were built of 23cm (9 in) brickwork, the one jutting into the lawn was constructed differently. Here we used pre-cast concrete paving slabs, set vertically. The surrounding paving was laid first and then the area of the new bed was excavated to a depth of 30cm (12 in). The slabs, that measure 90×60cm (3×2 ft), were then placed side by side around the perimeter of the bed, being held firmly in place with concrete and checked frequently with a spirit level to ensure they were upright. When the sides were completed the joints were covered with sheets of polythene to prevent water seeping between. The bottom of the bed was then filled with 45cm (18 in) of graded hardcore and topped with good quality topsoil. It is worth bearing in mind that any bed filled with soil will subside over the course of the first year and will need a subsequent top dressing to adjust matters. So it is best to delay permanent planting until the second year and concentrate on bulbs and annuals during this initial season.

In order to allow access around the bed we need to cross part of the lawn and here it can be a good idea to lay down screen blocks of the kind that are normally used for ornamental walls; such blocks measure $30 \times 30 \times 10$cm ($12 \times 12 \times 4$ in). To lay the path dig a trench 15cm deep and 90cm wide (6 in $\times$ 3 ft) around the two sides of the bed in question. Fork over the bottom of the excavation and lay 5cm (2 in) of coarse aggregate or gravel. The blocks can then be laid flat, side by side, so that they are flush with the existing lawn surface, finally being filled with sifted

Below: Clematis montana, *a good climber*

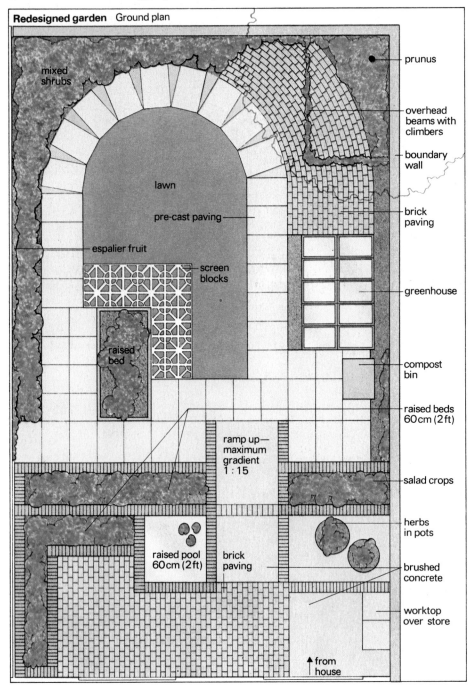

Redesigned garden Ground plan

- mixed shrubs
- lawn
- pre-cast paving
- espalier fruit
- screen blocks
- raised bed
- ramp up— maximum gradient 1 : 15
- raised pool 60 cm (2 ft)
- brick paving
- prunus
- overhead beams with climbers
- boundary wall
- brick paving
- greenhouse
- compost bin
- raised beds 60 cm (2 ft)
- salad crops
- herbs in pots
- brushed concrete
- worktop over store
- from house

topsoil. Sow grass seed and the finished product will merge into the surrounding surface and be able to support a wheelchair with ease.

Finishing touches

The existing prunus in our garden was an attractive specimen, and as it cast light shade we felt that it might form the basis for a secluded sitting area, given a suitable surface. Here we felt brick would form an ideal link with the existing walls and the pattern of courses matches the radius of the path, giving access to the greenhouse on one side. The other end is softened by planting and can be allowed to finish in a random sequence before it reaches the wall. White overhead beams frame the trunk of the tree and could be smothered with a climber such as *Clematis montana* Tetrarose.

The greenhouse could be fitted with a sliding door for easy access and there are many internal systems that can reduce maintenance and increase productivity at the same time. The small paved area between the greenhouse and the raised bed could house a compost bin, while the bed itself might be ideal for just a few salad crops.

Espalier fruit, as already mentioned, can be a real boon and the long fence on the left of the garden makes a suitable support.

Planting completes the picture and as the beds are relatively small, and the surrounding boundaries dominate, climbers will play an important part. In order to reduce maintenance it is a good plan to discard the idea of trellis which usually requires a regular coat of paint. Neat wiring is the answer here, being both permanent and unobtrusive, while self-clinging plants naturally need no support whatsoever.

As with any garden, try to select plants that will give colour and interest throughout the year, and remember that, after watering, a hose should be neatly stowed away, as one that lies at random on a path can be a real hazard.

Left: cross-section of raised bed in the lawn, constructed from pre-cast concrete slabs. Grass grows through the ornamental screen blocks laid at right
Below: cross-section through the curved path running round the lawn. Flush joints must be very carefully pointed
Bottom: cross-section of pool raised with 23cm (9 in) brick retaining walls, together with raised flowerbed built in the same fashion. The new height of 60cm (2 ft) is ideal for maintenance as it requires little awkward bending

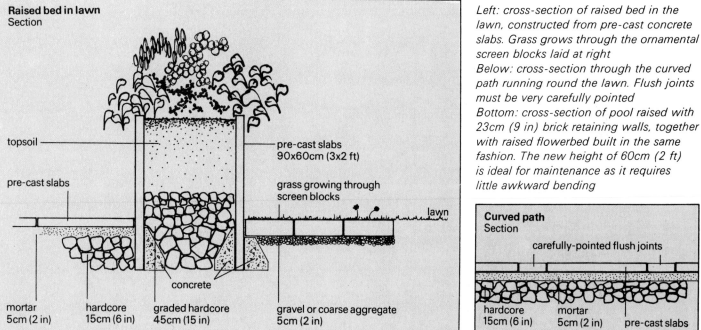

Raised bed in lawn
Section

topsoil

pre-cast slabs

pre-cast slabs 90x60cm (3x2 ft)

grass growing through screen blocks

lawn

concrete

mortar 5cm (2 in)

hardcore 15cm (6 in)

graded hardcore 45cm (15 in)

gravel or coarse aggregate 5cm (2 in)

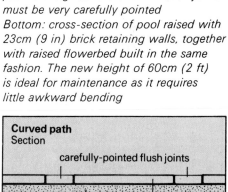

Curved path
Section

carefully-pointed flush joints

hardcore 15cm (6 in)

mortar 5cm (2 in)

pre-cast slabs

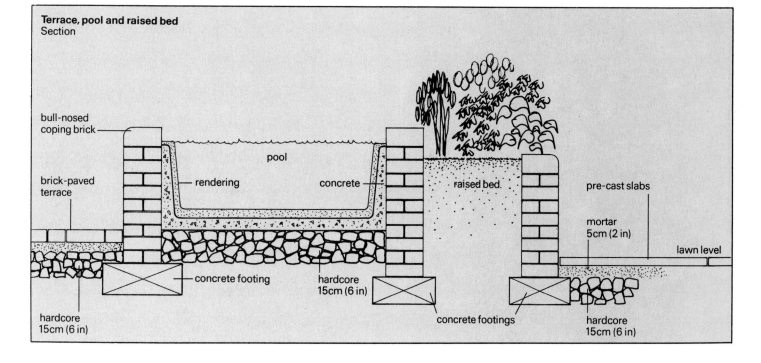

Terrace, pool and raised bed
Section

bull-nosed coping brick

pool

brick-paved terrace

rendering

concrete

raised bed

pre-cast slabs

mortar 5cm (2 in)

lawn level

concrete footing

hardcore 15cm (6 in)

hardcore 15cm (6 in)

concrete footings

hardcore 15cm (6 in)

A PROBLEM PLOT

Problems arise in various forms – neglected gardens, a waste ground left by developers, or a plot with curious contours – but with imagination they can all be overcome.

There is no doubt that most gardens can be planned with relative ease provided that basic design criteria are followed – largely a matter of common sense.

A very few gardens, however, are rightly called impossible – or very nearly so – conjuring up pictures of near-vertical slopes, quagmires, buried concrete paths and other equally daunting prospects. Fortunately, developers today are becoming far more conscious that the garden is an intrinsic part of the house it adjoins and that offering a building surrounded by a difficult site is not sound sales policy.

A steeply-sloping site, though not a design problem, can certainly be a financial one by the time some areas are levelled, others graded

and retaining walls are built. A garden that falls away, or slopes up, from a house in two directions is an altogether different proposition and can tax the owner's ingenuity to the utmost. Add to this a virgin site strewn with builder's rubble, devoid of topsoil, and without a whisker of vegetation, and you have a problem indeed.

Our 'problem' garden was just this – a plot of average size that fell steeply both away and across the back of the house. This was of split-level construction, with French windows leading onto a relatively level area to one side and the garage and utility room situated on the other side at the bottom of a steep bank.

The 'original site' artwork quite clearly shows the state of the site before work started. The brief called for a number of quite specific requirements: provision of a sitting and dining area, a small pond, room to grow vegetables, a greenhouse, lawns, space to park a caravan, and screening from the service road that ran along the right-hand boundary.

Although we were prepared for a good deal of initial hard work, and also to spend a sensible budget to complete the garden, subsequent labour and expense were to be kept to a minimum. This called for sound planning with an eye to both short- and long-term requirements.

The first and most important job was to carry out an accurate survey, checking existing levels and plotting these onto a scale drawing. We quickly found that the site fell into four distinct areas, upon which we could base our design. The real secret in planning a garden of this type is to recognize the existence of such divisions and to work with them to minimize expensive earth-moving and other major upheavals. We could thus create four 'garden rooms', each having its own purpose and each detracting from the long, rectangular boundaries. The back of the house was fortunate to be in full sun for most of the day and the

main sitting area could lead straight out from the sliding doors. Here we decided on a sensible combination of pre-cast paving and brick, the latter giving a visual link with the house and forming an interesting composition with the raised pond.

The existing bank was graded smoothly down to the lower level, the wall at the back of the pond giving both privacy from the service road and shelter, forming a perfect suntrap. Herbs soften the hard line of brickwork and give a pleasant aroma near the living-room.

Moving farther from the house, the low walls focus attention on the steps that drop down to the first small lawn, and from this point stepping stones cross the grass to reach the second, broader, flight. This was the point where the levels were most confused, falling sharply down and across the garden. By building a retaining wall and steps, and linking these in turn to the carefully-shaped bank, we created a series of features that were both attractive and practical.

It is worth bearing in mind that the steps in this garden, as in most others, benefit from being generous; a mean, narrow flight tends to 'fuss up' a design that is already complicated.

The lowest part of the garden was again given over to grass, the strong, flowing curve of the path giving the area a feeling of space and movement.

The vegetables and greenhouse fitted neatly into the corner, screened by either climbing roses or espalier fruit – the latter

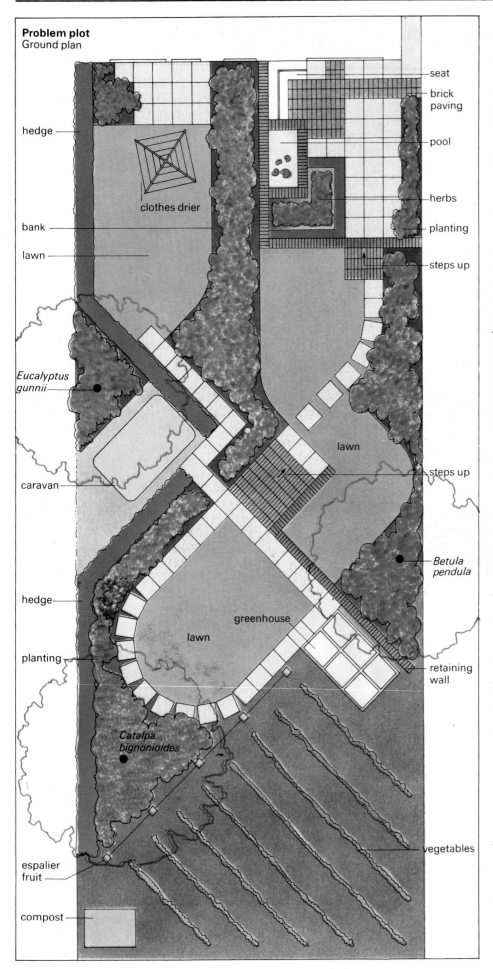

Problem plot
Ground plan

hedge

bank

lawn

Eucalyptus gunnii

caravan

hedge

planting

espalier fruit

compost

clothes drier

greenhouse

lawn

lawn

lawn

Catalpa bignonioides

seat

brick paving

pool

herbs

planting

steps up

steps up

Betula pendula

retaining wall

vegetables

undoubtedly saving space in a small garden where too many fruit trees could become oppressive. It's also worth bearing in mind that a garden full of retaining walls can be ideal for a host of climbing plants, and we took the opportunity to plant a fan-trained peach on the southern aspect of the wall to one side of the steps.

Caravans are not easy items to fit into a garden scheme, and the secret of success is to site them purposefully so that the position looks and feels intentional. There is nothing worse than a caravan, or a car for that matter, dumped at random wherever access is available.

As the service road ran the full length of the right-hand boundary we were able to make use of a flat section just to one side of the steps. A beech hedge, that echoes the main design lines of the garden, acts as an effective screen and can be clipped to just above the height of the caravan. Shade would be useful here as well, so we planted a fast-growing *Eucalyptus gunnii* that would overhang the caravan without becoming too heavy and oppressive. Such a tree is not only practical, its glaucous evergreen foliage is also a perpetual delight and invaluable for flower decoration.

With such an architectural garden there are bound to be a few hard edges, particularly during the initial seasons. This is where planting is really important, and with a sunny south-facing slope there is every opportunity for a superb display. As with all planting design, use bold groupings and drifts, the larger 'skeleton' shrubs holding the composition together. Of these, *Buddleia davidii*, *Cotinus coggygria* (*Rhus cotinus*) Royal Purple, *Choisya ternata* and *Cistus × cyprius* would be ideal. The infill planting should be more delicate and usually smaller. *Potentilla fruticosa* Tangerine, *Spiraea × bumalda* Anthony Waterer and *Hydrangea macrophylla* Blue Wave are some of the shrubs that might be used. Herbaceous material can be invaluable to highlight and brighten certain areas, and if used in conjunction with supporting shrubs needs little staking and tying.

Remember, too, that grey foliage is a great harmonizer, tying various elements of the design together. Many such plants thrive in hot, sunny positions and we could include *Senecio laxifolius*, *Phlomis fruticosa*, *Genista hispanica* and *Stachys lanata*, this last being an excellent carpeter at the front of the border.

As a final point, it's always worth including annuals to fill the gaps between the young, permanent plantings. These will add colour and maturity to the composition, as well as fragrance on a warm summer evening.

PLANTS IN DESIGN

AN INTRODUCTION TO GROUND COVER

Ground cover is a wide-ranging and diverse subject. Here we suggest two different planting schemes and with each give a comprehensive list of suitable plants.

'Gaultheria is apt to form handsome evergreen ground cover' wrote Clyde Bailey in 'The Cyclopedia of American Horticulture', published in 1900. This is the first noted use of the expression 'ground cover' that now has become a 20th century gardening cliché.

What is ground cover?

In nature the soil always becomes covered with some kind of vegetation. We choose that vegetation in a garden, or else we decide to use paving, gravel or a lawn, and our choice will determine just how much time we will need to spend working in our garden to keep it tidy and interesting. Some plants need constant attention while others virtually look after themselves, keeping the ground over which they spread free of weeds.

Ground cover plants have several attributes: the first and most important is that their foliage or branches make a covering dense enough to prevent weeds from germinating and growing through them. They can be ground-hugging plants that form a thick carpet, like saxifrage, alpine phlox, *Dianthus deltoides* (maiden pink) and thyme, or low evergreen shrubs such as prostrate juniper, santolina, erica and *Cotoneaster horizontalis*. Taller shrubs such as berberis, choisya, elaeagnus and potentilla have branches low and thick enough to stifle most weeds.

Obviously, if they are evergreen they will be more effective than if they are deciduous, but then the latter do a good job. *Spiraea × arguta*, *Elaeagnus × ebbingei*, an evergreen berberis, and *Pyracantha atalantoides* will fill a border well that acts as a break between two parts of a garden. Apart from occasional clippings and raking of dead leaves, this area needs no attention for years. In fact, this choice makes perfect ground cover.

Evergreen perennials make effective and pretty ground cover. Tiarella (foam flower), pulmonaria, *Lamium maculatum* (spotted dead nettle) and bergenia are a number of examples. Planted in groups between shrubs, or at the front of your border, they will all help to stop the weeds growing. Many perennials that lose their leaves in winter make a dense enough

mass of roots to discourage weeds. Mints, marjoram, *Alchemilla mollis* (lady's mantle), *Campanula carpatica* (bellflower) and some of the hardy geraniums will do this. Others with large leaves cover the soil so successfully all the summer that the ground under them keeps weed-free. Examples are hostas, acanthus, gunnera and *Ligularia dentata*.

A very important quality, especially in the warmer months, is help in conserving moisture. Everyone who has done any gardening must have noticed how the ground under a low, spreading plant is often still moist while the surrounding bare earth may be bone dry. So, thickly-filled borders stand up to dry conditions far better than sparsely-planted ones. The plants themselves create shade and thus help to prevent loss of moisture.

impossible to disentangle them.

If the soil is full of perennial weeds and grass then give them a dose of weedkiller that contains paraquat and diquat, and kills only through the leaves that absorb the weedkiller and pass it down to the roots. The moment it touches the soil it is neutralized and so cannot spread to nearby plants. After the weeds have died, break down the soil by digging or rotavation. If another crop of weeds come through, dig again, carefully removing as many roots as you can. It is essential to do this preliminary work thoroughly so do not be impatient and plant too soon.

As for manures, newly-dug ground is sure to need an addition of organic material. If you can get it, farmyard manure or good-quality compost is ideal for digging in. Otherwise you should use

Above: santolina in the foreground, geraniums in bloom, tradescantia and euphorbia mixed with Stachys lanata
*Far left: a border at Barnsley House, Gloucestershire, with (from front to back) senecio, a variegated symphoricarpos, taller, golden forms of privet, and elm
Left:* Asperula odorata *(woodruff) and large-leaved bergenias shaded by a horse chestnut tree at Syon Park, outside London*

Getting ready to plant

The preparation of your borders is of the utmost importance. Just because you intend to use weed-suppressing, ground cover plants, do not leave the roots of perennial weeds such as nettles and dandelions in the ground. Before you start planting, remove them all very thoroughly or they will grow up through the roots of your new shrubs and it will be

an organic fertilizer containing peat that you fork into the top few centimetres of your soil. Both come in handy-sized bags with full instructions for quantity per square metre (or yard). By the time you have bought several bags and carried them home, you will probably want to make your own compost for future use.

Some warnings

When planning to use ground cover plants, you must bear in mind the rate at which they will increase and the manner in which they do it. You can easily find out about the ultimate height and spread to which shrubs grow. But some plants increase by underground roots, such as *Hypericum calycinum* (rose of Sharon) and the mints. These should be treated with caution or put in the right place where they cannot invade your more treasured specimens. Hypericum can be prevented from becoming a nuisance if bordered by a stone wall and, say, the drive. In these circumstances its complete vigour is an advantage but elsewhere it could be disastrous.

Herbaceous plants that spread quickly by their roots are best planted beside each other; then it is a case of survival of the strongest, and eventually they will merge together. *Campanula glomerata*, *Euphorbia robbiae* (spurge) and *Anaphalis triplinervis* are three tough spreaders. Other plants increase by rooting as their new shoots touch the ground. These are usually easy to control as all you have to do is to pull up any new shoots where they are unwanted. Tiarella, *Symphytum grandiflorum* (comfrey), *Stachys lanata* (lamb's tongue) and ajuga (bugle) go into

Above: the rampant Lamium galeobdolon
Right: well-developed border of Stachys lanata, *santolina, red-flowered* Monarda didyma, *delphinium, acanthus, elaeagnus*

this category. Others like *Alchemilla mollis* increase at quite a formidable rate by seeding. No harm is done if you know where the seedlings are and pull them up while they are young.

As long as you know a plant's potential before you use it, all will be well. We all make mistakes and ones to avoid at all costs are putting *Saponaria officinalis* (soapwort) among shrub roses, and *Mentha gentilis* (ginger mint) in the herbaceous border. They are both so invasive that they should only be used where nothing else will grow. *Lamium galeobdolon* (yellow archangel) has the same habit and should be banned from the flower garden, except perhaps when it is used as a cascade round the edge of a tub.

The following suggestions will give you ideas for different situations where you can use ground cover.

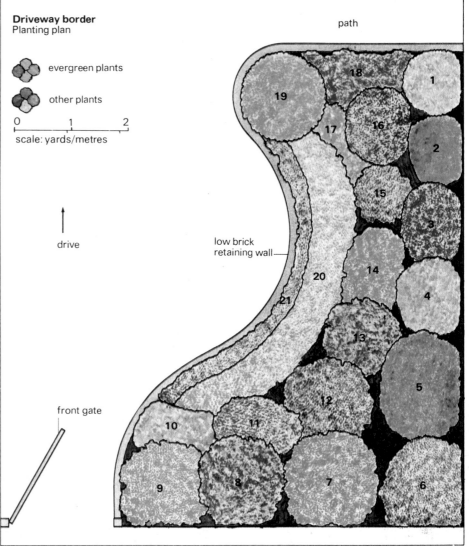

Driveway border
Planting plan

path

⬡ evergreen plants

⬡ other plants

0   1   2
scale: yards/metres

↑

drive

low brick
retaining wall

front gate

Key to planting plan

1 *Salix alba* Vitellina (golden willow)
2 *Mahonia japonica*
3 *Viburnum × bodnantense* – specimen
4 *Sorbus* Joseph Rock
5 *Virburnum tinus* (laurustinus)
6 *Chamaecyparis lawsoniana* Lutea
  (Lawson cypress) – specimen
7 *Cryptomeria japonica* Elegans
  (Japanese cedar)
8 *Potentilla* Elizabeth (cinquefoil)
9 *Juniperus sabina tamariscifolia*
10 *Tiarella cordifolia* (foam flower)
11 *Cytisus × kewensis* (broom) underplanted
  with *Ceratostigma plumbaginoides*
12 *Hebe* Autumn Glory

13 *Acer palmatum* (Japanese maple)
  – specimen – on acid soil, or *Cotinus
  coggygria* Royal Purple (smoke tree) on
  alkaline soil
14 *Hebe* Mrs Winder
15 *Pieris floribunda* on acid soil, or
  Taxus baccata Adpressa (common yew)
  on alkaline soil
16 *Cotoneaster* Hybridus Pendulus
  – specimen
17 *Helleborus corsicus* (Corsican hellebore)
18 Hostas and ferns
19 *Juniperus horizontalis* Glauca
  (creeping juniper)
20 *Erica* (heaths); select winter-flowering
  varieties according to soil
21 *Cotoneaster dammeri*

DRIVEWAY BORDER

The impression you get as you walk
through the front gate into a garden sets
the tone for what you will expect to find
farther round the corner, so you want to
try to make this area as well furnished and
interesting as you can. Bedded-out
wallflowers and petunias look fine when
they are in flower but you need to do
better than this in order to sustain year-
long interest. Foliage ground cover, with

an inter-planting of bulbs, flowers and
berries, can give something to catch the
eye each month of the year.

Make a list of the evergreen 'shapes'
that you like, such as the low-spreading
junipers and golden upright false cypresses, chamaecyparis, then go to a
nursery and have a good look around,
checking ultimate heights and spreads.
Next, make a plan on paper to scale and
fit in your various choices. Once you have

defined the shape of your bed, then mark out the position of each shrub or plant with bamboos and look at your border from the front gate and again from a window to make sure that everything is sited to best advantage. It is really just like creating a picture. Do not be tempted to plant too close; for the first summer or two you can always infill with annuals or biennials.

MIXED BORDER

Today few of us have the time or inclination to look after a straightforward herbaceous border, hopefully full of colour from mid summer to late autumn (June to October). It involves too much work and the plants remain in their glory for too short a time. With experience you may arrive at a labour-saving compromise that gives a good effect virtually all the year round, that is the mixed herbaceous and shrub border. Here, with careful planning, shrubs, perennials, conifers and even annuals are incorporated to create an interesting com-

bination of shapes, colours and textures. Deep borders are much easier to make than long, narrow ones, for then you can create vistas in depth as well as length.

In order to minimize your maintenance work you must choose a framework of ground-covering shrubs and then infill between them with a few perennials and low, mat-forming plants. This infilling process is essential, and should be thought of as expendable. As your shrubs grow they will encroach on the infillers and partly take over from them.

It is interesting that the great English gardener Gertrude Jekyll (1843–1932), famous for her superb colour schemes in herbaceous borders, did not neglect these mixed types. When you are planning, remember to develop contrast using leaf shape, texture and shrub form. Round, dome-shaped bushes are soothing and lead your eye on. Upright conifers with a clear-cut edge act as exclamation marks and tend to hold your attention, taking your gaze upwards. Standard trees with light foliage are useful and need not be

put at the back. Do not despise the golden forms of ligustrum (privet) or lonicera (honeysuckle), as they both make a wonderful contribution to foliage effect.

While waiting for your shrubs to develop, you can use digitalis (foxglove), verbascum (mullein) and onopordons that make flat, weed-suppressing rosettes the first year and then flower in the second. *Polemonium coeruleum* (Jacob's ladder) and aquilegia (columbine) look good between taller shrubs. When you have found out which lilies suit your soil, invest in a few and use them in small groups. The shrubs will act as support and give the bulbs the shade they need.

If you are fond of deciduous, summer-flowering shrubs like syringa (lilac), weigela and philadelphus (mock orange), you can improve their winter and spring appearance and save weeding under them by using ground cover underplanting. Try the tough comfrey *Symphytum grandiflorum*, a rapid spreader that flowers prettily in mid and late spring (March and April) and is quite easy to control.

Mixed border Planting plan — back of border — stepping stones — scale: yards/metres 0 1 2

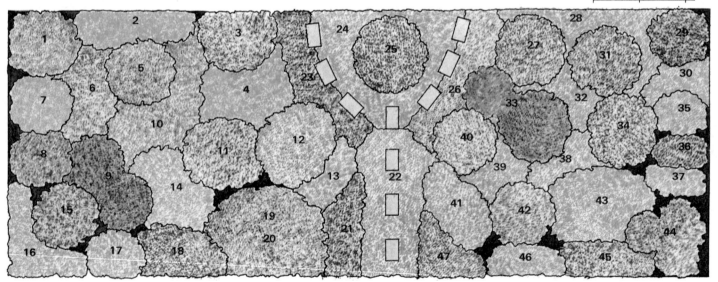

Key to planting plan
1 Hebe
2 *Atriplex halimus* (tree purslane)
3 *Elaeagnus pungens* Maculata
4 *Euonymus fortunei* (spindle tree)
5 *Gleditschia triacanthos* Sunburst (honey locust) – specimen
6 *Ruta graveolens* (rue)
7 Acanthus (bear's breeches)
8 *Juniperus communis* Depressa Aurea (common juniper)
9 *Potentilla* Elizabeth (cinquefoil)
10 Lavandula (lavender)
11 *Symphoricarpos orbiculatus* Variegatus (variegated coral berry)
12 *Lonicera nitida* Baggessen's Gold (honeysuckle)
13 *Cheiranthus* Bowles Variety (wallflower)
14 *Anthemis cupaniana*
15 *Santolina chamaecyparissus* (cotton lavender)

16 *Stachys lanata* (lamb's tongue)
17 *Hebe armstrongii* (hebe)
18 *Viola cornuta* Alba
19 *Jasminum humile revolutum* (jasmine) – specimen
20 *Lonicera japonica* Aureoreticulata (Japanese honeysuckle)
21 *Origanum vulgare* Aureum (marjoram)
22 *Lavandula spica* Munstead (dwarf lavender)
23 *Euonymus fortunei* (spindle tree)
24 *Euphorbia robbiae* (spurge)
25 *Sorbus hupehensis* – specimen
26 *Vinca minor* (lesser periwinkle)
27 *Cryptomeria japonica* Elegans (Japanese cedar)
28 *Convallaria majalis* (lily of the valley)
29 *Iberis sempervirens* (candytuft)
30 *Ajuga metallica* (bugle)
31 *Philadelphus* Belle Etoile (mock orange)
32 *Symphytum grandiflorum* (comfrey)
33 *Weigela* Bristol Ruby

34 *Syringa microphylla* Superba (rose-lilac)
35 *Dorycnium hirsutum* (canary clover)
36 *Polygonum affine* Donald Lowndes (knotweed)
37 *Saxifraga umbrosa* (London pride)
38 *Prunus glandulosa* (Chinese bush cherry) – specimen
39 *Helleborus orientalis* (Lenten rose)
40 *Berberis thunbergii* Rose Glow (barberry)
41 *Geranium endressii* Claridge Druce
42 *Acer palmatum* (Japanese maple)
43 *Salvia officinalis* Purpurascens (common sage)
44 *Berberis thunbergii* Atropurpurea Nana (barberry)
45 *Campanula carpatica* (bellflower)
46 *Lamium maculatum* Roseum (spotted dead nettle)
47 *Ajuga reptans* Burgundy Glow (common bugle)

Above: the aromatic Origanum vulgare Aureum *(marjoram) likes a well-drained position*

Convallaria (lily of the valley) make a thick mass of roots that deter all weeds, and they bloom before the shrubs come into leaf.

The evergreen *Euonymus fortunei* (spindle tree) varieties make splendid mounded humps that look especially good in the winter sunshine. Hellebores are perfectly happy when tucked away under shrubs; in fact it is an admirable place for them as their seedlings are then undisturbed. Bulbs cannot be classified as ground cover, but a drift of blue muscari (grape hyacinths) or scilla (squill) look just right under deciduous shrubs.

The plants suggested in the mixed border plan illustrated opposite will all grow on acid or alkaline soil.

DRY, SHADY AREA
Most gardens have a dry, shady patch under deciduous trees where planting is a problem. Grass is a possibility, but a poor one, as it would not thrive and mowing could be awkward. So what are the alternatives?

Hedera (ivy) is one obvious answer. This may sound dull and unexciting but if you choose one with a large shiny leaf such as *Hedera helix* Hibernica or *H. colchica* Dentata Variegata, you will have a year-long interest and the only maintenance will be to keep it within bounds and trimmed. Ivy can thrive in the driest of places and still look good. Small trees can be underplanted with the smaller-leaved

H. helix varieties many of which have pretty markings. They are a versatile group, as our Victorian gardening ancestors, who used them with great imagination, knew. They take quite a while to get their roots down and their top-growth on the move but once started will form an impenetrable carpet against weeds.

Another idea for the same situation would be *Cotoneaster horizontalis* underplanted with variegated periwinkle, *Vinca major* Variegata. This cotoneaster is not evergreen but in winter its mass of thin branches make a good weed barrier. The periwinkle needs a yearly clip back, which is best done just before its companion comes into leaf.

Bupleurum fruticosum is a wonderfully obliging evergreen shrub of great distinction. It manages to thrive in a really dry, shady situation, and considering its potential, it is surprising it is not better known. A group planted around a tree bole makes a heartening sight in winter. All flower-arrangers fall for its unusual green flowers and, later on, seed-heads. It would be expensive to buy enough plants for a group so why not try to make it up from seed or cuttings? You might feel it would take too long to achieve, but this is not true if weighed against the long-standing success of your plan.

The evergreen *Mahonia aquifolium* (Oregon grape) is another star performer under trees. The rich yellow flowers open in spring and are followed by black

berries; the leaves turn scarlet in winter.

Underplanting birch trees can present a real problem. They are gross feeders, taking every bit of moisture from the surrounding topsoil. One good solution is the rather coarse-leaved *Lithospermum purpureo-caeruleum*. It has eye-catching blue flowers in early summer (May) after which the stems fan out and take root wherever they touch down. The more refined lithospermums will only tolerate an acid soil, but this particular species is best on lime.

Whatever you choose, do use groups of the same plant; do not be tempted by a mixture as this greatly lessens the effect.

DRY, SUNNY BANK
Banks are always hard to mow, so if you do not want a flowery mead (which in itself can be very rewarding) you must find suitable plants to cover the ground. This should be quite easy if you consider the conditions – dry and in full sun, in fact typical of Mediterranean hillsides. Here you find *Anthemis cupaniana*, ballota, cistus (rock rose), dorycnium, rosemary, lavender and santolina, and others that revel in the sun and a dry root-run.

These all need very little attention and will make solid, evergreen or grey clumps in their second year. If necessary, rosemary can be cut back immediately after flowering. Never cut the old wood of lavender; instead, prune it back to the new growth in late spring (April) and, of course, remove the flower-stalks before they fade completely – for the sake of tidiness; these can then be dried and used for pot-pourri. Spring-prune santolina and ballota back to the new growth; this is essential if you wish to prevent them from becoming straggly. Ballota flowers in late summer (July), and can be cut for dry decoration.

Leave the flower-heads on dorycnium as they make good seed-pods, but deadhead the anthemis; give both a spring grooming.

Cistus need no attention except for an occasional tidy. The hardiest are *Cistus × corbariensis*, with pale crimson buds that are pure white when open, *C. × lusitanicus* Decumbens, white with a maroon blotch, *C. × purpureus*, and *C.* Silver Pink. A close planting of a selection of these shrubs will make a lovely aromatic carpet by the second year.

During the first summer it would be a good thing to use simazine between the plants to prevent weeds from germinating; or you could apply a thick mulch of peat, sterilized compost, leaf mould or lawn mowings. This last will heat up, so do not put it too close to stems of shrubs.

ISLAND BEDS FOR HARDY PERENNIALS

Island beds have long been a feature of public and private gardens, but until quite recently they were used for the display of bedding plants to include roses and dahlias, as well as short-lived or tender subjects for a limited period – known as spring (or summer) bedding.

While beds with all-round access and vision continue to be used for bedding plants, they are not described as 'island beds' any more, this term being reserved for beds planted with hardy perennials.

The conventional herbaceous border of the past was invariably backed by a wall, hedge or fence, against which the tallest hardy perennials were grown, grading down to the shortest at the front, for access and visibility. However, observations over many years revealed the harmful effect of the backing, which so often reduced light and air that plants grew excessively tall, and weakly. Even with a vast amount of tedious and expensive staking, the taller plants tended to overhang the shorter, and the general effect was often disappointing and displeasing to the eye as the plants were denied natural growth and freedom in their competition for light and air.

Experimental island beds appeared at Bressingham Gardens in Diss, Norfolk in 1952. Since then, it has been proved beyond all doubt that plants respond to the light and air of an island bed with shorter but sturdier growth and need minimal staking. In over forty beds of various shapes and sizes at Bressingham, delphiniums are virtually the only plants in need of support.

While accepting island beds as the most natural and pleasing means of growing hardy perennials, there are still environmental factors to consider, including the space available, soil and situation, and, to some extent, climate. There are gardens where a severe or limited rectangular shape may appear to lend itself more readily to a boundary-backed border, with a lawn as the central feature, but an open mind and a willingness to break with convention can be the start of a new and much more satisfying dimension in gardening.

What are hardy perennials?

In the context of island beds, hardy perennials are plants (other than bulbs or shrubs) that can be relied on to survive winter, and flower year after year. Not all are truly 'herbaceous' (the strict meaning of which is 'dying back to dormancy during winter') since some retain their foliage. There is an immense selection and with careful planning, a long succession of flowering – from early spring to mid winter (February to December) – can be achieved, or alternatively a full and varied display at almost any time of year.

The majority of hardy perennials prefer an open situation and relatively few are fussy as to soil. There is a wide range of height and habit, so taller, robust plants can be used as space-fillers in large gardens, while dwarf or slow-growing ones are more suitable where space is limited. Many so-called 'rock plants', that are actually dwarf hardy perennials, are ideal for frontal positions in island beds.

Key to planting plan

1 *Anemone japonica* White Queen (Japanese anemone)
2 *Heliopsis scabra* Golden Plume
3 *Papaver orientale* Goliath (Oriental poppy)
4 *Helenium autumnale* Coppelia (sneezeweed)
5 *Sidalcea* Rose Queen
6 *Salvia × superba* East Friesland
7 *Phlox paniculata* Mount Fujiyama
8 *Hemerocallis* Pink Damask (day lily)
9 *Eryngium bourgatii*
10 *Crocosmia masonorum*
11 *Dicentra spectabilis* (bleeding heart or Dutchman's breeches)
12 *Phlox paniculata* Starfire
13 *Agapanthus* Headbourne Hybrids (African lily)
14 *Molinia caerulea* Variegata
15 *Sedum spectabile* Autumn Joy
16 *Lythrum salicaria* Robert
17 *Rudbeckia fulgida* Goldsturm
18 *Campanula carpatica* (bellflower)
19 *Solidago* Queenie (golden rod)
20 *Erigeron speciosus* Foerster's Liebling (fleabane)
21 *Oenothera tetragona* Fireworks
22 *Stokesia laevis* Blue Star
23 *Doronicum caucasicum* Spring Beauty
24 *Potentilla atrosanguinea* Wm Rollisson (cinquefoil)
25 *Geranium pratense* Johnson's Blue (meadow cranesbill)
26 *Aster novi-belgii* Jenny (Michaelmas daisy)
27 *Kniphofia galpinii* Bressingham Comet (red-hot poker)
28 *Achillea* Moonshine (yarrow)
29 *Armeria maritima* Dusseldorf Pride (sea pink)
30 *Aster thomsonii* Nana
31 *Coreopsis grandiflora* Goldfink
32 *Veronica teucrium* Crater Lake Blue
33 *Dianthus* Sam Barlow

Island Bed
Planting plan

Scale: yards / metres | 1 | 2

Planting plan layout (numbered positions):
28, 29, 30, 31, 32, 33
27, 13, 14, 15, 16, 17, 18
12, 1, 2, 3, 4, 5
26, 11, 10, 9, 8, 7, 6, 19
25, 24, 23, 22, 21, 20

Below: Ameria maritima, *good for edging*

Shape and site

The shape of the bed should be in keeping with the surrounding features. Use a free-form shape if the features are informal, but in most cases a rectangle or oval fits in best with a formal garden outline. The most appropriate location for an island bed is normally somewhere fairly central, in a lawn or at one end of it.

You may already have a bed that you have been using for 'bedding' arrangements, necessitating replacing the plants once and often twice a year. Although the initial outlay for perennials is higher than for bedding plants, the former group's range of form and colour, returning year after year, more than compensates for the extra cost.

Selecting your plants

Once you have decided on a site, prepare the soil by digging it over, weeding it, and – if it is of poor quality – enriching it with well-rotted manure, compost or peat, and organic fertilizer. This done, you will be ready to think about planning and selecting the contents of the bed. The vital factors to consider are varying colours and heights for contrast and continuity of flowering times. Aim to place the tallest plants roughly in the centre, and the shortest around the perimeter. Flowering time, height and habit are given in most catalogues produced by specialist firms, and in books on hardy perennials. For a maximum display of colour within a limited area you will have to sacrifice variety – and to some degree continuity – concentrating on larger groups of fewer varieties. There is no doubt that grouping gives a better general effect but if variety is what appeals to you most then you should select plants for variety.

An island bed of, say, 17 sq m (about 20 sq yd), while not large, would hold about 100 plants of the kind that produce a modest spread of growth. All the plants could be different, but three of a kind to make 33 groups would not only be effective visually but also give a fair variety to cover several months of flowering. For such a relatively small bed, space five plants over roughly 1 sq m (or 1 sq yd). This will allow for an average planting distance, within a group, of 38cm (15 in), but several centimetres more should be left between the individual groups. By this means, the vital light and air space is allowed for along with ease of access for maintenance. With larger beds you can choose more robust plants requiring larger planting distances for healthy growth.

The importance of adequate, but not wasteful, spacing will be appreciated when it is realized that on a plant per square metre basis, growth varies so that in the case of a few plants you will have to restrict yourself to one plant in the same area of space where 12 dwarf kinds can be planted as they have little outward spread. Some segregation will obviously be desirable if your selection involves plants of widely-differing growing habits. It is important, therefore, that you know what growth to expect *before* you start to order your plants.

Preparing the planting plan

It is a simple matter to make your selection if you first prepare a planting plan as in this way errors in placing are minimized. Avoid plants that grow disproportionately tall for a given space: a safe rule is to restrict heights to half the width of the bed. So if your bed is 2·4m (8 ft) wide, the tallest plants for the centre areas should not exceed 1·2m (4 ft) in height, while intermediate plantings should be from 38–90cm (15–36 in) and

Below: section of island bed, with salvia (sage) at front, geranium (cranesbill) in centre, and campanula (bellflower) on the left at back, crocosmia on the right

Hardy perennials in informally-shaped island beds at Bressingham Gardens
Left: well-planted example has helenium (sneezeweed) at front, kniphofia (red-hot poker) and hemerocallis (day lily) in centre, and phlox, crocosmia and heliopsis at back. Below left: bed includes aster at front, geranium and sedum in centre, and campanula at back. Below: island beds as seen in landscaped environment of Bressingham's Dell Garden. Note effective use of specimen trees and shrubs between beds

dwarf plants on the outside edge from 15–40cm (6–16 in) in height.

To a large extent, the habit of hardy perennials – especially those suitable for the inner parts of a bed – falls into two categories: those that flower at more or less one level, like *Aster novi-belgii* (Michaelmas daisy) and other members of the extensive daisy family, and those that are more spiky, like lupins. To achieve the most pleasing results, and to break up uniformity or flatness, it is best to intersperse the two groups. Here and

there, something erect and spiky can be placed nearer the front than the height-to-width rule suggests, to provide focal points. However, so much depends on personal taste or choice. If at the outset you prefer to stick to the guidelines, adjustments can be made after the first season, and any errors in the planning and planting corrected.

Having made your selection, the planning is quite simple. Mark the height, colour and flowering time against each plant on your list, and add an

identification number. Transcribe these details onto labels on sticks that you can then place on the empty island bed to represent each variety. In this way, you can decide on the best planting positions before the plants arrive. It cannot be over-emphasized that you should only buy from specialist producers. They will not only have the necessary variety, true to name and type, but their plants will be of a quality that will pay off in the long run.

When to plant

The best time to plant hardy perennials is late autumn (October). Given sufficient moisture in the soil, its warmth will encourage immediate root action. However, planting may have to be deferred until the following spring, for nurserymen are sometimes unable to cope with all the orders on hand. Early winter (November) is still safe for planting out all but a few hardy perennials, but if you are planting in the spring, the earlier the better. Where the soil is dry, either in autumn or spring, surface watering should be done using a fine spray. Don't begin planting until any soil stickiness has evaporated. To avoid harmful treading in wet weather, or on sticky soils, you should stand on boards, moving them as planting proceeds.

How to maintain

After-care is not very demanding of time and energy. Weeds must be controlled, of course, and though chemicals cannot be used, the hoe will cope with seedlings, and retain the loose tilth that is so helpful to growth. Perennial weeds, if they appear, should be forked out ruthlessly. Mulching is good practice, and peat or pulverized bark is the best material to use. Apply the mulch in spring or early summer (May), 2–5cm (1–2 in) thick, and it will act both as a weed-deterrent and moisture-preserver.

Island Bed planting plan

Our own Island Bed planting plan is designed for a mainly sunny position, but its contents represent only a small fraction of the range available. It is intended to serve merely as a guide, and reliable, colourful alternatives would be possible so long as the height, habit and colour are similar. Arrangements for colour contrast or blend are likewise a matter of preference or taste. It is the basic principles that matter, and these can be reduced to the fundamental objective of allowing the plants to give of their best by providing the right conditions for growth, and making a sensible selection for whatever site you choose.

HERBACEOUS BORDERS IN THE GARDEN

There is an old-fashioned ring about 'herbaceous borders' and here we illustrate some typical ones. We then follow up with planting plans and lists of plants that would suit different seasons of the year and varying situations.

The herbaceous border has been much maligned in the labour-saving cult of recent years, admittedly with a degree of justification. But why condemn something of beauty if there are still keen gardeners prepared to undertake the work involved? A herbaceous border requires plenty of preparation and constant maintenance, but then so does a shrub border.

The herbaceous garden
The preparation for a border is not complicated and involves straightforward digging, although this isn't everyone's favourite gardening task. If the soil is sandy then you only need to dig out a single 'spit', that is, the depth of the spade being used. You should then incorporate manure in the bottom of this spit; if the soil is heavy, it may be necessary to double dig it (that is two spits deep), to give the extra drainage required. drainage required.

Again, incorporate manure into the bottom spit. Before planting, it does no harm to scatter a general chemical fertilizer and rake it in. Spring planting is firmly recommended for herbaceous plants. There is a critical period during late spring (late March and April) when it is best to plant and this can sometimes be extended into early summer (May) if the spring season has been a wet one.

Choosing plants
There are plenty of opportunities for making notes on possible selections during the summer, when visiting gardens or flower shows. Alternatively, you could choose from books on perennials or from specialist catalogues. Personal preference must count, of course, but it is as well to consider the factors that really matter where garden worthiness is concerned. Reliability, adaptability and display potential, together with freedom from trouble, the ability to grow without a support, and not encroaching on less vigorous neighbours are the qualities to

look for. Under the heading of 'display potential' preference should be given to plants that have a long flowering period, together with a reasonably good appearance when the flowers have passed.

One other category of worthiness includes plants with attractive foliage, and those that remain evergreen – for example, certain ornamental grasses and low-growing perennials. Some plants are still favourites despite the fact that they make a bright display only for a very brief period. Irises and paeonies are among these, while others – such as delphiniums and Michaelmas daisies – can be quite troublesome if you try to make them give of their best.

Most perennials prefer an open situation, but the range available is so immense that there is virtually no position in any garden – whether sunny or shady, dry or moist – where some will not grow. It goes without saying that a selection should be made in accordance with the site and soil type. A north-facing border with a high backing would best be stocked with plants that like – or will

adapt to – some shade, but choose sun-lovers for a south-facing border.

These would also need to be drought-resisting plants, so any observations on behaviour during past dry spells would be worth remembering. Fore-knowledge of plant behaviour, including habit of growth, height, spread and time of flowering, is a great advantage when making a selection. Those of you who feel the urge to give perennials the chance to grow as naturally as possible will find their study fascinating. Knowledge leads to anticipation, and on to realization of the joys that perennials can bestow.

Staking and tying
One drawback to having herbaceous plants is that they need support, and staking not only takes a long time but gives an ugly appearance to the border. The least attractive form of staking is with canes and string; pea sticks are best and should be used in early summer (May),

Below: herbaceous border at Barrington Court in Somerset

Above: hardy perennials in midsummer

when growth is just beginning to rise. For a week or two, the border will look as if it is merely a collection of pea sticks. The pea sticks should be inserted close to each clump with the tops bent inwards above the clump, just below the height at which the plant will flower; the plant will continue to grow through the bent-over twigs and eventually conceals them entirely. This style of staking will withstand the onslaught of the worst weather that even a traditional British summer can produce.

An alternative is to use a form of metal support based on the same principle as the bent-over pea stick, with the plants growing through a ringed wire meshing. The rings vary in diameter but may not be large enough for bigger clumps.

Planning a herbaceous border

At this stage a precise definition ought to be given as to what exactly is a herbaceous perennial. A perennial plant is one that lasts for an indefinite period, and this applies to trees and shrubs, but they do not die down to the ground each year. Thus it can be said that a herbaceous perennial has an annual stem and a perennial rootstock. However, many plants that are very useful in the herbaceous border, such as kniphofia (red hot poker), do not die down altogether, so, by way of a looser definition, a herbaceous perennial is one that flowers perennially, but has soft stems.

The herbaceous border is probably the most artificial form of gardening that has ever been devised, but if cleverly planned it can be one of the most spectacular and colourful features in a garden. Planning the planting of the border is fairly straightforward provided one or two principles are observed: first, it would be tempting to have in a border, say 7·3m (24 ft) long by 1·8m (6 ft) deep, three rows of plants – tall at the back, medium in the middle and dwarf in the front. But this would give too uniform an effect and so, in our plan, we bring forward some back-row plants to the middle and some middle-row plants to the front to provide a variation. You should have three, five, seven or nine plants in each clump as this enables it to have an irregular rather than a rounded shape; you can also arrange the plants to run into each other rather than leave gaps in the grouping.

In the planning you can organize an early border or an autumn border. However, unless you are especially fond of one particular group of plants, it would be inadvisable to have a border devoted to, say, delphiniums, irises or Michaelmas daisies, as the flowering period would be so brief. You might make an exception of paeonies; they do very well in a shady corner where little else will grow, and there can be few gardens that do not possess such a corner.

Widening a border

Where an old narrow border has become troublesome through competition from the backing, or because plants left in it are too tall in relation to the width, consider widening it if this is practical. If extra width can be gained by sacrificing a strip of lawn, there is no real problem. The turf removed can be used elsewhere perhaps; if not, it should be chopped up into small pieces and buried in the process of digging. If the border is fronted by a gravel path, this too can be dug and used, for not even dug-in gravel – unless it is too thick – will deter plants from growing, provided the soil is enriched and weathered. Such digging should always be done in the autumn, a rule in keeping with good husbandry in every respect.

It may occur to some readers that an old, unthrifty border – probably troublesome and unlovely as well – needs to be completely renovated and replanted with more suitable things. In such cases, the best plan would be first to mark any plants already in the border that are worth keeping. Take these out and heel them in somewhere else, so that everything remaining can be treated as weeds. Clear, and deeply-dig, the ground and shake out anything of a weedy nature: this should be burned, or made into a well-rotted compost by the addition of something that will increase fertility, such as manure or peat with organic fertilizer. Spade off any encroaching roots from the backing hedge or screening.

This kind of work is best done in mid or late autumn (September or October), especially if the soil is liable to become sticky when wet. On such soils it often pays to defer replanting until spring, but in any case start thinking about your selection of plants as soon as possible.

PLANTING HERBACEOUS BORDERS

Having, perhaps, visited other gardens and assessed the types of plants you would like in your own, you can now look at some catalogues and draw out the plan for your border. Here we detail individual plants and suggest particular border designs, and conclude this section with an alphabetical list of species and their characteristics.

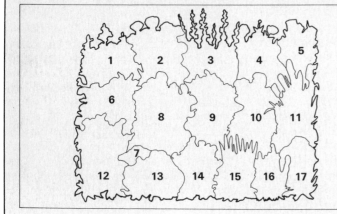

ALL SEASONS BORDER

Allow three plants of each species unless otherwise stated in brackets.

Key to border – 6 × 1·5m (20 × 5 ft)

1 *Anchusa italica*
2 *Rudbeckia subtomentosa*
3 *Delphinium*
4 *Helianthus decapetalus*
5 *Aster novi-belgii*
6 *Monarda didyma*
7 *Gypsophila repens* (1)
8 *Echinops ritro*
9 *Achillea*
10 *Chrysanthemum maximum*
11 *Kniphofia*
12 *Trollius ledebourii*
13 *Sedum maximum*
14 *Potentilla atrosanguinea*
15 *Salvia × superba*
16 *Liatris callilepis*
17 *Achillea filipendulina*

You may find it helpful to have some idea of the number of plants that will be required to fill 30 sq cm (1 sq ft) adequately. For instance, *Anchusa italica* Opel is 1·5m (5 ft) tall, with an individual spread of up to 1·2 sq m (4 sq ft). *Macleaya cordata* is 2m (6–7 ft) and has a 'thinner' style of growth, so you would plant three anchusas as against five macleayas. As a general indication, a border 12 × 1·2m (40 × 8 ft) would need 160 plants, and this can be reduced or increased in proportion as needed: for example, you would require 40 plants to begin with in a border 5 × 1·2m (20 × 4 ft). In order to provide you with a reference, we have compiled a useful chart giving you concise information, and from which the plants have been chosen for grouping in the borders as illustrated here.

As you can see from the chart details, borders can be planned for whatever time you require them and of whatever colour you want, although towards the end of the season the predominant colour, Michaelmas daisies apart, seems to be yellow. Here are three ideas for borders – for all seasons, in shade and late-flowering. If you have a particular colour or combination of colours in mind, it is easy enough to pick out from the list those you like and to make a border plan that will suit your own taste.

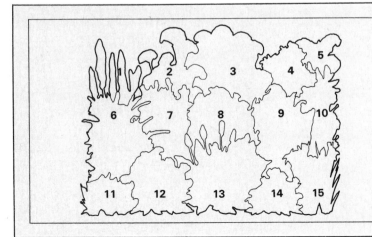

SHADED BORDER

Allow three plants of each species.

Key to border – 6 × 1·5m (20 × 5 ft)

1 *Aconitum arendsii*
2 *Thalictrum glaucum*
3 *Eupatorium purpureum*
4 *Campanula lactiflora*
5 *Thalictrum aquilegifolium*
6 *Dicentra spectabilis*
7 *Campanula persicifolia*
8 *Geranium psilostemon*
9 *Lysimachia clethroides*
10 *Anemone japonica*
11 *Liriope graminifolia*
12 *Doronicum caucasicum*
13 *Polygonum mileti i*
14 *Doronicum cordatum*
15 *Iris foetidissima*

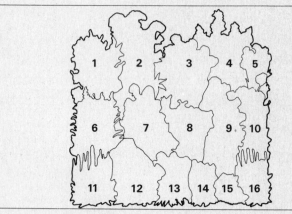

LATE-FLOWERING BORDER

Allow three plants of each species.

Key to border – 6 × 1·5m (20 × 5 ft)

1 *Aster novi-belgii*
2 *Eupatorium purpureum*
3 *Rudbeckia fulgida*
4 *Artemisia lactiflora*
5 *Vernonia crinita*
6 *Solidago × canadensis*
7 *Eryngium × oliverianum*
8 *Campanula × burghaltii*

9 *Heliopsis scabra*
10 *Anemone japonica*
11 *Veronica spicata*
12 *Sedum spectabile*
13 *Stokesia laevis*
14 *Potentilla atrosanguinea*
15 *Anaphalis triplinervis*
16 *Physostegia virginiana*

The Gardener's Seasons

early spring (February)
mid spring (March)
late spring (April)

early summer (May)
mid summer (June)
late summer (July)

early autumn (August)
mid autumn (September)
late autumn (October)

early winter (November)
mid winter (December)
late winter (January)

NAME OF PLANT	FLOWERING SEASON/REMARKS	HEIGHT
Acanthus mollis (bear's breeches)	Late summer to early autumn. White and pink. 'Architectural' leaves. Does not like winter wet.	1–1·2m (3½–4 ft)
Achillea eupatorium (or *filipendulina*) Coronation Gold	Mid to late summer. Flat yellow heads.	90cm (3 ft)
A.e. Gold Plate	Mid to late summer. Bright yellow.	1·2m (4 ft)
A. ptarmica The Pearl	Mid to late summer. Double white.	1m (3½ ft)
A. taygetea	Mid to late summer. Primrose yellow.	45cm (18 in)
A.t. Moonshine	Mid to late summer. Bright yellow.	45–60cm (18–24 in)
Aconitum arendsii	Mid summer to early autumn.	1·2m (4 ft)
A. napellus Bressingham Spire	Late summer to early autumn. Violet-blue.	90cm (3 ft)
A. variegatum bicolor	Late summer to early autumn. White and blue.	1m (3½ ft)
Agapanthus umbellatus (or *orientalis*)	Late summer to mid autumn. Mid-blue.	60cm (2 ft)
Alchemilla mollis (lady's mantle)	Mid summer to early autumn. Lime yellow.	45–60cm (18–24 in)
Anaphalis margaritacea	Early autumn. White, grey foliage.	45cm (18 in)
A. triplinervis	Late summer to mid autumn. White, sturdy.	30cm (12 in)
A. yedoensis	Early to late autumn. White, everlasting.	60cm (2 ft)
Anchusa azurea (or *italica*) Loddon Royalist	Early to mid summer. Gentian blue.	90cm (3 ft)
A.a. Opal	Early to mid summer. Soft opal blue.	1·5m (5 ft)
A.a. Royal Blue	Early to mid summer. Rich royal blue	90cm (3 ft)
Anemone japonica (or *hupehensis*) *alba* (Japanese anemone)	Early to late autumn. White.	60cm (2 ft)
A.j.a. Profusion	Mid autumn. Soft pink.	60cm (2 ft)
Anthemis tinctoria (ox-eye chamomile) Grallagh Gold	Mid summer to early autumn. Rich golden flowers.	90cm (3 ft)
A.t. Wargrave Variety	Mid summer to early autumn. Sulphur-yellow.	75cm (2½ ft)
Artemisia lactiflora (white mugwort)	Early to late autumn. Creamy-white.	1·2m (4 ft)
A.l. Lambrook Silver	Bright foliage, sprays of grey flowers.	75cm (2½ ft)
A. nutans	Feathery silver foliage. Sunny place.	60cm (2 ft)
A.n. Silver Queen	Silver foliage. Good for cutting.	75cm (2½ ft)
Aster novi-belgii (Michaelmas daisy)	See border plans for selected named species and varieties.	
Astilbe varieties	Mid summer to early autumn. Plant in a damp spot.	
Amethyst	Lilac-purple	90cm (3 ft)
Bressingham Beauty	Rich pink.	90cm (3 ft)
Ceres	Pink and rose.	1m (3½ ft)
Fanal	Bright red.	75cm (2½ ft)
Red Sentinel	Brick-red spikes.	75cm (2½ ft)
White Queen	White.	60cm (2 ft)
Astrantia carniolica Rubra	Mid summer to mid autumn. Crimson-green flowers.	38cm (15 in)
A. maxima	Mid summer to early autumn. Rose-pink.	90cm (3 ft)
Baptisia australis	Mid summer. Blue pea flowers.	90–120cm (3–4 ft)
Brunnera macrophylla	Late spring to mid summer. Blue forget-me-not flowers.	45cm (18 in)
Campanula × burghaltii	Mid summer to mid autumn. Large mauve bells.	60cm (2 ft)
C. glomerata Superba	Mid to late summer. Purple-blue.	45cm (18 in)
C. lactiflora Loddon Anna	Mid summer to early autumn. Pink.	1·2–1·5m (4–5 ft)
C. latiloba Peter Piper	Mid to late summer. Deep blue.	90cm (3 ft)
C. persicifolia	Mid summer to early autumn. Blue. Rather weedy.	90cm (3 ft)
Centaurea dealbata John Coutts	Early summer to early autumn. Clear pink.	60cm (2 ft)
C. macrocephala	Mid summer to early autumn. Large yellow flowers.	1·2–1·5m (4–5 ft)
Chelone obliqua	Early to late autumn. Pink.	60cm (2 ft)
C.o. Alba	White form.	60cm (2 ft)
Chrysanthemum maximum (shasta daisy)	Choose well-established varieties, such as these, from catalogues.	
Dairymaid	Late summer. Cream.	90cm (3 ft)
Esther Read	Late summer to mid autumn.	60cm (2 ft)
Wirral Supreme	Late summer to mid autumn. Reliable double white.	90cm (3 ft)
Clematis recta Grandiflora	Late summer to early autumn. White.	75–90cm (2½–3 ft)
Coreopsis grandiflora Goldfink	Mid summer to mid autumn. Deep yellow.	25cm (9 in)
C. g. Badengold	Late summer to early autumn. Orange-yellow.	90cm (3 ft)
C. verticillata	Mid summer to mid autumn. Starry yellow flowers.	45cm (18 in)

NAME OF PLANT	FLOWERING SEASON/REMARKS	HEIGHT
Crambe cordifolia	Early to late summer. Panicles of white flowers.	1·5–1·8m (5–6 ft)
Crocosmia masonorum	Late summer onwards. Montbretia-like orange.	90cm (3 ft)
Cynglossum nervosum (hound's tongue)	Mid summer to early autumn. Gentian blue.	30cm (12 in)
Delphinium varieties	Mid summer onwards. Good for cuttings. Choose varieties according to desired height and colour. Belladonna group are shorter, require no staking.	
Dicentra formosa Bountiful	Mid spring onwards. Pink 'bleeding heart' flowers.	45cm (18 in)
D. eximia	Late spring onwards. Pink.	45cm–60cm (1½–2 ft)
D.e. Adrian Bloom	Late spring to early summer. Vigorous.	30cm (12 in)
D.e. Alba	Early summer to mid autumn. White form.	25cm (9 in)
D. spectabilis	Late spring. Pink, the true 'bleeding heart'. Needs deep soil.	60cm (2 ft)
Dictamnus fraxinella (or *albus*)	Mid summer to early autumn. Spikes of lilac or white spider-like flowers.	75cm (2½ ft)
Dierama pendulum (wand flower)	Late summer to mid autumn. Pink flowers on graceful stems.	75–90cm (2½–3 ft)
Doronicum caucasicum Miss Mason	Late spring to mid summer. Bright yellow.	45cm (18 in)
D. cordatum	Mid spring to early summer. Golden daisies.	15–25cm (6–10 in)
D.c. Spring Beauty	Late spring to mid summer. Double yellow flowers.	38cm (15 in)
Echinacea purpurea	Early autumn. Rose to crimson.	1m (3½ ft)
E.p. The King	Early autumn. Reddish-purple on stiff spikes.	1·2m (4 ft)
Echinops humilis (globe thistle) Taplow Blue	Mid summer to mid autumn. Dark blue globes.	1·5m (5 ft)
E. ritro	Mid summer to mid autumn. Rich blue.	1m (3½ ft)
Erigeron speciosus (fleabane) Charity	Mid summer. Light pink.	60cm (2 ft)
E.s. Darkest of All	Mid summer. Deep violet-blue.	60cm (2 ft)
E.s. Dignity	Mid summer. Mauve-blue.	60cm (2 ft)
E.s. Foerster's Liebling	Mid summer. Deep cerise-pink.	60cm (2 ft)
E.s. Rose Triumph	Semi-double, deep rose-pink.	60cm (2 ft)
Eryngium bourgatii	Mid summer to early autumn. Silvery-blue.	45cm (18 in)
E. × oliverianum	Mid summer to early autumn. Blue.	90cm (3 ft)
E. tripartitum	Mid summer to early autumn. Metallic blue.	
Eupatorium purpureum	Early to mid autumn. Purple.	1·5–1·8m (5–6 ft)
E. rugosum	Late summer to mid autumn. White.	90cm (3 ft)
Euphorbia griffithii	Mid summer. Orange-red.	75cm (2½ ft)
E. polychroma (or *epithimoides*)	Late spring to early summer. Yellow.	45cm (18 in)
E. sikkimensis	Mid late summer. Purple shoots, yellow flowers.	1·2m (4 ft)
E. wulfenii	Late spring to late summer. Yellowish-green, evergreen foliage.	90cm (3 ft)
Geranium psilostemon	Late summer. Cerise.	75cm (2½ ft)
G. renardii	Early to mid summer. Light mauve.	38cm (15 in)
Geum × borisii	Early summer. Tangerine-scarlet.	30cm (12 in)
G. chiloense Fire Opal	Early summer to early autumn. Orange-red.	60cm (2 ft)
G.c. Prince of Orange	Early to mid summer. Double orange-yellow.	60cm (2 ft)
Gypsophila paniculata Bristol Fairy	Mid summer to mid autumn. Double white.	90cm (3 ft)
G. repens Rosy Veil	Mid summer to mid autumn. Double shell pink.	25cm (9 in)
Helenium autumnale Bruno	Early to late autumn. Mahogany-red.	1m (3½ ft)
H.a. Butterpat	Early to late autumn. Pure yellow.	90cm (3 ft)
H.a. Mahogany	Late summer to early autumn. Golden brown-red.	75cm (2½ ft)
H.a. The Bishop	Mid summer. Bright yellow, dark centre.	60cm (2 ft)
Helianthus decapetalus Loddon Gold	Late summer to mid autumn.	1·5m (5 ft)
H.d. Lemon Queen	Graceful lemon flowers.	1·5m (5 ft)
Heliopsis scabra Ballerina	Mid summer to early autumn. Warm yellow.	90cm (3 ft)
H.s. Golden Plume	Mid summer to mid autumn. Double deep yellow.	1·2m (4 ft)
H.s. Sunburst	Late summer. Double orange-yellow.	1·2m (4 ft)
Heuchera sanguinea Greenfinch	Early to late summer. Greenish sulphur-yellow.	75cm (2½ ft)
H.s. Pearl Drops	Early to late summer. Almost white.	60cm (2 ft)
H.s. Scintillation	Bright pink, tipped with coral-carmine.	60cm (2 ft)
Inula ensifolia	Mid summer to early autumn. Bright yellow, long-lasting.	25cm (9 in)
I. hookeri	Mid summer to mid autumn. Rayed, yellow flowers.	75cm (2½ ft)

NAME OF PLANT	FLOWERING SEASON/REMARKS	HEIGHT
Iris varieties	Named varieties of *Iris sibirica* and the flag iris, *I. germanica*, should be seen to judge for preference of height and colour.	
Kniphofia galpinii	Late summer to mid autumn. Delicate orange.	45cm (18 in)
K. nelsonii major	Early to mid autumn. Bright orange.	60cm (2 ft)
K. uvaria (red hot poker) Bee's Lemon	Late autumn. Citron yellow.	75–90cm (2½–3 ft)
K.u. Maid of Orleans	Mid summer to early autumn. Ivory-white.	90–100cm (3–3½ ft)
K.u. Royal Standard	Late summer. Bright red and yellow.	1m (3½ ft)
Liatris callilepis	Late summer to mid autumn. Fluffy lilac-purple.	75cm (2½ ft)
L. pycnostachys	Early to late autumn. Rosy purple.	90–150cm (3–5 ft)
Libertia formosa	Mid to late summer. White. Iris-type leaves.	75cm (2½ ft)
Ligularia clivorum Desdemona	Late summer to mid autumn. Orange flower, bronze foliage.	90cm (3 ft)
L.c. Greynog Gold	Late summer to mid autumn. Golden flowers.	90cm (3 ft)
L.c. Sungold	Mid summer to early autumn. Golden-yellow.	90cm (3 ft)
Liriope graminifolia	Mid autumn. Violet, grape hyacinth-like flowers.	15cm (6 in)
Lobelia cardinalis Queen Victoria	Mid to late summer. Good red. Not hardy. Needs a damp spot.	60cm (2 ft)
Lupinus (lupins) varieties	Early to mid summer. Choose variety according to desired colour. Place towards the back, where late-flowering plants can come up in front. Do not over-feed soil with farmyard manure.	
Lychnis chalcedonica (campion)	Late summer to early autumn. Brilliant scarlet.	1m (3½ ft)
L. flos-jovis	Mid summer to early autumn. Delightful combination of pink flowers and grey foliage.	25cm (9 in)
L. viscaria Splendens Plena	Mid to late summer. Cerise.	25cm (9 in)
Lysimachia clethroides	Early to mid autumn. White.	90cm (3 ft)
L. punctata	Mid to late summer. Bright yellow.	60cm (2 ft)
Lythrum salicaria (purple loosestrife) Robert	Late summer to mid autumn. Bright carmine.	75cm (2½ ft)
L.s. The Beacon	Late summer to mid autumn. Rosy-crimson.	1m (3½ ft)
Macleaya (or *Bocconia*) *cordata*	Early to mid autumn. Cream-white.	2·1m (7 ft)
M.c. Coral plume	Early to mid autumn. Buff.	2·1m (7 ft)
Monarda didyma Cambridge Scarlet	Mid summer to early autumn. Red.	90cm (3 ft)
M.d. Croftway Pink	Mid summer to early autumn. Soft pink.	90cm (3 ft)
Nepeta gigantea (catmint)	Mid summer to early autumn. Lavender-blue.	75cm (2½ ft)
N.×mussinii	Mid summer to early autumn. Lavender-blue.	38cm (15 in)
N.×m. Six Hills Giant	Mid summer to early autumn. Deeper blue.	60cm (2 ft)
Oenothera tetragona Fireworks	Mid summer to early autumn. Orange-yellow, red buds.	45cm (18 in)
O. glaber	Mid summer to mid autumn. Golden, bronzy foliage.	38cm (15 in)
Origanum laevigatum	Early to mid autumn. Purple.	38cm (15 in)
Paeonia (paeony) varieties	Late spring to early summer. Single or double, pinks to reds. Adapt to any soil or conditions.	
Papaver orientalis (oriental poppy) Lord Lambourne	Mid summer. Bright red.	90cm (3 ft)
P.o. Mrs Perry	Mid summer. Pink.	90cm (3 ft)
P.o. Perry's White	Mid summer. White with black blotches.	90cm (3 ft)
Phlomis samia	Mid summer to early autumn. Yellow, greyish leaves.	75cm (2½ ft)
Phlox	Late summer to early autumn. Choose according to colour preferences. Prefer good rich soil with plenty of moisture.	
Established varieties	Balmoral (rosy-lavender); Brigadier (brilliant orange-red); Hampton Court (blue); Pastorale (large pink); White Admiral (the best white).	
Physostegia virginiana Summer Snow	Late summer to mid autumn. White.	75cm (2½ ft)
P.v. Vivid	Early to late autumn. Deep rose.	45cm (18 in)
Platycodon grandiflorum	Late summer to early autumn. Blue.	45cm (18 in)
P.g. Snowflake	Late summer to early autumn. White.	45cm (18 in)
Polemonium foliosissimum (Jacob's ladder)	Late spring to early autumn. Lavender-blue.	75cm (2½ ft)
P.f. Sapphire	Early to late summer. Blue.	45cm (18 in)

NAME OF PLANT	FLOWERING SEASON/REMARKS	HEIGHT
Polygonum amplexicaule atrosanguineum (snake weed)	Mid summer to mid autumn. Deep red spike.	1·2m (4 ft)
P. bistorta Superbum	Early summer onwards. Does well in moist places.	90cm (3 ft)
P. millettii	Mid summer to mid autumn. Deep red. Slow-growing, likes moisture.	45cm (18 in)
Potentilla atrosanguinea (cinquefoil) Gibson's Scarlet	Mid summer to early autumn. Brilliant scarlet.	38cm (15 in)
P.a. Mons. Rouillard	Mid summer to early autumn. Deep crimson, orange blotched.	45cm (18 in)
P.a. William Rollisson	Mid summer to early autumn. Semi-double, orange.	38cm (15 in)
Prunella webbiana (self-heal) Loveliness	Early summer onwards. Pale mauve.	25cm (10 in)
Pyrethrum	Early to mid summer; if cut back at once, will repeat in the autumn. Choose from pinks to salmons and scarlets. Useful for cuttings.	
Rhazya orientalis	Mid summer to early autumn. Blue.	45cm (18 in)
Rudbeckia fulgida Deamii	Early to late autumn. Deep yellow, dark centre.	75cm (2½ ft)
R.f. Goldsturm	Late summer to late autumn.	45cm (18 in)
R. laciniata Goldquelle	Early to late autumn. Double yellow.	90cm (3 ft)
R. nitida Herbstsonne	Early to late autumn. Bright rich yellow.	1·8m (6 ft)
R. subtomentosa	Mid to late autumn. Deep yellow.	1·2–1·5m (4–5 ft)
Salvia haematodes	Mid summer to early autumn. Light lilac-blue, grey-green foliage.	90cm (3 ft)
S. × superba	Late summer to mid autumn. Violet-purple.	90cm (3 ft)
S. × s. East Friesland	Similar, except for height.	45cm (18 in)
S. × s. Lubeca	Mid summer to mid autumn. Violet-purple.	75cm (2½ ft)
S. × s. Lye End	Mid summer to early autumn. Blue.	1m (3½ ft)
S. turkestanica	Late summer. Rose and pale blue.	1·2–1·5m (4–5 ft)
Scabiosa caucasica Clive Greaves	Mid summer to mid autumn. Mid blue.	75cm (2½ ft)
S.c. Loddon White	Mid summer to mid autumn. White.	75cm (2½ ft)
S.c. Penhill Blue	Mid summer to mid autumn. Deep blue.	75cm (2½ ft)
Sedum maximum Atropurpureum	Early to late autumn. Deep purple flowers, creamy foliage.	45cm (18 in)
S. spectabile	Early to late autumn. Pale pink.	38cm (15 in)
S.s. Autumn Joy	Early to late autumn. Bright rose-salmon.	60cm (2 ft)
S. spurium Ruby Glow	Late summer to early autumn. Rose-red.	30cm (12 in)
S.s. Vera Jameson	Late summer to early autumn. Pale pink, purplish foliage.	38cm (15 in)
Sidalcea malvaeflora Elsie Heugh	Mid summer to early autumn. Soft pink.	90cm (3 ft)
S.m. Mrs Alderson	Mid summer to early autumn. Large clear pink.	75cm (2½ ft)
S.m. William Smith	Late summer to mid autumn. Warm salmon-pink.	1m (3½ ft)
Solidago canadensis (golden rod) Goldenmosa	Early to mid autumn. Large heads of golden-yellow.	75cm (2½ ft)
S.c. Golden Radiance	Early to mid autumn. Bright heads.	75cm (2½ ft)
S.c. Lemore	Early to mid autumn. Soft primrose.	75cm (2½ ft)
Stachys lanata (lamb's tongue)	Mid summer to early autumn. Pink flowers. The entire plant is woolly-grey and spreads.	30cm (12 in)
Stokesia laevis Blue Star	Late summer to early autumn. Lavender-blue.	45cm (18 in)
Thalictrum aquilegifolium Album	Late spring to late summer. White.	1·2m (4 ft)
T.a. Purpureum	Late spring to late summer. Purple-mauve.	90cm (3 ft)
T. dipterocarpum Hewitt's Double	Late summer to mid autumn. Double mauve.	90cm (3 ft)
T. glaucum	Early to mid summer. Bright yellow, grey foliage.	1·5–1·8m (5–6 ft)
Trollius europaeus (globe flower) Superbus	Early to mid summer. Light yellow.	45–60cm (1½–2 ft)
T. ledebourii Imperial Orange	Mid summer to early autumn. Orange.	1·5–1·8m (5–6 ft)
Verbascum bombyciferum (mullein)	Mid to late summer. Yellow, silvery leaves.	90–120cm (3–4 ft)
V. hybridum Cotswold Queen	Mid summer. Terracotta.	1·2m (4 ft)
V.h. Pink Domino	Mid summer. Deep rose.	1m (3½ ft)
V. thapsiforme	Mid summer. Deep yellow.	1·2–1·5m (4–5 ft)
Vernonia crinita	Mid autumn. Purple.	1·5m (5 ft)
Veronica incana Wendy	Mid summer to early autumn. Deep blue, silver foliage.	30cm (12 in)
V. spicata Barcarolle	Mid summer to early autumn. Deep rose-pink.	45cm (18in)
V.s. Minuet	Pure pink, grey-green foliage.	38–45cm (15–18 in)
V. teucrium Royal Blue	Mid to late summer.	45cm (18 in)
V. virginica Alba	Early to mid autumn. White.	1·5m (5 ft)

PLANTS: SOIL TYPES AND SITUATIONS

GARDENING ON SAND

What an inspiration it is to wander round the Royal Horticultural Society's garden at Wisley – surely one of the great gardens of England – that has been patiently created in a notoriously poor sandy area. It is a garden that has everything – from flowering plants and shrubs, fruit and vegetables, to a rock garden and wild garden. So if you are on sand take heart from this example, which proves that with the right approach you can grow almost anything. We then give advice on the best plants for sandy soils.

Gardening on a sandy soil does have its problems, but they can be overcome by using the quite simple techniques described here. First, though, let us take a close look at sand itself.

What is sand?

Sand is composed of minute fragments of weathered rock, usually quartz. Its colour is due to chemicals present in the natural formation, iron in red sandstone, for example. Such a sand would not support plant life unless it had decaying plant remains mixed into it. Over the centuries, primitive and then more advanced organisms have lived and died on the earth's surface, forming humus in the process. Once incorporated with sand this gives us what we call sandy soil. An average soil of this type might have 60 per cent sand and 40 per cent earthy matter or humus.

Grains of sand vary in size, but are large compared with particles of loam and clay, the other main soil groups. The size of the individual grains gives sand its character, making it too loose for good root anchorage, and resulting in large air spaces through which water rapidly drains away, taking with it any soluble plant food in the soil.

Humus, on the other hand, has a large capacity for holding water, and is granular and springy. It does not stretch the imagination much to realize that its addition to sand immediately solves some of the worst problems.

The number of microscopic bacteria and other micro-organisms present in one tablespoon of good soil is said to equal the human population of the world. If you are fully to understand what is going on beneath your feet, and thus make sensible decisions that solve problems, you must appreciate something of the role of these organisms.

The microscopic population chiefly comprises bacteria (30 billion weigh approximately 30g, or 1 oz), that break down organic matter, releasing the plant foods upon which your garden depends.

Our friend the earthworm also plays an important part in the conditioning of your soil. Worms aerate the soil; their burrows provide drainage and admit air to heavy soils, but this is of less concern on sand. Their main importance is that they eat soil for the purpose of digesting the vegetable debris in it; sometimes the process ends with a wormcast on the surface. If you have ever touched a wormcast when dry you will appreciate how finely divided it is. Thus, soil and vegetable matter are thoroughly mixed.

The worms dig your soil for you. It is estimated that in a 40–50 year period the whole of the top 25cm (9 in) of soil in any garden goes through the gut of a worm and is much improved by it. So encourage the worms, and put up with a few casts on the lawn – on sandy soils they will disappear with the touch of a besom.

Although a gross simplification, it is broadly true that if you do not supply the humus and moisture that nourish the earthworm and micro-organisms, there is little chance of your garden flourishing.

How to improve sand

Since it is clear that the best way to promote happiness when gardening on sand is to change the nature of the soil, making it less sandy by adding humus, let us look at a few ways this can be done.

Fresh soil Adding fresh soil to your garden is not often considered, but it is the real short cut if you are lucky enough to find a supply. Building sites often have a surplus of topsoil if an extensive area has been stripped for a large building. But do make sure that it is topsoil and not

and colder, and generally the best on sand; and pig manure is the least popular, although it can do a good job. There is nothing wrong with a mixture of all three if you are offered it. Poultry manure is not the best way to improve sand as it is primarily droppings that can be wet, smelly and caustic to plant roots, but mixed ten parts to one with your own compost it can be useful.

If buying manure by the load ask what weight the lorry will hold before you agree quantity and price per 1000kg (1

Left: a typical corner of the RHS garden at Wisley, where all manner of plants flourish on a sandy soil
Above: formation of sand – coarse sand beneath a weathered rock face

subsoil, that it is much better soil than your own, and that it can be tipped on or very near your garden. Spread an even 15cm (6 in) over your soil and dig it in.

Animal manure Although animal manure is supposedly a thing of the past, this is probably not true save in the centre of big cities. Look in your local papers for advertisements, or ring up a stables.

You can buy it as fresh, or *long*, manure (that is, with mainly long straw), which means you have to compost it for about four months; or you can get well-rotted or *short* manure, which is the better buy.

Quality and character are much affected by the animal that has lived on the straw. Horse manure is 'hot' and rots quickly, but is the lightest and least suitable for sand; cow manure is wetter

ton), and make sure the lorry arrives full.

Spent mushroom compost Useful for helping to rot the straw if you are using horse manure. It contains very little food value, but it does provide valuable organic matter, helping with water retention on light soils.

Municipal compost A few local authorities produce this by composting paper and vegetable waste. Do not confuse it with sewage sludge, which is much cheaper but such a variable product that one hesitates to recommend it. With sludge, it is necessary to check locally that it is free from disease organisms, and from injurious metals such as cadmium, copper or lead.

Spent hops Make an excellent bulk water-retaining manure, but they do smell. Buy them straight from a brewery.

Seaweed This is only for those who live near the sea. It has a dreadful smell if you rot it down, so dig it in fresh some months before you are ready to plant.

Leaf mould Some local authorities will

deliver loads of this when the streets are being swept clear of leaves in the autumn. In 6–9 months it makes a splendid humus.

Peat Very good but expensive.

Garden compost For the cheapest and one of the best forms of organic manure there is garden compost. Keep everything rottable from the house or garden, separating those things that are quick rotting (such as lettuce leaves and grass mowings) from those that are slow rotting (hedge and shrub prunings, for example). Both make useful compost, but are ready for use many months apart.

Cultivation

The materials mentioned are of little use in improving sand unless they are thoroughly mixed in. This is best done by double digging, incorporating as much compost or manure as you have – or can afford – into the second spit, thus creating the possibility of food and moisture retention.

You are unlikely to make a good soil in one year. The measure of your success will be the colour of your sandy soil. As it darkens you will know its fertility is increasing. In digging, you may find a strange, impervious rock-hard layer. This is known as an 'iron pan', and is caused by an excess of iron salts washed down from the upper layers sealing together grains of sand. The only answer is to break up the layer, and it may well take a pick and a strong arm to do it.

Mulching

While not improving the soil directly, this highly desirable practice most certainly improves the lot of plants growing in sand. It has two forms.

1 Dry mulching, that is keeping the Dutch hoe going so that there is a layer of dry, loose soil on top of the ground. This breaks contact between soil moisture and the dry air above, and materially reduces the amount of evaporation.

2 Covering of the soil and plant roots with a layer of non-conducting material such as litter, 'long' manure, leaves, peat or partly-decayed compost. Any convenient material will do, provided it makes a dry layer that stops loss of moisture.

Conserving moisture is one of the main objectives of mulching, but it also keeps the roots cool in summer, especially surface-rooters like raspberries or rhododendrons. It provides a mild feed after rain if you have used manure as a mulch and, if applied to tender plantings like fuchsias before frost, will protect them from low temperatures. It is particularly helpful when transplanting evergreens – ideally done in late spring (April) – as it

reduces the chances of the soil drying out before the plants have been able to make a new root system.

Ground cover

This is nature's way of providing a mulch. It is not for flowerbeds or the vegetable plot, but for most other places there are plants that will cover the soil around larger plantings to the benefit of both, and incidentally reduce your work by smothering weeds.

Nature abhors bare ground and will soon fill spaces with something, so you need to be selective. You might regret planting such charmers as *Convallaria majalis* (lily of the valley), that when happy brooks no opposition, or *Campanula poscharskyana*, that can be all too much of a good thing if incautiously used on the rock garden.

There are many dozens of good plants that are both ornamental and useful in the role of ground cover. For example, on a hot, dry bank try *Hypericum calycinum* (rose of Sharon) or *Helianthemum nummularium* Rhodanthe Carneum or, if you have room, the climbing *Hydrangea petiolaris* that, if treated as a scrambler, will easily cover 1·5 sq m (2 sq yd).

Remember that ground cover only works when the plants touch each other. Therefore until they are big enough you have to keep the ground clear by ordinary

Right: leaf mould makes a useful humus
Below: spent hops – obtained from a
brewery – make a good water-retaining
manure around this apple tree

methods, but it is indeed worth it. The subject of ground cover is a wide one, and has already been dealt with earlier in the section on page 106.

Taking stock

Before you select plants for your garden you need to know whether it is acid or alkaline, as rhododenrons, for example, will not grow on alkaline sands. You can usually find out what the local soil is like by ringing your local authority or parks department, and a local horticultural society might also help.

Alternatively, you could buy a soil-testing kit, usually consisting of a fluid that changes colour when mixed with soil. You then compare this colour with a colour chart (supplied with the kit) that gives a reasonably accurate idea of the

degree of acidity or alkalinity in your soil. If acidity is excessive you can correct the balance using lime at 270g per sq m ($\frac{1}{2}$ lb per sq yd); if alkalinity is excessive any of the soil-improving forms of humus described earlier will help.

Advantages of sandy soil
By now you may well think it a good thing to move somewhere else if you have a sandy garden, but there are distinct and very definite advantages to such a soil. It is the easiest of all soils to manage. In a world where spare time is becoming increasingly more difficult to arrange, the boon of being able to dash out and cultivate at a moment's notice is incalculable. Sand is light because of the large air spaces between grains, so digging is not the back-breaking job it is on clays, and

Above: peat, though expensive, is an excellent mulch for sandy gardens
Above left: the compost heap provides good organic manure at little cost
Left: well-rotted stable manure can help to improve a sandy soil

can be carried out at any time except during, or immediately after, rain.

Given the absence of an iron pan, drainage is superb, making plant losses due to waterlogging in winter most unusual. And tender plants appreciate the absence of ice around their stems and roots in frosty weather.

The greatest advantage of sandy soil is its 'earliness'. In mid spring (March) the gardener on clay is still wondering when it will be dry enough for him to complete the winter digging, but sandy soils are already taking early sowings such as peas and lettuce. Given food and moisture, plants grow quickly and easily, and cuttings root readily in the naturally well-aerated conditions of a clean sand.

PLANTS FOR SANDY SOILS

After our look at the problems of gardening on sand, no one who has a sandy soil needs to be told that it is dry and poor in plant food.
But over many thousands of years nature has been busy adapting the physical structure of some plants to enable them to thrive in different unpromising conditions.
Making the right choice of plants if your garden's soil is sandy will therefore save you a lot of disappointment, and here we provide a selection of suitable trees, shrubs and vegetables, describing in each case the growing habit and, where relevant, giving the flowering season.

Many and ingenious are the adaptations nature has made to certain plants to reduce loss of water. In extreme cases, for example *Ulex europaeus* (common gorse) or *Spartium junceum* (Spanish broom), leaves have virtually been abandoned, but the plants remain attractive, if a little short on elegance, using green stems to carry out the function of leaves.

To make the best of gardening on a sandy soil there are a number of simple points to remember.

1 Do start with small plants, for they are much easier to cosset and nurse to the stage where they can look after themselves than larger plants. Once they are well established they will thrive virtually unaided.

2 Use pot-grown plants where possible. Prepare the planting hole with a generous supply of moist humus, then water in well, and continue to water until a root system is established.

3 Mulch well to reduce water loss.

Far left, top: Populus alba *(white poplar) is very attractive in autumn*
Far left, bottom: Betula pendula *(weeping silver birch) has an attractive shape*
Left: Acer negundo *Variegatum*
Above: Robinia pseudoacacia *Frisia*

TREES

Although trees and shrubs are the foundation of most gardens they should be used sparingly in a small area, especially on sand. A large tree is said to evaporate 1000kg (1 ton) of water on a hot sunny day, so the moral is obvious. However, you may wish to provide shelter or hide something unsightly with one of the following trees.

Acer (maple)

Being the largest plants, trees can be used to give point to a layout or to provide a shady spot for your deckchair. A neglected small tree suitable for both purposes is the box elder *Acer negundo*. It looks like

neither a box nor an elder, but is attractive and medium-sized, although you will need a stem of at least 1·8m (6 ft) if you wish to sit under it, as its boughs tend to droop. Try one of its very good gold- or silver-leaved forms – *A.n.* Auratum is bright gold and *A.n.* Variegatum a most attractive green and white.

Ailanthus

The tree of heaven *Ailanthus altissima* is extremely tolerant, even of a smoke- or fume-polluted atmosphere. Its leaves resemble an enormous ash leaf up to 90cm (3 ft) long and with as many as 20 leaflets. It makes an extremely handsome lawn specimen and can easily be kept to a desired size by careful pruning.

Betula (birch)

It is difficult to leave out the birch from any list, for it is a supremely graceful tree that succeeds in any soil. A good form of the British silver birch *Betula pendula*

(lady of the woods) is hard to beat, but you must choose it yourself in the nursery as the quality of the silver stem is very variable. If you prefer a golden stem then the yellow birch *B. lutea* may suit.

Pinus (pine)

In particularly windy spots pines, such as the Austrian *Pinus nigra* in one of its forms, are excellent.

Populus (poplar)

The quickest-growing of the choice of trees included here, poplars can be used both as 6–9m (20–30 ft) trees or cut back and made into a thick suckering screen, say 4·5m (15 ft) high. Excellent species are the aspen *Populus tremula*, whose leaves shimmer in the slightest breeze, and the white poplar *P. alba*, whose leaves with their white, felt-like underside are conspicuous when ruffled by the breeze. Both species have a golden autumn colour.

Robinia

All false acacias (*Robinia pseudoacacia*) will do well but you should think especially of the small but brilliant golden *R.p.* Frisia, that makes a handsome picture mixed with the purple foliage of such as *Berberis thunbergii* Atropurpurea.

SHRUBS

The following selection covers the shrubs that have adapted best to sandy soil and are therefore most likely to succeed.

Berberis (barberry)

Berberis × stenophylla comes near to being the best of the informal evergreen hedges. It forms a dense barrier up to 3m (10 ft) high out of which it throws slender arching sprays dressed in narrow, dark green leaves that in late spring (April) are clothed with small, rich golden flowers.

There are good dwarf forms like *B. × s.* Irwinii and *B. × s.* Coccinea, with one of the parents of the latter, the evergreen *B. darwinii*, making a superb formal hedge or individual specimen in its own right. Of much stiffer habit, this has shining, dark green, holly-like leaves and is profuse in its spring bloom of richest orange-yellow. It is often laden with plum-coloured berries in the autumn.

Of the deciduous berberis there are well over 100 species that could be described. Three outstandingly reliable ones are *B. aggregata*, *B. thunbergii* and *B. wilsoniae*. All are invaluable small shrubs of 90–120cm (3–4 ft) height, compact in growth, and unsurpassed for the profusion and brilliance of their scarlet, coral and red berries and spectacular autumn foliage colouring.

Calluna and erica

Acid sands are the ideal base for a heather, heath, or ling garden, as can be seen in many commons, moors and heaths in Britain. Calluna and erica provide ground cover as well as floral beauty, and with a suitable choice of species your garden need never be without colour in any month of the year.

No heather garden would be complete without the ling native to Britain, *Calluna vulgaris*. *C.v.* Serlei is as good as any and who has not worn a bit of this white form for luck? Among the crimsons is *C.v.* C.W. Nix, and you cannot be without the double-flowered charmer *C.v.* H.E. Beale, that bejewels its long sprays with bright pink clusters.

There are golden-foliaged forms, too – *C.v.* Golden Feather, that turns a gentle orange by the time winter arrives, and the remarkable *C.v.* Robert Chapman, that is golden-foliaged in spring, orange come the summer, and red by the autumn.

The winter heath *Erica carnea* is particularly welcome, forming dense

Above: heather garden at the Royal Horticultural Society gardens at Wisley
Left: Erica carnea *Springwood White*

hummocks of rosy-pink flowers from early winter to early spring (November to February). It is the originator of innumerable varieties that span early winter through to late spring (November to April). Among the best are *E.c.* King George, with carmine flowers; *E.c.* Vivellii, with deep red flowers and bronzy-red foliage in winter; *E.c.* Springwood Pink and *E.c.* Springwood White; and the very late-flowering *E.c.* Ruby Glow, that also has bronzy foliage.

Should you live on a limey sand – and there are some, especially near the sea – then only a few heaths are for you. These include *Erica carnea*, that has the most colour variants, and the excellent, slightly taller *E.* × *darleyensis*, *E. mediterranea* and the Corsican heath *E. terminalis*, that all bear rosy-coloured flowers.

For height among the heaths, it is worth taking a chance on the hardiness of *E. arborea* Alpina, a tree heath, from whose root briar pipes are made. 'Briar' is

a corruption of *bruyère*, the French vernacular name for tree heaths. The form *E.a.* Alpina (that you should insist upon) produces a dense, upright bush that cheers you into mid spring (around March) with masses of ash-white panicles, 30cm (12 in) long, and heavy with honey fragrance on a warm day.

The common British bell heather *E. cinerea* (also known as Scotch or grey heath) is widely distributed and has produced a number of attractive varieties. Among the best are *E.c.* C.D. Eason, with flowers of a deep glowing pink, and *E.c.* Rosea, with flowers of a soft pink. Two varieties that scarcely have a flower at all, but are well worth a place in any garden for their golden summer foliage turning to red in winter, are *E.c.* Golden Drop and *E.c.* Golden Hue.

Cistus (rock or sun rose)

These rock roses are exceptionally free-flowering around mid summer (June), fast-growing, evergreen and really happy on a hot, dry bank in full sun. Many have aromatic foliage and gummy leaves that enable them to retain moisture. They associate well with heather and broom.

Low-growing *Cistus palhinhaii*, discovered on Cape Trafalgar in Portugal, is compact, unexpectedly hardy and bears 10cm (4 in) wide flowers. *C.* × *cyprius* is vigorous, hardy, some 1·8m (6 ft) tall and has 7–8cm (3 in) wide flowers, white in colour with five splashes of crimson around the base of each petal where it joins the central boss of yellow stamens. *C.* Silver Pink is a lovely natural hybrid.

Most rock roses rapidly become sprawling bushes and are best replaced with younger plants every seven or eight years rather than trying to keep them under control by pruning, which they dislike.

Cytisus (broom)

Brooms are remarkably well adapted to life on a hot, dry sand. A poor soil seems a positive advantage, and in full sun they will seed freely, even among rocks, and soon become as tough and unassailable as gorse. The shoots of many are green, which enables them to function as food producers when the leaves are out of action for any reason, such as storm damage or drought. They are very rapid growers, particularly the forms of the common broom *Cytisus scoparius*. Accordingly, it is a good plan to prune back the shoots regularly just after flowering so that 'legginess' is avoided.

C. albus (or *C. multiflorus*) is known as the white Spanish broom, and is a 3m (10 ft) high plant of slender grace that is best seen emerging in a fountain of white bloom from darker, more dwarf shrubs.

The common broom *C. scoparius* is an admirable plant in its own right, but unless very sheltered it needs a sound stake. We recommend *C.s.* Cornish Cream, *C.s.* Firefly, with yellow and bronze flowers, and *C.s.* Golden Sunlight, plus the sub-species *C.s.* Sulphureus, with cream and pale sulphur flowers, tinged red in the bud: all flower in early and mid summer (end of May and early June).

C. × beanii is a charming, semi-prostrate hybrid bearing golden flowers, and a great favourite is *C. × kewensis*, whose stems are only 30cm (12 in) high but that can cover a square metre or yard with myriads of creamy-yellow, pea-like flowers in late spring (April).

Genista

Botanically very close to the brooms, this is another yellow, pea-flowered family that in practical use takes over from them by flowering in late summer (July), as the brooms fade.

Genista aetnensis, the Mount Etna broom, is a tall plant of around 3–3·5m (10–12 ft) that cascades its pendant green shoots almost to the ground and studs them from end to end with tiny golden pea flowers in late summer (July).

G. hispanica, the Spanish gorse, is essential for any dry, exposed garden. It is not unlike a dwarf, close-knit gorse. Planted on a hot, dry bank (and kept watered), it rolls out an undulating carpet of green mounds that, in early and mid summer (May and June) of each year, turn bright yellow. Odd plants do die without any apparent reason, so it is as

Two plants particularly well suited to sandy conditions are Cytisus scoparius Sulphureus *(top), and the brilliantly-coloured* Genista tinctoria Royal Gold

well to have a young plant or two in reserve to fill any gaps.

The British *G. tinctoria* (dyer's green-weed) was used for the famous Kendal Green dye, and a selection from this, *G.t.* Royal Gold, is one of the best dwarf flowering shrubs available and should not be neglected.

Juniperus (juniper)

This is a most useful and long-suffering family. *Juniperus communis* (common juniper) contains *J.c.* Hibernica (Irish juniper), a column of grey-green that is admirable to give point to a formal layout; *J.c.* Effusa, a prostrate carpeting plant for a bank; and many diverse forms. The shore juniper, *J. conferta* is another

Right and far right: Mahonia aquifolium – *its berries are good for jam – is a decorative subject for underplanting*
Below right: Spartium junceum *(Spanish broom) is at home in a dry, sandy soil*
Below: Juniperus communis *(common juniper) and* Ulex europaeus *(common gorse) are hardy specimens*

excellent cover for sandy banks and originally came from Japan.

Mahonia

Mahonias are related to berberis but can be distinguished by their large pinnate leaves and spineless stems.

Mahonia aquifolium, known as the Oregon grape – after its bunches of most decorative blue berries – is one of the best plants for underplanting in dry places. It has bright yellow, honey-scented flowers in dense, short clusters. Prune back after flowering if you want to keep it low-growing.

M. japonica is 1·8–2·4m (6–8 ft) tall, and bears clusters of lily-of-the-valley-scented flowers in chains of pendant bells in early and mid spring (February and March); there can be up to 12 chains each with up to 100 flowers. Flowering as early as it does, and growing in the most inhospitable places, it is indeed a valuable plant to have in your garden.

Spartium

Any plant such as *Spartium junceum*, that has been growing in Britain since the first Elizabeth was on the throne, must have proved its worth. The common name, Spanish broom, indicates its place of origin, where it inhabits regions of very restricted rainfall; as a result, it has almost entirely dispensed with leaves and relies on round, green, rush-like stems to carry out their function. So it is a more than useful plant for an arid sand. It is broom-like in growth up to 3m (10 ft) and apt to be 'leggy' unless hard-pruned.

One good plan is to plant in groups of an even number some 1·2m (4 ft) apart; prune every other plant close back to the crown each year. Thus the bright yellow fragrant flowers are borne in 45cm (18 in) racemes from mid summer to mid autumn (June to September) on alternate plants. This is quite sufficient to clothe the planted area, and prevents the shrubs ever becoming too large for a small garden.

Ulex europaeus (common gorse)

The plant *par excellence* for a sandy soil, and a sight to be remembered as a golden glory of gorse clothing the shelving cliffs of Guernsey against a background of blue sea. It is rarely without blossom, hence the saying 'when gorse is out of flower, kissing's out of season'. Its early flowers offer a rich bee pasture. It has a scent that to some is of coconut and to others of honey and almond; this scent hangs in the air in good weather, and to a countryman must bring back the memory of warmth, high summer and hay making.

If you have a large area to cover it may be best to sow seed in groups some 60cm (24 in) apart.

VEGETABLES

Some of the finest vegetable-growing areas are on sandy soil, due to earliness and ease of cultivation, but of course water and adequate food materials are supplied. There is no reason why you, too, should not grow vegetables successfully, provided you practise the principles already described. The following tips may also help.

Lettuce, radish and spinach These must never lack water or they become hard and run quickly to seed. A quite small area of specially-prepared soil with a high humus-content situated close to the water supply helps enormously. Don't forget that few families eat more than three or four large lettuce per week so sow short rows, say of 1·8m (6 ft), every ten days;

A fine crop of mixed vegetables thriving in the sandy soil at Wisley

make the rows even shorter for radish.

Brassicas, marrows/courgettes, tomatoes When planting, after firming well, make a hole 5–8cm (2–3 in) deep a few centimetres away from the stem. Fill this when watering; it places the water where it is needed around the plant's roots.

Runner beans It is sometimes difficult to make a framework really strong on sand. Stout individual poles, say 1·2m (4 ft) apart, each with two to three plants on it may help, but drive them in quite firmly so that the wind can pass between the columns of beans.

Onions It is difficult to get the firm seedbed beloved of onions. Sets planted in mid spring (March) do better. A row of Express Yellow onions sown in early autumn (mid August) is a good bet to bridge the onion 'gap'. They harvest in mid summer (June) of the following year. Thin to six per 30cm (12 in).

Mulching This is just as important for vegetables as for other plants on sand.

GARDENING ON CLAY

Many people might despair when faced with the prospect of gardening on a clay soil, but in fact this is unnecessary as there is a great deal that can be done to alleviate the problem.
Here we give some suggestions, explaining how to double dig and trench, and also how to improve the drainage; we then describe some of the plants that will grow happily on clay.

What we mean when we speak of clay soils are mixtures of clay and ingredients such as sand, humus, and sometimes chalk; pure clay alone cannot be used for cultivation. To some extent, the proportions of the materials in a mixture determine the character of the soil: a high percentage of clay would give a 'stiff' or 'heavy' soil, meaning that it would cling together and be difficult to cultivate, whereas a large amount of sand and humus would mean a 'light' or even 'loam' soil – the last being ideal. There are, however, other differences, and these are due to the nature of clay itself.

Potential problems

Not all clays are formed in exactly the same way, and different varieties behave in dissimilar ways when alternately wetted and dried. With some clays, the particles are so tightly bonded that their structure is not greatly altered by water, but in others the particles are more loosely attached, and as a result are forced apart when wet and close up again when dry. The effect is one of constant expansion and contraction.

When clay of this shrinkable type predominates in a soil, trouble can arise with buildings: as the soil moves, so foundations are disturbed and walls may crack – or, in extreme cases, fall down. Trees and large shrubs could well increase the rate of water removal in dry weather, so aggravating the movement of the soil, and this is why it is unwise to plant too many of them near buildings that are situated on shrinkable clay.

So much for the drawbacks of clay as a soil ingredient. But, of course, it also has many advantages, including the ability to hold moisture and plant foods – particularly those such as calcium, magnesium and potassium, the ions of which are positively charged and so are held on the negatively-charged particles of clay. So clay soils are potentially fertile, and in the words of one expert 'in most climates the most productive soils contain at least 20 per cent clay'.

Difficulties only really begin when there is so much clay in the soil, or it is of such a closely-bonded character, that it is difficult for water to pass through it or for a spade, plough or cultivator to move it.

Waterlogging can result after heavy rain if a soil contains too much clay

Then the soil may become so completely waterlogged in winter that all air is driven out, and roots, worms and beneficial micro-organisms in the soil are drowned. Even if no such disasters occur, it may be physically impossible to cultivate the soil until it has at least partially dried out in spring, and so sowings and plantings are unduly delayed. Moreover, excess water chills the soil and delays seed germination and plant growth.

Suggested solutions

All the problems so far described are physical ones, and can be reduced in severity, even if not entirely removed, by various means. Digging helps, especially if done early in the autumn, when it will expose the soil to air and frost that will help to dry it and break it up. All manner of dressings can be added to give the soil a more open texture: coarse sand and grit are excellent, and so are well-weathered boiler ashes – but not ashes from a domestic fire, as these are too fine in texture and simply become as slimy as the clay itself.

Any rotting organic matter will help, including leaves, garden refuse, partially-decayed straw, old mushroom compost, and peat or bulky animal manure – particularly the horse variety that contains a lot of litter. All of these can be worked into the soil at any time it is vacant, or – if it is permanently planted – can be spread on the surface, and left to be pulled in by worms, washed down by rain, or hoed into the top 2–3cm (1 in).

Another possibility is to use lime – though not with fresh animal manure as the two interact unfavourably. The addition of lime turns the fine, colloidal particles of clay into larger granules, and so the soil becomes more open in texture and less pasty. Fresh, hydrated lime is the best form to use, and provided the soil is not already markedly alkaline and there are no lime-hating plants (and none are planned) then it can be applied at rates of up to 1kg per sq m (2 lb per sq yd). In practice, it is usually better to give considerably less, say about 250g per sq m (8 oz per sq yd), and to repeat annually until the desired improvement has been brought about. It is seldom possible or desirable to change the character of a soil suddenly, and usually in gardening you must be prepared to be patient and make gradual improvements.

Providing drainage

Drainage should either be done thoroughly or not at all. The problem in small gardens is usually what to do with the water that has been removed by land-drains. It is generally illegal to run it into a sewer, but if a soakaway for roof water is available it may be possible to turn the garden surplus into this. An alternative is to dig a special soakaway, preferably at the lowest point in the garden and sufficiently deep to penetrate through the underlying impervious layer that is holding up the water. But that can easily prove to be a counsel of perfection impossible to achieve.

A small hole cleanly dug with a spade to a depth of one metre (or yard) or more will expose what is called a 'profile' of the soil, showing fairly clearly where the relatively fertile topsoil gives way to poorer subsoil, and where the impervious layer of clay is – and maybe even how thick it is.

In a country garden, drainage may be no problem at all if a ditch or stream is available into which the land-drains, or at any rate the main drain that takes the flow of subsidiary drains, can be run.

The best way to make land-drains is to purchase the special earthenware pipes produced for the job, and to lay these end to end and about 45–60cm (18–24 in) deep. By this means they will collect water more efficiently and are less likely to become blocked with silt if laid in stones, clinkers, or large, loose gravel. If there is a considerable area to be drained, pipes laid in a herringbone pattern will probably cover it most economically and efficiently. Drains usually need to be not more than 2·4m (8 ft) apart, and all should have a fall of at least 30cm in 12m (1 ft in every 40) so that water can flow steadily away to whatever outlet has been provided.

Double digging and trenching

Drainage can also be improved by two special methods of deep digging known as double digging and trenching. To carry out the former, excavate a trench 30cm (12 in) wide and 25–30cm (10–12 in) deep across one end of the plot, and remove the spoil to the far end of the garden. Then turn over the soil in the bottom of the open trench with a fork or spade, so that altogether soil to a total depth of 50–60cm (20–24 in) is then broken up.

Dig a second trench, adjacent to the first and to the same proportions, and again turn over the soil in the bottom. However, this time use the spoil to fill in the first trench. Continue with more trenches, each time placing the spoil in the preceding trench, until you reach the end

Left: a 'true lute' can be used to work in top dressings
Below: a herringbone drainage system with a soakaway will assist in the removal of surplus water

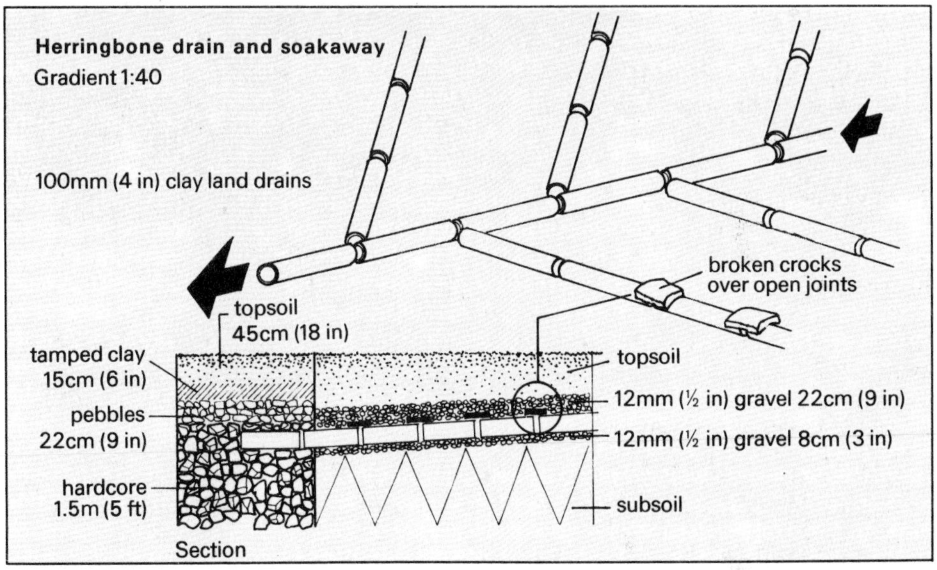

Herringbone drain and soakaway
Gradient 1:40

100mm (4 in) clay land drains

topsoil 45cm (18 in)

tamped clay 15cm (6 in)

pebbles 22cm (9 in)

hardcore 1.5m (5 ft)

broken crocks over open joints

topsoil

12mm (½ in) gravel 22cm (9 in)

12mm (½ in) gravel 8cm (3 in)

subsoil

Section

of the plot. The last trench is then filled in with the spoil from the first.

Trenching is a little more complicated. Make the first trench at least 60cm (2 ft) wide and 25–30cm (10–12 in) deep, and remove the spoil to the far end of the plot, as before (see **2** in diagram opposite). Next dig a second trench, 30cm (12 in) wide, on the far side of the first trench, to form a step into it (**3**); this smaller quantity of soil is also left at the far end of the garden, but separate from the first pile. Then turn over the soil in the bottom of the deep, narrow trench, breaking it up to a total depth of 75–90cm (2½–3 ft) (**4**).

Now turn over the step of soil in the wide trench and place it on top of the broken-up soil in the bottom of the narrow trench (**5**), so exposing an additional 30cm (12 in) wide strip of subsoil, which in turn is broken up where it lies with a spade or fork (**6**).

The next stage is to mark out, with a line, a further strip of surface ground, but this time only 30cm (12 in) wide. Then throw the topsoil from this over the

second-spit soil in the first trench (**7**), throw the second-spit soil over the broken subsoil in the second trench (**8**), and break up the newly-exposed strip of subsoil (**9**), leaving it where it is. Proceed in exactly the same manner, with 30cm wide strips, until you reach the far end of the plot (**10–12**); then fill the last trench with the soil from the first trench – second-spit soil underneath (**13**), topsoil on top (**14**).

Double digging and trenching produce much deeper cultivation than is possible by simple digging – still without bringing the relatively infertile subsoil to the surface or burying good topsoil where it is of little or no value to feeding roots. Deep cultivation is of some direct value because it lets in air and allows surplus water to escape, but it is much more effective if bulky organic matter can be worked in at the same time to the full depth of the disturbed soil. It also allows lime to be distributed more deeply than when plain digging is practised, and this helps to improve the texture and drainage of the lower soil where most problems occur.

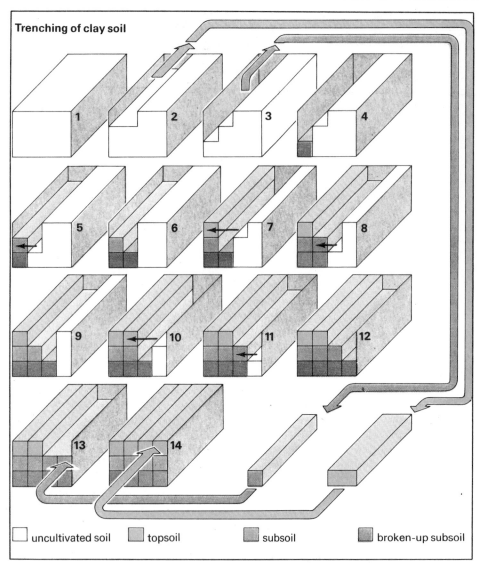

Trenching of clay soil

uncultivated soil □   topsoil ▨   subsoil ▨   broken-up subsoil ▩

Above: trenching improves texture and drainage of lower soil. Above right: lawn aeration and drainage are improved by spiking regularly with a hollow-tined fork

What not to do

There are some things you should never do with clay soils. As far as possible, avoid walking on them when they are very wet as this may consolidate them so much that, when they eventually dry out, they will be set hard like a brick. It is particularly important not to walk on newly-prepared seed or planting beds that have become wet; it may be necessary to put boards on the surface, even when digging, to distribute weight and avoid compacting the clay.

It is necessary to be extra cautious in the use of rollers on lawns grown on clay soils. If the lawns are not used for ball games requiring a very true surface, it is best not to roll at all, but if rolling is essential it should be as light as practicable and confined to periods when the surface is no more than just moist.

Lawns on clay are likely to need spiking, pricking, slitting, or similar means of aeration, more frequently than lawns on naturally porous soils. If hollow tining can be done, as soon as the work is completed sharp grit or sand can be brushed into the little holes that are made; finely-milled peat can be applied in the same way. Repeated treatments of this kind will produce a marked improvement in the texture of the top 5–8cm (2–3 in) of soil where most grass roots are found.

Avoid the use of nitrate of soda as a quickly-available source of nitrogen on clay as it aggravates the close texture of the soil. Try sulphate of ammonia instead, as it is almost as fast-acting, but doesn't have the same unwanted effect.

Garden features below soil level should not be attempted on clay because of the poor drainage, so steer clear of sunken gardens and paths, as these can easily become pools or streams of water. Raised features, however, are a different matter and can be very satisfactory. Among the possibilities are raised beds, banks, rock gardens built up above normal soil level, and – in the vegetable and cut flower plots – wide ridges where plants can be grown along the top. Even pyrethrum, which is very sensitive to excess water in winter, can be grown successfully on ridges.

It can be difficult to plant in clay soil, at any rate during the seasons usually recommended – that is, autumn (August to October), late winter (January) and early spring (February). In these months, clay can be so sticky that it is impossible to break it up into fragments sufficiently fine to be worked between and around roots. Of course, you could leave planting until late spring or summer (April to July) and then do it from containers, but that can be inconvenient and expensive, and will almost certainly limit your choice.

The alternative is to prepare a planting mixture, either of the best of your own soil, or of imported soil that is less binding, plus peat and sand in sufficient quantity to make it crumbly. Add a little bonemeal to the mixture, or better still some John Innes base fertilizer, to make it richer and to stimulate growth.

Once prepared, cover this heap of planting mixture with polythene or store it under cover so that it remains moist but never becomes sodden. Then a bucketful can be worked around the roots of every tree or large shrub, and a similar quantity around rose bushes and herbaceous perennials, as they are planted. It can mean the difference between success and failure.

PLANTS FOR CLAY SOILS

**Earlier we looked at the make-up of clay soil and gave some suggestions for its improvement.
Here we list some of the many trees, shrubs and herbaceous perennials that can be grown easily and successfully on clay.**

Soils that contain a moderate amount of clay are usually highly fertile, especially if they've been well cultivated, and so there are no particular problems in selecting plants to suit them. In fact, it is easier to make recommendations about what to avoid than what to choose since the list of undesirables is quite short, and confined mainly to plants that need perfect drainage and a loose, open soil. Many alpines come into this category, but their requirements are usually so specialized anyway that they have to be grown in special beds.

There are numerous grey- and silver-leaved plants that resent excess soil moisture, especially in winter, and so they may be less satisfactory on a clay soil than on one of a more porous character unless special care is taken to ensure that there is no waterlogging.

It must be remembered that whether a clay soil is alkaline, neutral or acid will to some degree determine what can be grown in it, but then the same applies to many soils that could not by any stretch of the imagination be called clay.

Clay soils are often cold, and this can make it unwise to use them for early crops or for plants that are on the borderline of hardiness. But again, this is not a problem exclusive to soils containing a lot of clay.

The greater the clay content, the greater the difficulty that will be experienced; near-pure clay would be unsuitable for any planting and is best either paved over or converted into a pool or lake. It is in the intermediate range between the stiff but fertile loams and the impossible clays that real problems of selection occur. You can observe how the natural flora of such a place differs from that growing in other areas.

Here, then, we offer a selection of plants for clay soil starting with trees.

TREES

Quercus (oak) may continue to thrive long after the soil has become too stiff and soggy for betula (birch) or the mountain ash sorbus. Some species of acer (maple or sycamore) will survive much better than others, the worst being the varieties of *Acer japonicum* and *A. palmatum*

The dwarf campanula, C. lactiflora Pouffe, *makes good ground cover on clay*

(Japanese maple), and the best the strong-growing kinds such as *A. platanoides* (Norway maple) and *A. pseudoplatanus* (sycamore), and all their varieties.

Platanus (plane) is another genus that can take a lot of clay, especially *Platanus × hispanica* (London plane), a good choice for heavy soils and a first-class tree for towns, being tolerant of industrial pollution. All the salix (willow) species and hybrids do well, likewise the white-flowered *Aesculus hippocastanum* (common horse chestnut) and *A. × carnea* (pink horse chestnut). However, some other species, such as *A. indica* (Indian horse chestnut) and the much smaller, shrubby *A. parviflora*, will grow on clay but do not like late spring (April) frosts, the damaging effects of which can be aggravated by cold, wet clay soil.

Other trees that grow well, even on quite stiff clay soils, include crataegus (hawthorn or may) in almost all its species, hybrids and garden varieties; the various species of fraxinus (ash); tilia (lime or linden); populus (poplar); and all kinds of laburnum. Some malus (flowering crab) succeed, though if drainage is bad they may suffer from scab and canker. *Magnolia × soulangeana* is often seen thriving on clay soils, and all varieties of *Prunus cerasifera* (cherry plum) are usually successful. Most popular are the purple-leaved plums, *P. cerasifera* Pissardii, *P.c.* Nigra, and varieties such as *P.c.* Trailblazer and *P.c.* Vesuvius.

Among conifers, all varieties of *Chamaecyparis lawsoniana* (Lawson cypress) and thuya (arbor-vitae) are reliable. Abies (silver fir) enjoys the moisture that clay ensures, and taxus (yew) also grows well in rich, damp clay soils.

SHRUBS

Many shrubs flourish on clay, even on very stiff soils. Almost all spiraea are reliable and so are the species, hybrids and garden varieties of philadelphus (mock orange). Weigela gives no trouble, nor does deutzia – provided the situation is not very frosty in late spring (April), as this can defoliate the plants and cause considerable die-back in some kinds.

All forsythia do well, and so do the garden forms of chaenomeles (ornamental quince) that, like forsythia, start flowering in early spring (February). Both *Corylus avellana* (hazel) and *C. maxima* (filbert) actually prefer rather moist clay soils. They can be grown either for their nuts or as ornamental bushes in their coloured-leaved and contorted varieties such as *C. maxima* Purpurea (purple-leaf filbert), *C. avellana* Aurea and *C.a.* Contorta (Harry Lauder's walking stick) – this last is also known as the corkscrew hazel because of its twisted branches.

Cotoneaster of all kinds usually succeed, as do pyracantha, another genus grown for highly-coloured berries as well as decorative flowers and good foliage. Ilex (holly) will thrive in very stiff soils, and there are a great many garden varieties and hybrids from which to choose, including some with handsomely-variegated leaves, and others with yellow or orange berries.

Another large genus is viburnum. Most species thrive on heavy soil, and there is a great deal of choice in foliage, flower, berry and habit. *Viburnum opulus* (guelder rose) actually seems to prefer soils that are rather wet and close textured, and so does the variety *V. opulus* Sterile, often called 'snowball tree', because of its large, globular clusters of white flowers. It is one of the handsomest and most easily-grown deciduous shrubs. However, *V. macrocephalum*, a smaller tree than *V. opulus* Sterile, is a little tender and in many northern areas needs the shelter of a sunny wall to make it grow and flower well. Not so *V. plicatum*, a species from China and Japan, with small, snowball-like blooms, for this is a tough and adaptable plant, as is its wild form *V.p. tomentosum*, that has flat, circular clusters of white flowers along more or less horizontal branches.

Ribes sanguineum (flowering currant) loves heavy soil and so do its garden varieties *R. sanguineum* Pulborough Scarlet and *R.s.* King Edward VII, both with deep red flowers, the pale pink *R.s.* Carneum, and *R.s.* Brocklebankii, with pink flowers and yellow leaves.

Cornus alba (red-barked dogwood) likes soil that is wet, and does not object if

it is also clayey. There are numerous varieties, including *C. alba* Sibirica (also known as *C.a.* Atrosanguinea), with bright crimson stems; *C.a.* Elegantissima, with light green and white leaves; and *C.a.* Spaethii, with light yellow leaves.

Aucuba japonica is a good evergreen to grow on heavy soils either in its green-leaved or yellow-spotted forms. The leaves are large like those of *Prunus laurocerasus* (common or cherry laurel), another evergreen that likes clay.

It is commonly said that roses love clay and this is broadly true, though it does not apply equally to all kinds. *Rosa (spinosissima) pimpinellifolia* (Burnett rose or Scots briar), for instance, is a species that in Britain is at its best on sand dunes close to the sea, though its garden varieties and hybrids will grow in heavier soil. However, *R. pimpinellifolia* has for many years been a fringe interest and all the really popular roses, such as the large-flowered hybrid teas, the cluster-flowered floribundas, and all the climbers includ-

With careful selection
you can still have a wide
range of trees and
shrubs, even on the
heaviest of clay soils.
Far left, top:
excelsior *Pendula,*
the weeping ash
Far left, centre: Aesculus
parviflora
Above left: spring-
flowering Magnolia ×
soulangeana
Above: Ribes
sanguineum
Pulborough Scarlet
(flowering currant)
thrives on heavy soil
Far left: all ilex (holly)
are happy on a clay soil,
so choose a variegated
one for colour value
Left: Acer platanoides
(Norway maple) is a
strong- growing species

ing the ramblers, thrive on clay soil provided it is well fed and reasonably well drained. No rose likes standing in water for long, and it is the potential richness of clay soils, not their wetness, that makes them congenial to roses.

HERBACEOUS PERENNIALS

Of herbaceous perennials for growing on a clay soil, it is those with strong, hungry root systems that are most likely to succeed, and also those that do not object to a good deal of moisture around their roots in winter and that are truly hardy.

All kinds of acanthus (bear's breeches) do well, anchoring themselves deeply in the clay and becoming quite difficult to remove once they have become established. Many species of polygonum (knotweed) do just the same, including the beautiful but notorious *Polygonum* (*sieboldii*) *cuspidatum* (also known as *Reynoutria japonica*), but this can become a nuisance, spreading far and wide, and often springing up where not wanted from underground stolons. However, the good forms of *P. amplexicaule* and *P. bistorta* (snake-weed) never give any trouble, and *P. campanulatum* (Himalayan knotweed) can be torn back quite easily if it begins to spread too far.

Several of the strong-growing campanula (bellflower) do well, none better than *Campanula lactiflora* (milky bellflower), that is normally a fairly tall plant though with one dwarf variety, named *C. lactiflora* Pouffe. *C. glomerata* is another excellent kind that spreads quite rapidly and looks delightful near the pink *Polygonum bistorta* Superbum.

Astilbe (false goat's beard) enjoys the moisture that clay brings but may not survive long if the clay dries out and

Many herbaceous perennials give excellent value on clay soils
Above left: Helleborus orientalis *(Lenten rose)*
Above: Polygonum bistorta *Superbum (snakeweed)*
Left: Phlox paniculata *Brigadier*
Top right: Aster novae-angliae *Harrington Pink*
Above right: a double variety of Hemerocallis fulva kwanso *(day lily)*
Above, far right: Doronicum plantagineum *(leopard's bane)*
Right: strong-growing Aruncus sylvester *(goat's beard) likes a damp spot*

cracks badly in summer. Its strong-growing relative *Aruncus sylvester* (goat's beard) is better able to look after itself but also prefers the damper spots.

Doronicum (leopard's bane) usually grows freely in clay soils, though it is the stronger-growing kinds, such as the varieties of *Doronicum plantagineum*, that will best be able to cope with really stiff clays. There are other good members of the daisy family, including *Aster novi-belgii* (Michaelmas daisy) and *A. novae-angliae*, most of the perennial helianthus (sunflowers) – but not *Helianthus atro-rubens* Monarch, that is rather tender – and all species and varieties of heliopsis. Some varieties of *Chrysanthemum maximum* (shasta daisy) succeed, the single-flowered varieties being, on the whole, hardier and more reliable than the double or semi-double varieties.

Solidago (golden rod) is capable of coping with the stiffest clay soils, and so is rudbeckia (cone flower), although *Rudbeckia (Echinacea) purpurea* prefers the lighter, better-drained loams. Most ligularia, still called by the old name of senecio in many gardens, prove successful, as does the less-well-known inula.

Some, but not all, achillea (yarrow) are good. It would be almost impossible to kill the garden varieties of *Achillea millefolium*, and that is also true of *A. (eupatorium) filipendulina* and *A. ptarmica* (sneezewort), but some of the grey-leaved kinds are less reliable.

Hosta (plantain lily) enjoys the moisture and richness of clay, but may need protection from slugs, as these have a fondness for hosta leaves. All the garden varieties of *Phlox paniculata* and *P. maculata* are good, and so are all lysimachia (loosestrife) and lythrum.

Hemerocallis (day lily) usually succeed, but if the soil is very stiff it will be wise to experiment first with some of the tough old varieties, such as *Hemerocallis fulva kwanso flore pleno*, before passing on to the choicer and more highly-coloured modern varieties, some of which seem to be a little less enduring. Much the same is true of iris. Old varieties of *Iris germanica* (purple or London flag) and *I. pallida* may survive where new varieties fail. The most likely of all to succeed is *Iris sibirica* in all its colour forms.

Most varieties of *Helleborus niger* (Christmas rose) and *H. orientalis* (Lenten rose) flourish on clay. The green-flowered species, *H. lividus*, *H. foetidus* and *H. corsicus* (Corsican hellebore) also manage very well. Paeonia (peony) actually prefers heavy soils provided it is not planted too deeply: the crowns should be barely covered with soil, *not* put down 5cm (2 in), as is usual on light soils.

Other possibilities are *Anemone hupehensis* (Japanese anemone), all varieties of which flower in late summer and early autumn (July and August); *Artemisia lactiflora* (white mugwort), a neglected plant with plumes of creamy white flowers; monarda in its several garden varieties; and *Galega officinalis*, an old-fashioned plant with clusters of small, vetch-like, blue and white, mauve and white, or all-white flowers that bloom throughout the summer.

Among hardy bulbs, all kinds of narcissus are very reliable, and so are both *Endymion non-scripta* (bluebell) and *E. hispanicus* (Spanish bluebell). Others that should do well are galanthus (snowdrop) – especially *Galanthus nivalis* (common snowdrop) and its varieties – and numerous species of allium.

GARDENING ON CHALK

Here we introduce our own design for a garden on chalk and describe a selection of suitable trees and shrubs; then on page 151 we turn to roses and herbaceous perennials. Given proper care and attention, a wide variety of plants will flourish in such conditions.

When grown on a chalk or lime soil, plants that originated in peat bogs or the deep leaf mould of the forest floor are inhibited by the degree of alkalinity present from taking up iron, magnesium and manganese. The result is that leaves turn yellow and the plants die back, suffering from what is known as lime-induced chlorosis. Among plants affected in this way are camellias, most heathers and other members of the ERICACEAE family, Japanese irises, rhododendrons (including azaleas), and some lilies and magnolias – they all prefer an acid soil.

However, if your garden happens to be on chalk or lime it is not the tragedy you might think. Most acid-loving plants were introduced to gardens comparatively recently as a result of botanical expeditions during the last 150 years – so if the Elizabethans in England could get along without rhododendrons, why shouldn't today's chalk gardeners? It is not all sour grapes to say that rhododendrons have their disadvantages: flowering time is short, most have no autumn colour, and the leaves – though evergreen – lack the healthy sparkle and well-polished look of holly, laurel or box.

You can grow a far greater variety of plants on chalk or limestone than on damp acid soil since the former is generally porous, dries quickly after rain, and does not get waterlogged in winter. Many reputedly tender plants only need good drainage, added to which chalk is warmer than clay soil. Lime-loving plants include a great number of lovely, medium-sized trees and shrubs, some excellent evergreens, numerous plants from the Mediterranean region, Australasia and the Cape (some of which have silver foliage), and all those that grow naturally on rocky cliffs by the sea or in the mountains. Bulbous plants, with very few exceptions, grow equally well. So while the ideal soil may be neutral, the chalk gardener is perhaps luckier than his opposite number on damp, acid soil. Remember that millions of pounds are spent yearly on liming soil, and that lime is good for most plants.

What is chalk?

Chalk is calcium carbonate ($CaCo_3$) and consists of the skeletons of minute marine animals that were laid down over millions of years at the bottom of the sea. Geological upheavals have raised these sea beds and erosion has exposed them. They run from Normandy in France to the south coast of England at Folkestone and Dover, along the South Downs, through parts of upland Dorset and the Isle of Wight, Wiltshire, Berkshire, east through the Chilterns and East Anglia, to the coast of Norfolk and up the spine of Lincolnshire to the Yorkshire Wolds. Limestone of various kinds appears all over the world, and you can safely say that anything that will grow on chalk will grow on limestone.

If you are in any doubt as to the soil structure of your garden, look at the local plants. Rhododendrons indicate acid or neutral soil, whereas campanula, clematis, dianthus (pinks) and scabiosa may mean limey *or* chalk soil.

Preparing the soil

Lime soil presents no difficulty where it has been worked as a garden or farm land. It may need feeding with well-rotted manure, compost or peat, but you can plant in it easily. Chalk is a problem when there is very little soil above it – such as you can see when driving through roadworks in chalk downs. The topsoil in a garden may vary in depth, especially if parts have been levelled or landscaped. The upper layer of chalk might already be broken, but lower down it could be solid. It is therefore vital, when planting a potentially large tree or shrub, to break up as deep and as wide a layer of chalk as you can. Use a pickaxe if necessary. Merely to scoop out a small hole to take the roots of a young plant is not enough. When the roots have filled the hole they will become pot-bound as if you had planted in a container, and the plant will suffer. There is no need to remove broken chalk: you can shovel it back and the roots will find their way between the pieces.

In a chalk garden you should feed the soil, using almost any form of humus: peat, leaf mould, animal or hop manure, or compost. A compost heap is most valuable to the chalk gardener, and good compost-making is worth studying. It is wiser to grow only calcicole plants than to try any that will be miserable. However, you can help those that are on the brink of

lime-tolerance by including 30g of Epsom salts per 5 lit (1 rounded tablespoon to the gallon) when watering. Rain water is better than that from a tap since lime is soluble and most reservoirs contain it. Once a year you can treat plants that are difficult to grow on chalk with some proprietary brand of sequestrene, but the cost is high.

Design for a chalk garden

As chalk gardens are frequently found on hillsides or near the sea our plan is designed so that it can be adapted to a sloping site. It faces south, the terrace linking house and garden being the driest, sunniest spot. This is filled with silver foliage, and the pink, blue or mauve flowers of succulents and other drought-resisting plants. A shallow, semi-circular step leads down to a level, almost circular area, gravelled for convenience, with a wooden seat built asymmetrically round a shady cherry tree.

A sloping site may have a view, but views tend to go with windy gardens – so shelter is provided by two mixed borders containing some of the shrubs and plants that grow best on chalk. The lawn starts as a wide grass path, curving in serpentine

As chalk is frequently found on hillsides or near the sea our garden is designed so that it can be adapted to a sloping site. The right-hand border screens a miniature 'gold' garden, while beyond the left-hand border is a vegetable plot. Prominent in the foreground is a flowering cherry tree Prunus *Accolade*, with a circular wooden seat built asymmetrically around it

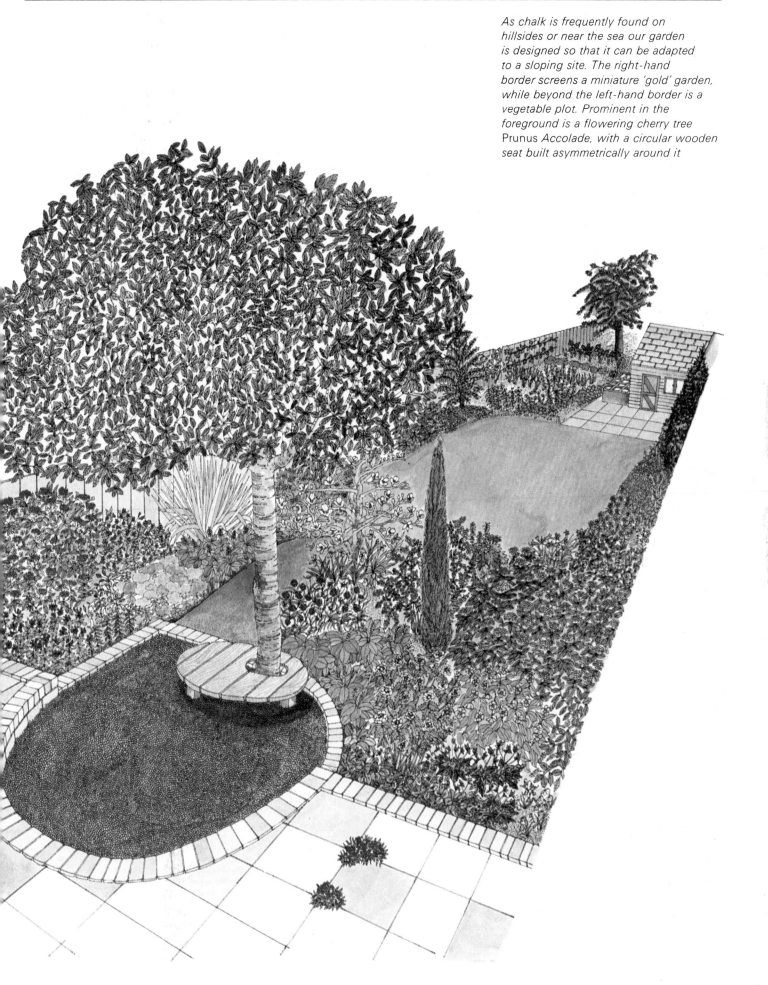

Ground and planting plan

Size: 21·6×9m (72×30 ft)

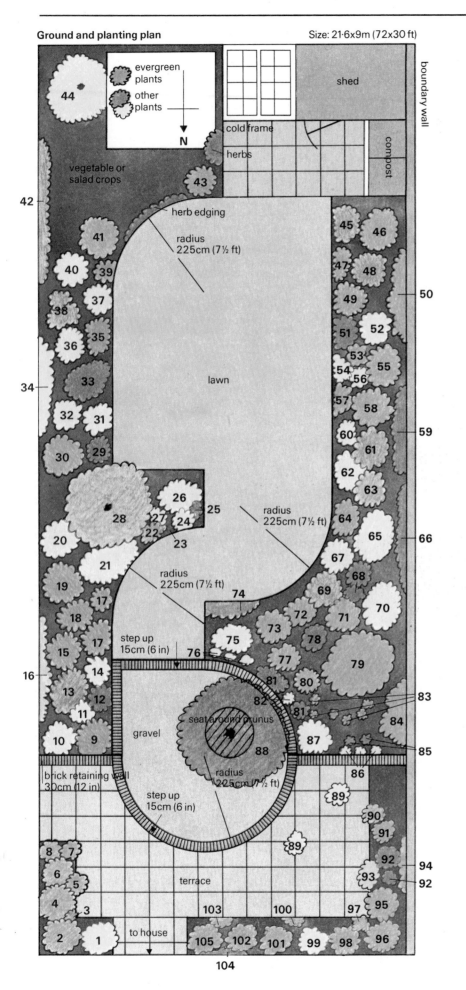

evergreen plants

other plants

N

44

vegetable or salad crops

42

shed

boundary wall

cold frame

herbs

compost

43

herb edging

radius 225cm (7½ ft)

41

45 46

40 39

47 48

37

49

38

51 52

36 35

53 55

54 56

33

57

34

58

32 31

lawn

30 29

60

61

62

63

28

26

25

64

27

24

22

65

20

23

radius 225cm (7½ ft)

66

21

67

radius 225cm (7½ ft)

68

19

74

69

17

72

71

70

18

73

17

75

78

step up 15cm (6 in)

76

77

15

16

79

14

81

80

13

82

83

12

81

11

84

10

seat around prunus

87

85

9

gravel

88

brick retaining wall 30cm (12 in)

86

radius 225cm (7½ ft)

step up 15cm (6 in)

89

90

91

8 7

89

92

6

94

5

terrace

93

92

4

95

3

103

100

97

2 1

to house

105 102 101 99 98 96

104

146

fashion between the borders, that extend from the boundaries to the central line, their relationships creating an ever-changing picture from viewpoints on the terrace. You can check on the last by holding the plan level with your chin and turning it from side to side.

The right-hand or western border screens a bed planted as a gold garden, a surprise that brightens the darkest day,

Key to planting plan

1 *Ceratostigma willmottianum*
2 *Cistus × purpureus* (rock rose)
3 Dianthus (pinks)
4 *Lavandula* (dwarf lavender)
5 *Hebe pinguifolia* Pagei
6 *Yucca filamentosa*
7 *Armeria maritima* (sea pink)
8 *Hebe pinguifolia* Pagei
9 *Escallonia* Apple Blossom
10 *Syringa × josiflexa* Bellicent (lilac)
11 *Lilium regale* (lily)
12 *Fuchsia* Monsieur Thibaut
13 *Hydrangea villosa*
14 *Sedum* Autumn Joy
15 *Abelia × grandiflora*
16 *Rosa* Zéphirine Drouhin (climbing rose)
17 *Bergenia purpurascens* Bellawley (pig squeak)
18 *Phormium tenax* (New Zealand flax)
19 *Hebe* Midsummer Beauty
20 *Buddleia fallowiana* Lochinch
21 *Viburnum tomentosum* Lanarth
22 *Berberis thunbergii* Atropurpurea Nana (barberry)
23 Viola (violets), underplanted
24 *Rosa* Felicia
25 Narcissus (daffodils)
26 *Forsythia suspensa*
27 *Campanula lactiflora* (milky bellflower)
28 *Pyrus salicifolia* Pendula (willow-leaved pear)
29 *Agapanthus* Headbourne Hybrids (African lily)
30 *Choisya ternata* (Mexican orange blossom)
31 *Fuchsia magellanica* Versicolor
32 *Hibiscus syriacus* Blue Bird
33 *Paeonia lactiflora* (paeony) hybrids
34 *Chaenomeles speciosa* Apple Blossom (ornamental quince)
35 *Penstemon hartwegii* Garnet
36 *Lavatera arborea* (tree mallow)
37 *Spiraea × bumalda* Anthony Waterer
38 *Eremurus himalaicus* (foxtail lily)
39 *Ruta graveolens* (rue)
40 *Kolkwitzia amablis* (beauty bush)
41 *Laurus nobilis* (sweet bay)
42 *Vitis vinifera* Brandt (ornamental grape vine)
43 *Rosmarinus officinalis* (rosemary)
44 *Sorbus hupehensis*
45 *Anemone (japonica) hupehensis* (Japanese anemone)
46 *Chamaecyparis lawsoniana* Stewartii (golden Lawson cypress)
47 *Helianthemum (chamaecistus) nummularium* The Bride (rock rose)
48 *Rosa* Maigold
49 *Helichrysum fontanesii* (everlastings)
50 *Hedera colchica* Dentata Variegata (Persian ivy)
51 *Salvia officinalis* Aurea (common sage)
52 *Weigela florida* Variegata
53 *Spartium junceum* (Spanish broom)

containing shrubs and plants with gold-variegated leaves, or white or yellow flowers. The left-hand or eastern shrub border hides the vegetable plot, that can be as large or as small as you like. The main lawn is 5·4 × 7m (18 × 23 ft), which is big enough for simple games, but can be reduced if you want to grow more vegetables. At the far end is a tool shed or small greenhouse and a compost heap.

54 *Euphorbia (epithymoides) polychroma* (cushion spurge)
55 *Euonymus japonicus* (variegated spindle tree)
56 *Lilium pyrenaicum* (yellow turks-cap lily)
57 *Helianthemum (chamaecistus) nummularium* Wisley Primrose (rock rose)
58 *Senecio greyi*
59 *Lonicera japonica* Aureoreticulata (Japanese honeysuckle)
60 *Anthemis cupaniana*
61 *Hypericum patulum* Hidcote (St John's wort)
62 *Alchemilla mollis* (lady's mantle)
63 *Rosa* Iceberg
64 *Genista lydia*
65 *Philadelphus coronarius* Aureus (mock orange)
66 *Rosa* Golden Showers (climbing rose)
67 *Potentilla arbuscula* (cinquefoil)
68 *Verbascum bombyciferum* (mullein)
69 Hemerocallis (day lily), yellow variety
70 *Cotinus coggygria* Royal Purple (smoke tree or Venetian sumach)
71 *Lonicera nitida* (Chinese honeysuckle)
72 *Santolina neapolitana* (cotton lavender)
73 *Acanthus mollis* (bear's breeches)
74 *Iris germanica*
75 *Magnolia* × *loebneri*
76 *Scabiosa caucasica* Clive Greaves (scabious)
77 *Escallonia* Donard Seedling
78 *Lilium regale* (lily)
79 *Viburnum rhytidophyllum*
80 *Juniperus virginiana* Skyrocket (pencil cedar)
81 Hosta (plantain lilies)
82 Narcissus (daffodils)
83 *Helleborus orientalis* (Lenten rose)
84 *Ceanothus rigidus*
85 *Cyclamen neapolitanum* and *C. coum*
86 *Galanthus nivalis* (common snowdrop)
87 *Paeonia suffruticosa* (moutan paeony)
88 *Prunus* Accolade (flowering cherry)
89 *Thymus serpyllum* (wild thyme)
90 *Sedum* Ruby Glow
91 *Ballota pseudodictamnus*
92 *Dianthus barbatus* (sweet William)
93 *Dimorphotheca ecklonis* (star of the veldt or African daisy)
94 *Rosa* Pink Perpétue (climbing rose)
95 *Centaurea gymnocarpa* (knapweed)
96 *Teucrium fruticans* (tree germander)
97 *Campanula poscharskyana* (rock campanula)
98 *Cistus* Silver Pink (rock rose)
99 *Caryopteris* × *clandonensis*
100 *Chrysanthemum haradjanii* (*Tanacetum densum-amani*)
101 Lavandula (lavender)
102 *Convolvulus cneorum*
103 *Dianthus alpinus*
104 *Clematis* Jackmanii
105 *Salvia officinalis* Purpurascens (purple-leaved sage)

PLANTS FOR CHALK SOILS

Here we describe a varied selection of trees, shrubs, and decorative herbs, roses and perennials to grow.

TREES

A plan can show only the horizontal plane of a garden. The verticals are provided by the walls with their climbers, and by the trees. The classic trees of the chalk downs are *Taxus baccata* (yew) and the *Fagus sylvatica* (common beech). While, fully grown, both would be too large for a small garden, it would be hard to choose which makes the better hedge. There are small-growing varieties of both, and of another good hedging tree, *Carpinus betulus* (common hornbeam).

Tilia (lime) can be pleached as a screen, and a large chalk garden might have other deciduous trees including fraxinus (ash), and most acers (maples) except the decorative Japanese ones. *Acer campestre* (field maple), *A. davidii* (snake-barked maple) and *A. platanoides* (Norway maple) are all good on chalk. *Quercus ilex* (evergreen oak) grows well, becoming a big tree in time, but makes a good, rigid hedge against sea winds. Among conifers the cypresses will flourish, as will *Cedrus atlantica* Glauca (blue Atlas cedar) and various pines and firs. Perhaps the best conifer for chalk is the juniper, that rarely grows too big. The large juniperus genus ranges from prostrate shrubs, through bushy shapes, to columnar trees – all of them in many shades of green.

When mature, Cedrus atlantica *Glauca (on right of* C. deodara*) reaches 30m (100 ft) or more in height and expanse*

Medium-sized flowering trees for chalk luckily include malus (crab apple), prunus (flowering cherry) and pyrus (ornamental pear). Smallish trees or large shrubs that have flowers and berries are cotoneaster, crataegus (hawthorn) and pyracantha (firethorn). You can also depend on the sorbus genus, with its flowers and berries, and leaf shapes that vary between the large, felted simple leaves of the aria (or whitebeam) group, and the small, pinnate leaves of the aucuparias (or mountain ashes) typified by *Sorbus aucuparia*. Laburnum is perfectly at home on chalk as are some rarer small trees like *Cercis siliquastrum* (Judas tree), with pink flowers springing from bare bark in spring, and an uncommon North American dogwood *Cornus nuttallii*, a slow grower that speeds up as it gets older, and has starry white bracts that last longer than the flowers.

In a small garden like the one illustrated here there is only room for a few trees. *Prunus* Accolade (flowering cherry) gives shade, and has masses of rose-pink cherry blossom in spring, with good colour in autumn. *Pyrus salicifolia* Pendula (willow-leaved pear) is a graceful, silvery tree, while *Sorbus hupehensis* is a pretty Chinese member of the aucuparia group with white flowers, autumn colour, and whitish berries tinged with pink that the birds ignore.

As representatives of the conifers we have a golden cypress, *Chamaecyparis lawsoniana* Stewartii (golden Lawson), and – as an exclamation point – the pencil-slim *Juniperus virginiana* Skyroc-ket (pencil cedar). Somewhere between a tree and a shrub comes the *Magnolia × loebneri*, one of the most reliable species of its genus on chalk.

SHRUBS

There is a group of large, early-flowering twiggy shrubs that grows well on chalk, but from which it is difficult to make a choice since it includes deutzia, forsythia, kolkwitzia, philadelphus (mock orange), syringa (lilac) and weigela. The best calcicole shrubs for year-round value are viburnums, some of which are evergreen and some deciduous, their flowers coming between early spring and mid summer (February and June) depending on the variety. Flowering from early to late summer (May to July) are abelia, buddleia, *Cotinus coggygria* (smoke tree or Venetian sumach), hibiscus, hypericum (St John's wort) and *Lavatera arborea* (tree mallow). *Hydrangea villosa* is the best species for chalk as it stands dry conditions, and produces blue flowers without the aid of chemicals.

The shrubs shown on our plan are closely planted for quick effect. Attention is given to leaf colour since gold, purple, silvery or variegated foliage are better value in the long run than shrubs like syringa (lilac), that flower for a few days and are dull for most of the year. However, one syringa, *S. × josiflexa* Bellicent, a delicate pink form, was chosen for its grace. Otherwise, there is gold-leaved *Philadelphus coronarius* (mock orange), set off by silver-leaved *Buddleia fallow-iana* Lochinch, purple-leaved *Cotinus*

coggygria Royal Purple, and gold-variegated *Weigela florida* Variegata. *Hypericum patulum* Hidcote (St John's wort) and *Potentilla arbuscula* (cinquefoil) provide golden flowers. Evergreens are represented by ceanothus, *Choisya ternata* (Mexican orange blossom), escallonia, euonymus (spindle), gold-flowered *Genista lydia* and hebe.

The buddleia should be cut down in late spring (April) to encourage new growth. This is called stooling and keeps many shrubs that flower on the current year's wood neatly in their station. It should be done with blue-flowered, grey-leaved *Caryopteris × clandonensis*, blue *Ceratostigma willmottianum*, fuchsia, pink *Lavatera arborea*, yellow *Spartium junceum* (Spanish broom), and

Above: wide-spreading Cercis siliquastrum
Above right: Cotinus coggygria *in flower*
Right: Ceratostigma willmottianum
Left: distinctive large bracts surround flowers of slow-growing Cornus nuttallii

Spiraea × bumalda. Some other shrubs – like deutzia and syringa – need the deadheads cutting back after flowering so that they will put their energies into new wood instead of seeds. If you do this with euphorbia (spurge), don't get the poisonous white juice on your hands – or if you do, wash very thoroughly – and don't cut lavandula (lavender) back into the old wood or it will die.

Some climbers are indicated on the fences or walls: *Vitis vinifera* Brandt (ornamental grape vine) for autumn colour; *Chaenomeles speciosa* Apple Blossom (ornamental quince) for spring; evergreen, blue-flowered *Ceanothus thyrsiflorus* for summer; mauve *Abutilon vitifolium* and *Solanum crispum* Glasnevin (Chilean potato tree) for the terrace; rose-pink and yellow climbing roses, and gold-leaved hedera (ivy) and lonicera to back the gold bed. Clematis, that grows so well on chalk, is represented by *Clematis* Jackmanii, the sturdy, purple favourite.

It is impossible here to cover all the plants and bulbs that grow on chalk or lime soil, but our plan includes representatives of most of the main types. Some have been omitted because they can be uncomfortable in a small garden. Among them are the prickly, thistly plants that grow in the driest soil, often by the seashore, such as eryngium (sea holly) and echinops (globe thistle), and tall, grey *Onopordon arabicum* (ghost thistle).

Conditions in a chalk garden seem to suit the shrubby plants from the warm, dry shores of the Mediterranean region. Many with aromatic foliage have been used as herbs (and still are), but are included here mainly for their decorative effect: for example, rosmarinus (rosemary), lavandula (lavender), blue-leaved *Ruta graveolens* (rue or herb of grace), and the culinary sage in its purple- and gold-leaved forms, *Salvia officinalis* Purpurascens and *S. o.* Aurea. *Thymus vulgaris* (common thyme), *T.* × *citriodorus* (lemon thyme) and *T. serpyllum* (wild thyme) can be used to fill gaps, the last-named – in bright-flowered varieties – being ideal for cracks in the paving, though it may ramp in a warm, dry flowerbed.

The cistus (rock rose) genus also comes from southern Europe, and does very well in dry conditions. There are two on the terrace in the plan, one being *Cistus* × *purpureus*, with bright cerise flowers 8cm (3 in) across, the other, *C.* Silver Pink, is a hybrid of great stamina. Helianthemums, too, are known as rock roses, and are similar plants in miniature, spreading to make ideal cover at the front of a border. We suggest *Helianthemum* (chamaecistus) *nummularium* The Bride, a white variety with grey leaves, and *H. n.* Wisley Primrose as being good for the gold border. Another shrubby plant that likes sunshine and sharp drainage, and is

well worth a place on the terrace, is the less well-known *Convolvulus cneorum*, a crevice plant from the southern Alps. Its grey, satiny leaves have been described as chromium-plated, and the white, pink-backed flowers come out for weeks.

Plant evergreen Ruta graveolens *(above left) as a scenting border shrub*
Mixed border (top) includes verbascum, dianthus (pinks) and stachys
Evergreen Convolvulus cneorum *(above) likes a well-drained soil in full sun*

ROSES

Roses are essential in any garden, but hybrid teas find the going on chalk too hard, so you will have to stick to the tough floribundas like Iceberg, or shrub roses such as the repeat-flowering musks, of which the most reliable is probably pink Felicia. Maigold, a hybrid with strong, glossy foliage and delicious fragrance, is shown in the gold border.

Climbing roses grow well on walls where they can find a cool root run, but many are strong enough for a fence or pergola. Two suggestions are Pink Perpétué, that echoes the colour of *Cistus × purpureus*, and the true rose-pink Zéphirine Drouhin, the rose without a thorn. Golden Showers is a fine repeat-flowering climber to back the gold border.

HERBACEOUS PERENNIALS

An enormous variety of herbaceous perennials grow well on chalk, and many have daisy-like flowers. There is the strongly-spreading, grey-green-foliaged *Anthemis cupaniana*, for example, the white flowers of which appear at the same time as cheiranthus (wallflower) – the latter being a useful filler. The *Anthemis tinctoria* E. C. Buxton (ox-eye chamomile) is a lovely, lemon-yellow 'daisy' for late summer (July), but it has been omitted from the gold border as it needs staking. *Dimorphotheca ecklonis* (star of the veldt or African daisy), 45cm (18 in) high, with white flowers and a blue disc, and *D. barberiae*, 30cm (12 in), with pink flowers, are two South African 'daisies' that are magnificent in a chalk garden and will not grow in a soggy site. Erigerons (fleabane) and *Aster novi-belgii* (Michaelmas daisy), both in the mauve/pink range, are other 'daisies' that do well.

All paeonies like chalk, although they benefit from a good dressing of leaf mould every year. There are the herbaceous named forms of *Paeonia lactiflora*, and the gorgeous tree paeonies or moutans, mostly hybrids of *P. suffruticosa* or the yellow *P. lutea*. Their flowering time is short but the elegant leaves make up for this and often have fine autumn colour. Scabiosa (scabious) is a typical flower of the chalk downs, and there are many kinds – from choice alpines to the excellent *Scabiosa caucasica* Clive Greaves, which has pale blue flowers, and the annual *S. atropurpurea* (sweet scabious or pincushion flower) in a variety of colours.

Two roses for the chalk garden are vigorous, lightly-scented floribunda Iceberg (above right) and double-flowered climber Pink Perpétué (right)

Above: spring-flowering Anemone blanda
Summer-flowering evergreen Euphorbia
wulfenii *Lambrook Gold (below right)*
reaches a height of roughly 1·2m (4ft)

Another comparatively large perennial plant is *Anemone (japonica) hupehensis* (Japanese anemone). This is one of the most useful flowers for a chalk garden as it starts to come into bloom in late summer to early autumn (late July to August) – after the mid summer flush – and goes on into mid autumn (September). It stands 60–90cm (2–3 ft) high and has pink or white flowers with great delicacy of form. *A. × hybrida* Louise Uhink is the one most often recommended, but several other anemones grow equally well, notably the brilliant blue or white woodland carpeter, *A. blanda* (mountain windflower of Greece), 15cm (6 in), and *A. fulgens*, 23cm (9 in), a scarlet flower, astonishing in spring. Spring anemones disappear in summer and care must be taken when weeding or planting around them. Pulsatillas used to be known as *Anemone pulsatilla*, but now have a genus of their own, and can form fine clumps on chalk.

Tubular-flowered penstemons are usually successful on chalk, though not considered reliably hardy in cold, damp gardens, where it is advisable to take cuttings in early autumn (September) for planting out the following year. A strong *Penstemon hartwegii* variety like Garnet or Firebird will flower from late summer to mid autumn, and has the advantage of being evergreen. Penstemons make good cover in early summer for that magnificent bulbous plant *Eremurus himalaicus* (foxtail lily), that can send its white spikes up to 1·8m (6 ft), but can also look rather silly if it is allowed to spring from an expanse of bare earth.

Many flowers loved by flower-arrangers will grow on chalk, among them *Alchemilla mollis* (lady's mantle), a good, perennial, front-of-the-border plant with acid-yellow clouds of bloom and sea-green leaves of interesting scalloped shape. All dianthus, including *Dianthus barbatus* (sweet William) and pinks, grow well on chalk. The former is not long-lived and should be treated as a biennial, but it would be a foolish chalk gardener who did not take advantage of the possibility of growing it really well.

A totally different type of plant is *Phormium tenax* (New Zealand flax). It has great, tough leaves that rise 1·2m (4 ft) from the ground like a bunch of swords, and makes a magnificent architectural focal point in a border. It needs protection from strong winds that can split and shred the leaves, and it flowers rarely – but when it does the effect is striking. Similarly the yuccas grow well on chalk, and are represented by grey-leaved *Yucca filamentosa*, that produces dramatic spikes of white bell flowers in most years and has a place on the terrace. *Y. flaccida* has leaves that curve down gracefully.

The large family of euphorbias (spurge) will grow elsewhere but is sometimes collected by chalk gardeners for its great decorative quality. *Euphorbia wulfenii* and *E. characias* are large plants with evergreen leaves of a good blue-green. The flower-buds appear from mid to late winter (late December) and slowly uncurl until the flowers, really bracts, unfold into great lime-yellow heads that remain until late summer. When these are dead, cut the stems down to the ground but do not get the white 'milk' on your hands as it can cause skin irritation. *E. (epithymoides) polychroma* (cushion spurge) makes a 45cm (18 in) mound of brilliant yellow in the spring and often has autumn colour. *E. myrsinites*, a rock plant that looks like a succulent, has sharply-carved, bluish-jade leaves that set off the acid-yellow flowers. Others include the taller *E. lathyrus* (caper spurge), 60cm (24 in), that is reputed to keep moles away, and the spreading *E. cyparissias* (cypress spurge or ploughman's mignonette).

While dealing with architectural plants we must not forget *Acanthus mollis* (bear's breeches), that gave the inspiration to the classic Corinthian capital. Its deeply-cut, glossy green leaves brighten the garden in winter and die off in late summer and early autumn, while the flower spikes are tall, prickly, and in colour a mixture of white petals (corolla) and purple outer leaves (calyx). Coming

Rampant Campanula poscharskyana *(above) flowers through summer and autumn*
Summer-flowering Sisyrinchium striatum *(below) prefers a sunny position*

from southern Europe they enjoy quick drainage and withstand drought without ill effects – but they like a winter mulch.

Coming down to smaller plants, the bergenias (pig squeak) are dependable, and hybridizers are producing many varieties of these huge evergreens with spoon-shaped, leathery leaves. *Bergenia stracheyi* Schmidtii flowers first, followed by *B. purpurascens* Bellawley, with rose-red flowers, *B.* Margery Fish, a nice pink, *B. stracheyi* Silberlicht, white and pink, *B. s.* Evening Glow, with purple flowers and purplish winter foliage, and many others. Most bergenias produce a few scarlet leaves in winter. Often bracketed with them because of their equally big leaves are the hostas (plantain lily) of which there are dozens. Their flowers are lily-like on strong stems and the leaves are ribbed longitudinally. As they die off completely in winter they are good companions for narcissus (daffodil) and other spring bulbs, including *Eranthis hyemalis* (winter aconite). Their leaves are dormant when narcissus are out, and then unfurl to hide the dying leaves.

Another showy plant for a chalk or lime garden that seems indifferent to sun or shade is hemerocallis (day lily). Again hybridizers have been at work and these can now be obtained with their 90cm (3 ft) stems rising from wide, strap-like leaves with a succession of flowers in every shade, from yellow – through apricot and orange – to deep mahogany.

Campanulas (bellflower) that flower in mid summer do well on chalk, tending to seed themselves all over the place, but they are easily controlled when small. They range from little rock plants that can be invasive, such as *Campanula poscharskyana* and *C. portenschlagiana*, to taller border plants, forms of *C. lactiflora* (milky bellflower), *C. latifolia* (great bellflower), *C. latiloba* and open-belled *C. persicifolia* (peach-leaved bellflower). *C. glomerata* is a magnificent rich purple but may ramp through other plants. All of the campanulas mentioned so far grow in sun or shade. *C. pyramidalis* (chimney bellflower), if it is brought inside the house and treated as a pot plant, will last longer than in the garden where the flowers fade as soon as they have been fertilized by the bees.

Many irises grow well on chalk, particularly *Iris germanica* and its many hybrids. This is the fleur-de-lis, its great, flambeau-shaped blooms having been known to heraldry since they became an emblem in Renaissance Italy. In Tuscany they can be seen everywhere, their pale, sword-shaped leaves springing from the dry soil. *I. sibirica* grows well as a border plant, while iris-like leaves but spikes of starry yellow flowers are found on another chalk gardener's friend, *Sisyrinchium striatum* (satin flower). This seeds itself freely so that once you have it you need never be without it. The same useful quality is shared by the verbascums (mullein), that produce attractive rosettes of pointed leaves in their first year, and spires of yellow flowers in the second year. *Verbascum bombyciferum* has white, woolly foliage that is most attractive.

Hardy succulents grow well on chalk, the two most useful groups being the sempervivums (houseleek) with neatly-spreading rosettes, and the sedums. The latter are a huge family, from tiny, ground-covering *Sedum spathulifolium*, to medium-sized *S.* Ruby Glow and blue-leaved *S. cauticola*, and to taller varieties like *S.* Autumn Joy, and the type species *S. spectabile*. Their showy red or pink flowers that appear in mid to late autumn are useful.

There are many bulbs that find chalk conditions ideal: galanthus (snowdrop), all the narcissi and crocuses, the little blue flowers of spring like muscari (grape hyacinth), chionodoxa (glory of the snow), scillas (squill) and puschkinias. There are also many early-flowering bulbous irises of the reticulata type, the earliest being *Iris histrioides* with the *I. reticulata* species following on. Cyclamen have corms not bulbs. *Cyclamen neapolitanum* flowering in autumn, and *C. coum* in spring are jewels of the chalk garden and grow best in dry shade.

Many lilies grow on chalk, particularly the beautiful, white *Lilium regale*, the shade-loving martagon group, the early *L. pyrenaicum* (yellow turks-cap lily), the orange *L. henryi*, flowering in late summer, and the hybrids of *L.* × *aurelianense*. Indeed most hybrids grow well on chalk but not those based on the Japanese kinds, like *L. auratum* (golden-rayed lily of Japan or goldband lily) and others.

Belonging to the lily family but growing from a fleshy root is perhaps the most beautiful chalk-loving flower, the agapanthus (African lily), with heads of glorious blue in late summer. Look for *Agapanthus* Headbourne Hybrids growing 45–75cm (18–30 in) high.

Chalk-loving plants come from many places, viola (violet) and helleborus (hellebore) from the woods, armeria (thrift) and mesembryanthemum (Livingstone daisy) from the seaside, and the brilliant blue *Gentiana acaulis* (trumpet gentian) from the Alps. If you know where a plant comes from it is often the greatest help when it comes to growing it, and its name sometimes gives you a clue.

Above: Sedum *Ruby Glow in foreground,* Centaurea gymnocarpa *and* Ruta graveolens *behind* Agapanthus africanus *(right) grows up to 60–75cm (2–2½ ft) tall*

ROCK GARDENING

Creating a focal point of interest in your garden can be a problem, particularly if you live on one of today's many housing estates. Often there are no fences between sites, and sometimes there are restrictions on having trees, or indeed any plant that grows above a certain height. One answer could be to create your own rock garden, and here we explain how to do it. Later on we tell you about scree gardens, and include a selection of rock and alpine plants.

Before you make any final decision on whether to proceed with a rock garden, you must first consider the conditions that will most suit rock plants and alpines. Ideally, a rock garden should be situated on a gentle slope, preferably facing south or south-west, and sheltered from strong winds. It should be close enough to any trees to benefit from the sunlight that will filter through the leaves in summer, but not so close as to suffer from the continual dripping of rain. A well-drained, sandy loam is the best soil for this type of garden.

Obviously, many sites will fail to meet at least one of these requirements, but don't worry. In fact, one of Britain's best-known rock gardens, at the Royal Horticultural Society's establishment at Wisley, is on a north-facing slope, but by clever construction parts of it have been 'turned' to face south. How this was done is explained in the section headed: Forming an 'outcrop' rock garden.

The worst places you can attempt to create a rock garden are in a dry corner, near a hedge, or in very dense shade. But the more determined you are, the more you can do to combat difficulties.

In this typical 'outcrop' garden large, weathered rocks have been set into a slope in an informal manner to create a series of 'steps' and colourfully planted

Preparing the site

Once you have settled on where to situate your rock garden you must turn your attention to the preparation of the site. First dig the area over and, if it is a heavy soil, trench it. Remove any perennial weeds, by chemical means if necessary.

Clay soils must be drained (see diagram next page), and to do this dig trenches approximately 45cm (18 in) deep and 90–180cm (3–6 ft) apart, according to the state of the clay. Half-fill the trench with rubble or large stones, cover these with upturned turf or very coarse compost, and fill up with soil.

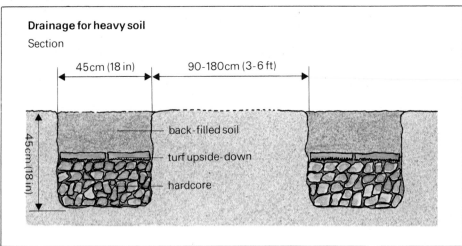

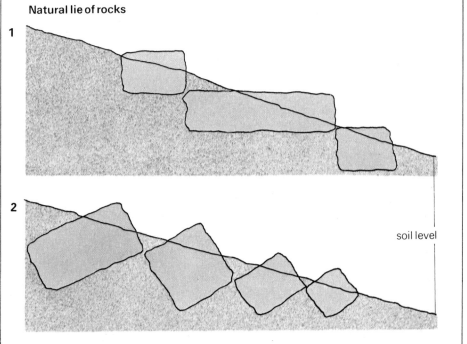

Rock used in the garden includes cold, hard granite (top) and mellow sandstone (above) which is soft in texture

Bed the rocks in a soil mound comprising 2 parts 6mm (¼ in) down rock or gravel chippings – to provide drainage – and 1 part each of loam and moss peat. If only 10mm (⅜ in) down chippings are available, these will suffice. The mound will subside after a while, even though you firm the soil down, so keep a reserve of the mixture for topping up after about ten days – or sooner if it rains.

Finally, add a top-dressing of 6mm (¼ in) down chippings, making it about 2–3cm (1 in) deep, and rake flat. The chippings have a three-fold purpose: to retain moisture; to protect the necks of plants from rotting; and to prevent rain splashing soil onto the flowers, some of which – although hardy – are delicate.

Other badly-drained sites will require the same approach. A rock garden built on chalk should present no problems, provided you follow the same drainage

*Above: an outcrop rock garden should imitate nature to be effective. In **1** rock lies flat in the earth's surface, but in **2** geological upheaval has set it at an angle of about 45 degrees*

procedure as for clay. But your choice of plants will be limited, and you may need to add a chemical agent to the soil to prevent the foliage turning yellow.

Choice of rock
You should give extremely careful thought to the choice of rock. It is not a cheap commodity, and you will have to balance aesthetic considerations with the availability of the stone you choose.

Two important factors to bear in mind when making your decision are the type of soil in your garden, and whether any local stone is available. Matching the rock with the soil is very important if your

rock garden is to look authentic. Nothing looks more out of place than, say, a water-worn limestone in a sandstone area or, indeed, vice versa. In some urban areas limestone tends to wash white and become rather glaring, although it will prove excellent if used in conjunction with a stream, pond or waterfall.

If you are unable to get any local stone, or if none exists, you will have to look around and see what you can find. Sandstone will be kindest to your plants, and is available in the south of England. Sussex sandstone is very popular, and Kentish Rag sandstone is quite easily obtained. Cotswold stone has a warm appeal, but although a sandstone, it contains an element of alkalinity, so a careful choice of lime-loving plants is necessary. Granite is cold, hard and heavy, and plants will not really grow well around it, but it can make quite an attractive garden.

As far as cost is concerned, the amount you will have to pay will be determined primarily by the distance the rock has to travel from the quarry and the quantities that are to be conveyed.

How much rock will you need?
When you have decided which rock to use, and discovered the cost per tonne, the next thing is to calculate how much you will need. For a rock garden measuring 4.5×3m (15×10 ft), $1\frac{1}{2}$–2 tonnes of rock should be sufficient. Individual pieces of different types of stone will vary in size, and you will get a slightly larger volume of sandstone per tonne than you will limestone. Ideally, of course, you should be able to pick out the particular pieces of stone that you want, but this is not always possible.

In a small garden, an economical use of stone is essential if you are to keep the overall effect in proportion. Judicious placement can often make the end result appear rather more than the number of stones might indicate.

Rock in nature
All rock starts life as a large lump – be it in the shape of a mountain or a range of mountains. The action of various strains and stresses in the earth's behaviour causes this lump to crack and split. Splitting occurs in parallel lines, vertically and horizontally, but not diagonally. Moisture which permeates into these cracks expands and contracts under the alternating effects of cold and heat, eventually causing the rock to split further and to crumble. Some parts disintegrate to the extent of forming soil, but others protrude from the earth's surface as an outcrop, and it is this that is often imitated in the rock garden.

Forming an 'outcrop' rock garden
The important thing to remember when forming an outcrop rock garden is that it should appear natural. In nature, geological upheavals can mean that rocks lie at an angle in the soil, so when positioning the stones in your garden make them slope gently into the ground: this will have the added effect of guiding moisture to your plants.

If you already have a slope suitable for a rock garden then clearly your task will be much simpler than if you don't. However, if your slope faces north, you would be well advised to turn it so that it faces south. This is achieved by setting large rocks into the slope at such an angle that they face north, thus providing a protected area behind them – facing south – where you can place your alpines and rock plants.

If your garden is flat, you will have to create an artificial slope, but at least you can point it in the right direction, and make it an appropriate size.

All rock has strata lines, that indicate successive layers of deposited substance, formed over millions of years. In some rocks, these lines are barely distinguishable, while in others they are fairly well defined. When arranging the rocks in your garden, try to ensure that the strata lines are horizontal and never vertical.

Remember, too, that if your particular design requires you to place one rock on top of another, you should follow nature's example and avoid the brick wall principle of overlapping.

Forming a tufa rock garden
Another type of rock used for building a garden is tufa. If weathered it will be grey in colour, but direct from the quarry it is bright creamy-white.

It is basically a porous limestone, formed by the action of water passing through limestone rocks and collecting particles that, together with decaying plant life of a primitive nature, form the original tufa. The porosity is brought about by the decaying and eventual washing away of the primitive plant life.

The advantages of tufa over the other types of rock mentioned are numerous. From the construction point of view, it has little or no strata lines. Many plants will actually grow *on* it, as roots can penetrate its porous form. Saxifrages and draba will both do very well here.

As with an outcrop rock garden, drainage is essential. Tufa should be arranged on an informal basis: you simply 'mould' the stone to the existing contours of your garden, or use it to create a rise and fall on flat ground. When you have laid the rocks and filled in with soil, the ground can be top-dressed with the left-over 'dust' from the rock, or with limestone chippings. The cost per tonne is rather high in comparison with other stone, but its porosity makes it light in weight and, therefore, good value for what you have to pay.

Below: densely-planted outcrop rock garden at Dinmore Manor, Herefordshire

SCREE GARDENING

When building an informal rock garden we compared different types when we compared the different types of stone available in Britain. Here we look at the use of stone chippings, or scree, in the rock garden, and include a selection of suitable shrubs and alpine plants.

A scree in the context of a rock garden is simply a reconstruction of the conditions in which rock plants grow in their natural habitat throughout the mountains of the world. Plants that will often prove difficult to cultivate in a normal environment positively thrive in a bed of stone chippings. The scree provides perfect drainage, a cool root run, and moisture during dry periods.

A scree can be created on any soil: alkaline or acid, heavy clay or light sand. It can form an integral part of a rock garden, or it can be a feature on its own, but always remember that in nature a scree emanates from a rock formation and usually 'fans out' from a fairly wide fissure or valley in the rocks. Examples of scree can be found in botanic gardens all over Britain, and there is a particularly good one at the Royal Botanic Garden in Edinburgh.

In a rock garden, the most suitable place to form a scree is between two rising outcrops, but it is also possible to lay special scree beds, either as an edge to a rock garden, or as a completely separate bed on a lawn.

Making a scree bed

To make a scree bed you must first mark out the area you propose to use and excavate it to a depth of approximately 90cm (3 ft) on a heavy subsoil, or 60cm (2 ft) on a light, well-drained soil. Slope the floor gently on a well-drained soil, but more sharply on a heavy soil, where you should also add a layer of rough drainage material – something like brick rubble or broken pot would do the job. Over this, place either rough peat, compost, half-decayed leaves or rotted turf, and tread firm. Finally, the scree itself is laid.

Opinions differ on the ideal make-up of a scree, but basically it is agreed that too much drainage is worse than too little. Make your scree of roughly 50 per cent chippings, 25 per cent sandy loam and 25 per cent peat or leaf mould, and you should be all right.

To add interest to the surface, as well as create a more natural finish, you could dot a few rocks here and there, building up the scree around them for greater effect. It is a good idea to add a modest top dressing of leaf mould or peat once a year.

The chippings should be no larger than the 6mm ($\frac{1}{4}$ in) variety if possible, although the standard 10mm ($\frac{3}{8}$ in) might be the only one available at your local supplier. If the colour of the chippings does not blend with the stone in your rock garden, you can cover the chippings with a thin top dressing of whatever will match, be it granite, limestone or tufa.

Raised scree beds

One form of rock garden leads to another. A raised scree bed can be constructed from broken paving stone comparatively cheaply, and can, in fact, form quite a feature in a garden that has been terraced. Alternatively, the raised scree can be free-standing, particularly in an environment containing a great deal of paving or concrete.

A raised scree won't usually exceed 45cm (18 in) in height, but a normal raised bed can be up to 90cm (3 ft). It makes an excellent form of gardening for the elderly, or those confined to wheelchairs, as it is not necessary to crouch to reach the planting area. It is also a controlled form of gardening, for the soil mixture can be specially chosen to suit whatever group of plants you plan to cultivate.

The construction of a raised scree bed differs from that of the other forms of rock garden so far described, in that, for strength and rigidity, the rocks or paving forming the wall can be interlocked on the brick wall principle.

The walls should not be exactly vertical; each stone should be set back gradually to form a slight slope. If you can also tilt the stones slightly to cause the rain to percolate through to the centre, so much the better.

You will have to insert plants for the sides of the bed at the same time as you build the wall. For extra security you might decide to cement the stones into

Top right: section of scree bed excavated to total depth of 90cm (3 ft) with a base slope at 20° to horizontal for poorly-drained soil, or 5° for well-drained soil
Centre: make hardboard, triangular template to measure the 20° angle of slope; for a 5° angle, the short side of the triangle should be 5cm (2 in) long
Right: section of raised scree bed with supporting side wall of paving slabs, tilted to allow water to run into bed

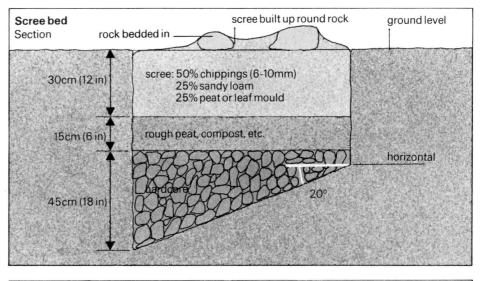

Scree bed
Section

rock bedded in — scree built up round rock — ground level

30cm (12 in)

scree: 50% chippings (6-10mm)
25% sandy loam
25% peat or leaf mould

15cm (6 in) rough peat, compost, etc.

horizontal

45cm (18 in) hardcore

20°

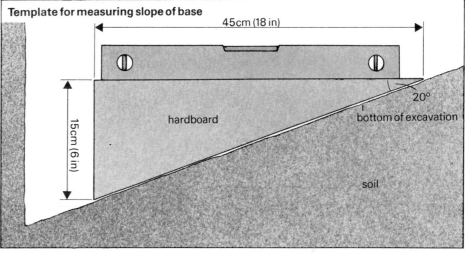

Template for measuring slope of base

45cm (18 in)

15cm (6 in)

hardboard

20°

bottom of excavation

soil

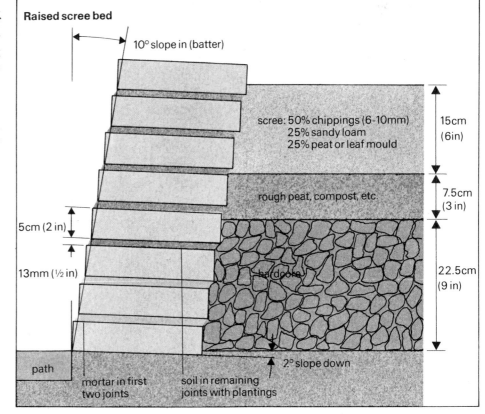

Raised scree bed

10° slope in (batter)

scree: 50% chippings (6-10mm)
25% sandy loam
25% peat or leaf mould

15cm (6in)

rough peat, compost, etc.

7.5cm (3 in)

5cm (2 in)

13mm (½ in)

hardcore

22.5cm (9 in)

path

mortar in first two joints

soil in remaining joints with plantings

2° slope down

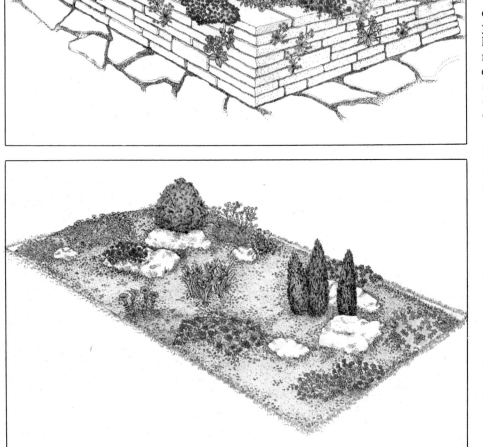

Top: free-standing, raised scree bed looks attractive in a paved area
Above: a finished scree bed, planted out

place, but the most satisfactory results will be achieved by setting them in soil, apart from perhaps the first few layers. This will allow plants like ramonda and lewisia to grow happily on their sides in the wall, rather than upright on the flat area below the wall, where they will collect rain in the centre of their rosettes.

Instead of paving or rock, you could use discarded railway sleepers to make the wall of the bed. Lay them one on top of another, to form a square or rectangle, and drive iron stakes into the ground around the edge to keep them in position.

Planting in rock and scree

There is an almost unlimited range of rock plants and shrubs, but it is important that, when making your selection, you also consider where you are going to put each plant. A visit to a specialist nurseryman is well worth the effort, as he will be able to advise you on what will be best for your particular soil. You will also be able to see the plants in flower. Alpines are always grown in pots and are thus easily transplanted at any time of year, although spring is naturally the best time for planting.

Never put fast-growing plants close to slow growers, otherwise the former will tend to overrun the latter. Try to arrange things so that your rock garden has some colour all through the year, rather than just in one season. The best plan is to plant the miniature shrubs first, and then select the most suitable positions for the other plants.

Evergreen conifers are particularly useful in the rock garden, providing variety in colour, height, form and texture. Often, a conifer can be used to enhance the appearance of another plant, but follow the directions of nature when deciding on the appropriate places for planting. You would never see a tall tree on top of a mountain – it will always be at the base – and so it should be in your garden. On the same principle, a prostrate conifer or shrub would best be planted to fall over the edge of a rock.

To provide a continuous and colourful display throughout spring and summer, you can plant aubrietia, alyssum, iberis, helianthemum, some campanula and the more vigorous dianthus: position them to cascade down a dry wall or bank. If you add *Polygonum affine* and *P. vacciniifolium* to this group, the display will continue through to the autumn.

Bulbs, in general, will not do well on a scree, but a selection of those which are suitable adds interest. Plant them so that they peep through mats of ground cover such as thyme or acaena. Tulips come in all sizes and colours, with the many hybrids and varieties of *Tulipa kaufmanniana* being particularly suitable. Then there are the numerous dwarf species and cultivars of narcissus. Crocuses will make an attractive show early in the year, and *Crocus speciosus* will start again in the autumn.

As already explained, it is not advisable to grow the more vigorous rock plants on a scree because they would soon choke more delicate and choice species. So while, for instance, *Campanula allionii, C. pulla, C. arvatica, C. cochlearifolia* and other small campanulas would all do well, larger plants such as *Campanula portenschlagiana* and *C. poscharskyana* would be out of place and a menace. The latter two would be best situated on a dry wall where it will not matter if they spread rampantly. Kabschia saxifrages are a good choice for a scree, particularly the yellow-flowered *Saxifraga × apiculata* and *S. burseriana*, with its many hybrids. Careful siting is vital, for unless they occupy a shady position in summer, they can be scorched in a single day. Autumn rains will tend to rot them, so glass protection may also be necessary. Otherwise they are completely hardy.

Of the other saxifrages, *S. aizoon* and its forms create silver-encrusted mats of rosettes, while *S. cotyledon* and *S. longifolia*, particularly the form of the latter called Tumbling Waters, provide handsome sprays of flowers, some 30cm (12 in) long.

The alpine aster *Aster alpinus* will thrive, and the alpine catsfoot *Antennaria dioica rosea* makes an attractive grey carpet with short pink flowers. *Armeria caespitosa*, a form of thrift, will form little

Above: scree at Edinburgh Royal Botanic Garden. Right: Cotyledon simplifolia *thrives on well-drained, rocky surfaces*

hummocks and produce heads of pink flowers. The European aretian androsaces would be too vulnerable in this sort of situation and is best kept in an alpine house, but the rock jasmine from Kashmir, *Androsace sempervivoides*, again with pink flowers, would enjoy scree conditions. Some of the gentians will give a good display, notably *Gentiana gracilipes* and *G. septemfida*, two summer-flowering species. The well-known *G. acaulis* and *G. verna* would also be happy, and although the latter is a short-lived plant, it will seed freely. A dwarf flax *Linum salsoloides* Nanum, bears slightly opalescent pearly-white flowers during the summer, and might also be considered suitable.

Among other bulbs that will do well

Above: the hardy Saxifraga × apiculata
Below: Erinus alpinus *with starry flowers that are borne throughout the summer*
Bottom left: *an alpine dianthus hybrid*
Centre: Ramonda myconii, *a native of the Pyrenees suited to north-facing slopes*
Bottom right: Linum salsoloides

in scree are the rhizomatous irises, including *Iris innominata, I. cristata* and *I. mellita*. The latter is a miniature flag iris, only 8–10cm (3–4 in) tall, and it can have either smoky-purple or yellow flowers. The other two are 13–15cm (5–6 in) tall, are natives of America, and – like most American iris – detest lime.

Dianthus go well in rock gardens. *Dianthus alpinus*, with its deep green, strap-shaped leaves, and its large, deep-rose flowers that appear in early summer, will like the cool side of a rock. Another European dianthus worthy of your consideration is *D. neglectus*, which has a distinctive light buff reverse to its petals, and will form a dense cushion of fine green linear foliage, almost indistinguishable from grass. *D. freynii* is yet another from Europe, and has more typical greyish foliage, and small pink flowers on 3–5cm (1–2 in) stems. Dianthus will not object to lime and neither will *Linaria*

alpina (toadflax), although the latter will be happier on a scree, where it will form a compact mat of blue-grey foliage and produce little mauve snapdragon flowers with orange markings.

Although it tends to seed itself freely, the pink-flowered *Erinus alpinus* and its hybrids will not become objectionable. An interesting miniature relative of the cabbage family is *Morisia monantha* (or *M. hypogaea*), which has a long taproot and will form a flat rosette of glossy, dark green leaves in which will nestle golden-yellow flowers in the spring. *Wahlenbergia serpyllifolia* Major and *W. pumilio* are two cousins of the harebells. They form prostrate mats and produce deep purple and lavender bells respectively in mid summer (June). They are sometimes considered temperamental plants and are often short-lived, but they are still worthwhile.

You can bring a touch of colour to the scree in the autumn by planting two cyananthus. *Cyananthus microphyllus* (also known as *C. integer*) can become over-large for a scree, but *C. lobatus* and *C. l. albus* will both do very well.

Shrubs can also be grown in the spartan conditions provided by a scree. *Daphne arbuscula* is a fragrant-flowered, 15–25cm (6–10 in) tall shrublet that will flower in June. *Juniperus communis compressa* (common juniper) is a greyish-foliaged conifer that will slowly reach to over 60cm (24 in) in a slim, columnar manner. Other suitable conifers are *Chamaecyparis obtusa caespitosa* and *C. o. minima*: both produce dense, dark green foliage, and are very slow growing, taking several years to reach 30cm (12 in).

This, then, is but a small selection of what will grow in rock and scree conditions. As already indicated, a visit to your local nursery will give you a much better idea of what is available and which plants grow best in your area.

GARDENING WITH PEAT

We have explained how scree can be used to enhance your rock garden and added a list of suitable alpine plants and shrubs. In this third part we tell you how you can build your own peat garden.

A further variation on the rock garden theme is the peat garden which, although less tidy than other rock gardens, should reflect nature just as keenly in its appearance.

Lime-hating, acid soil plants, such as erica, that are too small for the wilder parts of a woodland garden, and some of the smaller rhododendrons, will all do extremely well in a peat garden, provided you create the right conditions. All of these plants will require a moist soil, and frequent overhead spraying will be essential during summer months to prevent any drying out. Adequate drainage is imperative – although don't overdo it. And there should be plenty of light around the peat garden with, ideally, a nearby tree to cast a dappled shade across the bed in summer, without completely overshadowing it.

Laying out your peat garden

The design of your peat garden should resemble that of other informal rock gardens. Aim simply to create a series of rising beds, each capable of accommodating peat-loving plants, and you won't go far wrong. You won't be able to achieve the same height as with other rock gardens, for a small block of peat will naturally lack the strength of a piece of rock.

The ideal site for a peat garden is a gentle slope, so if your garden is flat you may wish to create an artificial slope. But remember that you must first ensure adequate drainage, so be prepared to trench the ground if necessary.

When you have formed a mound of suitable height and shape, you will have to consolidate the soil thoroughly before starting to position the blocks of peat.

On the matter of aspect, it is very important that your garden faces north – a southern aspect could prove disastrous for peat-loving plants in the heat of summer, especially if there is no tree to cast a shadow over the beds.

A moderate-sized peat garden made from large peat blocks that have been rounded, set one on top of another and covered with a selection of moisture-loving plants

163

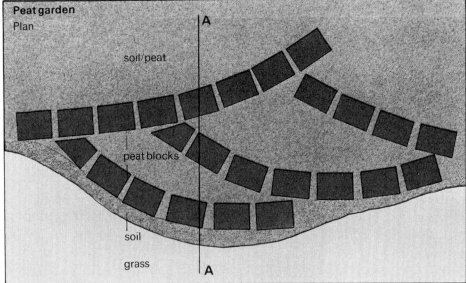

Above: the RHS's peat garden at Wisley
Right: bed peat blocks into soil mound
to form series of gradually-rising beds

Peat garden
Plan
soil/peat
A
peat blocks
soil
grass
A

Peat blocks

In Britain blocks are available from suppliers in Somerset and Scotland, and you can order them at most garden centres. Frequently, you will receive the blocks in a dry state; as it is important that they be wet before you bed them in the soil, you should give each block a soaking prior to use.

Firm placement will be necessary when you set the blocks in position, so ram moist peat between them for rigidity.

Although you can adapt an ordinary rock garden to the needs of peat-loving plants, this will never be entirely satisfactory; rocks can become very hot in the summer, and at such times plants will be happier in the cooler environment of a peat garden, where they can spread their roots through the peat blocks.

Plants for your peat garden

Two groups of plants immediately spring to mind: one the rhododendron, the other the erica, including heaths and heathers. Take care if you buy the latter, for while a small heather can look most attractive, particularly if purchased in flower, when it has covered an area of some 3000 sq cm (3 sq ft) and engulfed other more choice plants, it will lose much of its appeal.

Erica can be used initially to fill in empty spaces but with one exception should not be regarded as permanent plantings. The exception is *Calluna* Foxii Nana (ling), that will form a tight symmetrical hummock 10–15cm (4–6 in) across.

The number of suitable rhododendrons is almost countless: the free-flowering pink *Rhododendron pemakoense* flowers in late spring (April) and grows to a height of 30–38cm (12–15 in). Unfortunately, because of its early flowering its blooms will sometimes be frosted. *R.*

scintillans, although officially reaching 75–90cm ($2\frac{1}{2}$–3 ft) height, does this slowly; it is upright in habit, evergreen, and has mauve-blue flowers that are quite hardy.

The dwarf *R. impeditum* has a tendency sometimes to ramp, but you can usually rely on the quality of its blue flowers. One of the most attractive of all rhododendrons is the deciduous *R. camtschaticum*, with pure-pink, saucer-shaped flowers appearing in early summer (May), and reaching only 20–25cm (8–10 in) in height. *R. repens* is not very free flowering, but its cultivar, Carmen, will

Peat garden
Section **A A**

peat rammed into joints

peat blocks

7–8cm (3 in)

soil/peat

subsoil

A   **A**

10cm (4 in)

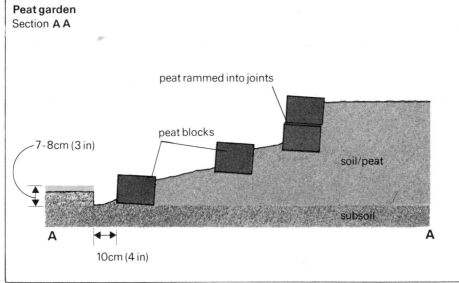

Plants for peat – above left: Gentiana
sino-ornata; *top:* Hylomecon japonicum;
and above: Rhododendron pemakoense
*Left: tilt blocks slightly to help retain
water, and ram moist peat between them*

develop a mass of dark red bells on a
fairly compact evergreen bush.

Cassiopes are attractive evergreens, in
particular *Cassiope lycopodioides*, which
produces a dense mat of whipcord-like
foliage and a mass of miniature white
bells.

Hylomecon japonicum, a native of
Japan, will display numerous golden-
yellow flowers on 20–25cm (8–10 in)
stems if grown in a rich soil.

Although all shrubs in the gaultheria
genus are dwarf, different species vary in
shape and size, and some species tend to
be invasive. *Gaultheria procumbens* (part-
ridge berry) has pinkish, globe-shaped
flowers and bright red fruits, while *G.
trichophylla* has deep pink, bell-shaped
flowers and blue fruits. *G. cuneata* is
rather more vigorous, reaching a height
of 30cm (12 in), and a spread sometimes
exceeding this. It has racemes of white
flowers and in the autumn produces
globose white fruits.

Of all gentians, *Gentiana sino-ornata*
will go best in shade and peat, but you will
need to divide the plants every second
year for continuous success. The clear

blue, trumpet-shaped flowers will provide
a spectacular display in the autumn.

Most phlox will only grow in an
outcrop rock garden, and as a general rule
you can take it that the smaller the leaf,
the more sun the particular species will
tolerate. *Phlox subulata* (moss phlox) and
P. douglasii, both prefer a well-drained
sunny site, but *P. stolonifera* Blue Ridge
will enjoy a peat garden, although it has
an untidy rampant habit, partially compensated for by the blue flowers on 10cm
(4 in) stems that will appear in the spring.

Of saxifrages, *Saxifraga moschata*
Cloth of Gold will add a patch of colour
to your peat garden if you can find it a
shady corner – it dislikes bright sunlight.

A plant that has had several names in
its time is *Cotyledon simplicifolia* (*Chias-
tophyllum oppositifolium*), that will be
happy in peat, and produces catkin-like
inflorescences of tiny yellow flowers in the
summer. Its succulent leaves are basal
and slightly coarse.

You can grow certain of the smaller
primula if your peat garden is damp
enough, but some Asiatic species will be
extremely difficult to cultivate in dry parts
of Britain, although they grow like weeds

in western Scotland. *Primula gracilipes*, *P. bracteosa* and *P. edgeworthii* are all very beautiful, with *P. gracilipes* perhaps the easiest to grow in Britain. The Balkan *P. frondosa* will be a simpler proposition to cultivate, and will produce lavender flowers and leaves with a covering of white hairs. *P. denticulata* (drumstick primrose), although even easier to grow than *P. frondosa*, has really too gross a form for the peat garden, and tends to seed freely.

An attractive native of Manchuria is *Jeffersonia dubia*, that produces large blue flowers very close to the ground, followed by kidney-shaped leaves.

Corydalis cashmeriana, as its name suggests, originated in Kashmir, and is reputed to be intractable, although it seems to do satisfactorily in peat conditions. It has delightful blue flowers similar to those of the British fumaria (common fumitory).

Some bulbs will do well in the peat garden. Erythronium are very colourful, with the easy-growing *Erythronium tuolumnense* a good choice, producing deep yellow flowers. The rose-pink-flowered *E. revolutum* (American trout lily) has a number of named forms, Pink Beauty being outstanding.

Cypripedium (lady's slipper orchid) are rather expensive, but worth it for the handsome display they can give. *Cypripedium calceolus* is a native of Britain, but rarely found growing in the wild. Its flower has chocolate sepals and, in common with all cypripedium, a distinctive pale yellow 'pouch'. *C. reginae* is of North American origin and has a rich rose pouch and pink-flushed sepals.

A charming miniature daffodil that will flower in early spring and grow to a height of no more than 15–20cm (6–8 in) is *Narcissus cyclamineus*. If it likes its situation it will seed and spread freely.

Among rhizomatous plants are the North American *Uvularia grandiflora*, a relative of the lily, displaying pale yellow, bell-shaped flowers on 25cm (10 in) stems in early summer (May), and *Iris gracilipes*, a small lavender-blue crested species with wiry stems and spear-like foliage.

Left: moisture-loving Primula frondosa
Below left: easy-growing Erythronium tuolumnense *will flower in spring*
Below: North American Cypripedium reginae

PLANTS FOR SUN

Most plants growing in a sunlit garden will revel in the experience, though problems can arise when there is too little moisture, such as during periods of drought. Add to this poor, hungry soil, as is found in sand, gravel and limestone districts, and gardening becomes a battle to keep things alive. The answer is to work with nature rather than against it, sticking to plants that flourish on hard living.

There are many plants adapted to hot, dry conditions that will furnish the garden throughout the year. Dry, sunny borders are often near the sitting-out area of the house – for example in the patio garden, that needs to look well dressed to provide a relaxed atmosphere. You can achieve this with proper planning and planting.

Preparing the soil

If drought is a problem, then thorough preparation before planting is essential, regardless of the type of soil. Incorporate whatever moisture-holding material you can lay your hands on. Well-rotted garden compost, old turfs, kitchen waste – even rotted-down newspapers, muck, and well-wetted peat with added bone-meal – any or all of these can be used. Most people know the value of these things, but the response from plants still seems little short of miraculous. No amount of watering, or sprinkling this and that on top, has the same result.

When the bed has finally been planted, a thick layer – 5cm (2 in) if possible – of a mulching material like peat or pulverized bark can be put down to stop excessive evaporation and smother germinating weed seeds. Thick straw spread around larger plants at the back of the border, such as trees and shrubs, makes a splendid mulch, protecting the roots with the most rewarding results.

Among the very small plants, especially some of the delicate silver ones, a good

Our island bed in the sun (above) has as centre-piece Genista aetnensis – *the Mount Etna broom tree – surrounded by a colourful selection of other plants suited to warm, dry conditions Planting plan appears overpage*

topping of local grit is best. It still preserves moisture and helps keep the ground clean, but it also ensures dry foliage in winter, thus helping to prevent the leaves rotting.

Choosing the plants

Now for the plants. Trees with large, soft leaves should be avoided. They won't do well, and look unsuitable with lavender and thyme. An upright juniper, or a blue-leaved conifer like *Cupressus (arizonica) glabra* (smooth Arizona cypress), would make a fine, upright feature, while the beautiful *Genista aetnensis* (Mount Etna broom) forms a large but delicate mass around which smaller shrubs such as cistus (rock or sun roses) can be grouped.

167

Plants for Sun
Planting plan

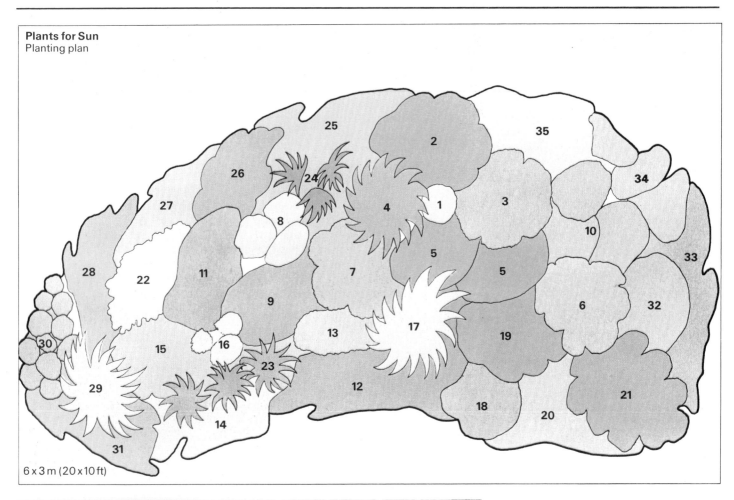

6 x 3 m (20 x 10 ft)

Ballota, blue rue, salvias and santolinas grow wild in countries bordering the Mediterranean. Their beautiful foliage is specially adapted to drought conditions, being either silky with soft hairs, felted with white 'wool', or wax-coated blue.

Other plants, like sedum and semper-vivum (houseleek), have thick, fleshy leaves that are themselves built-in water storage units. Others still, such as cistus, lavender and thyme, contain aromatic oils that preserve the leaves from excessive dryness. Planted round the house, their perfume fills the air on still summer evenings. And all these plants remain in winter, covering the bare soil and maintaining a picture.

This picture becomes the background in summer to many vivid flowering plants that flourish in full sun. Euphorbias (spurges), with their acid yellow-greens; helianthemums (rock roses) making cushions of pink, apricot and yellow; saponaria and mat-forming phlox, both buried beneath their carpets of flowers – all these do well in open, sunny sites with the minimum of assistance. And when they have finished flowering, they will still contribute to the colour and design of the garden with their permanent foliage.

To keep this type of gardening controlled and fresh it is important to tidy up

Striking, woolly-textured foliage of Ballota
pseudodictamnus *(above) is specially
adapted to drought conditions*
Flower spikes of Salvia × superba *(below
left) are much admired in late summer*
Eriophyllum lanatum *(right) makes useful
ground cover for sun-parched soil*

and prune the plants once a year. A cut-back, usually after flowering, will induce new growth that quickly covers bare stems, and makes a tidy cushion for the rest of the year. For other plants, among them ballota and blue rue, a trim in mid spring (March) will prevent an open, sprawling heap.

Extra colour from spring to autumn can be provided by bulbs. Iris and tulips are ideal, while crocus look delightful in flower though their long, grassy leaves can be a nuisance among smaller plants, smothering some of the mats, and so letting in weeds later in the year.

In the following list, numbers preceding plant names correspond with those on the accompanying planting plan.

1 *Genista aetnensis* (Mount Etna broom) forms a dainty tree up to 4½m (15 ft) tall, casting little shade, its dainty, leafless branches smothered in scented, golden yellow, pea-like flowers in mid summer (June).

2 *Cistus × corbariensis* has crinkled, leathery green leaves, bronze-tinted in winter, and pink buds that open to small white flowers in mid summer (June). It grows to a height of 45–75cm (18–30 in).

3 *Senecio laxifolius* is an excellent background shrub, with grey, white-backed leaves and sprays of pretty, silvery buds

that open to yellow daisies during mid and late summer (June and July). It needs to be pruned after it has flowered if plenty of young growth is to be ensured. Height is 1·2–1·8m (4–6 ft).

4 *Euphorbia (venata) wulfenii* makes a magnificent feature all the year round, and is made up of many strong stems clothed cylindrically with narrow, blue-grey foliage. The huge heads of lime-green flowers light up the garden for months from mid spring to mid summer (March to June). An established plant can be 1·2 × 1·2m (4 × 4 ft).

5 *Ruta graveolens* Jackman's Blue (rue) makes mounds of blue, filigree foliage 60–90cm (2–3 ft) high, and has yellow flowers from mid summer to early autumn (June to August). Prune it in mid spring (March) to keep it tidy.

6 *Salvia officinalis* Purpurascens (purple-leaved sage) has soft, greyish purple, velvet foliage when young, and spikes of blue flowers in summer. It can form a lax bush 1·2m (4 ft) across, and should be pruned in spring.

7 *Salvia officinalis* Icterina (golden sage) is a coloured form of cooking sage, and comes in shades of primrose, gold and sage-green. It flowers in summer and grows about 60cm (2 ft) tall.

8 *Salvia haematodes* is a tall-stemmed,

handsome-flowered sage that adds height and a soft lilac-blue colour to the garden. It flowers in early summer (May) and reaches a height of 1·2m (4 ft).

9 *Salvia × superba* (*S. virgata* Nemorosa) is shorter than *S. haematodes* and valued in late summer (July) for its stiff spikes of intense violet-purple flowers with crimson bracts. It reaches a height of some 60–90cm (2–3 ft).

10 *Eryngium tripartitum* is one of several sea hollies that could be used. Its graceful, branching stems are topped with metallic-blue flowers in summer. Height is about 90cm (3 ft).

11 *Achillea taygetea* Moonshine makes good clumps of silvery grey foliage, resembling soft plumes. 90cm (3 ft) branching stems carry many flat heads of clear yellow flowers in mid and late summer (June and July), and again in autumn.

12 *Geranium grandiflorum* Alpinum forms dense mats of pretty, finely-cut leaves that are covered with cupped, violet-blue flowers in mid summer (June). Grows to approximately 23cm (9 in).

13 *Othonnopsis cheiriifolia* has lax stems carrying paddle-shaped, blue-grey leaves of a waxy texture, that are topped in early summer (May) with fresh yellow daisies. Height is about 30cm (12 in).

light a sunny border for six months. It dies down in winter, to reappear in the following spring. Blue flowers appear in early and mid summer (May and June). Grows to approximately 60cm (2 ft).

25 *Phuopsis stylosa* has refreshingly green, ferny foliage that makes a spreading carpet. The flowers look like pink pin cushions stuck with pink pins. Height is about 15cm (6 in).

26 *Hebe* Carl Teschner forms low mounds of small, shiny, evergreen leaves on purple stems smothered with purple-blue flowers in mid and late summer (June and July). Height is around 23cm (9 in).

27 *Saponaria ocymoides* (rock soapwort) is a vigorous trailer completely smothered in bright pink, campion-like flowers between early and mid summer (May and June). Grows to approximately 15cm (6 in).

28 *Cerastium columnae* has irresistible white foliage that makes foraging mats covered with white-cupped flowers in early summer (May). Reaches only about 10cm (4 in) high.

29 *Artemisia purshiana* runs about sending up tall stems covered with grey, mealy, willow-like leaves, topped with spires of small, pale, mimosa-like yellow blossoms in autumn. It dries well. Grows up to 90–120cm (3–4 ft) high.

30 *Arabis albida* Flore Pleno forms spreading mats of green rosettes from which stand 25cm (10 in) stems clothed in clotted-cream double flowers resembling tiny stocks in early summer (May).

31 *Stachys lanata* Silver Carpet (lamb's tongue) makes unbeatable ground cover in full sun, creeping stems carrying silky silver foliage. This variety rarely flowers, so the neat effect is long lasting. Has a height of 30–45cm (12–18 in).

32 *Sedum maximum* (ice plant) has green, fleshy foliage touched with bronze. From mid to late autumn (September to the end of October) it sends up 45cm (18 in) stems of lime-green flowers with bronze buds.

33 *Thymus* Doone Valley (thyme) is exceptionally attractive, with close mats of dark green foliage heavily marked with gold, and large heads of mauve flowers in late summer (July). It has a lemon scent and a height of about 8cm (3 in).

34 *Helianthemum nummularium* Wisley Primrose (rock rose) has mounds of silvery grey leaves and large flowers of primrose yellow in summer. Reaches around 15–30cm (6–12 in) in height.

35 *Eriophyllum lanatum* never fails in sun-scorched ground, and quickly makes large patches of silvery white, finely-divided leaves. In summer there is a show of orange-yellow daisies. Height is approximately 15cm (6 in).

14 *Oenothera (macrocarpa) missouriensis* has large, yellow flowers that smother the foliage, and lax, sprawling red stems for weeks between summer and early autumn (June and August). Reaches a height of around 23cm (9 in).

15 *Ballota pseudodictamnus* is another superb foliage plant. From a woody base spring long, curving stems of round leaves, whitened in summer with 'felt'. Curious, white, purple-spotted flower bobbles appear in late summer (July), and these dry well. Grows to 60cm (2 ft).

16 *Verbascum chaixii* has 60cm (2 ft) stems that are tightly packed with yellow or white flowers, each of which has a mauve eye. Its upright form makes it useful as a contrast with the mound shape of other plants.

17 *Kniphofia galpinii* Slim Coral Red has fine, grassy foliage, and slender spikes of a deep coral red. Height is about 90cm (3 ft).

As an alternative to Slim Coral Red there is *K. galpinii* Little Maid, with dainty foliage and delicate ivory and green spikes. It flowers for about eight weeks, from mid to late autumn (September to October), and is ideal for the edge of the border, growing to a height of about 75cm (2½ ft).

18 *Helianthemum nummularium* Wisley Pink has soft pink flowers over silvery-grey mounds during mid summer (June), and grows 15–30cm (6–12 in) tall.

19 *Santolina virens* forms a neat, round bush of vivid green, aromatic foliage,

Mat-forming Phlox subulata *Benita is at home in rock garden and border alike*

making it a good contrast among silver-foliaged plants. Its yellow, button-like flowers appear in late summer (July). About 45–60cm (18–24 in) tall.

20 *Phlox subulata* Benita is one of many valuable carpeting phlox, with flowers of a pale lavender-blue with a dark eye in early summer (May). Height is only about 10–15cm (4–6 in).

21 *Bergenia cordifolia purpurea*, with its rosettes of large, green, wavy-edged leaves, that become burnished a purplish-red in winter, contrasts well with many small- or cut-leaved, drought-resisting plants grouped together. There are flowers of a bright magenta in early and mid summer (May and June). Height is approximately 30cm (12 in).

22 *Eryngium maritimum* (sea holly) is an English native from coastal sand dunes. It has beautiful, waxy, blue-grey leaves, and blue flower-heads and stems between late summer and mid autumn (July and September). The flowers dry well. Reaches a height of around 60cm (2 ft).

23 *Euphorbia niciciana* is a superb plant, in bloom for three months between mid summer and mid autumn (June and September) with brilliant lime-green flower-heads on 45cm (18 in) stems. Narrow, blue-grey leaves in winter.

24 *Iris pallida* Variegata, with boldly-striped, green-and-white leaves, will high-

PLANTS FOR SHADE

Shady areas in the garden can vary enormously: some are favourable to growth, others next to impossible. For example, a woodland garden with plenty of good leaf mould and in an area of ample rainfall is worlds away from the poor, dry conditions to be found at the base of a privet hedge, or beneath the shade of an immense horse chestnut tree. Here we describe a selection of plants that could be grown beneath a north- or east-facing wall, in a garden that doesn't get too much rain.

The shady area on the north- or east-facing side of a house or garden wall can be dry unless the soil is very good and there is adequate rainfall. You will probably need to add extra humus before planting, and also old muck, well-rotted garden refuse, old turfs, and well-wetted peat with a little bonemeal – any or all of which will help plants to grow well and cover the soil quickly.

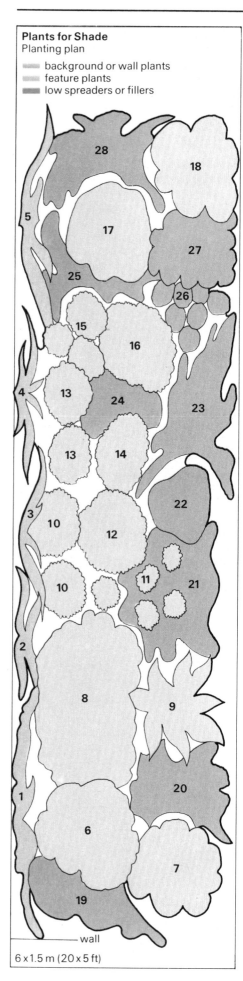

Plants for Shade
Planting plan

background or wall plants
feature plants
low spreaders or fillers

6 x 1.5 m (20 x 5 ft)

wall

Above: decorative, ivory-veined leaves of
Arum italicum marmoratum
Above left: attractive, soft-leaved hop
Humulus lupulus *Aureus*
Left: seeds of Iris foetidissima *make an*
eye-catching display in autumn

It is pointless trying to grow conventional flowering plants like pelargonium or petunia in a shady border. However, if you begin to consider plants that have interesting foliage, many of which provide colour and interest for the greater part of the year, then such a border can become a most attractive part of the garden. A thick covering of peat or crushed bark put down after planting is completed is an added attraction that has the practical value of suppressing weeds and conserving moisture.

Provided the rainfall in your garden is reasonable, you could include hemerocallis (day lily), hosta (plantain lily), *Humulus lupulus* Aureus (golden hop), pulmonaria (lungwort) and tradescantia, in addition to the plants shown on our planting plan. Ornamental grasses can be grown for a change of texture and colour – among them *Milium effusum aureum* (Bowles' golden grass), that provides vivid bunches of pale golden ribbons in spring, and *Holcus mollis* Albovariegatus, that makes low carpets more white than green in autumn, and has new growth of running tuffets striped green and white.

Dry shade at the base of a hedge is not easy to contend with. Whenever possible, have a path alongside the hedge so that the border is at least a little way from the dense root system. If that is not possible, then you must do everything you can to enrich the soil before planting. In a narrow border composed mostly of ground coverers, try some of the following: *Euphorbia cyparissias* (cypress spurge), *E. robbiae, Hedera helix* (ivy) varieties, *Lamium maculatum* (spotted dead nettle), *Vinca minor* (lesser periwinkle) and *Viola labradorica*, with *Iris foetidissima* for contrast.

At the Royal Botanic Gardens, Kew, there are some enormous old trees underplanted with great circles of *Hedera hibernica* (Irish ivy), with its very large, dark green leaves – they look splendid. In fact, all hedera make good ground cover. A mixture of several coloured varieties of *H. helix* could look attractive under smaller trees. Cyclamen, too, thrive under trees where little else will flourish, and there is a very useful kind of bramble called *Rubus tricolor* that, when established, sends out long, prostrate stems up to 3m (10 ft) long, furred with soft, reddish hairs, and closely set with beautiful, polished green leaves that are bronze-bordered in autumn. It will form a complete, weed-proof cover under trees.

Many spring bulbs enjoy a shady border. Eranthis (winter aconite), galanthus (snowdrop), *Hepatica triloba* (or *Anemone hepatica*), *A. blanda* and the species daffodils will all help to make this a favourite part of the garden.

The following selection will stand shade and a certain amount of drought, provided some humus is added to the soil. Lush conditions are not necessary – the plants will thrive along a north- or east-facing wall, or among small trees and shrubs. The background climbers could be on a wall, or trained over ugly stumps.

Plants are numbered as they appear on the planting plan.

Climbers

1 *Hedera canariensis* Variegata (variegated ivy) has large, grey-green leaves marbled with white, and pink-tinted in winter. It is not good in draughty places, but is quite hardy on a wall, and looks splendid draped over a stump.
2 *Clematis montana* Rubens is a glorious sight in early summer (May), smothered in deep pink flowers and purplish-tinted foliage.
3 *Jasminum nudiflorum* (winter-flowering jasmine) has bright yellow flowers for weeks in mid winter (December). The buds are undamaged by frost, but the plant needs regular pruning to keep it tidy and encourage long sprays of flowers.
4 *Hedera helix* Cristata has long sprays of pelargonium-shaped leaves that are heavily crimped at the edges. It is a very attractive plant, especially in autumn, when young, pale green leaves contrast with dark, mature ones.
5 *Lonicera periclymenum* Serotina (late Dutch honeysuckle) is sweetly scented and flowers well into autumn, setting trusses of currant-like red berries.

'Feature' plants

6 *Helleborus corsicus* (Corsican hellebore) has magnificent, jade-green foliage and stiff stems 90cm (3 ft) tall, that are topped with large clusters of pale, apple-green cups from late winter to mid summer (January to June). It will cover an area of approximately 1 sq m (3 × 3 ft).
7 *Alchemilla mollis* (lady's mantle) sprays out long stems of frothing, lime-green, starry flowers from a mound of velvety, rounded leaves in mid summer (June). It is invaluable for flower arrangers, and grows to a height of 60cm (24 in).

8 *Polygonatum multiflorum* (Solomon's seal) spreads slowly by underground rhizomes, and sends up arching stems 90cm (3 ft) long, set with pairs of dark green leaves. In early summer (May) white-and-green-flushed bells hang beneath the leaves.

9 *Hosta lancifolia* is not used as much as the variegated varieties, but is a very attractive and useful plant. Narrow, shining, dark green leaves form tidy mounds above which stand tall stems of dark lilac bells for weeks in autumn (August to October). It grows 45cm (18 in) tall.

10 *Dryopteris filix-mas* (male fern) survives in dry shade and is very useful. It reaches a height of 75cm (2½ ft).

11 *Arum italicum marmoratum* is a superb foliage plant with new leaves that begin to unroll from leaf-mouldy soil in late autumn (October), and continue to grow throughout the winter undamaged by bitter frost. By late spring (April) the elegant, spear-shaped leaves are poised on 45cm (18 in) stems of a dark glossy green, marvellously veined in ivory.

12 *Hypericum × moserianum* Tricolor is a slow-growing little bush prettily variegated in white, pink and green. It reaches a height of about 75cm (2½ ft).

13 *Iris foetidissima* is a splendid evergreen with strong, shining clumps of fresh green foliage that are invaluable as a feature for flower arranging. The small flowers are a soft ochre-yellow, and followed in autumn by great, bursting seed pods packed with vivid orange seeds. The height is 75cm (2½ ft).

14 *Liriope muscari* forms clumps of narrow, dark evergreen leaves that last the year round. The long spikes of curious violet-blue flowers on violet stems are a feature for weeks in autumn.

15 *Thalictrum aquilegiifolium* (meadow rue) is graceful and very compact. Its 1·2m (4 ft) purplish stems rise up from a base of delicate sprays of leaves, and are topped with large heads of fluffy lilac flowers in mid summer (June). The seedheads are attractive either green or dried.

16 *Valeriana phu* Aurea is an unusual plant that matures green but is topped with tall stems of small white flowers in mid summer (June). Its new spring foliage is a clear yellow, rivalling daffodils.

17 *Lonicera nitida* Baggessen's Gold is a bright golden variety of the familiar hedging honeysuckle that forms a beautiful specimen shrub and makes a delicate filigree accent among darker greens. It covers an area of around 1 sq m (3 × 3 ft).

18 *Bergenia cordifolia* Purpurea is not widely loved, although – with large, round, wavy-edged leaves that become

Bright spring flowers of Waldsteinia ternata *contrast with evergreen foliage*

burnished a purplish red with winter frost – it makes superb contrast to other plants in the border. In early summer (May) tall, rhubarb-red stalks carry vivid magenta flowers and reach about 45cm (18 in).

Ground cover

19 *Tiarella cordifolia* (foam flower) has running trails of pointed green leaves that make total cover. In spring, there is a mass of foaming, creamy-white flower spikes. Height about 23–30cm (9–12 in).

20 *Ajuga reptans* Atropurpurea (bugle) spreads rapidly with rosettes of very dark, chocolate-purplish brown, shining leaves.

21 *A. r.* Burgundy Glow has unusually beautiful foliage suffused rose, magenta and cream. Its 15cm (6 in) spikes of blue flowers provide strong contrast in spring, and often again in autumn.

22 *Epimedium × versicolor* Sulphureum (barrenwort) has heart-shaped leaves on wiry stems. The leaves are delicate shades of copper in early spring (February), turning to green for all of the summer, and becoming bronzed by the winter cold. Sprays of tiny yellow, columbine-like flowers appear in mid spring (March).

23 *Hedera helix* Manda's Crested (ivy) quickly makes excellent ground cover of very attractive, curling foliage. The pale, copper-tinted, new autumn leaves contrast with the mature summer foliage.

24 *Tellima grandiflora* Purpurea is an all-year-round foliage plant with spreading clumps of round, scalloped leaves that become bronze-tinted in winter, and are a rich carmine-red beneath. The stems of tiny green, pink-fringed bells are pretty in spring. The plant grows to a height of approximately 60cm (24 in).

25 *Viola labradorica* makes a creeping mass of small, dark purple leaves that set off quantities of lighter-coloured, scentless flowers. Height is around 10cm (4 in).

26 *Saxifraga umbrosa* Variegata (variegated London pride) makes excellent ground cover, its richly-mottled, gold and green rosettes being a feature all year. Pink flowers appear in early and mid summer (May and June), and the plant grows to a height of approximately 23cm (9 in).

27 *Waldsteinia ternata* is a useful carpeter, with spreading, dark-lobed leaves, evergreen and glossy, that contrast with bright yellow flowers in late spring and early summer (April and May).

28 *Vinca minor* Bowles' Variety is the best of all periwinkles, making close mats of small, dark green leaves, that in spring are lost beneath quantities of large blue flowers. It grows about 15cm (6 in) tall.

PLANTS FOR DAMP

A damp garden must remain moist for much of the growing season, for plants that don't flower until late autumn or early winter (October or November) – such as tricyrtis (toad lily) – will not put up with drought in late summer (July). As the soil will inevitably be heavy, probably like plasticine, it is vital that you do something to make life easier for both the plants and yourself before planting. A layer of mixed sand, peat, compost, well-rotted manure and leaf mould – as many of these as you can obtain – piled on top of the soil or lightly forked in, will help plants to establish quickly, before their roots penetrate the clay. Remember that weeds never stop growing in damp soil, so you must plant strong growers to cope with native competition.

When planting is done, a 5cm (2 in) layer of peat or crushed bark is much more than a luxury – it really will prevent that rash of germinating weed seeds that otherwise seem to appear overnight. Any knob of soil left exposed will grow a mat of water weed 90cm (3 ft) across, smothering your fine primulas in no time.

Where there is room, salix (willow) and cornus (dogwood) make a splendid effect planted *en masse*, while taxodium and metasequoia (dawn redwood or water fir) are both dramatic feature plants. For a small area where trees and shrubs would be unsuitable, phormiums are ideal, with their great sheaves of blade-like, evergreen leaves.

Blessed are those people who have a bit of ill-drained soil, especially if it is spring-fed. Soggy land is a haven for bog-loving plants, and with a little digging and damming a small – or large – pond can be created that will transform the site immediately.
Heavy, low-lying soil, with plenty of humus added – and possibly a little shade – can also provide a home for many lovely plants that prefer cool, damp conditions, and we describe some of these here.

Most plants suited to damp soil disappear in winter, so those few that do remain are very useful – without them, a bog garden in winter would be nothing but a patch of mud with a few withered remains. *Phormium tenax* (New Zealand flax) and its dwarf counterpart *P. colensoi* add form to the winter landscape, and there are several sedges that last. *Carex morrowii* Variegata provides welcome colour with its tuffets of brilliant gold leaves edged with a narrow green band, while *Luzula maxima* Marginata, another rushy plant, also keeps its dark green clumps. Try to have a few bergenias (pig squeak) nearby – but not too close to the water's edge, as they do not like bog conditions.

Polygonum affine (knotweed) makes a warm carpet of foxy brown foliage in its winter state, while the ajugas (bugle) provide colour unless the weather is exceptionally hard. Gunneras thrive magnificently in damp soil if there is room, but peltiphyllum (umbrella plant) would suit a smaller site, provided it is not allowed to spread its rhizomes too far. Rapid colonizers like myosotis (forget-me-not), *Lysimachia nummularia* (creeping Jenny), and the many forms of mimulus (musk) will run around the main feature plants and in only one season produce a lush effect.

Astilbe (false goat's beard), *Euphorbia palustris* (fen or bog spurge), ligularia and trollius (globe flower) will all grow without a pond present, but there must be ample moisture throughout the season.

Conditions around a pool are ideal for bog-loving plants and others liking cool, damp soil

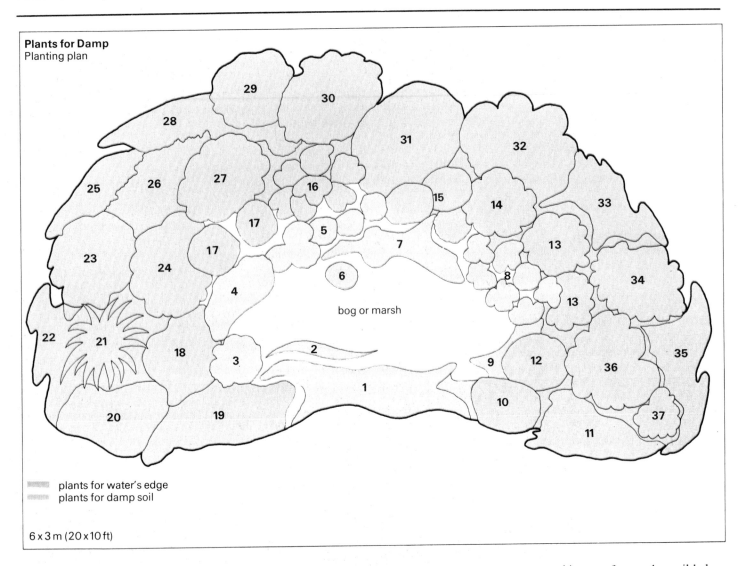

Plants for Damp
Planting plan

bog or marsh

plants for water's edge
plants for damp soil

6 x 3 m (20 x 10 ft)

Partial shade will sometimes retain the necessary coolness, but in dense shade the plants will be spindly and will probably not flower at all.

For damp woodland conditions there is a host of lovely things to grow, among them rhododendrons and other moist mountain shrubs. Some can be raised successfully in small gardens, but the controlling factor is always moisture. Being willing to cart the odd can of water is not enough. Among flowering plants that like partial shade and will thrive where there is enough rainfall are actaea, astrantia (masterwort), hardy geraniums (cranesbill), hosta (plantain lily), meconopsis and primula. Interesting foliage plants include *Filipendula ulmaria* Aurea, *Scrophularia nodosa* Variegata (variegated figwort) and rodgersia.

Many ferns add delicacy and charm to woodland plantings, *Polystichum setiferum* Acutilobum and *Matteuccia struthiopteris* for example, while by the waterside, *Osmunda regalis* (flowering royal fern) dies down in a glory of autumn shades.

The planting plan shows the different zones of planting around a pond or boggy area. Numbers preceding plant names in the following selection correspond with those on the plan.

The water's edge

Conveniently, some plants enjoy water-logged soil, and would not survive in dry conditions: these are the ones to put round the edge of a natural pond where they will push out into shallow water.

1 *Mimulus* Wisley Red spreads quickly, and has beautiful, ruby-red flowers that appear in mid summer (June). Height is about 30cm (12 in).

2 *Calla palustris* (bog arum) sends out long shoots that root into wet mud. Tiny, arum-like white flowers appear in spring, and the plant reaches a height of around 30cm (12 in).

3 *Mimulus ringens* (lavender water musk) is an unusual musk with branching stems of approximately 75cm (2½ ft) and, in summer, lilac flowers that last for weeks.

4 *Caltha palustris* Plena is the double-flowered form of *C. palustris*, and grows about 38cm (15 in) tall.

5 *Primula bulleyana* comes in shades of

orange, and is one of several possible bog primulas. Height is around 75cm (2½ ft).

6 *Scirpus palustris* Zebrinus is *the* striped rush, green and white in colour, and makes a handsome feature in water, but it needs plenty of room. Height is approximately 105cm (3½ ft).

7 *Myosotis palustris* (water forget-me-not) makes sheets of blue along the pond edge, flowering in early and mid summer (May and June). Height is about 15–30cm (6–12 in).

8 *Peltiphyllum peltatum* (umbrella plant) is a splendid feature plant, with each leaf resembling a scalloped parasol 30cm (12 in) across. The plant reaches a height of around 75cm (2½ ft).

9 *Lysimachia nummularia* Aurea (golden creeping Jenny) makes a bright carpet beneath water iris, flowering in the summer.

Damp soil

The following selection of plants prefer soil that is better drained than that by the water's edge, but which still has plenty of moisture and humus.

10 *Molinia caerulea* Variegata is one of

the loveliest grasses, with dainty tuffets variegated green and white. It grows to a height of approximately 45cm (18 in).

11 *Astilbe chinensis* Pumila pushes out spreading clumps of weed-smothering foliage, and slender spikes of rose-lilac flowers. Height is about 30cm (12 in).

12 *Iris laevigata* comes in several colour forms, and does not mind being in water. Height is around 60cm (2 ft).

13 Astilbe hybrids have beautiful foliage and feathery flower-heads in all shades from white to red in summer. Plants grow 30–90cm (1–3 ft) high.

14 *Lobelia cardinalis* Queen Victoria has chocolate-coloured leaves, and stems 75cm (2½ ft) long, that carry vivid scarlet flowers during mid and late autumn (September and October).

15 *Trollius europaeus* (globe flower) grows wild in wet mountain meadows. Bowl-shaped flowers of pale gold appear in early and mid summer (May and June). Height is approximately 75cm (2½ ft).

16 *Ligularia clivorum* Desdemona is a giant groundsel with large, heart-shaped, purple-bronze leaves, and orange-rayed daisies in early and mid autumn (August and September). It reaches a height of about 90cm (3 ft).

17 *Matteuccia struthiopteris* (ostrich feather fern) forms a perfect shuttlecock of lacy, pale green fern fronds.

18 *Scrophularia nodosa* Variegata (variegated figwort) has richly marbled leaves of cream and green, and grows to a height of around 90cm (3 ft).

19 *Astilbe simplicifolia* Sprite is charming: dark green, ferny foliage sends up wide sprays of shell-pink flowers in mid summer (June). Height is 25cm (10 in).

20 *Carex morrowii* Variegata is another foliage plant that is effective as a feature, especially in winter, radiating tuffets of narrow, gold-and-green leaves. Height is approximately 40cm (16 in).

21 *Phormium colensoi* (dwarf New Zealand flax) does not grow too large, and is useful for smaller pond sites. It flowers in summer and reaches a height of 90–120cm (3–4 ft).

22 *Prunella webbiana* Pink Loveliness is the raspberry-pink form of 'self heal', and makes a vivid carpet of colour between mid summer and mid autumn (June and September). It is good ground cover, and grows to a height of around 23cm (9 in).

23 *Campanula lactiflora* (milky bell-flower) makes a great show in rich soil, with milky blue, bell-shaped flowers in summer on 1.5m (5 ft) stems.

24 *Euphorbia palustris* (fen or bog spurge) grows into a large plant, 1.2 × 1.2m (4 × 4 ft), and is spectacular all summer with great heads of gold-green flowers.

Caltha palustris *Plena (above) grows in water of up to 15cm (6in) in depth, but does better with the crown submerged.* Calla palustris *(below) has exquisite spring flowers*

25 *Veronica gentianoides*, with its spreading rosettes of glossy green leaves, makes good ground cover. The 30cm (12 in) spikes of ice-blue flowers in early summer (May) are a bonus.

26 *Physostegia virginiana* Summer Spire provides colour in early and mid autumn (August and September) with rich lilac, trumpet-shaped flowers in spires. Height is about 38cm (15 in).

27 *Filipendula palmata* Elegans is a first-class meadow sweet with deep rose flowers throughout the summer, followed by showy, bronze-red seed-heads. It grows to a height of some 90cm (3 ft).

28 *Viola cornuta* has moundy mats of small, blue and white flowers all summer, and again in the autumn. Height is around 15cm (6 in).

29 *Gentiana asclepiadea* (willow gentian) has arching, 38cm (15 in) stems, wreathed in blue trumpet flowers in mid autumn (September).

30 *Eupatorium purpureum* has 1.8m (6 ft) purple stems carrying flat-domed heads of fluffy, cinnamon-pink flowers in mid autumn (September).

31 *Miscanthus sinensis* Zebrinus is a zebra-striped grass making good contrast in form. It can develop to a height of more than 1.5m (5 ft).

32 *Hosta sieboldiana* has crisp, robust, bluish grey leaves, heavily wrinkled and veined, that make a huge, overlapping mound. It is a spectacular feature when well grown, and reaches a height of 60–90cm (2–3 ft).

33 *Ajuga reptans* Burgundy Glow makes a vivid carpet all winter, with foliage suffused rose and magenta, and edged with cream. During summer, too, it is an eye-catching sight, with 15cm (6 in) spikes of blue flowers.

34 *Tricyrtis stolonifera* (toad lily) makes spreading clumps of 60–90cm (2–3 ft) stems topped, in late autumn (September), with small, white, lily-like flowers, so heavily spotted with purple that they appear lilac.

35 *Mentha rotundifolia* Variegata (apple mint) has green, woolly leaves heavily splashed with white, and – in summer – purplish white, flowers. Height is about 90cm (3 ft).

36 *Hosta fortunei* Albopicta has lilac flowers in late summer and early autumn (July and August), and large leaves magnificently marbled in shades of bright yellow, primrose, soft green and olive. It grows to approximately 45cm (18 in) in height.

37 *Geum* Lionel Cox forms clumps of soft green foliage with summer sprays of nodding cream cups, touched with apricot. Height is around 30cm (12 in).

Top: Iris Laevigata *Atropurpurea. Above (left): inner, fertile fronds of* Matteuccia struthiopteris. *Above (right):* Gentiana asclepiadea, *a good choice for shade*

FLOWERING TREES AND SHRUBS

INTRODUCTION

A well-laid-out garden presents an exquisitely beautiful tableau in which flowering trees and shrubs, ably accompanied by a supporting caste of herbaceous plants, hardy annuals and bulbs, are the principal performers. Perhaps everybody is now so used to seeing them in public parks and private gardens that there is a tendency to take them for granted. This can be offset by thinking of what a landscape would look like if it was devoid of such plants, and after all a garden is the gardener's landscape.

Apart from the natives, trees and shrubs were introduced into western gardens from the wild in early times. There is little doubt that the Romans brought over quite a number when they settled in Britain. From a gardening aspect they have endured many vicissitudes over the years. Before the 14th century people were too preoccupied with war to cultivate trees and shrubs. In the more settled times that followed and after the Black Death, noblemen and cottagers planted them in their gardens. Because of the popularity of the knot garden and other topical features during Tudor times they were generally banished to the deer park, outside the confines of the castle.

Trees and shrubs became of real interest from the mid-17th century onwards, undoubtedly inspired by the publication of John Evelyn's *Sylva, or a Discourse of Forest-Trees*, in 1664. Great impetus was given to the introduction of trees and shrubs. This continued through the 18th and 19th centuries into the early years of the 20th century when, sponsored by wealthy patrons, the Royal Horticultural Society, other learned bodies and prominent nurserymen, numerous intrepid plant hunters sallied forth to distant lands and brought to Britain and other western countries the many flowering trees and shrubs that grace our gardens today.

Not unnaturally, in the course of time, competing types of plants and forms of gardening – herbaceous borders, wild gardens, Victorian ferneries, formal beds and so on – have caused the fortunes of tree and shrubs to fluctuate. Now, after two World Wars and rapid changes in economic conditions over the past sixty years, bringing higher costs, lower availability of labour, and exorbitant prices of building land, gardeners have been forced to find more labour-saving means of gardening. This meant that the incidence of features, such as herbaceous borders and formal bedding out, while not completely abandoned, have been reduced to a minimum. Their place has been taken by trees and shrubs, with other types of plants playing a lesser, though still important role.

There is also an ecological reason why trees and shrubs, perhaps not by design, have assumed a greater significance. Essential changes in agricultural policy and development in some countries have destroyed many miles of trees and hedgerow, leaving many birds homeless. In many cases these have taken refuge in the thousands of trees and shrubs, hedges and climbers that

181

adorn the many gardens. From an aesthetic viewpoint this has brought great advantages to gardeners because the birds have tended to move from the country more into the residential areas, where they give immense pleasure to townsfolk and where, in gardens, they introduce movement – a most valuable factor in making a garden attractive.

The bulk of this section consists of a dictionary of trees and shrubs. Under each item their countries of origin are included. Quite a number are native to Britain or they have been growing here so long that they have become naturalized. It will be found, however, that the greater proportion has been brought from foreign climes, largely China, Japan and nearby Far East countries, while others have been introduced from the continent of Europe and many more from Canada, the United States and South America. Although this particular information appears to be of academic interest only, there is a more practical relevance which can be useful when selecting trees and shrubs, particularly from a catalogue. For example, numerous shrubs such as the hebes come from New Zealand, which has a long coastline, usually ensuring that its plants flourish in coastal districts; on the other hand there are some, like *Rosa pimpinellifolia altaica*, that are natives of Siberia and it is reasonable to suppose that they are very hardy and withstand severe cold. Some of the most beautiful climbing shrubs are indigenous to tropical or sub-tropical areas, such as the glorious *Eccremocarpus scaber*, which hails from Chile and needs to be planted against a warm sheltered wall in a southern garden if it is to flourish.

As already mentioned, the end result when planting out a garden is to obtain the effect of an attractive tableau which is three-dimensional. It is the intention of this section to equip the reader for this purpose, irrespective of whether he is planting out a whole garden or a shrub bed or border, or whether his garden is relatively large, or small, or just a patio. In the following chapters he is given detailed characteristics of thirty-five groups of plants containing a total of nearly 600 species, hybrids and varieties, which can be combined in many different ways to produce a variety of planting schemes. In addition details about origin, history, specific uses, cultivation, pruning, methods of propagation and other relevant information are supplied, together with attractive illustrations of many trees and shrubs invaluable in making a selection. These individual plant profiles are prefaced by a number of chapters dealing with more specialized aspects of handling trees and shrubs.

Many plants can contrive to produce a beautiful garden. According to one nurseryman's catalogue, there are up to 8000 trees, shrubs, conifers and bamboos available in Britain, of which the majority are flowering trees, shrubs and climbers. These form the backbone of all gardens, large and small and give enormous scope for garden-making on any scale.

It should be superfluous to state that trees and shrubs are decorative but this is the obvious quality that attracts people. One particular factor that all take notice of is floral colour, followed by the range of fruit colours after flowering and, often, brilliant autumn tints. Study of the plant profiles below shows that it is possible to sustain floral colour in a garden by selection during the greater part of the year. To do so must be the object of any gardener when he is planting out. The heyday of flowering trees and shrubs comes in the spring when Japanese cherries, prunus, crab apples, magnolias, rhododendrons, laburnums and philadelphus follow one after the other.

Summer and autumn bring their quota of colour too, slightly more sober in colour, with such lovely plants as the hydrangeas, buddleia, hypericum, hebes, *Magnolia grandiflora*, potentilla, fuchsias and many others.

Even in winter there can be a cavalcade of colour bravely produced by stalwarts like *Prunus subhirtella* 'Autumnalis', witch hazel, *Viburnum farreri*, the winter flowering rhododendron Lee's Scarlet, and *Daphne mezereum*.

As a bonus to this spectacle of colour many trees and shrubs produce berries that are mostly red, but also blue, white, black, brown, yellow, orange, pink and mauve.

Trees and shrubs have other valuable functions. Trees can give privacy, shade and screening, form wind-breaks and filter out sea salt at the seaside. A tree can be usefully planted as a focal point around which the garden is planned; it can be used to direct the line of vision over the greater distance and create a sense of spaciousness. Equally as valuable, shrubs can screen an ugly fence or shed, shroud a manhole, give excellent ground cover and provide blackdrops for more forward planting. Most important they make excellent boundary or division hedges. Trees and shrubs, with their varying shapes and sizes, create great 'architectural' interest in the garden. This is something which is supplemented by their variation in texture and the size of their leaves. Lastly, climbers or climbing shrubs and wall plants, while exceedingly decorative, can cover walls and sheds; left unsupported they sprawl over the ground, hang down over walls or clothe a dead tree trunk.

The pruning of flowering trees and shrubs is a concern of many gardeners. Actually most do not need regular pruning, but some should be cut back occasionally. Thinning is often a problem but this is really quite simple, if two rules are followed: trees and shrubs that bloom on the previous year's growth of wood (which generally flower early) should be pruned immediately after flowering; those blooming on the current year's wood, (and generally flowering during summer) should be pruned in late winter or early spring. Winter-flowering trees and shrubs should be pruned in the spring.

Most of the trees and shrubs described later can easily be propagated. This, of course, affords an inexpensive way of increasing stock. Some, like hebes and holly, seed freely. Self-sown seedlings are a bonanza and they should be transplanted to a nursery bed.

SELECTION, CULTIVATION AND USES

CHOOSING A SPECIMEN TREE

One of the best ways of showing a tree to advantage is to plant it as a specimen in a carefully-chosen site. Appearance, however, is by no means the only factor that must be considered; by following the guidelines given below you should be able to choose a tree that will both look attractive and serve a useful purpose.

Choosing a tree for a garden of any size needs careful consideration. Trees can have a functional role quite apart from their decorative appearance, and there are practical considerations to be taken into account, such as the local soil conditions. Bear in mind that large trees give a great deal of often unwanted shade and that their roots deprive other plants of nutrients. Trees with spreading canopies keep the rain off anything planted underneath: this area will therefore be of limited use for flowers or shrubs after the tree becomes established.

In siting a tree you must take care that neither its top growth nor its root system encroach in any way on to your neighbour's property. If the tree is likely to cast shade over the next-door garden, for example, you must get permission from the neighbours before planting it. It is important not to plant large trees too close to the house as their roots could undermine the foundations, and interfere with drains, electricity cables or gas pipes. Members of the salix and populus genera, in particular, have very thirsty roots that spread a great distance in search of moisture, penetrating and blocking drainage systems even.

What is required?
Choose the right tree for the specific purpose you have in mind. Perhaps the most frequent requirement of a tree is to form a screen; in this case it is better to choose one, or a group, that will break up the line of vision rather than form a solid block – a comparatively low-growing tree with a spreading head is often sufficient as it will not block out too much sun.

A very important function of a tree, particularly a columnar one, is to give a focal point around which the garden design can turn. A tree that has branches growing low down from the trunk can be planted between the house and the entrance or driveway, to give the effect of length by obscuring the actual distance involved. Similarly, a tree can be an accent or high point in an area where the

garden is fairly flat. A tree such as *Salix babylonica* (weeping willow), planted on the brow above a dip in the ground can give an illusion of a pool underneath it.

You can also use trees to create the illusion of movement, which is important to a good design. Introduce actual movement by selecting trees with flexible leaf-stalks and leaves that tremble in the breeze. Habit and form also play an important part; trees with arching or pendulous branches give a great sense of serenity, while those with very large leaves impart an exotic, sometimes subtropical touch.

Selecting a specimen tree
Trees have five main qualities – colour, habit, shape, size and texture – that must be considered when you are selecting a specimen. One of the first decisions to

Above: slow-growing Acer palmatum *has glorious autumn foliage*
Right: Gleditschia triacanthos *Sunburst can reach a height of 9m (30 ft)*

make is whether you want an evergreen or a deciduous tree. After that, the factor which most often predominates is colour. With this, the colour of the flowers is often the least important because it is short-lived in comparison to the leaves. Remember that fruits and bark can also provide colour throughout the summer and autumn and even into winter.

Geometric shape, coupled with habit, is the next important element to be considered. There are round-headed, pyramidal and columnar trees, and also those with fastigiate growth and arching or weeping branches and those with a wide-spreading habit. There are trees for almost any purpose or position in the garden, but you must study catalogues and books to find them, and visit gardens and parks to see them *in situ*. Columnar trees, for example, are often more suitable in a small garden as they do not throw too much shadow. And bear in mind when choosing a deciduous tree what sort of shape its bare branches will give in winter.

Trees with a bold texture have the same sort of visual effect as strong, bright colours – they appear to push themselves forward. Fine-textured trees (with small leaves) are like blue or greyish colours that visually recede into the background, and create an illusion of distance. These characteristics, if used with care, can give a feeling of movement that always adds interest.

The size that a tree is going to be after, say, 20 years' growth must be considered. Be sure that the eventual height and spread will not overwhelm your garden in years to come; even in a large garden it can be a mistake to plant forest trees such as elm and beech. There are many ornamental acers, birches, cherries and other prunus, ornamental crabs, and sorbus that graduate in size, making them suitable for the largest down to the smallest gardens. You will find more details about many of these later in the section, and also, of course, in catalogues from specialist growers.

Although there are few trees that are really suitable for very tiny gardens, their design functions can often be fulfilled by a weeping standard rose, such as Dorothy Perkins. In addition, it is possible to obtain a low-growing shrub, such as *Cotoneaster* Hybridus Pendulus, grafted on to a standard stem, that is very suitable for this purpose.

A choice of specimen trees

Unless otherwise stated, assume that the trees listed will grow satisfactorily under normal garden conditions, and in ordinary, good soil. The first dimension given is the average height and the second is the spread, both after 20 years' growth.

COLOUR

Red foliage

Acer palmatum Linearilobum Atropurpureum — Has bronze-red leaves that are divided to the base into long, narrow, serrated lobes. 4·5 × 2·5m (15 × 8 ft).

Acer platanoides Crimson King — A big, vigorous, deciduous cultivar with large leaves. 10 × 6m (33 × 20 ft).

Malus Jay Darling — Has large, wine-red flowers produced before or with its similarly-coloured leaves. Bears purplish red fruits. 6 × 5m (20 × 16 ft).

Gold/yellow foliage

Catalpa bignonioides Aurea — Has a rounded habit and is a vigorous grower, with large, velvety leaves. Excellent for town gardens, particularly in a mild climate. 9 × 8m (30 × 26 ft).

Gleditschia triacanthos Sunburst — Unlike the type species, this form has thornless stems. 9 × 8m (30 × 26 ft).

Laburnum anagyroides Aureum — A much-branched tree that prefers light soils and dislikes wet or heavy ones. Spreads with age. 4·5 × 3m (15 × 10 ft).

Purple foliage

Malus Profusion — An upright tree, producing wine-red flowers in late spring and early summer (April and May), succeeded by red fruits. 6 × 5m (20 × 16 ft).

Prunus × blireana Moseri — Has pale pink blooms in late spring (April). 4·5 × 3m (15 × 10 ft).

Quercus robur Atropurpurea — A slow-growing cultivar of the common oak, with stems that are purple when young and become greyish on maturity. 9 × 9m (30 × 30 ft).

Grey/silver foliage

Eucalyptus coccifera — A fast-growing, hardy, gale-resistant tree, with bluish green, elliptical juvenile leaves that become lanceolate and greyish on maturity. Grows in acid soil. 10 × 6m (33 × 20 ft).

Pyrus nivalis — An attractive tree with ascending branches, producing white flowers in late spring (April), followed by yellow-green fruits. 4·5 × 2·5m (15 × 8 ft).

Pyrus salicifolia Pendula — A slow-growing, weeping tree. 8 × 9m (26 × 30 ft).

Variegated foliage

Acer pseudoplatanus Nizetii — Has variegated yellow and white leaves, suffused pink, purplish beneath. 4·5 × 2·5m (15 × 8 ft).

Ilex × altaclarensis Golden King — Has almost spineless green leaves with a golden margin and bears large red berries. 8 × 4·5m (26 × 15 ft).

Liriodendron tulipifera Aureomarginatum — A variegated variety of the tulip tree, with leaves bordered with yellow. 10 × 6m (33 × 20 ft).

Autumn-tinted foliage

Amelanchier canadensis (snowy mespilus) — Has white flowers in late spring (April), followed by black berries. The twigs are purple in winter. It likes a moist position. 3·5 × 3m (12 × 10 ft).

Liriodendron tulipifera (tulip tree) — A large tree with leaves that are cut off square at the top, and become bright yellow in autumn. Its tulip-shaped, yellow-green flowers, borne in late summer (July), first appear after about 15 years' growth. 15 × 10m (50 × 30 ft).

Malus tschonoskii — A strong-growing, deciduous tree with pink-tinted and white flowers appearing in early summer (May), followed by yellowish fruits that are tinged reddish purple. 9 × 3m (30 × 10 ft).

Coloured fruits

Ailanthus altissima (tree of heaven)

A large, round-headed tree with compound leaves and conspicuous bunches of reddish, key-shaped fruits. Tolerates polluted atmosphere. 18 × 12m (60 × 40 ft).

Malus Golden Hornet

Has white flowers appearing in late spring (April), followed by persistent, bright yellow fruits. 8 × 6m (26 × 20 ft).

Prunus cornuta (Himalayan bird cherry)

Has white flowers in early summer (May), followed by grape-like bunches of brownish crimson glossy berries. Prefers soil with a little lime. 8 × 8m (26 × 26 ft).

Sorbus Joseph Rock

An erect, deciduous tree that produces leaves with autumn tints and clusters of yellowish amber fruits. Dislikes chalk. 12 × 8m (40 × 26 ft).

Coloured stems and bark

Fraxinus excelsior Aurea (or Jaspidea)

Has yellow leaves and yellowish bark. It can tolerate chalk, and exposed and coastal conditions. 4·5 × 3·5m (15 × 12 ft).

Parrotia persica

The bark of the older trees flakes off, giving a patchwork effect. Its large leaves have brilliant autumn colours, and it likes chalk. 6 × 4·5m (20 × 15 ft).

Tilia platyphyllos Rubra (red-twigged lime)

A large deciduous tree with reddish young stems. It does not suffer from aphid attack, so its leaves do not drip honeydew – which can be a problem with common lime. 12 × 9m (40 × 30 ft).

SHAPE AND HABIT
Round-headed

Acer pseudoplatanus (sycamore)

A large deciduous tree, with leaves that turn yellow in autumn. Forms a good windbreak, and tolerates seaside conditions. 13·5 × 6m (45 × 20 ft).

Crataegus monogyna (hawthorn, may, quick)

This thorny, deciduous tree produces clusters of scented white flowers in early summer (May), and crimson berries later on. 8 × 5m (26 × 16 ft).

Malus coronaria Charlottae

Has pink, violet-scented flowers in mid summer (June), and orange and yellow autumn tints. 4·5 × 4·5m (15 × 15 ft).

Ornamental flowering trees are suitable for almost any size of garden. Prunus
Hokusai *(above) grows 6m (20 ft) high;* Crataegus monogyna *(left) reaches 8m
(26 ft) and* Amelanchier canadensis *(far left) only 3·5m (12 ft)*
Below left: Pyrus salicifolia *Pendula has unusual variegated leaves*

Prunus cerasifera (cherry plum or myrobalan)	Has white flowers in early to mid spring (February to March), followed by yellow fruits. It likes some lime in the soil. 8 × 8m (26 × 26 ft).
Sorbus Mitchellii	Has mature leaves about 15cm (6 in) across, green above and white-felted beneath. 11 × 12m (36 × 40 ft).

Pyramidal

Acer rubrum Girling	Has dark green foliage that becomes vivid orange-red in autumn. 6 × 2·5m (20 × 8 ft).
Magnolia kobus	Produces white flowers in late spring (April) after about 12 years' growth. Can tolerate chalk. 3 × 3m (10 × 10 ft).
Malus tschonoskii	See under Autumn-tinted foliage.
Populus candicans Aurora	Has young leaves that are white, often pink-tinged, becoming green later. Grows well in chalky soil. 11 × 6m (36 × 20 ft).

Spreading

Acer negundo Elegans	Has leaves with a bright yellow margin, and young shoots with a white bloom. 6 × 6m (20 × 20 ft).
Malus Chilko	Has purplish leaves, and produces blooms 5cm (2 in) across in early summer (May), followed by crimson crab apples. 6 × 3·5m (20 × 12 ft).
Mespilus germanica (medlar)	A much-branched, deciduous tree with dull green leaves that become russet and yellow in autumn. It bears medlars in autumn, and likes a sunny position. 8 × 6m (26 × 20 ft).
Prunus Hokusai	A vigorous, wide-spreading Japanese cherry that produces large, semi-double, pale pink flowers in late spring (April). Likes chalk. 6 × 9m (20 × 30 ft).

Erect-growing (columnar)

Carpinus betulus Fastigiata	Has a narrow shape when young, but tends to broaden with age. 6 × 1·8m (20 × 6 ft).
Eucryphia × nymansensis Nymansay	A quick-growing evergreen with cream flowers borne during early and mid autumn (August and September). It is

Above: bold-foliaged Aralia chinensis *accents the line of the house nearby, as well as the columnar conifer in the background*
Above left: Carpinus betulus Fastigiata *is erect-growing when young, but broadens with age.*
The fine foliage of Betula pendula *Youngii (far left) and* Robinia pseudoacacia *Frisia (left) gives the impression of distance to a garden*

hardy in milder areas and tolerates chalk. 4.5×1.8m (15×6 ft).

Morus alba Pyramidalis — An erect-branched, slow-growing tree similar to the Lombardy poplar. 9×1.8m (30×6 ft).

Populus nigra Italica (Lombardy poplar) — A large, deciduous tree with close, upright branches. It is covered almost to its base with leaves. 24×5m (80×16 ft).

Prunus Amanogawa — Has fragrant, pink flowers during early summer (May). Can tolerate some lime in the soil. 6×1.8m (20×6 ft).

Prunus Umineko — Has white flowers that appear in late spring (April), and foliage that turns to brilliant autumn colours. 6×1.8m (20×6 ft).

Pendulous (weeping)

Acer saccharinum Pendulum — A form of the silver maple, with weeping branches, and leaves that are silver-white below. 11×4.5m (36×15 ft).

Betula pendula Youngii — A mushroom-headed, weeping tree that will grow on thin, acid or sandy soil. 8×9m (26×30 ft).

Caragana arborescens Pendula — Produces yellow, pea-like flowers in early summer (May), and succeeds in exposed positions and in poor, dry areas. 4.5×4.5m (15×15 ft).

Laburnum × watereri Alford's Weeping — Produces long racemes of yellow blooms in mid summer (June), and has a wide-spreading head. 5×3.3m (16×11 ft).

Salix × chrysocoma — A weeping tree with arching branches terminating in slender, very long, golden branchlets. Produces yellow catkins in spring. 8×4.5m (26×15 ft).

Tilia petiolaris (weeping silver lime) — Has mid green leaves that are downy above and silvery below. It produces highly-scented white flowers in late summer (July). 8×4.5m (26×15 ft).

TEXTURE

Bold foliage

Ailanthus altissima — Has leaves about 90cm (3 ft) long. See Coloured fruits.

Aralia chinensis (angelica tree) — Has leaves up to 1.2m (4 ft) long and 60cm (2 ft) wide, and white flowers borne in huge panicles during early and mid autumn (August and September). 3.5×3.5m (12×12 ft).

Catalpa bignonioides (Indian bean tree) — A tree of rounded habit with large, heart-shaped, bright green leaves. Its white, foxglove-like flowers have yellow and purple markings and appear in late summer to early autumn (July to August). These give way later to long, slender seed pods. 11×13.5m (36×45 ft).

Magnolia macrophylla — A slow-growing tree with large, thin-textured leaves. It yields large flowers that are fragrant and parchment-coloured with purple centres, and appear in early and mid summer (May and June). It will not tolerate alkaline soils, and ideally should be given a sunny position sheltered from wind. 8×4.5m (26×15 ft).

Parrotia persica — See under Coloured stems.

Paulownia tomentosa — Bears heliotrope-coloured flowers during early summer (May), and leaves that are often 60cm (2 ft) across. It needs protection from frost. 6×3.5m (20×12 ft).

Fine foliage

Azara microphylla — Has tiny, vanilla-scented, yellow flowers that appear in mid and late spring (March and April). 3×1.5m (10×5 ft).

Betula pendula (silver birch) — A white-stemmed, deciduous tree that thrives on thin, acid and sandy soils in sun or shade. 8×3m (26×10 ft).

Laburnum anagyroides (common laburnum) — Bears racemes of yellow flowers in early summer (May), and has trifoliate, dull green leaves. 4.5×3m (15×10 ft).

Nothofagus antarctica (Antarctic beech) — A fast-growing, deciduous tree, often having a distorted trunk and main branches. Its small, rounded, heart-shaped, dark green leaves turn yellow in autumn. It cannot tolerate chalk. 9×6m (30×20 ft).

Robinia pseudoacacia Frisia — A deciduous tree with small leaflets that are golden in summer, becoming a yellow-tinted apricot in autumn. 12×12m (40×40 ft).

CHOOSING CONTAINER-GROWN SHRUBS

As all keen gardeners know, the modern way to buy shrubs is in containers – generally polythene bags, but sometimes rigid polythene or plastic pots. These are all available from the many garden centres that have sprung up all over the country in recent years.

Reputable garden centres sell only good-quality plants, but nevertheless it pays the customer to know how to recognize top-quality as well as inferior-quality plants.

In Great Britain many garden centres have been approved by the Horticultural Trades Association. These centres sell plants of the highest quality only and are easily recognized as they fly a blue flag bearing the emblem of the International Garden Centre Association.

Too young or too old?
Shrubs should be well rooted and established in their containers, otherwise they may not 'take' successfully. A good test is to lift up a plant by the stems; it should

remain firm and secure in the pot. If a shrub is not well established, the container and soil are liable to fall away from the roots: the soil ball should remain intact when planting so that the roots are not disturbed.

Beware of shrubs that have rooted through the base of the containers and established themselves in the underlying medium; this is an indication that they have been in the pots for too long. In order to move such plants from the containers, you would have to cut the

roots away and this, of course, would check growth and mean that the shrub would take longer to establish itself in your garden. If, however, just a few roots show through the base of the container when you lift it up, the plant is well-established in its container and this can be taken as a sign that it is ready for transplanting.

Shrubs that have been containerized for a long time may also be showing signs of nutrient deficiencies – looking generally sickly and rather stunted. Leaves may be unusually small and yellowish, perhaps with marginal scorch or browning, or show abnormal red coloration.

Plants to avoid
Never buy shrubs that are not clearly labelled. Each shrub should have an

individual label, in which case you can be reasonably sure you are buying the right plant. Do not buy any shrubs that are in very dry soil and are obviously suffering from water shortage. This will result in a severe check to growth and even premature leaf fall.

Try to pick shrubs that have a generally healthy appearance, and that seem to be growing well. Avoid any plants with wind or frost damage; again this shows up in the leaves, which may have brown scorch marks, and also in the buds which, if dry and brown, will never spring into life. Reliable nurserymen will keep the more tender shrubs – some of the camellias, magnolias, rhododendrons and azaleas – in a suitably protected area like a lath structure, a polythene or netting tunnel, or a cold glasshouse.

Many people think they are getting better value for money if they buy really tall shrubs from a garden centre or nursery. But these are suspect, especially those with only a few 'leggy' stems, that are devoid of foliage at the base. Instead buy shorter plants that are well branched from the base – really bushy specimens with plenty of strong stems. These plants will already have been stopped; a 'leggy' plant will generally remain so unless you cut it back hard.

Avoid any plants with pests on the foliage as it is foolish to introduce any more trouble into your garden. Likewise beware of containers full of weeds: there is always a risk here of introducing a particularly pernicious weed to your garden, which may prove difficult to eradicate. And perennial weeds cannot be extracted from the soil ball without a great deal of root disturbance to the shrub. You may sometimes find liverwort

Far left: buy your shrubs from a good garden centre. Above left: shrub being removed from its container prior to planting
Left: conifer suffering from erratic watering
Below: azalea with lime-induced chlorosis

(flat, green, plate-like growth) on the surface of the soil, but this is harmless and can easily be scraped off before planting.

Flowering shrubs
One of the ideas behind containerized shrubs is that the customer can buy them when they are in flower. You can thus be sure that the plants have reached flowering age and that you will not have to wait several years for a display. It probably goes without saying that you should choose well-budded plants, or those with plenty of flowers. For instance, rhododendrons and camellias are generally offered when in bud, so ensure that they have plenty of fat flower-buds.

If you decide to buy some shrubs that show no signs of flowering, ask the sales assistant or nurseryman to give you an idea when you can expect the particular specimen to come into flower. Some subjects, for example chimonanthus (winter-sweet), take a number of years to reach flowering size.

Climbing plants
Climbing plants are generally supplied with some kind of support such as a stout bamboo cane, and are regularly trained in by the nursery staff to prevent plants becoming entangled with each other. But if this has not been done, do not attempt to untwine them; your plant's stem may well be damaged in the process. You will find that clematis are often grown in a netting sleeve to contain them; remove this immediately after planting.

Diseased shrubs
Reliable nurserymen would never offer diseased plants. But there is one serious disease of shrubs whose symptoms you should be able to recognize. Conifers and heathers are prone to attack by a fungus called phytophthora that causes the roots to rot and the plants to die. It affects some other shrubs too, such as rhododendrons, and is highly infectious – it can spread like wildfire in a nursery. Obviously you do not want to introduce it into your garden. Conifers suffering from this disease lose their natural foliage and turn greyish. They start to die from the base upwards. Heathers have similar symptoms and also the tips of the shoots wilt in the early stages of infection. Rhododendrons generally show a somewhat stunted appearance, the leaves being smaller than normal and often of a pale colour.

Rhododendrons, camellias, heathers and other lime-hating shrubs with yellowing foliage are probably not diseased but suffering with chlorosis from being potted in a compost containing lime.

PLANTING TREES AND SHRUBS

Here we describe the steps taken in planting trees and shrubs to achieve the best results. During the dreary winter months, when many plants die down or at least lose their leaves, the evergreens come into their own. They provide a welcome touch of colour when the garden is at its barest and are effective all year round as screens or hedges.

In prepared soil, dig a hole a little wider than the rootball of new shrub

Remove plant from container, taking care not to disturb its roots or soil ball

Put plant in centre of hole, adding a supporting stake at this stage if necessary

Replace soil carefully round shrub, but no higher than soil mark

Firm each layer of soil with your heel before adding the next

192

Planting time

Nowadays trees and shrubs are either in plastic or bitumenized paper-containers or the root-ball is wrapped in hessian when they are bought. Shrubs especially must have their roots kept moist.

It is important to be sure that no plants are planted where there is a severe frost or the ground is soggy. In the former case they should be stored unopened in a frost-proof place, watering those wrapped in hessian, or in the latter, heeled under in a sheltered spot until the weather improves.

Regarding planting time, evergreen trees and shrubs never become completely dormant in the winter, unlike deciduous ones that drop their leaves and rest during a cold period. Evergreens should therefore be planted when the ground is warm and not too dry so that their roots will grow and become established. This is best achieved in mid-to-late autumn (September to October) and late spring to early summer (April to May). Deciduous plants should be planted between late autumn and mid spring.

Preparing the ground

Prior to planting, the ground should be thoroughly dug to the depth of a spade or fork, or if you have the energy, double dig it to two spits. Add a good quantity of organic matter, such as well-rotted farmyard manure, garden compost, peat, leaf mould or spent hops. A top dressing of sterilized bonemeal at 135g per sq m (4 oz per sq yd) can then be forked into the surface. Firm down the soil with your heels and the site is ready for planting. Dig a hole, a few centimetres wider than the diameter of the soil ball and deep enough for the top of the ball to be slightly below the level of the soil surface after planting – about 13mm ($\frac{1}{2}$ in) is enough.

Planting

Remove the plant from its container or hessian wrap, taking great care not to disturb the roots or the soil ball around them, otherwise there may be a check to the plant's growth. The ties securing a hessian wrap should be cut, and then the wrap can be pulled back and the plant carefully lifted out. If your plant is in a flexible plastic bag, the bag should be slit two or three times with a knife, the plastic pulled right back, and the plant lifted out. Bitumenized containers are often held together by staples and these make it easy to pull them apart and lift out the plant. If a plant is in a rigid plastic pot you will have to invert it and sharply tap the rim on the edge of a bench, at the same time holding the base of the stem and the top of the rootball with your other hand. The rootball should then slide cleanly out of the pot with no disturbance.

The plant should be placed in the centre of the hole and the soil returned, firming all round with your heel as you go. The soil must be level with the soil mark on the stem.

If a plant requires a stake, this should be inserted first, for if you drive it into the ground after planting, it may go straight through the soil ball and damage the roots.

Shrubs such as cytisus, genista, spartium and some conifers, that have weak root systems, would benefit from staking for the first few years until they become really well-established. This applies particularly if they are in a windy situation. A stake would help prevent them being buffeted by the wind and so not rooting properly.

Care after planting

Correct care of newly-planted evergreens is of vital importance if they are to become properly established. On no account must the plants be allowed to become dry at the roots, otherwise they are liable to drop their leaves and die. Water them well immediately after planting and continue to do so whenever the surface soil starts to dry out. Until they are well-rooted in the surrounding soil, the evergreens may lose a lot of water through their leaves and be unable to replace it. To counteract this you can give them a good spray all over twice a day – early morning and in the cool of the evening. A less time-consuming method is to spray the leaves with a product called S.600. This forms a film over the surface of the leaves and so prevents rapid water loss. It may have to be re-applied after heavy rain. This product (usually available from garden centres and shops) need only be used until the plants have rooted in the soil – a matter of four to six weeks.

To ensure that the soil does not dry out too rapidly, it is a good idea to mulch the plants after planting. Place an 8cm (3 in) deep layer of organic matter around the plant, over the root area, but not quite up to the stems or trunk. Suitable materials for this purpose are well-rotted farmyard manure, garden compost, peat or spent hops. Fresh lawn mowings, provided they have not been contaminated by weedkiller during the past six weeks, could be used for mulching.

Young evergreens should be well protected from the prevailing wind, especially in the winter, as cold drying winds and gales often cause the edges of the leaves – and sometimes the entire leaf – to turn brown. If the plants are protected on the windward side by larger well-established plants, they will be better off. Otherwise it is a good idea to erect some form of temporary windbreak on the windward side. This could be a sheet of hessian stretched between two posts, or a wattle hurdle or fencing panel would give good protection if securely fixed to wooden posts. A windbreak should be higher than the plant it is protecting. With most shrubs, wind protection may only be necessary until they are well-established – say for the first two or three years, and then generally only in the winter.

If shrub is in exposed position, erect a windbreak to shield it

TRANSPLANTING LARGE TREES AND SHRUBS

There is a trend nowadays to transplant large or semi-mature trees and shrubs. This is often done by local authorities to provide an immediate effect in streets, parks and open spaces, or new housing estates. There may be occasions, however, when the private gardener wishes to move a fairly large established tree or shrub from one part of the garden to another. Here we look at the preparation that is necessary, and describe how to carry out the operation.

Although many trees and shrubs can be moved when fairly large without suffering any ill effects, there is also the question of whether or not you are physically capable of moving a mature tree from one position to another. Think carefully about this problem before you begin, and be sure that sufficient people are available to help you.

Preparation

Trees should preferably be prepared for transplanting one or two growing seasons before lifting, depending on the genus. Some trees – such as acer (maple), aesculus (horse chestnut), alnus (alder), platanus (plane), populus (poplar), fibrous-rooted rhododendrons, tilia (lime) and ulmus (elm) – move easily and re-establish themselves quickly. These can therefore be got ready only one season in advance.

Difficult and coarse-rooted genera, however, should be prepared over two seasons. In this category are abies (silver fir), betula (birch), carpinus (hornbeam), castanea (chestnut), cedrus (cedar), chamaecyparis (false cypress), crataegus (thorn), cupressus (cypress), fagus (beech), fraxinus (ash), ginkgo, ilex (holly), laburnum, larix (larch), liquidambar (sweet gum), malus (flowering crab), metasequoia (dawn redwood), nothofagus (southern beech), picea (spruce), pinus (pine), prunus, pyrus (pear), quercus (oak), robinia, salix (willow), sorbus, taxodium, taxus (yew), thuya (arborvitae) and tsuga (hemlock or hemlock spruce).

A plant with a good quantity of fibrous roots has a far greater chance of survival than one with coarse roots. Some pruning is necessary, therefore, and this is done by excavating a trench around the tree, about 90cm (3 ft) from the trunk and 60cm (2 ft) deep. This will sever coarse lateral roots, thus encouraging a fibrous root system. Fill the trench with topsoil and firm the surface area.

For trees needing two seasons' preparation, *don't* cut a trench right the way round in one operation; instead, remove half of the circle in the first year and the other half the following year.

In the case of deciduous trees or shrubs, this operation can be carried out while they are leafless – that is, between early winter and mid spring (November and March); for evergreens, the best time is late spring or mid autumn (April or September).

Transplanting

First, prepare the planting hole, so that the tree can go right in when it is ready. Dig a hole wider than the rootball and break up the subsoil, incorporating well-rotted farmyard manure or other organic matter; then firm the base well. The prepared hole should be deep enough to allow the tree to be replanted to its original depth. Place a layer of good topsoil in the bottom to assist rooting.

Now you are ready to move the tree. First dig out another trench around the base, making it the same size as before, but being careful not to damage too much of the fibrous root system. Then sever any down-growing roots beneath the tree.

Carefully tease away soil from the soil ball until you think you will be able to lift the tree; the more soil you are able to leave around the roots, the higher the chances of a successful transplanting. Once you have reduced the soil ball to manageable proportions, wrap it tightly with hessian and twine to prevent soil falling away during the move. Try to take

To encourage fibrous root system in tree to be transplanted, 1 mark out trench around trunk; 2 excavate to adequate depth; 3 sever coarse lateral roots; 4 refill trench and firm; 5 replace turfs
Left: mulching after the tree has been transplanted will help conserve moisture

the hessian underneath the soil ball if possible, and also over the top, right up to the trunk.

Now you will need as many willing hands as possible to raise the tree out of the hole and move it on to its new site. Set it in the planting hole, remove the hessian, and then backfill with good-quality topsoil, firming really well with your heels as you go.

After-care

The tree will probably need supporting for a few years until well established. This could be done by guying. Insert three angle-iron stakes, evenly spaced, around the tree and attach a length of seven-strand, galvanized wire to each stake through an eyelet or hole. Loop the other end of each wire around the lower branches; thread a piece of rubber or plastic hosepipe onto the wire to protect the bark. Try to get the wires as tight as possible, making sure that you pull the tree into a perfectly upright position.

Alternatively, you could insert three stakes around the tree an equal distance apart, about 60cm (2 ft) from the trunk, and secure the tree to them by means of proprietary, heavy-duty tree ties. These should be available at good garden centres. Use 75mm (3 in) chestnut stakes, at least 2m (7 ft) in length, and insert them about 45cm (18 in) into the ground.

Mulch the tree with well-rotted farm-yard manure or some other organic matter. Keep it well watered during dry spells, at least for the first season after transplanting.

For evergreens, an anti-transpirant spray, such as s.600, used immediately after transplanting would help to reduce water loss from the foliage until the plant has rooted into the soil. Otherwise, spray the plant with plain water every morning and evening for a few weeks after the move.

If you plant in a lawn or other grassy area, don't allow the grass to grow right up to the trunk until the tree is really well established. For a few years leave a circle of cultivated soil around the trunk, about 90cm (3 ft) in diameter.

To sum up, then: provided you move the tree or shrub at the correct season, with as much soil as possible around the roots, and keep it well watered after transplanting, there is every reason to expect it to survive.

SHRUBS FOR SMALL GARDENS

It is often difficult to make small gardens look really decorative, especially in built-up areas where there is a preponderance of buildings and walls. In such gardens, where too many annuals and bedding plants can look messy, the many attractively-foliaged, flowering shrubs provide the ideal answer.

In a very small garden, the first consideration is to ensure privacy. This is not always easy, since many tiny gardens exist in built-up areas and are consequently surrounded and overlooked by walls and buildings. Light, ornamental trees are often planted to screen the garden area, but even these block out a substantial amount of sunlight and rain from other plants – particularly when they are also in the shadow of neighbouring houses. In spite of these drawbacks, trees are used in purely functional ways – to form screens or focal points, or to divert attention from the ugly, permanent eyesores that exist in congested urban areas.

This is not to say, of course, that trees have only functional value – most are decorative and some are exceptionally beautiful. Nevertheless, small gardens cannot always afford the space necessary for trees. This is where shrubs come in.

Shrubs for cover and concealment
Although grown primarily for decoration, shrubs, like trees, can have a utilitarian purpose. The most common uses made of them are to hide bare boundary walls and fences, to conceal ugly objects such as sheds and to form a generally decorative background.

Unfortunately, there is a drawback to the indiscriminate use of some shrubs. Since the walls surrounding a small garden are often high, large shrubs are needed to cover them; after a fairly short time, such plants encroach on ground space and sap the nutrients and moisture from the soil, leaving it infertile for other decorative plants. Shrubs planted to cover or conceal have, therefore, to be chosen with care, and with an eye to their eventual size and spread.

Evergreen climbers
As some bushy shrubs grow too large for the small garden, it is better to cover walls and fences with evergreen climbing

shrubs trained along wires or trelliswork. Some climbers send out shoots that can be trained horizontally on either side of the stem for a distance of at least 2m (6½ ft). One climber can cover the same wall area as three or four shrubs, and in much the same time – consequently the demand on the soil is much smaller. Most such climbing shrubs are amenable to regular light trimming, so there is little encroachment on precious ground space. Two evergreen climbers that are particularly good for this purpose are *Pyracantha atalantioides* (firethorn) that has long-lasting scarlet berries, and the fragrant *Lonicera japonica* Halliana (honeysuckle).

Decorative infilling
Once the trees and shrubs for constructional and functional purposes have been planted, the remaining area can be infilled with decorative plants. Of course,

Small shrubs come in a wide range of foliage colour and texture

there is a considerable amount of overlapping between the shrubs classed as functional and those classed as decorative. A single plant can be utilized for either purpose, depending on the conditions available. These infilling shrubs are the plants, that, ultimately, will form the body of the garden and impart colour and form to it.

Before placing any plants, it is worthwhile studying the layout of larger gardens. Many of the large-growing shrubs that are so valuable in big gardens have rather less vigorous dwarf counterparts that will give much the same effect in a smaller space. Careful visualization and planning is really all that is needed to make a 'pocket-handkerchief' area as relaxing and pleasant a place to be in as a much larger garden.

Colour, shape and texture

To create a garden that is pleasantly varied and yet well organized, first consider the 'three harmonies' of garden design – shape, colour and foliage texture. These are particularly valuable for a small garden where there is normally very little room for error.

The harmony of shape is perhaps the most important; shrubs can be round, conical or pyramidal, and prostrate, erect or spreading – all in a variety of dimensions. Careful mingling of these different sizes and shapes in a border can produce a pleasing, contoured effect. To avoid monotony, an occasional upright-growing, pyramidal shrub can be planted to form an accent point.

The second harmony to consider is that of colour. Here it is important to bear in mind that the foliage of many shrubs lasts much longer than the blooms. Therefore, intermix leaf colours – green, purple, gold, grey and variegations – rather than flower colours. Some very striking combinations can be achieved just through foliage alone. The subtle use of colour will, of course, add emphasis to shape and form.

The third harmony – foliage texture – is often not as easily recognized as the other two. Optically, plants with large, bold foliage seem to push themselves forward, while those that have very tiny leaves appear to recede. By judicious positioning of these two types you can create a sense of gentle movement and flow that compliments the shape and colour of the chosen shrubs. This illusion of movement can also be obtained by planting blue-foliaged and gold-foliaged shrubs in close proximity.

Some varieties to choose

The shrubs listed below are excellent for planting in combination in a small area. The first dimension given is the ultimate height and the second is the spread.

SMALL SHRUBS

Of the plants listed below, some are naturally low-growing and spreading, while others can be kept in check by regular trimming.

Andromeda polifolia Compacta (bog rosemary)
Round, evergreen shrub with small leaves that turn purple in winter, and pink flowers borne in early summer (May). 30 × 30cm (12 × 12 in).

Berberis × *stenophylla* Corallina Compacta
Low-growing, evergreen shrub with dark olive-green, close-set leaves and orange flowers that appear in early summer (May). 45 × 60cm (18 × 24 in).

Ceratostigma plumbaginoides (plumbago)
Low-growing, round sub-shrub with mid green leaves that assume red tints in autumn. Blue flowers open from late summer to mid autumn (July to September). 30 × 38cm (12 × 15 in).

Cytisus × *beanii* (broom)
Semi-prostrate, deciduous broom. Bears golden flowers in early summer (May). 45 × 90cm (18 in × 3 ft).

Euonymus fortunei Emerald Cushion
Dwarf, mounded, evergreen shrub with dark green leaves. 30 × 30cm (12 × 12 in).

Euonymus fortunei Silver Queen
Variegated evergreen shrub with grey, silver and white small leaves that are tinged pink in winter. 45cm × 1·2m (18 in × 4 ft).

Helichrysum splendidum
Globular, silvery-grey, deciduous shrub. Bears yellow everlasting flowers from late summer to mid autumn (July to September). 60 × 90cm (2 × 3 ft).

Hypericum × *inodorum* Elstead
Erect-growing, semi-evergreen shrub with deep green leaves. Produces small, pale yellow flowers from late summer to mid autumn (July to September). Its size can be controlled by pruning back to the ground in spring. 90cm × 1·2m (3 × 4 ft).

Laurus nobilis (bay laurel)
Dense, pyramidal, evergreen, aromatic shrub with mid green leaves. It stands clipping well, so its size can be controlled; but if not, it will reach 4·5m (15 ft).

Pachysandra terminalis
Dwarf, evergreen, carpeting shrublet with deep green leaves, carrying white flowers during early and mid spring (February and March). Variegata is an attractive form with mottled white leaves. 30 × 45cm (12 × 18 in).

Below: Hypericum *Elstead can be kept under control by hard pruning*
Below left: dwarf Pachysandra terminalis
Bottom left: lovely deciduous Cytisus ×beanii *takes up a minimum of space*

Below: aromatic Laurus nobilis, *the laurel crown plant, is perfect for all-year-round cover*

Right: tiny Ceratostigma plumbaginoides

Potentilla Elizabeth
Dome-shaped bush with small, silver-green leaves and single rose-like yellow blooms borne from mid summer (July) onwards. 60cm × 1·5m (2 × 5 ft).

Potentilla fruticosa mandshurica
Dwarf, semi-prostrate, grey-leaved shrub with white flowers appearing from early summer to late autumn (May to October). 30 × 75cm (12 in × 2½ ft).

Rhododendron microleucum
Tiny-leaved, dwarf species with clusters of white flowers opening in late spring (April). 23 × 60cm (9 × 24 in).

Rosmarinus Jessop's Upright (rosemary)
Strong, erect-growing evergreen shrub with green leaves that are white on the undersides. 1·2 × 1·2m (4 × 4 ft).

Syringa velutina (Korean lilac)
Dwarf, deciduous shrub with 5cm (2 in) long, rounded, velvety, dark green leaves. Produces lilac-pink flowers in early and mid summer (May and June). 90 × 90cm (3 × 3 ft).

DWARF CONIFERS
The selection given below is very limited, since there are many different dwarf conifers available today. You should be able to find a reasonably good selection at any reputable nursery, or alternatively write to one of the specialist growers.

Chamaecyparis lawsoniana Gimbornii (Lawson cypress)
Globular, compact bush of slow growth. Has foliage that is bluish-green, tipped mauve. 60 × 60cm (2 × 2 ft).

Chamaecyparis obtusa Pygmaea (Hinoki cypress)
Low, spreading dwarf conifer with fan-shaped green foliage that reddens at the tips in winter. 45cm × 1·5m (18 in × 5 ft).

Juniperus communis Compressa (juniper)
Column-shaped, compact, slow-growing dwarf conifer with dense, tiny, bluish-grey foliage. 60 × 15cm (24 × 6 in).

Picea glauca albertiana Conica (Alberta white spruce)
Attractive dwarf, conical, slow-growing bush with leaves of bright grass green. 1·2m × 75cm (4 × 2½ ft).

Taxus baccata Standishii (yew)
Very slow-growing and columnar, with golden leaves. 1·8 × 30cm (6 ft × 12 in).

Above: compact Chamaecyparis obtusa *Pygmaea is a good conifer for small areas*

SHRUBS AND CLIMBERS FOR SUNLESS WALLS

Although north- and east-facing walls are traditionally difficult to cover with plants, there is, in fact, quite a range of hardy shrubs and climbers – most with good foliage and flowers – that can be grown very successfully in such positions. A selection taken from the list given below will ensure more than adequate coverage of almost any house or boundary wall.

Generally, walls with a north- or east-facing aspect are regarded as difficult to cover, whether with wall plants or climbers. This is unfortunate, since many houses have north- or north-east facing walls at the front or back – usually the most important walls.

Of these two different aspects, there is little doubt that the north-east facing walls are the most difficult to clothe satisfactorily. In general only the very toughest of shrubs and climbers can grow in such a position. Almost any rose, however, will be quite happy either standing against or climbing up a wall with an eastern aspect – mainly because they like some shade during at least part of the day.

Although all walls facing directly towards the north will certainly be dark and dreary, particularly when the days are short, they are somehow not quite as bad for plants as east-facing ones. Generally, but particularly in the summer, the wall of a house that has a northerly outlook – provided it is a fairly flat one without any deep recesses – seems to get a little (possibly reflected) sunshine on it very early in the morning and last thing before sunset. Also, any plants positioned against such a wall are exposed to a north light that seems to be of benefit to them. Fortunately, there are a good number of interesting shrubs and climbers that will grow quite contentedly in such a position.

If the bed to be planted is overshadowed by a tall building or a group of trees farther to the north, then the problem becomes even greater. Under such circumstances it will be necessary to fall back on the 'toughies' – such as *Fatsia japonica* (fig leaf palm), skimmia, elaeagnus and *Ilex altaclarensis* (holly). There are also some hardy rhododendrons and cultivars of *Camellia japonica* and *C. × williamsii* that are tolerant of comparatively heavy shade.

Camellias for north walls
Camellias, almost without exception, are excellent as plants for a sunless wall. They can be chosen to flower from early

Shade-tolerant camellia Donation does well against a north-facing wall

winter to early summer (November to May). During the rest of the year they provide an attractive appearance with their shiny, mid green, moderately large leaves. For clothing walls most varieties of *C. japonica* and *C. × williamsii* are most suitable – as is *C.* Inspiration, with its large, deep pink blossoms. Although camellias are fairly slow-growing, it is possible to obtain good wall coverage after a number of years; their ultimate height and spread can attain 4m (13 ft). At all times these shrubs are shapely, bushy, and very decorative plants.

You must, however, bear in mind that although camellias will flourish against a north-facing wall, they must not, on any account, be placed at the foot of one with an easterly aspect. This is because camellias come into bloom when severe frosts are likely; the real danger lies in the damaging effect of the warmth of the early morning sun on the frozen tissues of the blossoms. An east-facing wall is, of course, particularly exposed to this.

Roses for walls

In a small garden the wall of a house is often the only space that can be spared to grow roses; fortunately many will grow vigorously on a north- and east-facing walls. If you decide to grow bush roses at the foot of a wall, it is best to choose those that are vigorous and tall-growing – floribundas are generally just a little bit stronger than hybrid teas and can withstand more adverse conditions. The tall, vigorous Queen Elizabeth, with clear pink blooms, or the golden yellow Arthur Bell are both worth trying. Other bush roses that have withstood the test of time are the rugosa shrub Conrad F. Meyer that produces very full, silvery pink blooms in early summer (May), repeating this colourful display in autumn, and the hybrid perpetual Hugh Dickson, that has full, globular, very fragrant, red blooms during the summer.

Climbing roses such as disease-resistant Hamburger Phönix (left and below) and the exceptionally vigorous, fragrant Maigold (below left and bottom) are excellent for clothing high walls. Kerria japonica *Pleniflora (above right) and* Desfontainea spinosa *(below right) can brighten up most shady corners*

The best choice of roses for growing on almost sunless walls will nevertheless come from among the large-flowering climbers and the *Rosa kordesii* climbers. The former are colourful and vigorous and will soon cover a good area of the wall of a house. Possibly one of the most spectacular large-flowering climbers is the flamboyant, fiery scarlet Danse du Feu. It is moderately vigorous, growing to a height of 2·5m (8 ft). Rather taller-growing is the bronze-yellow, fragrant, free-flowering Maigold, which attains a height of 3·4m (11 ft), and the very fragrant, free-flowering Guinée, with dark scarlet, shaded black, full flowers. The *R. kordesii* climbers Hamburger Phönix (crimson) and Parkdirektor Riggers (blood red, semi-double flowers) are more modest-growing.

Hints on general cultivation

Remember that very often a foundation bed at the foot of a wall is very dry; therefore dig it as deep as possible and incorporate into it a good deal of humus-making material such as well-rotted manure, garden compost or peat. Plant nothing closer than 38cm (15 in) to the wall, and train climbers to the wall along a sloping bamboo cane. Water well before and after planting, and mulch.

Bear in mind also that the soil in such a bed often contains a lot of mortar, dropped during building. It is therefore likely to be alkaline, so if you intend to grow lime-haters, first neutralize the soil by adding plenty of peat.

Some plants for north and east walls

Any selection from the plants listed below should give adequate coverage of a north- or east-facing wall. It is a good idea to choose an evergreen to go next to a deciduous flowering plant, so that coverage is maintained throughout the year.

SHRUBS

Berberis × stenophylla

This is a graceful bush with long, arching branches and small, evergreen leaves. It has orange-yellow blooms, opening during late spring and early summer (April and May). 2·5m (8 ft) high.

Chaenomeles speciosa Moerloosii
(flowering quince)

A deciduous shrub with an arching, spreading habit that enables it to cover the lower half of a house wall very effectively. It has delicate pink and white blooms, borne in thick clusters between early and late spring (February and April), followed by fruits that are flushed pink. 1·8m (6 ft) high.

Choisya ternata (Mexican orange blossom)

A beautiful evergreen with glossy foliage. It produces sweet-scented, white, star-like flowers in clusters in early summer (May). 2·5m (8 ft) high.

Desfontainea spinosa

This somewhat less well-known evergreen appreciates the shelter of a wall. It has small, holly-like leaves and tubular, scarlet flowers that bloom from late summer to mid autumn (July to September). 1·8m (6 ft) high.

Jasminum nudiflorum (winter-flowering jasmine)

Has golden-yellow blooms carried on bare stems throughout the winter. It looks most attractive if planted so as to grow through the branches of an evergreen pyracantha. East-facing aspects should be avoided, however, because early sun after frost damages the flowers. 4m (13 ft) high.

Kerria japonica Pleniflora (jew's mallow)

A graceful, deciduous shrub with dainty, arching, bright green stems, that becomes garlanded with golden-yellow ball-like flowers during mid and late spring (March and April). 3m (10 ft) high.

Pyracantha (firethorn)

There are several very attractive species of pyracantha that can be trained to cover a wall. They are all evergreen, and are covered with masses of hawthorn-like flowers during the spring and early summer months. They reach a height of 4m (13 ft). Suitable forms for virtually sunless walls are *P. atalantioides*, with crimson berries during the winter, *P. coccinea* Lalandei with orange-red berries, and *P. rogersiana* Flava with bright yellow berries.

CLIMBERS

Akebia quinata

This semi-evergreen, twining climber can reach a height of 3m (10 ft). It produces very dark purple, scented flowers in late spring (April), followed by peculiar, 8cm (3 in) long, dark purple sausage-shaped fruits that are quite decorative.

Celastrus orbiculatus (climbing spindle berry)

A strong, deciduous, twining climber, reaching 3m (10 ft) high. Its leaves turn clear yellow in autumn, forming a splendid backcloth to its brownish seed capsules that split open to show a yellow lining and red seeds.

Hydrangea

H. anomala, reaching 4m (13 ft) high, with slightly domed, up to 20cm (8 in) across, corymbs of yellowish-white flowers, has brown, peeling bark when it is mature. *H. petiolaris* is a deciduous, strong-growing, self-clinging, climbing hydrangea that reaches 4m (13 ft) in height. It bears white flower-heads 15cm (6 in) across, and serrated leaves, in mid and late summer (June and July).

Top: well-grown Choisya ternata *and* Rosa banksiae *at Kiftsgate Court*
Winter-flowering Jasminum nudiflorum *(above) prefers a northerly aspect*
Above left: Hydrangea petiolaris

Parthenocissus quinquefolia (Virginia creeper)

This tall, self-clinging deciduous vine is treasured for its rather dull green leaves that turn orange and scarlet in autumn.

FLOWERING TREES
AND SHRUBS

AZALEA

Type	mostly hardy, deciduous, semi-evergreen and evergreen flowering shrubs
Family	ERICACEAE
Planting season	mid spring (March); container-grown plants at any time
Flowering dates	late spring–mid summer (April–June)
Mature size/shape	usually round, sometimes erect; height 10cm–2·5m (4 in–8 ft), spread 60cm–3m (2–10 ft)

Modern garden azaleas are a group of attractive and useful deciduous, semi-evergreen and evergreen flowering shrubs, created by extensive interbreeding. At one time botanists considered them to be a separate genus, but now they are included as a group, known as Series (S) Azaleas, of the rhododendron genus.

There are at least 40 species of azalea available commercially in Britain; of these about a dozen are cultivated for garden use. Several of the remainder have played an important part in producing the many decorative hybrids so popular today. These include the deciduous Ghent, Knap Hill and Exbury, mollis and occidentale types that have been developed in Europe since the early 19th century. The majority of the evergreens originated from a collection of kurume azaleas from Japan, and were known as 'Wilson's Fifty' because they were introduced by the plant collector and explorer, E. H. Wilson, in 1920; a further range was developed in Europe and the United States.

Azaleas are characterized by brightly-coloured flowers that appear, according to type and variety, in late spring and early summer (April and May), occasionally extending into mid summer (June). Some of the deciduous Knap Hill hybrids have bronze-tinted or coppery red young leaves, and others – such as the mollis group, the species *Rhododendron arborescens*, *R. calendulaceum*, *R. occidentale* and *R. reticulatum*, the Ghent azalea Corneille and the kurume Hinodegiri – follow their flowers with brilliant autumn tints. Quite a number are also pleasantly scented. They range in size from prostrate forms such as *R. nakaharai*, to the occidentale hybrids that grow to 2·5m (8 ft) high and 3m (10 ft) wide. Normally the evergreen hybrids are smaller, with a height and spread of about 1·2m (4 ft) after 20 years' growth. They are usually rounded or erect in shape.

Deciduous azaleas

Ghent hybrids are a popular category, originally produced in Belgium in the middle of the 19th century. Their variously-coloured, fragrant blooms have long, tubed flowers rather like those of the honeysuckle – and so are popularly known as 'honeysuckle azaleas'.

Knap Hill hybrids were originally raised at Anthony Waterer's nursery at Knap Hill in Surrey, hence their name, but their development was continued afterwards on a much larger scale by the late Lionel de Rothschild at Exbury, Hampshire. Those raised there, although similar in character to the original cultivars, are often called 'Exbury' azaleas. This group has large, trumpet-shaped, usually unscented flowers in varying colours.

Occidentale azaleas, a most valued race of garden hybrids, are characterized by pastel-coloured flowers – a quality possibly derived from *R. occidentale* that has creamy white to pale pink flowers with a pale yellow or orange basal stain.

Rustica hybrids, created by crossing double-flowered Ghent azaleas with *R. japonicum*, have sweet-scented, double, brightly-coloured flowers that are profusely produced and daintier in flower and growth than other deciduous azaleas, as well as being shorter and more compact.

Evergreen azaleas

The kurume group of evergreens, very widely grown in present-day gardens, and usually of comparatively small dimensions, has small, brightly-coloured flowers, and is eminently suitable where space is restricted.

Kaempferi hybrids are modest-growing azaleas, created in Holland around 1920 by crossing *R. kaempferi* with the cultivar *R. Malvaticum* (a seedling of the evergreen Hinodegiri). The Oldhamii group are also hybrids of *R. kaempferi*, but their other parent is *R. oldhamii* (the Formosan azalea); most have large blooms.

Satsuki hybrids, with medium to large flowers, have been produced mainly by crossing *R. indicum* with *R. simsii*, but there have been other crossings involving some of the Belgian hybrids.

Vuyk hybrids, with large flowers, are frequently grown in gardens today; their parentage is probably *R. molle* crossed with the kurume hybrids.

Glenn Dale hybrids, raised by B. Y. Morrison of the US Department of Agriculture at Glenn Dale, Maryland, are characterized by very large flowers, and are dwarf in growth.

Indian azaleas are mainly tender hybrids with very large flowers, bred chiefly in Belgium and Britain during the 19th century. Some varieties are specially forced by florists for the Christmas trade.

Hardy azaleas are excellent for shrub and mixed borders, and are particularly valuable because of their wide range of sizes. Possibly their greatest garden asset is that many bloom from early to mid summer (May to June) and sometimes into late summer (July), thus avoiding damage from frost. Another advantage, particularly with the deciduous Knap Hill hybrids and *R. luteum*, is their ability to exist in industrial areas.

Evergreen azaleas such as Hatsugiri, Izayoi and Rosebud are particularly useful for ground cover; *R. luteum* is sometimes planted as a hedge because of its yellow, honeysuckle-like flowers and the rich red hues of its leaves in autumn. The dwarf evergreen azaleas also make excellent – but rather expensive – low-growing division hedges. There are several species that are valuable for shrubberies; these wild species are largely indigenous to Japan and North America, but a few originate from the Caucasus, China and eastern Europe. Most were introduced to Britain during the 19th century, but earlier ones were *R. viscosum* (1734), *R. canadense* (1767) and *R. luteum* (1793).

Cultivation and propagation

Deciduous azaleas do best in moist, partially-shaded positions. The evergreen types are rather more tender than the deciduous and need to be sheltered from cold winds. They will grow in full sun provided they are kept moist. The best soil is a light, acid one; you can create such conditions by adding peat or leaf mould to existing soil. On no account must the soil be chalky or limey.

Provided the weather is good, you can plant bare-root azaleas at any time during the winter, but the best time is probably mid spring (March), when the soil is warming up. Plant container-grown ones at any time in good weather. Determine planting distance by adding together the spreads of two adjacent plants and then dividing by two.

Dig a hole large enough to take the rootball comfortably; on no account must this rootball be disturbed. When planted, the azalea should not be any deeper in the soil than it was before. Fill in the soil round the roots and firm gently. After planting, mulch with leaves, well-rotted compost or peat. Position early-flowering cultivars where they will be protected from the early morning sun, to avoid damage from frost on the petals that might thaw too fast.

Mulch the plants with leaves, well-rotted compost or peat in early summer (May) every year. Feed with 135gm per sq m (4 oz per sq yd) of J.I. base fertilizer, or rhododendron or rose fertilizer every spring. Where possible, dead-head the flowers as they fade.

Propagate deciduous azaleas by layering at any time when the shoots are young. Evergreens are grown from cuttings taken in late summer and early autumn (July and August). Root them in cutting compost in a cold frame for the winter, then pot them on and transplant them to a nursery bed in spring.

Pests and diseases

White fly particularly infest azaleas; treat with nicotine used according to the manufacturer's instructions. Azalea gall causes the young leaves and flowers, particularly of the kurumes, to form small swellings that are red or pale green, then white and eventually brown. Remove the galls if there are only a few of them, before they turn white; if there are a great many, spray them with Bordeaux mixture.

Left: deciduous azalea Coccinea Speciosa grows best if planted in a partially-shaded position Below: the evergreen foliage of Kaempferi azalea Willy provides good ground cover during the winter

The jewel-bright blooms of evergreen azaleas Vuyk's Scarlet (right) and Blue Danube (far right) make a magnificent display in early summer (May) Centre right: the foliage of R. luteum turns to spectacular shades of crimson, purple and orange in autumn Below right: Knap Hill azalea Persil blooms from early to mid summer (May to June)

Some varieties to choose

The following is a list of some of the most popular varieties of azalea grown today. A careful selection of plants will ensure a continuous display of flowers throughout the summer months.

DECIDUOUS HYBRIDS

Ghent hybrids

Flower in early and mid summer (May and June). Height and spread usually about 1·8m (6 ft).

Bouquet de Flore	Bright pink, deepening at the edges of the petals, with a white stripe down the centre of each.
Coccinea Speciosa	Brilliant orange-red; one of the best.
Corneille	Cream, double flowers, flushed pink outside, with pink buds and excellent autumn foliage tints.
Daviesii	Creamy white, flushed pale apricot on the reverse side, with orange-yellow blotches; buds are buff pink. Late-flowering.
Nancy Waterer	Golden yellow with orange-yellow top petals. Compact.
Pucella (Fanny)	Deep rose with top petals blotched orange.
Sang de Gentbrugge	Bright red.
Unique	Orange-yellow, in globular trusses. Tall-growing.

Mollis hybrids

Flower in early summer (May), and have good autumn tints. Height and spread of about 1·5m (5 ft).

Directeur Moerlands	Golden yellow with an orange flare. Also known as Golden Sunlight.
Dr. M. Oosthoek	Orange-red.
Floradora	Orange-red, spotted.
Goldball (Christopher Wren)	Orange-yellow, flushed flame and spotted a dark orange.
Hortulanus H. Witte	Brilliant orange-yellow.
Hugo Hardyzer	Bright rose-pink, strongly blotched orange.

Knap Hill and Exbury hybrids

Bloom from early to mid summer (May to June). Have a height and spread of 1–1·8m (3–6 ft).

Gibraltar	Orange-flame, with orange-yellow blotch.
Harvest Moon	Amber-yellow.
Persil	White, with an orange flare.
Satan	Geranium-red.
Seville	Brilliant orange.
Tunis	Deep crimson, with an orange flare.

Occidentale hybrids
Flower in early and mid summer (May and June). Have a height of up to 2·5m (8 ft), and a spread of up to 3m (10 ft).

Exquisitum	Cream, flushed pink, with an orange flare.
Graciosa	Creamy pink, with an orange-yellow basal blotch.
Irene Koster	Rose-pink; late-flowering.
Superbum	Pink, blotched apricot, with fringed petals.

Rustica hybrids
Have double flowers in early and mid summer (May and June). Height 1·8m (6 ft), spread 2·5m (8 ft).

Byron	Double white, tinged pink.
Freya	Pale pink, tinted salmon-orange.

EVERGREEN HYBRIDS
Kurume azaleas
Bloom from late spring to early summer (April to May). Height 1·2m (4 ft), spread 1·5m (5 ft).

Addy Wery	Deep vermilion-red.
Benigiri	Bright crimson.
Blaauw's Pink	Salmon-pink. Early.
Hatsugiri	Bright crimson-purple flowers. Dwarf habit.
Hinodegiri	Bright crimson.
Shin-seikai	White. Dwarf habit.

Kaempferi hybrids
Bloom during early summer (May). Height 75cm (2½ ft), spread 1·2m (4 ft).

Alice	Salmon-red.
Arendsii	Pale purple, with red spots.
Fedora	Deep pink.
Kathleen	Rose-red.
Orange Beauty	Salmon-orange.
Willy	Soft pink.

Vuyk's hybrids
Flower in early summer (May). Height about 90cm (3 ft), spread 1·5m (5 ft).

Blue Danube	Bluish violet.
Palestrina	White.
Vuyk's Rosyred	Deep rose.
Vuyk's Scarlet	Bright red.

Glenn Dale hybrids
Flower in early and mid summer (May and June). Height and spread about 1·2m (4 ft).

Buccaneer	Brilliant orange-scarlet.
Martha Hitchcock	White, edged with magenta.
Polar Sea	White.

SPECIES AZALEAS
Deciduous

R. albrechtii	Green-flecked, deep rose flowers appearing in late spring and early summer (April and May). Height 1·2m (4 ft), spread 90cm (3 ft).
R. luteum	Rich yellow, very fragrant blooms appearing during early and mid summer (May and June). Height 2·5m (8 ft), spread 1·5m (5 ft).
R. vaseyi	Pink or white flowers appearing during late spring and early summer (April and May). Has beautiful autumn tints. Height 4m (12 ft), spread 1·8m (6 ft).
R. viscosum (swamp honeysuckle)	White or pink fragrant flowers in late summer (July). Height 2·5m (8 ft), spread 1·8m (6 ft).

Semi-evergreen

R. kiusianum	Deep pink or purple flowers borne in early summer (May). Height 90cm (3 ft), spread 1·5m (5 ft).

BERBERIS

Type
evergreen and deciduous flowering and fruiting shrub

Common name
barberry

Family
BERBERIDACEAE

Flowering season
spring

Planting date
outdoors: deciduous varieties late autumn to mid spring (October–March); evergreen varieties mid to late autumn (September–October) or early to late spring (February–April); anytime from containers

Mature size/shape
prostrate to 3·6m (12 ft) high; round, dome-shaped, pyramidal or erect

Although only a fraction of them are widely available, berberis (barberries) are members of a large genus containing over 400 species. Some of these are deciduous, while others are evergreens but, irrespective of this, most of them have similar rosette-like clusters of leaves and generally spiny stems. In some instances the evergreens have holly-like leaves, and despite their smaller size, they can be equally uncomfortable to the touch.

Some of the evergreen species and their cultivars are grown for their very handsome glossy leaves. The deciduous species, on the other hand, are more particularly cultivated for the autumn colour of their foliage and their brightly-coloured berries (or fruits). These usually last well into the winter to enliven the somewhat duller garden scene. The production of berries in autumn is not, however, entirely the prerogative of the deciduous shrubs because many of the evergreens also have them. With several important exceptions, the evergreen shrubs generally yield berries of black, blue, purple and violet while those on the deciduous types are brilliant scarlet, orange-red, coral-red, crimson, pink and, in at least one instance, orange.

Apart from a few species that come from South America, all berberis are hardy and can be grown in most gardens without difficulty.

Most berberis flower in the spring and at that time their blossoms vary in colour largely from pale yellow to orange, occasionally with a touch of red. They are often borne singly, when they sometimes wreathe the arching branches of the shrubs, but can also grow in panicles, spikes or racemes or in flat or dome-shaped flower-heads. Whatever their form, they are always beautiful, but the loveliness of their spring blossoms is only a curtain raiser to the brilliance of their autumn tints and the plethora of vividly-coloured berries of varying shapes and sizes that follow later.

Most berberis are excellent for present-day gardens, being reasonably small in stature, labour-saving and largely trouble-free. They range in size from dwarf – up to 30cm (12 in) in height – to large shrubs – but most of these do not exceed 3·6m (12 ft) in height. A large number of them have ultimate heights and spreads from 60cm to 1·5m (2–5 ft), which makes them fairly reasonable for planting in somewhat restricted spaces. It is usually possible to find a berberis to suit almost any situation, be it sunny or shady, by the sea, in country or town and whatever the soil might be (as long as it is not waterlogged).

The native habitats of the various species of this large family are pretty widespread. Many were brought to Europe from China and Japan; others were carried from central Asia by plant explorers; a few valuable species originated in South America and at least one, *B. chinensis*, hails from Russia. The latter was first cultivated in gardens in 1808. The name berberis comes from the Arabic word for berries. There is one species which is native to the British Isles (or possibly was naturalized a long time ago). This is the common barberry, *B. vulgaris*, which grew widely in hedgerows until it was discovered that it acted as a host plant to the wheat fungus disease, black rust. Since then farmers have so effectively attacked it that it has become very scarce.

While dealing with the origins of the various species, there is one group of very valuable and colourful berberis that came into being as the result of a crossing between *B. aggregata* and *B. wilsoniae* that was made in the Royal Horticultural Society's gardens at Wisley. It produced a hybrid, *B. × carminea*, which in turn has given rise to a number of clones, several of which will be described later. These cultivars are categorized as the Carminea group.

Apart from the wide height range, berberis also come in a range of shapes – rounded, pyramidal, domed, compact, prostrate – all of which are valuable for giving interest and variation in a garden. Similarly, they display between them a number of different habits, such as elegant, arching branches (often weighed down in autumn under enormous crops of berries), drooping branches, or upright growth. Some have dense growth, while most of their shoots bear sharp spines. There are some berberis that are dwarf and wide-spreading, making good ground cover, such as *B. tsangpoensis* and, in particular, *B. sieboldii*, which suckers freely and spreads rapidly.

Berberis are excellent for shrub borders and mixed beds, where the changing colours of their foliage, flowers and berries give a beautiful display. Many of them make good hedges – either dwarf for interior divisions or taller for the boundary. For the former there is little better than *B. thunbergii* Atropurpurea Nana. While excellent subjects for higher hedges are *B. Buccaneer, B. darwinii, B. julianiae, B. stenophylla* (which makes a tough, dog-proof hedge), and *B. verruculosa*.

Cultivation

It is doubtful whether there is any race of plants more tolerant of their environment than berberis. The evergreens flourish in sun and light shade, but to get the fullest development of the autumn tints and vivid berries, the deciduous ones are better in the sun. They are happy in industrial areas and town gardens. Some, particularly *B. Buccaneer, B. darwinii, B. × ottawensis* Superba and *B. × stenophylla* thrive beside the sea, even if there is some exposure.

Berberis grow easily and are not fussy about soil. All of them grow in clay, providing it is not so heavy that it becomes waterlogged. In such a case, take steps to improve the drainage. They will grow well in dry, acid soil and, equally, with no objection in a shallow topsoil over chalk, which will be alkaline in reaction. Their only real dislike is permanently damp soil, which would have to be drained for them. Usually this defect can be corrected by digging a trench across the ground, partially filling it with rubble and finally filling it up with some of the excavated topsoil. If this action fails, then a more drastic scheme of drainage will have to be introduced.

The deciduous species and their cultivars are best planted any time in the winter from late

Left: Berberis thunbergii *Harlequin forms a rounded and compact deciduous shrub*
Below left: Berberis darwinii *is chiefly grown for its outstanding display of abundantly-borne spring flowers*
Below: Berberis darwinii *fruiting in autumn*

autumn to mid spring (October–March), when the weather is mild and the ground not excessively wet. The evergreens should be planted either in mid or late autumn (September or October) or else from early to late spring (February–April) so that the risk of exposing them to too much severe weather is lessened. Container-grown plants, of course, can be planted at any time.

Planting distances

To get an idea of how far apart shrubs should be planted, check on the ultimate spread of each (usually from a nurseryman's catalogue). The distance that two shrubs should be planted apart can be calculated by adding their two spreads together and dividing by two.

Dig a hole large enough in diameter to allow the roots of the shrub to be spread out in it, after cutting away any extra long or broken roots. To determine its depth, examine the stem of the new shrub for a mark or stain a few centimetres above the point where the roots start to spread out. This is where the soil reached to when the shrub was growing in the nursery. Make the hole to such a depth that when the roots are spread out, this mark will once again be just at the soil surface.

Careful planting makes a lot of difference to the well-being of a shrub. When the hole is dug, work some garden compost or manure into the soil at its bottom and put in the shrub, spreading out its roots. Mix more compost or manure with some of the excavated soil and cover the roots. Gently move the plant up and down a little to remove any air pockets that might have been formed and gently firm in the soil with your heel. Put in a second layer of soil, tread that in, and then fill the hole with the remaining soil. Level the surface, but do not tread the last layer of soil down.

The method of planting each shrub for a hedge is exactly the same. In order to form a good solid hedge, the planting distance between shrubs should be 45–60cm (18–24 in). The most effective-sized plants to use for this purpose are 30–38cm (12–15 in) high. After planting, give the plants about a fortnight to settle down and then prune each shrub back by about a quarter. This will encourage them to make really bushy growth and quickly produce a solid base to the hedge.

Fortunately most berberis need very little attention in order to flourish.

About 14 days after planting check that the wind has not made them loose in the soil. If it has, tread them in firmly again. (This attention should be given to *all* shrubs at the end of each winter, because frost, wind, snow and rain are likely to loosen them in the ground.)

Hoe regularly round the shrubs in order to eliminate the weeds. In dry weather particularly, berberis must be kept well watered. Give each one about 4 lit (1 gal) of water once a week during dry weather. While the soil is still moist give it a mulch with an 8cm (3 in) layer of garden compost, farmyard manure, damp peat or spent hops. A spray with cold water in the evening is also a help, particularly for the evergreens.

Berberis need no regular pruning. It is beneficial, however, periodically to remove old branches by cutting them down to the ground or a healthy bud. This encourages the growth of new wood from the base. All cutting back should, in any case, be directed towards keeping the bush an attractive shape by shortening any lengthy, untidy shoots and to maintaining it at a size appropriate to the space allotted to it. Deciduous varieties should be pruned in early spring (February), while evergreens should be cut back soon after flowering.

Trim hedges annually to keep them in shape: evergreens after flowering, deciduous ones in early or mid autumn (August or September).

Propagation

Although all species can be readily raised from seed, the resulting plants show considerable variation as berberis hybridize freely and hybrids do not come true from seed. In consequence it is more satisfactory to propagate them by rooting cuttings or layering. Some species like *B. sieboldii* that sucker freely can be reproduced by cutting off rooted suckers and replanting them where they are to grow, preferably between late autumn and mid spring (October–March).

To raise new plants from cuttings, take heel cuttings 8–10cm (3–4 in) long from lateral shoots in early or mid autumn (August–September). Plant them in a cold frame in an equal mixture of peat and sand. The following spring plant them out in a nursery bed, where they should be allowed to remain for one or two years before being transplanted to their final positions. Often cuttings of evergreen berberis are better if they are initially rooted in small pots of J.I. No 2 and then plunged in the soil outdoors, from which position they can be planted out.

The alternative method of propagating is by layering which consists of selecting a low-growing, non-flowering, flexible shoot that can be pulled down to the ground. Make an incision behind a bud at the point where it touches the ground, bury this point in the soil, firming it well in and holding the tip upwards. Fix the bend in position by means of a stone and hold the tip vertically by tying it to a stake. A shoot should be layered in mid autumn–early winter (September–November). In about a year's time, roots will form and the shoot can be severed at a point close to the root on the nearside and planted out.

Pests and diseases

Berberis are fairly free from pests, nor are they very prone to disease, but they are sometimes attacked by honey fungus, which can be detected by the presence of honey-coloured toadstools in the vicinity and by digging the surrounding soil and finding long black threads like bootlaces. The latter give this fungus its popular name of 'bootlace fungus'. If a plant is badly affected, dig it up and burn it.

Right: Berberis aggregata *heavily laden with coral-red berries; this shrub originated in W. China*

Some varieties to choose

As can be appreciated with such a large plant family as that of the berberis, only a small number of them are readily available. The first figure given under each variety description is the ultimate height and the second figure the ultimate spread of the plant.

EVERGREEN

B. candidula	Dome-shaped shrub with dark green leaves with silvery white beneath. Bright yellow flowers, blue-black berries. 60 × 60cm (2 × 2 ft).
B. verruculosa	Compact, slow-growing shrub with dark leaves, white underneath, golden-yellow flowers and black berries. 1·2 × 1·2m (4 × 4 ft).
B. hookeri	Compact shrub with leaves, glaucous underneath. Berries green at first, turning black. 1·5 × 1·5m (5 × 5 ft). Nana is a dwarf form. 75 × 75cm (2½ × 2½ ft).
B. gagnepainii	Erect branches and black berries. Good for hedges. 1·8 × 1·4m (6 × 4½ ft).
B. darwinii	Holly-like leaves, clusters of rich yellow or orange tinged with red blooms. followed by blue berries. 2·7 × 2·7m (9 × 9 ft). Prostrata is a useful dwarf form.
B. × stenophylla	Outstanding shrub with arching branches laded with golden flowers in spring, followed by somewhat sparsely-produced purple berries. 2·7 × 3·4m (9 × 11 ft).
B. linearifolia	Erect shrub with rich orange-red blooms, followed by black berries with a white bloom. 3 × 1m (10 × 3½ ft). Orange King is an outstanding form. 1·8 × 1·2m (6 × 4 ft).

DECIDUOUS

B. wilsoniae	Dense, mound-forming shrub with sea-green leaves, giving autumn tints and coral-red berries. 90 × 90cm (3 × 3 ft).
B. sieboldii	Compact, suckering shrub with bright green leaves, borne on red stems, turning rich carmine in autumn. Yellow flowers and red berries. 1 × 1m (3½ × 3½ ft).
B. thunbergii	Compact bush with brilliant autumn foliage and bright red berries. 1·2 × 1·8m (4 × 6 ft). Atropurpurea has reddish-purple leaves that become more intense in autumn. Atropurpurea Nana is a charming dwarf form of the last named. 38 × 38cm (15 × 15 in). Erecta is an upright-growing version. 1·5m × 45cm (5 × 1½ ft).
B. aggregata	Dense shrub with yellow flowers in late summer (July) with red and orange leaves and coral-red berries in autumn. 1·5 × 1·5m (5 × 5 ft).
B. buxifolia	Dark green leaves, grey underneath, yellow flowers, purple-black berries. 1·8 × 1·8m (6 × 6 ft). Nana is a dwarf variety. 45 × 45cm (1½ × 1½ ft).
B. dictyophylla	Leaves, white beneath, are carried on white bloom-covered red stems and turn red in autumn. Yellow flowers are followed by large red berries. 2 × 1m (7 × 3½ ft).

CARMINEA GROUP

B. Buccaneer	Erect-growing shrub with large, deep red berries. 1·2 × 1·2m (4 × 4 ft).
B. Pirate King	Dense-growing bush with fiery orange berries. 1·8 × 1·2m (6 × 4 ft).

BUDDLEIA

Type	deciduous, semi-evergreen and evergreen flowering shrubs, hardy and half-hardy, with a few greenhouse varieties
Family	LOGANIACEAE
Flowering season	mainly between early summer and mid autumn (May and September)
Planting date	late autumn–early winter (October–November), or mid–late spring (March–April); from containers at any time
Mature size/shape	bushy, and rounded or upright; height 1–6m (3½ –20 ft), spread 1·5–5·5m (5–18 ft)

The buddleia genus is comprised of 100 species of deciduous, semi-evergreen and evergreen shrubs and small trees. *B. davidii* is not native to the British Isles, although found growing wild, particularly in the southern parts of Britain. The 'wild' plants are strays from cultivated gardens. Its habitat is China, from where many of the species cultivated in Western gardens originate. Of the rest, *B. asiatica* comes from the East Indies, *B. colvilei*, *B. crispa* and *B. tibetica* from the Himalayas and regions north of India. The more delicate species, *B. auriculata* and *B. salviifolia* come from southern Africa, and *B. madagascariensis* originates from Madagascar. *B. globosa* is a native of Chile and Peru. With the exception of *B. globosa* and *B. salviifolia* (that came to Britain in the 18th century), buddleia were mostly introduced during the 19th and 20th centuries. The name was given in honour of Adam Buddle, an English botanist of the late 17th century.

Some buddleia are of great value in the garden since they can tolerate almost any soil conditions, and also grow very well in hot sunshine. Many make decorative garden plants because of their profusion of flowers and long flowering span that stretches throughout summer into autumn. Some are completely hardy and easily grown, while others are half-hardy. Most of those commonly grown in gardens are deciduous, but species such as *B. globosa* and *B. asiatica* are semi-evergreen or evergreen. Generally, it seems that these varieties become less hardy in proportion to how evergreen they are. For instance, *B. colvilei*, which is tender as a young plant is semi-evergreen, and the greenhouse or conservatory species *B. madagascariensis* is evergreen.

Most of the popular species flower in summer and some continue into the autumn. *B. tibetica*,

Above: its long flowering period and fragrant blooms make B. davidii *one of the most popular buddleias grown today. Buddleias were named after the Reverend Adam Buddle (1660–1715), English botanist and vicar of Farmbridge, Essex*
Top left: Buddleia alternifolia *can grow to a height of 6m (20 ft) but is usually pruned back every year to maintain a compact, neat look*
Bottom left: the hardy, unusual B. × weyerana *is excellent for growing in exposed coastal areas*

with their strong growth and comparatively large leaves, make excellent screens, while some of the relatively tall-growing species (particularly the more delicate shrubs) are good as wall plants. Several, *B. alternifolia* and *B. colvilei* in particular, will grow into small trees. A much-valued quality of *B. davidii* is the attraction it has for bees and butterflies – giving rise to its common name of 'butterfly bush'.

Cultivation and propagation

The hardier species and their varieties grow in full sun in most gardens, but the half-hardy ones do better planted against a warm wall with a western aspect. Buddleia like good garden soil and will tolerate lime.

Plant them in late autumn and early winter (October and November), or mid to late spring (March to April), and from containers at any time. Determine the planting distance by adding the spreads of adjacent shrubs and dividing by two.

Dig a hole large enough to take the rootball comfortably, and of such a depth that the original soil mark on the main stem will be just on the surface. When the shrub is in position, cover the roots well with soil, firm in by treading, and finally fill the hole. Once planted, no special care is needed.

No regular pruning is needed, except to keep the vigorous shrubs neat and bushy – particularly *B. davidii* that can be pruned to about 8cm (3 in) from the old wood in mid spring (March). Prune those that flower on the previous year's wood, such as *B. globosa* and *B. alternifolia*, after the blooms fade.

For propagation, take heel cuttings from half-ripe, lateral shoots in late summer and early autumn (July and August), and insert them in compost in a cold frame. Plant out in their permanent growing quarters in late autumn (October) of the following year.

Buddleia are fairly free from pests and diseases.

Some varieties to choose

The following is a selection of some of the most popular buddleia grown today. The first figure given in the dimensions is the height and the second is the spread.

B. alternifolia

This species is the only one that does not have opposite leaves; instead, they are positioned alternately on either side of the shoots. Bears fragrant lilac flowers in mid summer (June). 6 × 5·5m (20 × 18 ft).

B. asiatica

An evergreen, tender shrub with scented white flowers appearing during the winter. 3 × 3m (10 × 10 ft).

B. colvilei

A half-hardy, semi-evergreen shrub, with rose-pink flowers borne on drooping terminal racemes 15cm (6 in) long, appearing in mid to late summer (June to July). *B.c.* Kewensis is a form with rose-red blooms. 4 × 2·5m (13 × 8 ft).

however, comes into bloom about mid or late spring (March or April). There are also several winter-flowering ones, particularly *B. asiatica* and *B. auriculata*, both needing protection when grown outside. The greenhouse species *B. madagascariensis* and *B. officinalis* also flower throughout the winter. The flower colour varies from white through violet and purple to red. Two notable exceptions to this are *B. globosa*, with orange-yellow globular blooms, and the hybrid *B. × weyerana* that has rather similar orange, ball-shaped heads just tinged with mauve. Quite a number are scented, particularly varieties of *B. davidii*, and *B. fallowiana*, and also the hybrids *B.* Lochinch and *B.* West Hill.

B. davidii and its cultivars will tolerate shallow soil on chalk and will also flourish in the polluted air of industrial towns.

Generally buddleia do not grow very big; among the largest is *B. alternifolia* that can have a height and spread of 6m (20 ft) after 20 years' growth. Perhaps the smallest is the comparatively new *B. davidii* Border Beauty, that, after 10 years, can have a height of 90cm (3 ft), after which it will hardly grow at all. Eventual size is not too important, however, because it is usual to prune back the more common species annually to a greater or lesser degree in order to maintain a neat and bushy appearance.

The more popular buddleia are grown in shrub and mixed borders because of their long flowering period. Some, such as *B. davidii* and its cultivars,

B. crispa (B. paniculata)

A smaller, half-hardy, deciduous bushy shrub with leaves covered with white 'felt' that gives a silvery appearance. Has fragrant, lilac-pink flowers with an orange eye, borne in 10cm (4 in) long, cylindrical panicles in late summer (July). 2·5 × 1·8m (8 × 6 ft).

B. davidii

A hardy, deciduous, vigorous, spreading shrub, commonly known as the butterfly bush, carrying fragrant, lilac-purple blooms in 38cm (15 in) long arching racemes from late summer to mid autumn (July to September). It has numerous cultivars, flowering at about the same period. 3 × 3m (10 × 10 ft).

B.d. Black Knight	Deep purple trusses of flowers.
B.d. Border Beauty	Crimson-purple flowers; a dwarf form of Royal Red. 90cm × 1·5m (3 × 5 ft).
B.d. Empire Blue	Violet-blue, with orange centres.
B.d. Fascination	Large, lilac-pink heads.
B.d. Fortune	Lilac with orange eye, borne in long cylindrical racemes.
B.d. Harlequin	The foliage is variegated creamy white, and the flowers are reddish purple. A small cultivar.
B.d. Mayford Purple	Deep purple blooms.
B.d. nanhoensis	Slender branched, with narrow leaves and mauve flowers. A small shrub with a height and spread of about 1·5m (6 ft).
B.d. Opera	Very large, blue-purple spikes; late-flowering.
B.d. Peace	A pure white variety.
B.d. Royal Red	Enormous red-purple panicles.
B.d. Salicifolia	A low-growing cultivar with willow-like, linear leaves and purple racemes.
B.d. White Cloud	Dense panicles of white flowers.
B.d. White Profusion	White blooms borne in large panicles.

B. fallowiana

Its stems and leaves have the appearance of being covered with white wool. Bears fragrant, pale lavender-blue flowers in panicles from late summer to mid autumn (July to September). Requires a sheltered site. An attractive cultivar is B.f. Alba that is creamy white with an orange eye. 2·5 × 1·8m (8 × 6 ft).

B. globosa (orange ball tree)

A fast-growing, erect shrub with almost evergreen leaves. The flowers are scented, spherical, and orange-yellow and appear in early summer (May). Will grow in exposed, coastal gardens. 4 × 3m (13 × 10 ft).

B. Lochinch

Has silvery grey leaves and dense conical panicles of scented, violet-blue flowers with orange centres, appearing between late summer and mid autumn (July and September). Has a compact habit. 1·5 × 1·5m (5 × 5 ft).

B. West Hill

A shrub with a spreading habit and long, arching stems. Its flowers are fragrant, pale lavender with orange centres, in curved panicles, appearing in early autumn (August). 2·5 × 3·5m (8 × 12 ft).

B. × weyerana

A hybrid of B. davidii and B. globosa, with ball-shaped heads similar to those of B. globosa, but often with a mauve tint. They appear during mid to late summer (June to July). An attractive cultivar is Golden Glow, flowering later than the species. 2·5 × 2·5m (8 × 8 ft).

Buddleia colvilei, originating from the Himalayas, is one of the more unusual species, and is tender when young, becoming half hardy as it matures. It does best if planted against a warm wall with a western aspect

CISTUS

Type	evergreen hardy and semi-hardy flowering shrubs
Family	CISTACEAE
Common name	rock rose or sun rose
Flowering season	mainly mid–late summer (June–July)
Planting date	cistus are always transplanted from containers, and can be planted at any time in good weather. The best time is late spring–early summer (April–May)
Mature size/shape	mainly rounded, bushy and compact, some low-growing, spreading and erect; height 45cm–2·4m (18 in–8 ft), spread 45cm–3m (18 in–10 ft)
Special use	useful for hot, dry positions where the soil is poor

Cistus are very useful as flowering shrubs for small modern gardens, and comprise about 20 species. They share their common names of rock rose and sun rose with the helianthemum, a member of the same family.

Many of the cistus found in present-day gardens are natural or hand-pollinated hybrids. The species originate mainly from around the Mediterranean. *C. ladaniferus*, for example, comes from south-western Europe and North Africa; *C. laurifolius* was found growing wild right across southern Europe to central Italy; and *C. parviflorus* comes from Italy and Greece. Greece is also the habitat of *C. × skanbergii*. One very distinct, tall-growing species, *C. symphitifolius*, with magenta blooms and golden anthers, originated in the Canary Islands. Although this was first introduced to British gardens in 1799, it can only be cultivated in the mildest districts in temperate countries. Other species that have been cultivated for an even longer time are *C. salviifolius*, introduced into Britain in 1550, *C. ladaniferus* (1629), and *C. populifolius* (1656).

Cistus blooms vary in size according to species and variety, and resemble single roses. They produce characteristic, saucer-shaped, papery flowers in profusion over a period from mid to late summer (June to July) and even later. Each bloom opens its petals in the morning and sheds them again by the evening. So many fresh buds are set that there is no break in the flowering period. The flowers come in many colours, including white, through pinks, to reddish purple. Often they are blotched or have bases in contrasting colours such as yellow, crimson and chocolate-brown. Some species and varieties have greyish leaves.

Cistus shrubs are all small and vary in size from the more low-growing and spreading types, such as *C. × lusitanicus* Decumbens, with a height of about 45cm (18 in), to *C. × cyprius*, with a maximum height of 2·4m (8 ft) after about 20 years' growth. Apart from the low-growing and

Plant cistus such as C. × purpureus (top). C. × aguilari (above) together in groups for best effect

215

C. ladaniferus *(above)*, C. salviifolius *(left)* and
C. × obtusifolius *(below)* are all somewhat tender
and should be grown in sheltered, sunny positions
against a wall or bank. The wide-spreading variety
C. × lusitanicus Decumbens *(below left)* is hardy,
but should also be given protection from frost

prostrate forms, there are a few, such as *C.* × *purpureus*, that grow erect. A large number of the other species are bushy, compact and round.

They grow extremely well in a sunny position and in poor, dry soil that can be either shallow over chalk, or dry and acid. They are very wind-tolerant, being quite happy in exposed gardens in coastal districts, and can resist the bad effects of polluted air in industrial towns. Frost, however, can damage them, and it is better to plant even the hardiest ones in a sheltered position and to give them protection during very severe weather. Some species are relatively tender and should only be planted outdoors in the mildest districts, though they have a chance of surviving against a warm, sheltered wall. Young plants resist frost better than older ones, so it is a good idea to make provision for replacements by propagating from cuttings whenever possible. The colourful flowers, set off by variously-hued foliage, make cistus especially useful for shrub and mixed borders, as well as banks and walls. To get the best effect, grow a number of them together in groups.

Cultivation

As cistus do not transplant well, it is usual to plant them from containers, at any time during the year when the weather is good. It is, however, best to plant them out during late spring and early summer (April and May), so that they become well established for the current growing season.

For planting distance, add together the ultimate spread of the plants that are to be adjacent and divide by two. Dig a hole about 4cm (1½ in) wider than the rootball, and deep enough so that the plant will be at the same depth in the bed as it was in the container. Remove the shrub from the container and, without breaking the rootball, gently pull out one or two root ends at the side and bottom. Place the rootball centrally in the hole, fill in with soil and gently firm in by treading carefully. Cistus need little care other than protection from very severe frosts. Little pruning is necessary, except to cut out diseased and frost-damaged shoots and any dead wood.

Propagation

Species can be propagated from seed. Hybrids will not come true from seed, and must be propagated from cuttings.

Take heel cuttings 10cm (4 in) long, of half-ripened, non-flowering shoots of hybrids and varieties during late summer and early autumn (July and August). Insert them in cutting compost in a propagator at 16°C (61°F). When they have rooted, transplant them individually to 8cm (3 in) pots. After overwintering in a cold frame, pot them on to 10cm (4 in) pots. After another winter in a cold frame, plant them in their permanent quarters in late spring (April).

Pests and diseases

Cistus are fortunately very healthy plants, little troubled with pests, and are also not particularly susceptible to diseases.

Some varieties to choose

The first figure under each item is the ultimate height, the second is spread.

C. × *aguilari*	Tender shrub of erect, bushy habit, with light green leaves and large white flowers, appearing during mid and late summer (June and July). 1·2 × 1·2m (4 × 4 ft).
C. × *a.* Maculatus	White-flowered variety that has a ring of crimson blotches at the base of each petal.
C. × *corbariensis*	Among the hardiest of the cistus, this forms a low-spreading, bushy shrub with dull green leaves that have wavy margins. Flowers are white, yellow at the base of each petal, and borne from early to mid summer (May to June). 90cm × 2·4m (3 × 8 ft).
C. × *cyprius*	Has olive-green leaves, sticky to touch, and clusters of white flowers with crimson-maroon blotches, in mid to late summer (June to July). 2·1 × 2·4m (7 × 8 ft).
C. Elma	Tender, sturdy, bushy shrub, with very large white blooms, appearing in mid and late summer (June and July). 1·5 × 1·8m (5 × 6 ft).
C. ladaniferus	Erect, tender shrub with white flowers that have bright yellow stamens and maroon blotches at the base, borne in early to mid summer (May to June). 1·8 × 1·2m (6 × 4 ft).
C. laurifolius	The hardiest species, with leathery, dark, glaucous-green leaves and white flowers with yellow centres, appearing in mid to late summer (June to July). 1·5m × 90cm (5 × 3 ft).
C. × *loretii*	A shrub of dwarf habit with large white flowers that have crimson basal blotches, appearing in mid to late summer (June to July). 60 × 90cm (2 × 3 ft).
C. × *lusitanicus*	Dwarf hybrid with dark green leaves and white flowers, blotched pink at the base, borne in mid to late summer (June to July). 45 × 45cm (18 × 18 in).
C. × *l.* Decumbens	Wide-spreading variety, with a maroon spot at the base of each petal and dark green, scented foliage. 45cm × 1·2m (18 in × 4 ft).
C. × *obtusifolius*	Rounded, dwarf, tender shrub. Flowers are white with yellow basal stain, and appear from mid summer to mid autumn (June to September). 60 × 90cm (2 × 3 ft).
C. palhinhae	Hardy, low-growing, compact species with sticky leaves and large white flowers, appearing in early to mid summer (May to June). 90 × 90cm (3 × 3 ft).
C. populifolius	Erect with poplar-like leaves and white flowers, yellow at the base, borne in mid summer (June). 1·8 × 1·5m (6 × 5 ft). *C. populifolius lasiocalyx* has larger flowers with inflated calyces. Very hardy.
C. × *pulverulentus*	Dwarf shrub with sage-green leaves and rose-red flowers appearing from early to late summer (May to July). 75cm × 1·2m (2½ × 4 ft).
C. × *purpureus*	Upright tender shrub with grey-green leaves and rose-to-purple blooms, dark maroon at the base, appearing from early to late summer (May to July). 1·5 × 1·2m (5 × 4 ft).
C. salviifolius	A low, tender shrub with sage-like leaves and white flowers, yellow at the base, borne in mid summer (June). 45 × 45cm (18 × 18 in).
C. Silver Pink	Very hardy shrub with clusters of silvery pink flowers in mid to late summer (June to July). 75 × 75cm (2½ × 2½ ft).
C. × *skanbergii*	Tender, upright shrub with grey-green leaves and clear pink blossoms, borne during mid and late summer (June and July). 1·2 × 1·2m (4 × 4 ft).

CLEMATIS MONTANA

Type	deciduous, woody climber
Family	RANUNCULACEAE
Flowering season	early summer to early autumn (May to August)
Planting date	late autumn to early summer (October to May) in mild weather
Mature size	up to 12m (40 ft)

Clematis montana is an extremely vigorous, deciduous climber, easily capable of reaching 7m (23 ft) and can, on occasion, extend even higher if trained into large trees. It ascends by means of its twisting leaf stalk that surrounds twigs in the wild. In cultivation, if you want to grow it up a wall, it is best to provide a trellis or plastic netting.

The plant is native to the Himalayas and was brought into cultivation in 1831 by that enterprising traveller Lady Amherst. When E. H. Wilson visited Szechwan, a province of China, in 1900, he sent back seed of the variety *C. m. rubens*. This has purplish petal-like sepals, known as 'tepals', and flowers a little later than the type. In addition to the purplish flowers, its young stems also have a purple colour and the young leaves have a purple-bronzy tinge. The leaves are somewhat downy while the Indian plants are more or less glabrous, or smooth. Wilson also sent back the variety *C. m. wilsonii* that bears smaller white flowers that do not open before late summer (end of June or early July). There are one or two named forms as well: Tetrarose has pink flowers up to 8cm (3 in) across; Alexander, with white flowers, and Elizabeth, with pink flowers, are also fragrant.

The plant bears leaves made up of three leaflets; these are lance-shaped, slightly lobed and each about 5cm (2 in) long, although there is some variation in their size. The flowers arise from the leaf axils of the previous year's growth and come in clusters of about six; each flower is on a stalk that may be 10cm (4 in) long and is made up of four white tepals. The flowers each measure about 5cm (2 in) across, produce very freely and open in early summer (May).

The plant is easy to cultivate and thrives in any soil, flowering well even if trained against a north-facing wall. Like all clematis, it is very intolerant of root disturbance, so you should only purchase pot-grown specimens. If possible, the roots and the base of the stem should be kept in the shade. The plant looks very effective if trained up into a tree and allowed to ramble at will. In some positions, its vigour may be excessive, but you can prune it hard each summer as soon as flowering is

Left: Clematis montana rubens, *one of the best forms of this vigorous grower*
Top: C. montana *produces its mass of flowers in early summer (May)*
Above: brought into cultivation at the same time as C.m. rubens, C.m. wilsonii *bears its smaller flowers towards late summer (July)*

over and remove all flowered shoots. *Clematis chrysocoma*, which looks much like *C. montana*, with rather large pink flowers and young leaves covered with yellow down, is far less vigorous, although equally attractive; it can be recommended as an alternative in cases where *C. montana* might prove too vigorous.

Propagation by cuttings is easy, but slightly different from the cuttings of most woody plants. These are generally finished just below the node, that is to say where the leaf joins the stem. Clematis cuttings on the other hand are called inter-nodal and are cut half-way between two leaves. Cuttings should be taken in late summer (late June or early July) and the stem should be firm, although not woody. It is probably sufficient to allow only one full-grown leaf to each cutting and it is not necessary to have a growing point on your cutting; as soon as the cutting is well rooted, a shoot will arise from the leaf axil and they should then be potted separately in 8cm (3 in) pots either in a soilless mixture or in J.I. No 1, and subsequently potted on into a 13cm (5 in) pot. Once this pot is filled with roots, the plant can be placed in its final position.

CORNUS

Type	hardy, mainly deciduous, flowering and fruiting small tree, shrub, and herbaceous perennial
Common name	dogwood, cornel
Family	CORNACEAE
Flowering season	mainly between early and late summer (May to July); a few species bloom in autumn and winter
Planting date	tree species – late autumn to early winter (October to November); shrubs for bark and foliage colour – mid to late spring (March to April)
Mature size/shape	ranging from 15cm high × 60cm wide (6 × 24 in), to 6m high × 6m wide (20 × 20 ft); mainly rounded, a few prostrate, spreading and upright

Above: Cornus florida rubra *with showy, rose-pink bracts in early summer although the loveliest of flowering trees, it can be injured by a late frost*

Cornus forms a genus of about 40 species. They are mainly deciduous (a small number are evergreen) and include small trees, shrubs and herbaceous perennials, belonging to the plant family CORNACEAE. However, recently some authorities have divided this genus into several families, in accordance with certain botanical differences. These changes do not appear to have infiltrated current nurserymen's catalogues, so it is more practical to deal with the subject on the old-fashioned basis.

The meaning of the Latin *cornus* is 'horned' and the genus derives this name from the fact that its species have wood of hard, firm texture. At one time it was frequently used for making small objects that also needed to be strong. In particular, it was used for making the now almost-extinct wooden meat skewers.

Although cornus are widespread in origin, their habitat is confined to the northern hemisphere. Various species are indigenous to Siberia, Manchuria, China, Japan, Korea and North America, and at least one is native to the British Isles – the common dogwood, *C. sanguinea*. Of the cornus introduced into Western gardens, *C. mas* is probably the earliest, because it is described authoritatively as 'long cultivated'. *C. stolonifera* first reached the Western world in 1656, and *C. amomum* in 1683, followed by *C. alba*, *C. alternifolia*, *C. canadensis*, *C. florida*, *C. racemosa* and *C. rugosa*, all of which came during the 18th century. Further introductions continued periodically throughout the 19th century.

Cornus is a genus of many parts: most of the species produce flowers during the summer months, although exceptions are *Cornus oblonga*, that flowers in autumn, *C. chinensis* (not to be confused with *C. kousa chinensis*), *C. mas* and *C. officinalis*, whose clusters of yellow blooms enliven their naked twigs during the winter, and the hybrid of *C. florida* and *C. nuttallii*, *C.* Eddie's White Wonder, that has large white flowers during spring. It should, however, be noted that in many cases the flowers of cornus are relatively inconspicuous, although they become prominent because they are subtended by coloured bracts. The flowers themselves are normally white, yellow, or yellow-green, and are borne on the last season's growth.

In some cases, the blossom is followed later by fruit. Examples include *C. capitata* and *C. kousa*, with their red, strawberry-like fruits; *C. mas*, with bright fruits like cherries; *C. controversa* with black fruit; *C. rugosa* and *C. amomum*, both of which have blue fruits, and *C. stolonifera* with white ones. The more common cornus with evergreen leaves are *C. capitata* and *C. oblonga*. Among the deciduous plants, there are some that have yellow foliage, of which *C. alba* Aurea and *C. mas* Aurea are particularly worth mentioning.

Quite a number have variegated leaves, but perhaps the loveliest is *C. alternifolia* Argentea, regarded by some as one of the best of the silver variegated shrubs. Its parent, *C. alternifolia*, gives the richest autumn tints; others that have this quality are *C. alba*, *C. baileyi*, *C. controversa* – the foliage of which turns purple-red – *C. florida* and *C. kousa*, with its rich bronze and crimson leaves. Still the cavalcade of beauty does not end, as we have yet to take account of those cornus that brighten beds during winter with their brilliant-coloured bark, such as *C. alba*, *C. baileyi*, *C. stolonifera* and the Westonbirt dogwood, *C. alba* Sibirica – all of them red – and *C. stolonifera* Flaviramea that is yellow or olive-green. To add to this, *C. officinalis* has attractive peeling bark.

Cornus shrubs are rounded, sometimes erect-growing or spreading in habit. After about 20 years, they reach 2·5–6m (8–20 ft) high, and some 2–6m (6–20 ft) in spread. An exception is *C. canadensis*, strictly a herbaceous perennial, but often listed among the shrubs; this is prostrate and has a height of 15cm (6 in) and a spread of 60cm (2 ft).

They are as tolerant of various environments as they are versatile in the qualities they possess. All cornus will flourish in clay. A chalky subsoil is tolerated by *C. mas*, while both *C. alba* and *C. stolonifera* and their cultivars, together with *C. baileyi*, will thrive on a damp site. Both *C. alba* and *C. stolonifera* and all their cultivars are also suitable for planting in industrial towns and, together with *C. baileyi*, they will withstand cold and exposure.

With all their virtues, it is evident that cornus are eminently suited to shrub and mixed borders although some, such as *C. kousa chinensis*, with their rich autumn foliage and colourful fruits might be effectively grown as a specimen in the lawn. Owners of comparatively small gardens should not be deterred from growing cornus because of their eventual size, especially those with coloured bark; it is the practice to cut these back to within a few centimetres of the ground in spring.

In addition, the prostrate *C. canadensis*, that also tolerates deep shade, is a charming and most effective ground cover plant.

Cultivation

It is important to position tree species in a sunny situation: this helps to mature their wood. Exceptions are those species grown for their colourful bark and foliage; these require to be in moist soil, either in sun or semi-shade. Cornus are happy in any good garden soil. *C. mas* and its cultivars will grow in chalky soil; but in the case of other more popular cornus, this should be avoided.

Plant the tree species in late autumn or early winter (October or November); however, those strong-growing bushy shrubs grown for the colour of their bark and foliage are best planted in mid or late spring (March or April). Container-grown plants may be planted any time, provided the ground is wet and is kept so after planting.

Right: silver variegated Cornus alternifolia *Argentea*
Below: Cornus nuttallii *flowering in early summer; named after the English botanist Thomas Nuttall in 1835*
Overleaf, left: Cornus kousa chinensis *bearing strawberry-like fruits; this Chinese type is larger and superior to its Japanese counterpart*
Overleaf, right: Cornus canadensis *prefers a peaty or woodland soil; strictly a herbaceous perennial but usually classified as a shrub*

Planting distance is determined in the usual way by halving the sum of the ultimate spreads of plants that are to grow in juxtaposition.

Before planting, dig a hole that is wide enough to take the rootball without disturbing it too much and that allows the roots to spread out after planting. It should be deep enough so that, after planting, the soil line indicating the level at which it was previously planted is level with the soil surface. If you need to stake it, put a stake into the soil between the loose roots without damaging them. Replace the soil and firm it by gentle treading.

Normally cornus need little attention, except those grown for bark or foliage colour that should be watered well during dry spells. Generally, cornus only need pruning to control their shape and size. Cut to the ground in late spring (April) those that you want to grow for their bark.

Propagation

Species may be raised from seed taken in early and mid autumn (August and September). Sow them in seed compost and then place them in a cold frame. When large enough, pot them up and then transplant into a nursery bed later. They should grow here for two or three years before being planted out; sometimes seeds will take 18 months to germinate.

Cornus may also be raised from 10cm (4 in) long, half-ripe cuttings taken in late summer or early autumn (July or August). They are placed in growing compost and put in a propagator. After rooting, plant them in 8cm (3 in) pots in potting compost and leave to overwinter in a cold frame; then place them in a nursery bed and plant them out two or three years later.

Suckers can be planted in early winter (November). Cornus may also be propagated by layering long shoots in mid autumn (September) and severing them a year or two later.

Some varieties to choose

In the following selections, the dimensions given under species and variety descriptions refer to ultimate height and spread respectively.

C. alba (red-barked dogwood)	Suckering foliage plant of upright habit with red stems in winter; often autumn tints. Inconspicuous flowers followed by white or blue-tinged fruits. 3 × 3m (10 × 10 ft).
C. a. Elegantissima	Has white-margined and mottled leaves.
C. a. Sibirica	Has brilliant crimson shoots in winter.
C. a. Spaethii	A good golden-variegated form.
C. alternifolia Argentea	Very beautiful, silver-variegated foliage; spreading. 3 × 4·5m (10 × 15 ft).
C. canadensis (creeping dogwood)	Herbaceous perennial with star-like, white flowers in mid summer (June), followed by vivid red fruits. Excellent ground cover. 10 × 60cm (4 × 24 in).
C. controversa	Has white flowers during mid and late summer (June and July). Blue-black berries. 4·5 × 4·5m (15 × 15 ft).
C. florida rubra	Leaves turn orange and scarlet in autumn. Inconspicuous flowers subtended by rosy pink bracts in early summer (May). 4 × 6m (12 × 20 ft)
C. kousa	Elegant shrub bearing insignificant purple-green flowers with white bracts in mid summer (June); strawberry-like fruits ripening in mid autumn (September). Autumn tints. 3 × 3m (10 × 10 ft).
C. k. chinensis	Has large bracts and crimson autumn foliage.
C. mas (cornelian cherry)	Large shrub producing yellow flowers in early spring (February). Red edible fruits. Autumn colours. 3 × 2·5m (10 × 8 ft).
C. m. Aurea	Has yellow leaves.
C. m. Elegantissima	Yellow and pink variegated foliage.
C. nuttallii	A handsome species with large white, flushed pink bracts in early summer (May). Strawberry-like fruits. Yellow autumn foliage. Needs a warm position. 5·5 × 3m (8 × 10 ft).
C. stolonifera	Suckering shrub with dark red winter stems and white fruits. 2·5 × 2·7m (8 × 9 ft).
C. s. Flaviramea	Has yellow or olive-green winter shoots.

COTONEASTER

Type	evergreen and deciduous flowering and fruiting shrubs
Family	ROSACEAE
Flowering season	mid summer (June)
Fruiting season	early autumn to late winter (August–January)
Planting date	late autumn to early spring (October–February); from containers, anytime
Mature size/shape	prostrate to 7m (23 ft); spreading, round or erect shrub

The cotoneaster genus contains a little over 50 species of shrubs all of which – with the exception of a comparatively few rarities – are obtainable without much difficulty. Among them are some of the most indispensable of hardy ornamental shrubs and even small trees. There is a cotoneaster for almost every site in the garden no matter what its environment. Large, medium, small and prostrate ones are available, evergreens and semi-evergreens, and varieties suitable for a warm, sunny position or a cold exposed garden, be it inland or on the coast. In tree form as standards and half-standards they are invaluable because they are almost the only evergreens available at this size.

Although they are an extensive and diverse race, most cotoneasters nevertheless have a strong family likeness. They all have hawthorn-like white or pinkish flowers that are either flattened or cupped in shape and often carried in clusters, mainly in mid summer (June). These blossoms are most attractive to bees, although almost insignificant compared with what, in most cases, follows them. The foliage often acquires the most beautiful rich autumnal colourings and, most striking of all, the branches become laden with attractively-coloured berries of different sizes and shapes, which can be scarlet, orange-red, purplish-red, yellow, pink-tinged yellow, crimson or black. It is in these lovely berries that the real glory of cotoneasters is to be found.

With some exceptions, the native habitat of these various species is the Far East – mainly China – while a few hail from places farther to the west – the Himalayas, Assam, Tibet, Burma, East Turkestan and Afghanistan. There are one or two species that are thought to have originated in areas still farther to the west: *Cotoneaster orbicularis* from the Sinai Peninsular and *C. lucidus* from the Altai Mountains in Mongolia – which would indeed be a testimony to its hardiness. Among the earliest to be raised successfully in Britain was *C. tomentosus*, now a very rare shrub indeed; it was taken from the European Alps in 1759.

C. simonsii, *C. horizontalis* and *C. microphyllus* can be found growing wild in the British countryside, but these are probably escapees from cultivated gardens, through birds eating the seeds and later spreading them in their droppings. There is, however, one species – *C. integerrimus* – which seems to be native to Britain. It was found growing wild on Great Orme Head above Llandudno in North Wales in 1783, but there are records of it growing in gardens in the 17th century, so even this might be a stray.

Understandably, there have been numbers of cultivars raised in Britain, but two of particular interest are *C.* St Monica, which was found in a convent garden in Bristol, and *C. splendens* Sabrina, which was raised in a garden in Somerset.

Apart from their attraction in any garden, the species have characteristics and variations that make them most valuable. They range in height from about 5–8cm (2–3 in) above the ground up to an ultimate height of about 4–5m (15 ft), with a few small trees reaching 6m (20 ft) tall. Among them there is a wide range of habits, such as prostrate, spreading, erect, arching, pendulous

Above: Cotoneaster microphyllus, *a low-growing evergreen that originated from the Himalayas, in flower during early summer* *Overleaf:* C. × Hybridus Pendulus, a low-growing shrub, grafted onto a stem to make a small, weeping tree

and so on, that make them indispensable in any planting scheme. The trailing forms make excellent ground cover and also help to suppress the growth of weeds. Some species and their cultivars, particularly the evergreens and semi-evergreens, are excellent for hedge-making and with their rich autumn tints and colourful berries they give a most pleasing ornamental effect on the boundary of the plot or as a division between two sections of the garden. Probably they are best of all used in a shrub or mixed border where their colour will prolong some of the fading glory of the summer.

Several species and hybrids, for instance *C. buxifolius vellaeus, C. franchetii, C. horizontalis, C. lacteus, C. salicifolius* Autumn Fire, *C. salicifolius rugosus* and *C. simonsii*, make excellent wall plants. Because of their tolerance of a wide range of conditions, the aspect of the wall does not disturb them at all; they are therefore particularly valuable for growing against a north wall.

Cultivation
On the whole, cotoneasters are so robust and undemanding that they will survive and flourish in almost any soil and conditions. Most are tolerant to the environment of an industrial area and by the same token they all grow well in town gardens, where the smaller ones are especially acceptable because of space restrictions. There are some, such as *C. simonsii*, that can be planted in full shade and still prosper. On the other hand, all of them will grow well in both partial shade and sun. Many of these most accommodating shrubs and trees also grow well in coastal areas, where they will stand up to a certain amount of exposure.

As far as their soil requirements are concerned, any planting guide will tell you that cotoneasters will grow well in 'ordinary' garden soil. But if your soil is out of the ordinary, you may need a little more guidance.

All species will grow in clay soil providing it is well drained and there is no possibility of it becoming waterlogged. As this is the risk with very heavy clay, it is important to prepare such soil very thoroughly before planting this shrub. Dig it well, to a depth of one spit, removing the topsoil so that the subsoil can be broken up to ensure good drainage. Mix the excavated topsoil with sand or grit to lighten it and help the free passage of water through it, and then replace it. This should stop water remaining on the surface in wet weather.

All species are quite happy in dry acid soils. They will flourish in a shallow soil covering a chalky subsoil, which will almost certainly be alkaline in reaction. There is just one place where a cotoneaster should not be planted, and this is on a damp site: the best course is to choose some other plant that likes the conditions. The alternative (particularly as many other choice plants also dislike a permanently damp soil) is to drain the land either by digging a trench across the site, almost filling it with rubble and replacing the topsoil, or, if the condition is very serious, you may have to resort to a more elaborate scheme involving laying drainage tiles.

Above left and above:
evergreen C. conspicuus
Decorus in flower and
fruit

When and how to plant

It is only natural that the space to be allowed between cotoneasters and their neighbouring shrubs in a border depends upon the ultimate size they are likely to reach in maturity. The correct planting distance can be calculated by adding the spans of two shrubs that are to be planted alongside each other and dividing the sum by two.

Soak the rootball well before planting. Dig a hole wide enough to allow the roots to be well spread out, and of such a depth that the previous soil level will be at the surface of the soil in the new quarters. Mix a little garden compost or manure into the soil at the bottom of the hole and put the plant in position. Place a layer of similarly-enriched soil over the roots and tread it firmly in with your heel. Then add a further layer of soil, tread it in and finally fill up the hole, levelling off the soil surface.

For planting as a hedge *C. franchetii, C. frigidus, C. henryanus, C. lacteus, C. simonsii, C. wardii* and *C. × watereri* all make excellent berried hedges. They are planted as described above for bushes in shrubberies, the first two at 45cm (18 in) and the remainder at 60–90cm (2–3 ft) apart respectively.

For use as wall plants, those suitable should be planted about 40cm (15 in) in front of the wall and trained back to it, because very often the soil at the base of a wall keeps excessively dry.

Generally speaking cotoneasters need little attention, but do keep the soil around them free from weeds with regular hoeing. In dry weather they appreciate being watered and mulched with an 8cm (3 in) layer of garden compost, manure or damp peat. The evergreens particularly like being sprayed with water during the evening.

No regular pruning is necessary. When the large-growing shrubs have outgrown their allotted space they can be pruned back: evergreens in late spring (April) and deciduous ones in early spring (February). Trim back evergreen hedges as necessary immediately after flowering by cutting out the more vigorous shoots and side growths. Prune back the current season's shoots to the berry cluster nearest to the tip of the branch. Hedges composed of deciduous cotoneasters should be trimmed in early or mid autumn (August or September).

Propagation

Fruiting cotoneasters can be propagated by removing the seeds from the ripe berries in autumn and sowing them in pans of J.I. seed compost or a soilless seed compost and placing them in a cold frame. They normally take about 18 months to germinate. After pricking out the seedlings, first into trays or pots and then into a nursery bed, allow them to grow on for 2–3 years before transplanting them.

Remember that only seeds from species will come true; cultivars must be propagated by cuttings. Take heel cuttings of ripe evergreen shoots, about 10cm (4 in) long, in early or mid autumn (August or September), and of semi-mature deciduous shrubs in late summer or early autumn (July or August). Plant them out in a nursery bed in the following late spring or early summer (April or May) and then leave them for 2–3 years before planting out in their final positions.

An alternative method is to layer shoots in late autumn or early winter (October or November) that will root within a year.

Pests and diseases

Apart from being infested with greenfly and scale insects in the summer, cotoneasters are fairly free from pests. Possibly the most frustrating are birds, that steal their berries in wintertime. Being members of the ROSACEAE family, cotoneasters are subject to possible infection with fireblight, which blackens the flowers and kills the branches. Other diseases that might possibly affect them are honey fungus disease and silverleaf.

Above and below: tall-growing evergreens
C. Exburiensis and C. Rothschildianus, both
are from the Watereri group

Some varieties to choose

Of the total number of species of fruiting cotoneasters and their varieties that exist, a very large proportion are readily obtainable from good nurseries, but the less common ones may be difficult to find in garden centres. The following list will help you to choose the best cotoneasters and their cultivars for your purpose. Many of these shrubs have fruits in varying shades of red, and any exceptions are indicated. Of the dimensions given, the first is the ultimate height, the second the ultimate spread.

PROSTRATE OR LOW-GROWING (EVERGREEN)

C. congestus	Attractive, densely-foliaged shrub, which forms mounds of small bluish-green leaves; red berries. 30cm × 2·7m (12 in × 9 ft).
C. dammeri	Very prostrate, trailing shrub, ideal for covering banks and ground cover; sealing-wax red berries. 5cm × 1·8m (2 in × 6 ft).
C. Donald Gem	Low, rounded, spreading bush with greyish leaves and long-lasting berries. 23cm × 1·5m (9 in × 5 ft).
C. microphyllus	Dwarf glossy-foliaged, spreading shrub; large, round scarlet berries. 5cm × 2·4m (2 in × 8 ft).
C. microphyllus cochleatus	Charming, slow-growing, creeping shrub with bright green leaves and scarlet berries. 2·5cm × 1·8m (1 in × 6 ft).
C. salicifolius Autumn Fire	Rather taller-growing, pendulous semi-evergreen shrub. Produces abundant quantities of bright orange-red berries. 30cm × 3·6m (12 in × 12 ft).
C. salicifolius Repens	Prostrate plant with very narrow leaves and small red berries, 30cm × 2·7m (12 in × 9 ft).
C. Skogholm	Vigorous, trailing hybrid with rather dark foliage and coral-red berries. 25cm × 1·8m (9 in × 6 ft).

PROSTRATE OR LOW-GROWING (DECIDUOUS)

C. adpressus	Dwarf, wide-spreading shrub, excellent for the rockery; bright red berries. Leaves turn scarlet in autumn. 40cm × 1·5m (15 in × 5 ft).
C. horizontalis Variegatus	Small, cream variegated leaves becoming suffused with red in autumn; red berries. 45cm × 1·8m (18 in × 6 ft).

MEDIUM-GROWING (EVERGREEN)

C. buxifolius vellaeus	Low, arching, spreading habit, with small leaves of frosted grey; bright red berries. 1·2 × 3m (4 × 10 ft).
C. conspicuus Decorus	Somewhat low-growing shrub, good for covering banks. Profuse red berries. 75cm × 2·7m (2½ × 9 ft).
C. Hybridus Pendulus	Prostrate, moderately low shrub; red berries. When grafted to a tall stem makes a beautiful weeping tree. 60cm × 3·6m (2 × 12 ft).

MEDIUM-GROWING (DECIDUOUS)

C. adpressus praecox	Vigorous, arching shrub with extra large, orange berries and brilliant autumn tints. 90cm × 1·8m (3 × 6 ft).
C. horizontalis	Branches in herringbone pattern. With its red berries and autumn colour it is invaluable for north- and east-facing walls and banks. 60cm × 3m (2 × 10 ft).

TALL-GROWING (EVERGREEN) — RED BERRIES

C. Aldenhamemsis (Watereri group)	Wide-spreading shrub with long, fan-like branches that bear bright red berries. 3·6 × 4·6m (12 × 15 ft).
C. Cornubia (Watereri group)	Vigorous, semi-evergreen. Its large red berries are so profuse that they weigh down its branches. 4·6 × 3·6m (15 × 12 ft).

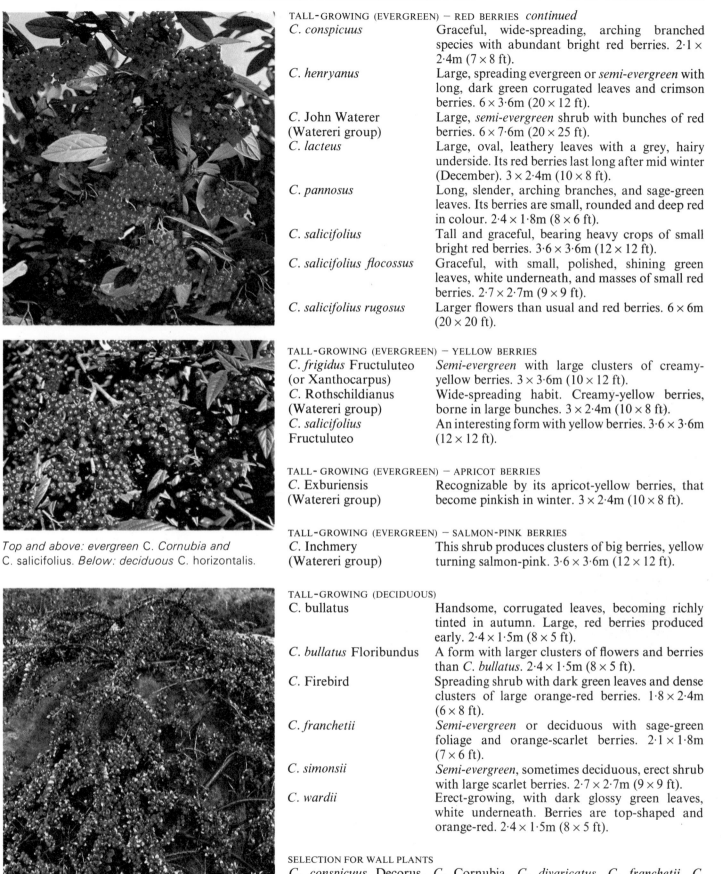

Top and above: evergreen C. Cornubia *and*
C. salicifolius. *Below: deciduous* C. horizontalis.

TALL-GROWING (EVERGREEN) – RED BERRIES *continued*

C. conspicuus	Graceful, wide-spreading, arching branched species with abundant bright red berries. 2·1 × 2·4m (7 × 8 ft).
C. henryanus	Large, spreading evergreen or *semi-evergreen* with long, dark green corrugated leaves and crimson berries. 6 × 3·6m (20 × 12 ft).
C. John Waterer (Watereri group)	Large, *semi-evergreen* shrub with bunches of red berries. 6 × 7·6m (20 × 25 ft).
C. lacteus	Large, oval, leathery leaves with a grey, hairy underside. Its red berries last long after mid winter (December). 3 × 2·4m (10 × 8 ft).
C. pannosus	Long, slender, arching branches, and sage-green leaves. Its berries are small, rounded and deep red in colour. 2·4 × 1·8m (8 × 6 ft).
C. salicifolius	Tall and graceful, bearing heavy crops of small bright red berries. 3·6 × 3·6m (12 × 12 ft).
C. salicifolius flocossus	Graceful, with small, polished, shining green leaves, white underneath, and masses of small red berries. 2·7 × 2·7m (9 × 9 ft).
C. salicifolius rugosus	Larger flowers than usual and red berries. 6 × 6m (20 × 20 ft).

TALL-GROWING (EVERGREEN) – YELLOW BERRIES

C. frigidus Fructuluteo (or Xanthocarpus)	*Semi-evergreen* with large clusters of creamy-yellow berries. 3 × 3·6m (10 × 12 ft).
C. Rothschildianus (Watereri group)	Wide-spreading habit. Creamy-yellow berries, borne in large bunches. 3 × 2·4m (10 × 8 ft).
C. salicifolius Fructuluteo	An interesting form with yellow berries. 3·6 × 3·6m (12 × 12 ft).

TALL-GROWING (EVERGREEN) – APRICOT BERRIES

C. Exburiensis (Watereri group)	Recognizable by its apricot-yellow berries, that become pinkish in winter. 3 × 2·4m (10 × 8 ft).

TALL-GROWING (EVERGREEN) – SALMON-PINK BERRIES

C. Inchmery (Watereri group)	This shrub produces clusters of big berries, yellow turning salmon-pink. 3·6 × 3·6m (12 × 12 ft).

TALL-GROWING (DECIDUOUS)

C. bullatus	Handsome, corrugated leaves, becoming richly tinted in autumn. Large, red berries produced early. 2·4 × 1·5m (8 × 5 ft).
C. bullatus Floribundus	A form with larger clusters of flowers and berries than *C. bullatus.* 2·4 × 1·5m (8 × 5 ft).
C. Firebird	Spreading shrub with dark green leaves and dense clusters of large orange-red berries. 1·8 × 2·4m (6 × 8 ft).
C. franchetii	*Semi-evergreen* or deciduous with sage-green foliage and orange-scarlet berries. 2·1 × 1·8m (7 × 6 ft).
C. simonsii	*Semi-evergreen*, sometimes deciduous, erect shrub with large scarlet berries. 2·7 × 2·7m (9 × 9 ft).
C. wardii	Erect-growing, with dark glossy green leaves, white underneath. Berries are top-shaped and orange-red. 2·4 × 1·5m (8 × 5 ft).

SELECTION FOR WALL PLANTS

C. conspicuus Decorus, *C.* Cornubia, *C. divaricatus, C. franchetii, C. henryanus, C. horizontalis, C. microphyllus, C. salicifolius* Autumn Fire, *C. salicifolius flocossus, C. salicifolius rugosus, C. simonsii, C. wardii.*

SELECTION FOR HEDGING

C. franchetii, C. frigidus, C. lacteus, C. simonsii, C. wardii.

CRATAEGUS

Type	deciduous flowering and fruiting shrubs and trees
Family	ROSACEAE
Common names	hawthorn, may or quickthorn
Flowering season	early–mid summer (May–June)
Planting date	any time in winter when the weather is good; from containers at any time
Mature size/shape	wide-spreading, occasionally erect; height and spread 4·5–6m (15–20 ft)
Special use	the berries and blossoms are used to make home-made wines

Crataegus is a genus containing 200 species of small, deciduous trees and shrubs, about half a dozen of which are in popular cultivation. They are collectively known by the common name 'thorn'. The name comes from the Greek word for hawthorn, that was itself derived from 'kratos' – strength – and was an allusion to the strength and hardness of hawthorn wood.

Two crataegus are native to Britain; these are *Crataegus monogyna* (common hawthorn, may or quickthorn) that is more commonly found, and *C. oxyacantha*, also popularly known as hawthorn or may. *C. monogyna* has been used very extensively for hedging in the British countryside, and its flowers and berries are still made into home-made wine. Most of the other species found in cultivation in Western gardens originate from the United States and Canada. A few have been cultivated for many centuries: *C. pedicellata* was first introduced into Britain in 1683, *C. intricata* in 1730 and *C. crus-galli* (the aptly-named cock-spur thorn) in 1691. The odd one, compared with these Western species, is *C. chlorosarca* that comes from Japan and is usually thornless.

In general, these plants have an ultimate height and spread of approximately 4·5–6m (15–20 ft). Since they respond quite well, on the whole, to being cut back, they are capable of being kept under control easily.

In most cases crataegus bear clusters of white, five-petalled flowers, with a characteristic haw-thorn scent, during early or mid summer (May or June). Some species and varieties have pink or red blooms. The popular common name of 'may' probably arises from the fact that the flowers are exceptionally prolific in early summer (May). The blossoms are followed by bunches of orange-scarlet fruits or haws that, combined with the brightly-coloured autumn foliage of some species, put up a superb display in autumn.

The other characteristic of most crataegus – an unpleasant one – is that their branches are armed with long, sharply-pointed spikes or thorns.

The more commonly-grown crataegus are excellent when planted as specimens in lawns; with their attractive blossoms, richly-coloured berries and, in some cases (autumn tints) they maintain interest for most of the year. They are also good plants for a shrub border, and can be grown in the dappled shade at the edge of a wide-spreading tree canopy. *C. monogyna* has long been proved to make just as good a hedge in the garden as it does in a field or hedgerow. It is quick-growing and once established forms an impenetrable barrier to man and beast.

Cultivation

As a group, crataegus will thrive in any normal garden soil. They do best in open ground, in a sunny position, but they are not averse to partial shade. They can be counted among the hardiest and most adaptable plants in the garden, being quite happy in industrial areas and tolerant of atmospheric pollution. Crataegus are equally

Right: the old country saying 'ne'er cast a clout til may be out' refers to the blossoms of C. monogyna *(common hawthorn, may or quickthorn) – not, as is often supposed, to the month of May.*
Below right: C. oxyacantha *with its bright, shiny fruits borne in autumn; below:* Crataegus prunifolia *thrives in partial shade or sun and tolerates polluted or exposed conditions*

amenable to exposure and severe winds in coastal districts, but it is wise to give the young shrubs protection for some time after planting. Another characteristic that makes crataegus so valuable in the garden is their almost unequalled ability to resist both excessive dryness and exceptionally moist conditions.

Plant crataegus at any time during the winter, provided there is not a severe frost and the soil is not excessively wet. If the plants arrive from the nursery when such conditions are prevalent, place them in a frost-free shed until better weather returns. They will be quite safe in their polythene or waterproof paper packing for two or three weeks. If, after this time, they still cannot be planted, undo the wrapping and keep the shrubs watered. If the ground is too soggy for planting, heel them in (in a dryish, sheltered spot) until conditions improve. Plant container-grown crataegus at any time of the year, provided that conditions are suitable.

As these shrubs usually grow quite quickly, allow a good space between each – at least 2·5m (8 ft) all round. Fortunately, they can be controlled in size quite easily by regular pruning back. If you are planting a hedge of *C. monogyna*, space each plant 30cm (12 in) apart. The best results are obtained if they are 30–38cm (12–15 in) in height when planted. Immediately after planting *C. monogyna* for a hedge, cut the plants back to about 10cm (4 in) from the ground, to encourage bushy growth.

For a bare-root crataegus it is important that the hole is large enough for the roots to spread out, and of such a depth that the original soil mark on the main stem will be just on the surface of the soil in its new position. As you fill in the hole, firm the soil well with your foot. It is a good idea to incorporate some garden compost or well-rotted manure in the soil at the bottom of the hole.

If the shrub is containerized, dig the hole so that its diameter is about 10cm (4 in) greater than the rootball, and of such a depth that the surface of the soil in the container will be just within the bed when the shrub is planted. Before planting, carefully remove the container by cutting off the bottom and making a vertical slit in its side with a sharp knife. Place the shrub centrally in the hole and fill in with well-firmed soil.

Crataegus are easy to grow and need little attention, other than having the soil immediately around them kept free of weeds by hoeing. No regular pruning is required, but hedges of *C. monogyna* are best trimmed between late summer and mid spring (July and March).

Propagation
Species are raised from berries that are picked as soon as they are ripe. The seeds take at least 18 months to germinate. After bruising the flesh of the berries slightly to facilitate rotting, sow them in small pots of seed compost, and then place them outside in a plunge bed. A thin layer of gravel on the surface of the compost prevents it being panned by heavy rain.

Alternatively, *C. intricata*, *C. pedicellata*, *C.* × *lavallei* and *C. prunifolia* can be budded in late summer (July), or grafted in early to mid spring (February to March) onto rootstocks of *C. crus-galli* or *C. oxyacantha*. Cultivars of *C. monogyna* and *C. oxyacantha* are budded or grafted onto rootstocks of *C. monogyna* in spring.

Pests and diseases

The most troublesome pests are caterpillars, and these should be picked off as they appear. If the infestation is serious, spray with a systemic insecticide such as fenitrothion.

In common with other members of the ROSACEAE family, crataegus are subject to fireblight that blackens and shrivels the flowers and causes the branches to die back and the leaves to turn brown and wither. To treat, cut back to clean wood – wood that does not show red beneath the bark. If much of the tree is infected, dig it up and burn it. In all cases, burn the infected wood to prevent the spread of the disease. Honey fungus is another disease that is fatal to crataegus. In the case of infection, dig the plant up and burn it.

Powdery mildew is a less deadly disease that can attack crataegus. It manifests itself by the presence of a white deposit on the leaves and, in very bad cases, by distortion of the tips of the shoots. Treat by cutting out infected growth. Another fungus disease is rust; it forms yellow or orange swellings on the young shoots, leaves and fruits at the beginning of summer. If the plant is seriously affected, spray with thiram or zineb.

Some varieties to choose

Although the following varieties are sometimes sold as trees, they can quite frequently be obtained in bush or feathered (branched) form. Of the dimensions given, the first figure is the ultimate height and the second is the ultimate spread. *C. coccinea*, though still listed as such in many catalogues, has now been divided by botanists into two separate species – *C. intricata* and *C. pedicellata*. It is the latter two names that are used in this list.

C. crus-galli (cockspur thorn)

This shrub is characterized by its vicious thorns, often up to 8cm (3 in) long. Its white flowers, appearing in mid summer (June), are followed by long-lasting red fruits. 4·5 × 5·4m (15 × 18 ft).

C. × *grignonensis*

Bears flowers that appear quite late, and are followed by large, bright red fruits. Both leaves and berries remain till winter. 6 × 5·4m (20 × 18 ft).

C. intricata

Often included in catalogues as *C. coccinea*. It has reddish-brown fruits. 4·5 × 4·5m (15 × 15 ft).

C. × *lavallei* (*C. carrierei*)

This species is almost thornless. Its leaves remain green until mid winter (December), and its white flowers, borne in mid summer (June), are followed by orange-red haws. 4·5 × 3m (15 × 10 ft).

C. monogyna (common hawthorn, may, quick-thorn)

Fragrant white flowers are borne in early summer (May), and masses of crimson fruits appear in autumn. It has several most attractive ornamental cultivars. 7·5 × 4·5m (25 × 15 ft).

C. oxyacantha

Bears clusters of sweetly-scented white flowers in early summer (May), and crimson fruits in autumn. There are several attractive hybrids, including Paul's Scarlet that has double, scarlet flowers. 4·5 × 5·4m (15 × 18 ft).

C. o. Rosea Flore Pleno	Double pink variety.
C. o. Toba	Double white flowers turning pink, and glossy leaves. 5m (15 ft).

C. pedicellata (scarlet haw)

Often included in catalogues under *C. coccinea*, this shrub has thorny branches that carry clusters of white flowers in early summer (May), followed by bunches of scarlet fruits; these are often accompanied by red leaves in autumn. 4·5 × 4·5m (15 × 15 ft).

C. prunifolia

This shrub bears 5–8cm (2–3 in) wide clusters of white flowers in mid summer (June), followed by scarlet fruits and leaves that are autumn-tinted. 4·5 × 4·5m (15 × 15 ft).

Below: C. oxyacantha, one of the two species native to Britain, is often used to form rootstocks for other species. It bears scented flowers in early summer (May)

CYTISUS

Type	hardy, deciduous, evergreen and semi-evergreen flowering shrubs
Family	LEGUMINOSAE
Common name	broom
Planting dates	from containers in mid–late autumn (September–October) or mid–late spring (March–April)
Flowering season	late spring–late summer (April–July)
Mature size/shape	prostrate, spreading and bushy with erect or arching branches; height 8cm–4·5m (3 in–15ft), spread 45cm–3m (18 in–10 ft)

The genus cytisus contains between 25 and 30 species of principally deciduous and semi-evergreen flowering shrubs, with a few evergreens. It is closely related to the genera genista and spartium – all three, in fact, belong to the family LEGUMINOSAE. A few species are tender and require greenhouse cultivation, but most are generally hardy. *Cytisus (candicans) monspessulanus* (Montpelier broom), however, is liable to be damaged by severe frost.

Cytisus species originate mainly from the areas surrounding the Mediterranean; exceptions to this are *C. grandiflorus* (woolly-podded broom) and *C. (multiflorus) albus* (white Spanish broom) that come from Portugal, *C. nigricans (C. carlieri)* that grows wild in central Russia and *C. ratisbonensis* that is a native of the Caucasus and Siberia.

The numerous hybrids and varieties that are available nowadays are of garden origin and have been developed mostly during the 20th century, although a number of species were introduced to Western gardens much earlier. The most outstanding of those introduced into Britain are *C. nigricans* that arrived in 1730, *C. monspessulanus* (1735) and *C. ratisbonensis* (about 1800).

In many species the foliage is somewhat insignificant and appears on the branches for only a few months of the year. Some, such as *C. battandieri, C. ardoinii* and *C. × praecox* (Warminster broom), have silvery or greyish leaves.

The flowers of cytisus, that are sweet-pea-shaped and usually produced in extreme abundance, appear mainly between late spring and late summer (April and July). Primarily, the species have flowers in various shades of yellow, cream or white, but many hybrids bear flowers that combine these colours with crimson, mauve-pink, cerise-red, orange-yellow, chocolate and salmon-red. Occasionally a cultivar appears that is self-coloured, such as *C.* Johnson's Crimson that has clear crimson blooms. Some cytisus are scented – examples of these are *C. battandieri, C. purgans* and *monspessulanus*.

Cytisus are, on the whole, fairly modest growers. After about 20 years' growth they range in size from the prostrate, rock-growing shrubs *C. decumbens* and *C. demissus* at about 10cm (4 in) high, to the tallest, *C. battandieri*, that reaches 4·5m (15 ft), with nearly as great a spread. In shape they vary from prostrate and spreading to bushy and upright. Some have arching branches.

These shrubs make excellent and colourful garden plants. Their variation in size gives them a wide range of uses in shrub or mixed borders. For instance, the taller ones can be used as background and the prostrate types in forward positions.

A number of cytisus, such as the low-growing, spreading *C. decumbens, C. demissus* and *C. scoparius prostratus*, are very good plants for the rock garden. *C. decumbens, C. scoparius prostratus, C. beanii* and *C. × kewensis* are excellent as ground cover. In addition, cytisus are effective as wall plants – in particular *C. battandieri*, and *C. monspessulanus* and its hybrid *C.* Porlock.

Cytisus × praecox bears creamy-white flowers during late spring and early summer (April and May), and makes an ideal border shrub or a small specimen bush

Cultivation

In general, cytisus are quite happy in ordinary, well-drained garden soil, but they prefer it to be on the poorer side rather than too rich. All cytisus will succeed in clay, provided it is near-neutral in reaction and most species are also lime-tolerant. Neither *C. albus* nor *C. scoparius* (common broom), however, will survive long in poor, shallow chalky soil, nor tolerate extremely acid conditions. Many cytisus are very happy grown in gardens by the sea and quite a few will tolerate the polluted air of industrial areas.

It is best to obtain container-grown plants because cytisus do not like to be disturbed once they have been planted. Container-grown cytisus can be planted at any time during the year, but the best results are obtained if this is done in mid–late autumn (September–October) or mid–late spring (March–April).

Determine the space to allow between neighbouring shrubs by adding together their ultimate spreads and dividing by two. Remove the rootball carefully from its container by cutting round the edge of the bottom and down the side.

Dig a hole that is a little larger in diameter than the rootball and of such a depth that the top of the rootball is level with the surface of the soil in the bed. With as little disturbance as possible, tease out a few roots at the side near the surface. Then place the rootball centrally in the hole and fill in with soil. Firm well by treading in and fill the hole completely with more soil. Once planted, cytisus are easily grown and need little attention.

For pruning purposes, cytisus can be divided into two types – those that flower on the previous year's wood, and those that flower on the current year's wood. The former are pruned by cutting back the stems by two-thirds immediately after flowering, and the latter by cutting the shoots back hard in the spring before growth begins. On no account cut back hard into the old wood – mature plants, particularly those of *C. scoparius* and its hybrids, do not respond well to such treatment.

Cytisus are not much affected by diseases, but can develop swellings on the stems that are due to gall mites. Remove the galls as they appear.

Propagation

Species are easily raised from seed. Propagate named varieties from 8–10cm (3–4 in) long, lateral shoot, heel cuttings taken in early–mid autumn (August–September). Insert these in rooting compost in a cold frame. When they have rooted, pot on the small plants into growing compost, in 8–10cm (3–4 in) pots and plunge them outdoors. Finally, plant them in their permanent quarters in mid–late autumn (September–October).

For a magnificent display of cytisus in early summer (May), plant low-growing species such as C. × kewensis *(right) and* C. purpureus *(above right) Far right: cytisus are exceptionally versatile plants for the garden because of their variation in height* C. battandieri *(above) reaches 3m (10 ft), while* C. × beanii *(below) grows only 90cm (3 ft) high*

Some varieties to choose

The dimensions given are first the ultimate height, and secondly the spread, after about 20 years' growth. Unless otherwise stated, the cultivars are approximately the same size as the species.

C. (multiflorus) albus (white Spanish broom)
A bushy, erect shrub with arching branches and grey-green leaves. Bears white flowers in late spring and early summer (April and May). 1·8 × 1·8m (6 × 6 ft).

C. ardoinii
A mat-forming, alpine shrub with grey-green leaves and bright yellow blooms that are borne in late spring and early summer (April and May). 8 × 30cm (3 × 12 in).

C. battandieri
Has silvery leaves and golden yellow, pineapple-scented blossoms borne during early and mid summer (May and June); has a tree-like habit. 4·5 × 3m (15 × 10 ft).

C. × beanii
A dwarf shrub that bears golden yellow flowers in early summer (May). 50 × 90cm (20 × 36 in).

C. decumbens
A prostrate-growing shrublet with bright yellow blooms borne in early and mid summer (May and June). 10 × 45cm (4 × 18 in).

C. demissus
A prostrate shrub suitable for the rock garden, with exceptionally large yellow-and-brown flowers that are borne in early summer (May). 10 × 45cm (4 × 18 in).

C. × kewensis
An attractive hybrid that has a prostrate habit, and an abundance of pale yellow flowers in early summer (May). 45cm × 1·2m (18 in × 4 ft).

C. nigricans (C. carlieri)
An erect-growing shrub with yellow flowers that first appear in mid summer (June) and continue blooming until mid autumn (September). 1·2m × 90cm (4 × 3 ft).

C. Porlock
A large, bushy shrub, bearing butter yellow, very strongly-scented flowers that appear in late spring and early summer (April and May). It needs wall protection in cold areas. 3 × 1·2m (10 × 4 ft).

C. × praecox (Warminster broom)
A pendant bush with arching branches that bear masses of rich cream flowers during late spring and early summer (April and May). Its cultivar *C. × p.* Allgold has rich, sulphur yellow flowers. 1·8 × 1·8m (6 × 6 ft).

C. purgans
Bears rich yellow, scented blossoms during late spring and early summer (April and May). This is a usually leafless, erect-growing bush. 1·2 × 1·2m (4 × 4 ft).

C. purpureus (purple broom)
A low-growing shrub that has lilac-purple flowers appearing in early summer (May). 45cm × 1·5m (18 in × 5 ft).

C. ratisbonensis
A small shrub with yellow flowers sometimes stained red, that grow along arching branches during early and mid summer (May and June). 1·5 × 1·5m (5 × 5 ft).

C. scoparius (common broom)
An upright-growing species with erect, bright green branches in winter. It produces rich yellow blossoms during early and mid summer (May and June). This species produces many very beautiful and colourful clones, some of which are given below. 2·5 × 2·5m (8 × 8 ft).

Andreanus	Yellow and chocolate-red blooms.
Burkwoodii	Rich crimson-red blooms.
Cornish Cream	Cream-coloured blossoms.
Donard Seedling	Purple-rose and orange blooms that are flushed pink.
Firefly	Yellow and bronze-crimson blooms.
Golden Sunlight	Rich yellow flowers.
Goldfinch	Purple, yellow and red blooms.
Hookstone Purple	Intense purple blooms.
Johnson's Crimson	Clear crimson flowers.
Killiney Red	Bright red flowers; a compact and low-growing shrub.
Killiney Salmon	Near-orange flowers.
Lady Moore	Rich red, buff and rose blooms.
Lord Lambourne	Unusual, bi-coloured flowers in cream-yellow and maroon-crimson.
Marie Burkwood	Pale rose flowers.
Mrs W. A. Slocock	Maroon and gold blooms.
Sulphureus (or Pallidus)	Deep cream blooms, tinged red in bud.
Windlesham Ruby	Ruby-red blooms; a bushy shrub.
C. scoparius prostratus	A dwarf, spreading shrub with large yellow blooms that open in mid summer (June).

DAPHNE

Type	hardy, deciduous and evergreen shrubs
Family	THYMELAEACEAE
Flowering season	certain species are in flower every month of the year
Mature size	up to 1.5m (5 ft) high, 60–100cm (2–3¼ ft) spread

The daphne genus is composed of 70 species of showy, sweetly-smelling shrubs that are usually small and suitable for a rock garden or the front of a shrub border.

The plant name 'daphne' is commemorative of Daphne, the daughter of the river god of Greek mythology, who was supposedly turned into a laurel bush to escape from the attention of Apollo, but the name itself may come from an Indo-European root word meaning 'odour'.

Daphne mezereum is found growing naturally in England from Yorkshire southwards, but not in Devon or Cornwall, and in Europe from Scandinavia to Spain and northern Greece. It prefers a calcareous (chalk or limestone) soil and the shade of woodlands, requires no pruning and flowers freely in early and mid spring (February and March) before the leaves appear. Its scented, rosy-purple flowers are followed by red, poisonous berries, while the variety *D.m.* Alba has white flowers and yellow berries; *D.m.* Grandiflora has larger flowers than the type that are produced throughout the winter.

Two evergreen species of daphne, *D. pontica* and *D. laureola*, have flowers that are not nearly so attractive as those of *D. mezereum*. Apart from Europe, *D. laureola* is also found in Asia Minor, the Azores and North Africa.

There are many shorter species, ranging from 15 to 45cm (6 to 18 in) high, that flower later in the year and are ideal for the rock garden. Some good ones include *D. alpina*, *D. blagayana*, *D. cneorum*, *D. collina* and *D. retusa*.

Daphne is propagated by sowing seed in autumn in boxes containing equal quantities of soil, peat and sand. These will germinate naturally in spring, or early spring (February) if brought into a warm greenhouse. Most types can be propagated by layering in the usual manner, but some rarer types can be grafted in spring to *D. mezereum*, if deciduous, or to *D. laureola*, if evergreen. Most daphnes will grow freely in colder climates, although some require temperate conditions.

Above right: Daphne retusa. *a slow-growing, alpine, evergreen ideally suited to the rock garden*
Right: Daphne mezereum Alba (mezereon), *a deciduous species bearing sweetly-scented flowers*

DEUTZIA

Type	deciduous flowering shrubs
Family	PHILADELPHACEAE
Planting date	late autumn–early spring (October–February); from containers at any time
Flowering season	early–late summer (May–July)
Mature size/shape	mainly rounded, but some with erect or arching branches; height 90cm–2·4m (3–8 ft), spread 90cm–2m (3–6½ ft)

The genus deutzia, that contains about 50 species of easily-grown deciduous flowering shrubs, was named after Johan van der Deutz, Dutch friend and patron of Carl Thunberg, the Swedish botanist and pupil of Linnaeus.

Many species of deutzia were discovered growing wild in China and Japan, but others, such as *Deutzia staminea*, come from the Himalayas. Quite a few species were introduced to Western gardens in the early years of this century, though a few came earlier. *D. scabra* was introduced to Britain in 1822, *D. gracilis* in 1840 and *D. purpurascens* in 1888. Many of the most attractive hybrid clones were raised at a rather later date, and owe their cultivation to the hybridist Lemoine of Nancy, France.

The leaves of deutzia are green, but several have foliage that is grey or white on the under surface. The brown bark on the stems – a very attractive feature – eventually peels off. The white, pink or purple flowers are prolific and the inflorescences vary from type to type, being carried in clusters, panicles, corymbs or racemes. The flowers themselves appear in different shapes – hawthorn-like, star-like, long-petalled, bell-shaped, single or double. The most magnificent is the Formosan *D. pulchra*, with racemes of white flowers that are reminiscent of the drooping heads of lily of the valley. The flowers of some deutzia, such as *D. maliflora* Avalanche, *D. compacta* and its forms, varieties of *D. × elegantissima*, and *D. sieboldiana* are sweetly perfumed. Deutzia flower between early and late summer (May and July).

These plants are modest growers: the compact shrub *D. × rosea* has a height and spread of some 90cm (3 ft) after about 20 years' growth, while the erect-growing *D. scabra* can reach a height of 3m (10 ft) and a spread of 2m (6½ ft). They mostly form neat, rounded bushes, but a few – *D. scabra* and *D. × elegantissima* for example – have erect branches, while *D. × kalmiiflora* and *D. × rosea* are arching in habit.

Cultivation

Because they are easy to cultivate, deutzia can be grown successfully in both town and country gardens, and be incorporated into the smallest planting scheme. They come into flower quickly and are excellent for shrub and mixed borders. All species and varieties will grow happily in any well-drained garden soil, but they will also succeed on clay or on a shallow soil over chalk. Many types are invaluable in industrial towns because they can withstand a polluted atmosphere.

Deutzia will thrive in both full sun and light shade, such as is found in woodlands and shrubberies: under such shade, plants with rather stronger flower colouring retain their tints better. Although the vast majority of deutzia are hardy, try to avoid planting them in open positions without some protection – particularly in colder districts or in frost pockets, or where late spring frost is likely to damage the young shoots.

Above: the fragrant, massed blooms of Deutzia × elegantissima *Fasciculata*

*Right: Upright-growing
deutzias Contraste and
Magicien (below right)
make ideal background
plants for a mixed border
Far right: compact
D. × rosea Carminea
has an attractive
arching habit*

Plant bare-root deutzia at any time between late autumn and early spring (October and February), provided there is no frost and the ground is not soggy. Those from containers can be planted at any time, as long as the ground is sufficiently moist. Water the deutzia well before removing it from its container, and again after planting if the weather is dry.

Determine the distance to be allowed between neighbouring deutzia or other plants by adding together the ultimate spreads of adjoining plants and dividing the sum by two.

Deutzia need little care after planting, except for annual pruning. Prune by reducing the old flowering shoots immediately after blooming, so as to thin the shrub, then cut the remaining shoots back to within a few centimetres (or inches) of the old wood.

Fortunately, as a rule most deutzia are little troubled by pests and diseases.

Propagation

To propagate these plants, take 8–10cm (3–4 in) long cuttings of semi-ripe, lateral shoots in late summer and early autumn (July and August) and insert them in rooting compost in a cold frame. Transplant the rooted cuttings into nursery rows the following late spring or early summer (April or May) and then plant them out the following autumn into their permanent positions.

Alternatively, take 25cm (10 in) long hardwood cuttings of lateral shoots in mid autumn (October). Insert them in a nursery bed and plant them out permanently a year later.

Some varieties to choose

The dimensions given for each shrub in the list below refer to its ultimate height and spread. Unless otherwise indicated assume that the cultivars of any species are about the same size as the parent.

D. discolor Major
In mid summer (June) bears flowers 2–3cm (1 in) across, that are white, and tinted pink on the outside. 1·5m × 1·5m (5 × 5 ft).

D. × elegantissima
Upright-growing, bushy shrub producing 5–8cm (2–3 in) wide, fragrant, star-shaped, pink to pale rose-purple blooms during early and mid summer (May and June). 1·5 × 1·5m (5 × 5 ft).
D. × e. Fasciculata   Bright rose-pink blooms.

D. gracilis
Carries racemes of white, star-like blossoms in mid summer (June). 1·2 × 1·5m (4 × 5 ft).

D. × hybrida
This species is the head of a group of hybrids that all bloom during mid and late summer (June and July). They are all 1·8m (6 ft) high, with a spread of 2·5m (8 ft).

D. × *h.* Contraste	Loose panicles of lilac-pink flowers. The outside of the petals is a rich wine purple.
D. × *h.* Joconde	Large, rose-purple blooms.
D. × *h.* Magicien	Large mauve-pink, tinted white and purple flowers.
D. × *h.* Mont Rose	Panicles of rose-pink blossoms.
D. × *h.* Perle Rose	Soft rose-pink blooms.

D. × *kalmiiflora*
Bears clusters of starry flowers, white inside and deep rose-pink on the reverse, during mid summer (June). 1·8 × 1·5m (6 × 5 ft).

D. longifolia Veitchii
Considered to be the finest of the *longifolia* shrubs. Its lilac-pink tinted flowers open in mid and late summer (June and July). 1·2 × 1·5m (4 × 5 ft).

D. × *magnifica*
Has rough, grey-green leaves and unusual, double, pompon-like flowers that open in mid summer (June). 2·4 × 1·8m (8 × 6 ft).

D. × *maliflora*
Strong-growing shrub producing large corymbs of white, purple-shaded flowers in mid summer (June). 1·8 × 1·8m (6 × 6 ft).

| *D.* × *m.* Avalanche | Has slender, arching branches laden with fragrant white flowers in mid summer (June). |

D. monbeigii
Characterized by dull green leaves with white undersides. Its flowers are small, star-shaped and white, and appear in mid summer (June). 1·8 × 1·5m (6 × 5 ft).

D. pulchra
Magnificent hardy shrub, characterized by racemes of white blooms, resembling the drooping heads of lily of the valley, and appearing in mid summer (June). 1·8 × 1·5m (6 × 5 ft).

D. × *rosea*
Compact, rather smaller shrub with arching sprays of rose-pink flowers borne in round clusters in mid and late summer (June and July). 90 × 60cm (3 × 2 ft).

| *D.* × *r.* Campanulata | White flowers with contrasting purple calyces. 1·5m × 90cm (5 × 3 ft). |
| *D.* × *r.* Carminea | Rose-pink blooms. |

D. scabra
Tall, erect shrub carrying large panicles of white blooms during mid and late summer (June and July). It has attractive brown bark that peels off. 2·4 × 1·8m (8 × 6 ft).

| *D.s.* Candidissima | Double white flowers. |
| *D.s.* Codsall Pink | Purple-pink blossoms. |

| *D.s.* Plena | Double white blooms suffused rose-purple. |

D. setchuenensis
Slow-growing species, not quite hardy enough for the coldest parts of Britain. It has brown, peeling bark and produces small, starry white flowers in mid and late summer (June and July). 1·8m × 90cm (6 × 3 ft).

| *D.s. corymbiflora* | Bears a profusion of white flowers and is a broader-leaved form. |

There is a deutzia for almost any size of garden. Erect D. scabra *Candidissima (top) reaches 2·4m in height, while arching* D. × rosea *Campanulata (above) is considerably more compact*

ESCALLONIA

Type	evergreen flowering shrubs, with a few deciduous exceptions
Family	SAXIFRAGACEAE
Planting date	late autumn–late spring (October–April); from containers at any time
Flowering season	early summer–early winter (May–November)
Mature size/shape	mainly rounded and bushy, some with erect-growing or arching branches; height 30cm–4·5m (12 in–15 ft), spread 1·2–2·5m (4–8 ft)

The escallonia genus contains about 60 species of evergreen and deciduous shrubs or trees, and was named after Señor Escallon, a Spanish traveller in South America.

All escallonia species come from South America, usually Brazil and Chile. Of the more popular species still grown today, *Escallonia rubra* was the earliest to be introduced to European gardens; it arrived in 1827, and was followed by *E. illinita* in 1830, *E. laevis* in 1844 and *E. macrantha* in 1848. With the exception of Exoniensis and Langleyensis, the many hybrids are almost certainly of 20th century origin. The beautiful 'apple blossom' series is of Irish garden origin, and the cultivar *E. macrantha* Bantry Bay was discovered growing in a rock crevice on Garnish Island in Bantry Bay.

There is only one deciduous species, *E. virgata* (or *E. phillipiana*), that generally features in present-day catalogues; it is hardy, but will not tolerate a chalky soil. Most evergreen escallonia are slightly tender and, in some inland positions in Britain, must be given wall protection. They grow quite satisfactorily in southern and western areas of England and Scotland, and in coastal districts everywhere.

Escallonia have attractive, dense foliage made of fairly small, light to deep green, shiny leaves. Many of the more popular ones bear foliage that is aromatic when crushed – C. F. Ball for example. In general, the flowers are small and tubular with widely expanded, rounded lobes, and are usually carried in panicles up to 10cm (4 in) long, that are lateral or terminal according to the species or hybrid concerned. They range in colour from white through blush- and rose-pink to cherry red. Some cultivars, Donard Gem in particular, have sweetly-scented blooms. Many of the present-day escallonia have a long flowering season, extending from mid summer to late autumn (June to October), and even early winter in the case of *E.*

macrantha. On the other hand, the flowering period of the comparatively new race of escallonia, known as the 'apple blossom' series, is from early to late summer (May to July).

The smallest of these fairly modest-growing shrubs is *E. rubra* Woodside, that after 20 years will not exceed 60cm (24 in) in height, but has an appreciably larger spread. On the other hand, its parent, *E. rubra*, towers to a height of 4·5m (15 ft) with a spread of 1·8m (6 ft). Many escallonia are somewhat rounded and bushy in shape, but they often have erect branches. Others, with arching branches – including Donard Seedling, Edinensis, Langleyensis and Slieve Donard – are sometimes called the 'cascade escallonias'.

Although the escallonia genus does contain quite a number of species, only a comparatively few true species are offered for sale today by nurserymen. The principal ones are *E. macrantha* and *E. rubra*. The reason for this lack of species is the tremendous number of hybrids – in many cases superior to the species – that have been raised from the hardier types.

Most escallonia flourish in ordinary, well-drained garden soil, and are lime-tolerant and drought-resistant – qualities making them particularly valuable in seaside gardens, where the proportion of sea-sand in the soil makes it not only less water retentive, but possibly alkaline because it contains the shells of many dead minute sea creatures. In addition, *E. macrantha*, Red Hedger and Crimson Spire are very resistant to high winds and salt-laden spray – again making them excellent for seaside gardens, or wind-exposed gardens in the milder districts. All escallonia will tolerate the conditions existing in industrial areas.

Escallonia can make excellent wall plants; the hybrids C. F. Ball, Donard Seedling, Slieve Donard and Iveyi are particularly good for this purpose. Some of the tall escallonia with upright growth, such as the hybrid Newryensis and the species *E. punctata* (*E. sanguinea*), make excellent

rootball and allow space for the roots to spread, and deep enough for the original soil mark on the main stem to be at the soil surface. Replace some of the soil and firm well round the root by treading, then add the rest of the soil to fill the hole. Plant hedges in the same way.

No regular pruning is needed, but it is wise to remove the spent flowers after blooming and to trim back established hedges at the same time. Newly-planted hedges should be reduced by one quarter immediately after planting to encourage bushy growth.

Escallonia are generally free from pests, but they might be attacked by silver leaf disease. This causes die-back of the branches and the leaves often turn a silvery colour. Treat by cutting back to clean wood, and paint the wound with a proprietary sealant.

Some varieties to choose
The first dimension given in the following list is the average height, and the second is the spread.

SPECIES

E. macrantha	Fine, glossy, aromatic, deep green leaves and crimson flowers, borne from mid summer to late autumn (June to October). 3 × 1·8m (10 × 6 ft).
E. rubra	Glossy green leaves, and red flowers produced in loose panicles in late summer and early autumn (July and August). 4·5 × 1·8m (15 × 6 ft). *E. r.* Woodside is a dwarf rock shrub with crimson flowers. 30–60cm (12–24 in) high.

HYBRIDS

Apple Blossom	Slow-growing plant, with pink and white flowers borne mid summer – late autumn (June – October). 1·5 × 1·5m (5 × 5 ft).
C. F. Ball	Upright shrub with dark green leaves and crimson blossoms between early summer and late autumn (May and October). 2·4 × 1·5m (8 × 5 ft).
Crimson Spire	Erect-growing, with very dark foliage and crimson flowers blooming from mid summer to late autumn (June to October). 1·8 × 1·8m (6 × 6 ft).
Donard Brilliance	Bushy, pendulous shrub with shiny green leaves and rose red blooms, appearing mainly during mid summer (June). 1·8 × 1·8m (6 × 6 ft).

Donard Star (above) and Donard Seedling (top) grow well in polluted areas Slow-growing Apple Blossom (above left) is worth persevering with for its unusual shape. Iveyi (left) needs wall shelter, while Pink Pearl (far left) makes a fine hedge

wind-breaks. Lastly, provided the conditions are correct for them, escallonia are excellent for hedging. Good choices for seaside hedges are Red Hedger, Crimson Spire, *E. macrantha* and Pride of Donard. For inland districts, try C. F. Ball and Edinensis as well.

Care and cultivation
Plant bare-root escallonia in open weather from late autumn to late spring (October to April); those in containers can be planted at any time.

Determine planting distance by adding together the ultimate spreads of plants that are to be neighbours and dividing the sum by two. For hedges, space the plants about 45cm (18 in) apart. Dig a hole of a sufficient diameter to take the

Donard Gem	Bears sweetly-scented pink blooms that open during mid and late summer (June and July). 1·2 × 1·5m (4 × 5 ft).
Donard Radiance	Shining, deep green foliage and large, rose red blooms flowering from late summer to mid autumn (July to September). 2·1 × 1·5m (7 × 5 ft).
Donard Seedling	Arching branches carrying dark green leaves and apple-blossom pink flowers that appear in mid and late summer (June and July). 2·1 × 1·8m (7 × 6 ft).
Donard Star	Compact shrub with rose pink flowers borne during mid and late summer (June and July). 1·8 × 1·5m (6 × 5 ft).
Donard White	White flowers, pink in bud, blooming from mid summer (June) to autumn. 1·5 × 1·5m (5 × 5 ft).
Edinensis	Shrub with cascading habit and bright green foliage. Bears rose pink blooms in mid and late summer (June and July). 4 × 4m (13 × 13 ft).
Glory of Donard	Large, deep carmine flowers produced in mid and late summer (June and July), with dark green leaves. 1·8 × 1·8m (6 × 6 ft).
Gwendolyn Anley	Small, very hardy, bushy shrub bearing flesh pink blooms from mid summer until mid autumn (June to September). 90cm × 1·8m (3 × 6 ft).
Ingramii	Rose pink flowers, borne between mid summer and early autumn (June and August). Fast-growing. 1·2 × 1·8m (4 × 6 ft).
Iveyi	Vigorous, rounded shrub with glossy, dark green leaves. Has white flowers in late summer and early autumn (July and August). Needs wall protection in colder areas. 3 × 2·5m (10 × 8 ft).
Langleyensis	Hardy shrub with rose pink flowers carried on arching branches in mid and late summer (June and July). 1·8 × 1·8m (6 × 6 ft).

Peach Blossom	Clear, peach pink flowers, appearing during mid and late summer (June and July). 2·5 × 1·5m (8 × 5 ft).
Pink Pearl	Soft pink, stained bright rose pink flowers, blooming in mid and late summer (June and July). 1·5 × 1·5m (5 × 5 ft).
Pride of Donard	Large, brilliant rose red, somewhat bell-shaped flowers, hanging in racemes between early and late summer (May and July). 1·8 × 1·5m (6 × 5 ft).
Red Hedger	Erect-growing shrub with glossy, mid green leaves. Produces bright crimson flowers steadily between mid summer and late autumn (June and October). 1·8 × 1·8m (6 × 6 ft).
Slieve Donard	Compact, very hardy shrub with long arching sprays, laden with apple-blossom pink blooms during mid summer and early autumn (June and September). 2·4 × 1·5m (8 × 5 ft).
St Keverne	Medium-sized shrub with arching branches, carrying large panicles of apple-blossom pink blooms during mid and late summer (June and July), and sometimes longer. 1·5 × 1·5m (5 × 5 ft).

Peach Blossom is one of the most attractive hybrid escallonia, both for flowers and foliage. To keep it looking at its best and to prolong the flowering period, remove the blooms as they fade

EUCALYPTUS

Type	evergreen flowering trees and shrubs
Family	MYRTACEAE
Common name	gum tree or ironbark tree
Flowering season	late spring to early winter (April to November) according to species
Planting date	mid to late summer (June to July); always from containers
Mature size/shape	4·5–116m (18–375 ft) high × 1·5–11m (5–35 ft) spread; usually sparsely-branched, pyramidal head on tall bare trunk
Special uses	affording partial shade; providing foliage for flower arrangements; as seedlings in summer bedding schemes; commercially to yield eucalyptus oil

This unusual genus is composed of between 600 and 700 species, varieties and hybrids of evergreen trees and shrubs. All eucalypts come originally from Australia and Tasmania, but have adapted well to conditions in most other parts of the world.

It is difficult to find a plant family that shows a greater variety in size when fully grown. Heights range from not more than 3m (10 ft) for low-growing shrubs and scrub plants, to the tallest known broad-leaved tree in the world, *Eucalyptus amygdalina regnans*, that reaches 116m (375 ft) and rivals the giant California redwoods. Never-theless many are fast-growing and can become too big for some gardens. Often they are stooled, that is, cut back yearly 2·5cm (1 in) from the base.

Eucalyptus is beautiful in outline, pyramidal with sickle-like leaves on a bare, slender trunk. Foliage has excellent shape, colour and texture. More generally their leaves are silvery-grey to blue-green in colour. The shape of the mature leaves on many of the species is like a sickle, often at the same time with an intriguing, almost in-describable, twist. What is most interesting is that their juvenile leaves are completely different – in size, shape, colour, arrangement and mode of attachment to the stem – from adult leaves. So attractive are these juvenile leaves that it is quite common to cut back more mature branches regularly in order to encourage their growth. All the foliage has an aromatic fragrance that, at the low concentration at which it is exuded, is quite refreshing.

Another outstanding quality of many euca-lyptus trees is the colour of their barks, that adds great beauty and interest to a garden. In the first place most species have twigs and branches with white or cream-coloured bark. As the wood matures, the smooth outer bark on their trunks and branches is cast annually. This shedding usually commences after they are four or five years old. At first new pale cream or white bark is revealed, but later this darkens to give a striking mottled effect.

It is not always appreciated that eucalypts flower quite prolifically after they are about four years old. The flowers are mostly white, with white or cream-coloured filaments, about 1–3cm ($\frac{1}{2}$–1 in) long, and sweetly scented.

Because of the climatic variations of their native habitat, eucalypts can become fairly readily adapted to almost any weather conditions – ranging from areas of tropical rains to the dryness of the desert and even freezing alpine regions, though the degree of adaptability does vary with the species. What is more, many of them are remarkably easy about where they will make themselves at home. All other conditions being equal, all of those available will flourish on clay soil, many of them are happy at the seaside, most

Many eucalyptus species shed their outer bark annually, adding an attractive mottled appearance to the garden even in winter

are able to resist pollution and so can be made to adorn industrial towns, and there is at least one, *E. parviflora*, that will tolerate chalky soil.

Among the earliest to be introduced into gardens from the wilds, in 1829, was the Tasmanian blue gum, *E. globulus*. It is a beautiful tree with blue-green leaves that are almost silvery when young. It can reach noble proportions.

Unfortunately, many of the species that flourish in temperate zones will grow too large for small gardens. They can, however, be very effective in larger gardens, where they give an exotic air that cannot be paralleled by any other plant. They may be grown as specimen trees, pruned shrubs and stooled plants, which normally only produce juvenile foliage. Planted in a woodland garden they give excellent partial shade to rhododendrons and other sylvan shrubs and plants.

Their foliage is excellent for flower arrangements. In winter, when dormant, the leaves will remain fresh for several weeks. Equally as lovely are the young summer shoots that will last fresh for several days if the ends are scalded.

The less hardy species when young make excellent foliage plants in summer bedding schemes. They can also be very beautiful if grown indoors as house plants.

Cultivation and propagation

Eucalypts should be given full sunshine, and sheltered from freezing winds and gales that are likely to cause root disturbance. They prefer an acid or neutral, well-drained soil that is moderately fertile and fairly moist, but not water-logged – and certainly not dry.

It is important *not* to plant a eucalyptus in soft, freshly-dug soil, because 'root-rock' is almost certain to kill it. The position should be prepared some time before, well firmed and allowed to consolidate thoroughly before planting.

Eucalypts must be planted when small, no more than 15–30cm (6–12 in) tall and from pots. The best time to plant is in mid or late summer.

The distance between eucalypts and neighbouring trees varies from 3–5·5m (10–18 ft) according to species. As the trees are mainly bare lower down, shade-loving shrubs may be put closer.

On no account must the roots of eucalypts be disturbed. Dig a hole that is no greater in diameter than the pot from which the eucalyptus is removed, but about 5cm (2 in) deeper so that the swollen root is well under the soil. Water the plant in well and then stake firmly. As the tree grows rapidly both in height and girth, the stake should be changed periodically for a longer one, each time moving it a little farther away from the trunk to allow for growth. Young plants should remain staked for up to six years.

Protect the basal stem of young trees against frost with straw or sacking during the first winter, though otherwise they need very little attention. Eucalypts do not need pruning, unless you want to have their juvenile foliage or stooled shrubs.

New trees can be propagated from seeds sown 3mm ($\frac{1}{8}$ in) deep in pots of sandy soil in a minimum temperature of 18°C (65°F). Sow them between early and late spring (February and April).

Pests
Mature trees are normally unaffected, but young shoots and juvenile foliage are susceptible to suckers (blue gum psyllid), which can be cured by spraying dimethoate, formothion or malathion.

Some varieties to choose
The following is a selection of some of the most useful and readily-available eucalypts. The dimensions given after the species listed correspond to height and spread respectively after 20 years unless otherwise stated.

E. coccifera
(Mount Wellington peppermint)
A wind-resisting sub-alpine species with oval-shaped green or blue-green juvenile leaves. The adult leaves are lance-shaped and green-glaucous in colour. Its trunk is mottled pale grey or white when newly exposed. Flowers in early and mid summer (May and June). 11 × 8m (35 × 25 ft).

E. dalrympleana
Attractive fast-growing species, which is among the hardiest. Its juvenile leaves last for two or three years and are ovoid and blue-green; the pendulous adult leaves are light green. Young shoots and foliage are bright orange and scarlet, with pink or red bark on the stems. The bark on the branches and trunk is white patchwork, becoming light brown. 14 × 3m (45 × 10 ft) after 10 years.

E. glaucescens
Very hardy. It has round juvenile leaves of brilliant blue-green that become glaucous and oblong and sickle-shaped when they mature. When young the adult leaves are sometimes tinted pink. The bark eventually becomes reddish-brown and shreds to expose white to grey. 8 × 4m (25 × 12 ft).

E. gunnii
One of the hardiest species. Its sickle-shaped adult leaves are sage green while the juvenile foliage is rounded and of a striking silver-blue colour. It makes a fine large tree or it may be pruned annually to form a bush. 14 × 4·5m (45 × 15 ft) after 10 years.

E. parviflora
This exceptionally hardy species will tolerate chalk soils. May be grown as a tree or stooled to form a bush. Its juvenile leaves, which are ovate, are green or sub-glaucous. They are carried on branching shoots giving a feathery foliage. These ultimately give way to long, narrow, blue-green adult leaves. 9 × 4·5m (30 × 15 ft).

E. pauciflora
(cabbage gum)
Has lance-shaped, thick and glossy green or glaucous leaves that are up to 20cm (8 in) long, with glossy, dark red to orange-yellow twigs. Can be stooled. 11 × 6m (35 × 20 ft).

E. perriniana
(round-leaved snow gum)
Juvenile leaves are blue-grey; after about two years these become long and pendulous. New leaves have an attractive lavender-purplish hue. Its glaucous or green bark shreds after about four years to give brown blotches. A more modest grower at 5·5 × 2m (18 × 6 ft) after three years.

E. pulverulenta
Another rather modest grower. Both its juvenile and adult leaves are glaucous and covered in a brilliantly silvery-white bloom. Its white bark eventually peels to reveal cream to light brown patches. Most spectacular grown as a stooled specimen. 5·5 × 1·5m (18 × 5 ft) after four years.

E. urnigera
(urn-fruited gum)
This hardy tree has juvenile and adult leaves of dark green. Its pale green or cream bark eventually becomes blotched with red-brown. The cream flowers are followed by urn-shaped, glossy green fruits. 5·5 × 3m (18 × 10 ft) after four years.

Far left, above: characteristically pyramid-shaped mature Eucalyptus gunnii
One of the most striking features of eucalypts is the contrast between adult and juvenile foliage: far left, adult, and left, juvenile, foliage of E. gunnii
Above left: juvenile foliage of the hardy E. coccifera

EUONYMUS

Type	deciduous and evergreen shrubs and small trees
Common name	spindle tree
Family	CELASTRACEAE
Planting date	evergreens: mid–late autumn (September–October); late spring–early summer (April–May) deciduous: late autumn–mid spring (October–March); from containers at any time
Flowering season	throughout the summer
Mature size/shape	bushy, prostrate, trailing and climbing; height 30cm–4·5m (12 in–15 ft), spread 90cm–3m (3–10 ft)

The euonymus genus consists of 176 species of deciduous and evergreen foliage shrubs. The name euonymus – meaning 'of good name' in Latin, and deriving originally from the Greek name for the plant, 'euonymon dendron' – was an ironic reference to the plant's poisonous nature.

Two species – *Euonymus europaeus* (common spindle tree) and *E. latifolius* – are native to Europe; the former is a native of Britain, where it is commonly seen growing in the hedgerows. All the other species are Asian in origin; *E. alatus* (winged spindle tree), *E. japonicus* and *E. fortunei* come from China and Japan, while *E. sachalinensis (E. planipes)* and *E. yedoensis* are native to north-east Asia and Korea respectively, as well as Japan.

For thousands of years, long before the invention of the spinning-wheel, thread for woollen cloth was spun by twirling a stick – called a spindle – that was made from the stems of *E. europaeus*. Its wood was also used for making clothes-pegs, knitting-needles and meat skewers; for the last use it was given the country name of 'skewer-wood'. Because of the many uses for the wood, euonymus has been grown in cottage gardens for many centuries.

Most of the species cultivated today were introduced to Britain within the last two centuries. Among the earliest to arrive, in 1730, was the European species *E. latifolius*. Other species still popular today came later – *E. alatus* in 1860, *E. yedoensis* in 1865, *E. sachalinensis* in 1892 and *E. fortunei* in 1907.

Euonymus flowers, generally greenish or purplish in colour, are insignificant. The evergreens bear shiny leaves that are green, purple or greyish-green, or variegated silver, gold or white, while the deciduous species are characterized by rich

autumn colouring. Some euonymus also bear distinctive fruits – coloured white, scarlet, rose-pink and crimson – that persist long into the winter. These are poisonous and should not be eaten. To ensure good cross-pollination for fruit production, plant several euonymus in a group.

The deciduous species are hardy, but the evergreen forms are somewhat tender and need to be grown in fairly mild localities if they are to do really well. Nevertheless, the evergreens thrive in coastal areas, where they are able to resist salt-laden winds. They are also quite at home in the chalky soil that is sometimes found in seaside gardens. *E. fortunei* and *E. japonicus*, along with their many cultivars, will flourish in industrial areas. *E. fortunei* and its cultivars, as well as *E. japonicus robustus*, although preferring milder conditions, certainly tolerate cold, exposed positions. *E. fortunei* will also grow well in deep shade – an extremely useful characteristic that is invaluable for sombre areas of the garden and for clothing north and east walls.

Above: the fruits of Euonymus latifolius *are poisonous – so be careful that children do not pick or eat them*
Top right: slow-growing E. alatus; *it is famous for its magnificent autumn colouring (far right)*
Right: to ensure fruiting on E. europaeus Red Cascade, *plant several specimens close together so that cross-pollination can take place*

Many of the species and their cultivars are modest-growing enough to be accommodated in small gardens. One of the largest of the more popular euonymus, the deciduous *E. yedoensis*, grows to a height of about 4·5m (15 ft), with a spread of 2·5–3m (8–10 ft); next in size come *E. latifolius*, *E. japonicus*, *E. alatus* and *E. fortunei* (when grown against a wall) – all having an approximate height of 3m (10 ft) and a spread of 1·8m (6 ft). Quite a number of cultivars of *E. fortunei* are very modest-growing; the largest is *E. f.* Carrierei with a height of 90cm (3 ft) and spread of 1·8m (6 ft), while *E. f.* Kewensis, *E. f.* Vegetus, *E. f.* Coloratus and *E. f.* Emerald 'n Gold vary in height between 30–60cm (12–24 in). Some members of this species appear to have both trailing and climbing forms. Another small euonymus of compact habit is *E. japonicus* Microphyllus (Myrtifolius).

Both the evergreen and deciduous species of euonymus are almost essential plants for a shrub or mixed border. With their shiny green or variegated leaves they can provide an excellent contrast to flowering or other foliage plants. Some, such as *E. fortunei radicans*, a trailing and climbing shrub, are excellent grown against north-facing walls. Such shrubs are also good for ground cover, particularly where it is sunless. Others, such as *E. fortunei* Kewensis, that is low-growing and prostrate in habit, are most valuable for forming small hummocks or covering bare stretches of rock garden.

Where the climate is reasonably warm, the evergreen species *E. japonicus* can be used to make a hedge. This is particularly the case in coastal districts, where this euonymus is undoubtedly the most commonly-used hedging plant due to its tolerance of salt-laden winds.

E. fortunei Variegatus (Gracilis) is often grown as a tub plant, while *E. japonicus* Ovatus Aureus (Aureovariegatus), the most popular of the golden euonymus, is frequently grown indoors as an ornamental house plant.

Cultivation and propagation

Generally, euonymus will grow in partial shade or sun. The evergreens will tolerate quite a lot of shade, but, as they are not quite so robust as the deciduous euonymus, should be given some shelter. The variegated forms are rather less hardy than any of the others, and therefore appreciate the protection of a wall or bank, or the shelter of overhead trees. Euonymus will flourish in any ordinary garden soil.

Plant the evergreens in mid and late autumn (September and October), or late spring to early summer (April to May), deciduous shrubs between late autumn and mid spring (October and March), and container-grown types at any time. Determine the distance to be allowed between shrubs by adding together the spreads of adjoining plants and dividing the sum by two. For a hedge, allow 38–45cm (15–18 in) between each plant; the shrubs for this purpose should not be taller than 30cm (12 in). When you have planted a hedge, pinch out the growing points to encourage bushing, and repeat this process as necessary during the first year.

Dig a hole large enough to take the rootball and allow the roots to spread. After placing the rootball in position, fill in the hole with soil and firm gently by light treading. No regular pruning is necessary for specimen shrubs, but any thinning should be carried out in early spring (February). Clip hedges in late spring (April), and trim further in early or mid autumn (August and September).

Aphides and scale insects are the most common pests to attack euonymus. If the infestation of either of these becomes serious, spray with malathion, taking care to spray the undersides of the leaves. Leaf spot disease, indicated by brown spots on the leaves, can cause serious disfigurement; if this occurs, spray with captan. Powdery mildew often affects *E. japonicus*, and all infected shoots should be cut out and burnt. Spray with dinocap if this disease is serious. Euonymus are also liable to attack from honey fungus which can cause rapid death of the plant.

To propagate euonymus, take 8–10cm (3–4 in) long heel cuttings in early and mid autumn (August and September), insert them in growing compost and keep in a cold frame until they have rooted. Then plant them out in rows in a nursery bed, in late spring or early summer (April or May). After one or two years transplant them to their permanent growing quarters.

Some varieties to choose

The first dimension given in the list below is the height and the second is the spread, both after about 20 years' growth. Unless otherwise stated, assume that a cultivar has about the same dimensions as its species.

DECIDUOUS

E. alatus (winged spindle tree)
Slow-growing shrub with many branches, and branchlets characterized by winged corky bark. Excellent autumn colouring. $2·1 \times 2·1$m (7×7 ft).

E. europaeus (common spindle tree)
Vigorous shrub with green stems and mid green, oval leaves. Insignificant green-white flowers are followed by numerous rose-red capsules that open to reveal orange-red seeds. $2·5 \times 1·8$m (8×6 ft).

E. e. Albus	Yields snowy-white fruits.
E. e. Atropurpureus	Leaves purple throughout spring and summer, but turn vivid red in autumn.
E. e. Fructu-coccineo	Characterized by bright red seed capsules.
E. e. Red Cascade	Arching, near-pendulous branches weighed down by a profusion of rosy-red fruits.

E. latifolius
Has brilliant scarlet autumn tints, accompanied by persistent, large, drooping, scarlet fruits containing orange seeds. $3 \times 2·5$m (10×8 ft).

E. sachalinensis (E. planipes)
Produces the most brilliant foliage tints and large, scarlet fruits in autumn. $3 \times 2·5$m (10×8 ft).

E. yedoensis
Mid green leaves that turn yellow and red in autumn. Cymes of insignificant white flowers yield to large, persistent, conspicuous, rosy-pink fruits containing orange-red seeds. $4·5 \times 3$m (15×10 ft).

EVERGREEN

E. fortunei
Very hardy, trailing evergreen that is good for ground cover or as a self-clinging climber. Its leaves are mid green, and it gives pink fruits enclosing orange seeds in autumn. It appears to exist in a prostrate (juvenile) form that grows 30–90cm (12–36 in) high, and a climbing form (adult) that reaches 3m (10 ft) if grown against a wall. The spread for both is about 1·5m (5 ft).

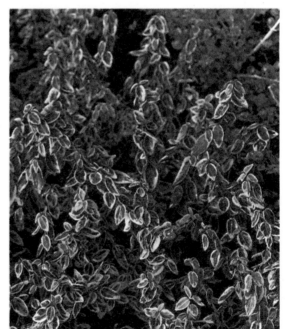

Above: E. japonicus *Ovatus Aureus needs a sunny site for its leaves to retain their colour. This variety can look particularly decorative even in winter (left) Far left: variegated* E. fortunei *Silver Queen needs the shelter of a wall or bank Below left:* E. fortunei *Emerald 'n Gold is one of the best small varieties, and its winter foliage (far left below) is especially attractive*

E. f. Carrierei	Has larger leaves than the species. 90cm–1·8m (3 × 6 ft).	
E. f. Coloratus	Produces deep red-purple leaves that persist through winter and turn green in summer. Height (climbing form) 2·5m (8 ft), (trailing form) 75cm (30 in), spread 1·2m (4 ft).	
E. f. Emerald Cushion	Dwarf, mounded, rich green shrub. 30 × 60cm (12 × 24 in).	
E. f. Emerald 'n Gold	Golden-variegated leaves, pink-tinged in winter. 30cm × 1·2m (12 in × 4 ft).	
E. f. Emerald Gaiety	Variegated white-leaved bush. 30cm × 1·2m (12 in × 4 ft).	
E. f. Kewensis	Prostrate form with minute leaves. Suitable for rock gardens. 30 × 60cm (12 × 24 in). Will also climb.	
E. f. Silver Queen	Green leaves with a creamy-white margin.	

E. f. Silver Queen — Green leaves with a creamy-white margin. Trailing form 45 × 90cm (18 × 36 in), climbing form 2·5m (8 ft) high.

E. f. Vegetus — Small, bushy, creeping, free-fruiting form. 60cm × 2·5m (2 × 8 ft).

E. japonicus — Upright bushy shrub. Excellent for hedges in milder districts. 3 × 1·8m (10 × 6 ft).

E. j. Aureopictus (Aureus) — Leaves have a golden centre and a green margin. 1·5 × 1·5m (5 × 5 ft).

E. j. Microphyllus (Myrtifolius) — Slow-growing, compact, green bush. Similar forms are *E. j.* Microphyllus Pulchellus (Aureus) with golden leaves and *E. j.* Microphyllus Variegatus that has leaves with a white margin. All 60 × 30cm (24 × 12 in).

E. j. Ovatus Aureus (Aureovariegatus) — A golden euonymus. 1·5 × 1·2m (5 × 4 ft).

FUCHSIA

Type	tender, half-hardy or hardy, deciduous flowering shrubs
Common name	fuchsia
Family	ONAGRACEAE
Flowering season	early summer to late autumn (May–October), sometimes longer
Planting date	outdoors: mid spring to mid summer (March–early June); repotting, as necessary, mid spring to mid autumn (March–September)
Mature size/shape	30cm–2m (1–6½ ft), mostly bushy; some prostrate, sprawling or semi-climbing to 4m (13 ft)

Fuchsias were named after a German physician, Professor Leonhart Fuchs (1501–1506), who is chiefly remembered for an early 'herbal' illustrated by unusually beautiful woodcuts. He never saw the plants called after him as he died long before the first fuchsia was discovered.

History and development
Although fuchsias were known and grown in Britain in the late 18th century, the fuchsia story, so far as gardeners are concerned, really began in the 1820s when a species called *Fuchsia magellanica* was introduced from Chile. It was far hardier and more variable than *F. coccinea* that was already in cultivation. Some forms were quite stiff and angular in branching, others more slender and lax. The flowers too, though fairly small, varied in colour and shape, some having short oval sepals, while others were short and narrow. One of these natural variations, *Fuchsia magellanica* Gracilis, is still a popular shrub for planting outdoors as are some other forms and hybrids. But what was important about the Magellan fuchsia was that it could be interbred with other species and was able to pass on to its offspring a greatly extended capacity for variation.

Very soon gardeners had crossed it with *F. coccinea* producing quite a showy shrub, which was christened *F. globosa* because of its much rounder flowers, particularly when in bud and half open.

The next and really vital step occurred in 1838 when Theodore Hartweg went to Mexico at the behest of the Horticultural Society (it had not yet acquired the prefix 'Royal') to look for new plants in the mountains. He discovered 'a most beautiful broad-leaved fuchsia'. It was sent home, named *Fuchsia fulgens*, and within a few years had been crossed with *F. magellanica*, *F. coccinea* and *F. globosa*. This resulted in a completely new race of man-made fuchsias, different from any of the parent species, with greatly increased flower size and diversity in colour, shape and plant habit.

Almost at a stroke, what we think of today as garden fuchsias were born. Although they have been developing ever since, nearly all the elements on which this advance was based were already there by the mid 1840s. Some early varieties are still grown and admired; for example the Chillerton Beauty, introduced in 1847, is still one of the dozen or so best fuchsias for planting out of doors.

Hybrids
As time went by, other species were introduced into the breeding programme, most notably *F. triphylla*, an especially elegant West Indian species that has passed on its long, slender, almost tubular flowers and its relative tenderness to fine garden hybrids such as Gartenmeister Bonstedt and Thalia.

Since *F. magellanica* was fairly hardy and *F. fulgens* distinctly tender, with *F. coccinea* occupying an intermediate position, it is not surprising that subsequent garden hybrids display a widely-ranging sensitivity to cold. In Great Britain, a few are purely greenhouse plants, many are half-hardy (can be planted outdoors in summer but need protection in winter), and some are hardy enough to be grown outside in most places though they may be killed during exceptionally severe winters.

Gardeners have been captivated by man-made hybrids on account of their great variety in form and colour. Some have single flowers, some semi-double, others fully double. A few varieties, such as Bon Accord, have quite small upward-facing flowers and, at the other extreme, giants such as Texas Longhorn have pendant flowers fully 15cm (6 in) across. The colour range is from white, palest pink and lavender, to salmon, scarlet, crimson and purple; colour in sepal and petal often contrasts and is sometimes different from the tube.

But it is not so much the colours themselves as their many different combinations, plus the variety of flower form and plant habit, that have made it possible for breeders to go on producing new cultivars for over a century, without yet appearing to have exhausted the resources of the fuchsia. This is well-illustrated by the long descriptive trade catalogues devoted exclusively to the plants. Some estimates put the present number of fuchsias at over 2,000.

Some tender species

Today about a hundred tender species are known, all from Central and South America, New Zealand and Tahiti. The flowers attract bees and humming-birds for pollination, and some are most beautiful, though not as a rule very showy, and they are quite different in character from the garden races. Not many are grown in gardens though *Fuchsia procumbens* is sometimes seen as a pot plant; this is prostrate and has small, upturned, purplish and green-tipped flowers and bright red berries. *F. arborescens* has larger leaves with clusters of narrowly-tubular flowers rather like those of a lilac; it can grow to the size of a tree and is occasionally seen trained on the back wall of a heated conservatory. *F. cordifolia*, a straggly bush with scarlet, green tipped flowers, will also train on a wall, either outside in a warm sheltered spot, or in a frost-proof greenhouse.

Flowering season

Fuchsias have an exceptionally long flowering season and some varieties would bloom all the year round if the temperature never dropped below about 13°C (35°F) and there were no more than twelve hours of darkness. These are mostly what the scientists call 'long day' plants, meaning that their flowering-mechanism is triggered by long days and short nights, in contrast to chrysanthemums, that are typically geared to short day and long night flowering.

Modern research, giving a fascinating insight into plant behaviour, has shown that fuchsias in the greenhouse can be made to flower earlier than normal. This is achieved by illuminating them for an hour or so in the middle of the night,

Left: broad-leaved Fuschia fulgens, brought from Mexico in the mid 19th century
Below: Fuchsia triphylla *Thalia, a West Indian species with slender tubular flowers*
Below right: Fuchsia procumbens, *a tender prostrate species, quite different from the garden races*
Bottom right: the arching Mrs Popple, one of the hardier, long-flowering varieties
Below, far right: aptly-named Mission Bells variety is strong and vigorous

thus breaking a long night into two short ones.

But in practice, most gardeners are prepared to settle for a five- to six-month flowering period from early summer to late autumn (May to October), involving little artificial heat even for the more tender varieties, and with no interference in normal day lengths.

Some of the hardier varieties, such as Margaret and Mrs Popple, will flower for that length of time outdoors or, if the weather is mild, may even go on flowering until Christmas. Others tend to bloom in a succession of flushes, or periods of flowering, rather like modern roses.

By their profusion and continuity of display in both garden and greenhouse, fuchsias are unexcelled by any other easily-grown plant.

Cutting and propagation

The plant can be propagated readily by cuttings 5–8cm (2–3 in) long, prepared from young shoots at any time from spring to early autumn (March–August). The cuttings root quickly in a propagator filled with sandy or peaty compost or even in a pot placed inside a polythene bag. Once well-rooted, they should be potted singly in small pots with John Innes No 2 or loamless/soilless compost, and then moved on to larger pots as necessary. Cuttings of half-hardy fuchsias should be taken from half-ripe wood and rooted in the late summer to mid autumn period (July–September). The young plants may be kept going slowly during the winter in a temperature above 9°C (48°F).

Pinching and training

Varieties of a sprawling or weeping habit, such as Cascade, Mrs Marshall, Marinka and Golden Marinka, are excellent for hanging baskets or window boxes. Many of the upright varieties can be trained quite easily to form pyramids; those slightly arching in habit also make fine standards (branched heads on bare but sturdy stems) and some kinds, with very long stems, can be spread out on trellis work or wires fixed beneath the greenhouse rafters.

If you want bushy fuchsias, you should pinch out the tip of each rooted cutting when the plant is 15–20cm (6–8 in) high. This will make it produce several sideshoots more rapidly than it would do if left to grow naturally, and these sideshoots can themselves be pinched when 15–20cm (6–8 in) long, to make them branch again.

Alternatively, if you want to form a standard, do not pinch the cutting but encourage it to grow straight up, removing all sideshoots back to one leaf and tying the main stem to a cane to keep it as straight as possible. Then, when the desired height has been reached, usually between 75–100cm (2½–3 ft), remove the tip of the stem and allow the sideshoots to develop freely from the uppermost buds. This will produce the bushy head mentioned above.

Fuchsias are easy to pinch and train and you can form other shapes quite readily, including what are known as pyramids (though they are really cones), and espaliers that have an erect central stem with branches trained in horizontal tiers.

Left: Fuchsia cordifolia, *a greenhouse species*
Below left: Golden Marinka, with its unusual and attractive variegated foliage
Below: Mrs Marshall, a sprawling variety much used in hanging baskets and window boxes

Planting out, pruning and winter care

From late spring (April) onwards, half-hardy fuchsias should be grown without artificial heat and, for the last few weeks before being planted outdoors in early or mid summer (May or June), they are better in a frame than in a greenhouse. By autumn, they can be lifted, repotted and returned to a frost-free greenhouse where they are allowed to rest and will drop their leaves.

Hardy varieties can be planted outside from mid spring to mid summer (March–June), and are best placed with their uppermost roots at least 5cm (2 in) below the soil level. In cold districts you can ensure protection by spreading a 5cm (2 in) layer of peat over the roots in early winter. Then, even if frost kills the top growth, as often happens, the plant will probably throw up new stems straight from the roots in the following spring.

In any case, you should prune all fuchsias in mid spring (March), shortening straggly stems and removing weak or damaged ones. Do not prune back in autumn as the old wood provides further protection to the root stock.

In winter, even the most tender fuchsias will survive as long as the temperature never falls below 7°C (45°F) and many will grow in unheated or almost unheated greenhouses.

Plants that have been trained as standards, or pyramids, or other interesting shapes, are valuable and should be kept going from year to year by being sheltered in the greenhouse during winter.

Watering and feeding

Fuchsias like all reasonably fertile soils and will grow in light or shade although they flower most freely in the sun. If they are under glass, you may have to shade them a little in hot weather, to prevent their leaves and flowers from being scorched. They need plenty of water while in full growth during spring and summer, but in winter, when days are dull and temperatures are low, keep the soil just moistened.

The plants require moderate feeding when growing from early summer to early autumn (May–April) so add a little liquid fertilizer to the water every 10–15 days. But do not use more than is recommended by the maker's instructions, for the soft foliage of fuchsia is easily damaged by over-feeding.

Pests and diseases

The plant can also be severely damaged by capsid bugs which are insects so small and active that they frequently escape detection. The injury they cause is distinctive; leaves distort and flower production falls off rapidly. Greenfly also attacks fuchsias and both pests can be controlled by the occasional spraying with an insecticide containing diazinon, BHC or malathion. Whitefly can be found on fuchsias, especially those under glass, and should be controlled with the same sprays.

Fuchsias are seldom subject to disease though grey mould may damage the plants in winter if temperatures are too low and the soil and atmosphere too moist.

HAMAMELIS

Type	hardy, deciduous shrub
Common name	witch hazel
Family	HAMAMELIDACEAE
Flowering season	mid winter–early spring (December–February)
Planting date	late autumn–mid spring (October–March); from containers, anytime
Mature size	1·8–3m (6–10 ft) high, 1·8–2·5m (6–8 ft) spread

The name hamamelis is said to come from *hama* and *mela*, the Greek words for together and fruit, because flowers and fruit can sometimes be found side by side on the same plant. It was discovered in China by the plant collector Charles Maries in 1878 but was relatively unused in Britain for about 20 years after this.

These deciduous plants need not be pruned, although if the side branches are cut back in the formative years a small 'trunk and tree' effect is produced, rather than the natural bush shape. The plants will withstand cold conditions and even the flowers will not be damaged by a touch of frost. A light, loamy soil suits them best, with an addition of peat or leaf mould at planting time.

Propagation is easiest from seed but they often do not germinate for two years. Sow seed in boxes of soil, peat and sand mixture. The Chinese and Japanese varieties of hamamelis are often grafted onto *Hamamelis virginiana* to give them a vigorous root-stock, as cuttings of these varieties are difficult to root. Grafting should be done under glass in the spring.

Hamamelis japonica from Japan has slightly-fragrant yellow flowers. The variety *H. j. arborea* is more vigorous and has darker-coloured flowers, while *H. j. zuccariniana* has lemon-yellow flowers that do not appear until mid spring (March).

Hamamelis mollis from China is often said to be the most beautiful. It has a primrose-like fragrance with golden-yellow flowers that proliferate from mid winter to early spring (mid December to mid February). *H. m.* Pallida, a recent variety, produces large, sulphur-yellow flowers in clusters.

Hamamelis virginiana, the American witch hazel, flowers in the autumn before the leaves fall, and as the flowers are altogether smaller than their Asian counterparts, they are not easily seen. The bark and leaves of this plant are the source of a medicinal oil used in the preparation of bay rum.

There are now several new forms and hybrids. Successful varieties include *Hamamelis × intermedia* Diane, a red-flowered cultivar, and *H. × i.* Jelena with large, coppery flowers and spreading habit; the leaves of both colour well in autumn.

Above: Hamamelis japonica arborea, *a tall-growing variety, flowering in spring*
Below: Hamamelis mollis, *most popular of witch hazels, in flower during winter*

HEBE

Type	hardy and semi-hardy evergreen flowering shrubs
Family	SCROPHULARIACEAE
Flowering season	mainly mid–late summer (June–July)
Planting date	mid–late autumn (September–October), or late spring–early summer (April–May); from containers at any time
Mature size/shape	mainly rounded, prostrate and erect-growing; height from 5cm–2·5m (2 in–8 ft), spread from 15cm–2·5m (6 in–8 ft)

These plants used to be included by botanists in the genus veronica, but in recent years the shrubby types have been separated from the annual, perennial herbaceous, and rock plants, and placed in separate genus – hebe – consisting of about 100 species of evergreen flowering shrubs. They are grown mainly for their decorative flowers and shapely foliage, and were given their name in honour of Hebe, the Greek goddess who was cup-bearer to the gods on Mount Olympus.

Some of the species originate in South America, but most come from New Zealand, which has a predominance of coastal areas. This has tended to make hebe develop as excellent plants for the seaside. They are exceptionally tolerant of high winds and salt-laden gales – one form, *H. × franciscana*, is regarded as the most wind-and-salt tolerant of all seaside shrubs. Unfortunately, these characteristics have the disadvantage of making hebe somewhat on the tender side, because the climate tends to be warmer in coastal districts than inland. It is therefore important to consider most hebe as half-hardy plants likely to thrive best in warm, sheltered gardens. Wherever they are planted they must always be sheltered from severe frost. In Britain many of the more delicate species and cultivars that do not thrive inland are quite happy if planted along the south and west coasts, even in exposed places.

The flowers are mostly coloured blue, lavender, mauve, purple, lilac, pink and red, with a few white exceptions. They are usually crowded in racemes or spikes that vary in length from one plant to another; the smallest is about 2·5–5cm (1–2 in) in length increasing to 15cm (6 in) long in the case of *H. salicifolia*. In addition there is great variation in the size of the flowers in the racemes or spikes.

Above: the summer-flowering Hebe Great Orme *is very resistant to seaside winds.* H. salicifolia *(right) can reach a height of 2·5m (8 ft)*

253

Hebe have a long flowering period that begins in early summer and continues until late autumn (May to October), and frequently much later. For instance, *H. × franciscana*, a very compact, rounded hybrid, produces its dense racemes of bright violet-blue, scented flowers intermittently throughout the year.

The foliage of hebe is a valued asset in the garden because it is often dense enough to make an excellent screen. The leaves are usually lanceolate or ovate, and very variously coloured, ranging from dark green through violet-purple, coppery-red and grey, and including the golden foliage of *H. loganioides*, the silver-edged leaves of *H. × andersonii* Alba Variegata and the sulphur-yellow, variegated ones of *H. × andersonii* Aurea Variegata. Some forms – called 'whipcord' hebe – have closely overlapping, scale-like leaves, re-sembling the foliage of cupressus (cypress).

The largest in size is *H. salicifolia*, with a height and spread of 2·5m (8 ft); at the other end of the scale there is the tiny, cushion-forming cultivar *H. buchananii* Minor with a height of 5cm (2 in) and spread of 15cm (6 in).

Hebe are most valuable in a shrub or mixed border, and prostrate and low-growing cultivars such as *H. Carl Teschner*, *H. carnosula* and *H. pinguifolia* Pagei make very good ground cover plants. The dwarf hebe used for this purpose are generally hardy and can therefore be grown in town gardens. The more tender species and cultivars usually have to be given wall protection when grown in inland gardens.

Another more unusual function of hebe is making informal hedges. For rather taller hedges, almost any variety of *H. speciosa* is suitable. For a hedge up to about 90cm (3 ft) or so high, choose *H. Alicia Amherst*, but if one twice this height is required, plant *H. Midsummer Beauty*. *H. brachysiphon* (*traversii*) will make an attractive 1·2m (4 ft) high hedge, and *H. anomala* is suitable for a hedge no taller than 60cm (2 ft).

Cultivation and propagation

All hebe should be planted in full sun, and they need some protection where exposure to frost is likely. They thrive in any well-drained soil, even chalk, and can be planted in industrial areas.

Plant bare-root hebe during mid and late autumn (September and October), or in late spring and early summer (April and May); container-grown plants can be established at any time. Determine the planting distance between two hebe shrubs by adding their respective ultimate spreads and dividing by two.

To propagate, take 8cm (3 in) cuttings of non-flowering shoots in late summer and early autumn (July and August) and plant them in a compost mixture suitable for cuttings in a cold frame (preferably in a frost-free position). The following late spring (April) pot the rooted cuttings into 8cm (3 in) pots and place them outdoors. Plant out the hardy species and cultivars permanently in mid autumn (September), and the more tender ones the following spring.

Some varieties to choose

In the following selection the first figure given is the height and the second is the spread after about 20 years' growth. When this is not shown for any cultivar, assume that its dimensions are similar to those of the species. All those listed are hardy in coastal areas.

Hardy

H. albicans	Rounded shrub with glaucous leaves that make it an excellent foliage plant. Its white flowers appear in mid to late summer (June to July). 60 × 60cm (2 × 2 ft).
H. brachysiphon (*traversii*)	Rounded shrub with dark green, narrowly oval leaves. It bears masses of white flowers in mid to late summer (June to July), and is excellent for hedging. 1·5 × 1·5m (5 × 5 ft).
H. Carl Teschner	Dwarf shrub of compact habit, admirable for ground cover. Its profusely-produced flowers are violet-blue with a white throat and are carried in short racemes. They appear in mid and late summer (June and July). 30 × 75cm (12 × 30 in).
H. Edinensis	Dwarf plant with tiny, bright green leaves, excellent for a rockery. It seldom flowers. 38 × 38cm (15 × 15 in).
H. Great Orme	Compact, bushy, upright shrub with dark green lanceolate leaves. It produces long, tapering racemes of pink flowers between early and late summer (May and July). Resistant to salt-laden winds. 90 × 90cm (3 × 3 ft).
H. pinguifolia Pagei	Grey-foliaged, low, bushy shrub that makes a very good ground cover and rock garden plant. Its profuse, short spikes of white flowers open during early and mid summer (May and June). 20 × 90cm (8 in × 3 ft).

Moderately hardy

H. armstrongii	One of the 'whipcord' species of hebe, with a dwarf, spreading, cupressus-like growth. Its foliage is the colour of old gold and is borne on olive green stems, and it produces white flowers from mid summer to early autumn (June to August). 75 × 75cm (2½ × 2½ ft).
H. Bowles' Hybrid	Pretty, low-growing shrub with crowded mauve-coloured racemes borne between early summer and mid autumn (May and September). 60 × 45cm (24 × 18 in).
H. × franciscana Blue Gem	Compact, dome-like shrub with rich green leaves and bright blue flowers that appear intermittently during the whole year. Very resistant to salt-laden winds. 1·2 × 1·2m (4 × 4 ft).
H. × franciscana Lavender Queen	Tall, erect bush with medium green leaves. It produces lavender-blue flowers from late summer to mid winter (July to December), and even later. 1·8 × 1·5m (6 × 5 ft).
H. Midsummer Beauty	This shrub has reddish undersides to its leaves, and its flowers are lavender-coloured, appearing continuously through the summer until mid winter (December). 1·8 × 1·8m (6 × 6 ft).
H. salicifolia	Moderately large species with pale green lanceolate leaves and lilac-tinged white flowers that appear from mid summer to early autumn (June to August). 2·5 × 2·5m (8 × 8 ft). The variety *H.s.* Spender's Seedling has fragrant, white blooms.
H. Waikiki	Bushy shrub with bronze-tinted young shoots. The flowers are blue and appear in mid to late summer (June to July). 60 × 60cm (24 × 24 in).

HYDRANGEA

Type	deciduous and evergreen flowering shrubs and climbers
Family	HYDRANGEACEAE
Flowering season	mid summer–mid autumn (June–September)
Planting date	late autumn–early winter (October–November), or mid–late spring (March–April); container plants, anytime
Mature size/shape	shrubs: 75 × 75cm (2½ × 2½ ft) to 4.5 × 4.5m (15 × 15 ft); climbers: up to 7m (23 ft) high

The name hydrangea comes from *hydor* and *aggos*, the Greek words for water and a jar, after the shrub's cup-shaped fruits.

The hydrangea genus, HYDRANGEACEAE, is composed of 80 species. It is a most valuable family of flowering garden plants and contains both shrubs and climbers. There are deciduous and evergreen plants among the species but the climber *Hydrangea serratifolia* is the only popular one that is evergreen.

The shrubs are quite hardy in milder climates such as are found in the south and west of England, but in other areas the gardens must be very warm and sunny to ensure success. They make excellent shrubs for town and mild coastal districts. In severe, exposed areas hydrangeas can only be grown in a greenhouse or indoors. Generally speaking the climbing species are hardier than the shrubs.

The majority of hydrangeas produce flowers in flattened or dome-shaped heads on the ends of the previous year's growth. They are composed of flowers of two different sorts. Most are fertile but rather small and almost insignificant, yet coloured. The second kind are conspicuous with rather large, coloured sepals. These larger type of flowers are sterile and they are known as ray-florets. They occur on the outside of the head and in some cases, such as the lacecap hydrangeas, the fertile flowers grow in a ring of coloured ray-florets. There are other cultivars, particularly the mop-headed, or hortensia, group of *H. macrophylla* completely made up of sterile ray-florets.

Among the earlier species to be introduced into Western gardens was *H. arborescens* that is native to the eastern part of North America. It was first cultivated in 1736. Another hydrangea that grows wild in the United States is *H. cinerea* – introduced somewhat later, in 1908. A third, originally collected from the New World, is the evergreen climber *H. serratifolia*, this grows in a wild state in Chile. For the rest, almost all have their homes in the Far East – western China, Taiwan, South Korea, Japan and the Himalayas. *H. macrophylla*,

Below: Hydrangea serrata *Bluebird, a small, robust shrub belonging to the lacecaps group, with stout shoots, abruptly acuminate leaves, and both fertile and sterile florets*

the common hydrangea, with its numerous varieties of hortensias and lacecaps, first came from China and Japan.

The origin of one of the most distinctive and unusual hydrangeas, however, is rather a mystery. This is Ayesha, also listed as Silver Slipper, and it produces dense, flattened heads of greyish-lilac or pink, cup-shaped florets that have a slight but definite fragrance. Although it is different, it is normally classified in the hortensia group of *H. macrophylla*.

Perhaps lacking in any other quality, hydrangeas do have one exceptional ability that makes them invaluable in a garden of almost any size during the summer. This is their capacity for enlivening the scene with their bright green leaves and large, colourful flowers sometimes 30cm (12 in) in diameter, particularly in a shrub border where evergreens predominate, at a time when the picture might be starting to become a little drab because their flowering time has passed. Fortunately they vary quite widely in size, from dwarfs not exceeding 60cm, up to 4.5m or more in height (2–15 ft). So you can find one that would be suitable for almost any position.

Lacecap and mop-head cultivars make excellent informal screens and hedges and are often seen at seaside resorts; they tend to be more unusual in inland gardens. They are very resistant to wind and salt. Given the right climatic and soil conditions, there is no reason why they should not be used similarly anywhere.

They grow well in semi-shade and often do best in the dappled shelter of trees where other flowering subjects may not prosper.

The climbing hydrangeas are very valuable in a garden because of their hardiness. They are equally happy in sun or semi-shade and are useful for clothing a north-facing wall. They withstand atmospheric pollution and are therefore excellent for covering walls and fences as well as buildings in industrial areas.

The hortensia and lacecap groups of *H. macrophylla* are ideal for tub culture. In severe weather they can be brought under cover. This quality makes them suited to paved areas.

Planting

As mentioned previously, hydrangeas require fairly mild conditions. The best soil for them is good, moisture-retentive loam, previously enriched with well-rotted manure, garden compost or peat. The naturally blue *H. macrophylla* varieties will not produce good blue blooms in alkaline soil and need dressings of peat and applications of sequestrene or aluminium sulphate if they are planted in it. Pink varieties become less clear or assume purple hues in acid soil and need an additional dressing of ground limestone.

Plant hydrangeas in late autumn and early winter (October and November) or in mid and late spring (March and April). Container plants can be established at any time.

Sufficient space is afforded between a hydrangea and its neighbour if you determine the

distance by adding the ultimate spread of each together and dividing the sum by two. When used for hedging, the planting distance should be 60cm–2m (2–6½ ft) according to variety.

For a bare-root hydrangea, dig a hole wide enough so that the roots, after being pulled apart gently, can be spread out in it, and of such a depth that the soil mark on the main stem, showing how far down it had been planted in the nursery, is level with the surface of the soil in its new quarters. Then place the plant into position, replace the excavated soil and firm it. In the case of a pot plant, it is advisable not to disturb the roots. The hole should be of such a depth that the soil at the top of the rootball is level with that of the bed.

For pot culture, plant in 15cm (6 in) pots of J.I. No 3 or a soilless compost. You must be careful not to use lime in the case of blue cultivars and so compost must be specially prepared for this purpose. Start the plants into growth in late winter (January) at a temperature of 9°C (48°F), keep them moist and, finally, water them well when they are in full leaf. Normally you grow hydrangeas in pots for one season after which you can plant them outdoors in a sheltered place.

Plant climbing types about 38cm (15 in) away from a wall or fence and train them back to the structure that they will climb by means of their aerial roots. You can also train them up a tree.

Cultivation and propagation

Keep hydrangeas well watered particularly during dry spells. They appreciate an annual mulch of well-rotted manure or compost in spring.

Most hydrangea species require no pruning but you should remove dead flower-heads in spring. Two exceptions are *H. arborescens* and *H. paniculata*; they should have their previous year's flowering shoots reduced to half in spring. The two or three-year-old shoots of *H. macrophylla* need to be thinned out at ground level to promote strong, new shoots.

Propagate hybrids by taking cuttings and putting them into sandy soil in a cold frame in early autumn (August).

Above, far left: low-growing Hydrangea macrophylla;
Above left: H. arborescens *Grandiflora, with large, globular heads of sterile florets*
Above: climbing H. petiolaris, *with large-flowered clematis*
Left: H. macrophylla *Hamburg*

Some varieties to choose

This genus contains numerous species, varieties and cultivars of which the following form a brief and easily-cultivated selection. The dimensions given after each one listed correspond to height and spread respectively.

Climbers

H. serratifolia (integerrima)
An evergreen species that grows in sun or shade. Creamy-white flowers in mid and late summer (June and July). 6×2m ($20 \times 6\frac{1}{2}$ ft).

H. petiolaris
A strong, self-clinging species that is excellent for growing in trees and on a shady wall. It also makes a very attractive large shrub. Has flowers in corymbs composed of white, sterile florets surrounding its greenish-white fertile flowers during mid summer (July). 7m (23 ft) high.

Shrubs

H. arborescens
A small species shrub of loose growth. It has corymbs, 15cm (6 in) across, of creamy-white flowers from late summer to mid autumn (July to September). 1.5×1.5m (5×5 ft).

H. aspera
It is massed in mid and late summer (June and July) with large heads of pale porcelain-blue flowers, surrounded by a circle of lilac-pink or white ray-florets. 2.5×2.5m (8×8 ft).

H. involucrata
A pretty dwarf species with blue or rosy-lilac and white blooms. 1.2×1.2m (4×4 ft).

Shrubs continued

H. macrophylla
This species covers two very important groups of hydrangeas – the hortensias or mop-heads, and the lacecaps. The dimension given with each variety below is the height: height and spread can be regarded as about the same as the height.

HORTENSIAS
Their florets are sterile, forming large round heads. They bloom from late summer to mid autumn (July to September). A good selection includes the following:

Altona
Deep pink, almost red. 1.5m (5 ft).

Amethyst
Pink or flax-blue double flowers. 1.5m (5 ft).

Ami Pasquier
Crimson. 1m (3¼ ft).

Hamburg
Deep pink to crimson. Deep blue, on blueing soil. 2.5m (8 ft).

Holstein
Pink. Sky blue, on blueing soil. Large flowers. 1.5m (5 ft).

Kluis Superba
Rosy-crimson or blue, on blueing soil. 1.5m (5 ft).

Madame Emile Mouillière
White becoming pink-tinted. 2.5m (8 ft).

Maréchal Foch
Rich rose or deep purple-blue, on blueing soil. 2.5m (8 ft).

Parsival
Deep rosy-pink. Violet purple on blueing soil. 1.5m (5 ft).

President Doumer
Deep crimson. 75cm (2½ ft).

Princess Beatrix
Clear red. Compact. 75cm (2½ft).

Westfalen
Rich crimson or violet. 1.5m (5 ft).

LACECAPS
Have flattened corymbs of fertile flowers surrounded by a ring of coloured ray-florets, between late summer and mid autumn (July and September). The following represent a good choice:

Blue Wave
Heads of blue fertile flowers surrounded by large ray-florets, coloured pink to blue. Best in semi-shade. 1.8m (6 ft).

Lanarth White
Dwarf with pure white florets surrounding blue or pink fertile flowers. 75cm (2½ ft).

Mariesii
Rosy-pink or blue. 1.8m (6 ft).

Tricolor
Pale pink to white flowers. Green, grey and pale yellow variegated leaves. 1.8m (6 ft).

Seafoam
Blue fertile flowers surrounded by white ray-florets. 1.8m (6 ft).

White Wave
Bluish or pinkish fertile flowers margined by large, pearly white ray-florets. 1.5m (5 ft).

H. paniculata
A large shrub with terminal panicles of white, sterile florets during early and mid autumn (August and September).
H.p. Grandiflora is a very hardy cultivar and is more frequently grown. 4.5 × 4.5m (15 × 15 ft).

H. quercifolia
A medium-sized hydrangea that gives beautiful autumn tints and white flowers during late summer (July). 2 × 1.5m (6½ × 5 ft).

H. serrata
An important dwarf species that, although charming in itself, has given rise to a number of beautiful small cultivars such as *H.s.* Bluebird, with blue fertile and sterile florets that become reddish-purple on chalk soil and blue on acid, and *H.s.* Rosalba with blue fertile florets and white sterile ones, quickly turning crimson. 90 × 90cm (3 × 3 ft).

H. villosa
One of the most beautiful late summer-flowering species. Medium-sized, it has 15cm (6 in) long, pale purple corymbs in early autumn (August); likes semi-shade. 2.5 × 3m (8 × 10 ft).

Left: Hydrangea macrophylla *Mariesii, with large, sterile, ray-florets around insignificant fertile florets; top:* H. paniculata, *with pyramidal inflorescences*
Above: the eye-catching H. villosa, *with hairy leaves and flower-stalks*

ILEX

Type	evergreen and deciduous, green and variegated, berried trees and shrubs
Common name	holly
Family	AQUIFOLIACEAE
Flowering season	late spring – early summer (April–May)
Fruiting season	early winter – early spring (November–February)
Planting date	late spring – early summer (April–May), or mid – late autumn (September–October)
Mature size/shape	height 45cm–9m (18 in–30 ft), spread 1–9m (3–30 ft). Various, from conical to weeping

To many people, holly bushes are merely plants that grow wild, with their brilliant red berries set deep among the rich green, spiny leaves providing the most lovely, colourful, welcoming decorations for our homes each Christmas. There are also moments when these same bushes, seen growing without any berries, are deadly dull. Yet when laden with fruit, particularly when it peeps through their leaves whitened with glistening snow, holly can present a beautiful sight.

However, this large genus – composed of 300 species of tender and hardy, deciduous and evergreen, trees and shrubs – provides many elegant specimens that are hardy in a temperate climate. It is doubtful whether any genus of trees and shrubs presents greater variety or is more versatile than ilex; beyond the bounds of the very popular green-leaved, red-berried species and their cultivars there are others with a wide range of leaf colorations and markings; berry tints, shapes, stem colourings and other variations give almost infinite opportunities for ringing the changes in the garden scene.

It is as well to mention at the outset that their somewhat inconspicuous white and green flowers that appear in late spring and early summer (April and May) display very little beauty and are likely to pass unnoticed. Male and female flowers are usually borne on separate trees; when these are planted side by side, the females yield masses of berries that last well into the winter until they are ultimately eaten by birds. Some cultivars, however, are self-fertile (or hermaphroditic); examples of these include *Ilex × altaclarensis* J. C. van Tol and *I. aquifolium* Pyramidalis.

Above: Ilex aquifolium, *common holly, a useful and attractive evergreen that makes excellent hedging or can be grown as a specimen tree in the garden*
Left: I. a. Aureomarginata, *an ornamental variety*

As far as shape is concerned it is possible to find ilex that grow as tall and wide pyramids, or miniatures, such as *I. crenata* Mariesii that makes an excellent subject for rockeries, and *I. c.* Golden Gem that grows to a height of 30–60cm (12–24 in) with a spread of 60–120cm (2–4 ft). Between these limits, there are round bushes, ones of conical and columnar shapes, and others with weeping and fastigiate habits.

In terms of size there is also a wide selection. Two of the smaller hollies have been mentioned already. At the other end of the scale are found heights of up to 9m (30 ft) and spreads of the same dimensions. Fortunately most hollies do not mind being pruned so that size can be largely controlled; although most hollies are naturally pyramidal, the shape too can be modified to a certain extent by judicious cutting back.

Much of the attraction of members of the ilex genus lies in the variously-sized coloured berries they produce that are so evident in winter. In the majority of species and hybrids they are red, but on *I. aquifolium* Amber they are bronze-yellow; *I. a.* Bacciflava's are yellow, while those of the deciduous *I. decidua* and the evergreen *I. latifolia*

are orange. The berries of *I. crenata, I. glabra* (the inkberry) and *I. macrocarpa*, another deciduous species, are all shiny black.

Although holly trees and shrubs are both evergreen and deciduous, the evergreen types are far more common.

Many of the holly cultivars have splendid foliage so varied in character that it is hard to do them credit in a few words. Some, such as *I. × altaclarensis* Camelliifolia, have reddish-purple hues in their green leaves when they are young. Quite a number of plants have reddish or purple stems. Among these are *I. × altaclarensis* Maderensis Variegata and *I. aquifolium* Madame Briot. There is at least one species, *I. serrata*, that is deciduous and has attractive tints in autumn.

Perhaps the most exceptional species is the Canary Island holly, *I. platyphylla*, that has dark green, leathery, short-toothed leaves, sometimes 13cm (5 in) long and 7cm (2¾ in) wide. These are closely rivalled by the large, bold leaves of *I. latifolia*. It is striking how holly leaves vary in shape. The most intriguing leaf forms are the bat's wing shapes of *I. pernyi*, rivalled only by the kite-shaped leaves of *I. cornuta* O. Spring. Most holly leaves have sharp spines but a few are spineless, or almost so, such as *I × altaclarensis* Camelliifolia and *I. aquifolium* Pyramidalis. Another curiosity in this respect is the silver form of the hedgehog holly, *I. aquifolium* Ferox Argentea, that has spines arising from the surface of the leaves. Lastly, and perhaps the most unholly-like of all, is the dwarf *I. crenata* Mariesii that is crowded with tiny round leaves.

The species and cultivars that have variegated foliage possibly constitute the crowning glory of the ilex genus. Many claim that it includes among the best of the variegated shrubs. A great number of shades and patterns have been woven on the leaves of this type of holly and the many combinations include splashings, mottling, blotching, stripes and, very often, edgings. These may consist of any of the following colours: green, pale green, gold, yellow, creamy-white, white and grey.

Hollies are very tolerant as a group. While *I. crenata, I. aquifolium* and their cultivars are content in dry-acid soil, all will grow in clay soil; in fact, *I. aquifolium* and its varieties are happy in both extreme acidic and alkaline conditions. One holly at least, the deciduous *I. verticillata*, with its autumnal, yellow-tinted foliage, flourishes on a damp site. Deep shade does not worry either *I. × altaclarensis* or *I. aquifolium* and their cultivars. Both the latter, together with *I. cornuta* and its hybrids, withstand atmospheric pollution in industrial towns. Exposure at the seaside is no problem to *I. × altaclarensis* and *I. aquifolium* and their cultivars; *I. × altaclarensis* Maderensis is especially resistant to strong winds.

I. aquifolium, the common holly, has a very widespread habitat throughout the world stretching from Europe to North Africa and China. It has been in cultivation since ancient times. Over the years it has been used to decorate cottages and mansions in the depth of winter, particularly at Christmas when so many other shrubs are leafless and colourless.

Many of the forms and cultivars grown today are of garden origins, but there are still a large number of species that have originated in widely-separated parts of the world: China, Japan, the Himalayas, North America and the Canary Isles.

With such variation and brilliance of colour, these plants are obviously of value to present-day gardens. They are fairly slow-growing and most of them can be readily trimmed, so size will not become a problem for a long time. Another great asset they possess is their ability to offer a wide range of shapes that help so much in creating a harmonious garden scene. They can be splendid when planted as specimens in a long stretch of grass. The more columnar forms make excellent markers for a gateway and might well supersede some of the conifers of similar habit. In a shrubbery, or simply a shrub border, you can use some of the brilliantly-coloured varieties most effectively to brighten up dark spots and create interest with their variety of size and shape.

Several species and their cultivars make good hedges that are easily kept in shape – and with the sharp spines of the leaves they are almost impenetrable to man and beast. *I. aquifolium* and its cultivars Argenteomarginata and Madame Briot make excellent hedges of this sort, while *I. × altaclarensis* Camelliifolia, *I. × a.* Golden King and *I. × a.* J. C. van Tol make very beautiful but less prickly ones. *I. crenata* Convexa, reaching 1·2m (4 ft) in height, makes a superb low hedge.

Cultivation

We have already referred to the tolerance shown by the ilex genus. Practically all its members are hardy so when they are established there is little fear of their meeting disaster. They will grow quite well in both sun and shade. However, it must be remembered that the variegated types need plenty of sun to colour well.

They can be grown in any ordinary garden soil but if something a bit moist and loamy can be provided the results are better.

The best times to plant hollies are late spring (late April), early summer (May), or mid to late autumn (September to October), although if the weather is good you can plant them at any time during the winter. You can, of course, plant containerized plants at any time of the year.

You calculate the distance that must be allowed between a holly and its neighbour in the normal way by adding the ultimate spread of each together and halving the sum. When planting a hedge, place hollies 60cm (24 in) apart.

It is best to plant holly (particularly the variegated forms of *I. aquifolium*) by digging a hole of such a diameter that it will take the rootball intact and of such a depth that the main stem is buried to the same extent as when it was growing in the nursery. When replacing the soil, firm it well by treading it in. When it is dry you must water the plants frequently. Always use young plants as

Left: Ilex aquifolium *Handsworth New Silver, a female clone with long, deeply-variegated, spiny leaves*
Below: Ilex × altaclarensis *Golden King, that has broad, nearly spineless leaves with bright yellow variegation*
Right: Ilex crenata *Mariesii, an unusual dwarf-growing form, compact, round-leaved and suitable for growing in a rock garden or trough*

I. × a. Balearica	Erect tree with almost spineless green leaves. Berries quickly. 7·5 × 3m (25 × 10 ft)
I. × a. Golden King	One of the best variegated, golden hollies. Red berries. 7·5 × 4m (25 × 12 ft)
I. × a. Hodginsii	Strong, vigorous male clone with purple stems. 7·5 × 4·5m (25 × 15 ft)
I. × a. Silver Sentinel	Erect, creamy-white and grey variegated, berry-producing tree. 7·5 × 2·5m (25 × 8 ft)
I. × a. Wilsonii	Dome-shaped tree with large clusters of red berries. 7·5 × 3·5m (25 × 11 ft)

I. aquifolium
Common holly, with an ultimate height and spread of 7·5 × 3m (25 × 10 ft); has numerous cultivars.

I. a. Angustifolia	Neat, pyramidal tree. Tiny red berries. 4·5 × 2·5m (15 × 8 ft)
I. a. Argenteomarginata Pendula	Perry's silver weeping holly has bright red berries. 3 × 4·5m (10 × 15 ft)
I. a. Aureomarginata	Has golden-edged leaves. Female trees bear red berries. 5·5 × 3m (18 × 10 ft)
I. a. Bacciflava	Has bright yellow berries. 5 × 5·5m (16 × 18 ft)
I. a. Golden Queen	Gold-margined leaves. No berries. Columnar 4·5 × 2·5m (15 × 8 ft)
I. a. Handsworth New Silver	Modest-growing tree with purple stems and grey and creamy-white colouring on leaves. Red berries. 4 × 2m (12 × 6 ft)

I. cornuta Burford Variegated
Leaves edged gold and suffused with varying shades of green. 3 × 3m (10 × 10 ft).

I. crenata
Small, slow-growing holly. Females have black berries. Excellent as a hedge. The cultivars are dwarf or modest growing. 2·5 × 2m (8 × 6 ft).

I. c. Convexa	100 × 75cm (3 × 2½ ft)
I. c. Golden Gem	45 × 100cm (1½ × 3 ft)
I. c. Mariesii	45 × 100cm (1½ × 3 ft)

I. pernyi
Has dwarf, pyramidal growth, near-triangular in shape; pale green leaves and small bright red berries. 2 × 1·2m (6 × 4 ft).

larger ones very much resent root disturbance. If they are exposed to high winds during winter give them some protection by erecting a screen of sacking, polythene or wattle on the windward side, until they are established – after which they will need little attention. No regular pruning is required but if you want to clip holly to size and shape it, this should be done in late summer or early autumn (July or August). Hedges should be kept trimmed every year, preferably in late spring (April).

Keep a watch to check that no shoots on variegated hollies revert to green. If you find any, remove them immediately.

Holly is fairly free from disease but may be attacked by leaf miners. The larvae of this pest tunnel into the holly leaves. They should be sprayed regularly with BHC between mid summer and late autumn (June and October).

Propagation
Hollies are propagated by means of cuttings taken in early autumn (August). In addition they may be layered in late autumn (October).

Some varieties to choose
The following is a selection of the most popular of the hollies grown today. The first figure given in the dimensions is the ultimate height, and the second is the spread.

I. × altaclarensis
Has dark green leaves. Produces red berries. Has many beautiful cultivars, some of which are given below. 7·5 × 4·5m (25 × 15 ft).

JASMINE

Type   tender and hardy, deciduous, semi-deciduous and evergreen flowering shrubs and climbers

Family   OLEACEAE

Planting dates   hardy: late autumn–early winter (October–November) or early–mid spring (February–March); tender: early–mid spring (February–March); from containers at any time

Flowering season   early summer–mid autumn (May–September) except *J. nudiflorum*–winter

Mature size/shape   shrubs: height and spread from 25 × 60cm (10 × 24 in) to 2·4 × 1·5m (8 × 5 ft); climbers: 1·2–9m (4–30 ft) high

Special use   perfume

Jasmine, or jessamine as they are sometimes called, are fairly popular as climbing plants, but the value of the ones that are self-supporting shrubs is not fully appreciated. This is a pity, because those sold in temperate areas such as the British Isles are hardy, whereas quite a number of the climbers are tender.

The jasminum genus is a large one, containing 300 species. The Persians called these plants 'yasmin', and the modern name is derived from the Latin version of this.

Many of the jasmine grown today originate from China. Notable exceptions to this are the shrubs *J. fruticans*, that grow wild in Mediterranean regions, and *J. humile wallichianum*, from north-east Nepal, and the climbers *J. dispersum* and *J. officinale* from the Himalayas, and *J. azoricum* that was introduced into Western gardens from Madeira. *J. officinale* has long been a favourite plant in Britain, and was grown in cottage gardens in Elizabethan times. Some of the others, however, are relative newcomers; the shrubs *J. humile revolutum* and *J. nudiflorum*, and the climbers *J. dispersum*, `J. floridum* and *J. polyanthum* were introduced to Western gardens at various times throughout the 19th century.

Jasmine flowers are tubular and often borne in terminal clusters, or emerge from the leaf joints; sometimes they form panicles. The flowers vary in

Jasminum mesnyi with semi-double flowers (top) and J. polyanthum *(right) are both tender climbers that can reach a height of up to 3m (10 ft)*

size from the tiny ones of the shrub *J. parkeri* to those of the tender climber *J. angulare*, that are 5cm (2 in) long. All the shrubby species have yellow blossoms; the climbers, however, are primarily white, cream and yellow, but there are exceptions such as *J. beesianum* that has deep velvet red flowers, and *J. × stephanense* with pale pink ones. The majority of the shrubs and climbers flower between early summer and mid autumn (May and September), but some, such as the tender climber *J. polyanthum*, flower from late spring to mid summer (April to June) when grown in a warm place in a mild district, and between early winter and late spring (November and April) when grown under glass.

All the shrubby species are more or less deciduous during a severe winter, but the stems maintain a green effect in most cases. The leaves of jasmine are usually trifoliate or pinnate with three to eleven leaflets. In some instances, such as the climbers *J. officinale* Aureovariegatum and *J. × stephanense*, the leaves are variegated. At least two of the more popular species, *J. fruticans* and the climber *J. beesianum*, bear black fruits after the flowers fade.

Jasmine are fairly modest growers and therefore suitable for smaller gardens. The smallest of the shrubs is the dwarf *J. parkeri*, that has a height of 25cm (10 in) and a spread of about 60cm (2 ft). One of the largest shrubs is *J. humile revolutum* that has maximum dimensions of about 2·5 × 1·5m (8 × 5 ft), after about 20 years' growth. The tender and hardy climbers range in height from *J. floridum* at

J. angulare *(above)* and J. officinale *(overleaf)* are both sweetly scented
Below: J. nudiflorum *must be pruned back hard as soon as it has flowered*

Some varieties to choose
The dimensions given for the shrubs are the height and spread after about 20 years' growth, and the ultimate height in the case of the climbers.

HARDY SHRUBS

J. fruticans	Semi-evergreen with erect growth. Has yellow flowers, in terminal clusters appearing from mid summer to mid autumn (June to September), succeeded by black fruits. 1·5 × 1·5m (5 × 5 ft).
J. humile	Semi-evergreen, semi-scandent shrub. Has bright yellow flowers in terminal clusters that appear in mid to late summer (June to July). 1·2 × 1·2m (4 × 4 ft).
J.h. revolutum	Has dark evergreen leaves and relatively large, yellow, fragrant blooms borne during mid to late summer (June to July). 2·5 × 1·5m (8 × 5 ft).
J.h. wallichianum	A shrub of scandent growth, with leaves that have up to eleven leaflets. It produces pendant clusters of yellow blossoms from mid summer until mid autumn (June to September). 3 × 2·5m (10 × 8 ft).
J. nudiflorum (winter jasmine)	Winter-flowering shrub producing bright yellow flowers on naked green shoots from early winter until early spring (November to February). 3 × 2·5m (10 × 8 ft).
J. parkeri	Dwarf shrub with tiny yellow flowers. Excellent for rockeries. 25 × 60cm (10 × 24 in).

HARDY CLIMBERS

J. beesianum

Has long, pointed, dull green leaves. Although they are rather small, the scented flowers have an unusual deep velvet red colour. They open during early and mid summer (May and June), and are followed by long-lasting black berries. 3m (10 ft).

J. officinale
(common jasmine)

Tall, twining climber with scented white flowers borne from mid summer to mid autumn (June to September). Plant in a sheltered position in cold districts. The form *J.o.* Affine is a greenhouse species. 9m (30 ft).

J. × stephanense

A vigorous climber with scented, pale pink flowers, borne in terminal clusters that appear during mid to late summer (June to July). Its leaves are often variegated. 6m (20 ft).

TENDER CLIMBERS

J. angulare

Has rather thick, dark, evergreen, trifoliate leaves. Its 5cm (2 in) long, scented white flowers are carried in large panicles and appear in early and mid autumn (August and September). 3m (10 ft).

J. floridum

Evergreen climber with yellow blooms that open between late summer and mid autumn (July and September). 1·8m (6 ft).

J. mesnyi
(*J. primulinum*)

An almost evergreen climber. It has semi-double, bright yellow flowers, 5cm (2 in) long, that appear successively from mid spring to early summer (March to May). 3m (10 ft).

J. polyanthum

Vigorous twining species. Its fragrant white blooms, flushed rose on the outside, are borne in panicles and appear from late spring until mid summer (April to June) outdoors, and between early winter and late spring (November to April) under glass. 3m (10 ft).

1·2m (4 ft) to *J. polyanthum* and *J. × stephanense* at 4·5m (15 ft).

One particular value of the hardy and slightly tender species is that they will flourish in industrial areas. Some of the shrubs, such as *J. humile* and its forms and *J. nudiflorum*, are quite suitable for a north-facing wall or in a sunless position.

The shrubby species are most effective grown in mixed and shrub borders, where the more scandent types (those with a tendency to climb) can benefit from being given some support. Jasmine are also suitable for ground cover on rockeries, and the hardy climbers are invaluable for training against outside walls and fences or for clambering over trellises, arbours and pergolas. The tender types make a fine display in a cool greenhouse.

Cultivation and propagation

Outdoor jasmine thrive in any ordinary, well-drained garden soil. The more delicate ones need to be planted in a growing medium composed of equal parts of loam, peat and leaf mould, with a little sand or soilless compost. Plant bare-rooted jasmine in mild weather either in late autumn and early winter (October and November) or in early to mid spring (February to March). Most jasmine are usually supplied from the nurseries in containers, so can, in fact, be planted at any time.

Pot or plant the more tender species in a cool greenhouse border during early to mid spring (February to March). Determine planting distance for shrubby, outdoor plants by adding together the ultimate spreads of adjacent shrubs and dividing by two. For climbing species, allow a distance of 1·5–2·5m (5–8 ft) according to ultimate height and vigour.

The hardy species need little attention except that some protection might be given when the weather is very severe. Tender species planted in a cool greenhouse should be watered freely from mid spring until late autumn (March to October) and then sparingly. Train shoots to the walls or a trellis. Potted plants that have their own support will benefit from being stood outside in the sun from mid summer (June) onwards.

Cut back the flowering shoots of *J. nudiflorum* and *J. mesnyi* to 5–8cm (2–3 in) long, after they have bloomed. Prune out all old, weak wood and tie in the new growths. Thin out the shoots of *J. officinalis* after flowering, but do not cut back. No regular pruning is necessary for the other species.

Propagate greenhouse species from cuttings taken between mid spring and mid autumn (March and September); plant them in rooting compost and put them in a propagator with bottom heat of about 16°C (61°F). For the hardy species, root 8–15cm (3–6 in) cuttings in a cold frame or a sheltered border between mid autumn and mid winter (September and December).

The most serious pests that attack jasmine are aphides and mealy bugs. If infestation becomes serious, spray with malathion. Jasmine are generally free from disease, but grey mould (botrytis) might attack after frost damage.

LABURNUM

Type	hardy, deciduous spring-flowering trees and shrubs
Family	LEGUMINOSAE
Common name	golden chain or golden rain tree
Flowering season	early–mid summer (May–June)
Planting date	late autumn–mid spring (October–March); from containers at any time
Mature size/shape	mainly broad-headed, a few erect-growing, pyramidal-shaped and weeping; height 6m (20 ft), spread 4·5m (15 ft)

The laburnum genus consists of six species of hardy, deciduous flowering trees and shrubs. Of this small genus, only two species, *L. alpinum* and *L. anagyroides*, are in general cultivation. Although they are sometimes found growing on the fringe of woodlands in Britain, they are not native but strays from gardens. These two common species were introduced into cultivation from central and southern Europe between the middle and end of the 16th century. The rest grown today are of garden origin.

The timber of laburnum trees is used for turnery, decorative wood carving and inlay, and also for making musical instruments including the chanters of bagpipes. Rootstocks of the common species are used for the grafting of cytisus.

Flowering during early and mid summer (May and June), these trees and shrubs are most suitable for small gardens. Unfortunately, all parts of the laburnum are poisonous, particularly the seed in the pods. These should be collected and burned as soon as they develop, if young children are likely to play anywhere near the tree. If you have the choice, avoid planting a laburnum until your children are older.

Laburnum trees of all types are characterized by long racemes of yellow, pea-like flowers, growing in dense, hanging clusters, and pale green, bean-like seed pods appearing in autumn. The flowers have some fragrance but do not seem to attract bees particularly. There is one hybrid, *Laburno-cytisus adamii* (a cross between *L. anagyroides* and *Cytisus purpureus*), that can have blooms showing three colours simultaneously – yellow, purple and a mixture of the two.

Magnificent laburnum avenue in full flower at Hampton Court. The trees have been trained over arches and provide a golden area of coolness and shade in the summer

The leaves are mostly green and trifoliate, but two notable exceptions are *L. anagyroides* Aureum, with golden leaves, and *L. a.* Quercifolium, with deeply-lobed, oak-like leaves. All laburnum are comparatively modest-growing: the trunk can reach about 30cm (12 in) in diameter, and after about 20 years' growth the tree will be some 6m (20 ft) tall. However, laburnum rarely exceed 9m (30 ft) in height during their whole life span of about 50 years. Their spread is usually 3·4m (11 ft), or a little more. They are particularly useful for screening in summer, and can be quite effective if planted at the rear of a shrub border that skirts the boundary of the garden. They start to bloom at a time when the spring-flowering camellias, cherry trees and rhododendrons are reaching the final stages of their display.

The erect-growing forms, such as *L. anagyroides* Erect, can be used as accent plants to give height to a garden. *L.* × *watereri* Alford's Weeping is

excellent grown as a specimen tree in the lawn. Similarly, laburnum of pendulous habit can make colourful focal points in a garden, especially if they are framed on either side by shrubs and trees with dark green foliage.

Cultivation and propagation

Laburnum are easily grown, flourishing in both sun and partial shade; they will grow in ordinary, well-drained soil, but show a preference for light soil, rarely being successful in a wet or heavy one. They can also tolerate conditions in cold, exposed gardens, in coastal areas and industrial towns.

Plant laburnum between late autumn and mid spring (October and March), or, if grown in containers, at any time. Space them about 3·7m (12 ft) apart, or the same distance from other neighbouring small trees.

Dig a hole large enough to take the rootball comfortably and allow the longer roots to spread, and of such a depth that the original soil mark on the trunk will eventually be just on the surface of the bed. Before replacing the soil, knock in a stake between the outspread roots, then replace the soil to fill the hole, firming it by gentle treading. Secure the trunk to the stake with tree ties, at points near

the ground, at the middle and at the top. Once planted, laburnum need little extra care and attention. In order to ensure regular flowering, and to maintain health and vigour, remove the seed pods after flowering. Newly-planted specimens often remain dormant until mid autumn (September). Little pruning is required.

Propagate species from seeds planted in pots in a cold frame in late autumn (October). Prick off the seedlings into trays, and then into nursery rows, and set them out in permanent quarters the following autumn. Hybrids and cultivars are propagated by being grafted in mid spring (March) on to seedling stocks of the two species cultivated.

Pests and diseases
The only pests that attack laburnum seriously are leaf-cutter bees and leaf miners, both of which damage the leaves. The trees are, however, subject

Both L. × vossii *(left) and* L. alpinum *(below left) make ideal small specimen trees*
Far left: laburnum seed pods are poisonous and should be picked and burnt as soon as they appear.
Below: avenue of L. anagyroides *at the Royal Botanic Gardens, Kew*

to attack by honey fungus, indicated by failure to flower properly, premature leaf fall and die-back of branches. If the infestation is serious, you must dig up the tree and burn it.

Some varieties to choose
In the following list the first figure given is the height and the second is the spread. Any small variation of size in the varieties compared with species or hybrids is indicated; otherwise you can assume that they are approximately the same.

L. alpinum (Scotch laburnum)
A broad-headed tree that usually becomes gnarled as it ages. Its leaves are a deep, shining green, paler beneath. Has racemes of yellow flowers 25cm (10 in) or more long, appearing from early to mid summer (May to June). It is drought-resistant. 4·8 × 4·5m (16 × 15 ft).

L.a. Pendulum	A lower, slow-growing tree that develops a dome-shaped head of stiff, pendulous branches.
L.a Pyramidale	Has erect branches.

L. anagyroides or *L. vulgare* (common laburnum)
A small tree that spreads with age. Compared with *L. alpinum*, it has shorter racemes of yellow flowers appearing in early to mid summer (May to June), with small, dull green leaves and rounder seed pods. Its racemes are about 20cm (8 in) long. 4·5 × 3m (15 × 10 ft).

L.a. Aureum (golden-leaved laburnum)	An unusual, colourful tree with soft yellow leaves borne throughout the growing season, becoming green in colour before or during autumn (August to October). As autumn nears they turn green, but they can revert to green at any time. Flowers in mid summer (June).
L.a. Autumnale	Useful cultivar with deeper green foliage than the species. Its yellow flowers, borne in racemes up to 38cm (15 in) long, appear about two weeks later than the species; often repeat-flowers in autumn. It is smaller than the species.
L.a. Erect	Has ascending branches.
L.a. Pendulum	Low-growing, elegant, weeping tree, excellent for small gardens.
L.a. Quercifolium	Has oak-shaped leaves.

L. × watereri
A hybrid of *L. alpinum* and *L. anagyroides*. It has small, glossy green leaves and long thin racemes of yellow flowers 30cm (12 in) long, appearing in mid summer (June). 4·8 × 3·4m (16 × 11 ft).

L. × w. Alford's Weeping	Vigorous, colourful tree with wide, spreading head composed of long, weeping branches. When in flower in mid summer (June), these carry pendulous racemes of yellow blooms. Makes an excellent specimen tree for the lawn.
L. × vossii (*L. × watereri* Vossii)	A profusely-flowering form with long racemes borne in summer.

LONICERA

Type	deciduous and evergreen flowering shrubs and climbers
Family	CAPRIFOLIACEAE
Common name	honeysuckle
Flowering season	early summer–early autumn (May–August) and mid winter–mid spring (December–March)
Planting date	late spring–early summer (April–May) and mid autumn–mid spring (September–March); from containers at any time
Mature size/shape	climbers: up to 6m (20 ft); shrubs: 1–3m (3½–10 ft) high × 60cm–3m (2–10 ft) spread

The lonicera genus is remarkable for its variety of types and their uses in the garden. There are altogether 200 species, some deciduous and others evergreen. Many are flowering shrubs (shrubby honeysuckles), while quite a few are climbers of varying vigour and height. The latter include *Lonicera periclymenum* (woodbine or common honeysuckle) that has been grown in cottage gardens in Britain since earliest times. The name was given in honour of Adam Lonitzer, a 16th century German botanist.

This species is one of the most widespread throughout the world – originating from such far apart places as Afghanistan, Burma, China, Iran, Japan, the Pyrenees and the United States.

Various members of the genus were first introduced into cultivation a long time ago. Possibly one of the oldest known is *L. alpigena*, that is of garden origin and has been cultivated since the 16th century. The rather tender greenhouse climber, *L. sempervirens*, was first introduced in the West in 1656; other climbers of early origin are *L. etrusca* and *L. implexa*, that first arrived in Western gardens in 1750 and 1772 respectively. Similarly, the very floriferous, vigorous shrub *L. tatarica* also arrived about the middle of the 18th century.

Two species of lonicera are tender climbing plants that, in temperate zones, will only survive in the very mildest of climates, but they are excellent for the greenhouse. One of them, *L. hildebrandiana*, is so vigorous, growing 18m (60 ft) or more in height, that only a large conservatory can house it. It is evergreen and has the largest leaf, flower and fruit of all the loniceras. The other, the aforementioned *L. sempervirens* is a semi-evergreen growing to a height of only 6m (20 ft).

Above: early-flowering
L. periclymenum
*Belgica has scented
blooms*
Left: shrub honeysuckle
L. tatarica *produces
red berries after
flowering*
Far left: the climber
L. × tellmanniana *is
ideal for covering a
sunny wall — but be
sure its roots are
shaded*

L. japonica *Halliana* (below) and L. j. *Repens* (below right), are *two climbing varieties with different-coloured but equally-scented flowers*

Lonicera flowers are mainly tubular with diverging lips, and are borne in close pairs. These pairs are often fused together (on the shrubby honeysuckles in particular) and so are the berries that follow them. This feature is characteristic of the family. In many cases, and particularly with the climbers, the flowers have a strong, sweet scent. There are at least three fairly common lonicera – *L. fragrantissima*, *L. × purpusii* and *L. setifera* – that flower during the winter.

With most species, both shrubs and climbers, the flowers are followed by berries that can be black, purplish-black, dark blue, red, coral, lilac-pink, violet or amethyst, pink suffused with yellow, and white.

It is possible to find a number of members of this large family that will tolerate some of the worst environments. The low-growing *L. pileata* will tolerate the polluted air of industrial areas and the salt-laden atmosphere of coastal districts, as well as cold, exposure, and heavy shade – making it excellent for underplanting and ground cover. *L. nitida* is another species suitable for heavy shade.

The vigorous, spreading shrub *L. involucrata* also withstands the adverse conditions of the seaside and industrial areas, and is suitable for cold and exposed gardens.

Shrubby loniceras are not generally very large-growing; the more popular ones range in size from *L. pileata* with a spread of 60–90cm (2–3 ft) and height of 1–2m ($3\frac{1}{4}$–$6\frac{1}{2}$ ft), to *L. tatarica* with a spread and height of 2–3m ($6\frac{1}{2}$–10 ft). The most common lonicera shrubs are erect and rounded in shape, although there are quite a few that have a spreading habit and arching branches, among other characteristics.

As might be expected with a group of shrubs that have so many variations, their uses in the garden are manifold. The cool greenhouse climbers, *L. hildebrandiana* and *L. sempervirens* have already been mentioned as being attractive for large and medium-sized conservatories. The outdoor species described below are hardy, twining climbers, ideal for clothing walls, fences, pergolas and archways, for climbing over unsightly sheds and concealing the ugliness of objects

such as telephone poles and tree trunks. The shrubs, with variations in size and habit, are excellent for planting in mixed borders and for growing against a wall. In the border, the green, and occasionally gold, leaves and the different-textured foliage, often studded with coloured berries, can make an invaluable contribution to the appearance of an ornamental garden.

A practical use for shrubby lonicera is hedge-making. Until recently the undoubted leader in this respect was *L. nitida*, but latterly some nurserymen are recommending its variety *L. n. Fertilis* instead. This makes a very effective hedge, with its box-like glossy leaves that cover its erect branches. Nevertheless, it is hard to fault the species that, with its dense habit and small evergreen leaves, quickly makes a good hedge that responds well to clipping. Another shrubby honeysuckle sometimes used for hedging is the light-green leaved, deciduous *L. involucrata*.

Cultivation

Lonicera grow quite well in any ordinary, well-drained soil, although it is advantageous to reinforce it with well-rotted manure or compost for the climbing species. The shrubs are happy in partial shade or sun, but the climbers do better in light shade. In particular, the climbers *L. × tellmanniana* and *L. tragophylla* like their feet to be in the shade and their heads in the sun.

Plant the evergreen climbers during late spring or early summer (April or May) and deciduous and shrubby ones between mid autumn and mid spring (September–March). Plant container-grown ones at any time.

Calculate planting distance by adding the sum of the ultimate spread of the lonicera being planted to that of its neighbour and dividing by two. When making a hedge, the distance between each plant should be 30cm (12 in). Dig a hole large enough so that the roots can be comfortably spread out, and deep enough so that the original soil mark will be just on the surface. Firm well after the soil is replaced. After planting, train the climbers back to their support. Keep well-watered and mulch lightly with leaf mould or compost each spring.

Prune out old wood when necessary after flowering. Cut hedges back by two-thirds after planting and tip back all new growth during the first summer. Cut all new growths back halfway each year until the desired height is attained, and clip in early summer and mid autumn (May and September).

Propagation

Take hardwood cuttings in mid autumn (September) and insert in a sheltered nursery bed. Plant out a year later. Layer branches between early autumn and early winter (August and November). They can usually be severed after a year.

Pests and diseases

Lonicera are sometimes attacked by aphides that cause distortion of the foliage. They are moderately free from diseases.

Some varieties to choose

CLIMBERS

L. japonica
A strong-growing evergreen or semi-evergreen species, reaching up to 9m (30 ft) high. *L. japonica* Aureoreticulata is now more commonly grown, and has small oval leaves, netted by golden yellow veins and mid-rib, and scented yellow flowers appearing between mid summer and early autumn (June–August). *L. j.* Halliana is an attractive variety with fragrant white flowers that change to yellow, while *L. j.* Repens has leaves and shoots that are flushed purple, and scented flowers purple-coloured on the outer side.

L. periclymenum (woodbine or common honeysuckle)
The varieties *L. p.* Belgica (early Dutch honeysuckle) and *L. p.* Serotina (late Dutch honeysuckle) are nowadays more frequently cultivated than the species. The former has scented tubular blooms, purple rose on the outside and lips yellow inside, and flowers from early to late summer (May–July); the latter blooms – red-purple outside, cream-white inside – from late summer to mid autumn (July–September). Both attain a height of 6m (20 ft).

L. × tellmanniana
This bears 5cm (2 in) long, trumpet-shaped flowers of golden yellow in mid to late summer (June–July), and grows 6m (20 ft) high.

SHRUBS

L. fragrantissima
A partially evergreen shrub that produces sweetly-scented, cream-coloured, bell-shaped blooms from mid winter through to mid spring (December–March), followed by red berries that ripen by early summer (May); attains a height and spread of 2m (6½ ft).

L. involucrata
A spreading, deciduous shrub with yellow flowers appearing in mid summer (June), and two red bracts that remain as the shiny black berries are forming. It has bright green leaves and reaches a height and spread of 2·4m (8 ft).

L. nitida
A dense evergreen, used for hedging; it has insignificant yellow flowers in late spring and early summer (April–May), that are followed by round, translucent violet or amethyst berries; it reaches a height and spread of 2m (6½ ft).

L. pileata
A low-growing, semi-evergreen shrub that will grow in heavy shade; it has light green foliage and bears insignificant yellow-green flowers in late spring and early summer (April–May), followed by translucent violet berries; it reaches a height of 1m (3¼ ft) and a spread of 1·5m (5 ft).

L. × purpusii
Another winter-flowering deciduous shrub that yields sweetly-scented, cream-coloured, short tubular flowers from mid winter to mid spring (December–March); height and spread 2m (6½ ft).

L. syringantha
A deciduous shrub with sea-green leaves, bearing hyacinth-scented, soft lilac-rose, tubular blooms in early to mid summer (May–June), followed by red fruits in autumn; it has a height and spread of approximately 2·4m (8 ft).

L. tatarica
A deciduous shrub with leaves that are dark green above and blue-green beneath. It produces 2–3cm (1 in) long pink flowers that clothe the branches in early to mid summer (May–June); following the flowers are red, globular berries that appear in late summer to early autumn (July–August); attains a height and spread to 2·4m (8 ft).

MAGNOLIA

Type	deciduous and evergreen, hardy flowering trees and shrubs
Family	MAGNOLIACEAE
Planting date	deciduous: late autumn to mid spring (October–March); evergreen: mid–late autumn (September–October) late spring to early summer (April–May); from containers at any time.
Mature size/shape	rounded, conical, erect, wide-spreading; height 2·1–5·4m (7–18 ft), spread 1·8–2·7m (6–9 ft)

There are eighty species in the genus, Magnoliaceae, all of which are evergreen and deciduous trees and shrubs. The family includes some of the most magnificent specimen trees. Of these *Magnolia denudata* (conspicus), which is slow-growing, and *M × soulangiana* are probably the most spectacular. Magnolias were originally named after the French botanist, Pierre Magnot, (1638–1751) professor of botany and director of the botanic gardens at Montpellier.

The foliage of magnolias is usually striking. Mostly the leaves are lanceolate in shape, sometimes broadly and occasionally narrow and willow-like as is the case with *M. salicifolia*. Perhaps the most beautiful of all the foliage among magnolias is that of *M. grandiflora*, 'The Laurel-leaved Tulip Tree of North America'.

They have lovely, well-formed blossoms which might be bowl- or chalice-shaped or star-like. They are largely white or cream, sometimes stained or flushed with purple. Exceptions are *M × soulangiana* 'Rustica Rubra' with blooms of rich rosy-red and the rather less common *M. acuminata* with greenish-yellow. Some magnolias have fragrant flowers. *M. sieboldii* follows its flowering by producing the loveliest pink capsules, which open in late autumn (October) to reveal orange-coloured seeds. Many magnolias unfortunately do not flower when they are small. An exception to this is *M. stellata*.

Most magnolias are hardy, but it is advisable to plant those that flower in the spring and that may have their blooms damaged by frost and cold winds, in a sheltered spot. Those that have large leaves would also benefit by being positioned so that they are not exposed to gales. Magnolias are particularly happy growing in heavy clay, but this is not essential; many prefer a slightly acidic soil, often abhorring chalk. A few, however, will tolerate an alkaline soil, among these are *M. ×*

loebneri and *M. wilsonii*. Magnolias are tolerant of atmospheric pollution; and especially suitable for growing in industrial areas are *M. × soulangiana* and *M. × loebneri* and their cultivars.

Magnolias are either large shrubs or small trees, often short-stemmed, and assume a variety of shapes and habit-rounded, conical, erect, wide spreading and so on. In stature the more popular ones vary from *M. liliiflora*, height 2·1m (7 ft), spread 1·8m (6 ft) to *M. × loebneri*, height 5·4m (18 ft), spread 2·7m (9 ft), after about 20 years.

Historically, probably the earliest to be introduced to western gardens were *M. virginiana*, *M. grandiflora* and *M. liliiflora* during the 17th century. After that there was a long succession during the 18th and 19th centuries. Many that grace present-day gardens are of garden origin, but most of the species are variously indigenous to China, Japan, Tibet and North America.

Magnolias may be planted advantageously in almost every position in a garden, where they can be accommodated. It is, however, as specimens and wall plants that they excel themselves.

Growing conditions and soil requirements

Magnolia are happy in any good well-drained, loamy soil. If it is heavy clay it should be admixed with peat or well-rotted garden compost. Generally alkaline soil should be avoided, although there are a few varieties that will tolerate.

Above: Magnolia × soulangiana, *named in honour of the chevalier Etienne Soulange-Bodin (1774–1846), French horticulturist and raiser of this splendid hybrid*

Planting distance

Magnolias should be planted so that they will eventually touch either their own kind or other types of shrubs after a period of years. (say. 10 to 20). The space that should be allowed them to achieve this is determined by adding together the eventual spreads of neighbouring plants and dividing the total by two.

How to plant

It is better not to disturb the roots of magnolia when planting. A hole should be dug of such a depth that the surface of the new bed will be finally at the level to which it it was planted in the nursery, and wide enough to take the root-ball leaving space for soil to be packed round it. This space is filled in with soil and well trodden in. Magnolia usually need staking when they are young.

Container plants should have their container carefully removed by cutting away the bottom and slitting down the side. They should be then treated as for bare-root plants.

Cultivation

During the first few years they should be top-dressed each late spring (April) with leaf mould. peat or compost.

Propagation

Species can be raised from seeds by planting them in peaty compost in a seed pan and allowing it to stand up to 18 months to allow for germination. Seedlings are then transferred to a nursery bed.

Magnolias can also be propagated by means of heel cuttings and by layering.

Some varieties to choose

The first figure given with each item refers to height. the second to spread.

M. grandiflora EXMOUTH	Polished evergreen leaves, soft above. reddish below. Large richly fragrant. creamy-white flowers late summer to mid-autumn (July to September). 3·6m × 2·4m (12 × 8 ft).
M. liliiflora	Mid-green deciduous leaves. Red-purple. chalice-shaped flowers between late spring and late summer (April and July). 2·1m × 1·8m (7 × 6 ft).
M. × soulangiana	Deciduous. mid-green leaves. White. chalice-like blooms. stained purple at the base, in late spring (April). 3·6 × 4·2m (12 × 14 ft).
M. stellata	Slow-growing, deciduous tree with pale to mid-green leaves. White. star-shaped flowers in mid spring and late spring (March and April). 2·7 × 3m (9 × 10 ft).

Below: Magnolia grandiflora
Bottom: Magnolia × soulangiana *Lennei*
Below right: Magnolia Stellata

MALUS

Type	deciduous flowering and fruiting trees
Common name	flowering crab apple
Family	ROSACEAE
Flowering season	late spring and early summer (April–May)
Mature size/shape	height 2–7·5m (7–25 ft), spread 2·5–6m (8–20 ft); round-headed, erect, or weeping tree
Special use	fruits of some varieties used in preserves

Left: Malus *Lemoinei*, one of the erect-growing hybrids. Its attractive blooms are followed by purple-bronze fruits *Below:* the fruits of M. *Golden Hornet* cling on late into the year

The genus Malus is composed of 35 species of hardy deciduous flowering and fruit-bearing trees together with a few shrubs. To this basic number, however, has to be added a mass of cultivars and forms that in many cases are even more beautiful than their parents. When it comes to loveliness, malus may be included with prunus (ornamental cherry) as being unexcelled in floral charm by any other trees.

Among the species of flowering crabs and their cultivars there are no less than five styles of flowers, which range in colour from the white of Dartmouth to the deep wine-red of Lemoinei and they have a wonderful display of colourful fruits in the autumn. Sometimes these are like small, brightly-coloured apples, or they can resemble cherries. There are some enthusiastic gardeners who plant flowering crabs almost entirely for the enjoyment that these fruits give when the days are shortening. You can first of all enjoy the marvellous show of variously-coloured blossoms that they give in late spring and early summer (April and May) and then the autumn tints of their fruits. The fruits of many of them are also suitable for making delicious preserves.

Malus are usually small trees, and nurseries generally offer them as standards with trunks ranging from about 1·25–1·8m (3½–6 ft) in height. On the whole they are modest growers and probably the maximum height reached by any of them is the 9–11m (30–36 ft) attained after many years by *Malus tschonoskii*, which compensates to some extent for this large vertical dimension by being an erect species of pyramidal shape with an ultimate spread of 1·8–3m (6–10 ft). When grown as a bush, *M. tschonoskii* is less attractive, and certainly requires more room than many small gardens today can afford to give it. There are, however, a small number of malus that are suitable for just such a situation. One of these is the very delightful shrubby species, *M. sargentii*, which has an ultimate height of 2·5m (8 ft) and spread of 3m (10 ft).

The origin of these beautiful ornamental trees is a somewhat complex subject. The habitat of the species from which many of them are derived covers widespread parts of the world – Europe, North America, the Mediterranean region, Siberia, China and Japan. Many of the most beautiful ones grown in gardens nowadays are garden-bred.

There is, however, little doubt that the existence of wild or crab apples goes back a long way in time. They were eaten by prehistoric man, who also brewed from them a primitive form of cider. As a further confirmation of its antiquity, the crab apple is claimed to derive its name from the old Norse word 'skrab' meaning a small, rough-barked tree. The many varieties grown in present day orchards originated with these wild crab apples. Some experts believe that *M. sylvestris* was the original, while others say it was *M. pumila*; and there are some authorities who claim the two species are identical. There is, however, evidence that they are separate entities and *M. sylvestris* is most likely the original flowering crab. It is obvious from the present-day varieties that several groups of species had an influence on their development. There are the purple-leaved forms, that all have the influence of *M. niedzwetzkyana* in them. The superbly-flowered Chinese species, *M. floribunda*, can claim to be an early parent of many of the most beautiful. Another strain originated in Canada, and its descendants are classed as the Canadian crabs or rosy blooms. Another line stems from the Arnold Arboretum in the United States, where *M. × arnoldiana* was raised in 1883 to become the parent of present-day cultivars. Finally there is the Pumila group that is derived from *M. pumila* and contains some of the best producers of fruit for jelly – among them Red Sentinel, Montreal Beauty, and John Downie.

Needless to say, few gardens can afford to be without such beautiful trees. They are superb grown as specimens in a well-mown lawn and are equally as beautiful in a shrub border. Possibly one of their greatest, but almost unrecognized, assets to a garden is the variety of shapes they present – pyramidal, vase-shaped, or round-headed, with erect-growing, spreading or pendulous habits. It is doubtful whether any species offers a greater choice.

Cultivation

Malus can be planted in sun or partial shade. It is not particular about soil and will grow in any ordinary garden soil, providing it is reasonably fertile, although it has a preference for one that has been enriched with well-rotted manure or good garden compost.

Like other deciduous trees, malus should be planted when the weather is mild and the ground not soggy, from late autumn until mid spring (October–March). Trees in containers can be planted at any time. As a general guide, each tree should be planted so that there is an all-round space between itself and its neighbours on all sides equal to its ultimate spread.

In order to give the tree a good start, it should be

Left: Malus *Dartmouth*
Below: M. *Echtermeyer, also known as* M. × purpurea *Pendula. Its fruits are purplish red*

Above: the aptly-named M. Profusion *produces a mass of flowers in spring*
Right: the fruits of M. Yellow Siberian *often last through most of the winter*

planted carefully by digging a hole of such a diameter that its roots can spread out, and of such a depth that the existing soil mark on the trunk will be level with the new soil surface. Place the tree in the hole and spread out the roots. As it is necessary to stake a standard until it is well established, drive a stake (one that reaches the top of the trunk) into the bottom of the hole between the roots. Then mix in a small amount of bonemeal or fishmeal into the excavated soil and gradually refill the hole with it, firming it gently with your heel. When it is completed, tie the trunk to the stake at the bottom, centre and top, preferably using tarred twine with a fabric or plastic band to protect the bark.

When planting a container-grown tree, remove the container carefully without disturbing the roots; use a sharp knife to cut off the bottom and again to make a vertical slit down the side. In their early years after planting, all malus benefit from an annual mulch in late spring of well-rotted manure or compost.

No regular pruning is needed, except to remove dead and straggly branches in autumn or winter. Anything particularly unruly can be hard-pruned in late summer (July) after flowering.

It is possible to propagate species (that almost always come true) by sowing seeds, but it is not a very satisfactory method for the amateur, as such seed-raised trees take ten or more years to reach the flowering stage. A better way is to bud them in mid spring (March) or to graft them in late summer and early autumn (July and August). This is essential in the case of all hybrids and varieties to ensure faithful reproduction. Both budding and grafting should be done on seedling apple stocks or root stocks of Malling II, Malling-Merton III or Malling xxv.

Pests and diseases

Malus is rather prone to attack from pests. Aphides, particularly the woolly variety, may attack the young leaves and fruits. The presence of these aphides is shown by the branches being covered with white, waxy, woolly tufts and the growth of galls.

Capsid bugs cause distortions by piercing the young leaf buds and fruit. Fruit tree red spider mites attack the undersides of the leaves, which turn bronze, wither and drop. The fruits of malus are sometimes holed by the larvae of the codling moth and apple sawfly.

Malus is liable to much the same diseases as the ordinary apple. These include apple mildew, which is shown by a white powdery layer on new growths and leaves.

Apple scab produces brown or black scabs on the fruits. In addition, the leaves become blotched with olive green and often they fall. Small blisters also develop on the shoots; these eventually crack the bark and can be seen as ring-like scabs.

Bootlace fungus could cause the rapid death of the tree unless it is brought under control in the early stages. An application of a chemical called Armillatox may save the tree.

Some varieties to choose

In the list that follows, the first figure given under the variety description is the ultimate height and the second the ultimate spread of the plant.

M. Aldenhamensis — Small tree with loose growth and purplish leaves that become bronze-green in late summer. It has wine-red blossoms and purplish-red fruits. 4·5 × 4·5m (15 × 15 ft).

M. Chilko — Canadian tree, with large purplish-red flowers and egg-shaped, shiny, brilliant crimson fruits. 6 × 4m (20 × 13 ft).

M. coronaria Charlottae — Broad-headed tree with autumn tints. Its large shell-pink flowers are violet-scented. Has globular, green to yellow fruits. 5 × 4m (16 × 13 ft).

M. Dartmouth — Mid green leaves, white flowers and a wealth of red and yellow fruits. 6 × 3m (18 × 10 ft).

M. Dorothea — Raised at the Arnold Arboretum in USA. Its flowers are pale crimson and its fruits golden yellow. 4·5 × 4·5m (15 × 15 ft).

M. Echtermeyer — Weeping variety with purplish leaves, whose drooping branches reach the ground. Rose-pale pink flowers and purplish-red fruits. 4·5 × 4·5m (15 × 15 ft).

M. Eleyi — Dark purplish-green leaves. Its flowers are deep red-purple and are followed by conical, purplish-red fruits. 4 × 4m (13 × 13 ft).

M. floribunda Japanese Crab — Small tree with arching branches. Very beautiful crimson buds opening to white flowers. Small red and yellow fruits. 4 × 4m (13 × 13 ft).

M. Golden Hornet — Strong-growing erect tree with pale green leaves and white flowers, followed by persistent bright yellow fruits. 5 × 4m (16 × 13 ft).

M. hupehensis — Stiff, spreading, vigorous species with plentiful fragrant, white flowers that are pink in bud. Yellow fruits, tinted red. 7·5 × 5·5m (25 × 18 ft).

M. John Downie — White flowers, with large fruits conical in shape, bright orange and red in colour. Possibly the best. 7·5 × 6m (25 × 20 ft).

M. Lemoinei — Erect-growing. Purple leaves and purple-crimson flowers followed by purple-bronze fruits. 5·5 × 4·5m (18 × 15 ft).

M. Montreal Beauty — Large, scented, white blossoms tinged with pink. Erect habit. Huge, brilliant orange-scarlet fruits. 6 × 6m (20 × 20 ft).

M. niedzwetzkyana — Vigorous, open-branched tree, with deep green leaves, flushed purple. Flowers are purple-red and conical fruits dark purple-red. 7·5 × 6m (25 × 20 ft).

M. Profusion — Profuse wine-red flowers. Young leaves coppery crimson. Has small ox-blood red fruits. 5·5 × 4m (18 × 13 ft).

M × purpurea — Round-headed tree with bronze-coloured young leaves and wine-red blossoms; most attractive because they usually appear simultaneously. Crimson-purple fruits 6 × 4m (20 × 13 ft).

M. Red Sentinel — White flowers and large clusters of deep red fruits, that persist throughout most of the winter. 4 × 3m (13 × 10 ft).

M. sargentii — Delightful, shrubby species, massed with pure white flowers with golden anthers in spring, and small bright cherry-like fruits in autumn. 2 × 3m (7 × 10 ft).

M. Yellow Siberian — Mid green leaves and single white flowers, followed by cherry-like, bright, deep yellow fruits that often persist during the winter. 4 × 3m (12 × 10 ft).

Top: blossoms of M. floribunda, *a small tree with arching branches*
Above: M. Eleyi *has unusual, dark purplish-green leaves*

PHILADELPHUS

Type	hardy, deciduous, fragrant flowering shrubs
Family	PHILADELPHACEAE
Common name	mock orange
Planting date	late autumn–mid spring (October–March); from containers at any time
Flowering season	mid–late summer (June–July)
Mature size/shape	mainly rounded bushes, some with erect or arching branches; height 60cm–3m (2–10 ft), spread 60cm–4m (2–12 ft)

Philadelphus shrubs are popularly known as 'mock orange' because their flowers have a perfume similar to that of the orange blossom. They have sometimes – incorrectly – been called 'syringa' (lilac). The philadelphus genus consists of 75 species of hardy, fragrant, deciduous shrubs that are grown mainly in shrub and mixed borders.

Philadelphus are widespread throughout the world: *Philadelphus coronarius* is of central European origin, *P. argyrocalyx* is native to New Mexico, *P. insignis* to California and *P. maculatus* to Mexico and Arizona. *P. delavayi* originated in China, Tibet and Upper Burma and *P. incanus* is native to central China. Some historians claim that *P. coronarius*, the most commonly-cultivated species today, was introduced to Britain by the Romans; it was certainly grown in cottage gardens in Tudor times. Most of the other species were brought from their native habitat to Western gardens during the 19th century – the earliest probably being *P. maculatus*, the parent of many fine hybrids growing today.

The flowers of these shrubs are mostly pure white, single or double, sweet-scented and cup-shaped, varying in diameter between 13mm and 5cm ($\frac{1}{2}$–2 in). A few exceptional hybrids, raised from *P. × purpureo-maculatus*, have white blooms blotched irregularly with purple. Examples are Beauclerk, Etoile Rose and Sybille. Another popular hybrid, Belle Etoile, has white flowers flushed maroon in the centre. The flowering season for all species and varieties lasts throughout mid and late summer (June and July).

Most philadelphus have mid green, ovate leaves with prominent veins. Two attractive exceptions are *P. coronarius* Aureus, with gold young foliage, and *P. c.* Variegata, with green and cream variegated leaves.

Although philadelphus are mainly bushy shrubs, some have an erect habit, and still others have arching branches that are laden with

Top: dainty P. microphyllus *grows some 60–90cm (2–3 ft) high*
Above: P. *Virginal – a strong-growing, superb double-flowered hybrid*

blossoms during the flowering season. Usually they are modest-sized plants that can be grown in gardens where space is somewhat restricted. One of the smallest in stature is the very dainty, small-leaved species *P. microphyllus* that has a height of 60cm (2 ft) and a spread of 90cm (3 ft). Among the largest are the hybrids Belle Etoile and Burfordensis, both growing up to 3m (10 ft) in height, with a spread of 4m (12 ft), after about 20 years.

Only a small number of the species are grown today, but there are a large number of very beautiful hybrids that are very popular. These are collected into groups that are distinguished by the appropriate parental name. Among the most common are the Lemoinei, Purpureo-maculatus, Virginalis, Cymosus and Polyanthus groups.

Cultivation and propagation

Plant philadelphus either in full sun or partial shade. They thrive in any ordinary, well-drained soil and do not object to chalk. They will even flourish in the poor conditions and polluted atmosphere of industrial areas, and help to sweeten the air with their rich, penetrating perfume. Many species will grow quite happily in cold, exposed gardens.

The best time to plant bare-root shrubs is between late autumn and mid spring (October and March); but those in containers can go in at any time. Determine the planting distance to be allowed between neighbouring shrubs by adding together their ultimate spreads and dividing the result by two.

For a bare-root philadelphus, dig a hole deep enough to take the undisturbed rootball comfortably and allow the roots to spread, and position the plant so that the original soil mark on the main stem will be on the surface of the soil.

Once planted, philadelphus are easily grown and require very little attention. Thin out old wood after flowering has finished, but retain the new young shoots because they will flower during the next season. Philadelphus are not usually troubled by pests, but can be attacked by leaf spot disease. This manifests itself on the leaves by yellow blotches with darker margins. If the attack is serious, spray with benomyl.

Propagate philadelphus by taking hardwood cuttings about 30cm (12 in) long in late autumn or early winter (October or November), and rooting them in a sheltered border. Plant these out the following year in their permanent positions.

Left: P. coronarius *Aurea is noted for its unusual foliage colour*

Some varieties to choose

The dimensions given in the list below refer to the height and spread after about 20 years' growth in both cases. Unless otherwise stated, the flowers are white or cream and fragrant, and appear in mid and late summer (June and July).

SPECIES

P. coronarius	Strong-growing, medium-sized bush, particularly good for dry soils. 2·4 × 2·1m (8 × 7 ft).
P. × lemoinei	A cross between *P. coronarius* and *P. microphyllus*, this species has produced numerous clones. It is a comparatively small shrub. 1·8 × 1·2m (6 × 4 ft).
P. microphyllus	Very dainty, small shrub with tiny leaves carried on twiggy branches. Flowers are very richly perfumed. 60–90cm × 60–90cm (2–3 ft × 2–3 ft).

Thin out the old wood after flowering to maintain shape of large-growing philadelphus like Burfordensis (above right) and smaller types like Bouquet Blanc (right)

HYBRIDS

Avalanche (Lemoinei group)	Loose-growing shrub with arching branches carrying single flowers in great abundance. Has small leaves. 1·2 × 1·5m (4 × 5 ft).
Beauclerk (Purpureo-maculatus group)	Medium-sized shrub bearing single flowers with white petals that have a maroon-cerise blotch near the stamens. 2·4 × 1·8m (8 × 6 ft).
Belle Etoile (Purpureo-maculatus group)	Compact shrub with single blooms that are white with purple blotches at the base of the petals. 3 × 4m (10 × 12 ft).
Bouquet Blanc (Cymosus group)	Moderately small shrub with double flowers carried in large, crowded clusters. Strongly orange-scented. 1·5 × 1·5m (5 × 5 ft).
Burfordensis (Virginalis group)	Magnificent shrub with erect branches. Bears large, single blooms distinguished by an outstanding boss of yellow stamens. 3 × 4m (10 × 12 ft).
Enchantment (Virginalis group)	Very vigorous, large bush, giving terminal clusters of double blooms in great abundance. 2·4 × 3m (8 × 10 ft).
Etoile Rose (Purpureo-maculatus group)	Blooms have a carmine-rose basal coloration. 1·8 × 1·5m (6 × 5 ft).
Favourite (Polyanthus group)	Moderate-sized shrub with single, very large blooms characterized by serrated petals and prominent yellow stamens. 1·5 × 1·5m (5 × 5 ft).
Manteau d'Hermine (Lemoinei group)	Dwarf shrub with double flowers borne in great profusion. 90 × 90cm (3 × 3 ft).
Silver Showers (Lemoinei group)	Upright-growing, small shrub producing abnormally large blooms in great abundance. 1·2 × 1·2m (4 × 4 ft).
Sybille (Purpureo-maculatus group)	Small shrub with arching branches loaded with single white flowers that are purple-stained. 1·2m × 90cm (4 × 3 ft).
Virginal (Virginalis group)	Strong-growing, erect shrub, considered to be the best double-flowered cultivar. 3 × 2·1m (10 × 7 ft).

POTENTILLA

Type	deciduous, flowering shrubs and sub-shrubs
Family	ROSACEAE
Common names	shrubby cinquefoil
Flowering season	late spring–early winter (April–November)
Planting date	late autumn–mid spring (October–March) when the weather is good; from containers at any time
Mature size/shape	prostrate, mound-shaped, bushy and erect-growing, height 30cm–1·5m (12 in–5 ft), spread 90cm–2·1m (3–7 ft)

The potentilla genus is a large one, containing about 500 species of plants. It belongs to the family ROSACEAE – a relationship that many potentillas, particularly the shrub types, demonstrate by their rose-like single or semi-double blooms. It derives its name from the latin *potens*, meaning 'powerful' – a reference to the reputed medicinal properties of the plant. The genus is made up of herbaceous perennials, hardy annuals, deciduous flowering shrubs and sub-shrubs. From a garden point of view the hardy annuals are of little interest, but the others, being fairly modest-growing and blooming profusely and continuously over a long period, are extremely valuable for a small garden.

Many of the shrubby potentillas grown nowadays are garden-originated varieties of *P. fruticosa* – a species that is widespread throughout the Northern Hemisphere. Of the other shrubby types, *P. arbuscula* is native to the Himalayas, the dwarf shrub *P. salesoviana* to Siberia, and the prostrate sub-shrub *P. tridentata* to the eastern part of North America.

Shrubby potentillas

The shrubby potentillas are all modest growers, ranging from an ultimate height of 30cm (12 in) and spread of 90cm (3 ft) for *P. fruticosa mandshurica*, to a height of 1·5m (5 ft) and spread of 2·1m (7 ft) for *P. f. grandiflora* Jackman's Variety. Some are prostrate in form, while others have an erect habit. Most are very amenable to being clipped back, particularly cultivars of *P. fruticosa* and some should be cut right down every mid spring to keep them bushy.

The vast majority of shrubby potentillas have yellow flowers, but a few types bear cream or white blooms. In more recent years there have been some interesting breakthroughs in colour. Among the new cultivars *P. fruticosa* Daydawn is peach-pink;

P. f. Tangerine is bright yellow to coppery red (according to the general temperature and whether it is grown in sun or shade); *P. f.* Sunset is deep orange to brick red; and *P. f.* Red Ace, the very latest available, is bright vermilion-flame.

With a few exceptions, the shrubby potentillas bloom from early summer to early winter. They are exceptionally hardy and will grow both in sun and partial shade. Although they are shade tolerant, there is no doubt that they flower best when grown in full sun. They flourish in light, well-drained soil and are reasonably drought-tolerant.

These potentillas are excellent for shrubberies in small gardens. They are bushy in shape, with tiny leaves coloured sage green, silver, dark green, and grey-green, and are smothered with brightly coloured flowers that persist over a long period. Some make very good ground cover.

Several of the shrubby potentillas can be grown to great effect as deciduous, informal, flowering hedges. Suitable forms for this purpose are *P. fruticosa grandiflora* Jackman's Variety, that makes an excellent 90cm (3 ft) high hedge; *P. f.* Katherine Dykes, that grows to 1·2m (4 ft) high; and *P. f.* Primrose Beauty, reaching 75cm (2½ ft).

Care and cultivation

Plants from all kinds of containers can be planted out at any time of the year, provided they are not allowed to dry out. All potentillas are generally free from pests and diseases.

Shrubby potentillas Plant these shrubs out in good

Below: keep Potentilla fruticosa mandshurica *in good bushy shape by clipping the stems back every spring*

weather, at any time from late autumn to mid spring. Determine the planting distance to be allowed between neighbouring shrubs by adding together their ultimate spreads and dividing the sum by two.

Dig a hole large enough to take the rootball comfortably and allow the roots to spread out, and of such a depth that the original soil mark on the stem will be just on the surface of the bed. Replace the soil after positioning the shrub and firm in by gentle treading. The shrubby species need little attention, except that it is advantageous to prune back the tall types to the ground each spring, to encourage bushing. After blooming has finished, remove the tips of the flowering shoots.

Propagation
Divide and replant long-lived herbaceous perennial varieties in late autumn or mid spring. Raise the short-lived types from 8cm (3 in) cuttings taken in late spring; insert them in cutting compost and keep them in a cold frame. Plant them out in a nursery bed when they have rooted, and transplant them to their permanent positions in the garden in mid autumn.

Propagate shrubby species from 8cm (3 in) long, half-ripe heel cuttings taken in mid autumn. Plant them in a cold frame, then put the rooted cuttings in a nursery bed; transplant them to permanent quarters in the following late autumn.

Some varieties to choose
The dimensions given for the shrubby potentillas refer first to the height and secondly to the spread.

Left: P. fruticosa arbuscula

P. arbuscula	Sage-green leaves, and yellow flowers that appear from mid summer to late autumn. 60cm × 1·5m (2 × 5 ft).
P. a. Beesii	Mound-forming, with silver foliage. 45cm × 1·5m (18 in × 5 ft).
P.a.rigida	A dwarf compact plant with bristly stems covered in striking papery stipules and small pretty leaves that have three leaflets. It has bright yellow flowers mid summer to mid autumn. 60 × 60cm (2 × 2 ft).
P. Elizabeth	A cross between *P. arbuscula* and *P. fruticosa mandshurica*. Dome-shaped bush with canary-yellow blooms flowering from early summer to late autumn. 90cm × 1·2m (3 × 4 ft).
P. fruticosa	Dense bush with yellow flowers borne from early summer to mid autumn. 1·5 × 1·5m (5 × 5 ft). It has numerous forms and cultivars; all of those listed below have yellow flowers unless otherwise stated.
P. f. glabra	Has red stems, and white flowers produced between mid summer and late autumn. 60 × 60cm (2 × 2 ft).
P. f. grandiflora Jackman's Variety	Flowers from mid summer to mid autumn. 1·5 × 2·1m (5 × 7 ft).
P. f. Katherine Dykes	Blooms from early summer to late autumn. 1·5 × 1·8m (5 × 6 ft).
P. f. mandshurica	Forms mats of greyish foliage and bears a continuous show of white flowers from early summer to late autumn. 30 × 90cm (12 in × 3 ft).
P. f. Tangerine	Mound-shaped shrub with pale coppery-yellow blooms if grown in partial shade or cool weather, otherwise yellow. They appear from mid summer to mid autumn. 60cm × 1·5m (2 × 5 ft).
P. f. Red Ace	New cultivar with vermilion-flame blooms, produced early summer to early winter. 60cm × 1·2m (2 × 4 ft).
P. salesoviana	Dwarf shrub with hollow, reddish-brown stems and white, pink-tinged blooms flowering in mid and late summer. 45 × 60cm (18 × 24 in).

PRUNUS

Type	deciduous and evergreen flowering shrubs and trees
Family	ROSACEAE
Flowering season	late winter to mid summer (January to June)
Planting date	early–mid autumn (August–September); from containers at any time
Mature size/shape	round, round-headed, conical, pyramidal, flat-headed, narrow-headed and dome-shaped; height 60cm–12m (2–40 ft), spread 60cm–11m (2–36 ft)
Special uses	cherrywood pipes and walking sticks are made from *Prunus mahaleb* blackthorn walking-sticks are made from the wood of *Prunus spinosa*, and the fruits of the same plant are used for preserves, wine-making and flavouring gin

The prunus genus is comprised of 430 species, and a wider range of these are grown today than of any other flowering tree species. For convenience, the genus is divided into five sections – almonds, peaches, plums, cherries and cherry laurels. Here we look at the largest section – flowering cherries – before going on to consider the remaining four.

Two ornamental cherries are native to Britain: *Prunus avium*, commonly known as gean, mazzard or wild cherry, is found throughout the British Isles, while the rather smaller *P. padus* (bird cherry) grows wild in Scotland and Wales. Some flowering cherries, such as *P. conradinae* and *P. serrula*, have come from China, while *P. cornuta* (Himalayan bird cherry) originates in the Himalayas. *P. incana* (willow cherry) and *P. prostrata* come from Europe, *P. subhirtella* (spring cherry) and *P. sargentii* from Japan, and *P. serotina* from the eastern part of North America, Mexico and Guatemala. Many of the most beautiful ornamental cherries are of garden origin.

Flowering cherries have been grown in Japan for a very long time, particularly *P. incisa* (Fuji cherry) and the small, slender shrub, *P. japonica*. These Japanese cherries form a large section of the prunus genus, and are usually treated as a separate

P. sargentii *is ideally suited to a garden with limited space. It bears single blooms (right, above) and has blazing autumn foliage (right)*

group. Some cherries have been cultivated in Western gardens for several centuries. *P. fruticosa* (ground cherry) was first introduced to Britain in 1587, *P. serotina* in 1629, *P. mahaleb* (St Lucie cherry) in 1714 and *P. glandulosa* Sinensis (Chinese bush cherry) – a favourite in Victorian and Edwardian gardens – in 1774.

These prunus are almost entirely deciduous, but a notable exception is *P. ilicifolia* (holly-leaved cherry), that has leathery leaves with spreading spines. Some forms, such as *P.* Pandora and *P. sargentii*, produce bronze-red young leaves that make a delightful foil to the buds in spring. Quite a few, including the two last-named, have foliage that turns brilliant yellow, orange and crimson in autumn. *P. incisa*, that has been used for centuries by the Japanese for bonsai, *P.* Okame, and *P. serotina* are notable for this quality.

All the ornamental cherries bear masses of blooms shading from white to purplish-pink or, in the case of the Japanese cherry *P.* Ukon, pale yellow. Most flower from mid spring to early summer (March to May), though a few flower at other times of the year: *P. subhirtella* Autumnalis (autumn cherry) blooms intermittently from early winter to mid spring (November to March), and *P. conradinae* produces its flowers during early spring (February).

Some ornamental cherries have attractive-coloured bark; these include the British wild cherry, *P. avium*, that has a grey trunk turning mahogany-red. This bark peels off and becomes deeply fissured with age. Possibly the most delightful of those with coloured bark is *P. serrula*, that has glistening, polished, red-brown mahogany-like new bark.

These trees are quite varied in size. Possibly the smallest is the dwarf *P. prostrata* (rock cherry), that forms a gnarled hummock not exceeding 60cm (2 ft) in height and some 1·8m (6 ft) in width. The largest is *P. avium* that has been found growing in Britain to a height of 30m (100 ft), but most of the ornamental cherries grown in modern gardens do not exceed 6m (20 ft) in either height or spread.

Among the different shapes found in this section of the prunus genus are round, round-headed, conical, pyramidal, flat-headed, narrow-headed and dome-like. Some are spreading with ascending or horizontal branches, while others are weeping, arching, twiggy or erect-growing. One of the loveliest of the erect-growing forms is the Japanese cherry *P.* Amanogawa, with a height of up to 7m (23 ft) and a spread of just over 2m (7 ft). Some species are pendulous: *P.* × *yedoensis* Ivensii, that has long, twisted branches and slender drooping branchlets, is a good example.

Quite a number of ornamental cherries, including the Japanese ones, can tolerate industrial atmospheres – a quality that is of great use in individual gardens and overall town designs alike, because with them considerable colour can be imparted to otherwise drab surroundings. Another advantage of these prunus is that they will all grow on clay soils.

The great value of the ornamental cherries is that they supply masses of blooms in spring when many other trees and shrubs are just stirring from their winter rest. They are effective planted as specimens in the lawn or when grown in shrub borders. In placing such trees in a garden layout, it is vital to remember that their shape and size is perhaps more important than the colour of their flowers. The blooms are transient, whereas the other factors are constant throughout the year. The columnar, erect-growing cherries, such as Amanogawa, *P.* × *hillieri* Spire, and Umineko, make excellent accent points in a garden design, and are more colourful than the conifers that are often used to obtain this effect.

Some of the ornamental cherries, particularly the Japanese forms, are so heavily foliaged that they make dense screens in summer, while others make excellent deciduous hedges. For this purpose the best choice is either the small-growing purple-leaved *P.* Cistena that reaches a height of 1·8m (6 ft) and has rich red leaves in autumn, or *P. incisa*, that is also magnificently tinted during autumn.

Cultivation

The majority of ornamental cherries are hardy and are easy to grow in an open, sunny position. There are, however, several that are suitable only for growing in the mildest areas. One of these is *P. campanulata* (Formosan cherry). All cherries will thrive in any ordinary, well-drained soil, but they prefer one that contains a little lime. The Japanese cherries are particularly suitable for planting in shallow soil over chalk.

Plant all cherry trees in early or mid autumn (August or September), while the soil is still warm. If the weather is mild, you can plant right through the winter. Those grown in containers can be planted at any time provided they are well-watered.

Determine the planting distance between prunus in the usual way by taking the ultimate width of the prunus to be planted, adding it to that

Far left: Prunus Pandora, *with a maximum height of 10m (33 ft), makes an excellent flowering specimen tree*
Left: the almond-scented P. × yedoensis *is smaller at 8m (26ft)*

of its neighbour and dividing by two. For a hedge, plant each prunus 60cm (24 in) apart.

Ornamental cherries are shallow-rooting plants, therefore it is important that the soil in which they are to be planted is not cultivated too often nor dug too deeply. The prunus should not be planted too deeply either. Dig a hole of such a diameter that the roots can spread out in it. When the hole is refilled, firm the soil by treading it well. At the time of planting, especially in exposed, windy positions, insert a stake into the soil and tie the young tree to it until it has become established.

Once planted, prunus need little attention apart from watering, and mulching with well-rotted manure or garden compost when needed. While the prunus are still young, take care to see that they are not loosened at their roots by high winds, and that their ties are secure.

No regular pruning is needed for these trees, but if it is necessary to cut any wood, do so in the summer because this reduces the risk of infection from silver leaf. Cherry hedges should be trimmed after flowering.

Propagation
The species are best increased from seeds sown outdoors immediately after they have been collected. Japanese cherries can be budded in late summer (July) and grafted in mid spring (March), using *P. avium* as the rootstock.

To propagate other flowering cherries, take 8–10cm (3–4 in) long heel cuttings from semi-ripe

Ornamental cherries are quite varied in height, so you should be able to find one to suit your garden, whatever its size and shape. P. avium *Plena (right) reaches a height of 12m (40 ft), while* P. glandulosa *(top right) grows only to 1.5m (5 ft) The popular, double-flowered Japanese cherry,* P. Sekiyama *(below), is medium-sized at about 7m (23 ft) high with a similar spread*

shoots of the smaller-flowered types such as *P. conradinae* and *P. incisa* in late summer (July). Insert these in a soilless cutting compost and place them in a propagating case giving a bottom heat of 16–18°C (61–64°F). When rooted, pot the cuttings into 8cm (3 in) containers of potting compost and place them in a cold frame for the winter. After winter is over plant them in a nursery bed. In a year or two, plant them out in their permanent growing quarters.

Pests and diseases
Birds, and bullfinches in particular, eat the flowering buds in winter. Aphides, cherry blackfly and mealy bugs can infest the leaves, and caterpillars feed on them. Treat by spraying with the appropriate proprietary insecticide.

Flowering cherries can be attacked by silver leaf – this is a fungus that causes the leaves to turn a silvery colour. You can minimize the risk by not cutting any wood away during winter – this should be done in the summer, when the wound is likely to heal quickly.

Some varieties to choose
In the list of ornamental cherries given below, the first dimension is the ultimate height and the second is the ultimate spread.

P. avium (gean, mazzard, wild cherry)
Has grey bark that turns mahogany-red, and bears white flowers in late spring and early summer (April and May). Its autumn foliage is crimson. 12 × 9m (40 × 30 ft).

P. conradinae Semiplena
An early-flowering spring cherry that produces its semi-double, soft pink blooms in early and mid spring (February and March). 8 × 4·5m (26 × 15 ft).

P. glandulosa Sinensis
Has double, bright pink flowers borne during late spring (April). It has a bushy, round habit and likes a warm, sunny position. 1·5 × 2·4m (5 × 8 ft).

P. × hillieri Spire
An erect tree with masses of soft pink, single flowers borne during late spring and early summer (April and May). It has rich, autumn-tinted foliage. 8 × 2·4m (27 × 8 ft).

P. incisa (Fuji cherry)
A bushy tree, bearing flesh-pink flowers in great profusion during mid and late spring (March and April). 3·7 × 6m (12 × 20 ft).

P. Kursar
Has a somewhat upright habit and clusters of deep rose-pink flowers on short stalks. It has orange autumn tints. 8 × 6m (26 × 20 ft).

P. Okame
A small tree that has masses of carmine-rose flowers blooming throughout mid spring (March). It has good autumn tints. 6 × 6m (20 × 20 ft).

P. Pandora
Has ascending branches that bear masses of shell pink blossoms during mid and late spring (March and April). It has rich autumn tints. 10 × 10m (33 × 33 ft).

P. sargentii
Rounded tree with dark chestnut-brown bark and single, pink blooms borne in mid spring (March). It has glorious autumn tints. 9 × 6m (30 × 20 ft).

P. subhirtella Autumnalis (autumn cherry)
Has semi-double, white flowers, borne intermittently from early winter to mid spring (November to March). 6 × 8m (20 × 26 ft).

P. × yedoensis (Yoshino cherry)
An early-flowering tree with arching branches and a profusion of almond-scented, bluish-white blooms borne during mid and late spring (March and April). 8 × 11m (26 × 36 ft).

JAPANESE CHERRIES

P. Amanogawa
Columnar tree that produces fragrant, shell pink flowers during late spring (April). 7 × 2·1m (23 × 7 ft).

P. Asano
Small tree with ascending branches that carry thick clusters of deep pink, double flowers during mid and late spring (March and April). 8 × 6m (26 × 20 ft).

P. Horinji
Small, upright tree with soft pink flowers set in purplish-brown calyces, blooming during late spring (April). 5·5 × 3m (18 × 10 ft).

P. Shirotae
Beautiful cherry with fragrant, snow-white blooms carried in long, drooping clusters during late spring and early summer (April and May). 6 × 10m (20 × 30 ft).

P. Sekiyama (Kanzan)
Popular cherry, with purplish-pink flowers borne during late spring and early summer (April and May). 7 × 7m (23 × 23 ft).

P. Shimidsu Sakura
Small tree with pure white blossoms appearing in early summer (May). 4·5 × 6m (15 × 20 ft).

P. Ukon
Spreading tree with semi-double, greenish-yellow, occasionally flushed pink flowers that are borne in late spring (April). 5·5 × 7m (18 × 23 ft).

The exceptionally attractive Japanese ornamental cherries will grow quite happily on clay or chalk, and in areas of industrial pollution. The scented, columnar, P. Amanogawa (right), and the fragrant P. Shirotae (top) are among the most popular

OTHER ORNAMENTAL PRUNUS

The deciduous ornamental almonds, peaches, apricots and plums, together with the flowering cherries shown earlier, are among the world's most popular and decorative flowering trees and shrubs. The cherry laurels (a group of evergreen shrubs), though not comparable as far as flowers are concerned, are yet very attractive for garden purposes – either as lawn specimens or as hedges.

Although several of these ornamental prunus were introduced to Britain as long ago as the 17th century, *Prunus spinosa* (blackthorn or sloe) has the strongest claim to being a native of Britain. This might be because of the long period over which it has been cultivated, but it has certainly naturalized to the extent that it is a common plant found in hedgerows throughout Britain. This species is found all over Europe and in North Africa and western Asia. Most of the others that are not of garden origin come from China and Korea – even *P. armeniaca* (common apricot) that now grows wild in southern Europe. *P. cerasifera* (myrobalan, cherry plum) comes from the Balkans, the Caucasus and western Asia, and *P. (amygdalus nana) tenella* (dwarf Russian almond) is native to south-eastern Europe, western Asia and Siberia.

P. laurocerasus (common or cherry laurel) is a native of eastern Europe and Asia Minor and was introduced to Britain in 1576; *P. lusitanica* (Portugal laurel) grows wild in Spain and Portugal and was introduced to gardens in 1648.

Deciduous ornamental prunus

Possibly the greatest virtue of the deciduous prunus is the prettiness of their single, semi-double or double white, pale pink, rose-pink, salmon-pink, rose-red, cherry-red and crimson blossoms. Many flower on bare branches long before their own leaves appear, and before many other deciduous trees start to show any signs of life after their winter dormancy.

Above left: peach trees make a spectacular display at blossom time.
Prunus persica *Klara Meyer is an excellent example*

Prunus persica *Klara Meyer*, an ornamental peach, follows its showy, double blooms with juicy, edible fruits

The first to flower, *P. davidiana* (Chinese peach), has single rose-coloured blooms, borne on bare branches, opening in late winter (January) and continuing into mid spring (March). *P. mume* (Japanese apricot) flowers in early spring (mid February), producing clusters of pale pink flowers; the next to open is *P. cerasifera* that crowds its thin branches with masses of white flowers. The majority of the other prunus (apricots, almonds, peaches) bloom during mid and late spring (March and April).

Some of these prunus yield fruits that are not only picturesque but also edible. *P. cerasifera* bears red or yellow 'cherry plums', the wild apricot, *P. armeniaca*, produces red-tinged apricots and the hybrid *P. cerasifera* Trailblazer gives bright, cherry-red plums during early and mid autumn (August and September). In addition, the Manchurian apricot *P. mandshurica*, a small, somewhat uncommon tree, bears pink blossoms and rounded yellow fruits.

The best known of all the flowering plums, however, is the blackthorn, *P. spinosa*, that abounds in the British countryside. Its small, damson-like, black fruits are familiar to most people. They are used in making preserves, wine and sloe gin.

The common almond, *P. dulcis* (*P. amygdalus* or *P. communis*), produces, later in the year, almond-green, soft velvety fruits. Unfortunately it does not usually produce good fruits in Britain, since it needs the warmer climate of southern Europe. One of the best of the edible cultivars is *P. dulcis* Macrocarpa.

The foliage of some of the deciduous prunus is quite attractive, the leaves mainly having a purple tinge. Among the ornamental plums, *P. × blireana* has leaves of a metallic coppery-purple; some of the cultivars of *P. cerasifera* also have purple-tinged leaves. Perhaps the most interesting of these is *P. c.* Pissardii (Atropurpurea); the young foliage is dark red turning to deep purple. The ornamental peach *P. persica* Foliis Rubis has rich purplish-red leaves when it is young, turning to bronze-green on maturity. The dwarf shrub *P.* Cistena (purple-leaf sand cherry) is another prunus with rich red foliage; *P. (triflora) salicina* (Japanese plum) has leaves that change to bright red in autumn.

The ornamental prunus are not exceptionally large trees; they take some years to reach their full size. Typical among the larger ones is the almond, *P. × amygdalo-persica*, with a height and spread of 6–8m (20–26 ft), while at the other end of the scale, *P. spinosa* has a height and spread of 3–4·5m (10–15 ft). Of the dwarfs, the almond *P. tenella* has a height and spread of not more than 60cm–1·2m (2–4 ft), and *P.* Cistena a maximum height and spread of 1·2–1·5m (4–5 ft).

Generally, all these trees look their best planted in a shrub border, along the boundary of the garden or, in the case of the more modest growers, as specimens in the lawn. The dwarfs, such as *P. tenella* and *P.* Cistena, are excellent shrubs for island beds and narrow borders. In addition, some prunus make very attractive, comparatively modest-growing, colourful hedges and screens. *P. cerasifera* and its purple-leaved cultivar *P. c.* Pissardii, *P. spinosa* Purpurea and *P. s.* Rosea are recommended for this purpose.

The cherry laurels
Both *P. laurocerasus* and *P. lusitanica* are evergreen and they both have dark green leaves and small white flowers that, with the exception of one or two varieties, are not particularly outstanding. The leaves of *P. lusitanica* have red stalks and, in some cultivars, are reddish as they unfold. After flowering, *P. laurocerasus* yields red fruits that turn black; the fruits of *P. lusitanica*, also red, become dark purple. A particular virtue of *P. lusitanica* is that it is quite happy in shallow chalk soil, whereas *P. laurocerasus* is not. Both are excellent for hedging.

Because *P. laurocerasus* is so frequently seen growing as a clipped hedge, it is not always realized that it can reach a height of 4·5–6m (15–20 ft) and a spread of 6–10m (20–30 ft). *P. lusitanica* is a rather more modest grower, with a maximum height and spread of 4·5–6m (15–20 ft).

P. laurocerasus is grown mainly for its outstanding value as a hedging and screening plant. This value is appreciably enhanced by its tolerance of shade. One variety, the almost prostrate *P. i.* Zabeliana, makes excellent ground cover. When allowed to develop freely both the species and its cultivars make beautiful specimen trees.

Cultivation
The deciduous prunus thrive in any ordinary, well-drained soil, but prefer one that contains a trace of lime. The soil must not be too dry or water logged, nor cultivated too frequently or very deeply, because prunus are mostly shallow-rooting plants. Neither *P. laurocerasus* nor *P. lusitanica* is very particular about soil, provided it is fertile and well-drained, except that the former does not thrive on shallow chalk soil.

Plant all types of prunus in early autumn (August), or throughout the winter during mild spells. Provided you water generously, you can plant them out from containers at any time.

Calculate the planting distance by adding together the spreads of the proposed adjoining trees and dividing by two. For hedges, *P. cerasifera* and its cultivars should be 60cm (2 ft) apart, *P. spinosa* 38cm (15 in), *P. laurocerasus* 75cm (2½ ft), *P. lusitanica* 60cm (2 ft) and *P.* Cistena 60cm (2 ft) apart.

Plant all types in a hole large enough in diameter to allow the roots to spread out, and of such a depth that the soil mark indicating the original depth will be at the surface of the soil in the new position. Replace the soil with gentle treading in. In windy positions, insert a stake at the same time as you plant, particularly for trees. After planting a hedge, cut back all shoots by one-third to promote a good bushy growth.

Apart from mulching and watering in order to

prevent the roots drying out, hardly any attention is needed. Little pruning is required, but you can clip back deciduous hedges at any time, unless you are growing them for the flowers. In this case prune after flowering. Prune laurels with secateurs, not shears, in late spring (April).

Fortunately, these prunus are fairly free from pests, except that greenfly and blackfly might be troublesome. Treat by spraying with the appropriate proprietary insecticide, used according to the manufacturer's instructions. These prunus are also fairly free from disease, except for the risk of silver leaf that can be avoided by always cutting back in the summer when the wound will heal rapidly. The ornamental peaches are liable to be affected by peach leaf curl. Treat by spraying just before bud-burst with lime sulphur, liquid copper fungicide or captan. Repeat the treatment a fortnight later and once again at leaf-fall.

Some varieties to choose
The first dimension given is the average height and the second is the spread. Unless otherwise stated, assume that the cultivars are approximately the same size as their parents.

ORNAMENTAL ALMONDS
P. × amygdalo-persica Pollardii
Vigorous hybrid between a peach and an almond. Rich pink blooms 5cm (2 in) across, opening in mid and late spring (March and April), before any leaves appear. 6–8m × 6–8m (20–26 ft).

P. (amygdalus or *communis) dulcis* (common almond).
Erect tree, producing clear pink flowers in clusters on bare branches in mid and late spring (March and April). 7 × 7m (23 × 23 ft).

P. d. Alba	White flowers.
P. d. Praecox	Pale pink flowers, in early spring (February).
P. d. Erecta	Variety with columnar habit.
P. d. Roseoplena	Double, pale pink flowers.

P. (amygdalus nana) tenella (dwarf Russian almond)
The best variety of this species is *P. t.* Fire Hill that is a dwarf plant with rose-crimson blooms borne during late spring (April). 90 × 90cm (3 × 3 ft).

ORNAMENTAL PEACHES
P. davidiana (Chinese peach)
Small, erect tree that needs a sheltered position because it produces its white or rose-coloured flowers from late winter to mid spring (January to March). 8·5 × 7m (28 × 23 ft).

P. d. Alba	White blossoms.

P. persica (common peach)
Smallish, bushy tree or large shrub with pale pink flowers and fleshy, juicy fruits. 6 × 6m (20 × 20 ft).

P. p. Cardinal	Glowing red, semi-double blooms.
P. p. Crimson Cascade	Weeping habit, crimson blossoms.

Above: P. dulcis
(common almond) needs
constant warm weather
to produce good fruits
Left: the fruits of P.
spinosa *(sloe) have*
many culinary uses
Top left: P. lusitanica
(Portugal laurel)
Far left: P. cerasifera
Pissardii *(cherry plum)*
makes   an ornamental
hedge

P. p. Iceberg	Semi-double, pure white blooms.
P. p. Klara Mayer	Double, peach-pink flowers and edible fruits.
P. p. Russell's Red	Carmine-red flowers.

ORNAMENTAL APRICOTS

P. mume (Japanese apricot)

Small tree with almond-scented, pink flowers, some borne in late winter (January), others during late spring (April). 6 × 6m (20 × 20 ft).

P. m. Alphandii	Semi-double pink blooms.
P. m. Beni-shi-don	Deep madder-pink blossoms.
P. m. Pendula	Weeping habit, with pale pink flowers.

ORNAMENTAL PLUMS

P. × *blireana*

Beautiful small tree with metallic coppery-purple foliage and double, fragrant, rose-pink blossoms opening in late spring (April). 5 × 4·5m (16 × 15 ft).

P. cerasifera (myrobalan, cherry plum)

The species has a height and spread of 7m (23 ft).

P. c. Pissardii	Deep purple leaves; an excellent hedging plant.
P. c. Trailblazer	Larger-leaved variety.
P. c. Pendula	White-flowered, weeping tree with bronze leaves.

P. Cistena (purple-leaf sand cherry)

Dwarf shrub characterized by deep red leaves, white flowers and black-purple fruits. A good hedging plant. 1·5 × 1·5m (5 × 5 ft).

P. spinosa (blackthorn, sloe)

Spiny, bare branches packed with small white flowers during mid spring (March) and succeeded by blue fruits. 4 × 4m (13 × 13 ft).

P. s. Plena	Double-flowered form.
P. s. Purpurea	Excellent purple-leaved form.

CHERRY LAURELS

P. laurocerasus (common or cherry laurel)

Characterized by dark, shiny evergreen leaves. In late spring (April) it bears small white flowers followed by red, subsequently black, fruits. It is very tolerant of shade and rain drips from trees. 5·5 × 8m (18 × 26 ft).

P. l. Otto Luyken	Compact, low-growing form.
P. l. Rotundifolia	Bushy variety.
P. l. Variegata	Variety with creamy-white, variegated leaves.

P. lusitanica (Portugal laurel)

Evergreen, with dark green leaves on red stalks. It has long racemes of white flowers in mid summer (June), followed by small red fruits that turn dark purple. 5·5 × 5·5m (18 × 18 ft).

P. l. Angustifolia	A neat, slightly smaller cultivar.
P.l. azorica	A large evergreen shrub.
P.l. Variegata	Attractive variegated form.

PYRACANTHA

Type	evergreen flowering and fruiting shrubs
Common name	firethorn
Family	ROSACEAE
Flowering season	early and mid summer (May and June)
Planting date	best mid and late autumn (September and October) and then late spring and early summer (April and May); container-grown: any time
Mature size/shape	2·4–4·2m × 2·4–4·2m (8–14 ft × 8–14 ft) round, sometimes erect

The pyracantha genus popularly known as firethorn, is one of the groups within the ROSACEAE family and is composed of 10 species of hardy evergreen shrubs. The reason for their popular name will be fully appreciated by anybody who has seen some of the species during the winter, almost on fire with their brilliant display of red berries, or who has attempted to pluck a branch to brighten up a floral arrangement and jabbed their thumb on one of the vicious spikes that cover the shoots. Pyracantha are unrivalled for their many uses and values in the garden; they have a cheerful, tidy appearance and add brilliance during the winter when things are getting a bit dull and a lot of the neatness has gone from the outdoor surroundings of the house. They are all relatively quick-growing, which is a great asset in these days of small gardens, where often there is an urgent need to cover ugly walls or fences, or for screens to obscure some neighbouring eyesore or to increase privacy.

The species all have great similarities. Of these the most obvious are the masses of very attractive, hawthorn-like, white or creamy-white blossoms that they bear in mid summer (June) and the plethora of brilliantly-coloured small berries, about 6mm (¼ in) in diameter, that they produce during autumn and winter. The colours to be found among the berries of the different species and their cultivars are red, coral-red, orange, yellow and creamy-yellow. It is unfortunate that because these winter colours are so outstanding only the most discriminating of gardeners fully appreciate the great quality of the firethorns as flowering shrubs. For beauty, abundance and perfume there are few evergreens to surpass them. When their branches are heavy with the myriad clusters of flowers nestling among their foliage – that sets them off so well – it is difficult to find a more beautiful sight in any garden.

Pyracantha are closely related to cotoneasters, producing much the same type of bloom and in many instances the same massive display of coloured berries. They are, however, distinguished from them by having thorny branches. Incidentally, the main differences between the various firethorns are largely found in their foliage. The leaves can be large, small, narrow, oval, broadly rounded at the apex and so on.

Most of the pyracantha species that adorn gardens at the present time originated in China. *Pyracantha atalantioides* was brought from that country in 1907 by the botanist and explorer E. H. Wilson, while another – *P. rogersiana* – was introduced from the same part of the world in 1911 by George Forrest. Exceptions are *P. crenulata*, whose habitat is in the Himalayas, and the very beautiful *P. coccinea*, that was discovered growing wild in southern European countries and Asia Minor and first brought to northern Europe round about 1629. In fact there are records that show that firethorn was quite well-established in English gardens from the early 17th century.

It can be imagined that a race of plants giving such a wonderful display of beauty and colour through more than one season cannot fail to have numerous uses in a garden. They are seen growing against walls so often that it is frequently accepted they are exclusively wall plants. This is certainly

Below: P. Orange Glow has very long-lasting berries

294

one of the purposes for which they are eminently suitable, particularly as many of them are indifferent to the aspect of their background. In addition to this quite valuable use they make excellent specimen shrubs, for with their solid mass of coloured berries from autumn onwards, there is little else in the garden to rival them. A single bush might be placed as a focal point in the corner of a rich green sward of neatly-mown grass, or you might grow one in a shrubbery border where the brilliance of its colourful berries and the clear greenness of its evergreen foliage would enliven the sombreness of its neighbours in winter. One in particular is highly recommended for this last task: *P. rogersiana* Flava follows its masses of creamy-white flowers in early summer with cascades of brilliant chrome-yellow berries as the summer gives way to the cooler days of autumn.

Another invaluable use of several species is for making hedges that, with the very vicious, long spines of the plants, become almost impenetrable. Perhaps the best for this job are Orange Glow, which is very dense, *P. rogersiana* and Watereri. Several of them, such as *P. atalantioides* that grows 4·5–5·4m (15–18 ft) high, make good screens.

To grow pyracantha against a wall, train the sideshoots horizontally along strands of wire, 15cm (6 in) or less apart, fixed to vine eyes driven into the wall. After a time these sideshoots knit together to form a solid mass of green at least 1·5m (5 ft) either side of the main stem. This characteristic affords an excellent, economical way of making a hedge in a small garden. You erect a post and wire fence with strands of wire 10–15cm (4–6 in) apart, either in the open or against an existing wooden fence, and plant the pyracantha at intervals along it. If you train the sideshoots carefully along these wires and cut out all shoots growing backwards and forwards as soon as they appear, it is surprising how quickly a good hedge can be made. When the shrubs are first planted to achieve this object, cut them back by about a quarter to encourage basal growths that should be trained horizontally as soon as possible to secure a good solid base to the hedge.

A pyracantha hedge has several virtues. The first is that it is quite inexpensive because it is only necessary to plant one bush about every 2·5m (8 ft) instead of every 45–60cm (18–24 in) as with a conventional hedge. With the cost of shrubs this is quite a consideration. The second important thing is that such a hedge does not take up much space, because it can be kept clipped back to a depth of under 30cm (12 in). Thirdly, as the hedge has been created by far fewer shrubs than is more conventional, the demand on the plant foods in the soil is much lower. Once again, this is invaluable in a small garden, because it does not become unduly impoverished and allows for other ornamental shrubs to flourish. You must remember, however, that it takes rather longer to get a good hedge this way, but the extra patience required is well compensated.

Right: espalier-trained pyracantha

Above: The very compact P. wateateri makes a fine hedge and is equally useful for screening an odd wall

Cultivation

Pyracanthas are hardy and can tolerate almost any conditions; they are even quite happy to be planted in seaside areas. When they are mature they are pretty tolerant of exposure, although in very cold areas they should be given some protection when they are young. Most of them are not very particular about the aspect of their position, and for this reason, they are especially valuable because they can be planted to cover a north wall. Some, such as *P. atalantioides*, will flourish in sunless spots and so give brightness with their blooms and berries to places, such as town gardens completely hemmed in by tall buildings, where no other plants would flourish. In addition pyracantha are quite indifferent to pollution and can thus be used in industrial areas.

They cause very little worry regarding soil, because they flourish in almost any soil, providing it is fertile. However, be sure that whatever its nature, the soil is well-drained. All pyracantha will grow very happily in clay, but you must take particular care here to see that water passes freely through it and there is no likelihood of it becoming waterlogged. As a very large number of other shrubs object to this condition you can drain the ground by putting a 45cm (18 in) deep trench across the site, and fill it with about 30cm (12 in) of rubble and a top layer of 15cm (6 in) of topsoil. Pyracantha will grow well in a chalky soil and equally in soil that is on the acid side without any signs of trouble.

All pyracantha resent being transplanted, so usually container-grown plants are sold by nurserymen; as we describe under When and how to plant, the seedlings or rooted cuttings are finally potted up before transferring them to their growing position outdoors.

Little attention is needed beyond watering during a period of drought, hoeing the surrounding soil to keep it free from weeds and mulching with garden compost, peat, manure or spent hops when the soil is moist in early summer (May). Being evergreens, they welcome being sprayed with cold water in the evening during dry weather.

When they are grown as wall plants, the sideshoots should be regularly tied in every year between late summer and mid autumn (July and September). To encourage side growths, any shoots growing forward that are not needed should be cut back to the stem from which they emerge between early and mid summer (May and June). When they are growing as specimens no pruning is necessary other than to keep them tidy and to size.

When and how to plant

Like other evergreen shrubs generally, pyracantha are best planted out between mid and late autumn (September and October) or during late spring and early summer (April and May) after the risk of the young plants being exposed to any severe winter weather and icy winds has passed. Although these periods are more usually recommended as being the safest, it seems that when they are container-grown (as they usually are), there is little reason why they should not be planted any time other than when the weather is likely to be severe. If this is done, however, it is important to see that they are kept well watered for a time after planting.

Since the majority of pyracantha have an ultimate spread of about 3m (10 ft), if several are planted in a group in a shrub border they need to be planted about 3m (10 ft) apart. When they are planted in a mixed bed of shrubs, the planting distance between a pyracantha and its neighbour is determined in the usual way by adding the ultimate spread of the former to that of its adjacent companion and dividing the sum by two. The ultimate spread of various shrubs is often given nowadays in nurserymen's catalogues or standard books on gardening.

Unless the previously-mentioned technique for making a pyracantha hedge is adopted, to get a good thick hedge quickly the planting distance should be 38–60cm (15–24 in).

As pyracantha are nearly always raised in containers, a hole for one that is intended as a free-standing bush should be dug so that it is about 10cm (4 in) greater in diameter than that of the rootball and of such a depth that the soil level in the pot is just at the surface of the soil in the bed when it is planted. Humus-making material, such as compost, manure or damp peat, should be mixed into the soil at the bottom of the hole. Tap the plant out of the pot and place it in the hole. Pack some of the excavated soil (not too tightly) round the rootball and firm it gently treading around the circumference of the hole. Finally level the surface of the soil, leaving it loose. Before planting, plunge the pot into water and keep it there until any bubbles cease to rise. At the time of planting insert a stake because pyracantha normally need some support in their early days.

When making a hedge, treat the plants similarly. When they are 20cm (8 in) tall, pinch out the growing tips to encourage basal growths. This should be done again later on.

If the pyracantha is intended to be a wall plant, it is best to plant it, leaning backwards slightly, about 30cm (12 in) in front of the wall and to train the young growths back to it in the first instance. This is because beds at the foot of a wall are so much under the eaves of the house that rain does not easily reach them and the soil keeps almost permanently dry. In this position it is important, prior to planting, to provide some wires spanning vine eyes driven into the wall or trellis, to which the young branches can be tied before they get disturbed.

Pyracantha can be raised from seed, but remember that only the species (not their cultivars) will be truly reproduced. Pick the ripe berries in late autumn (October) and squash them to obtain the seeds. Sow them in trays of J.I. seed compost or a soilless compost and put into a cold frame. When the seedlings are large enough to handle, prick them out into several seed trays. Ultimately they are transplanted into 8cm (3 in) pots and kept in the cold frame. The following late spring or early summer (April or May) plunge them into the soil or a specially-made bed of peat outdoors. In late autumn (October) you can make a start on planting out the young shrubs in their permanent growing quarters.

The alternative is to grow from cuttings that should be of hardwood and about 10–15cm (4–6 in) long. Take the cuttings in late autumn (October) and insert them in a bed of equal parts sand and peat in a cold frame. Pot them up in the following late spring or early summer (April or May) and plunge the pots into an outdoor bed of soil or peat. Finally, plant out the small plants in late autumn (October).

Pests and diseases
Stems and leaves are sometimes affected by aphides, particularly woolly aphides, that are detected by the presence of white, waxy tufts; spray with derris or malathion to control them. Scale insects are another menace. They make the plant sticky and sooty moulds develop. Spray with diazonin or malathion if the infestation is heavy.

As with other species belonging to the ROSACEAE family, pyracantha are likely to be attacked by fireblight, that blackens and shrivels the flowers and causes the leaves to wither and the branches to die back. If this happens there is nothing to do but dig up the infected plant and burn it.

A disease peculiar to pyracantha is pyracantha scab, indicated by an olive-brown or black coating on the leaves and berries. Spray with captan as soon as you see these symptoms.

Above right: two varieties intermingling will give even more colour interest

Some varieties to choose
The selection that follows lists excellent shrubs, that are easily available, to grow free-standing, or as wall plants, or for hedging. The figures given for ultimate height (first figure) and spread (second figure) relate to pyracantha growing as bushes. On a sheltered wall they normally reach greater height.

P. angustifolia	Grey-green leaves, with conspicuous clusters of orange-yellow berries that do not ripen until mid winter (December) and are sometimes retained until spring. 3×2.7m (10×9 ft). Will do best against a west wall.
P. atalantioides (*P. gibbsii*)	Considered to be the best red-berried wall plant. Good for sunless walls. Birds seldom eat the fruit. 3.6×3.6m (12×12 ft). Aurea has rich yellow fruits.
P. coccinea	Flowers in mid summer (June), followed by red berries. 3.6×3.6m (12×12 ft). Lalandei is possibly the most popular pyracantha. It has larger orange-red berries that smother the branches. 4.2×4.2m (14×14 ft).
P. crenulata	Orange-red berries. 2.7×3.9m (9×13 ft).
P. Orange Glow	Branches are inundated with long-lasting, bright orange-red berries. Good for hedging, as a bush, or on a north-facing wall. 2.4×3m (8×10 ft).
P. rogersiana	Freely produces reddish-orange berries. Makes an excellent hedge. 2.4×2.4m (8×8 ft). Flava is a very attractive bright yellow-berried version.
P. Shawnee	Comparatively recent introduction from America. Its masses of white flowers are succeeded by an abundance of yellow-to-orange berries as early as early autumn (August). Good for wall or border. It is claimed to be resistant to fireblight and scab. 3×3m (10×10 ft).
P. Watereri	Compact-growing shrub with masses of bright red berries. Good for a wall as a specimen, or as a hedge. 2.7×3.6m (9×12 ft).

RHODODENDRONS

Type	evergreen and deciduous flowering shrubs
Family	ERICACEAE
Flowering season	late winter to late summer (January–July)
Planting date	outdoors: mid to late spring (March–April) or autumn (September–October); from containers: anytime
Mature size/shape	prostrate to 12m (40 ft) spreading or bushy
Special use	Permanent ornamental foliage and flowering shrubs or small trees

Between them, the rhododendron and the rose have revolutionized British gardens, and it has all happened in the last hundred years or so. Rhododendrons were grown long before that but they were a rather dull lot and made no impact on ordinary gardeners. The first to arrive from Asia Minor in 1763 was *Rhododendron ponticum*, and it liked the British climate and soil so much that it soon escaped from gardens and began to naturalize itself. It is now the common rhododendron of many woodlands and some moorlands, a shrub much used as cover for game and also as a windbreak or hedge, but seldom nowadays as an ornamental garden shrub. Its purplish-mauve colour is too restricted, its flowers insufficiently impressive, to stand competition with the beauties that have since arrived. Nevertheless it is still a very common rootstock for other rhododendron cultivars. The name is derived from the Greek *rhodon* (a rose) and *dendron* (a tree).

The revolution began with the discovery in the mid-19th century of previously unknown rhododendrons in the Himalayas and in the mountain ranges and valleys of Burma, Assam and southern and south-western China. What started as a trickle became a flood and today botanists recognize 500–600 distinct species.

Not all the newcomers were beauties or even of much use to gardeners, but a great many were. What was really remarkable was the astonishing range of shapes, sizes and colour to be found among them. There were prostrate rhododendrons that crept along the ground and, at the other extreme, tree rhododendrons that could reach 10–12m (up to 40 ft); some with huge, and some with tiny, flowers in all manner of colours including scarlet, crimson, pink, salmon, apricot, yellow, purple and very nearly pure blue.

Because of the parts of the world from which they came, a good many of the new species were rather tender. Some needed greenhouse protection

in winter, some grew well in places where the climate was exceptionally mild. But many were completely hardy everywhere and even the tender kinds provided the plant breeders with some magnificent material on which to work.

Looking back to the latter part of the 19th century it is possible to distinguish two distinct types of hybrid. One came from the nurserymen who kept their breeding programmes completely secret and crossed species and existing hybrids with the sole object of producing hardy, reliable, free-flowering shrubs. The other came from wealthy amateurs willing to record and publish the crosses they made and anxious to outvie one another in size of bloom, novelty of colour, richness of scent and everything else that made the new rhododendron so exciting.

The amateurs cared little if some of their seedlings were tender. The nurserymen, by contrast, concentrated on utility, and since, even in the hardiest rhododendron, the flowers and opening flower-buds can be completely spoiled by frost, they selected in the main varieties which flowered only in summer (mid May to mid June). So the amateurs produced hybrids of great beauty and variety with a flowering season from mid winter to late summer (January to July) and the nurserymen produced hardy hybrids which tended to look much alike in shape and size, had a concentrated flowering season, and differed chiefly in flower colours and quality.

The two races are still with us, the pedigree hybrids and the hardy hybrids, plus a great many species just as they grow in the wild. But we now know a great deal more about rhododendrons than we did, can select for gardens from all three groups with every expectation of success, and have developed means of growing rhododendrons even where it would have seemed impossible to do so a generation or so ago. The rhododendron has arrived as a shrub which does for the ordinary garden in spring and early summer what the rose can do so well for it from midsummer to autumn—fill it with colour and perfume and do it with a minimum of trouble or risk of failure.

In one respect rhododendrons are still at a disadvantage to roses. Most of them dislike

Right: magnificent view of hardy hybrid Mrs Furnival
Below: flower detail of hardy hybrid Gomer Waterer

alkaline soils so much that they can only be grown in chalk or limestone soils with special precautions or treatments. But those precautions are now fully understood and the treatments are available, and anyone can grow rhododendrons today.

Nearly all the shrubs that gardeners would regard as 'true' rhododendrons are evergreens, but botanists extend the genus to include what gardeners know as azaleas, some of which are evergreen and some deciduous. Most garden centres follow this horticultural practice and list azaleas separately, but a few adopt the botanical classification and put them under rhododendron, though with the garden varieties in a separate group under appropriate sub-headings. It is quite likely that botanists will one day also give the azaleas generic rank (they already fill a separate section or 'series' of the huge rhododendron genus) and there is so much to be said about them that we have already given them a section in their own right on page 204.

All rhododendrons prefer acid soils but they differ in their sensitiveness to it. For most, pH 5·0 to pH 6·0 is ideal, but many will grow well even up to pH 6·5 and some, including *Rhododendron ponticum* and some of the hardy hybrids, will get along quite nicely in neutral soils (pH 7·0) without special help. But usually, beyond pH 6·5, it will be necessary either to import acid soil and peat to make up beds for the rhododendrons, or to feed them two or three times a year with 'chelated' iron and manganese.

Chelates are complex chemical compounds which are now available in most garden shops, ready for mixing with water according to label instructions and applying to the soil. If special beds are prepared it is an advantage if they can be built up 30cm (12 in) or more above the level of the existing soil so that lime does not wash from this into the rhododendron bed. However, this means that another danger must be guarded against; raised beds can become very dry beds in summer. Rhododendrons can be watered, but if the mains water is 'hard' (alkaline), as it may well be in a chalk or limestone locality, this can introduce the very element you are trying to exclude. Rainwater is the ideal solution, and it is worthwhile putting a rain barrel where it can collect water from something like a shed or greenhouse roof.

All rhododendrons make masses of fibrous roots which bind the soil together into a tight ball. This makes them very easy to move even when they are quite big – a bonus for the gardener who can move them to other places if the original arrangement proves unsatisfactory, or can deliberately overplant at the outset to get a quick effect and then thin out later on.

If rhododendrons are to be moved from open ground, autumn (September–October) and mid to late spring (March–April) are the best planting seasons, but if they are obtained in containers rhododendrons can be planted at any time of the year provided they are properly looked after. But they should never be planted in exposed positions during wintry weather.

Bushes do not normally require pruning, but if they grow too large the branches can be cut back even to within a few inches of the soil level, although this will prevent flowering for at least one year. The best time for such hard pruning is in early summer (May) or immediately after flowering.

Rhododendrons, especially the species, usually set seed freely. This is almost dust-like and a pod can contain thousands of seeds, which is why the breeders were able to produce new varieties so quickly. But such tiny seeds are rather difficult to manage, seedlings take a number of years to reach flowering size, and those raised from hybrid plants are likely to differ greatly both from their parents and from one another. So in practice seed is not much used as a method of propagation except by specialists and breeders.

Nurserymen propagate mainly by grafting, usually onto seedlings of *Rhododendron ponticum*, and to a lesser degree by cutting and layering. Grafted plants have good roots and grow well, but if they produce suckers (shoots direct from the roots), these will be of the same character as the stock, not of the garden variety grafted on it. This accounts for many of the big bushes of *Rhododendron ponticum* to be seen in gardens. Their owners have failed to notice and remove the suckers which, because of their greater vigour, have gradually swamped and killed the garden variety. Ponticum suckers have narrower, darker green leaves than most of the hybrids, but the important point to watch for is any growth that is clearly of a different character from the rest of the bush. Trace such stems to their source and if this is at the roots or very low down on the main stem, more or less at soil level, they are almost certainly suckers and should be cut out with a sharp knife or secateurs.

By contrast rhododendrons raised from cuttings or layers are 'on their own roots' to use the gardener's phrase. The whole plant, stems and roots, is of the same kind, and suckers will bear just as beautiful flowers as stems from above ground and should be retained.

Most rhododendrons like to grow in dappled shade—the kind of shade provided by fairly thin woodland. If the cover trees are mixed deciduous

and evergreens, say some oaks and some pines, this is ideal. But these conditions are not essential and the hardy hybrids in particular will usually grow well even in full sun, provided the soil does not get too hot and dry in summer. One of the advantages of digging-in plenty of rotted leaves or peat before planting is that they both help to keep the soil cool and moist without making it too wet in winter; this should also be done each spring.

In addition to the 500–600 species there are now thousands of hybrid rhododendrons. Some nurserymen specialize in them and all garden centres offer quite a good selection. Here is a short selection of pedigree species and hybrids, together with some non-pedigree hardy hybrids which are still the toughest and easiest to grow (they are certainly the best where the air is smoke-polluted).

Bottom left and left: hardy hybrids Pink Pearl and Sappho

HARDY HYBRIDS

These average 3–4·5m (10–15 ft) in height and diameter when fully grown, or considerably more in moist, sheltered positions. Most of them flower in early to mid summer (May to June). The flowers are widely funnel-shaped, and measure 5–7·5cm (2–3 in) across.

Beauty of Littleworth	White-spotted crimsons.
Blue Peter	Violet-blue, the best of its colour.
Britannia	Scarlet with wavy-edged flowers. Slow growing and compact.
Christmas Cheer	Pink buds opening to blush-white flowers in mid spring (March).
Cynthia	Rose-red, very vigorous, hardy and reliable.
Doncaster	Crimson-scarlet, below average height.
Goldsworth Yellow	Apricot-pink buds opening to primrose-yellow flowers.
Gomer Waterer	White flushed mauve with yellow blotch.
Loder's White	Mauve-pink buds opening to pure white flowers in early summer (May).
Mrs Charles E. Pearson	Mauve-pink becoming nearly white.
Mrs Furnival	Rose-pink blotched with brown and crimson.
Mrs G. W. Leak	Similar to last in colour but a little earlier and a looser flower truss.
Pink Pearl	Rose buds opening to very large pink flowers. Rather lax habit.
Purple Splendour	Rich deep purple.
Sappho	Mauve buds opening to white flowers with almost black blotch.
Souvenir de Dr S. Endtz	Rose buds opening to pink flowers. Vigorous in growth.
Susan	Lavender-blue.

PEDIGREE HYBRIDS

These are best planted in thin woodland with dappled shade (sharp de-frosting caused by early morning sun may damage buds) and shelter from cold winds.

Angelo	Huge, sweetly-scented white flowers in mid summer (June). 3–4m (10–13 ft) when full grown.
Blue Diamond	Clusters of small lavender-blue flowers in late spring (April). 1m (3 ft).
Elizabeth	Large, deep red flowers in late spring (April). 1m (3 ft). Very hardy.
Hawk	Large pale yellow flowers in early summer (May). Up to 3m (10 ft). Crest is a particularly fine form.
Lady Chamberlain	Clusters of drooping, almost tubular orange-red flowers in early summer (May). Up to 2m (7 ft).
Loderi	Huge trusses of white- or pink-flushed, richly scented flowers in early summer (May). 3–4m (10–13 ft).
Naomi	Large pink- or mauve-tinted sweetly scented flowers in early summer (May). To 3m (10 ft).
Polar Bear	Large white flowers in late summer (July). 3–4m (10–13 ft).
Praecox	Magenta flowers in early spring (February–March). To 1·5m (5 ft).
Tally Ho	Brilliant red flowers appearing mid summer (June). About 2m (7 ft).
Temple Belle	Bell-shaped rose-pink flowers in early summer (May). 1m (3 ft).

SPECIES

As with the pedigree hybrids, species are best planted in light shelter such as thin woodland.

R. arboreum	Red, pink or white flowers from late winter to late spring (January to April). To 12m (40 ft).
R. augustinii	Blue or mauve flowers in late spring (April–May). 2 to 3m (6–10 ft). Electra is a fine blue form.
R. cinnabarinum	Cinnabar-red (vermilion) tubular flowers in early summer (May–June). To 3m (10 ft). The variety Blandfordiflorum has flowers yellow inside, and the variety Roylei purplish-red flowers.
R. discolor	Large pink flowers in mid summer (June–July). 3–4m (10–13 ft).
R. falconeri	Huge leaves and large cream flowers blotched with purple in late spring (April–May). 4–6m (13–20 ft).
R. fortunei	Scented lilac-pink flowers in early summer (May). 4–5m (13–17 ft).
R. leucaspis	Saucer-shaped creamy white flowers in early spring (February–March). About 50cm (20 in).
R. racemosum	Small pink flowers in mid to late spring (March–April). Up to 2m (7 ft). Forrest's Dwarf is a shorter form.
R. russatum	Small violet-blue flowers in late spring (April–May). Up to 1m (3 ft).
R. thomsonii	Blood-red flowers in late spring (April). 4–5m (13–17 ft).
R. wardii	Saucer-shaped yellow flowers in early summer (May). 3–4m (10–13 ft).
R. williamsianum	Bell-shaped pink flowers in late spring (April). Neat heart-shaped leaves. About 1m (3 ft).
R. yakushimanum	Rose-pink buds opening to white flowers in early summer (May). 1m (3 ft). There are numerous hybrids of this species, most of which retain its dwarf compact habit but extend its range to include all the rhododendron colours. These are very good garden plants.

Top: R. wardii, *an early summer-flowering species*
Centre: the pedigree hybrids Blue Diamond and Lady Chamberlain
Below: cluster of spring-flowering R. falconeri

Choosing and Buying Roses

The first step towards growing first-class roses is to select the right plants. It's something that deserves time and thought – your roses may be with you for many years, so don't rush into buying inferior plants simply because they are cheap and easy to get.

Choosing the right rose varieties for your garden is best done after seeing the plants in garden conditions. If you can be patient, follow their progress in a friend's garden over an entire season. In this way you can judge how big and strongly they will grow, how well and often they will flower, how resistant they are to disease, and how well they will stand up to the elements.

Your friends may have some roses that you like in their garden but by restricting yourself to these you can miss something better. A good local nursery will always be helpful with advice, but as most nurseries stock only a limited range, your choice may still be restricted. Also, you may not be able to see the roses in their mature state. It is particularly unwise to choose shrub roses in this way unless you have already seen them in a garden. It is quite impossible to visualize the sheer mass of a large shrub without having actually seen it. You could buy a rose

60cm (24 in) tall and end up with one 1·8 × 1·8m (6 × 6 ft). Actual size may not be so important if the habit of growth is light and airy, but a very leafy, dense-growing bush will make its presence felt in no uncertain manner. It's worth remembering that some of the bigger nurseries and many of the specialist rose nurseries have display beds – as distinct from nursery fields – where well-established bushes can be seen.

Where else can you see a variety of roses growing? Many city parks have beds of roses properly labelled and there are fine displays in public gardens elsewhere, and at stately homes and houses owned by the National Trust, many of which are famous for their collections of old roses. Examples include: Hardwick Hall in Derbyshire, Hidcote Manor in Gloucestershire, Mottisfont Abbey in Hampshire, Nymans in Sussex, Sissinghurst Castle in Kent, Wallington in Northumberland.

The Royal National Rose Society has special display gardens in Cardiff, Edinburgh, Glasgow, Harrogate, Norwich, Nottingham, Redcar, Southport and Taunton, and in these you can see the latest and best varieties. But the finest collection of all is at the Society's headquarters near St Albans in Hertfordshire. Another fine place to visit in order to 'pick' your favourites is the famous Queen Mary's Rose Garden in Regent's Park, London.

Far left: a flourishing rose garden with floribundas Iceberg and Evelyn Fison at front, climbers Golden Showers and Chaplin's Pink at back
Above: Royal National Rose Society garden at St Albans, essential viewing for any serious rose buyer
Left: a true container-grown rose has moss or algae growing on soil surface

Container-grown roses

Another popular way of buying roses is to get them as container-grown plants from garden centres and nurseries. The advantage of this is that roses can be planted out at almost any time and with the minimum of root disturbance; but they must be container-*grown*. The roots must also be well-established and a good way to determine this is to lift up the container and see if any have worked their way through to the bottom; if they have, it is a good sign. The presence of moss and algae on the soil surface is another way of seeing that your chosen rose has not recently been pushed into the container with a bit of earth rammed over the roots. An unscrupulous supplier may simply take the bare-root roses, usually the weakest ones that he was unable to sell in the autumn, and chop off enough of the roots (which can mean most of them) to fit them into the container, putting them on sale in the spring as 'container-grown'. If in doubt, always make sure by asking, as you will be paying quite a bit more for roses grown in this way. Do not be misled by a show of leaves, or even flowers; any rose that is not actually dead will produce some of these, but the plant itself may be second rate and take ages to establish itself properly, if it ever does.

Choosing from catalogues

If you order from a catalogue through one of the big, specialist nurseries you will be fairly sure of getting good-quality plants. But picking what you want from a catalogue alone has its hazards. The colour printing may not be top quality, and therefore misleading, and often the descriptions are far too brief. Only a few of the big growers mention if a particular rose is prone to disease; this is because the incidence of disease varies enormously in different parts of the country. One area may be terribly bad for black spot, strangely enough because of the purity of the air; another may be quite free of it because the air is polluted by sulphur fumes from factory chimneys. Or again, one variety may suffer from mildew on one type of soil or in one situation in a garden, but not in another. No nursery will want to put customers off by warning them against something that may never happen. However, there is no excuse for not warning about a rose that will not stand up to rain, and, regrettably, there are roses like this on many lists. If you see the words 'good under glass' beware: it really means that a downpour will reduce the flowers to a sodden mass.

Bargain buys?
Hundreds of thousands of roses are sold each year through stores, supermarkets, and greengrocers' shops. They are usually cheaper and you can find real bargains in this way, but you can also get rubbish and even dead plants if you don't know what to look out for. Some of the varieties sold in this way may never have been very good while others have long been superseded by better ones, but are sold because it is easy to propagate from them.

Unless temperature and humidity are right, the polythene packs in which the roses are sold can act like miniature greenhouses, forcing some of the buds into premature growth. These white and sickly-looking shoots will be killed off as soon as the rose is planted out. Avoid roses like this, along with any that look dried up or have wrinkled bark on the stems. This means they have spent too long in a dry atmosphere and, if they survive, will be a long time recovering.

You must be very cautious in following up the 'bargain' offers in newspapers as you are most unlikely to get first-rate plants. Special offers in growers' catalogues are another matter. These are usually made up of ten or a dozen roses chosen by the seller. The grower can market them at a cheaper rate as he can make up the selection in advance instead of having to pick out varieties according to customers' orders. These offers are most useful to a beginner who wants the minimum of trouble in choosing and ordering his roses; they also make good presents for a young couple just starting out with a garden.

However, it is worth checking the varieties against the description of them in the main part of the catalogue to make sure that they are not too disparate in size and character. Selections have been offered ranging from Queen Elizabeth, which can top 2·4m (8 ft), to Zambra, an orange floribunda at 30cm (2 ft), and taking in on the way Lavender Lassie, which is generally reckoned to be a shrub rose. There is nothing wrong with these roses individually, but planted as a group by somebody who did not know them they would look strange to say the least.

How to recognize a good rose
We have given the black side of choosing and buying roses and emphasized the pitfalls simply to ensure that you will know whether you are getting the best and what to complain about if you are not. At most times you will obtain good roses from all

Vigorous floribunda Queen Elizabeth

sources mentioned but it is safest to go to one of the big, specialist growers. They may be a little more expensive but you will get quality and there are few suppliers of any kind who will not exchange bad or wrongly-labelled plants.

You will only learn to recognize good or bad varieties by experience, by seeing them grow, or by reading about them. Knowing a good rose is not enough. You also want to make sure that you are getting a healthy plant, and there are certain points to look out for.

No good rose bush should have less than two firm, green, wrinkle-free and unbroken canes, *at least* as thick as a pencil. Preferably they should have three or four canes and they should not be discoloured by greyish or brown patches of disease.

There should be a strong root system with plenty of fibrous roots and you may have to unpack the rose to check this. Despite the disapproving frown of the sales assistant, you are perfectly entitled to inspect what you are buying, and if in any doubt you would be wise to do.

There is even a British Standards Institution specification for roses, stipulating, in addition to the above, that the neck between the roots and the point where the canes branch out should be at least 16mm ($\frac{5}{8}$ in) thick. This is only applicable to plants sold as First Grade, although if you keep your eyes open you will generally find some plants that comply with this BSI specification, even if they are not so described.

The top awards
Awards won by roses are sometimes shown in catalogues, but the only ones of real value to growers in Britain are those given by the Royal National Rose Society and the Royal Horticultural Society. The Rose Society is the main body concerned with roses, but you occasionally see the RHS awards, FCC, AM or AGM (First Class Certificate, Award of Merit or Award of Garden Merit) after the description of a rose. The Rose Society holds most thorough trials over a period of three years and in ascending order of merit the awards they give are: Trial Ground Certificate, Certificate of Merit and Gold Medal. In some years, a really outstanding rose may win the President's International Trophy, in addition to the Gold Medal; but any rose with even a Trial Ground Certificate would be a sound choice for your garden. Overseas awards have little relevance in Britain where growing conditions and, in some cases, judging rules are very different.

Hybrid Teas and Floribundas

Anyone interested in roses will want to be able to recognize the various forms and to be aware of their advantages and disadvantages. Here we tell you about the famous hybrid tea and floribunda roses.

Hybrid teas (HT) are the most popular roses in Britain because of the size, scent and beauty of their flowers.

It is often said that modern roses lack scent. This is true of floribundas, to a large extent, but they make up for this with their extra vigorous character and profuse flowering.

HYBRID TEAS

The first hybrid tea rose, raised in 1867, was the silvery-pink La France. This was the result of crossing the older hybrid perpetual roses with tea roses from the Far East, thus combining the greater refinement of shape and more recurrent blooming habit of the latter with the robust constitution of the hybrid perpetual. Few tea roses could survive the climate of the British Isles except under glass. Their name, rather a strange one, supposedly comes from the fact that they smelled like the newly-opened tea cases that arrived from the East.

Their colour range is probably only exceeded by that of the iris, for there are no blues among the roses, nor is it likely there ever will be, for they lack the necessary pigment – delphinidin. The lilac-mauve of the HT Blue Moon is the nearest approach there is. Unlike the floribundas, there is an abundance of HT varieties that are just as strongly-scented as any rose of the past. Several come to mind, such as Alec's Red, Blessings, Bonsoir, Ernest H. Morse, Fragrant Cloud, John Waterer, Lily de Gerlache, Mala Rubinstein, My Choice, Prima Ballerina, Red Devil, Wendy Cussons and Whisky Mac, and there are many more. The HT Peace, the most popular rose ever raised, seems scentless, although some people claim to detect a trace of something in it.

Advantages of the hybrid tea

Hybrid teas are most often used in the garden for bedding, and for this they certainly have advantages over other plants. They are permanent, or at any rate they should last for twenty years or more, so that you do not have to replant each year as you do with annuals. Their range of colour has already been mentioned, and they will bloom for five to six months with only the briefest of resting periods. Some varieties have coppery-red foliage when they first come out, so the beds can look appealing even before the first flush of bloom in mid summer (June). There is even a modern HT called Curiosity, a red and yellow bi-colour and 'sport' (chance variation) of the older Cleopatra, that has variegated leaves of deep green, splashed yellowish-white.

Finally, they make wonderful flowers for the house, though it is largely true that those lasting longest in water are often the most prone to rain damage outside. Gavotte, Red Devil and Royal Highness come into this category, but Alec's Red,

Right, and below: vigorous, upright HT varieties Alexander, and Fragrant Cloud

Fragrant Cloud, Gail Borden, Grandpa Dickson, Piccadilly and Troika are a few that can be recommended for both indoors and out.

Planting distances

It is impossible to be exact about how far apart HT types should be planted for bedding; 45cm (18 in) is a good average,

but some varieties, Peace for example, are far more vigorous than others and need fully 75cm (2½ ft). Others, like Perfecta, are strong growers but tall, narrow and upright, and yet others, like Josephine Bruce and Percy Thrower, tend to sprawl outwards. The important thing is that the roots should not be so close as to rob one another of nutrient and water, and there should be room between them for hoeing, mulching and proper spraying. The beds should not be so densely packed that air cannot circulate freely as this would encourage disease and probably insect pests as well. On the other hand, nothing looks worse than a rose bed with huge spaces of bare earth between the plants.

If you have seen your chosen types of rose growing before you buy them, you will probably know their spacing requirements, but some people favour ground-cover plants between their roses and space must be left for sunshine to reach these. Violas and pansies, particularly the blue varieties, are the most frequently recommended, and there is no doubt that they can look very attractive. On the other hand, it is hard to reconcile the use of these with good rose cultivation. Roses need to be well mulched to give of their best, or, failing this, the beds should at least be hoed regularly to keep them free of weeds, and neither of these activities would make violas or pansies very happy about their living conditions.

Plants for edging rose beds
The use of edging plants is another matter. Small, or smallish, grey or silver-leaved kinds like anaphalis (pearl ever-lasting), lavender, nepeta (catmint) and dwarf sage, most of which have reasonably discreet mauve flowers, are excellent for this purpose. They blend in beautifully with roses and there is no colour clash, but you may wish to use plants that flower earlier and so give colour to the bed before the roses are out. In this case, polyanthus and primroses are hard to beat.

You can also use miniature roses; many are almost evergreen in a mild winter and most start flowering before the HT. They are best suited to the edge of a south-facing border, or at least where their bigger neighbours will not overshadow them and keep the sun away. Even the greatest rose enthusiast could not claim that a newly-pruned rose bed was a thing of beauty and some form of edging does divert the eye from unsightly stumps.

Mixing varieties and heights
It is generally supposed that you should not mix several different varieties or colours of roses in one bed. It is really a matter of choosing what you like. The plants of one variety will be more or less uniform in height and can look marvellous in the mass, but with some roses there may be quite a long rest period in the middle of summer, when little or no colour is showing. A mixed bed can look spotty, with some varieties blooming and some not, but there will be long periods

Left: small mixed border with HT roses and a floribunda in the background
Below: Whisky Mac, a strong-growing HT

when all are out together and a spectacular riot of colour can result. Plant mauve, white or cream roses between any two colours that might otherwise clash. You can divide a round bed into segments like an orange, each one planted with a different variety of rose, and possibly add a standard or half-standard HT in the centre to give height.

The question of height is an important one, particularly if your garden is flat. Trees and shrubs carry the eye upwards and break up something that could otherwise seem rather monotonous. Standard roses, either in the centre of a round bed, or spaced out at about 1·8m (6 ft) intervals along the centre of a long one, can have the same beneficial effect. Use a rose of a contrasting colour for these.

Varieties for hedges and shrubs

The standard HT can also be used to line a path or a drive, which suggests another use for the bush varieties. Not nearly enough use is made of rose hedges, and tall robust kinds, like the vermilion Alexander, Peace, Chicago Peace, and many others are first-rate for this. Some, if not pruned too hard, can be built up into fine specimen shrubs to stand on their own, perhaps in the middle of a lawn or by the corner of a patio.

FLORIBUNDAS

Most of the general principles outlined for the hybrid tea rose apply equally to floribundas, so with these it is enough to point out where they are better or worse, how they differ, and to recommend varieties suited to different purposes.

The floribunda, as opposed to the HT, grows with large heads or trusses of comparatively small flowers. These are often only single or semi-double, and open to show their stamens. Modern breeding tends towards larger, HT-shaped flowers with fewer in a truss so that in some instances it is difficult to say to which class a rose belongs. Pink Parfait and Sea Pearl are examples of this and have the rather clumsy official classification of 'floribunda – hybrid tea type'. In Germany, its country of origin, Fragrant Cloud is classed as a floribunda, though it is rather difficult to see the justification in this case, as the flowers are so large. Floribundas have a different ancestry from the HT and, because of the scentless roses in it, few have a worthwhile fragrance. Arthur Bell, Chinatown, Dearest, Elizabeth of

Above right: this low-growing floribunda, Paddy McGredy, is a good edging variety
Right: Iceberg, a bushy floribunda

Glamis, Escapade, Harry Edland, Michelle, Orange Sensation and Pineapple Poll do have scent, but breeders are conscious of the lack in most others and are trying, with mixed success, to remedy it.

Advantages of the floribunda

As a race, floribundas are very vigorous and make more new growth in a season than most HT types. They flower more continuously and are very quick to repeat should they rest at all, which gives them an advantage for bedding. And because most have fewer, smaller and tougher petals, they will open better in wet weather. This also means that most floribundas make good cut flowers. The bright vermilion Anne Cocker, with its blooms in tight little rosettes on the truss, will last fully ten days in water – central heating permitting – and many others are almost as good.

Varieties for edging

It is probably best not to mix floribunda and HT in one bed because of the difference in their growth. However, there are a number of low-growing, bushy floribundas coming onto the market that will make excellent edging for a rose bed. Meanwhile, the brilliant scarlet Topsi (rather prone to black spot in some areas), dark red Marlena, pink Paddy McGredy and the brand new orange-scarlet Stargazer are all suitable for this, or for lining paths or drives. They are excellent, too, for a small bed.

For some years now, both types, HT and floribunda, seem to have been getting taller and taller and, in some cases, even lankier; so this new breeding tendency towards what might be called the rounded, cushion effect is welcome, especially in the smaller garden. It almost constitutes a return to the poly-pom roses from which the floribundas are descended, but the flowers are much better and the plants healthier.

Varieties for hedges and shrubs

The stronger-growing floribunda has a particular advantage over their HT counterparts as hedges and as shrubs. Their growth is more branching and bushy as a rule and the sheer mass of flowers they produce is difficult for anything else to match. Some have tremendous vigour and will reach 1·2–1·5m (4–5 ft) in two seasons, if not overpruned. If you want a tall, narrow hedge, try yellow, disease-free Chinatown, the equally healthy Queen Elizabeth, Southampton or Dorothy Wheatcroft. The Queen Elizabeth can be kept quite bushy and between 1·5–1·8m (5–6 ft) in height if you prune it to about 90cm (3 ft) each year, and this will avoid the 2·2 or 2·7m (8 or 9 ft) specimen that you see so often with all its flowers at the top.

There seems no way to prune the supremely beautiful Fred Loads to curb its reach for the sky. Unlike Queen Elizabeth, it has huge trusses of large flowers in soft vermilion-orange, not all at the top. Although it might be more rightly classed as a shrub rather than a floribunda, officially it is known as a 'floribunda-shrub'.

The following lists of recommended varieties will serve as a guide but go and see them growing before you decide which ones to buy.

Some varieties to choose

HYBRID TEAS

Alec's Red	cherry red
Alexander	vermilion
Blessings	light pink
Ernest H. Morse	turkey red
Grandpa Dickson	pale yellow
John Waterer	deep red
Just Joey	coppery-orange
Pascali	white
Peace	pale yellow, pink edges
Piccadilly	scarlet, yellow reverse
Troika	apricot-orange
Whisky Mac	orange-yellow

FLORIBUNDAS

Allgold	yellow
Anne Cocker	vermilion
City of Leeds	salmon-pink
Elizabeth of Glamis	salmon-pink
Escapade	lilac-mauve, white reverse
Evelyn Fison	scarlet
Iceberg	white
Lili Marlene	dusky scarlet
Matangi	orange-vermilion, white eye and reverse
Orange Sensation	vermilion
Orangeade	orange-vermilion
Queen Elizabeth	pink
Southampton	apricot-orange
Topsi	orange-scarlet

Right: Peace, the most successful HT cultivar ever grown

Climbing and Rambling Roses

The important thing to understand straight away is the difference between a rambler and a climber. Their habit of growth is different and, in some cases, their uses are too. They are not always interchangeable and, to make matters a little more complicated, there are two main groups of ramblers.

Ramblers

Most ramblers are either wild or species roses, and their fairly close relatives. By far the greatest number of those grown in the garden are hybrids of *R. wichuraiana*. They produce massed clusters of small flowers, single, semi-double or double, and they bloom in late summer or even early autumn (July or August) and they do not repeat later on. The leaves are attractive and very glossy before mildew claims them as it does with so many ramblers. Like the wild roses of the hedgerows, ramblers send up long, pliable canes from the base of the plant each year. It is on these that the flowers grow so it is best to remove the old canes when blooming is over. Examples of the first rambler group are American Pillar, Crimson Shower, Dorothy Perkins, Excelsa and the very lovely and relatively healthy Sander's White.

Ramblers like the scented Albertine are different. They are also once-flowering, but the blooms are larger and appear much earlier in mid summer (June). While new canes may come from the base, enormously long and vigorous ones will also grow from some way up the main stems; these stems should be shortened back above one of these new growths after flowering. It is much harder to tell this kind of rambler from a climber that flowers only once a year.

Because of the likelihood of mildew, never plant ramblers against a wall or a close-boarded fence, as air circulation there will be poor. Instead, use them for arches or pergolas.

Climbers

Purists maintain that climbing roses are misnamed and that they are not climbers at all. They have no tendrils, certainly, and do not twine round their supports, or cling to the trunk of a tree in the way that ivy does. In nature, they reach aloft by thrusting their way into shrubs, hedges and trees, hooking their often formidable thorns over the twigs and branches. They get up there somehow, even if in the garden they usually have to be tied in to their supports.

Climbing roses, whether incorrectly titled or not, have larger flowers than ramblers as a rule. Once again, they can be single, semi-double or double, but are often as big and shapely as those of a hybrid tea. They may appear in small clusters (though there may be hundreds of these) or they may come out singly, and a large number of climbers are repeat-flowering. This is particularly so with the newer varieties such as Bantry Bay, Casino, Compassion, Danse du Feu, Golden Showers, Grand Hotel, Handel, Pink Perpétue, Schoolgirl and Swan Lake; but old favourites such as Caroline Testout, Gloire de Dijon, Mme Grégoire Staechelin and Mermaid, come into this category, too.

Climbers only occasionally send up new canes from ground level and in some cases virtually never. From this they form a sturdy main framework and concentrate on producing sideshoots and laterals from this. Sometimes a climber can become very bare and gaunt looking at the base but proper training can help to keep it clothed with leaves and flowers low down. With some of the more pig-headed varieties it may be necessary to plant a low-growing bush, preferably an evergreen, in front of it to hide the often rather ugly, gnarled bare stems.

Apart from natural climbers, you should be able to identify the climbing sports of a number of the HT and floribunda races. A 'sport' occurs when a quirk in a bush rose's make-up, probably due to its mixed ancestry, causes one of two things to happen: it will either produce flowers on its stem quite different from those on the rest of the bush (Super Sun, an orange-yellow sport of the red and yellow bi-colour Piccadilly, is an example of this), or else the flowers stay the same but the habit of growth will change. Suddenly the odd bush will develop the long canes of a climber and, as it is possible to propagate from both kinds of sport, a new rose is born. The prefix 'climbing' appears in catalogues before the variety name if the rose is a climbing sport, e.g. Climbing Iceberg.

These climbing sports used to be much more popular than they are today, although they are still sold in large quantities. It has been found that a very large number of them flower with far less freedom than their bush equivalents and some, whether from HT or floribunda, only flower once. So be careful when

Glossy-foliaged and large-flowered Chaplin's Pink Climber

making your choice and ask your supplier about the variety you are thinking of choosing before you commit yourself. Roses that usually do come up to expectation as climbing sports include Allgold, Crimson Glory, Ena Harkness, Etoile de Hollande, Fashion, Iceberg, Lady Sylvia and Shot Silk. Climbing Peace can grow to an enormous size yet have only one flower in five years; this is typical in Britain though it will flower better in a warmer climate.

Use in the garden

How can you best use climbing roses in the garden? Climbers, as distinct from ramblers, can be trained on walls, but however good the repeat performance of a rose, there will be periods when it is out of flower. Many climbers are described as 'perpetual flowering' but few, if any, really are; at best they are recurrent, so why not grow them up through some other wall shrub that will bloom before they do or when they are resting?

Forsythia suspensa or *Chaenomeles japonica*, for instance, will give colour to the walls of your house in mid and late spring (March and April). Or you can choose a shrub that flowers when the roses do, but in a contrasting colour. The

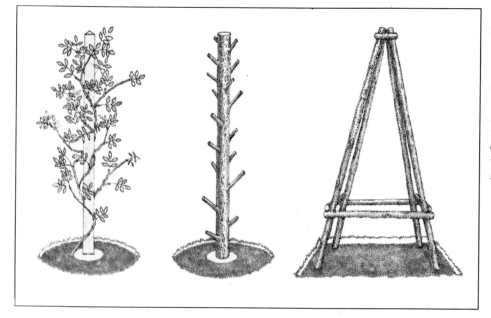

soft blue of a ceanothus looks wonderful combined with the pale, primrose yellow of the repeat-flowering rose Casino, or with white Swan Lake. Mid summer flowering clematis, grown up through roses, is another way of achieving extra colour in between the first and second flush of rose bloom. Choose kinds that are cut hard back each early spring (February) and do this without fail, or you will end up with the rose struggling pitifully to peer through an impenetrable tangle.

Training the less vigorous climbers and ramblers on pillars is an effective way of using them, provided that the pillar is a substantial one and preferably set in concrete so that its base will not rot. It should be round, or at least have any sharp corners planed away, so that the rose stems are not chafed.

A variant of the straight up-and-down pillar is to use part of the trunk of a small tree, such as a larch, that has branches coming out of it at fairly regular intervals all round. If these branches are sawn off about 30cm (12 in) from the trunk, they are very easy to tie the rose to. For either sort of pillar, train the canes around it in a spiral; this will make it more likely to send out flowering sideshoots low down.

Training techniques
The secret of training climbers and ramblers is, paradoxically, to keep the main growths as horizontal as possible. If they go straight up, the sap flows up them freely, and most of the new growth and flowers will be at the top. If, when used against a wall or fence, the canes are fanned out to each side and tied in to horizontal wires, the effect of bending the

canes will be to restrict the sap flow and to divert it into the side buds along their entire length. These buds develop and form flowering laterals, which in turn are fanned out and tied in, so that the rose moves upwards, gradually, and is covered with flowers and leaves from tip to toe.

The supports should consist of strong, galvanized wire, the strands about 30–45cm (12–18 in) apart, threaded through 15cm (6 in) vine-eyes, so that, allowing for a few centimetres of the eye to go into the wall or fence, the wires will be 13cm (5 in) from the wall surface. This allows some air to circulate between the wall and the rose. You should tie the canes not too tightly (so as to allow for growth) to the outside of the wires with plastic-covered garden wire.

Up pillars Training roses in a spiral on a pillar has something of the same effect as fanning them out, but start the training straight away, as some climbers have very stiff canes that, once developed, are quite difficult to bend.

Up pyramids Probably even better than a pillar is a 2m (7 ft) tall, upright pyramid of either three or four rustic poles, joined at the top and with crosspieces bracing the sides about half-way down. The rose will be much less restricted in its growth on a pyramid than on a pillar, and it is even possible to grow two roses of blending colours at the same time on one support.

As hedges You can form a hedge of almost any height you like with climbers and

Above: climbers can be trained up a pillar (left) or larch trunk (centre), but vigorous varieties will prefer a pyramid (right)
Right: free-flowering rambler R. wichuraiana Excelsa

ramblers. Link upright posts at approximately 1·8m (6 ft) intervals with galvanized iron wires 30cm (12 in) apart, and on these the roses are trained. In time, they will make a fine and very colourful screen, but only in the summer, for in winter the leaves will fall.

As weeping standards Rambling roses make the best weeping standards if you choose them from the first group previously mentioned. Their canes are pliable and hang down all round as they should, laden with blossom, but whatever rose you use, make sure it is supported above the ground by a very strong stake, about 1·8m (6 ft) tall. Wind pressure on a weeping standard can be very great, so something substantial is needed to keep it upright. Nurseries supply suitable wooden stakes, but an old metal gas pipe, painted green, is a good alternative and it will last almost for ever if galvanized as well as painted. The top should go right up into the head of the rose to give it extra support and the rose should be tied to it with plastic ties, one at the top and two equally spaced further down.

Sometimes a wire 'umbrella' frame on the top of the stake is recommended. This should not be needed with ramblers like Excelsa, but with the more rigid canes of Albertine, that is frequently sold as a weeping rambler, you may need an umbrella to persuade its canes to go in the right direction.

Up trees A very lovely way of using the more strong-minded ramblers and climbers is to train them up trees. Many of the old species such as *R. filipes* Kiftsgate and *R. longicuspis* are first-rate for this, as are the old ramblers Rambling Rector, Seagull and Wedding Day. With a little guidance at the beginning, they will ramble quite happily on their own with no tying in, and produce waterfalls of

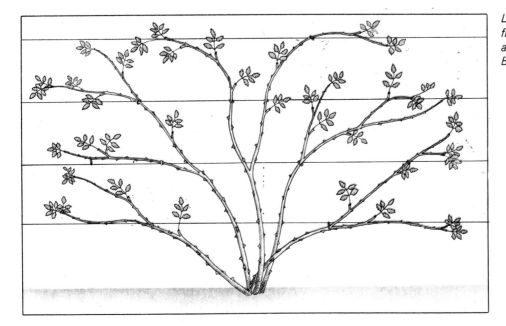

Left: to restrict sap flow and encourage flowering, canes of climber growing against a wall should be trained outwards
Below: climber, Alchymist

immensely fragrant, small white flowers in mid summer (June). Don't plant them too close to the trunk of the tree, because the rain must be able to reach the roots.

However, a warning is needed about the kind of tree you choose. If your rose is described as reaching 9m (30 ft), it is obvious that you must not pick a tree of 4.5m (15 ft) up which to grow it. An old apple tree can be ideal, but it must not be too old or have rotting branches, for after a year or two the weight and wind resistance of the rose may bring the whole lot down in a gale.

Covering up and ground cover Climbing and rambling roses are invaluable for covering old, unsightly sheds (as well as new, unsightly houses), and ramblers belonging to the *wichuraiana* group can be used for ground cover. *R. wichuraiana* itself will grow quite flat along the ground, spreading out in all directions, rooting as it goes and covered in late summer (July) with star-like, single white flowers. A similar hybrid called Max Graf has pink flowers and in time both roses will grow dense enough to smother weeds. Wandering over a bank that you have been wondering how to cover and that is difficult to keep tidy, they make a really different and attractive feature in the garden.

Some varieties to choose
CLIMBERS

Allen Chandler	bright crimson
Aloha	pink
Altissimo	blood-red
Compassion	apricot
Danse du Feu	orange-scarlet
Golden Showers	daffodil yellow
Handel	cream, edged pink
New Dawn	pale pink
Parkdirektor Riggers	blood-red
Pink Perpétue	pink
Schoolgirl	apricot-orange
Swan Lake	white

RAMBLERS

Albéric Barbier	creamy-white
Albertine	coppery-pink
Excelsa	red
Sander's White	white

Miniature Roses in the Garden

Miniature roses need to be well displayed to look their best, and can be grown in beds by themselves or be put into window boxes or pots.

Miniature roses are thought to be related to the long-flowering China roses, and their Latin name is *R. chinensis minima*. They are sometimes referred to as Rouletii after a Dr Roulet who found some, quite by chance, growing in pots at a village called Onnens in Switzerland in 1918. Nobody remembered seeing anything like them before or could find out how they got there, though one theory is that they were a lost offspring of a much older French rose known as Pompon de Paris.

Yet another species name for the miniatures is *R. lawrenceana*, after the 18th century writer on roses, Miss Molly Lawrence, and this multiplicity of names reflects the uncertainty as to where they really originated. However, they are first-rate little plants; *R. rouletii* itself is only about 13cm (5 in) tall, with small, delicate rose-pink flowers.

In the true miniature rose, everything should be on the same scale. The flowers, the leaves and the stems should be in the same proportion to the rest of the plant as those on a hybrid tea or floribunda, but with a number of recent varieties, such as Gold Pin, this is not so. Miniatures are gaining in popularity all the time, particularly in the United States, and in the race for more and more novelties, a number of full-sized floribundas are being crossed with the miniatures, and the result is that the flowers are relatively too large for the plant. This does not always happen, but depends on which strain comes out on top in a particular cross.

This inter-breeding with floribundas can have another effect, too, as seen in a rose such as Baby Masquerade, that will certainly reach 38cm (15 in) and sometimes more. The flowers and leaves are still small, duplicates of the floribunda Masquerade on a tiny scale, but the whole plant in itself is not small as a miniature

Miniature roses massed in a bed at the Royal National Rose Society's gardens

should be. In fact, though appearing in most nursery catalogues as a miniature, Baby Masquerade is classed officially as a floribunda-dwarf.

One other thing can affect the size of miniature roses, and that is whether or not they are grown on their own roots. Miniatures take very easily from 8cm (3 in) cuttings, planted out in mid autumn (September), which is most useful if you want to increase your stock. Grown in this way, they make good, strong plants, but they will be considerably smaller than if they are budded onto a vigorous root-stock. They will be the size they should be, and the closer in their ancestry to the original *R. rouletii* the likelier they are to keep small.

General characteristics
Each leaflet on a miniature rose will probably be no more than 13mm ($\frac{1}{2}$ in) long, the flowers no more than 3cm (1 in) in diameter. The blooms can be single or semi-double, but they can also be as packed with petals and as fully double and shapely as a hybrid tea. The minute blooms of Cinderella, for instance, have up to 60 petals, each as perfectly formed as a baby's toenail.

Some miniatures are fragrant, though this only really becomes significant when they are grown in pots at eye-level. The colour range is as wide as for any other class of rose, and there is an extremely good selection of those in the mauve and lavender shades, like Lavender Lace. They all last well in water.

Miniatures are, in the main, very rain-resistant and recurrent flowering, repeating quickly. They also flower early, and the first blooms will probably show colour in early summer (mid to late May). By this time the plants will be fully clothed with leaves, for these will start to develop in mid to late spring (February or March). In fact, in a mild winter, many miniatures are practically evergreen.

The health of these tiny roses is probably better than that of larger ones, due perhaps to the healthy China rose strain in their make-up, but such spraying as may be needed is very quick and easy. One or two squirts deal with each plant.

No real pruning is needed, but with some varieties there is so much growth that the shoots can become rather congested and will benefit from thinning out in early spring. Otherwise it is simply a matter of removing, as and when necessary, the small number of twigs that may die back each year, and perhaps having to shorten the odd vagrant, extra-vigorous growth that throws things out of balance. It is easier to use sharp scissors rather than secateurs for thinning.

Growing outdoors
There are many attractive ways of growing miniature roses in the garden, but probably the way that most people see them first is when they are sold as pot plants in shops and garden centres. This has given rise to the myth that they are pot plants for the house, not suitable for growing out of doors, and that they are more delicate than other roses. They are, in fact, every bit as tough, and are sold in pots because they are small and easy to handle like that; they can also be kept alive indefinitely, unlike bare-root roses.

Miniatures are not house plants. If they are kept indoors all the time, the dry air will cause the leaves to drop, and the plant will be weakened. Bring the roses into the house when they are coming into flower, and take them out again immediately afterwards. Stand them in a spot shaded from the midday sun, or plunge the pots into damp ashes or peat, and keep them well watered at all times. Leave them out of doors for the winter, or they can be

Below: terraced beds display miniatures well on a slope. Bottom: they can also be used to advantage as edging plants

brought into a cool greenhouse in late autumn (October), when slight heat (and good top ventilation) applied in spring will bring them into flower in late spring (April) or even a week or two earlier. After this, stand them out of doors once more to build up their strength again in their natural environment. Use J.I. No 2 potting compost for your pots.

For the rockery They make excellent rockery plants, but they must have reasonably large pockets of good soil, 30cm (12 in) deep at least, for they will not thrive on the starvation diet that suits some rock plants. On a rockery, they are likely to have good drainage, which they like, and the big stones will give them a cool root-run, which they possibly like even more. One rose on its own may look a little lost on a big rockery but groups of three or four together make a good show.

As edging If you are looking for something with which to edge your rose beds and give you early – or fairly early – colour, miniature roses can be the answer. The important thing to remember here is that they need sun to give of their best, so that the other roses must be far enough back from the border edge not to overshadow them. You can use miniatures, too, for edging paths, but for something as wide as a drive, it is probably best to plant some of the taller-growing, stronger-coloured of the miniature varieties. Orange-salmon Corain or yellow Rosina would be suitable. These roses look well in front of (and on the sunny side of) other shrub plantings.

In raised beds If you do want to smell your roses and appreciate the tiny beauty of their individual blooms as well, grow them in a raised stone sink at least 30–38cm (12–15 in) deep, perhaps placing it on a patio or using it as a backing for a garden seat. As an alternative, try long, narrow, terraced beds, built up with dry-stone walling or brick, and planted entirely with miniatures, each bed rising one tier above the last and perhaps planted with a contrasting colour. This is a good way to use a bank where the garden changes its level, but drainage in both a properly-constructed sink or on terracing is likely to be better than roses like, so water regularly.

Miniature rose garden

Each of the terraces described above will form a complete miniature rose bed, but it is possible to try something even more ambitious than this – a complete miniature rose garden. For these there are nowadays not only bush varieties but miniature standards and climbers,

though both the latter tend to be on the large side. In America even miniature moss roses have been developed.

Mark out the beds in whatever pattern and to whatever size takes your fancy or that you have room for, but remember that miniature roses are relatively expensive in comparison to their larger relatives and that you will not need more than about 20cm (8 in) between each bush. A bed 1·2 × 1·2m (4 × 4 ft) may not seem large, but it would take about 36 of the smaller-growing miniature roses, that are the best for this kind of planting.

You should not need to double dig the

ground. In time, miniature rose roots can go quite deep, but not as deep as this. However, the soil should be well broken-up to a depth of 30–38cm (12–15 in), and some fertilizer added before planting.

Paths between the beds can be either very narrow, to be in proportion to the roses, or as wide as an ordinary garden path, so that you can stroll along them more easily. The wider paths, if they are of grass, can be easily cut with a lawn-mower. Narrow grass ones may create problems in keeping them neat, and the grass itself, if it is anything other than very closely shaved, may actually look out of scale with the roses. Nothing looks better than grass for surrounding rose beds, but this is one case where small paving stones or fine gravel (contained within thin, damp-proofed, wooden edging) may be the most practical solution, and is a very good second best. A paved, sunken garden of miniature roses makes a most pleasing feature for any garden.

The following selection of varieties is divided into the dwarf and the taller-growing kinds. Dwarf here means about 15–20cm (6–8 in) and taller means

23–25cm (9–10 in), but remember that height will depend a lot on the conditions in which the roses are grown.

Some varieties to choose

DWARF

Baby Gold Star	yellow, flushed apricot
Colibri	orange-yellow, flushed pink
Frosty	white
Humpty Dumpty	carmine-pink
Lavender Lace	lavender-mauve
Pixie	white, tinted pink
Pour Toi	creamy-yellow
Peon	crimson, white
(or Tom Thumb)	centre
Simple Simon	deep pink
Toy Clown	white, edged pink
Yellow Doll	yellow

TALLER

Cinderella	shell-pink
Coralín	orange-salmon
Little Flirt	flame-yellow, red reverse
Maid Marion	scarlet
Oakington Ruby	crimson
Perle de Montserrat	rose-pink
Rosina	golden-yellow
Starina	red, flushed gold, carmine reverse

Shrub Roses

All roses are shrubs, so why is the term 'shrub rose' used, and what exactly does it mean? It is not easy to give a precise answer to either of these questions, and perhaps the nearest you can get is to say that 'shrub roses' are not normally used in the way that hybrid tea and floribunda roses are. Some shrub roses can be so used but they are the exception and are quite different in appearance from the more modern varieties. What shrub roses are, as opposed to what they are not, should become clear from the descriptions that follow.

They are made up from a number of families or groups, the oldest being the wild or species roses and their near relatives. Next in historical order come the gallicas, the oldest family of cultivated roses, and then follow the damasks, albas, centifolias, moss roses, Bourbons, hybrid perpetuals, China roses, rugosas, hybrid musks and the modern shrub roses.

Examples from any of these groups can be bought today without great difficulty and they add a dimension to rose-growing undreamed of by those who have never tried them. Think of the charm of the single rose or huge, many-petalled blooms, rich in scent, their soft pastel or rich purple colours often changing as the flower ages, and with their petals infolded or quartered in a way that recalls the prints from Victorian albums. Their informal growth contrasts strongly with the sergeant-major uprightness of the hybrid tea; in some cases they display great beauty of foliage and in autumn have branches laden with heps like drops of scarlet sealing wax. They also mix happily with shrubs.

After each of the following groups, we suggest a few varieties from which to choose and give first the ultimate height and then the spread for each plant.

Species

The species native to Britain, like the dog rose, have very fleeting flowers but many from overseas, particularly from the Far East, make excellent, if rather large, garden shrubs, flowering early and staying in bloom for weeks on end. Only one or two are recurrent, and they are not perhaps the first choices for garden display, unless you are forming a compre-

Above: Rosa gallica versicolor
Below: the alba Königen von Dänemark

hensive collection. All but one of the true species have single flowers of five petals, but a number of what you could term 'sub-species' (natural crosses made by species in the wild) have semi-double or double flowers. Generally, they are carried in enormous profusion along the whole length of great arching canes and smother the shrubs with colour in early and mid summer (late May and June). Plant them as specimens in a lawn, or in general shrub planting, always in full sun.

No pruning should be carried out or the natural shape of the shrub will be spoiled. A little trimming to develop a balanced bush is allowable early on, but avoid drastic cutting later simply because you have not left enough room for the rose to reach its full size. Just remove the dead branches as they occur.

Diseases and pests are rarely a problem to species. They are tough and shrug off any mild touch of mildew or black spot they may get without needing spraying.

Here are a few varieties to help you make your choice.

Canary Bird. Brilliant, single yellow flowers in early and mid summer (May and June). 2×2m (7×7 ft).

Complicata. Huge, single pink flowers with white eye and gold stamens. Very vigorous and will scramble into surrounding shrubs. $1\cdot8 \times 2\cdot4$m (6×8 ft).

R. moyesii Geranium. Crimson-red, single flowers and tall, open growth; huge heps. $3 \times 2\cdot4$m (10×8 ft).

R. × paulii Rosea. Pink, single flowers. Low and spreading for ground cover. $1\cdot2 \times 4\cdot5$m (4×15 ft).

Gallica

Most gallicas are small, upright shrubs, not often exceeding $1\cdot2–1\cdot5$m ($4–5$ ft), and they carry their single crop of flowers well above the foliage. They make a very pretty showing if used in small clumps in front of a planting of other shrubs, or they can be used effectively for a low hedge to line a drive or path, where their tendency to sucker if on their own roots does not matter too much. A great advantage is that they can be clipped over – though not too drastically – rather than pruned. The canes have few thorns, but are covered with stiff, hairy bristles. Some mildew is likely on most of them.

As will become clear from the descriptions that follow, there are some gallica hybrids that do not conform to type and are much larger and lax-growing.

Belle de Crécy. Very fragrant flowers, cerise-pink, turning to Parma violet. $1\cdot2$m $\times 90$cm (4×3 ft).

Camaieux. Crimson-purple flowers, striped white and fading to lilac-grey.

Below: species rose Canary Bird
Above: Pink Grootendorst, a hybrid musk

90×60cm (3×2 ft).

Cardinal de Richelieu. A lax grower with dark, maroon-purple, double flowers. $1\cdot5 \times 1\cdot2$m (5×4 ft).

Charles de Mills. Flat, quartered blooms in cerise-crimson to wine-purple. $1\cdot5 \times 1\cdot2$m (5×4 ft).

Rosa Mundi (*R. gallica versicolor*). Deep pink, striped palest blush. $1\cdot2 \times 1\cdot2$m (4×4 ft).

Scarlet Fire. Massed, single scarlet blooms in late summer (July). 2×2m (7×7 ft).

this is not essential. Of this comparatively small group the following are typical:

Celsiana. Flowers large, loose and blush-pink. 1·5 × 1·2m (5 × 4 ft).

Mme Hardy. Flat, pure white, double and quartered flowers with a green eye. 1·8 × 1·5m (6 × 5 ft).

Alba

Some of the alba roses, despite their name – meaning white – have pink flowers. As a group, their characteristic and attractive grey-green foliage makes them distinctive additions to a general shrub planting. The more vigorous varieties, that can be very large, scramble happily up through their neighbours quite happily. Some degree of suckering is possible.

Alba Semiplena. Double, ivory-white flowers against typical alba grey-green leaves. The white rose of York. 3 × 1·5m (7 × 5 ft).

Céleste. Soft pink. 1·8 × 1·2m (6 × 4 ft).

Félicité Parmentier. Pale yellow buds, opening to flowers of soft, blush-pink. 1·5m × 90cm (5 × 3 ft).

Königin von Dänemark. Buds scarlet-pink on opening, turning soft pink, quartered. 1·5 × 1·2m (5 × 4 ft).

Centifolia and moss

The centifolia and moss roses can really be taken together, as the latter, in its original form, was a sport from the former and, apart from the mossy, glandular growth on the flower-stalks and calyx of moss roses, they are similar in habit. All of them, except for a few very

Above: the Bourbon La Reine Victoria
Below: Rosa damascens Mme Hardy

Below: Henri Martin, with characteristic 'moss' on the stem and calyx

Damask roses

It is difficult with damask roses to pinpoint specific characteristics for the whole group, except for scent, the fact that they form large, bushy shrubs, and that none of them is the rich, damask purple that you associate with the name. Their colour range is from white to deep pink, and they should be used for general shrub plantings or as specimens.

Little pruning is needed, except for the removal of dead wood and the shortening of laterals before flowering, though even

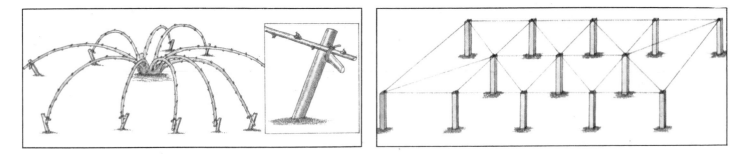

Above: peg down a hybrid perpetual for an ordered display in early summer
Above right: fasten canes of several hybrid perpetuals to a wire cage
Below: Roger Lambelin, a hybrid perpetual

small ones that can be used as rockery plants, will need the support of stakes. They are lax, rather untidy growers if left on their own and have big, drooping leaves. The weight of the very beautiful, many-petalled flowers will weigh down the canes. The taller varieties can be used as pillar roses.

The centifolia was the origin of the term 'cabbage rose', though the cupped blooms do not much resemble the cabbage as we know it today.

Chapeau de Napoleon. Deep-centred, globular, scented pink blooms with a unique 'cockade' of greenery around the bud that makes it look like Napoleon's hat. 1·5 × 1·2m (5 × 4 ft).

Fantin Latour. Very lovely, soft pink flowers in clusters opening flat. 1·8 × 1·5m (6 × 5 ft).

Henri Martin (moss). Green moss and pure crimson double flowers. 1·5 × 1·2m (5 × 4 ft).

Common Moss. Pink, globular blooms in great profusion. 1·2 × 1·2m (4 × 4 ft).

Bourbon

Most Bourbons are large, vigorous shrubs with sumptuous double flowers, that in a number of cases flower again in the autumn when they may be even better than in the first flush. The support of a pillar or a tripod will probably be needed, particularly with the more lax growers. Little pruning is needed, except for the shortening back of the sideshoots in early spring.

Honorine de Brabant. Blooms pale lilac-pink, spotted and striped mauve and crimson; recurrent. 1·8 × 1·8m (6 × 6 ft).

La Reine Victoria. Pink, cupped, shell-like, fragrant blooms; needs support; recurrent. 1·8m × 90cm (6 × 3 ft).

Pierre Oger. Sport of the last, paler creamy pink, deepening in hot sun. 1·8m × 90cm (6 × 3 ft).

Mme Isaac Pereire. Huge, richly-scented, cerise-crimson blooms. Will reach 3–3·3m (10–11 ft) when trained up wall or pillar. 2 × 1·5m (7 × 5 ft.)

Hybrid perpetual

The hybrid perpetuals are in many ways like the Bourbons, though more of them flower again well in the autumn. At that time they send up very long canes that, if left to themselves, will bear flowers mainly at the top in the following year. These can either be shortened back at pruning time in spring to encourage branching lower down or, if you have room for it, they can be pegged down. To do this, remove the soft tips and simply bend the canes over in an arch, tying the ends to wooden pegs driven into the ground all round the bush. This has the same effect as training the canes of a climber on horizontal wires, and in the early summer all the sideshoots will develop and produce flowers.

If you have a whole bed of hybrid perpetuals, as an alternative to pegging them, you can make a low 'cage' of galvanized iron wire, strung between stakes about 30cm (12 in) long, and tie the rose canes down to the wires. This may not be the most beautiful structure in the winter, but in summer the effect is spectacular.

Pegging down can also be done with many of the Bourbons and other tall-growing roses.

Frau Karl Druschki. A lovely, pure white rose that, unfortunately, has no scent. 1·5 × 1·2m (5 × 4 ft).

Georg Arends. Strawberry pink with a cream reverse to the petals. 1·5m × 90cm (5 × 3 ft).

Mrs John Laing. Silvery-pink very recurrent; fragrant. 1·5m × 90cm (5 × 3 ft).

Reine des Violettes. Scented, lilac-purple flowers, recurrent, opening flat and quartered with a button eye. 1·8 × 1·5m (6 × 5 ft).

Roger Lambelin. Double, crimson-purple fragrant flowers. 1·2m × 90cm (4 × 3 ft).

China

The China roses are distinguished by their light and airy growth, pretty flowers that repeat well right through to the autumn, and by attractive, pointed leaves that are exceptionally healthy. Some of the smaller varieties can be used for bedding, but as their colours are mostly pastel pinks to white, expect a restrained rather than an eye-catching display. Because of this,

small beds probably suit them best. The bigger varieties can reach 1·8–2m (6–7 ft) and mix well with other shrubs. Little if any pruning is needed.

Bloomfield Abundance. Tiny, pearl-pink, hybrid tea-shaped blooms in enormous flat-topped clusters. 1·8 × 1·8m (6 × 6 ft).

Cécile Brunner. Flowers like the last. The climbing form is, surprisingly, enormously vigorous, but not so recurrent. 90 × 60cm (3 × 2 ft).

Perle d'Or. Not unlike Cécile Brunner in habit, but with egg yolk-yellow flowers. 90 × 60cm (3 × 2 ft).

Rugosa

The name of this type of shrub, the most versatile of roses, derives from *rugosus*, the Latin for wrinkled. Mostly large and bushy, with magnificent, disease-proof, wrinkled foliage that colours in the autumn, they can be mixed with other shrubs, make (very thorny) hedges, or can be used as specimens, and are resistant to the salt-laden winds of the seaside. They will grow well even in poor soil and carry their flowers, scented in most cases, from mid summer to mid autumn (June to September). The kinds with single flowers form large red heps that look like small tomatoes and the ones from early flowers appear on the bushes alongside the later blooms; if you want heps, don't dead-head.

One or two hybrid rugosas, like Conrad F. Meyer and its sport Nova Zembla are not really typical of the family. Lovely in bloom, they can become bare at the base and need something else planted in front of them. They are also less healthy than the others, and are susceptible to rust.

Alba. Single white flowers on a dense shrub; orange-red heps maturing to tomato red. 1·8 × 1·8m (6 × 6 ft).

Frau Dagmar Hartopp. Single, pale-pink flowers and huge, crimson heps. 1·5 × 1·5m (5 × 5 ft).

Roseraie de l'Hay. Velvety, wine-red, scented flowers all summer; no heps. 1·8 × 1·5m (6 × 5 ft).

Pink Grootendorst. Small, clear, pink flowers in big clusters, the petal edges frilled like a carnation; no heps. 1·8 × 1·5m (6 × 5 ft).

Hybrid musk

Many of the hybrid musk roses are like giant floribundas in a way. However, they are much more widespreading, reaching in some cases 1·8–2m (6–7 ft) tall and wide. The scented blooms come in large, free-ranging sprays or trusses, and they make wonderful colourful hedges if you have the space. They can also be used for

bedding in a large plot, but do not expect the regularity of growth that you get with a floribunda. There is a fine autumn flowering as well as one in early summer and some flower in between.

Buff Beauty. Apricot-yellow blooms, fading to cream. 1·8 × 1·8m (6 × 6 ft).

Cornelia. Coppery-apricot, fading to cream. 1·5 × 2m (5 × 7 ft).

Penelope. Penelope Semi-double flowers, creamy-pink, shaded light orange in colour; very robust. 1·8 × 1·5m (6 × 5 ft).

Modern shrub roses

These are very diverse in appearance and habit. Some, like Chinatown and Fred Loads, are actually extra-vigorous floribundas and grow in exactly the same way. Others, like Constance Spry, are hybrids of old roses and usually take after one or other of the parents in habit of growth or flower form.

Cerise Bouquet. Cerise-crimson flowers in large sprays. 2·4 × 3m (8 × 10 ft).

Chinatown. Very large, scented, canary-yellow double flowers in clusters. 1·5m × 90cm (5 × 3 ft).

Constance Spry. Huge, pink cupped blooms in old style. 1·5 × 2·4m (5 × 8 ft).

Fred Loads. Huge trusses of semi-double, pale vermilion-orange flowers; prune hard and regularly to restrain growth. 2·4 × 1·2m (8 × 4 ft).

Fritz Nobis. Clove-scented, blush-pink, semi-double flowers; very free. 1·8 × 2·1m (6 × 7 ft).

Frühlingsgold. Huge, arching canes, bearing 10cm (4 in), semi-double, light yellow blooms. 2·4 × 2·1m (8 × 7 ft).

Golden Wings. Non-stop flowers with single, yellow, scented blooms; very healthy. 1·8 × 1·5m (6 × 5 ft).

Marguerite Hilling. Sport of Nevada, pink. 2·1 × 2·4m (7 × 8 ft).

Above: Buff Beauty, a fragrant hybrid musk
Below: the magnificent arching habit of Fruhlingsgold, a modern shrub rose

Nevada. Completely smothered in ivory-white, semi-double flowers in mid summer (June) and later. 2·1 × 2·4m (7 × 8 ft).

History of the Garden Rose

Modern roses bear little resemblance to the original wild roses – with their rather fleeting flowering season – that go back millions of years to a time long before Man inhabited the earth. Fossils of some have been found in France, the Middle East and in America.

Many of these old species roses survive today. There are probably about 150 true species, but a number of roses that appear to be species because they have been given Latin names are really hybrids that have crossed by chance with other roses in the wild. Many of them have semi-double or double flowers whereas, with one exception, genuine species roses have simply five single petals.

Accidental crossing was responsible for the creation of all the early families of rose, for it was not until the late 18th century that anyone began to realize that cross pollination between plants by bees and other insects was the way in which new varieties were created. The intentional breeding of new plants by man is a comparatively new science and in the case of roses, because of their very mixed ancestry, a very unpredictable one. The poet Keats knew about this when he wrote in his 'Ode to Psyche':

With all the gardener Fancy e're could feign,
Who breeding flowers, will never breed the same

Gallica

The gallica or French rose is the oldest cultivated rose we know and the first records of it go back to the 16th century though they were not then grown as garden plants in the way they are now.

Much earlier the gallica, and possibly a form of damask rose, was grown in enormous quantities at Paestum in Italy to decorate and perfume Roman feasts and other festivities. Damasks, and another race of roses, the albas, were also grown on a massive scale for the production of attar of roses in the Balkan countries and Turkey and, to a lesser extent, in France. Dating back hundreds of years, this industry still exists.

As can be seen from a reading of the old herbals, the rose was long considered a plant with almost unlimited medicinal properties. The Romans thought that a preparation made from a British wild species, *Rosa canina*, was a cure for hydrophobia, a symptom of rabies, and this is how the dog rose got its name.

One of the early gallicas, *R. gallica officinalis*, was cultivated near the town of Provins in northern France as well as in other places, for the medicines and magic potions to be distilled from it. Thus it earned the popular name of the apothecary's rose. To this day it is known as the rose of Provins and has also gained fame as the red rose of Lancaster, from England's 15th century Wars of the Roses. Its lasting qualities are such that it is still stocked by nurseries.

Alba

The gallica, of course, was far from being the only one chosen as a symbol. *R. × alba*, another you can still buy, was the white rose of York, and variety Alba Maxima was the Jacobite rose of Bonnie Prince Charlie. Heraldry featured the 'Tudor' rose, and the rose has long been a symbol of purity in many religions.

HYBRID TEA ROSE—"LA FRANCE"

Opposite page: La France, the first hybrid tea, from an 1896 botanical book. Top left: the dog rose, R. canina, *was known to the Romans. Top right:* R. chinensis Old Blush, *one of the repeat-flowering China roses. Right: hybrid perpetual Reine des Violettes dates from 1860. Far right: Zigeunerknabe (Gypsy Boy), Bourbon rose raised in 1909. Below: one of the earliest known,* R. gallica officinalis

19th century development

Napoleon's wife, the Empress Josephine, was a dedicated gardener and at Malmaison, her villa near Paris, she collected together all the roses then known to be in cultivation, making what was probably the first rose garden. Such was its attraction that the idea caught on amongst her fashionable contemporaries and the rose, as a popular garden plant, had arrived. From about this time, you can begin to see the breeding lines that were to lead to the modern hybrid tea, though the first step came about purely by chance.

At this time, many missionaries and government and trade officials worked in China and other parts of the Far East. A number of them, fascinated by the strange plants they saw, became keen collectors and sent specimens and seeds back to interested friends and botanical gardens in Europe.

Almost all the roses known in the West were once-flowering – in early summer – but a number from China were fully recurrent and when these began to arrive there was great excitement in the gardening world. In themselves, the roses were not the most spectacular varieties to look at, or particularly robust, but they were welcomed for their long flowering period alone. Nobody knew how to pass this quality on to the existing Western roses, but Nature did it for us.

Bourbon

On the Ile Bourbon (now Réunion) in the Indian Ocean, some China roses were planted in a hedge with a rose called the Autumn Damask. This was a very ancient and strong-growing Western rose that had gained its name because it usually did produce a few flowers after the first flush but could not really be called recurrent. Insects, flitting from one rose to another in the mixed hedge on the Ile Bourbon, fertilized the flowers, and seedlings resulted that were strong-growing, strong in constitution, and flowered well into the autumn. They combined the best qualities of both parents and were noticed in the first quarter of the 19th century by a visiting botanist called Bréon. He took some back to France and the Bourbon rose, with its characteristic huge, many-petalled flowers, was born. Its merits quickly made it popular.

Portland

Almost at the same period a similar chance cross between a China rose and a damask – nobody knows if they were actually the same varieties – was taking place in Italy, and produced a small group called Portland roses, named after the Duchess of Portland of the time. They did not catch on to the same extent as the Bourbons but nevertheless they are an important group in the history of the hybrid tea rose.

Hybrid perpetual

Bourbons, crossed with the Portlands, resulted in the hybrid perpetual roses so loved by the Victorians that the catalogues of large growers might contain well over 1000 varieties. This may seem difficult to believe and it is probably as well to be sceptical. Even in nurseries cross pollination was still taking place largely at random and it is pretty certain that many of the so-called new varieties were as nearly identical to those already in existence as makes no matter. Two rival nurseries might well call exactly the same rose by different names of their own choosing.

Hybrid tea

The early hybrid perpetuals had short centre petals that made for a flower of globular form. This faded out and the high-centred bloom we admire today began to appear after the introduction of the recurrent tea rose from China. Not really hardy in the northern European countries, this was a rose of great elegance of form, with long centre petals and with the outer ones reflexing symmetrically all round. Crossed with hybrid perpetuals, it produced the first hybrid tea, named La France, in 1867.

The yellow rose

Some of the tea roses were of a pale, creamy-yellow colour but, apart from a few species, there were no bright yellow ones. One of these species, the Persian *R. foetida*, had – and still has – glowing yellow single flowers. A sport from it, *R. foetida bicolor*, was brilliant scarlet, with the petal reverse yellow, and there was also a double yellow form. A French nurseryman from Lyons, called Pernet-Ducher, worked for many years trying to cross the latter with hybrid perpetual roses and at long last his great patience was rewarded by the production of Rayon d'Or, leading in turn to the better Soleil d'Or, a double yellow rose, flushed with orange and red, and this was put on the market in 1900. From this rose all our yellow, flame and orange roses are descended, and our bicolours from crosses with *R. foetida bicolor*. These early yellow roses were known as Pernetainas after their raiser but as they became merged with other roses the name was dropped.

Top: very old centifolia variety Fantin Latour. Above: R. rugosa rubra *shrub rose gives a fine display of heps*

The susceptibility of *R. foetida* to black spot disease was also, unfortunately, passed on to its many grandchildren and through interbreeding with other-coloured roses this same tendency has been firmly established in practically all modern varieties.

Floribunda

As we know, floribundas have a different habit of growth, the blooms being smaller and coming in trusses as they do on many ramblers, unlike the large blooms, one to a stem, of many hybrid teas. It is not surprising, therefore, to know that floribundas have come down to us as a result of crosses between China roses and the rambler *R. multiflora*. Crossed with bush roses, these produced first of all the poly-pom roses that were quite popular before World War II. They were small, bushy plants with small flowers in clusters that made a colourful display before succumbing to mildew – something they were very prone to do.

In 1924, the Danish hybridist Svend Poulsen put Else Poulsen and Kirsten Poulsen on the market; he had bred them

by crossing poly-pom roses with hybrid teas, and they became known as hybrid polyanthas or simply as polyanthas. They were the first to resemble floribundas as we know them today, though it was not until after World War II that they became really popular and the name floribunda was adopted. Present breeding tendency is towards floribundas with bigger, HT-shaped flowers, with fewer on a truss, and they are known as floribunda-hybrid tea type. It is getting more and more difficult to distinguish some of them from hybrid teas and this development is so marked that the World Federation of Rose Societies is debating the use of a new term – 'cluster-flowered' – that will embrace all those roses that do not have single flowers to a stem.

Other types

So much for hybrid teas and floribundas, but there are a few strands of rose development that have not been mentioned. Rambling roses came from species like *R. wichuraiana*, sometimes crossed with hybrid teas and other roses, and climbers from the Chinese *R. gigantea* and other natural climbers.

The centifolia roses, that were enormously popular at one time, are thought to have been the result of a cross between an alba rose and the dog rose. They were developed largely in the Netherlands and appear with their globular, 'very double' blooms in the pictures of many of the old Dutch flower painters. A centifolia sported the first moss rose, a group pretty well identical to the centifolias except for the mossy, glandular growth on the pedicals and calyx. The novelty of this appealed greatly to the Victorians and in our thinking the moss rose is closely linked with that period. There has been little recent development with them except for the production of a yellow moss rose and, in the USA, miniature moss roses.

Rugosa roses, the Ramana rose of Japan, have gone their own way producing a number of first-rate shrub roses but, strangely for something so good, playing a very small part in the history of the rose.

The Royal National Rose Society

Earlier on, we left the Empress Josephine spreading the word about the rose as a garden plant. But, for many years, rose gardens were the preserve of the rich and in Britain it was not until the foundation of the National Rose Society (now Royal) in 1876 by Canon – later Dean – Reynolds Hole and the Reverend H. Honeywood D'Ombrain that the rose began to be the flower for everyone, rich or poor. Beginning by encouraging rose shows all over the country, they worked hard to popularize the flower they loved so well. How well the society has succeeded in the 100 years it has been in existence, can be seen in every garden today.

Modern breeding programmes

Looking forward, what pointers are there to the way the rose will go? Healthier roses must and will come and this is something to which many of the best breeders are giving thought. However, it can take up to eight years to breed and market a new rose, so a great deal of patience on the part of both growers and the public is called for.

There is a constant striving for a blue rose. Whether or not this would be a good thing must remain a matter of opinion but one is only likely to develop through a freak of nature. The make-up of the rose does not include delphinidin, that essential ingredient of blue flowers, so it is most unlikely that we will get anywhere nearer the target than, say, the present-day hybrid tea, Blue Moon, which is really lilac-mauve in colour.

Comparatively few of the species and old roses have played much part in the breeding programmes of modern hybridists. Using them can be a long and frustrating job, especially for a firm that has to make money to stay in business, but the constant search for novelties has brought a few into the picture recently.

The floribunda Picasso, with unusual deep cerise blotches on the petals of its light cerise flowers, has a species in its recent pedigree. News, another floribunda, is beetroot-purple, its colours coming from the gallica rose Tuscany. These two are just beginnings: before long we may see yellow garden roses with a red eye, grandchildren of the Iranian species rose *R. persica*, and currently the subject of experimental breeding programmes.

Above: R. foetida bicolor, *ancestor of modern bicoloured varieties*
Left: Blue Moon, nearest yet to a true blue rose

Above: R. foetida bicolor, *ancestor of modern bicoloured varieties. Left: Blue Moon, nearest yet to a true blue rose.*

Choosing the Site and Planting Your Roses

Having looked at the roses themselves we now tell you where and how to plant the various groups for best results and we go on to routine care and propagation.

Roses like plenty of sun, though there are some climbers that will do quite well on a north-facing wall. They will grow in most types of soil, though are far from their best on chalk. A good, medium loam suits them best of all, so you can help them on light soils by adding as much humus as possible, and peat and other materials on heavy ones, both to lighten them and to improve drainage. The latter is important, for no rose likes being waterlogged. They should have plenty of water if they are to flourish as they should, but they will survive drought far better than they will constant flooding.

Choose, if possible, an open but not a windswept site. Avoid narrow, draughty wind-tunnels such as you find between houses, or shady places under trees, where the roses will grow tall and spindly looking for the light and have to compete with the tree roots for water and food.

How many roses you will need to fill your chosen beds depends not only on how many you can afford, but also on the varieties you select. If you have seen the same varieties growing elsewhere beforehand, you will know just how large they get, and whether they are spreading or upright growers. As a rough guide, it can be said that an average distance between plants of about 45cm (18 in) will suit most hybrid teas and floribundas. This will allow for air circulation, and make spraying and hoeing between them not too difficult a task.

Do not plant new roses in a bed that has grown other roses for some years. The soil will have become what is known as 'rose sick' and the new roses will never do well. You must either replace the soil from another part of the garden, which is a job few people care to tackle if the bed is a big one, or else choose another spot altogether. However, if you are simply replacing a rose that has died in the middle of an established bed, it is not too big a job to dig out a 45cm (18 in) hole, about 30cm (12 in) deep, and put new soil in – still hard work but it should be done.

Preparing the site

Roses will give you twenty years or more of their beauty, so it is only fair and

A fine display of mixed roses resulting from careful siting and planting

sensible to give them the best home possible to live in. The preparation of the site will vary to a greater or lesser extent according to your type of soil. In extreme cases where, for instance, drainage is almost non-existent and the ground waterlogged, it may be necessary to put in land drains, or at the very least put in materials to make it more porous. Light, sandy soils need the opposite approach for, though good drainage is essential, a correct balance must be struck between this and some degree of water retention. Roots need air as well as water to function properly, which is the reason heavy soils need to be broken up so as to make them more friable.

This breaking-up should be done by double digging and keeping the fertile topsoil where it should be, at the top. It is a good idea to put chopped-up turfs, grass side downwards, along the bottom of each trench and, when filling in, add well-rotted compost, leaf mould, granulated peat or stable manure – or a mixture of all of them – whatever organic material you can get hold of, together with a generous dressing of bonemeal.

All this digging and manuring should be done some time in mid autumn (September), about three months before your roses arrive. The ground will have time to settle down and you can recover from a back-breaking job. Heavy work it may be, but you will be more than glad in years to come that you faced up to it, for with good cultivation roses will not only grow and bloom well, but will be much more resistant to diseases.

Finally, a few tips for special conditions. About 1½kg per sq m (3 lb per sq yd) of gypsum (calcium sulphate) added to the bottom of a double-dug trench will help to break up a clay subsoil, though only over quite a long period. On very light, sandy soils, deep digging should not be needed, as both water and roots can penetrate it easily in its natural state. In fact, disturbance of the lower spit will make it even easier for the water to get away, which is the last thing needed on this kind of soil. Plenty of humus in the top spit is the answer here.

If you are gardening on solid chalk, with only a few centimetres of soil over it, it will be necessary to dig out the chalk to a depth of at least 45cm (18 in), and to add plenty of peat to the soil that replaces it. Roses do best in a slightly acid soil, of a pH value between 6·0 and 6·5.

When and how to plant
Your roses will probably arrive from the nursery in early winter (November). This is the best month for planting them, as the soil will still be warm enough for the roots to get established.

If you have to wait a few days before planting, either because you are too busy with something else, or the ground is frost-bound, or soggy from prolonged rain, do not unpack the roses but keep them in a cool, frost-proof shed. If there is likely to be a longer delay, heel them in as soon as weather conditions permit. To do this, unpack the plants and put them along a trench in a spare corner of the garden, burying them so that at least 15cm (6 in) of soil covers the roots. They can remain like this for some weeks if absolutely necessary, but it is always best to get them into their final quarters with the least delay so that they can start to make themselves at home.

Whether you are planting straight away or heeling in, inspect the roses carefully as soon as you have unpacked them. Check the labels to make sure that they are what you ordered, as even the best of nurseries can make mistakes and will always exchange a wrong variety. If the plants are described as being First Grade, they should have a minimum of

two firm, healthy canes (stems), at least as thick as a pencil and with smooth, unwrinkled bark. The neck joint between the rootstock and the budding union should be at least 16mm (⅝ in) thick, and there should be a good, fibrous root system. Cut off any leaves remaining on the canes, and cut back any of the latter that are diseased or broken to a point

1 *Dig hole wide enough to spread roots*

2 *Carefully remove wrapping material*
4 *Work planting mixture around roots*

3 *Settle roots in hole and check level*
5 *Fill in and firm down before watering*

just below the damaged portion. Shorten any very long, thick roots by a third; this will encourage the thinner, feeding roots to grow from them. If the roses look dry, put them in a bucket of water for at least an hour.

While they are sucking up the water, you can make up your planting mixture which, while not absolutely essential on good soil, will certainly help to give your roses a good start. You will need about one large shovelful for each rose, consisting of equal parts of soil and moist granulated peat, with a handful of bonemeal or rose fertilizer per plant mixed well in. It is advisable to wear gloves when handling fertilizers.

Dig your first planting hole wide enough for the roots to be spread out as evenly as possible all round, and deep enough so that the budding union comes about 13mm ($\frac{1}{2}$ in) below the soil level. Carry your bucket of roses to the rose bed so that you can lift them straight from it and the roots have no chance to dry out again. Put your first rose in its hole, spread out the roots and check the level by putting a cane across the top of the

hole. Put a shovelful of planting mixture over the roots, tread lightly, and then fill in the hole with soil, treading again rather more firmly. Finally, give each rose at least 8 litres (2 gal) of water. It may be as well to tread the soil once more after a few weeks, especially if there has been a frost that may have loosened the plants.

Climbers
Climbing roses against a house wall, where the soil is certain to be very dry, need slightly different treatment. Plant them at least 45cm (18 in) out from the wall and fan out their roots *away* from it towards the damper ground. If they are long enough, tie in the canes straight away to the lowest support wire to help prevent wind-rock.

Standards and shrubs
Standard roses should have the stake that will support them driven into the hole before planting, so that it will not damage any roots. The stake should be long enough so that it just goes into the head of the bush to give it extra support, but should not show above it. Tie the two together with plastic ties that have a buffer between the plant and stake to prevent chafing, but only fix them loosely at first as the rose may sink a little as the soil settles. After a week or ten days, you can tighten up the ties enough to hold the stem firmly, but not to strangle it.

When planting the larger-growing shrub roses, make sure that you really have left room enough all round for them to achieve their full size.

Container-grown plants
Many people buy container-grown roses from nurseries and garden centres, and these plants should be carefully inspected before buying to make sure that they are up to standard and have genuinely been grown in a container and not just put in one for selling purposes. They have the

Left: a good soaking helps dry plants
Above: standards should be firmly tied

great advantage that they can be planted at any time, even in full flower, provided the rootball is not disturbed too much.

However, don't just dig a hole big enough to take the container, particularly if your soil is heavy. By doing this you might simply be making a sump, that would fill with water after rain and whose sides the roots might find it hard to penetrate. Dig a hole at least 30cm (12 in) across, breaking up the subsoil for drainage. Water your rose well while still in its container, and put it in the hole to check that the depth is right. If it is, slit down each side of the container with a sharp knife, ease it out from under the rootball, fill the hole with planting mixture, tread firm and water well. Should the container be of metal, you will, of course, have to remove the rose before putting it in the planting hole.

Growing under glass
Roses are not hothouse plants, but they can be grown successfully in a greenhouse, at least for part of the year, so that you can have spring blooms long before the garden roses are out.

Use 20 or 25cm (8 or 10 in) pots with 2–3cm (1 in) of broken crocks in the bottom; their size depends on the vigour of the variety. J. I. potting compost, either No 2 or No 3, is a suitable growing medium, with perhaps a small amount of well-rotted garden compost or small pieces of chopped turf immediately on top of the crocks.

Plant the roses in early winter (early November), making sure that the soil level is about 2–3cm (1 in) below the pot rims to allow for watering and liquid fertilizers if you wish to use them. You may well have to cut the stronger roots back quite hard to fit the whole thing into the pot, but they will soon form new, finer ones. Firm planting is important, and all leaves and flower-buds should be removed and long shoots shortened a little.

Leave the pots out of doors until mid winter (early December), and then bring them into the greenhouse.

A cold greenhouse will produce flowers in early summer (May), but some heat will be needed for flowers earlier than that. Good ventilation is important at all times, particularly from above, and some form of shading will be needed if the sun is hot. Prune them at the end of mid winter (December), and do not introduce heat into the house until at least ten days after it has been done.

Prune hard, to the first two or three eyes (buds) or you will get tall, straggly plants. Watering should not be too generous at first, but gradually increased as the plants start into growth. Give a thorough weekly soaking once they are really away, with a liquid feed added to the water two months after pruning.

Pests such as caterpillars and greenfly can be removed by hand if you only have a few roses. Mildew can be largely avoided by good roof ventilation, but if any spraying of the plants has to be done, it is much safer to take them out of the greenhouse so that you do not breathe harmful chemicals.

When the plants finish flowering, towards the end of early summer (May), turn off the heating if this has been used, and open the ventilators to prepare the roses for a move outdoors in two weeks or so. Once outside, sink the pots to their rims in ashes in a sheltered spot, where they can be left until brought indoors again in early winter (December), when re-potting should be done if necessary.

Routine care of Roses

If you are to get the best results from your roses, whether they be tiny miniatures or giant ramblers,
then regular attention is most important. Here we tell you about the routine jobs, such as when to add
fertilizer and how to disbud.

Starting with winter, when there is least to do by way of maintenance, your first job is to spray the dormant roses at least once, but preferably two or three times, with Bordeaux mixture to kill over-wintering disease spores. It has been found that this spraying makes quite a difference to the health of roses later in the year.

Fertilizing and mulching

After spring pruning, apply a proprietary rose fertilizer round each bush at the rate recommended by the supplier, probably between 70–140g per sq m (2–4 oz per sq yd), and hoe it in lightly so that the fine, surface-feeding roots are not disturbed or severed. Water well afterwards if there is no rain about.

Late spring (mid April) when the soil has begun to warm up, is a good time to mulch the rose beds, but there is no point in putting on a mulch in the middle of a dry spell. A mulch serves three purposes: to keep the weeds down, to fertilize the soil when it breaks down, and to form a blanket to keep in the moisture. But it cannot do the latter if there is little or no moisture there in the first place, and if the mulch itself dries out, it will absorb an enormous amount of rainwater before any moisture penetrates to the soil beneath. Grass mowings in particular, unless spread very thinly, form an almost impenetrable mass.

Remove any persistent perennial weeds before mulching, and then spread a layer about 5–8cm (2–3 in) thick of well-rotted farmyard manure over the whole bed, keeping it just clear of the rose stems. This is the ideal mulch as it has in it many of the nutrients that roses need, and makes good humus as well. If you cannot get

Looking after your roses pays off with a colourful display such as the one below

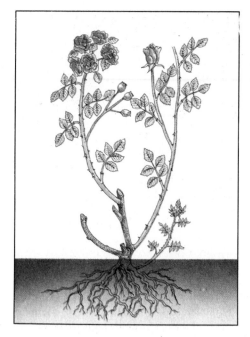

manure, use well-rotted compost or leaf mould, which is almost as good. Other alternatives are hop manure or granulated peat (the most attractive-looking, but getting more and more expensive), but these have no manurial value, though peat is an excellent soil conditioner when it is eventually hoed in. It helps to lighten heavy soils and to make light soils more water-retentive.

Early summer (mid to late May) is the time for a second application of fertilizer, and if you wish to add a third to boost the

Left: identifying parts of the rose bush
Below left: as with all flowering plants, dead-heading will encourage a rose to continue blooming; on a floribunda cut off the entire truss down to a good bud
Below right: pinch out side buds to get one large bloom on each stem
Bottom: suckers come up around the stem

roses for autumn blooming, this should be done no later than late summer (the end of July). Otherwise growth will be encouraged that will not have time to ripen before the winter and is likely to be killed by frost.

When and how to dead-head
In the natural way of things, roses produce seeds after flowering, and a good deal of the plant's energy goes into this rather than into the production of new flowers. If the seed-heads (heps) are removed the rose tries again and more flowers are the result. This removal is known as dead-heading or summer pruning, and serves a double purpose in that it also removes the sometimes unsightly, dying blooms of the varieties whose petals do not drop cleanly or those that may have become sodden with rain.

Do not just pull the heads off, however. It is far better, and will produce new flowers more quickly, if you cut back to a good strong bud below the old flower or below the spent truss of a floribunda. Remove as little wood and as few leaves as possible in doing this, however, or the rose will be weakened.

How to recognize suckers
Roses, unless they are growing on their own roots (which is unusual with nursery-bought plants), will have been budded on to an understock or rootstock of a more vigorous species or near species, such as *Rosa canina* in one of its many forms. Suckering is an attempt by the rootstock to start a life of its own by sending up shoots. These shoots are called suckers, and if they are not dealt with promptly, all the strength of the roots will be diverted into them. The rootstock will take over, and your own chosen rose will die.

How to distinguish a sucker growth presents problems for a beginner, particularly as a number of different roses are used as rootstocks, and their shoots vary in appearance. Sometimes a sucker is easy to recognize, as some stocks produce very light green shoots that will probably have several leaflets. They look entirely different from the growth of hybrid tea or a floribunda, but this is not an infallible guide. After you have had some experience, you will be able to recognize any sucker immediately, but to be on the safe side until you are sure, trace the suspected sucker back to its source.

This will probably mean scraping a little soil away from the base of the plant to see where the sucker comes from. If it comes from below the budding union (a thickening of the main stem just above the roots, from which the canes of your rose

Above: always plant roses so the budding union (that you can see clearly on new shrubs) is beneath the soil surface
Left: suckers grow from the rootstock and should be removed by clearing away soil to their start point and pulling hard

sprout) it is a sucker. It should be pulled away from the root rather than cut, stopping short, of course, of pulling your rose up in the process.

This is the only way of making sure that no dormant buds are left behind to form new suckers. Never just cut a sucker off at ground level. All you will be doing then is pruning it and encouraging more strong growth.

Treated like this, they should come away quite easily, provided that they are dealt with promptly and not allowed to mature. The only real problem is when one comes from right under the rose, or from the middle of a tangle of old roots. Then there is probably nothing to be done except to cut it back as far as possible and to keep an eye open for it emerging again – as it is certain to do.

The stem of a standard rose is part of the rootstock, and any shoots that appear on the stem are the equivalent of suckers and should be broken off.

Disbudding for bigger blooms

Many HT roses have clusters of buds at the end of each cane. For general garden display, this does not really matter, but if you want to get bigger blooms (and fewer of them), remove some or all of the side buds as soon as they are large enough for this to be done without damaging the main bud. If you are going to show your roses, you will have to disbud them. One or two varieties, like Pink Favorite, have so many closely-packed buds that, to get the best of the rose for garden display, at least some of the buds should be pinched out carefully between finger and thumb.

Autumn pruning

This is not pruning to encourage new growth. It simply means shortening the

canes of HT and floribunda types by about one-third early on in winter (early November) to prevent the bushes being rocked by the winter winds and probably loosened in the soil. This is especially important for tall-growing varieties.

Tidying up

This is another autumn job, consisting of raking up and burning the fallen rose leaves from the beds, to help destroy disease spores that may winter on them. Also, pick off the plants and burn all remaining leaves that are showing signs of black spot disease. This may be quite a job if you have a lot of rose bushes and is really a task that should be started earlier in the summer if you want to keep it under control, and continued right through to this stage of the autumn. If you can face up to this programme, it pays dividends the following summer.

Finally, hoe the beds lightly to destroy weeds and to accelerate the breaking down of the spring mulch into the soil.

Taking cuttings

You can increase your stock of roses by taking cuttings, but it should be remembered that not all types of rose take equally well and some, even if they do take, will not have the same vigour on their own roots as when budded onto rootstock. As a compensation, you will not have to cope with suckers from the roses, and they will cost you nothing.

A large number of HTs are reluctant to root from cuttings, though it is always worth a try. Floribundas, generally speaking, are much easier and miniature roses take readily. So do most climbers, ramblers, and shrub roses. Among the latter, families like the gallicas, albas, rugosas (if on their own roots when bought), and species like the spinosissima group, sucker quite freely, and root cuttings can be taken by easing out the sucker and cutting off a portion that has roots attached.

For the other roses mentioned, cuttings can be taken any time between mid autumn and early winter (September and November). Choose a strong, well-ripened and unbranched shoot – one that grew early in the summer – and make a clean cut immediately below the lowest eye. Make another cut directly above a bud about 25cm (9 in) away from the first, sloping the cut downwards and away from the bud as you would in pruning. Remove all but the top pair of leaves, and your cutting is ready for planting. From long shoots, you can obtain two or even three 25cm (9 in) cuttings. Do not try to take one from the very soft, pithy tip of the shoot however.

Once you have a selection of cuttings label them if they come from different roses and put them in a polythene bag so that they will not dry out.

Dig a narrow trench about 15cm (6 in) deep and, if your soil is at all heavy, sprinkle a mixture of sharp sand and granulated peat along the bottom. Place your cuttings in this, about 15cm (6 in) apart and so that 15cm of their length are below soil level, fill in the trench and firm well. If you moisten the ends of the cuttings before planting and dip them into a hormone rooting powder their chances of rooting will be increased.

On light, sandy soils it may not be necessary to dig a trench or even to use sand or peat. Simply make a long, straight, 15cm (6in) deep slit by pushing a spade into the earth and working it backwards and forwards. The cuttings can be inserted into this, and treading along the sides of the slit will push the

earth back into place around them.

Leave the cuttings until the following autumn, when those that have taken can be transplanted to their final quarters, but do not expect to have fully-grown plants for two or three years. Taking cuttings is an easy but not a very quick way of increasing your stock.

For miniature roses, the cutting can be about 8cm (3 in) long and everything else is scaled down in proportion. Miniatures will grow to full size relatively quickly.

Propagation by budding

This is a much speedier method of increasing the number of your roses. It is the way nurseries create new plants and consists of inserting a bud or eye from one of your existing roses into the neck of a rootstock, where, with luck, it will grow away. It is a rather more complicated process than taking cuttings, and the actual budding does require a knack, though this is not too hard to acquire (see Budding and Grafting, page 41).

Your local rose nursery may well be prepared to let you have a few rootstocks, or there are several specialist firms that supply them, though often in quantities of not less than twenty-five. In the autumn, plant your stocks about 60cm (24 in) apart in a spare piece of ground. During the winter, they will settle in and, in the spring, start to grow. Late that same summer prepare to do your budding and choose a showery spell of weather if possible.

Cut some ripe shoots with strong, plump, dormant buds from the roses you wish to increase. Shoots that have flowered in mid or late summer (June or

To propagate a rose from a cutting, cut off a new shoot below the lowest eye, then cut above a bud 25cm (9in) away. Trim off all but top two leaves. Place 15cm (6 in) apart in a narrow trench 15cm deep and leave until following autumn

July) should be ripe in mid autumn (early September) and are very suitable. Place all but one of the shoots in a plastic bag while you work on the first one, to prevent them from drying out.

With a very sharp knife, make a scooping cut into the shoot, starting about 13mm ($\frac{1}{2}$ in) above a bud and coming out about the same distance below it. Trim off the leaf but leave the leaf-stalk to act as a handle for holding the bud. With your thumbnail, twist out the small, boat-shaped piece of pith and wood behind the bud, trim the bottom and top ends of the bark, and put the bud carefully to one side.

Now prepare the stock. Scoop away a little soil at the neck, where it enters the earth, and wipe the neck clean with a damp rag. With the sharp point of your knife, make a T-shaped cut in the bark of the neck with the down-stroke of the T about 19mm ($\frac{3}{4}$ in) long. Very gently, taking care not to damage or detach them, ease out the triangular flap of bark on either side of it.

Now, holding it by the leaf-stalk, slide the bud downwards into the T-cut, under the bark flaps. Bind the whole thing gently but firmly with raffia, except immediately over the bud itself. As an alternative to this you can buy special budding ties that are very easy to use. They are flexible and expand when the bud does. Raffia will simply rot away at about the time when the bud has taken and it is no longer needed.

By the following spring, the bud should have taken, though you must allow for a number of failures – at least until you have mastered the knack of preparing and inserting the bud. When the new shoot is growing strongly, you can cut away the whole top growth of the stock immediately above it, and all the strength from the roots will go into the new rose. For a while, even though it is growing from it, the shoot will not be very firmly anchored into the stock, so it is wise to support it by tying it to a short cane pushed into the ground beside it to guard against the buffeting of the wind. Be very careful when doing this, or you may snap off the shoot. By the following autumn your new rose should be growing strongly and be ready for transplanting to its permanent home.

If you are budding standard roses and want to get a balanced head, insert two buds (double budding) at least, each about 2–3cm (1 in) above the last and on different sides of the stem. This applies to rugosa stock; for canina stock, insert the buds into good strong lateral growths, as close to the stem as possible.

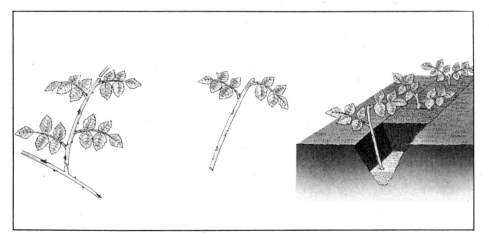

Pruning Roses

The profusely-flowering floribunda Iceberg responds well to good pruning

It is unfortunate that when writing about pruning it tends to sound so complicated. There is no doubt that the best way to learn is to get an experienced rose grower to show you how to do it, provided that he takes the time to explain just why he is doing each operation. If you understand what you are doing and why, pruning all at once loses its mystique and suddenly you wonder what all the fuss was about.

So, first of all, why do we prune? In the wild (and you can see this for yourself in the hedgerows) roses send up new canes each year from the base of the plant or from very near it. The old canes will gradually deteriorate and eventually die off. The best blooms come on the new growth, and all you are doing when you prune is speeding up this natural process of replacement. Also, some of the old canes may very well be diseased, so you are getting rid of these as well.

There are two other things to aim for in pruning. One is to achieve a reasonably balanced bush, though this may not be too important if the roses are growing close together in a bed, and the other to keep the centre of the bush fairly open so

that light and air can reach it. A thick tangle of canes in the middle should be thinned out and, if two are crossing so that they will rub together, one of the pair should be removed or at least shortened enough to prevent this happening.

It pays to buy a good pair of secateurs as they will last you for many years. They should always be kept clean and sharp. If they are not, you will bruise the stems of the roses and make rough, ragged cuts, that will encourage the entry of disease spores.

Hybrid teas
The first thing to do is to cut away all weak, twiggy growth – everything, in fact, that is thinner than a pencil. This includes the very small, matchstick-like twigs that often sprout from the main canes, and that will produce no more than a few undersized leaves if left. Cut right out any dead wood, including stumps and snags that may have been left from poor pruning in the past. Some of these may be too tough for secateurs and for them you should use a fine-toothed saw. Dead wood will be brown or greyish, with

gnarled and wrinkled bark.

Next, remove any diseased canes, or shorten them back to the first healthy bud below the diseased portion. If you cut through a cane and the centre of it is brown, this is a sign of die-back, so move down, bud by bud, until you reach healthy white wood.

You may find some quite thick and apparently healthy canes that were pruned the previous year, but from which only a few spindly twigs have grown below the old pruning cut. If this is all the canes have produced in a season, they will do no better in the next, so remove them.

All of what might be termed 'rubbish' has now been disposed of, and the remaining green and firm, healthy canes should be shortened to about 15–20cm (6–8 in). The cuts should be made about 6mm ($\frac{1}{4}$ in) above a bud, and at an angle, sloping down away from the bud. If you cannot find a bud where you want one, choose the nearest, preferably an outward-facing one, to encourage the new shoots to grow away from the centre of the plant. But once again, if you cannot find an outward-facing bud, do not think that inward growth will make the rose moody and introspective. In fact, it is not unusual, even if you do cut to an outward-facing bud, for the one below it, facing inwards, to be the one that starts away first and makes all the running. You try to point the way, but the rose does not always follow.

That is really all there is to the yearly pruning of HT roses for the average gardener. Harder pruning will produce larger flowers, but fewer of them. Rather lighter pruning is probably advisable on poor, dry soils. Unless these have a regular and massive application of fertilizer and humus, there will not be the goodness in them to promote vigorous new growth on the same scale.

Newly-planted roses
Always prune these more severely, to perhaps 8–10cm (3–4 in). This will ensure that top-growth starts later and there is more time for the energy of the plant to go into developing a sound root system early in the year. If you plant your roses in the spring, prune them at the same time.

Everybody argues about the best time to prune. Each expert has his own theory, so who is right? The answer is, of course, everybody. As long as the bushes are dormant, or nearly so, which will probably be from early winter to mid spring (end of November to end of March) in mild areas, and provided that there is no frost about, it does not matter very much

*Top left and right: pruning rules for
a standard depend largely on whether it
is an HT or floribunda variety; be sure
to keep the head a good, even shape
Above left: hard pruning will produce
larger blooms on HT varieties
Bottom right: cut out old wood at source*

when you prune. If there is a severe winter, autumn pruning may mean that you lose a few canes through frost damage; these can be trimmed back later. But this can happen with a bad spring frost, too. In colder districts, it is wiser to leave your pruning until well into mid, or even late, spring (late March or April).

Floribundas

These are grown mainly for their mass effect and continuity of bloom rather than, as with an HT, the beauty of their individual flowers. For this reason, and because they naturally make more new growth than an HT without the encouragement of hard pruning, they can be treated more lightly.

Basically, however, the approach is the same. Weak, dead or diseased wood is removed, and then healthy growths shortened by between one-half and one-third, cutting just above a bud as before.

Strong laterals or sideshoots should be shortened to the first or second bud.

With very strong and tall-growing varieties, like Iceberg or Chinatown, which may be wanted for specimen planting or for the back of a border, a strong framework of wood can be built up over several years. If the main canes are cut back only moderately, they will produce strong laterals that are shortened in turn the following year, producing yet further branching. Gradually, a very large bush takes shape, from which the main shoots need only be removed as they lose their vigour and are replaced by others.

Ramblers and climbers

As the methods of pruning are different, it is as well to be able to distinguish between the two, but the position is complicated by the fact that there are two types of ramblers, one being much closer to a climber in its habits than the other.

Ramblers With a few exceptions, these only flower once, some varieties doing so as late as late summer or even early autumn (July or August). The first group, that includes varieties like American Pillar, Dorothy Perkins, Excelsa and Sander's White Rambler, have large

clusters of small blooms, and throw up new canes 2m (6 ft) or so long from the base of the plant each year. Pruning consists of cutting the old canes to the ground as soon as they have finished flowering and tying the new ones in their place. With a vigorous, thorny rose, this can be a rather fearsome job, and strong, thorn-proof gloves will be needed. It is often easier to remove the old canes by cutting them into short lengths and pulling these out individually.

If new growth is poor one year, a few of the old canes can be shortened by about one-third and left in place. They will produce some flowers but not with the profusion of new ones.

The second type of rambler, that includes varieties like Albertine, has rather larger flowers and tends to produce enormously vigorous new canes, branching out from anywhere along the length of the old ones. Prune after flowering by cutting away the old just above where a new cane has sprouted. Remove unproductive or diseased old wood as and when it occurs.

Climbers As a class, climbers generally have larger flowers than ramblers, some as big and as shapely as HT roses. Many of the newer introductions and a number of the older ones flower twice. Do not prune any of them until the first year after planting. This is especially important with the climbing sports of HT and floribunda, as hard pruning then may cause them to revert to their bush form.

Many climbers do very well with little or no pruning except what is needed to keep them in bounds, but all will do much better if the laterals are shortened by about two-thirds in winter. Some varieties are extremely stubborn about producing new growth low down, and can become very bare at the base. Apart from training the canes as horizontally as possible to encourage new sideshoots to break, strong cutting-back of a main cane may help to produce others from the bottom. If this does not work, there is nothing for it but to plant something else in front of it, though not so close that it will rob the rose of the goodness in the soil.

Standard roses

Usually these are varieties of HT roses or floribundas, and pruning should be done in the same way as for the equivalent bushes. It is always important to bear in mind the balance of the head and to keep it as even as possible, as with a standard you are more likely to be seeing the rose from all sides.

Weeping standards Both of the rambler

Guide to pruning roses

HYBRID TEA **FLORIBUNDA** **STANDARD**	**Hard pruning** Newly-planted, and HT roses for exhibition blooms	**Moderate pruning** Established HT and floribunda	**Light pruning** Roses growing on poor, dry soils
RAMBLER **WEEPING STANDARD**	**Small-flowered** Cut old canes down to ground after flowering Treat head of standard as small-flowered rambler	**Large-flowered** Cut out old flowered wood to base of new lateral	
CLIMBER	Don't prune when first planted, but shorten laterals by two-thirds in subsequent years		
MINIATURE	Thin out dense, twiggy growth and discard dead wood; trim to shape		
SHRUB	Thin out dense growth, discard dead wood, trim to shape; shorten laterals up to two-thirds		

groups are used for these standards, though there is no doubt that the first, small-flowered, group are the best as their long, pliable canes weep naturally. Once again the pruning is the same as if they were growing in their natural rambling form. That is, completely remove old canes after flowering for group one; for the second type, cut back old wood above – or, perhaps, below as the canes should be hanging downwards – the point where a strong side-growth has sprouted.

Miniatures
This involves the thinning out when needed of the varieties that produce dense, twiggy growth and the removal of the few shoots that may die back each year. Some of the more vigorous varieties may send up extra-strong shoots oc-casionally that unbalance the bush, and these should be shortened. Nail-scissors are best to use for pruning miniatures.

Shrub roses
Species roses, except in their formative years when a limited amount of cutting back may be needed in order to produce a reasonably balanced shape, should be left alone apart from the removal of dead wood. This can be taken out at any time. Pruning would destroy the natural habit of growth and this is one of the main charms of a species rose.

Apart from the removal of diseased or dead wood (that applies to all of them), most other shrub roses – damasks, albas, centifolias, moss roses, Bourbons, hybrid musks, hybrid perpetuals and modern shrub roses – need their laterals shortened by about two-thirds at the most after flowering to encourage new growth, though they will do quite well even without this attention. Occasionally a strong main shoot can be cut hard back to encourage new growth low down.

If used in hedges, both rugosas and gallicas can be clipped over lightly in winter, rather than pruned, but this should be done following in the main their natural outline. If you are using roses you cannot expect (and should not want) the squared-off regularity of a privet or box hedge.

Varieties of shrub roses that bear heps, other than species, can be trimmed in early spring if they need it, and the pruning of tall floribundas that may be used as shrubs has already been described under the floribunda heading.

Rose Pests and Diseases

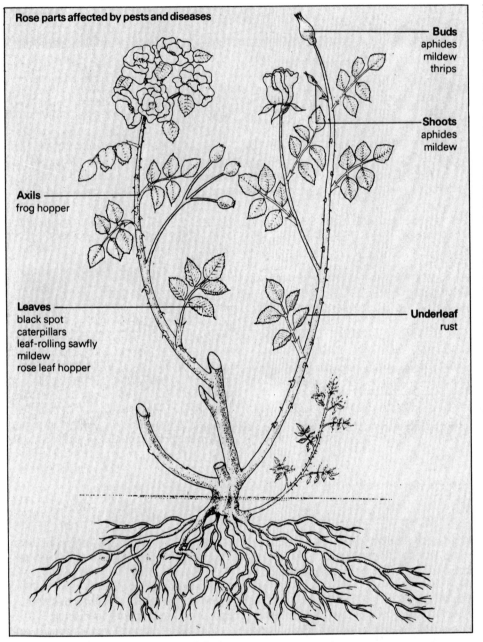

Rose parts affected by pests and diseases

Buds
aphides
mildew
thrips

Shoots
aphides
mildew

Axils
frog hopper

Leaves
black spot
caterpillars
leaf-rolling sawfly
mildew
rose leaf hopper

Underleaf
rust

could be added to the list given above, based on individual growers' experience in particular gardens or in particular districts. Even moving a variety as prone to mildew as Rosemary Rose from one part of a single garden to another has been known to bring about a cure. Dryness about the roots and lack of proper air circulation often encourages mildew, and the purer the air the more black spot flourishes. In industrial areas, where there is sulphur in the atmosphere from factory chimneys, black spot will be no problem, and it is ironic that the creation of smokeless zones, so beneficial to most things, has caused this rose disease to spread into areas where it was not known before.

So the experience of a grower of a particular variety in one part of the country may be very different from one elsewhere, but the roses named above have been found to be some of the best in all conditions.

Not everyone, however, will want to grow just these varieties, and if you have an established garden, you will have to deal with the roses already growing there, that may not be so disease resistant.

Chemical fungicide sprays are expensive, and spraying itself is not the most enjoyable of occupations. Many people feel, too, that it is risky to use chemicals, about whose long-term effects we really know very little. One has only to think back to the time, not so long ago, when DDT was used on a world-wide scale against insect pests and then was suddenly found to be harmful and withdrawn from sale, to see the force of this argument. All of which adds up to not spraying more than you have to.

If there is no sign of black spot in your garden, do not spray against it; or wait until you see the first signs of mildew before you take action. In some years it will be much less prevalent than others and only touch one or two roses.

However, there are areas, and the south-west of England is one, where black spot is always a serious problem, and there it is usual to have to carry out preventative spraying each year before the disease appears, and probably to top up regularly as often as every ten days or so for the rest of the summer. In other places, rust is the trouble, but find out from local growers what diseases your roses are likely to get, and judge from your own experience before acting.

How and when to spray

Wherever you live, you are unlikely not to have to spray against anything at all, be it insects or disease spores, so a few general

There are a number of roses that, under most garden conditions, can be said to be reasonably or almost completely free from disease. The hybrid tea roses in this category include: Pink Favorite and Honey Favorite (both outstanding), Peace, Grandpa Dickson, Wendy Cussons, Rose Gaujard, Ernest H. Morse, Red Devil, Fragrant Cloud, Chicago Peace and Gail Borden.

Some healthy floribundas are: Southampton, Matangi, Sarabande, Escapade, Chinatown and Evelyn Fison, and among the climbers are Aloha, Mermaid and Golden Showers.

The rugosas, Chinas and a number of the species are outstanding among the shrub roses, but many of the others are so tough that they can shrug off attacks by mildew and black spot without coming to any harm, though this will not prevent them looking rather unsightly in late summer if they remain unsprayed.

Quite a large number of other roses

points about spraying should be born in mind. It is best to use a spray that produces a fine mist. Do not spray in hot sunshine, or the leaves of the rose may scorch – evening is the best time; spray sufficiently to wet the plants all over, but not to the extent of leaving them dripping, which is an awful waste of expensive liquid. Do spray the undersides of the leaves as well as the upper surfaces.

Systemic sprays
These penetrate into the tissue of the plant. In some cases they will circulate with the sap, but not all sprays do this equally well, which is why it is important to wet the whole rose. Systemics have the great advantage, of course, that they are not washed off by rain and so will remain effective for several weeks.

Pesticides and fungicides
Great strides have been made in recent years with pesticides and fungicides. Greenfly infestation should not be a serious problem any more; mildew is largely under control; an oxycarboxin spray such as Plantvax 75 is a certain treatment for rust, and black spot, while not mastered, can at least be controlled to a large extent in all but the worst areas.

Our chart, based on one prepared by the Royal National Rose Society, should prove a useful guide as to the best sprays to be used for the different diseases and insects. As indicated, many of these chemicals can be mixed together, so that you can spray against everything (if you are unlucky enough to suffer from everything) at one and the same time. The warning given in our Note below should, however, be stressed. Make quite sure that your particular sprays are compatible. Otherwise you run the risk of losing all the leaves from your roses.

Mildew
This is the most prevalent of the rose diseases, and is carried by airborne spores from one plant to another. The first signs are generally small, grey, powdery-looking patches on the leaves and on the flower-stalks and undersides of the buds. In bad cases, the mildew will spread over the entire plant, distorting growth and preventing the second crop of flowers from opening properly. Mildew will not kill a rose, but it will ruin its appearance.

If treated promptly, mildew can nowadays be controlled, but the spraying of vigorous climbers can be a problem if they are high up on the wall of a house. Ramblers, which as a class are subject to mildew, should preferably never be planted against house walls

Aphides massed on rose stems

Black spot
This is also carried by airborne spores, and usually appears first around the middle of the summer on the older, lower leaves of rose bushes. The small, circular black spots rapidly grow in size, the rest of the leaf yellows, and eventually dies and drops off. Bad attacks can completely defoliate a rose and this lack of leaves, apart from being unsightly, weakens the plant and can kill it over several seasons of repeated attacks. Spraying will help control, but no real cure has been found. Ideally, affected leaves should be picked off and burned to prevent the black spot spores from spreading.

Spores of both black spot and mildew can overwinter on leaves left on the ground, and also on the rose stems and stumps that have not been properly pruned back.

Rust
Fortunately, this is not as widespread as mildew or black spot, and only certain varieties are usually liable to attack, for a serious invasion of your garden by rust can kill the roses. Until quite recently it was recommended that badly-affected plants should be dug up and burned, but now a spray of oxycarboxin gives complete control. Rust can be recognized by

Rust affects leaves

the formation of orange pustules on the undersides of the leaves, and it should be dealt with without delay.

These, then, are the rose diseases that most rose growers will have to deal with at some time. There are also insect pests, against which modern insecticides give very good protection, but as with diseases, you also need to be able to recognize the insect enemies to be able to deal with them. The following are the most common and troublesome.

Aphides or greenfly
Probably too well known to need description except to say that those that infest the young shoots and buds of roses can be brown and pink as well as green. They suck the sap of the plant and exude a sticky substance known as honeydew, on which a sooty mould forms. Increase is incredibly rapid, so spray promptly.

Thrips
Small, black insects that move with great

Black spot appears only in clean-air districts

speed over the plant and drop off if disturbed, only to climb back later. Hot, dry summers seem to suit thrips; nibbled-looking buds are likely to be their work and distorted flowers the outcome. Some varieties of rose are, for some reason, much more prone to attack than others, notably Ophelia and its descendants, Mme Butterfly and Lady Sylvia. One cure for thrips is said to be the covering of the beds under the roses with metal foil, as the thrips do not appear to like the reflected light coming from below! Hardly the ideal solution for most gardens.

Frog hopper or cuckoo spit
Small, green insects that hide themselves in a blob of white froth, usually at a joint between a stem or leaf and a side shoot. The nymph sucks the sap of the rose. Either the fingers (if the attack is limited), or a jet of water, should be used

to remove the froth before spraying.

Rose leaf hopper
Very small, pale yellow insects, that leap high in the air if disturbed. They cause mottling of the rose leaves, and the presence of their cast-off white skins on the undersides of the leaves is a sure sign that leaf hoppers are about.

Caterpillars
In a mild attack, these can be removed by hand but Dipterex is a most effective spray. It will penetrate the leaf, and so will deal with caterpillars that have doubled a leaf round themselves, as some do when they are feeding on it.

Leaf-rolling sawfly
This pest appears to be on the increase. The name is very descriptive, for the sawfly lays its eggs on the leaves that then curl up lengthwise, protecting the grub feeding within. This makes it difficult to reach with sprays, which are only really effective if applied before an attack, which in itself is difficult to predict. Otherwise, tedious though it may be, removal of the rolled-up leaves is recommended to prevent the larvae moving on from one leaf to another when they have had enough of the first one.

Note Capsids, scale insects, chafer grubs and leaf miners can also be a problem on roses and should be controlled with the appropriate insecticide.

Roses: guide to fungicides and insecticides

FUNGICIDES FOR OUTDOOR ROSES

Active ingredient	Proprietary name	Powdery mildew	Black spot	Rust
maneb	Maneb WP		★★	★★
zineb	Dithane		★★	★★
thiram	ICI Garden Fungicide		★★	★★
captan	Orthocide or Captan		★★	
dinocap	Karathane or Dinocap	★★		
folpet	Murphy Rose Fungicide	★	★★	★
benomyl	Benlate	★★★	★★	
triforine	Gesal Rose Mildew Treatment	★★★	★★	□
oxycarboxin	ICI Plantvax 75			★★★
thiophanate-methyl	Mildothane	★★	★★	
mancozeb	Dithane		★★	★★

Home greenhouse insecticides
For all pests except mites, either: resmethrin+pyrethrum (Sprayday), or bioresmethrin (Copper Garden Spray). Against red spider mites, only water or white oil (e.g. Volck) are recommended. The following have systemic action: formothion, dimethoate, menazon and fenitothion (e.g. Fentro, Accothion). Trichlorphon (Dipterex), while not systemic, can penetrate the leaf-blade.

Compatability guide
Any two wettable powder (WP) fungicides can be mixed with one liquid insecticide, or two if one is Dipterex 80 (a solution). More than two liquid pesticides should not be mixed together unless a trial has shown them to be compatible. For this generalization ICI Garden Fungicide (a colloidal liquid) can be considered a WP. When three or more pesticides are to be sprayed together they should be diluted separately and mixed together immediately before spray application.

INSECTICIDES FOR OUTDOOR ROSES

Insecticide	Aphides	Thrips	Capsids	Leaf hopper	Scale Insects	Caterpillars	Leaf-rolling sawfly	Chafers	Leaf miners
formothion dimethoate	★★★			★★★	★				
malathion diazinon	★★	★	★	★★	★★	★			
menazon	★★★			□					
gamma-BHC	★	★	★★	★		★		★★	★★
trichlorphon						★★★	★★		★★
fenitrothion	★★	★	★	★★	□	★★	★★	★	★□

★★★ very active   ★★ moderately active   ★ slightly active   □ more evidence required   WP wettable powder

Roses for Exhibition

We end this section on roses with a look at growing for exhibition. By showing your best blooms you share their beauty with others as well as competing for perfection.

Everyone who grows roses in their garden can exhibit them at a local show and, if they are prepared to take just a little bit of trouble, win prizes with them. Getting your roses ready for showing, and eventually staging them on the day, gives an added interest to your gardening and provided that you do not take it too seriously, it can be great fun. Our advice for preparing hybrid teas and floribundas is given separately.

Hybrid teas

For local showing it is not even necessary to grow special roses. It is often said, in some cases rightly, that you should not choose HT roses for your garden from the varieties in competitive classes at shows. This is because a number of fine exhibition roses either do not stand up to rain well, or perhaps only produce a very limited number of flowers at one time. Dedicated exhibitors do not mind this and use special bloom-protectors when necessary to keep off the rain. Varieties such as Bonsoir, Gavotte, Isabel de Ortiz, Memoriam, Montezuma, Red Devil and Royal Highness only give of their wonderful best when the sun shines continuously, and Princess has fine show blooms, but not too many of them.

However, there are many roses that will produce flowers that will win in any company and are good garden roses as well. Some of these are: Alec's Red, Chicago Peace, Embassy, Ernest H. Morse, Fragrant Cloud, Fred Gibson, Grandpa Dickson, Honey Favorite, Peace, Pink Favorite, Silver Lining and Wendy Cussons. Rose Gaujard can also be a winner but has a lot of split-centred blooms, and Gail Borden and My Choice are fine if you get your timing right, as they tend to open quickly. The blooms of Perfecta, a rose that has won countless show awards, stand up to rain in themselves but tend to have some rather weak flower-stems. In the 'very double' flowers these may bend over or even snap with the weight of water after a heavy shower. A show rose should have good, strong stems and hold its flower upright.

The actual growing of your exhibition roses needs no special skill for anything other than the biggest shows. Obviously,

A magnificent show rose – this perfectly formed hybrid tea Blessings

if they are well looked after, they will produce bigger and better blooms, so do not neglect to use the fertilizer recommended in the feature on routine care and garden cultivation in Week 34. Keep the roses well-watered and spray regularly, if this is needed, against insect pests and diseases. Healthy foliage is important in a show, as it is in the garden.

Disbudding

The only other thing that you may have to do with some varieties to get the best out of them is to disbud. A single bloom to a stem, with no side branches, is required in almost all classes for HT roses at a show. Some kinds grow naturally like this, but others – Pink Favorite and Stella are examples – often have clusters of buds at the top. Other roses do this, more in the second flush than in the first, so if you want to exhibit them, pinch out all but the main, central bud as soon as the others are large enough for you to do so. You can leave a second bud to develop a little lower down the stem if it looks as if the main one will open long before the show.

The perfect show bloom

For the actual exhibition, the bloom of an HT rose should be half to three-quarters open at the time of judging. A blown bloom will not win a prize. It should have a high, pointed centre of petals, with no sign of splitting, and the other petals should reflex as evenly as possible all round it. It should be fresh, true to colour for the variety, and as free as it can be of blemishes from weather or other damage. The size should be typical of the variety, though many judges, wrongly, give an oversized bloom preference over a typical one. Extra size should only really count where the class is for specimen blooms. Foliage should be healthy, and the stem should be firm and straight.

SORBUS

Type	deciduous flowering and fruiting tree or shrub
Family	ROSACEAE
Flowering season	early or mid summer (May or June)
Planting date	late autumn to mid spring (October to March); from containers: anytime
Mature size/shape	60cm high × 45cm wide (2 × 1½ ft) to 7·5m high × 4m wide (22 × 12 ft); round-headed, conical, pyramidal, fastigiate

The genus sorbus is composed of 100 species of hardy, deciduous trees that were formerly included in the pyrus (pear) genus. The name comes from the Latin for the fruit of the service tree. Sorbus are easily grown on the whole and not particularly choosy about the soil or the position they are offered. Many of the species and hybrids are tolerant of shade and do not object to atmospheric pollution; this makes them very suitable for gardens in industrial areas. There are some members of the genus that are equally happy in coastal areas and exposed cold districts. They range in size from dwarf shrubs to larger trees. Unfortunately the most charming of the former, *Sorbus reducta*, is rare these days. It is an erect growing shrub with a height of between 30–60cm (1–2 ft) and has round, pinkish berries.

Sorbus trees reach heights of 6–9m (20–30 ft) and are largely sold as standards or as feathered trees. Numbers of them are very upright in their growth which enables them to be fitted into restricted areas but in many cases they are not really suitable for smaller gardens. However, in a built-up area, if there is space, *S. aucuparia* (mountain ash or rowan) is excellent for screening from sight any ugly or undesirable neighbouring object. Because of its mid-green, feathery leaves, with grey underneath, it provides a cheerful effect.

In order to facilitate the description of these species, it is necessary to consider briefly how their family is made up.

The sorbus genus is made up of three groups, and most of them belong to the first two.

Aria Members have simple leaves that are either toothed or lobed. In the main, they do well on chalky soil. The head of this group is the well-known *S. aria* (whitebeam).

Aucuparia The leading member of this category is the familiar *S. aucuparia*, or mountain ash. Plants in this group have pinnate leaves with numbers of leaflets. Quite a number of its members – species and cultivars – are short-lived on shallow chalk, preferring richer, deeper soils.

Micromeles The members of this much smaller class are different from those of the aucuparia in that the calyces of their fruits fall seasonally like deciduous leaves.

At this point it is appropriate to mention that there is a group of hybrids known as the 'Lombarts hybrid Sorbus'. This race has been raised by a famous Dutch nursery since the 1950s. It is made up of vigorous, elegant trees of upright habit, chiefly characterized by having larger and more unusually-coloured berries. They are not stocked by all nurserymen but they are worth searching out.

Regarding the habitat of these many species, a few such as *S. aria*, *S. aucuparia* and *S.*

Far left: Sorbus hybrida, *one of the whitebeams, forms a compact small tree*
Left: S. aucuparia *Xanthocarpa, a rowan or mountain ash*
Below S. a. *Beissneri is especially noted for the warm colouring of its bark*

bristoliensis are natives of the British Isles. So far, the latter has only been found growing wild in the Avon gorge near Bristol. The origins of the rest are widespread throughout the world – the mountains of Europe, Scandinavia, North America, Kashmir, Tibet, Manchuria, China, Japan and elsewhere. In addition, quite a number of the most attractive sorbus are hybrids or cultivars raised in gardens and nurseries.

With its autumn tints and coloured berries – that often ripen while the leaves are still green – sorbus can add a particularly beautiful touch to your garden. If you have the space you can grow some of the more slender, fastigiate species or cultivars as a specimen in the lawn or as an accent point in a shrubbery.

The small, upright, slender whitebeam species *S. minima* that does not grow to a greater height than 3m (10 ft) in ten years is a possibility in a smallish garden, as is the very upright, small tree *S. alnifolia submollis* (*zahlbruckneri*), a contrasting form to other whitebeams. It reaches a height of 2·5m (8 ft) or so in about the same time.

When a screen is required a mountain ash or whitebeam might fit the purpose most effectively.

Although the general tendency among the groups of trees is to grow upright branches, some are to be found with various shapes and habits that are valuable in creating a pleasing elevation in the garden. A few are rounded in outline, others are pyramidal, and columnar shapes are included among them. Also, a selection of habits such as horizontal branching, spreading limbs and arching branches all help to create an attractive design.

Cultivation and propagation

Sorbus will thrive in ordinary garden soil, provided it is well drained. If there is a fairly deep layer of topsoil they will grow satisfactorily on chalk. They prefer a sunny position but can grow quite well in partial or full shade. They are very accommodating as a whole and can withstand exposure to cold, high winds, salt-laden gales and atmospheric pollution.

As they are deciduous trees and shrubs, sorbus are best planted during suitable weather between late autumn and mid spring (October to March). One exception is when they are containerized – then they may be planted at any time. A second is when they are being planted at the seaside; it is better to postpone planting in this case until spring so as not to expose them to salt-laden gales just as they are starting to grow.

Bare-root trees are a problem in this respect because nurserymen are sometimes sold out so late in the season. So if you have an exposed garden it is advisable to buy good stock in the autumn and heel it under in a sheltered place until the worst weather has passed.

Fortunately, many sorbus are fairly slender, although they have some height, so the space allowed between them in a group or between neighbours is comparatively small. The best guide to spacing is to average the ultimate spread of the sorbus, and that of its neighbour.

Above: S. aria *Lutescens showing its silvery-white spring foliage. It produces bunches of deep red berries in the autumn*

Left and right: two forms of the rowan or mountain ash, S. hupehensis. *At right, the species and at left, the variety Pink Form*

When planting a bare-root sorbus tree, dig a hole large enough in diameter to allow its roots – after you have cut away all damaged and extra-long ones – to be spread out in the bottom of it. It should be deep enough so that when planted the soil mark on the main stem, indicating the depth to which it was growing at the nursery, just shows above the soil surface in its new quarters. Mix a little garden compost or well-rotted manure with the broken-up soil at the bottom of the hole and, before filling it, insert a good stake between the roots so they do not get damaged, giving the tree support during its early years. As you replace the excavated soil, firm it well with your heel.

If the plant is pot-grown, remove the container and bury the rootball to a depth of the surrounding soil level without breaking it up and make sure that the soil round its edges is well firmed.

You can propagate species by planting seeds extracted from ripened berries in late autumn (October) right away in J.I. seed compost, using a cold frame. Transplant them a year later to a nursery bed and after three to five years plant them out in their permanent growing positions.

Hybrids and cultivars can be propagated by layering; rare kinds can be budded or grafted on to *S. aucuparia* stocks.

Disease

Apple canker produces severe cankers on the bark of sorbus and sometimes kills large shoots.

Fireblight, which blackens and shrivels the blooms and gradually kills the branches that carry brown and withered leaves, is likely to attack them, so cut it out and burn the infected wood.

Honey fungus may also attack sorbus and destroy it quickly.

Some varieties to choose

Sorbus adds an attractive feature to your garden if you can afford the space. They usually have white flowers appearing early to mid summer (May to June). The dimensions given are for the ultimate height and spread respectively.

Whitebeam

S. aria	Compact round-headed tree. Its leaves are greyish-white at first, then green above and densely white below, and finally golden-russet in autumn. Its berries are deep crimson in colour and it has a number of very attractive cultivars. 5·5 × 4m (18 × 13 ft).
S. a. Lutescens	Young leaves are a striking silvery-white in spring, becoming a greyish-green in summer. Its berries are a deep red and grow in large bunches on the more mature trees.
S. hybrida	Compact tree with green leaves and grey tomentose (dense covering of matted hairs) underneath. Its berries are globular and red and they grow in large clusters. 5·5 × 4m (18 × 13 ft).
S. h. Gibbsii (or *S. pinnatifida* Gibbsii)	An attractive cultivar that bears a good crop of dark red berries, too large for birds to tackle.
S. intermedia (Swedish whitebeam)	Round-headed tree that is very hardy and resistant to wind. It has large clusters of orange-scarlet fruits. 5·5 × 4m (18 × 13 ft).
S. minima	Small, slender tree with leaves that are green and have grey tomentose underneath, and speckled, scarlet berries. Suitable for a small garden. 3 × 2m (10 × 6 ft).

Mountain ash or rowan

S. aucuparia	Familiar tree with attractive greyish, downy winter buds that give pinnate leaves that turn orange and yellow in late autumn (October). It bears bright red berries. 6 × 3m (20 × 10 ft). It has several very fine varieties.
S. a. Aspleniifolia	Has fern-like leaves.
S. a. Beissneri	The young shoots are dark coral-red and the bark is a warm copper colour. It has bright red berries.
S. a. Edulis	Larger than usual sweet and edible berries.
S. a. Xanthocarpa	Berries are amber-yellow.
Lombart hybrids	These hybrids of *S. aucuparia* surpass all the other mountain ash varieties. They reach between 2·5–4·5m (8–15 ft) in height and from 2·5m (5–8 ft) in spread after being planted about ten years. The figures given for the individual plants in the following list are approximate heights.
Apricot Queen	Pale, orange-yellow berries. 4·5m (15 ft).
Carpet of Gold	Golden-yellow berries. 4·5m (15 ft).
Coral Beauty	Coral-red berries. 3·5m (11 ft).
Lombarts Golden Wonder	Large, golden-yellow berries. 4·5m (15 ft).
Old Pink	Large clusters of pink berries and pink-tinted leaves. 3m (10 ft).
Orange Favourite	Light, orange berries. 3·5m (11 ft).
Red Tip	Cream-white berries showing a red tip and red-tinted foliage. 2·5m (8 ft).
S. Embley	Small to medium-sized, erect-growing shrub whose former botanical name was *S. discolor*. It has sticky buds yielding leaves with up to 15 leaflets. Its leaves are longlasting and turn to a glowing red, giving a superb display in autumn. This beauty is enhanced by its glistening, orange-red berries. 6 × 2·5m (20 × 8 ft).

Left: bright yellow berries of S. Joseph Rock, an attractive small tree
Below left: S. sargentiana *forms a small, pyramidal-shaped tree*

S. hupehensis	Slow-growing tree with purplish-brown branches and slightly bluish leaves of up to 17 leaflets, and white berries. 5 × 3m (17 × 10 ft).
S. h. Pink Form	Has persistent, glistening pink berries.
S. Joseph Rock	Small tree with foliage that turns a superb crimson-purple colour in autumn. Its berries are yellow. 5·5 × 2·5m (18 × 8 ft).
S. prattii	Elegant large shrub or small tree with leaves composed of up to 30 leaflets. Its small, globose berries are pearly-white. 3 × 2·5m (10 × 8 ft).
S. sargentiana	Pyramidal tree with sticky, crimson winter buds, red leaf-stalks, producing clusters, 15cm (6 in) in diameter, of late-ripening, small, scarlet berries. 4·5 × 3m (15 × 10 ft).
S. scopulina	Slow-growing, columnar shrub or small tree with sealing-wax-red fruits. 3 × 2m (10 × 7 ft).
S. vilmorinii	Beautiful small tree or medium-sized shrub. Its fern-like leaves have up to 30 leaflets, and turn red to purple in autumn. Its berries are rose-red at first, then pink, and ultimately white, flushed rose. 3 × 2m (10 × 7 ft).

Micromeles

S. alnifolia submollis (or zahlbruckneri)	Very upright, slender, small tree. Its green leaves are deeply-veined, and turn golden-brown in autumn. Its berries are bright red and egg-shaped. 4·5 × 1·2m (15 × 4 ft).

SYRINGA

Type	hardy, deciduous flowering shrubs with fragrant flowers
Family	OLEACEAE
Common name	lilac
Planting date	late autumn–early winter (October–November); from containers any time
Flowering season	early–mid summer (May–June)
Mature size/shape	1·5–4·5m (5–15 ft) high and 1·5–4m (5–13 ft) spread; mainly rounded bushes, but a few are erect-growing

Syringa has been known for a long time. The Elizabethans called it the pipe tree because its wood was made into a musical instrument similar to that traditionally used by the god Pan known as pan-pipes or syrinx. The latter name has given rise to the genus name syringa.

Among the earliest species grown in gardens in England were *S. vulgaris*, brought from the mountains of eastern Europe during the 16th century, and *S. × persica*, that is said to have been cultivated in English gardens in 1640. In habitat the species is fairly widespread throughout the world. Like *S. vulgaris*, *S. josikaea* comes from eastern Europe; *S. microphylla*, *S. reflexa* and *S. sweginzowii* originated in China, while *S. amurensis* grows wild from Manchuria to Korea. Despite its name, *S. × persica* (Persian lilac) appears to have been brought from Afghanistan.

The genus syringa consists of 30 species of hardy deciduous shrubs and some small trees. Syringa – or lilacs – are much prized for their large, pyramidal panicles of flowers that are often very fragrant. They succeed the ornamental peaches, cherries and other spring-flowering shrubs and trees and continue flowering into mid summer (June). Syringa never form a true tree, although as bushes some species will grow as tall as 4·5m (15 ft) or sometimes even 6m (20 ft). This is because each growing shoot often ends in two hard buds of equal size that in spring sprout equally and vigorously, repeatedly producing forks. Syringa therefore rarely form a straight central stem and so remain long-lived bushes rather than trees.

Do not make the mistake of confusing the philadelphus (mock orange) with syringa. Although the philadelphus is often referred to as syringa this is quite erroneous since they do not even belong to the same plant family.

Although easy to grow, syringa often require a season or two to settle down, and are even then comparatively slow-growing. In many cases they are not true to colour until they have been in the garden for three years.

While some species grow fairly big after about 20 years, they never become unduly large. They are very suitable for small gardens because, in most cases, they are quite amenable to being cut back. In fact, you can rejuvenate overgrown bushes by pruning them back during the winter to about 75cm (2½ ft) above the ground. The larger-growing syringa, such as *S. × chinensis*, *S. josikaea*, *S. vulgaris* and *S. × prestoniae* (the Canadian hybrids) have heights and spreads up to 4·5m (15 ft) and 4m (13 ft) respectively. Among the several other species that are appreciably smaller are the rounded bush *S. × persica* with all-round dimensions of about 2m (6 ft), the beautiful, slender-branched, spreading shrub *S. microphylla* and the slow-growing, dense, compact, free-flowering bush *S. (palibiniana) velutina* – both with

Syringa vulgaris *Souvenir de Louis Spaeth is one of the best and most consistent single lilacs for the garden, having attractively-coloured, scented flowers and good, shrubby growth* dimensions not exceeding 1·5m (5 ft); these can give the same effect in small gardens as the larger versions.

Although syringa are grown primarily for their large, colourful, scented blooms and their distinctive green leaves (that in the case of *S. vulgaris* are dark brown in autumn), there are at least two that have ornamental bark. One is the less common *S. reticulata* that can be readily trained to a short, stout tree with an attractive trunk. The other is *S. amurensis*, the older bark of which peels off to show dark chestnut brown. Also, one cultivar, *S. emodii* Aureovariegata has yellow variegated leaves.

Syringa thrive well in town gardens, particularly on industrial sites where their fragrant and prominent clusters of flowers enliven what might otherwise be a sombre environment.

Many of the choicest varieties grown at the present time are of garden origin. Particular mention must be made of the very lovely Canadian hybrids that were raised originally by Miss Isabella Preston of the Canadian government's Division of Horticulture in Ottawa in 1920.

Syringa make very handsome and colourful specimen shrubs. Alternatively, they are effective grown in shrub or mixed borders where, apart from their colourful flowers, their rather lighter, sometimes heart-shaped, green leaves make a much-appreciated contrast to darker foliage. The more dwarf species *S. microphylla* and *S. (palibiniana) velutina* are very good in a large rock garden.

The more bushy species and varieties are excellent for planting as informal hedges and also make good summer screens. Many varieties of *S. vulgaris* are particularly good for this purpose. In order to get the best out of them it is important to let the shrubs grow and flower freely. Some experts advocate allowing such a hedge to go its own way for one year and lightly pruning it the next, and so on.

Cultivation

In order to ensure maximum flower production, plant syringa in full sun. Although they will grow in partial shade they will not then be so floriferous. They thrive in any good fertile garden soil and can tolerate chalk.

Plant at any time in late autumn or early winter (October or November), provided the ground is not excessively wet. Those grown in containers can be planted at any time, but if it is in summer, take care to water well at the time of planting and also subsequently if the weather is dry.

Plant larger-growing syringa 3–4m (10–12 ft) apart if they are to be adjacent; allow a distance of about 1·5m (5 ft) with the smaller species. When planting them with other shrubs in a shrub border determine the planting distances in the usual way by adding the spread of the syringa to that of its neighbour and dividing by two. For a hedge plant the bushes about 2·5m (8 ft) apart, unless you are using a smaller type of syringa such as *S. microphylla*, when the planting distance should be

only about 60cm (2 ft).

Dig a hole wide enough to take the rootball comfortably and to allow the roots to spread out. Its depth should be such that the soil mark already on the main stem is level with the surface when it is planted. Fill the hole with soil and firm it well. As soon as growth becomes evident, cut back the shoots to a pair of buds so that a good bushy shape develops. Syringa need little attention once they are established. During the first season it is a good idea to pick off most of the flowers as they appear. In mid summer (June) they appreciate a dressing of sulphate of potash scattered around them and hoed in.

Remove all flowers as soon as they start to fade. After late autumn (October) and throughout the winter remove any crossing and weak shoots. Cut back all suckers as near as possible to the main stem or the root as soon as they appear.

Propagation

Syringa are propagated from 10cm (4 in) long heel cuttings or half-ripe shoots taken in late summer or early autumn (July or August). For the Canadian hybrids, take cuttings in early or mid summer (May or June). Insert them in potting compost either with mist propagation, or in a propagator at 16°C (61°F). Pot rooted cuttings into 10cm (4 in) pots and put in a cold frame. Transplant them to a nursery bed the following mid spring (March) and finally to their permanent home two or more years later.

Named varieties can be layered in spring and autumn. *S. vulgaris* varieties are sometimes budded or grafted on species seedling stock or privet; the advantage is that the latter does not sucker so much as the former, but it is better to grow them on their own roots because die-back and even death sometimes happen, especially with privet, owing to the basic incompatibility of stock and scion.

Pests and diseases

Leaves are sometimes tunnelled by lilac leaf miners. Also, shrubs are open to attack by willow scale insects. If the infestation of either of these is serious, spray with nicotine.

Flowers are sometimes killed by late frost, that also causes young shoots to die back. Such affected tissues are liable to become covered with a greyish-brown fungus due to grey mould (botrytis). Cut out any shoots affected with this. Honey fungus is also liable to attack and kill syringa. If this gains a really strong hold you will probably have to dig the tree out and burn it. Brown spots on leaves and blackened, withered shoots are due to lilac blight; treat by cutting affected branches back to healthy tissue. A spray of Bordeaux Mixture, repeated if necessary, can also help.

Silver leaf is another disease that might attack syringa and their varieties. It causes die-back of the branches that then carry leaves with a silvery tinge. Again, cut back to healthy tissue and paint the cut with a fungicidal paint. If the tree is badly affected dig it out and burn it.

Some varieties to choose

In the following selection the first figure given is the height of the shrub after about 20 years' growth and the second is the spread. Unless otherwise stated, the size of a variety is approximately the same as the species from which it derives.

S. × chinensis (Rouen lilac)
Broad, erect pyramidal panicles of fragrant purple flowers that appear in early summer (May); 3 × 2m (10 × 6½ ft).

S. × hyacinthiflora
This is a variable hybrid, but the cultivars mentioned below are excellent. Flowers mainly in early summer (May), with single blooms; dimensions generally 2·5 × 1·5m (8 × 5 ft) after about ten years.

S. × h. Blue Hyacinth	tubular blue flowers with petals like hyacinths, that are mauve in the bud.
S. × h. Clarke's Giant	erect shrub with rosy-mauve to lilac-blue blooms in 30cm (12 in) long panicles.
S. × h. Esther Staley	carmine-red buds, opening to pure, bright pink.

S. × josiflexa Bellicent
An outstanding clone associated with the Canadian hybrids; has enormous panicles of fragrant, rose-coloured flowers; 4 × 2m (13 × 6½ ft).

The Canadian hybrid cultivars are among the choicest syringas grown today.
S. × josiflexa Bellicent (above) is a fine clone associated with them, and S. × prestoniae Isabella (top left) is a particularly vigorous and beautifully-coloured example
Bottom left: S. vulgaris Maud Notcutt, with large, erect-growing panicles is typical of the best single-flowered varieties available today

S. microphylla (small-leaved or little-leaf lilac)
Has small leaves and erect panicles of fragrant lilac flowers during mid summer (June) and again in mid autumn (September); 1·5 × 1·5m (5 × 5 ft).

S.m. Superba	freely flowers from early summer to late autumn (May to October), with rose-pink blooms; 2m (6½ ft) high.

S. × persica (Persian lilac)
Bushy, rounded shrub producing 10cm (4 in) long, erect pyramidal panicles of fragrant lilac flowers in early summer (May); *S. × p.* Alba is a white version; 2·25 × 2·25m (7 × 7 ft).

S. × prestoniae (Canadian hybrids)
This is the species of a vigorous hardy race of cultivars flowering in early and mid summer (May and June); 4 × 2m (13 × 6½ ft). Some of the most attractive varieties are listed below.

S. × p. Audrey	erect heads of deep pink.
S. × p. Elinor	semi-erect, slender, panicles of dark purple buds opening to pale lilac.
S. × p. Hiawatha	rich reddish-purple in bud, opening to pale pink.
S. × p. Isabella	30cm (12 in) long, slender, semi-erect panicles of mallow pink blooms; vigorous.
S. × p. Virgilia	compact shrub with 23cm (9 in) long, loose panicles of lilac flowers, deep lilac-magenta in bud.

S. sweginzowii
An open shrub of graceful habit that produces sweetly-scented, flesh-pink blooms in long, loose panicles in early and mid summer (May and June); 4 × 3m (13 × 10 ft).

S. (palibiniana) velutina (Korean lilac)
A modest-sized shrub of dense, compact habit with small, rounded, dark green leaves that are carried on slender, twiggy branches; bears numerous elegant panicles of lavender-pink blossoms in early and mid summer (May and June); 1·5 × 1·5m (5 × 5 ft).

S. vulgaris (common lilac)
An attractive shrub in itself, with heart-shaped leaves and erect, pyramidal panicles of lilac flowers; this species is the parent of the more popular syringa grown today; 3 × 2·5m (10 × 8 ft). These below flower in early summer (May).

SINGLE VARIETIES

S.v. Congo	large compact panicles of lilac-red flowers.
S.v. Marechal Foch	bright rose-carmine flowers in broad, open panicles.
S.v. Massena	late flowering with deep reddish-purple flowers.
S.v. Maud Notcutt	exceptionally large white flowers in 30cm (12 in) long, erect-growing panicles.
S.v. Primrose	very free-flowering, compact bush yielding small, dense panicles of primrose blooms.
S.v. Souvenir de Louis Spaeth	a very popular consistent lilac with wine-red blooms.
S.v. Vestale	a shrub of compact habit producing broad, crowded panicles of white flowers.

DOUBLE VARIETIES

S.v. Charles Joly	popular syringa with dark purplish, late-flowering blooms.
S.v. Katherine Havemeyer	broad, compact panicles of pure lavender.
S.v. Madame Antoine Buchner	loose, narrow panicles of rosy-mauve blooms.
S.v. Madame Lemoine	creamy-yellow buds opening to pure white.
S.v. Michel Buchner	large panicles of pale rose lilac.
S.v. Monique Lemoine	late flowering, pure white.
S.v. Mrs Edward Harding	popular, very free-flowering with claret-red, shaded pink late-blooming flowers.
S.v. Paul Thirion	late flowering, carmine buds opening to claret-rose, then turning lilac-pink.

In addition to the double blooms that make S. vulgaris *Madame Antoine Buchner an attractive specimen shrub, its light green leaves can provide an effective contrast to darker-foliaged plants*

VIBURNUM

Type	evergreen and deciduous fruiting shrubs
Family	CAPRIFOLIACEAE
Flowering season	mainly early–late summer (May–July), some bloom in winter and spring
Planting date	deciduous: late autumn–mid spring (October–March); evergreen: mid–late autumn (September–October), and mid spring–early summer (March–May)
Mature size/shape	bushy, round, spreading and erect; height 90cm–3·7m (3–12 ft), spread 1·5–4·5m (5–15 ft)

Above: V. sargentii *one of the most decorative of all viburnum, flowers in summer and is followed by long-lasting fruits*

The genus viburnum contains some 200 species of evergreen and deciduous shrubs that are fairly widespread throughout the Northern Hemisphere. The famous plant explorer E. H. Wilson discovered a number of most attractive species in China, which he introduced into Western gardens during the early years of this century. *V. japonicum* hails from Japan and *V. dentatum* (arrow wood) was found growing wild in North America.

Several species have been discovered growing in Europe, in the Mediterranean region. These include the very lovely *V. tinus* (laurustinus) that flowers over a long period during winter, and has been cultivated in Britain since the late 16th century. Perhaps the most beautiful fruiting viburnum, however, is *V. opulus* (guelder rose or water elder), that grows freely in Europe, north and west Asia and Algeria, and in the moist hedgerows and edges of woodlands in the British Isles. *V. lantana* (wayfaring tree) is also a familiar hedgerow plant, particularly in the chalky downlands of Britain.

There are three distinct categories among viburnum species, all of which have a special beauty and value of their own. Some produce their flowers on bare wood in winter, while others flower in the spring and summer on fully-leaved stems. The third group follow their flowers in autumn with very decorative fruits ranging in colour from black to brilliant scarlet. A very large proportion of species fall into this category. Most viburnum have white flowers that are sometimes tinged pink in the bud, and carried in flat heads or rounded corymbs.

Fruiting viburnum make excellent small or medium-sized plants of varying shape for the shrub border. They are able to tolerate partial shade, and some species make good lawn specimens or ground cover. *V. tinus*, flowering from mid winter to early summer (December to May), makes a most attractive informal hedge, particularly for a shady position and in coastal areas. *V. japonicum* is useful grown as a wall plant.

Cultivation

Viburnum species must be grown in moist positions – dryness should be avoided at all costs. For this reason, they do not object to partial shade. They do best, however, in full sun, provided the soil is moist.

Usually, viburnum grown for their fruits should be planted in groups of two or three, so that pollination can take place without difficulty. All species grow well in any good, moist garden soil but do prepare the site by double digging and incorporating plenty of humus-making, moisture-retaining material such as well-rotted manure, garden compost, or peat, so that it is as rich as possible.

The deciduous species can be planted any time between late autumn and mid spring (October and March), provided the weather is favourable. Evergreens are best planted between mid and late autumn (September and October), and again from mid spring to early summer (March to May).

If you are planting in groups, place the larger shrubs about 3m (10 ft) apart, and the more modest growers, like *V. davidii*, about 1·2m (4 ft) apart. Plant *V. tinus* shrubs for hedging about 60cm (2 ft) apart. Water the plants well before planting, and incorporate garden compost or rotted manure in the excavated soil before replacing it.

The deciduous shrubs, flowering in summer, need little regular pruning. Any that are overgrown can be thinned after flowering and any dead wood removed at the same time. Deciduous, winter-flowering viburnum are pruned in spring to remove flowered shoots and maintain the shape.

Evergreen species do not need regular pruning except to control size and remove old and dead wood. This should be done in early summer (May).

Leaf-curling aphides and whiteflies sometimes infest viburnum. The presence of whitefly is indicated by the undersides of the leaves being covered with black scales and fringed with white wax. *V. tinus* is particularly prone to attack from these pests. Both aphides and whiteflies can be controlled by sprays of a systemic insecticide.

Grey mould disease can be troublesome on viburnum and should be treated by cutting out and burning the infected wood, then painting the wound with protective paint. Sometimes pale or

purple spots appear on the leaves, due to a fungus disease called leaf spot. If the disease is severe, spray with a fungicide such as captan or zineb. Occasionally, viburnum are attacked by honey fungus, which usually causes speedy death of the plant. The only treatment is to dig up the affected plant and burn it.

Propagation

Take heel cuttings about 8–10cm (3–4 in) long in mid or late summer (June or July). Insert them in a soilless compost in a propagating case with a bottom heat of 16°C (61°F). When they have rooted, pot in J.I. No 1 in 8cm (3 in) pots, and place in a cold frame for the winter. Alternatively, take softwood cuttings in early and mid autumn (August and September) and root them in a cold frame. In either case, transplant them to a nursery bed in late spring or early summer (April or May) and leave them for two or three years until planting them in their permanent home in winter.

Another method of propagating is to layer low-growing shoots in mid autumn (September). They will have rooted and can be ready for severing after a year. Species can be raised from seed, but it is a long process and it could take four to six years before flowers are produced.

Some varieties to choose

In the list given below, the dimensions for each shrub refer first to the height and secondly to the spread, both after about 20 years' growth.

V. betulifolium

One of the best fruiting, deciduous shrubs, this has an erect habit and long branches that are weighed down with bunches of redcurrant-like, persistent berries. Bears flat heads of small white flowers in mid summer (June). 2.4×1.5m (8×5 ft).

V. corylifolium

Medium-sized, deciduous shrub with white flowers that appear in early and mid summer (May and June) and are followed by good autumn colours in the foliage and long-lasting bright red fruits. 2.4×2.4m (8×8 ft).

V. davidii

Small, compact, evergreen shrub with deeply-veined dark green leaves. Small white flowers carried in terminal cymes appear in mid summer (June) and are followed by turquoise-blue, egg-shaped fruits. 90cm $\times 1.5$m (3×5 ft).

V. henryi

Erect-growing, evergreen shrub with pyramidal panicles of white flowers produced in mid summer (June) and followed by bright red, then black, fruit. 1.8×1.2m (6×4 ft).

V. japonicum (macrophylla)

Handsome, evergreen shrub with leaves 15cm (6 in) long and 10cm (4 in) wide. Produces fragrant, white, rounded trusses of blooms in mid summer (June), and then red fruits. 2.5×3m (8×10 ft).

V. lantana (wayfaring tree)

Deciduous shrub with creamy white flowers opening in early summer (May) and followed by red, turning black, oblong fruits. Likes a chalky soil. 3×2.1m (10×7 ft).

V. opulus (guelder rose, water elder)

Large, vigorous, spreading deciduous shrub with leaves that colour richly in autumn. Produces white, lacecap hydrangea-like flowers in mid and late summer (June and July), and copious bunches of brilliant red fruits. 3.7×4.5m (12×15 ft).

V.o. Compactum	Smaller variety. 90×90cm (3×3 ft).
V.o. Fructuluteo	Pinkish, lemon-yellow fruits.
V.o. Notcutt's Variety	Larger fruits than the parent. Autumn tints.

V. rhytidophyllum

Fast-growing evergreen shrub that bears cymes of small, creamy white flowers during early summer (May). Its fruits are oval, and red, turning black. 3.7×3.4m (12×11 ft).

V. sargentii

Resembles *V. opulus* but has larger leaves, corky bark and purple instead of yellow anthers. Its fruits are long-lasting and bright, translucent red in colour. 3.7×4.5m (12×15 ft).

V.s. Flavum	Bears yellow berries.

V. tinus (laurustinus)

Winter-flowering evergreen with metallic blue, fruits, turning black. 1.8×2.1m (6×7 ft).

V.t. Gwenllian	Has small blue berries. 2.1×2.4m (7×8 ft).

Left: V. davidii, at 90cm (3 ft) high, is an ideal shrub for a small border
Far left: the fruits of deciduous V. lantana change colour dramatically as they age
Top left: in addition to its bright berries, V. opulus Compactum has splendid autumn colour
Far left, above: magnificent fruits of V. opulus Nottcutt's Variety
Far left, top: V. opulus flowers in mid and late summer (June and July)

YUCCA

Type	hardy and tender evergreen small trees and shrubs
Family	LILIACEAE
Planting dates	late spring–late autumn (April–October); from containers at any time
Flowering season	early summer–late autumn (May–October)
Mature size/shape	mainly rounded, foliage sometimes surmounting a short trunk; height 75cm–1·8m (2½–6 ft), spread 90cm–1·8m (3–6 ft)

There are 40 species in the yucca genus, consisting of evergreen, hardy and tender shrubs and small trees. Despite their sub-tropical appearance, a number are quite hardy in temperate districts. The name comes from the Carib word for cassava, though this is not related to the yucca plant.

These plants are natives of Central America, Mexico and the southern districts of the United States. The earliest to be introduced to cultivation in Britain, in about 1550, was *Yucca gloriosa*; this was followed by *Y. filamentosa* in 1675. The next to be cultivated in Britain was *Y. recurvifolia*, introduced in 1794, followed during the 19th century by *Y. glauca* (about 1811), *Y. flaccida* (1816), *Y. parviflora engelmannii* (1822) and *Y. whipplei* (1854).

Yucca produce very formal rosettes or clumps of narrow, usually rigid, bold leaves and tall racemes or panicles of drooping, bell-shaped, lily-like flowers. The inflorescence sometimes grows as much as 1·2–1·5m (4–5 ft) above the main body of the shrub or tree. This gives an effect of great stateliness and beauty, and an 'architectural' quality that is of great value in the garden. In California the shape has given rise to their popular name 'candles of the Lord'.

The real magnificence of yucca lies in their large, spiky, bold leaves. Some species, such as *Y. recurvifolia*, have extremely sharp spines at the ends that can very easily draw blood or damage an eye. It is therefore a wise precaution not to plant any of these in gardens where young children play. In any case, they should be positioned where they are unlikely to come into close contact with people. Some species have leaves of exceptional length and breadth: those of *Y. parviflora engelmannii*, for example, are 2–3cm (1 in) wide and 1·2m (4 ft) long, while those of *Y. recurvifolia* are up to 90cm (3 ft) in length. The leaves of *Y. gloriosa* (Adam's needle) are rather shorter, at

Above: Y. recurvifolia *can be impressive in a border. Its column of creamy-white flowers with spiky leaves at the base gives it a fountain-like appearance*
Right: Y. gloriosa *has white flowers tinged with red*

between 30–60cm (12–24 in) long, but they can range from 8–10cm (3–4 in) in width.

The leaves of most of the species found in present-day gardens are greyish-green in colour, but notable exceptions with bright green foliage are *Y. brevifolia* (Joshua tree) and *Y. parviflora engelmannii*. *Y. gloriosa* Variegata has leaves that are striped and margined creamy-yellow, and *Y. recurvifolia* Variegata has foliage with a central band of pale green. In many species the leaves have white threads along their margins.

The flowering season of the yuccas varies from species to species. In general they fall into two groups – late summer to early autumn (July to August) and mid autumn (September) onwards. An exception is *Y. whipplei*, that produces blooms during early and mid summer (May and June).

exposed to salt-laden winds. They do well in full sun and are quite happy in poor soil, even tolerating shallow soil over chalk.

Plant yucca during late spring or late autumn (April or October), and container-grown plants at any time. Determine the space to be allowed between a yucca and its neighbouring shrub by adding together their ultimate spreads and dividing by two.

Although most of the yucca available from nurseries in Britain are hardy, it is wise to give them protection against frost in really severe weather. No pruning is necessary.

Yucca are not seriously affected by pests, but sometimes large brown spots with grey centres, due to leaf spot, appear on the foliage. If this infection is serious, spray with a fungicide such as captan or zineb.

To propagate yucca, cut off suckers with roots during mid or late spring (March or April) and plant them out at once in their permanent growing quarters.

Some varieties to choose
In the varieties listed below, the approximate dimensions given under each item are the height and spread after about 20 years' growth; they exclude the height of the flowering stalk. Assume, unless otherwise stated, that the size of any cultivar is approximately the same as its parent.

Y. brevifolia (Joshua tree)
Looks like a miniature tree with a small trunk. It has narrow, green, recurved leaves that are channelled on their upper surface and have small, tooth-like serrations along their margins. Its cream flowers often have a greenish tint and appear in early and mid autumn (August and September). 1.5×1.5m (5×5 ft). It needs careful protection from frost and is really suitable only for the most sheltered areas.

Y.b. jaegerana is a form that is rather shorter than the type and has smaller leaves and panicles.

Y. filamentosa
Stemless yucca that is useful for more forward positions in a shrub or mixed border. It produces dense clumps of leaves that are spreading or erect-growing and greyish-green in colour, with many curly white threads along their edges. Its 5–8cm (2–3 in) long, creamy-white flowers are carried in erect, smooth, conical panicles that grow up to 1·2m (4 ft) tall, and appear in late summer and early autumn (July and August). Flowering begins when a plant is between two and three years old. 75cm × 1·2m ($2\frac{1}{2}$ × 4 ft). Y. f. Variegata has leaves that are edged and striped with yellow.

Y. flaccida
Stemless species that forms clumps of long, lance-shaped, green or greyish leaves, characterized by sharply-pointed ends that bend downwards. They have curly, white, filament-like threads on their margins. Creamy-white flowers, carried in erect, downy panicles 1·2m (4 ft) above the foliage, are

Usually the flowers are creamy-white or creamy-yellow, sometimes with a greenish hue, but an outstanding exception is *Y. parviflora engelmannii* that has aloe-like, tomato-red blooms. *Y. whipplei* has greenish-white flowers edged with purple. There is a legend that yucca flower only once every seven years, but this is not true; they will bloom nearly every year once they commence.

In size yucca range from 60–75cm (2–2½ ft) high with a spread of 90cm–1·2m (3–4 ft) for *Y. glauca*, to the 1·8m (6 ft) height and spread of *Y. recurvifolia*. A particular exception is the rather spreading *Y. parviflora engelmannii* that can extend horizontally to about 1·8m (6 ft), at a height of about 1·2m (4 ft). All these dimensions are reached after about 20 years' growth.

Cultivation and propagation
Yucca are long-lived, and flourish in ordinary, well-drained garden soil. They will also thrive at the seaside, even in sand dunes that are fully

borne during late summer and early autumn (July and August). 1·5 × 1·5m (5 × 5 ft). The most commonly-seen variety is *Y. f.* Ivory.

Y. glauca
A low-growing plant with a short stem. It forms a rounded head of long, narrow, glaucous leaves that have a white edging with a few marginal white threads. Its 5–8cm (2–3 in) long, greenish-white flowers, appearing in late summer and early autumn (July and August), are carried in racemes that are 1·2m (4 ft) tall. 90 × 90cm (3 × 3 ft).

Y. gloriosa (Adam's needle)
The leaves of this species emerge in rosettes at the head of a slow-growing, woody trunk. They are recurving and about 45cm (18 in) long and up to 10cm (4 in) wide. The leaves are slightly glaucous and viciously spiked. The blooms, that first appear when the plant is five years old, are creamy-white and tinged red outside. They appear between early and late autumn (August and October). 1·5 × 1·5m (5 × 5 ft).

Y. parviflora engelmannii
This yucca is exceptional in having aloe-like, tomato-red flowers with gold inside; they are produced in long, slim panicles in late summer (July). Its thick, tough, bright green leaves are long and narrow. Again, this plant is susceptible to cold and needs a sheltered spot in order to survive. 1·2 × 1·8m (4 × 6 ft).

Y. recurvifolia
One of the most popular of the genus; it has greyish-green, long, narrow leaves that emerge at ground level when the plant is young, but appear later at the top of the slow-growing trunk. The outside leaves recurve, but the central ones remain erect. They have sharp spines on their ends. Panicles of creamy-white flowers grow on stalks up to 90cm (3 ft) high, and appear from early autumn (August) onwards. This species rarely blooms until the trunk is about 60cm (24 in) high. 1·8 × 1·8m (6 × 6 ft).
Y. r. Variegata is an attractive cultivar with leaves that have a pale green central band.

Y. whipplei
Stemless species that forms a round clump of greyish leaves. It has greenish-white, scented flowers, margined with purple, growing on a stem that sometimes reaches a height of 3·4m (11 ft). These blooms appear in early and mid summer (May and June). This species needs a warm, sunny position to survive. 1·5 × 1·5m (5 × 5 ft).

Top right: flowers of Y. flaccida *Ivory*
Top far right: Y. filamentosa *has a less formal appearance than some varieties of yucca*
Right: a fine specimen of Y. recurvifolia. *Its grey-green leaves top a thickish, fibrous trunk*

PART 3

FLOWERS

Enjoying the beauty and fragrance of flowers is one of life's more rewarding pleasures. We give flowers to each other on special occasions and we like to have them in our homes. Many of us visit the great public gardens where we can see flowers grown to perfection. Add to all this the creative act of growing them and the joy of flowers is brought to a higher level of intensity.

Some people are daunted by what they see as the complexity of the subject but extremely satisfactory results can be achieved even by the newcomer to gardening. The key question for each type of flower is what group it falls into: annuals, perennials or biennials. This classification is based on botanical realities but is also a matter of horticultural convenience, enabling the grower to determine what can be expected from a flower and how best to treat it.

An annual grows from a seed, reaches maturity, produces flowers (and more seeds) and dies – all in one season. Possibly because these plants only have one chance to reproduce, they are mostly extremely prolific in their flower production and tend to have a long flowering season. Also, many of them come from the warmer parts of the world, where their vivid colours attract the insects and other creatures that help to pollinate them. The brilliantly coloured 'bedding' plants, like French marigolds, petunias, lobelia and the rest that are sold in such quantities in the early summer are mostly annuals. A few plants, such as antirrhinums, are not strictly speaking annuals at all, but they are grown afresh each year from seed as they flower much better when they are in their first season. Annuals are invaluable for a quick, colourful effect and, as many are easy to grow from seed they need not cost very much.

The term 'perennial' refers to border plants that live for several years. Typically they have a permanent root system from which stems, leaves and flowers emerge each year. This topgrowth usually dies off at the end of the season. In the past, whole borders were devoted to plants of this kind ('herbaceous borders') and superb examples may still occasionally be seen. However this practice has largely fallen out of favour nowadays. To be really effective, herbaceous borders should be on a generous scale and most people simply don't have the room. Also, many perennials demand a lot of work, needing to be staked for support and cut down at the end of the growing season. But by no means all of this very large group need such attention and even a small garden should contain some well-chosen perennials. The group, after all, contains some of the most stately and beautiful of flowers.

Intermediate between these two groups are the biennials. As their name implies, they require two seasons to mature. They grow from seed in the first year, overwinter in a more or less static condition and resume growth and come into flower in the second year. Some of the most charming old-fashioned flowers are included in this group – Canterbury bells, foxgloves and hollyhocks, for instance. Here again, many are easily grown from seed and once established they will often seed themselves freely in unexpected corners of the garden.

There is another important class of plants that are separated by gardeners from the rest. These are the bulbs, a group that also includes plants that develop other bulb-like roots. Some of these, such as the crocus, have corms. Others, like the dahlia, develop fleshy tubers, while a third group, including many of the irises, form rhizomes. Bulbs include some of the most dazzling of flowering plants and a walk on a warm spring day among flower beds planted with tall tulips and underplanted with violas, forget-me-nots and polyanthus is an unforgettable experience. Bulbs, of course, are usually associated with spring, but there are many others, too often overlooked, that flower in the summer or autumn. Most bulbs are relatively easygoing about their growing conditions and, given that many kinds will spread readily, they are not generally exorbitantly expensive. It was not always so. In the seventeenth century, at the height of the 'tulipomania' that was sweeping Europe, thousands of pounds changed hands for single bulbs of particularly highly prized varieties!

Provided that the right conditions of soil, light, temperature and moisture exit and that flowering plants are used imaginatively, there is no reason why the beginner as well as the more experienced enthusiast should not make a success of growing flowers. Many of the more commonly used plants do not require particular soil conditions but some, particularly the majority of the annuals, do demand sun. A few kinds will even show their displeasure on overcast days by closing up their flowers. As far as planting imaginatively is concerned, it is important to remember that in the wild, plants are usually found in colonies and it is a wise gardener who takes the hint. The temptation to buy one of everything is hard to resist and even the smallest garden should have room for individual specimens of favourite flowers. But these will be set off to much better advantage against bold groups of plants. A spotty effect should be avoided at all costs and restricting the range of colours and plants used really does pay off. The gardens that make passers-by stop and look are invariably the ones where this kind of discipline has been exercised.

A garden should always be a joy rather than a burden another good reason to think carefully about what to plant. A little planning can save a lot of disappointment and the gardener's most essential tools are possibly a pencil and paper. A final, encouraging thought – 90 per cent of the work will be done by nature.

Bulbs in the Garden

Now is the time to start planning your bulb display for next year. Bulbs in friends' gardens and in public display are still in full bloom and, seeing them in the open air and in natural surroundings (rather than the isolation of the bulb-grower's catalogue), you can more easily decide upon the varieties and colours that you would like to have.

GENERAL WORK

Late spring (April)

If weather conditions are favourable and the soil is dry enough to work without it sticking to the rake or your boots, make the first outdoor sowings of hardy annual seeds. Thoroughly prepare the ground for chrysanthemums, add a general fertilizer, such as Growmore, and set the plants in position within two weeks.

Finish planting bare-rooted trees, shrubs and hardy herbaceous plants. Container-grown types can be planted at any time of year provided conditions are suitable and the plants are regularly watered.

Pot-grown clematis can be planted now. The soil level from the pot should be set 2–5cm (1–2 in) below ground level and the roots firmly pressed down. Prune the new plants back to about 30cm (12 in).

Carefully tie in to their supports new shoots of shrubs trained as climbers or those climbers that need assistance. Keep an eye open for greenfly and blackfly and spray as soon as they appear with malathion or a systemic insecticide.

It is at the far end of our Flower Garden that we have decided to make a special feature of bulbs, where they can be seen at their best during spring from the upper windows of the house. The word 'bulb' is, of course, used here rather loosely, as the term is intended to cover also corms and tubers.

The function of the bulb itself (or corm, or tuber) is to be a form of food storage, to help the plants survive not only the long cold winter, but also the hot dry summer that is common in the parts of the world where these plants grow wild. Most

bulbs are found naturally in mountainous regions, where they are covered with snow for much of the winter. Directly the snow melts the leaves and flowers appear; and during this period, although they get plenty of water, the soil in which they grow drains quickly.

There are, of course, exceptions to this. The various members of the narcissus family often grow in alpine water meadows, and there are one or two bulbs that have no objection to quite marshy conditions, such as the spring and summer snowflake, *Leucojum vernum* and *L. aestivum* and the big summer-flowering Peruvian squill (*Scilla peruviana*).

Where to plant

Generally, however, it is safe to assume that bulbs do best where the soil is reasonably light and well-drained. In practice, they will thrive in most gardens. And since bulbs will have made most, if not all, of their growth by early summer (mid May), they will be perfectly happy under deciduous trees and shrubs, where they can get enough light for their growth before the leaves have developed too much. They should not be planted beneath evergreens, however, as they will not get enough light to produce food to store for the coming year.

How to plant

There are a lot of old gardeners' tales about the correct planting depth for bulbs: one of the favourites is that the top of the bulb should be the same distance from the surface as the length of the bulb. But in the wild, bulbs are almost always considerably deeper than this, and you can safely say that the tops of small bulbs should be at least 10cm (4 in) below the surface, while larger bulbs should be 15cm (6 in) below. If they are less deep there is always a risk that hoeing or some other operation will bring them to the surface. Small bulbs can be planted close together, say 5–8cm (2–3 in) apart, but the larger ones should have 15–20cm (6–8 in) between them.

Most spring bulbs should be put in the ground as soon after early autumn (August) as you can obtain them, and they will start making roots within a month. Narcissus, in fact, are scarcely ever without roots and must inevitably receive a slight check if they have been lifted and dried off, although it may be barely noticeable.

The main exception to this generalization is the tulips, which can well be left until early winter (November) before planting.

Above: nivalis *(snowdrops). One of the earliest flowers of the year.*
Bottom right: crocus, easy-to-grow and free-flowering for several years
Bottom left: the scented Iris reticulata, *Harmony has prominent gold markings*

Soil or sand?

If your soil is very damp and heavy there is probably some advantage in planting your bulbs on a layer of sharp sand, which drains fast and will prevent water from lodging immediately around the basal plate of the bulb, the part most suscep-

tible to fungus rot. This makes considerably more work: it is fine if you are only planting 10 or 12 bulbs, but quite another matter if you are planting hundreds. Nevertheless, it is certainly worth doing with expensive bulbs.

It is of even greater importance to make sure that the base of the bulb is in contact with the soil (or the sand). With rather large bulbs it is only too easy to take out a trowel full of soil and put your bulb in so that it lodges halfway down the hole with its base suspended in air. When the roots emerge they are unable to find any nourishment, and they may well perish. There is enough nourishment stored in

Above: Narcissus pseudonarcissus *(daffodil)* Penrose *and (below) narcissus* White Lion

the bulb to produce leaves and possibly even a flower, but the bulb cannot renew itself and will eventually die. Seeing that plants get off to a good start is one of the main secrets of success in gardening.

Dividing the clumps

If your bulbs are doing well they will, in the course of five or six years, form clumps. These will eventually get so crowded that flower production suffers.

When this happens you must lift the clumps and divide them up. The best time to do this is in the early summer, when you see the leaves just starting to yellow. The bulbs should be good and plump by then and the new corms should have been formed. Some bulbs, most notably snowdrops, never seem to become overcrowded and there is no need to lift and divide them unless you wish to increase the area of these bulbs. To help you plan your 'calendar of bulbs' for the early spring we suggest a selection of winter aconite, snowdrops, iris, crocus, narcissus and tulips.

Winter aconite

The first to appear is usually the winter aconite *Eranthis hyemalis*. This has a tuber from which springs a little ruff of leaves, in the centre of which is a yellow flower not unlike a buttercup. The plant grows wild in woodland and does best in a shady position. If it is happy it spreads quite extensively and will also seed itself, but it is not happy everywhere. It seems to like the sort of woodland soil that has plenty of leaf mould and if you have either a very sandy or a very clayey soil you may well find that it does not persist for more than two or three years. *E.* × *tubergenii* is a hybrid between the ordinary winter aconite and the larger species from western Asia, *E. cilicica*. It has larger flowers which, however, never set seed, and is somewhat more expensive.

Snowdrop

After the winter aconite come the snowdrops. There are many species of these, all looking rather similar and chiefly distinguished by the way their leaves emerge from the ground. The one most widely grown is *Galanthus nivalis*, that is available with either single or double flowers. We are always told that snowdrops should be moved when they are still in active growth. This is fine if you are moving them from one bed to another, or if you can get some from your friends, but firms only sell the dried-off bulbs and when you are buying new snowdrops you will have to make do with these. They seem to grow adequately, although the display the first spring after planting may not be quite as good as you would expect. However, do not lose heart, it will almost certainly be much more satisfactory the following year.

Among other species, *Galanthus elwesii* is supposed to be a much larger-flowered snowdrop, but the large flowers are seldom maintained for long in cultivation and after a few years you can only distinguish *G. elwesii* from the ordinary snowdrop by its broad glaucous leaves. If you can obtain *G. caucasicus*, particularly in its double form, you will find that it flowers earlier than *G. nivalis*, usually in late winter (January), and has the added advantage of increasing faster.

Iris

We come now to the dwarf bulbous iris, of which three are worth having. The most spectacular is *Iris histrioides* Major. This produces blue flowers up to 10cm (4 in) across, which usually open in late winter (mid January) and, although they look very exotic, are completely unmoved by the worst that the winter can unleash. They are often frozen and covered with snow without showing any ill effects. They are not, alas, cheap, but they persist and increase, although not very rapidly.

Then there is the charming little yellow *I. danfordiae*. In most gardens, after flowering, it splits up into several smaller bulbs which take a long time to flower again, so frequently they have to be replaced each year. It is said that if the bulbs are planted very deeply, at least 23cm (9 in), they are less liable to split up.

The commonest of the early iris is *I. reticulata*, which flowers usually in early spring (February). It has rather narrow violet flowers (although purple or blue in some forms) with an exquisite violet scent. Provided they have well-drained soil all these bulbous iris are very easy to grow. An infection to be watched out for is the dreaded fungus disease known as ink-spot, which causes the bulbs to rot. There is no simple cure for this, if indeed there is any. It has been suggested that if the bulbs are lifted, dried off completely and then soaked for two hours in a very weak solution of formaldehyde (one part in 300), they can be protected, but this only applies to healthy bulbs, not to infected ones.

Crocus

Perhaps of all the spring bulbs the crocus is the favourite, and here we have an enormous choice. For many of us the first sign of spring is the Dutch yellow crocus. This is a sterile form of the eastern Mediterranean *Crocus aureus*, which has been known in gardens for nearly 300 years. Since it never sets seed it increases rapidly by producing extra corms, and soon makes large clumps. The true *C. aureus* flowers slightly earlier and has rather richer coloured flowers, as well as increasing by seed.

However, if you want a crocus that increases by seed the best is *C. tomasinianus*, a very slender plant with grassy leaves and a thin flower, which is nearly invisible until the sun opens the lavender petals. There are also some darker purple varieties, such as Taplow Ruby, Barr's Purple and Whitewell Purple. *C. tomasinianus* increases at a prodigious rate, both from extra corms and from self-sown seedlings, which may flower the second year after germinating. Very similar, but with a larger flower, is *C. dalmaticus*.

C. chrysanthus has a large number of forms, all characterized by bunches of rather globular flowers, mainly in varying shades of yellow, but including some very good blues, which unfortunately are usually very slow to increase, while the yellow and cream forms are vigorous.

The Cloth of Gold crocus, *C. susianus*, is prodigal with its rather small yellow flowers which have dark brown stripes on their outside. A very attractive crocus is *C. etruscus*, that is usually only obtainable in the form known as Zwanenburg and that flowers in early spring (late February). The flowers are quite large and a very fine shade of lavender-mauve. Another very popular crocus is the deep mauve *C. sieberi*. Finally there are the huge Dutch hybrids, that flower in mid spring (March) but some people find rather gross. Best of these is the showy silver-lavender Vanguard.

Narcissus

Daffodils (with a trumpet centre) and narcissus (with flatter, cup centre) all belong to the genus *Narcissus* and they all like ample water when they are growing. They are exquisite in flower, but they have very long leaves, which persist until mid summer (June) and tend to look unsightly. They are probably best placed between shrubs, where their leaves will not be so noticeable. Whatever you do, do not cut the leaves off or plait them into dainty bundles, as that will wreck your chances of good flowers in the next season. You must just make up your mind that when you grow narcissus, you must put up with these disadvantages.

Tulip

Most tulips come rather late, but the water-lily tulip, *Tulipa kaufmanniana*, is usually in flower by mid to late spring (March–April) thus linking early and late spring displays. Many tulips tend to deteriorate after a year or so, but *kaufmanniana* is fairly reliable, although rather slow to increase. The wild plant has a flower that is long and pointed, cream outside, with a broad crimson stripe down each petal, and ivory inside. The flower opens nearly flat in sunlight. It has now been hybridized, producing blooms in deep yellow, pinks and even scarlets.

The Darwin hybrid variety Apeldoorn, up to 75cm (2 ft) tall, is good for display

Bulbs in bowls

Early bulbs planted indoors can bring added colour to your home in winter. Order them in early autumn (August) to plant in bowls or pots indoors or in the greenhouse in mid autumn (September). Bulbs, corms and tubers that are generally grown in pots for early flowering are hyacinths, daffodils (narcissi), tulips, crocuses and cyclamen.

Always plant top-size bulbs as you will get more and better bulbs from these and they are well worth the extra cost. You can buy 'prepared' bulbs. These are treated with refrigeration to speed up the period before flowering.

Plant in potting compost so that the upper third of the hyacinth bulbs are exposed and the noses of crocuses and daffodils.

After planting, place the bulbs in darkness and in a cool place. Leave for six to eight weeks until they produce shoots. To start with keep the bowls in a subdued light, then, after a week, transfer them to a full light and a temperature of 10°C. Keep the compost or fibre moist but do not over-water and they should flower beautifully.

Herbaceous Plants

Our gardens would look rather sad places without the herbaceous plants that flower, most particularly in the late summer (from mid July onwards), when there are few flowering shrubs left and we must depend on perennials and roses for colour in the garden.

All annuals and biennials are strictly speaking herbaceous – all the word means is that the stems are of only annual duration and die down each autumn, so that in that sense even bulbs are herbaceous – but the term is usually used of herbaceous perennials. Perennials are plants that go on growing for many seasons, increasing in dimensions as they

do so. They are normally planted either in the autumn or in the early spring, although there are one or two exceptions.

When to plant

Ideally autumn is the best time to plant, if you do so early enough. This enables the plants to root into the fresh soil before winter comes, so that they will be in a good condition to grow away as soon as the days lengthen and the air warms up. Plants that are transplanted in the spring have to start to grow away at once, so that if the spring is exceptionally cold or exceptionally dry their initial growth can be checked quite considerably. However there are one or two plants which seem to make very little growth after being transplanted in the autumn, with the result that they often die during the first winter and for these spring planting is obviously better. The most well-known of

these is that large scabious, *Scabiosa caucasica*, one of the best herbaceous plants to grow for cutting.

When to transplant

There are a number of plants that really loathe any root disturbance, either because they have long tap roots, which may cause the death of the plant if they are damaged, or for less recognizable reasons. There seems no obvious reason why hellebores should dislike being moved, but they certainly do and may sulk for a year or so after they are transplanted. We find the same thing with paeonies, but this may be because they have such a vast amount of tubers underground that it is almost impossible

to move a good-sized plant without seriously damaging the root system. Plants with long tap roots, such as lupins or oriental poppies, should only be moved as young plants and once planted should be left.

In any case it is always best to start off with small plants, whether they be seedlings or divisions from other plants. Such plants usually arrive with their roots more or less undamaged and soon grow on to make vigorous specimens.

Caring for herbaceous plants

You can find herbaceous plants to fit any soil or situation, but the majority will be perfectly happy in a soil that is reasonably deep and not inclined to water-logging. Most like full sunlight, although it is possible to grow bog plants and shade-lovers where conditions allow.

After a time some herbaceous plants may become very large, in which case they should be lifted and divided up. Some plants get their roots so interlocked that it is by no means easy to divide them; the answer is to get two garden forks and insert them back to back in the clump and then lever them apart. The centre of the clump is probably impoverished, due to the fact that it will have exhausted the soil where it was originally planted; also the centre tends to get overgrown by the stronger outside parts which are in fresh soil; so when clumps are split up the centre is usually discarded and the plantlets on the outside are preserved.

There are many hundreds of herbaceous perennials to choose from, so for our Flower Garden we have selected a number of plants which are easy to grow and which will establish themselves in the border quickly.

Hellebore

Helleborus niger (the Christmas rose) is the earliest-flowering of our selection. It grows on the edge of woodlands in the wild, so a position giving dappled shade is ideal. Almost all the hellebores are somewhat greedy plants, so the soil cannot be too rich. The white flowers will emerge from the ground at any time from early winter to early spring (November–February) and the new leaves start to emerge at the same time. Later the leaves are going to be quite large, so a position among or just in front of shrubs should prove very suitable. Some Christmas roses have the unfortunate habit of producing only very short stems, so that the flowers easily become splashed with mud in bad weather. If you are ordering plants by mail there is not much you can do about this; but if you go to a nursery, pick out the long-stemmed plants.

Otherwise you might prefer to grow one of the hybrids of *H. orientalis* (the Lenten rose). These all have long-stemmed flowers, which usually do not open before early spring (February). There are a few whites among them, but most are some shade of pink or greenish-pink, while a few are a very deep maroon. They require the same treatment as the Christmas rose, but have very much larger leaves, which take up a lot of room later in the season. There are also a number of hellebores with green flowers.

Hellebores may be transplanted in the autumn (September), and the earlier the

better. The old leaves of the Lenten rose often persist while the flowers are opening, but the plants seem to come to no harm if you cut these off before the flowers open: the leaves begin to look rather tattered by that time. This is not a problem with the Christmas rose.

Alyssum

Our next plant is *Alyssum saxatile*, which flowers in late spring (April). Strictly

Above: double dianthus. Pink Diane
Top: Helleborus niger, *the Christmas rose*
Above left: delicate Scabiosa caucasica *is best planted in the spring*
Left: the leaves of Alyssum saxatile *give winter interest, the flowers appear in late spring. Right:* Hosta albo-marginata, *the plantain lily, thrives in shade*

speaking it is not herbaceous at all, but a small shrub, which carries its grey leaves throughout the winter and makes the border interesting during the dreary season. In the spring it covers itself with golden, sweet-smelling flowers. It likes full sun and has no objection to rather poor soil. After about four years it gets somewhat leggy, but it is very easily propagated by cuttings or by seed.

Senecio cineraria

The grey-leaved cineraria (which you might otherwise know as *Cineraria maritima*) is a good example of the sort of plants that are grown for their foliage colour rather than for their flowers. Such plants are very valuable since they remain attractive for more than six months; this is more than can be said for most flowering plants, which seldom carry their flowers longer than three weeks and

often considerably less. The grey (or, in the variety White Diamond, the silvery-white) leaves are very attractive, and they gain much of their appeal from their contrast with more usual green leaves. Don't try to overdo this effect, because unfortunately the cineraria bears rather crude yellow daisy-like flowers which are not very appealing.

Most grey or silver-leaved plants will not survive in soils that retain too much wet and our grey cineraria is also liable to perish during particularly severe winters. Fortunately cuttings root very easily, so it is always a good idea to root a few in late summer (July) and keep them in pots under cover during the winter, in case disaster strikes. In any case, the plants become rather gaunt after a few years and are best replaced.

Hosta
Another plant with unusual foliage but also with quite attractive lily-like flowers, is the plantain lily, a species of hosta (sometimes known as funkia). This vanishes completely during the winter

and the new shoots can often be wrecked by slugs, so it is as well to mark their positions and put down bait in late spring (April) when young leaves are emerging.

The leaves vary in size and in colour and some are variegated with ivory, but they are all handsome plants, which get more effective as they get larger. There is

Above: peach-leafed Campanula persicifolia Telham Beauty is easy to grow

really no need to split up their clumps at any time, as they can go on getting larger and larger without any ill effects. In summer (June–July) they send up spikes of lily-like flowers, usually about 5cm (2 in) long, trumpet-shaped and white or mauve in colour. These plants thrive in dense or partial shade.

Dianthus (pinks)
These plants also have pretty grey leaves, but they are grown mainly for the sake of their small, fragrant, carnation-like flowers. They prefer a limey soil and, if you have the sort of soil that will grow rhododendrons, you will probably have to add some lime before you plant your dianthus. These again are evergreen and look interesting during the winter, but they very soon become gaunt and need frequent replacing. This is done by means of cuttings, usually known as pipings, which are ready in late summer or early autumn (July and August).

Dianthus are not particularly showy flowers, but their heady scent makes them worth all the trouble. They look attractive

Bottom left: pompon chrysanthemum London Gazette, give welcome autumn colour
Bottom right: pyrethrum chrysanthemum with daisy-like flowers in early and mid summer

massed together or along the front of a border. The flowers are usually white, pink or crimson, and popular varieties are Mrs Simkins, Red Clove, and the newer Imperial Pink.

Campanula

Two species of these nice trouble-free plants are generally grown in borders. One is the peach-leafed *Campanula persicifolia*, which grows about 45cm (18 in) high and has flat blue or white flowers in mid summer (June). These are only slightly bell-shaped and reach about 5cm (2 in) across. The other is the tall *C. lactiflora*, which can grow to 1·2m (4 ft) and has a huge head of small mauve, rather spidery flowers in late summer (July). Although the individual flowers are only about 2–3cm (1 in) across, they are borne in large numbers and a plant in full flower is a wonderful sight. There are shorter forms of *C. lactiflora* and also some pinky-purple ones.

Agapanthus (African lily)

An attractive plant flowering in late summer (July and August). The plants to

obtain are called Headbourne hybrids and are all hardy, whereas the larger *A. africanus* generally requires wintering under cover. The Headbourne hybrids have quite small strap-shaped green leaves, but throw up stems to 75cm (2½ ft), bearing at their tops heads of blue trumpet-shaped, lily-like flowers about 5cm (2 in) long. They like as warm a position as you can give them and full sunlight, but they are very tolerant about soil, so long as it is not waterlogged.

Chrysanthemum

For late autumn (October) we have chrysanthemums. The cut flower types, *C. maximum*, are not the most beautiful plants and are best raised each year from cuttings, but the Korean chrysanthemums are excellent for the border. These bear daisy-like flowers in the greatest profusion, usually some shade of red in colour, and are completely trouble-free. The little pompon chrysanthemums add needed colour in autumn (early October) and are now available in various pastel shades which are preferable to the rather dull colours which they used to be. The ordinary chrysanthemum can be grown as a border plant, if the flowers are not disbudded, but it is less attractive than either the Korean or the pompon types.

Japanese anemone (wind flower)

The Japanese anemone, in pinky-purple or in white, is a marvellous plant, being completely trouble-free and increasing with ease, and always flowering well in mid to late autumn (September–October). It does not really like being moved, so it is best left undisturbed as long as possible.

Pyrethrum

Botanically derived from *Chrysanthemum*

roseum, these are invaluable for their single white, pink or carmine daisy-like flowers on long stems in early and mid summer (May–June). They like a sunny position and deep well-drained soil.

Lupins

Excellent companions for the pyrethrums are *Lupinus* (lupins) which like the same conditions and produce their spires of pea-like flowers above decorative leaves about the same time. They are available in a wide range of colours of white, pink, yellow, red and lavender-blue, and are often bi-coloured. The Russell hybrids are a good strain but there are many varieties from which to choose. If you remove the old flower-heads as they fade, you will encourage a second season of blooming.

Oriental poppy

A third perennial to plant with the two foregoing is *Papaver orientalis* (the Oriental poppy), which also likes the sun and flowers at about the same time. It is available in pink, white, scarlet or crimson flower shades. Incidentally, it likes water if there is a drought period immediately prior to its flowering season in early to mid summer (May–June).

Thyme

This, the first of our two dwarf plants, is the creeping *Thymus serphyllum*, which makes a mat of aromatic foliage covered with crimson or purple flowers in mid summer (late June). These are also fragrant. Thyme spreads rapidly and the plants should be at least 30cm (12 in) apart to avoid congestion.

Sempervivum (houseleek)

Looking like a little cactus with rosettes of fleshy leaves, which are often attractively coloured, this dwarf plant has rather odd looking daisy-like pink flowers

on 10cm (4 in) stems. The houseleek produces numerous offshoots each year, so do not place new plants too closely together. The cobweb houseleek has its leaves covered with cobwebby grey hair.

Nepeta (catmint)
A spreading plant, catmint has feathery masses of small, grey-green fragrant leaves, with lavender-coloured feathery flower spikes in summer and autumn (June–September).

These last three plants like rather gravelly soil and it is worthwhile incorporating some gravel if the soil is rather slow-draining.

Papaver orientale, *the poppy with pronounced colour contrast in its markings*

Dahlias, Lilies, Gladiolus and Iris

Some of the most popular flowers in the garden are tuberous – dahlias, which give a glorious show of colour throughout the autumn, as well as lilies, gladiolus and iris. This week we tell you how to care for these plants so as to get the best display.

GENERAL WORK

Early summer (May)

Continue to remove all the dead flower-heads from bulbs to save the plants wasting energy on seed production and encourage them to build up strong bulbs for next year.

Put stakes in position alongside herbaceous perennial plants for tying in the young shoots as they grow.

Plant evergreen trees and shrubs, water in thoroughly and put a mulch over the root area. Keep the soil moist and spray the plants each day until they start making new growth.

Tie in climbing plants, and shrubs treated as climbers, to their supports as the young shoots grow.

Roses may produce too many spindly shoots so cut some out to prevent a tangled mass of unprolific stems.

Clip evergreen hedges, such as privet, to keep them tidy. Repeat as necessary.

Mow the lawn regularly, each week, cutting it to 2·5–4cm (1–1½ in).

Pests, particularly greenfly, blackfly and red spider mite can start attacking many plants now. Spray with insecticide regularly according to manufacturer's instructions.

Certain plants in our garden are characterized by some sort of underground swelling that acts as food storage. In the dahlia it is a swollen root, called a tuber; in the lily it is swollen leaves that form a bulb; in the gladiolus it is the swollen base of the stem, which is called a corm; while in the case of the iris it is a creeping underground stem, the rhizome, which bears roots on its underside.

Popular dahlias

Of these plants the dahlia is probably the most important and popular so far as garden ornament is concerned.

There are a vast number of varieties in each group from which to choose and it is essentially a matter of personal preference for shape and colour, and the area they are to occupy in the garden.

The main types of dahlia grown are:
decoratives (flat broad petals)
cactus and semi-cactus (quill-like petals)
show or pompons (globular heads of

tubular petals)
collerettes (single flowers with the larger outside rays set off by inner 'collars' of petals in contrasting colours)
anemone-flowered (central coral-coloured disc florets)
singles or dwarfs (single circles of petals).

In the case of the first three types, the size of the flower-heads can vary considerably and the heads are often referred to in catalogues as giant (over 25cm/10 in), large (20–25cm/8–10 in), medium (15–20cm/6–8 in), small (10–15cm/4–6 in), or miniature (less than 10cm/4–6 in), or miniature (less than 10cm/4 in). Some useful varieties are listed or shown here.

DECORATIVES

Lavender Perfection (giant)	lavender pink
Majuba (large)	deep red
Snowstorm (medium)	pure white
Terpo (medium)	scarlet
Gerrie Hoeck (medium)	pure pink
Glory of Heemstede (small)	deep yellow
Procyon (small)	scarlet and yellow
David Howard (miniature)	orange-bronze
Rothesay Pippin (miniature)	deep scarlet

CACTUS AND SEMI-CACTUS

Colour Spectacle (large)	red and white
Golden Crown (large)	orange and yellow
Clarion (medium)	orange-red
Golden Autumn (medium)	golden yellow
Morning Kiss (medium)	pink and white
Orfeo (medium)	deep purple
Rotterdam (medium)	blood red
Hit Parade (small)	scarlet
Popular Guest (small)	lavender pink
Preference (small)	salmon-pink
Park Princess (miniature)	bright pink

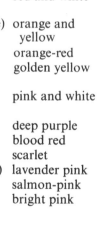

Top left: dahlia Symbol, large decorative
Top right: dahlia Twiggy, medium decorative
Right: single dahlia, Coltness, is available in a good mixed colour range

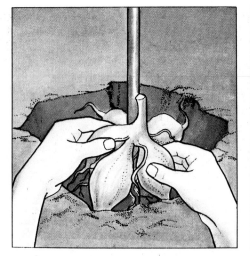

Above: planting dahlia tuber in ground previously dug and manured
Below: digging up tuber with fork

Above: cutting stem after frost
Below: storing tubers in boxes, with stems uppermost, at end of season

Below: cactus dahlia, Klankstad Kerkrade

Starting from seed

Single or dwarf dahlias are mainly grown from seed sown in heat as early in the year as possible, pricked out when large enough and gradually hardened off, to be planted out in mid summer (June). They flower fairly freely from early autumn (mid August) until the frosts come, but often they fail to produce any tubers, so cannot be kept from one season to the next unless the plants are lifted before the frosts come, potted up, and kept under cover. They are very useful plants for late flowers, but they do require heat in the early stages, although a warm airy room may be sufficient if you haven't a greenhouse.

Starting with plants

All the other types of dahlia can be considered together because they all require the same treatment, and in the first year it is best to start by buying plants. It is difficult to overfeed dahlias, so there is every advantage in preparing the place where you intend planting them by thorough digging and incorporating plenty of humus or, alternatively, very well-rotted manure.

As they are susceptible to even slight frost—they are always the first to suffer in the autumn—they should not be planted out until all risk of frost can be considered past and even mid summer (June) is not too late. Dahlias are somewhat brittle plants so they will probably require staking and it is a good idea to put the stakes in at the same time as you plant. They make large plants and can be planted at least 90cm (3 ft) apart, although a little less will be all right for the smaller pompons.

At one time people used to grow enormous dahlias, such as Crawley Beauty, which made plants 2m (7 ft) high with flowers up to 25cm (10 in) across, but these are not so popular now as they used to be. Such giant plants have to be put 1·80m (6 ft) apart.

Routine care

Although the dahlias will branch naturally many people pinch out the growing point when the plant is about 15cm (6 in) high to encourage branching to take place earlier. This should not be done until the new plant has clearly rooted into the soil. Then all you have to do is tie in the branches as they elongate, so that the plant is always kept fairly rigid.

Dahlias do not care for prolonged drought and should be watered copiously and the leaves sprayed well during dry spells. Otherwise your only worries are

POMPONS	
Brilliant Eye (medium)	glowing scarlet
Pride of Berlin (medium)	lilac-rose
Amusing (small)	orange-scarlet
Little William (small)	red and white
Nero (small)	velvety-red

COLLERETTES	
Grand Duc	red and yellow
La Cierva	purple and white
Libretto	velvety-pink and white

ANEMONE-FLOWERED	
Fable	dark red
Guinea	pure yellow
Roulette	pink

SINGLES OR DWARF	
Coltness hybrids	many colours
Firebird	bright red
Sneezy	pure white
Murillo	pink

pests. Greenfly can be a bore in the early stages of growth but your worst pest will probably be earwigs, which attack the flowers just as they are about to start. Straw or hay in an inverted flowerpot at the top of the stake is a useful way of trapping them, but this must be inspected daily and the earwigs burnt.

End-of-season care
With the first autumn frosts your dahlias will blacken. This is when you remove as much soil from the roots as you can and put them in a place that is dry and frost-free. Some people dust the tubers with a copper-lime dust to keep off a sort of mildew that sometimes attacks resting tubers, although provided they are kept perfectly dry there seems to be little risk.

In the second year
In the spring you have three choices. You can just replant the tubers as you lifted them and this is probably best done about early summer (mid May). Alternatively you can bring the plants into a cool greenhouse or warm room in early summer (May) with the roots in soil or peat, which is kept moist; after a time shoots will start to appear around the rootstock (but not from the tubers themselves) and you can cut the plant up into as many plants as there are shoots.

The way that is most preferred, provided you have the facilities, is to bring the tubers into heated greenhouses in early spring (February), again with the roots in moist soil or peat, and wait for shoots to appear. Once they have two joints they can be detached and rooted but quite considerable heat is needed for this. Since shoots are continually produced you can get a large number of plants from a single rootstock. Once rooted, the cuttings are potted up individually, if necessary potted on, and gradually hardened off to be planted out in mid summer (June) when the whole cycle starts up again.

LILIES
Of all the bulbs that beautify the herbaceous department it is arguable that the lilies are the loveliest. They are certainly the most difficult to manage successfully. In nature they are usually found in open scrub, where their lower leaves are shaded, while the flowers emerge in full

Above: Lilium tigrinum; *the popular tiger lily is unfortunately prone to virus disease.*
Right: modern hybrids –
Golden Splendour, Emerald Strain,
Black Dragon, Pink Perfection

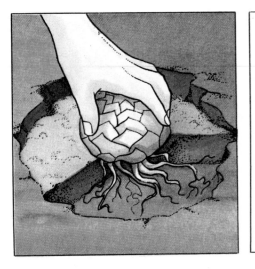

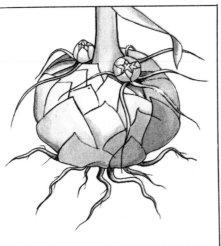

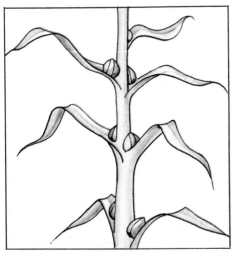

Top: planting lily bulb on sand
Top right: lily bulb with offsets
Above: lily plant with bulbils

sunlight sometime between mid summer and early autumn (June to August). Also, unlike other bulbs, the underground portions of the stems are liable to produce roots. This means that they do best in a fairly open soil with ample compost or leaf mould and that they should be planted fairly deeply, so that there is a good length of stem underground. It is probably best if the top of the bulb is 15cm (6 in) below the surface.

Preparing the ground

Since lily bulbs are expensive it is best to take considerable trouble, digging out the soil to a depth of 30cm (12 in), breaking it up well and incorporating compost or leaf mould, levelling out at a depth of about 20cm (8 in) and putting down a good layer of sharp washed garden sand to improve the drainage immediately around the bulb, and then filling up with the rest of the soil.

In the garden, lily bulbs scarcely rest at all and there is often ample root growth going on at times when nothing can be seen above ground, so the bulbs should be planted as early as possible, say in late autumn (October), if the bulbs can be procured at that time. The bulbs may have travelled a long way – even from as far as Japan – so that the roots will have dried off altogether and the plants may take some time to get going again. It is not unknown for a whole season to pass before any leaves are seen, so don't despair until the second year.

Some varieties to choose

Lilium candidum (madonna lily) – pure pearly white – and its popular hybrid *L. × testaceum* (Nankeen lily) – pale yellow – are exceptional in that they are more or less evergreen and should be planted in early autumn (August or the first week in September). Once they have been planted in suitable soil there is little you can do, except wait and hope for the best. If it likes you, the madonna lily will thrive, but it is a choosy plant and it is not clear quite what it needs, but it seems to do best where the roots are crowded.

Virus disease is very common in lilies, although less common with plants that have been raised from seed. It is apparently always present in *L. tigrinium* (tiger lily) – orange red with black spots – so if you grow that you will probably be wise not to grow any other lily. The lilies that seem easiest to grow are *L. regale* – white, *L. henryi* – orange, and the Mid-century, Harlequin and Bellingham hybrids – mixed colours, followed by *L. umbellatum* (now called *L. × hollandicum* but frequently listed under *L. maculatum*) – in many varieties and different colours. Also easy and rewarding to grow are *L. hansonii* – orange-yellow, *L. pardalinum* – orange-red, and *L. speciosum* – pure white.

Of the modern lilies raised in recent years that are generally reliable, hardy and free-flowering, the following offer a good selection:

Citronella	golden-brown
Connecticut Dream	yellow
Connecticut Yankee	orange
Earlibird	apricot
Enchantment	red
Firebright	currant-red
Geisha Girl	lemon-yellow
Golden Splendour	gold
Green Magic	white and green
Limelight	yellow
Orange Light	orange
Pink Champagne	yellow and pink
Redstart	wine
Red Velvet	deep maroon
Shuksan	light orange
Tabasco	ruby-red
White Princess	ivory

Increasing your stock

Lilies are very slow to produce offsets, but some come rapidly from seed, notably *L. regale*; and some produce bulbils on their stems, which can be grown on outdoors in a specially-prepared seedbed. Otherwise you have to remove bulb scales, put them upright in a box of sand and peat with only the tip protruding, and keep in a temperature of 15°C (60°F) until a bulblet forms at the base; this can then be grown on.

GLADIOLUS

Gladiolus present few problems. They like to be in full sun and can be planted from mid to late spring (March to April); even later will be quite satisfactory. The top of the corms should be about 10cm (4 in) below the surface and slightly deeper will do no harm at all. There is no point in purchasing the very large corms as the smaller ones will give just as good flower spikes from mid summer to late autumn (July to October) and are cheaper to buy.

By and large they are fairly trouble-free, but it is possible that they may be attacked by thrips, which distort the leaves. They are pests easily controlled by malathion or other insecticide.

Once the leaves begin to yellow, which is some time after flowering, the corms should be lifted and dried as fast as possible, as by hanging up in an airy, frost-free situation. Later they can be cleaned and stored in open slatted trays until the time comes to plant them again. You clean them by removing the old growths above the corm as well as the old corm and roots below it.

Large-flowered gladiolus
Early:

Bon voyage	azalea pink
Flower Song	yellow and carmine
Life Flame	vivid scarlet
Mabel Violet	velvet purple
Peter Pears	orange and red
White Friendship	cream

Mid season:

Albert Schweitzer	salmon-orange
Blue Conqueror	violet blue
Deciso	salmon-pink
Green Woodpecker	lime green
Hochsommer	orange and yellow
Memorial Day	rose magenta
Snow Princess	white

Late:

Bloemfontein	apricot-pink
Trader Horn	crimson-scarlet

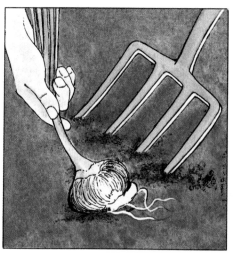

Tropical Sunset	red and purple
Zenith	shell-pink

Primulinus varieties
Early:

Canopus	cyclamen pink
Harmony	lilac-purple
White City	white

Mid season:

Apex	scarlet
Comic	smoky-brown
Yellow Poppy	yellow

Late:

Pretoria	coral-red

Miniature varieties

Delphi	rose, salmon shading

Butterfly varieties
Early:

Red Spot	yellow and red
Riante	peach-rose

Mid season:

Greenwich	greeny-yellow

Top right: lifting gladiolus corm with fork
Above: corms drying fast, hanging up
Right: storing corms over winter
Bottom left: large-flowered mixed gladiolus Atlantic, Memorandum, Shakespeare. Bottom right: large-flowered gladiolus Red Cascade

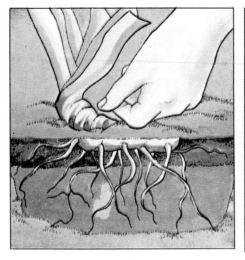

They have fans of leaves springing from a fleshy underground stem, which should never be completely buried, and flower on stems about 1m (3 ft) tall. Although they appreciate good soil, they will grow in ground that is rather poor.

Routine care
Their treatment is easy enough. The best time to move them is after flowering and new plants should be received in late summer (late July) or early autumn (August). If the rhizomes are bearing roots, just these should be buried, leaving the rhizome on the surface; if the rhizome has no roots, you must half-bury it, so that the top half is above the ground. As you want to encourage rooting, after planting you must water if there is a very dry spell, until the rhizome has anchored itself well. The plants can then be left for three years, after which lift them, break up the clumps and start again.

Your only real cause for concern is rhizome rot, which is caused by bad drainage or by the rhizomes getting buried. If you see the rhizomes rotting and the fans dying off, lift the plant, cut off the infected parts, dust the cut ends with powdered charcoal and replant in a new situation. This must be done as soon as you see symptoms, whatever time of the year it is.

Melodie	pink and orange
Southport	ivory white
Late:	
Bright Eye	yellow and red
Dancing Doll	yellow and pink

FLAG IRIS
Flags or, as we now call them, tall bearded iris, are among the most spectacular of all garden flowers, although their season is disappointingly short – only early and mid summer (May and June).

Left and below left: planting iris, with top of rhizome showing above soil
Above: flag iris Amethyst Flame
Bottom: flag iris Golden Alps

Some varieties to choose
There are so many excellent tall bearded iris now on the market that it is difficult to recommend what to buy to begin with. Many gardeners start with a mixed selection, and then gradually add to their collection. Among some of the outstanding modern hybrids are:

Blue Shimmer	blue and white
Braithwaite	lavender and purple
Cleo	chartreuse green
Cliffs of Dover	milk-white
Golden Planet	golden yellow
Green Ice	greenish-cream
Headlines	white and purple
Helen McGregor	clear, light blue
Lady Mohr	oyster, yellow and red
Lothario	bi-colour blue
Mabel Chadburn	yellow
Mulberry Rose	mulberry
New Snow	snow-white
Pinnacle	white and yellow
Prairie Sunset	pink, apricot and gold
Ranger	crimson
Sable	blue-black
Zantha	golden yellow

There are other forms of iris, such as the beardless, cushion and bulbous-rooted, but these flower at various times of the year and require different cultural conditions. They will be described later.

Chrysanthemums

The specialist will spend endless time over his chrysanthemums to get large and perfectly-shaped blooms, probably for exhibition, but there is no good reason why you should not have more, though smaller, flowers to decorate the border in the autumn and early winter (September to November). There is a choice of four different groups.

GENERAL WORK
Early summer (May)
Continue to hoe weeds regularly to prevent them getting a hold and making the borders unsightly. Take care not to damage any shallow-rooting cultivated plants.

Dig a spare corner in the garden, firm it by treading, and rake the soil to a fine tilth to make a seedbed for sowing biennials for flowering next year.

To help healthy growth of hardy herbaceous perennials, as well as spring-flowering bulbs, water them from time to time with liquid fertilizer.

Start planting out chrysanthemums in positions prepared for them previously.

Climbers that have finished producing their spring flowers should have their flowering wood pruned out.

If there are any weeds on the lawn, either treat it overall with a weedkiller or spot-treat individual weeds if there are only a few.

Complete the sowing of hardy annuals where they are to flower.

Single
True singles have only one row of outer petals (called ray florets) – which are long and thin – and an eye (which consists of disc florets). The species that forms this group is *Chrysanthemum rubellum*, sometimes known as *C. erubescens*. It covers itself with masses of pink daisies about 5cm (2 in) or more across. Each flower is on a long stem, so that the plant is also

Above and top right: two decoratives – anemone-flowered Raymond Moundsey and spider-flowered Martha, excellent for town use and giving welcome autumn colour
Above right: a true single, Clara Curtis

useful for cutting. The whole plant may grow about 90cm (3 ft) high. There are a number of different coloured forms now available.

Korean

The Koreans are similar to singles in that they have a central eye, but in fact they are semi-doubles – that is, they usually have more than one row of outer petals.

The flowers are again about 5cm (2 in) wide, and come in a number of colours, of which crimson and dark purple are the most common, though shades of apricot, salmon pink, yellow and bronze are also available. These are not always easy to obtain but if you can get them they usually make a very brilliant display in mid autumn (September).

Pompon

As far as display in the border goes, you probably cannot do much better than the pompons. These produce large numbers of small, tight flowers, looking rather like powder puffs, that can be obtained in almost all colours from white to pink, red, purple and yellow. There are now some very attractive pastel shades in pale shell-pink. It is a little difficult to suggest particular varieties as so-called 'improved' types are constantly being introduced and any list of names can soon become out of date. It is best to visit a chrysanthemum show, join a chrysanthemum society, or visit a specialist nursery. You can also study catalogues, so long as you bear in mind that nurserymen tend only to mention the most desirable features in their particulars. If you live in a town, a talk with someone in the Parks Department could well prove informative.

Decorative

Ordinary chrysanthemums that are grown for border ornament are becoming increasingly hard to obtain and you may

well find that you have to get the outdoor decoratives. These have actually been bred to make many-petalled, large show blooms, which must be specially grown and disbudded. On the other hand, if you do get a chance to get hold of varieties such as Garden White or Memento (white), Golden Orfe or Solley (yellow), and Hilde or Pink Glory (pink), then do so without hesitation.

Routine care

Whatever plants you select the treatment is the same. The nursery will supply rooted cuttings, preferably in late spring (April). These will have come out of a greenhouse and so will be very soft and particularly appetizing for snails and slugs. Pot them up separately and harden them off by standing the pots outside where slugs cannot reach them. Be sure to sprinkle slug pellets around the pots as an added precaution. After about three weeks they should be ready to go into the border – and ideally should be there before mid summer (by the end of May).

Although the cuttings are small the plants will get quite large, so plant them at least 75cm (2½ ft) apart. About a week after you have planted them out, remove the growing tip *only*, so as to encourage the plant to throw out side growth. Do not remove any of the stem, however, as this will reduce the amount of sideshoots that a plant will produce. Removing the tips of the new sideshoots about a month later will encourage further bushing. After this all you have to do is sit back and wait for the plants to come into flower.

Chrysanthemums are fairly greedy plants, so top-dressing with a chrysanthemum fertilizer in late summer and early autumn (July and August) can do nothing but good, although it is by no means essential. Apply the fertilizer in the evening and give the plants a good soaking directly afterwards if the soil is at all dry. If you have a sprayer with a really fine spray, use a foliar feed instead. In any case you should stop feeding the plants during early autumn (after the second week in August).

Plants from cuttings

Once flowering is over, cut the stems down to within about 5cm (2 in) of the ground and leave them over the winter. You now have two choices: you can either leave the plants as they are, thinning the new growths out to about four per plant, or you can take cuttings and do exactly as you did the year before.

To root cuttings all you have to do is to pull up the shoots, which will appear in late winter or early spring (January to February), and cut them off just below a node (where you will see one or more leaves). The cuttings should be about 8cm (3 in) long. Dip the ends into a rooting powder and put them in a potful of cutting compost, which can either be purchased or made up of equal portions of peat and sharp garden sand.

Very little heat is needed to root the cuttings, so if you have no greenhouse you can do it perfectly well on a windowsill in a warm room. You can envelop the pot in a polythene bag, but in that case you should turn the bag inside out every three days. The compost should be watered after you have inserted your cuttings, to ensure it is in contact with the base of the cuttings, but after that no further watering should be necessary unless the compost dries out.

The cuttings should root in two or three weeks and if you give a gentle tug and find that they do not feel loose, you can be fairly sure that they are rooted. Once they are, pot them up in 8cm (3 in) pots in either J.I. No 1 or any growing compost and gradually harden off as before.

If you choose the easy way and leave your clumps in the border, you will need to lift them about every three years and split them up. This is best done in mid spring (March) when you should replant the new, outside growths in another part of the border.

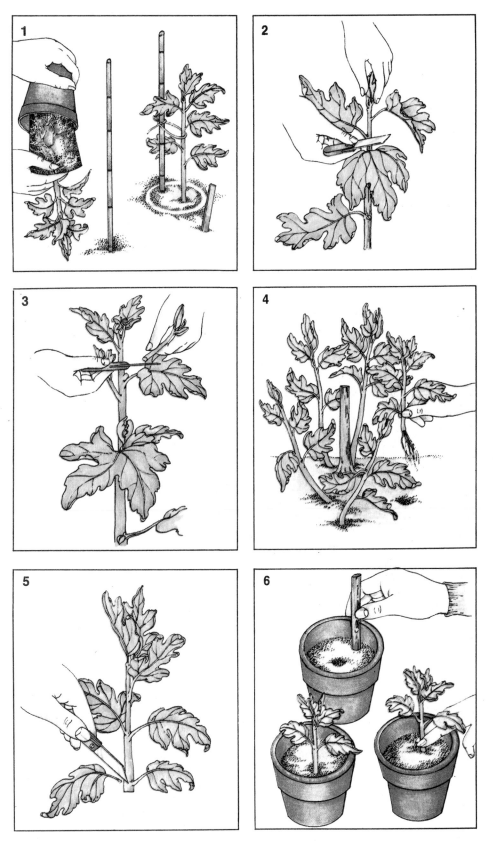

1 *Planting out from pots;* 2 *cutting out top shoot and* 3 *sideshoots;* 4 *thinning out new growth to four plants* 5 *Cutting off new shoots below the node for propagation;* 6 *planting cutting with dibber — one centrally, or first of several cuttings around the pot*

Above right: pyrethrum Evenglow
Above and right: double and single types
of shasta daisy, C. maximum *Esther Read*

If the leaves are discolouring in patches, then eventually yellowing and turning limp, the plants have probably got chrysanthemum eelworm pest. In this case you might just as well give up growing chrysanthemums altogether for at least three years. Dig out all the plants and burn them. However, eelworm attacks outdoor chrysanthemums comparatively rarely, although it likes the more showy types.

SOME OTHER CHRYSANTHEMUMS
There are a number of other chrysanthemums that you can grow in the garden.

Shasta daisy
Esther Read, such a stand-by of the flower arranger, is a double form of the shasta daisy, which used to be called the Edward VII chrysanthemum and is, botanically, *Chrysanthemum maximum*. This is so easy to grow that if anyone you know has it, they can probably let you have some of their divisions (see Division and layering). All you have to do is plant them in the border and divide the clumps every three or four years. The shasta daisy itself is just an enormous white daisy, but there are quite a few double forms besides Esther Read.

Pyrethrum
There is also an old friend, *Chrysanthemum coccineum*, but you may not recognize the name. This is the pyrethrum, that crimson daisy which is so much used for cut flowers in mid summer (late May and June). This is not quite so easy to grow as *C. maximum*, as slugs are likely to do great damage when the new leaves appear in the spring; but if you use plentiful slug pellets or surround the plants with soot, you will find them quite trouble-free. They appear to exhaust the soil rather quickly, so many people split the clumps up and transplant every other year. At one time there were many forms of pyrethrum, both single and double, in various colours from deep crimson to pale pink and white, but the choice is now much less and you will probably have to settle for either the deep crimson or the semi-double pale pink.

Annual chrysanthemums
Finally there are the annual chrysanthemums, which have been bred from three wild species, *C. carinatum, C. coronarium* and *C. segetum*. These can be started from seed sown in warmth in mid spring (March), pricked out in boxes and eventually planted out, or sown outside in late spring (after the middle of April). There are both singles and doubles and they range in colour from white to sulphur, yellow, pink and red. They grow to about 60cm (24 in) high and may be expected to flower from mid summer to mid autumn (late June until September). They are thus useful for filling up any gaps or for inserting between spring bulbs, so as to give a display after they have died down. They like sunny situations, and will thrive in all soils, although they prefer it to be fairly dry and well-drained.

Summer Bedding Plants

GENERAL WORK

Early summer (May)

If the bulb area is to be used for summer flowering bedding plants, lift the bulbs and put them in a trench in a spare part of the garden, where the leaves can die down naturally and the bulbs ripen thoroughly.

Spring bedding plants should be pulled up and discarded.

Half-hardy annuals can be set out where they are to flower.

As they die, cut off the flower-heads of rhododendrons and azaleas, taking care not to damage the leaves and buds below.

Cut back hard the stems that have carried flowers of spring and early summer shrubs, to encourage new shoots to grow for next year. Also remove any dead and spindly growth.

Climbers that finish flowering this month should have their old flower-stems cut out.

During drought periods water the lawn thoroughly, preferably with a sprinkler. This is particularly important with new lawns which are still getting their grass roots well down into the soil.

To fill gaps in the borders and to make containers decorative during the summer, some of the tender perennials are ideally colourful and useful. Most of these plants are frost tender, but have a very long flowering season. This means that to keep them through the winter you must have some place which can be kept free of frost. This is usually all that is necessary and no great heat is involved, although it may be helpful to have a little more warmth in the spring for raising cuttings. However, it is possible to take cuttings of most sorts towards the end of summer, when no artificial heat at all is required.

Filling up the spaces

Very few of us nowadays have enough space, time, or money to reserve special beds for designs using bedding plants. Most people usually plant such beds with hybrid tea or floribunda roses, which will flower throughout the summer, but can be left from year to year. It is, therefore, in the mixed borders of our Flower Garden that we shall be putting in bedding plants, particularly where there were clumps of spring-flowering plants. They are also excellent for planting in containers for the patio, and are ideal for window boxes.

A display of mixed summer bedding plants in the Flower Garden—from taller heliotrope and verbena to fibrous-rooted begonias in the foreground

Top right and above right: two varieties of zonal pelargonium, Paul Crampel and Mrs Quitter, like poor soil and full sun
Top left: mix heliotrope with calceolaria
Above: ivy-leaved pelargonium L'Elegante, free-flowering, long-stemmed trailing species, effective in hanging baskets
Opposite: combined pelargonium hybrids, variegated regal and zonal varieties

There is a very large choice of bedding plants, including a number of annuals which will require some heat in the spring to raise the seedlings. Alternatively, you can buy young plants from a nursery, although this is rather more expensive. To begin with, we have chosen plants that can be kept going from year to year.

Heliotrope

An old favourite is heliotrope, or 'cherry pie'. This is around 45cm (18 in) high with rather dark leaves and large heads of violet or bluish flowers with one of the loveliest scents of all garden plants. You will probably have to start by buying in some plants and there is no point in doing this much before mid summer (June) as you cannot plant them out until all risk of frost has gone. They can be raised from seed sown in gentle heat, around 15°C (60°F) in mid spring (late February or early March), but the results may be a rather mixed bag, although Lemoine's Giant is said to come true from seed.

In early autumn (mid August) side-shoots or growing tips may be taken for cuttings. Make them about 5cm (2 in) long, from just below a leaf joint and put them in a cutting mixture, either a ready made-up bought compost or equal parts of peat and sharp garden sand. If only a few are being taken, insert the cuttings in a pot and put the potful inside a polythene bag. The cuttings should be put in a position shaded from direct sunlight and should root in two or three weeks. Once rooted they are first hardened off by removing the polythene bag and leaving them for a few days, and then either potted up separately in 8cm (3 in) pots or planted out about 8cm (3 in) apart in trays. At this stage you should use either a soilless growing compost or J.I. No 1.

Before there is any risk of frost bring them under cover, in a frame or a greenhouse if possible, otherwise into the house, and keep them as dry as possible. Water only when the leaves wilt and always use water warmed to 15°C (60°F) when you do. Towards late spring (at the end of March or early April) you will need to water more frequently. You can put your plants outside during the day to harden them off, but remember you will have to bring them back under cover if there are any late frosts. Plant them out in mid summer (June).

Zonal pelargoniums

The most popular bedding plant for over a hundred years has been the geranium, which should really be called the zonal pelargonium. This is one of the most useful of all garden plants, although in very wet summers it may produce masses of leaves and only a few flowers. You also have to be somewhat selective as to what sorts you obtain as some of the most handsome only give of their best in a cool greenhouse and do not flower very freely out of doors.

Some of the blazing scarlets, such as the ever popular Paul Crampel and the double-flowered Gustav Emich, are somewhat harsh in colour and not too easily combined with other plants, but if you find this you can always go in for the delightful salmon-pink King of Denmark or the orange-tinged Maxim Kovaleski or Orangesonne. Doris Moore is an attractive cherry red, Vera Dillon is almost magenta and Hermione is pure white. All these are old and trusted varieties, but fresh ones are brought out each year.

There is also a race of zonals with showy leaves that are their main attraction. These include the yellow-leaved A Happy Thought and Golden Harry Hieover and the astonishing Henry Cox, in which the leaf is variegated in deep maroon, red, green and cream. The flowers of these variegated types are not produced particularly freely and they are not very attractive in any case; the interest lies in their leaves.

Ivy-leaved pelargoniums

Very different in habit, but flowering very freely, are the trailing ivy-leaved pelargoniums, which are splendid for putting around the sides of containers or in hanging baskets, as the growths hang down and hide their containers. Although there is quite a range of colours, you will have to find a specialist nursery if you require anything other than the pink Madame Crousse or the purple-veined white L'Elegante. The latter has the advantage of leaves margined with pale cream and purple, so that it is handsome at all times of the year.

Assuming that you have to start by buying in pelargonium plants, it is usually best not to plant them out at once, as they have probably been growing in a fairly warm greenhouse. So leave them in their pots for a fortnight, bringing them in at night if there is a risk of frost. The beginning of mid summer (June) is a good time to plant them out, so early summer (mid May) is a good time to purchase plants. One of the great advantages of pelargoniums is that they do best in very

poor soil, so see that they have the poorest soil in your border and full sunlight. If the soil is too rich they grow prodigiously, but concentrate too much of their energies on stems and leaves and not enough on flowers.

Cuttings are taken in early autumn (mid August). Take growing points about 8cm (3 in) long, remove any flower buds if necessary and let them lie in the sun for 24 hours. Now cut them off just below a leaf joint and insert them in a cutting mixture. There is no need to envelop the pot in a polythene bag.

The cuttings usually root fairly quickly and they can be potted up singly. During the winter they should be kept just free of frost, on the dry side and in as much light as possible. Sometimes the cuttings produce flower buds very soon, but these must be removed. About mid spring (the end of March) you will have to start giving more water, and this is quite a good time to nip out the growing point to encourage a bushy plant.

Stand the plants outdoors in late spring (the end of April), but remember to bring them back in if late frosts are expected. Plant them out finally towards mid

summer (June). Provided they have been hardened off, pelargoniums will take a degree or so of frost without damage, but is not advisable to expose them to it. It is possible to pot the plants on in late spring (early April), but not really necessary.

Viola

A bedding plant that is rather rarely seen nowadays, even though it is hardy, is the viola. This is much like the pansy to look at, but has the advantage of a much longer flowering season. These are sown in early spring (February), pricked out when large enough in boxes, hardened off and planted out usually in early summer (May). Alternatively it is possible to buy named sorts such as the mauve Maggie Mott or the yellow Golden Bedder. You can also buy the apricot Chantreyland but this will come true from seed as will the reddish Arkwright Ruby.

With named sorts, or with any seedlings you want to perpetuate, you take cuttings in late summer or early autumn (July or August). To find the cuttings you have to lift the plant up, when you will see small shoots coming from the rootstock. These are detached from as near the root as possible when about 5cm (2 in) long, and treated like any other cutting.

Once rooted they are pricked out in boxes and then planted out either in their permanent positions or in some reserve ground. The original plants will survive the winter, but they never flower so well the second season. All these violas are about 15cm (6 in) high.

You may well be wondering why so excellent a plant should be so rarely seen and the answer is that there is one snag. Once the viola has set seed it will stop flowering, so you have to keep on nipping off the faded flowers, which can be quite tedious and time consuming. However, if you do this you have flowers all through the summer so it is worth it if you can find the time.

Verbena

Verbenas are usually treated as half-hardy annuals, being sown in gentle heat, around 13°C (55°F) in early spring (late February), pricked out into boxes, hardened off in early summer (early May) and planted out about two or three weeks later. Most of the seeds produce mixed colours so that if you want to preserve a particularly good form you will have to resort to cuttings.

These are taken from sideshoots in early autumn (August) and usually root readily enough. They can then be planted out in boxes, kept frost-free throughout the winter, brought back into gentle heat towards mid spring (the end of March) and then treated as the seedlings were. You start to harden them off at the end of

Below: Viola×wittrockiana *Jungfrau useful for bedding out and edging paths*
Right: verbena Lawrence Johnston
Below right: Viola cornuta *Dartington*

and stopped by pinching out the growing tips in early spring (February). As soon as you see sideshoots appearing you can pot the cuttings up in 8 or 10cm (3 or 4 in) pots, and once established they are gradually hardened off and planted out. They like a rather rich soil and often resent prolonged drought. On the other hand they will do equally well in full sun or in partial shade. They are becoming scarce, so are worth cultivating.

Fibrous-rooted begonia

Finally we should mention *Begonia semperflorens* (the fibrous-rooted type), a dwarf plant, often with deep purple leaves and flowers of some shade of red, pink or white. It can be treated as a half-hardy annual, but needs at least 25°C (70°F) to start the minute seeds and it is probably best to buy in plants. Shoots growing from the base of old flowering stems of plants lifted in the autumn (October) can be used for cuttings in the spring (March or April), but the plants need a temperature of around 10°C (50°F) throughout the winter. The cuttings are cultivated in the same way as the others.

Begonia semperflorens may be a bit expensive to keep over the winter, but it does have the advantage of continuous flowering, whether the weather be wet or dry, and does equally well in full sun or in shade, so it can be a really useful plant.

spring (the beginning of May), as usual seeing that they are not damaged by late frosts, and plant them out before mid summer (at the beginning of June).

Verbena are trailing plants with round heads of flowers in various shades of red from scarlet to pale pink, or with white or violet flowers; often the flowers have a white eye. It is also possible to keep plants through the winter in the greenhouse and continue to take cuttings in mid and late spring (March and April) if you want to build up a large stock. With all these bedding plants it is a great help to have a frame in which to harden off the plants. It can be kept open at all times except when late frosts are forecast.

Calceolaria

Verbena is seen only rarely nowadays, but it is more common than the so-called shrubby calceolaria. This may be slightly woody at the base, but looks like a herbaceous plant about 30–45cm (12–18 in) tall with purse-shaped flowers that are usually yellow, though at one time a deep brown form was popular. The variety Sunshine is a good hybrid. The plants will take a few degrees of frost without damage, but prefer to be protected.

Colourful display

If you prefer a show of colourful flowers, choose ones that will flower over a long period. Begonias will last from year to year if you bring them under glass during the winter.

Heliotrope is not very showy, but it diffuses an exquisite perfume and does flower over a long period. Zonal pelargoniums are not confined to the rather fiery-coloured Paul Crampel; you can also obtain delightful salmon-pink ones, such as King of Denmark, the orange Maxim Kovaleski, the almost magenta Vera Dillon, the white Hermine and the red-edged white Lady Warwick. Nor should you overlook those with variegated leaves, such as Henry Cox, whose leaf is shaded black, red, green and cream and is very showy. Happy Thought has a large yellow zone in the leaf, while Golden Harry Hieover has a gold and red leaf. They produce red or crimson flowers, though not very freely, and it is their leaves that are the main attraction.

If the containers are quite high off the ground, ivy-leaved pelargoniums trailing over the sides, with perhaps a fuchsia in the centre, make a pleasant planting. One of the best is L'Elegante, with silvery variegated leaves and white, purple-striped flowers. The more popular pink Mme Crousse, or its purple sport Claret Crousse, are also attractive and both of them are easy to grow.

All of these plants would do best planted directly into a soil that is not too rich: J.I. No 1 is quite sufficient. The first hard frost will kill all the pelargoniums and heliotropes, at which time you can just pull them up and throw them on your compost heap. However, with both these flowering plants it is very easy to root cuttings in early or mid Autumn (August or September) and they can be over-wintered on the kitchen windowsill. Fuchsias can also be rooted then, but most people prefer spring-struck cuttings.

The marguerite, *Chrysanthemum frutescens*, with grey-green leaves and white daisies that seem to go on flowering for ever, is still excellent value for money. Here again cuttings root easily, but if you lift the plant and pot it up, it will probably go on flowering all through the winter indoors.

Half Hardy Annuals

Annuals are the great stand-by in our Flower Garden. With careful planning, they help to provide that 'riot of colour' throughout the flowering season that every gardener dreams of. Although slightly more difficult to raise, the half-hardy annuals are particularly valuable for colour in the borders.

Half-hardy annuals can be very useful in the garden, especially for summer bedding and filling up gaps in the border. The only conceivable objection to them is that they need some heat when the seeds are germinating, so that if you have no greenhouse, you will have to raise them in the home, or sow them outside rather late in the season, or buy plants in.

Why 'half-hardy'?
The reason we call a plant half-hardy is that it is liable to be damaged by frost. This means that in most parts of the United Kingdom, for instance, it will not be safe to put the plant out in the garden before the last week in early summer (May) or the beginning of mid summer (June). As the plant is also an annual it is in a great hurry to flower and set seed. Since, once its seeds are ripe, it is going to die in any case, it is not much concerned with making a large root system; the important thing is for it to flower and set seed before the winter comes.

Buying plants
What this means in practical terms is that once an annual starts to flower it has, almost certainly, ceased making growth, so do not choose any plants that show either buds or flowers. It is possible to encourage further growth by taking off all the visible flowers and buds, but they will

Left: Cleome spinosa *need a warm spot*
Top right: callistephus Milady Blue, a single species of half-hardy annual that likes a loamy soil; decorative as pot plants
Above: dimorphotheca, or African daisy, whose flowers do not open in the shade

never make really satisfactory plants.

Half-hardy annuals are liable to come into flower quickly if their root space is at all constricted, so you will be wise to avoid boxes of seedlings with a crowded mass of plants growing closely together. Look for a box where the plants are at least 5cm (2 in) apart in each direction. This gives the roots room to expand and so will stop the plant coming into flower prematurely. The point is that although annuals can come into flower with very few roots, if they are given the opportunity to make a sizeable root system they will make larger plants and produce more flowers, and so continue flowering over a longer period. Thus, ideally, you want to purchase plants that are well-spaced in their boxes and not showing any signs of flowering.

The best time to buy

The next question is when to buy them. As you will probably not want to plant them out before mid summer (end of May), take no notice of anyone offering you plants in late spring (April). (This, of course, only applies to half-hardy annuals, since hardy annuals can be purchased at any time if you are unable to grow them from seed.)

The plants will probably have come out of the nurseryman's greenhouse and will be what some gardeners call 'lishy'. The leaves are very soft and practically irresistible to slugs and insect pests, and you will need to harden them off before you plant them out. This usually takes 10–14 days, so around the middle of early summer (mid May) is an excellent time to purchase the seedlings of half-hardy annuals. All you have to do is stand the boxes outside, preferably propped up on some support to keep the slugs away, water the soil if it gets at all dry (but not otherwise), and put the plants wherever you want them after 14 days.

Of course, if there is a risk of frost during this fortnight, you will have to bring the boxes indoors overnight. Anywhere in the house will be frost-free at that time of year, so it does not matter where you put the boxes, which can go out again during the daytime. If you have a frame you can, of course, harden your plants off in that, opening the lights at all times, except when frost is expected.

Raising from seed indoors

With the exception of *Begonia semperflorens*, most half-hardy annuals require very little heat to germinate. About 15°C (60°F) is quite adequate so, if you lack a greenhouse, you can probably germinate them on a windowsill indoors. In this case sow the seed in mid spring (towards the end of March) in a seed compost. When the seedlings have produced about two pairs of leaves, prick them out 5cm (2 in) apart in trays in a growing compost, either J.I. No 1 or a soilless mix, and put them in a slightly cooler place after ten days.

Then harden them off as already described. There is not much point in starting the seeds too early, as either the weather is too cold or the plants get too advanced by planting out time. The same routine applies if you have a greenhouse.

Sowing 'in situ'

One other possibility is to sow the seeds in position outside in early to mid summer (the end of May), for flowering in late summer and early autumn (July and August). This will not be possible with plants that flower in early and mid summer (May and June). as they will not have enough time to make their growth.

Care after planting out

Once they have been planted out – with tall plants about 30cm (12 in) apart and the shorter ones 15–25cm (6–9 in) apart – there is not much that needs doing. You should bear in mind that the annual's main object in life is to set seed, so if you can find the time to nip off all flower-heads as soon as they have finished flowering, you will encourage the plant to produce more flowers and so prolong the season. If, at the same time, you give a very light dressing of a balanced fertilizer or a foliar feed you will aid this process, although probably not very significantly.

Some plants to choose

The first four plants in the following list are all known as 'everlastings', that is, they can be dried and used for flower arrangements throughout the year.

Acrolinium, Helichrysum, Lonas and **Xeranthemum** have mixed colour, single or double, daisy-like flowers and grow up to 60cm (24 in). They can all be started early or sown direct out of doors, and flower from late summer to late autumn (July to October).

Ageratum These are usually low-spreading plants rarely more than 15cm (6 in) tall, although there are some taller ones. They bear heads of small bluey-mauve powder puffs over a long period, if regularly dead-headed. Seed sown outside in early to mid summer (the end of May onwards) produces good, autumn-flowering (August to October) plants.

Alonsoa A rather unusual plant about 30cm (12 in) tall with masses of small bright red flowers. Sow outside early to mid summer (late May) for late summer to late autumn (July to October) flowering.

Antirrhinum The popular snapdragon is not strictly half-hardy at all, but the plants need quite a long growing season, so seedlings must be raised early. There is little point, therefore, in sowing in early to mid summer (late May), but you can sow outside in early autumn (August) and let the plants overwinter *in situ*. In fact you can treat antirrhinum as a biennial.

Begonia semperflorens A marvellous little plant about 20cm (8 in) tall, sometimes with purple leaves and an endless succession of red, pink or white flowers from mid summer (the end of June) onwards. There is no objection to buying flowering plants as it is really perennial and can be kept through the winter in heat. Nor is it necessary to remove the faded flowers. It will also, rather unusually, grow in semi-shade, whereas most annuals require full sun. A temperature of at least 22°C (70°F) will be needed to germinate the dust-like seeds, so most gardeners will have to buy plants at the appropriate time.

Callistephus (Chinese aster) This decorative plant is highly popular. The flower-heads, usually in various shades of pink and blue, yellow or white, come in a number of shapes – daisy-like blooms, doubles, quills, pompons or chrysanthemum shape – and are always interesting. It will grow to a height of approximately 15–60cm (6–24 in), and can be sown outdoors in early summer (May). Its flowering season lasts from late summer (May) onwards.

Celosia (cockscomb or Prince of Wales feathers) This plant possesses rather odd, feathery heads that are coloured crimson or yellow. It can grow up to 90cm (3 ft) tall, and it will flower from late summer (July) onwards.

Cleome (spider flower) This grows as a tall bushy plant with pink and white flowers. It can reach a height of 1·2m (4 ft), although usually it will grow to less than this. It produces flowers from late summer (July) onwards.

Cosmea (cosmos) This has fern-like leaves and dahlia-like flowers that come usually in some shades of pink or red. It will grow up to 75cm (2½ ft) in height, and its flowering season occurs in the autumn (August and September).

Dimorphotheca (star of the veldt) Probably best left until early summer (May) and sown where you want it to flower. It grows about 30cm (12 in) tall and has masses of bright orange, yellow or white daisies which appear right through summer and into autumn.

Felicia bergeriana (kingfisher daisy) Is again best left until near mid summer (late May) and sown *in situ*. It only reaches a height of 10cm (4 in) and has daisies of a brilliant kingfisher blue from mid summer to mid autumn (June to September).

Gaillardia The annual variety. Has large daisies in various shades of yellow and orange with almost black cones in the centre. Grows about 60cm (24 in) tall, and flowers from mid summer to late autumn (June to October).

Lobelia Has such tiny seeds that it is almost essential to start them in pots, although you will get nice plants from seed sown in early summer (May). Mainly blue flowers but some red or white, from late summer (July) onwards. The plants grow about 10cm (4 in) tall.

Mesembryanthemum (Livingstone daisy) Has fleshy leaves and daisy-like flowers in a bewildering assortment of colours. Grows only about 10cm (4 in) high, but spreads widely and flowers from late summer (July) until the frosts come. It also likes dry conditions. Seed sown outside in early to mid summer (late May) starts to flower rather later, but is quite satisfactory.

Nemesia Showy South African plants growing about 25cm (10 in) tall with clusters of flowers in varying shades of red, orange, yellow, and even blue. The flowering season is rather short, so late-sown seeds will provide you with a second display.

Nicotiana The popular tobacco plant, usually 45–90cm ($1\frac{1}{2}$–3 ft) tall has white or red night-scented flowers from late summer to mid autumn (July to September).

Perilla This is grown not for flowers, but for its dark purple, almost black, indented leaves. Grows to about 60cm (24 in).

Petunia Possibly the most reliable half-hardy annual for continuous display. It does require starting fairly early in the year, but is usually trouble-free, flowering through summer and autumn until the first frosts. The flowers come in a wide range of single or bicolours and may be simple and bell-like or a mass of petals (multifloras). It grows to a height of 10–25cm (4–10 in).

Far left, above: Cosmos Sunset loves sun
Above right: celosia Belden Plume, a fiery tropical plant, thrives in warm conditions
Right: ageratum North Sea, its clusters of neat flower-heads last for a long time

Above left: Salpiglossis sinuata *blooms in profusion and has beautiful veined markings. It originally came from Chile*
Above right: Lobelia erinus, *a dwarf spreading plant, flowers from early summer*
Top: Phlox drummondii *should be planted out in a moist, sunny border*

Annual phlox A very attractive annual with heads of flowers from deep crimson to white and yellow. Can well be sown outside at the end of May. Grows to 15–20cm (6–8 in) and flowers from late summer (July) through the autumn.

Portulaca Rather rarely seen nowadays as it can be unsatisfactory in wet summers, but gorgeous in a dry, warm one. Grows to 15cm (6 in) with large single or double red and yellow flowers from mid summer to mid autumn (June to September).

Ricinus (castor oil plant) Grown for its ornamental bronze, dark purple or green leaves and stately habit, it reaches 1·2m (4 ft). You will probably have to grow this yourself, as nurserymen rarely offer it in plant form. Be careful if you have small children, as it is highly poisonous.

Salpiglossis The plants are unpleasantly sticky to touch but the flowers, which are trumpet-shaped and about 8cm (3 in) long in many rich colours, are amongst the most spectacular of all annuals. The plants grow to 60cm (24 in) and flower from late summer to mid autumn (July to September).

Salvia The bedding salvia, well known for its scarlet flowers, though there are now forms with the spiky flower-heads in purple or pastel shades. Grows between 23–30cm (9–12 in), flowering in late summer and early autumn (July and August).

Statice About 30–45cm (12–18 in) tall with large heads of everlasting flowers in a wide selection of colours. Can be sown outside, and flowers in late summer (July).

Tagetes French and African marigolds. The French makes perfectly good plants from seeds sown in mid summer (June), but the African, which is taller, needs a rather longer season, although it flowers from mid summer seeding in a good year. Usually yellow and orange flowers from late summer (July) onwards; the bushy plants grow to about 15cm (6 in).

Ursinia Another orange South African daisy, best sown outside in a sunny position. Grows to 23cm (9 in) and flowers from mid summer to early autumn (June to August).

Venidium (monarch of the veldt) Large daisy in pastel shades, with a dark blotch in the centre. Height-wise, it will grow up to 75cm (2½ ft), and its flowering season lasts from mid summer to late autumn (June to October).

Verbena (vervain) Still a valuable bedding plant with heads of bright flowers in pink, crimson, scarlet or violet from mid summer (June) until the first frosts. Height about 30cm (12 in).

Zinnia One of the showiest annuals for late flowering either in tall forms up to 60cm (24 in) or in dwarf forms not taller than 30cm (12 in). The flowers are multi-petalled in shades of orange, yellow, red or white. They should not be planted out before mid summer (mid June), long after most other half-hardy plants, and even so may prove unsatisfactory should the summer be either cold or wet.

Raising Annuals under glass

When you grow your own plants from seed you have better control of their quality and timing. Most of the favourite bedding plants can be sown in the greenhouse from about mid to late spring (March to April). It is a good idea to sow seeds from the packet over a period of time so you can enjoy a long flowering period.

How you sow can be varied to suit the cost, quantity and size of the seed. Large seeds (like zinnia) should be sown individually in small pots. Finer seed should be sown in a tray or pan; prick out the seedlings into more trays when they are large enough to handle. Instead of pricking out you can then thin the seedlings by pulling out the excess and discarding them.

For germinating seed use a sterilized seed compost such as John Innes Seed Compost and make sure that it is moist. A useful rule is to cover the seed with its own depth of compost. Very fine or dust-like seed, however, should not be covered.

After sowing cover the seed containers with glass and then a sheet of brown paper or newspaper. Some form of propogator will be most helpful for germinating the seeds. For bedding plants high temperatures are undesirable. Too much heat will force the seedlings and they will become spindly, pale and weak. A temperature of 7–18°C (45–65°F) is adequate for most plants. There are inexpensive small electric propogators for warming only one or two seed trays, and designs that are heated by paraffin oil lamp. Many people manage to germinate the odd trays of seeds in their homes on the window-sill of a warm room.

Germination time may vary from a couple of days to several weeks depending on the type of seed and temperature. Remove the containers cover when the first seedlings are through – but exposure to bright sunlight in the early stages can be harmful.

Pricking out should be done as soon as

the seedlings are big enough to handle easily. In the case of very tiny seedlings such as lobelia, small groups can be 'patched out' since it is impossible to separate them. When pricking out be generous with your spacing so the roots do not become entangled and damaged when the young plants are divided for planting out. After pricking out, water the seedlings with a Cheshunt compound to help prevent damping-off disease.

All bedding plants must be given a

Above left: Nemesia strumosa suttonii, *whose cut flowers last well in water*
Above right: clarkia, used mainly as border *decoration, or can be grown for cutting*
Top: Zinnia elegans, *Envy, a showy plant*

period of gradual acclimatization to the open air before planting out – 'hardening off'. In the greenhouse itself move the seed trays to cooler spots and move the trays to frames outside three weeks before you intend to bed them out.

Hardy Biennials

Biennial flowering plants can be the stand-by of every judicious gardener as their extended life cycle enables you to organize your bedding schemes and keep design and colour in mind for the following year.

True biennials are plants that grow one year, overwinter, then flower, seed and die in the following year. Among them are many of the popular garden plants such as Canterbury bell, honesty and foxglove, also a number of plants usually grown as biennials which are really perennials, such as wallflower, pansy and sweet William.

Some have such large seeds that it is possible to sow them in their flowering positions, but others will need to be sown in a part of the garden reserved for raising seedlings, such as in our seedbed in the north-west corner. They can be thinned out subsequently into rows where they can remain until it is time to plant them in their flowering positions in mid autumn (September). With very fine seeds, like those of foxglove, it is probably better to sow in a flowerpot left outside; once they have germinated they can be transplanted 15cm (6 in) apart into rows in the seedbed and then planted into their flowering positions in the autumn.

When to sow

The time for sowing depends to a large extent on when the plant will flower the following year. Plants that flower fairly early in the spring, such as wallflower, honesty and pansy, have to make all their growth before the winter so the longer they are given the better it will be. Later-flowering plants, such as hollyhock, stock, sweet William or Canterbury bell, will make some further growth after the winter before they start producing flowers so they can be sown somewhat later.

Far left: plantagieum *Blue Bedder*
(viper's bugloss); above: Cheiranthus cheiri
(wallflower) with profuse showy blooms
Below: richly-coloured giant pansies

GENERAL WORK

Mid summer (June)

Hoe weeds regularly in all parts of the garden where there is bare earth, to prevent the weeds getting established, seeding and spreading. Always take care not to damage any shallow-rooting cultivated plants.

Continue to plant out half-hardy annuals and sow some in positions where they are to flower to give a longer season of colour.

As climbing plants, and those shrubs treated as climbers, continue to grow and produce new shoots, tie in to the supports where necessary.

From now until early autumn (August) the lawn will probably require mowing twice a week. Cut the grass to 13mm ($\frac{1}{2}$ in) high. Unless the lawn has been treated with a weedkiller, the grass cuttings should be added to the compost heap.

Above and above right: Lunaria annua *(honesty) flowering, and seeding in autumn to leave flat silver pods that can be used to make excellent winter decoration*

Keep an eye open for any attacks of pests or diseases on plants and take prompt action by spraying or dusting with the appropriate pesticide according to the manufacturer's instructions. Watch out for signs of reinfestation.

Annuals treated as biennials
There are also some hardy annuals that will produce much larger plants if they are treated as biennials and sown in the autumn (September). The plants that like this treatment include godetia, calendula, candytuft, echium (viper's bugloss), sweet pea, cornflower, larkspur, Shirley poppy, eschscholtzia and annual clary sage. Just sow the seeds in rows in drills and leave the young plants until the following spring, when you can transplant them to wherever you want them to flower.

Preparing to sow
Before considering sowing times, you should first think of preparing the ground. The most important things for a young seedling are plenty of light, so that it can manufacture energy, and a fairly light soil so that the roots can penetrate quickly and anchor the plant.

The light will normally be there, unless you sow in the shade of evergreens, but you will have to prepare the soil. It will need loosening up, even if it is a light, sandy one. A very stiff soil is hard for the roots to get into so, if your soil is heavy, dig it, break it up and incorporate some sand or peat into this broken-up soil. If the soil is dry, give it a thorough soaking with water before you start your sowing. If the soil has been well soaked the young roots will soon get down to the moisture, even though it may be dry on top.

How to sow
Having got your soil prepared, make a small drill, not more than 2–3cm (1 in) deep and sow your seeds as thinly as possible. Rake some soil over them and sit back and wait.

After sowing, biennial seeds usually germinate rapidly enough and you should not have to wait more than a fortnight before you see the seedlings appear; usually you will get results even sooner.

With the large-seeded plants, which you can put where they are expected to flower, it is wise perhaps to put two seeds in every place and pull out the weaker of the two if both germinate. The distance between the plants when you line (plant) them out will vary according to type and the recommended distances are given below under each plant individually.

Thinning and transplanting
Apart from those seeds sown *in situ*, you now have two choices. If you do not want

many plants, you can just thin the seedlings out and leave them where they are. Alternatively, you can transplant them as soon as they are large enough to handle and leave them in rows until about the middle of autumn (mid September) when you lift them and put them where you want them to flower.

Be sure that the young plants do not dry out when you line them out. The simplest way is to puddle them. You dig a hole to the required depth with a trowel – the required depth will be such that the roots can be as deep in the soil as they were before you moved them. Then pop in the plants, fill the hole with water and then push the soil back around the roots. This enables your small biennials to get away without much check, and you want to keep them growing with as few checks as possible.

The plants should be in their final positions by mid autumn (mid September), to give them a chance to make a little growth and anchor themselves in the fresh soil before the onset of winter. However, this may not always be possible. You may, for example, want to put wallflowers where you now have dahlias. These will not be lifted before late autumn (the end of October), so it may well be early winter (November) before you put in your wallflowers.

The result will be that you won't get quite such a good display in the spring as you would have done if you could have

moved the plants earlier, but, failing an absolutely appalling winter, you should still get quite good results.

Some plants to choose
Here we list some good biennials, in order of flowering.

Pansy Sow in late summer (July) and prick out 15cm (6 in) apart. They start to flower in late spring (April) and can go on until late summer (late July). The blooms come in a variety of rich shades, either single or bi-coloured.

Wallflower Sow either in mid or late summer (June or July). Line out 15cm (6 in) apart. In flower from late spring (late March) to mid summer (June) in reds, oranges and yellow colours.

Honesty Should be sown in mid or late summer (June or July), preferably where the plants are to flower. If you do prick them out they should be 25cm (9 in) apart. The purple or white flowers appear in early to late summer (May to July). The flat and round silver seed pods which follow are very sought after for winter flower decorations.

Top left: the familiar digitalis (foxglove)
Below and bottom right: two Papaver
nudicate *(iceland poppies), suitable for
rock gardens as well as mixed borders*
Bottom left: Verbascum bombyciferum
(mullein)

Sweet William Sow in late summer (early July) and prick out to 25cm (9 in) apart. They flower mid to late summer (June to July) in mixtures of red, white, pink or salmon colours.

Stock It is the Brompton and East Lothian strains that are biennial; the ten-week and the night-scented are annuals. Sow in late summer (early July), and prick out 30cm (12 in) apart. It is possible to leave them in the rows until the following spring, in which case they must be put in their final positions in mid spring (March). Flowers are shades of pink, red, lilac, yellow or white, with the Bromptons appearing in early summer (May) and the East Lothians during summer and early autumn (July and August).

Foxglove These digitalis seeds are so minute that they are best started in a pot. Prick out the seedlings to 30cm (12 in) apart and, again, they can be left in the rows until late spring (early April) if it is more convenient. The flower spikes of white, pink, purple and yellow appear in mid summer (June).

Canterbury bell Sow in summer (May or June). The seeds are very small, so it may be easier to start them in a pot. Prick out

Below: matthiola (Brompton stocks)
Left: Althaea rosea *(hollyhock)*

the seedlings at least 30cm (12 in) apart and once more you can wait to plant them in their final positions until the following late spring (April). They flower in summer (June and July) in white, pink, blue or mauve shades.

Iceland poppy This needs rather different treatment. All poppies (or papavers) dislike transplanting so you can either sow them where they are to grow, or start them in a pot, prick out or transplant about 5cm (2 in) apart into trays and then put them in their final positions the following spring (April). The trouble with sowing them *in situ* is that the seeds are very tiny, so it is not easy to differentiate between the young seedlings and weeds when thinning them out. Some people treat these poppies like any other biennials with complete success, but it can be a bit tricky. Sow in mid to late summer (late June or early July). They flower from mid summer (June) until the frosts come, in various shades of pink, orange, red or yellow.

Mullein The one you find catalogued most often is either called *Verbascum* Broussa or *V. bombyciferum*. It makes an enormous silver rosette of leaves the first year and the following year sends up a great golden spire 1·2m (4 ft) high. Sow in mid to late summer (June to July) and prick out 30–45cm (12–18 in) apart. These again can be left until the spring before being put in their final positions. They flower from mid summer to early autumn (June to August). There are other mulleins which are perennials, but they all want the same treatment.

Hollyhock These have such large seeds that you can put them where you want them to flower. Sow in mid to late summer (June or July) and, if you are pricking out, put the plants 30cm (12 in) apart. They flower in shades of pink, white, red, yellow or purple from late summer to mid autumn (July until September).

Herbaceous Perennials

Herbaceous perennials form the basis of your summer flower display. Rooted cuttings are expensive but some varieties are simple to grow from seed.

GENERAL WORK

Mid summer (June)

Spring-flowering bulbs that have finished flowering and whose leaves have yellowed, and which are in positions required for summer bedding plants, should be dug up now, placed in a box containing soil or peat in a dry place and left to complete ripening and drying.

Herbaceous perennials, annuals and bulbous plants that are tall growing and have not already had stakes or twigs put alongside them, should have this done now. Tie in as the plants grow.

Put a 2–5cm (1–2 in) layer of mulching material such as compost or peat round the root areas of gladiolus and lily if not already done. This will help to discourage weeds and conserve essential moisture.

Sow seeds of herbaceous perennial plants in the open ground or in pots outdoors.

With a rake, preferably a spring-back wire one, rake the lawn now to lift up creeping stems of weeds for cutting off with the mower. If possible, rake twice, once in each direction.

Water all plants, including the lawn, regularly and thoroughly once or twice a week during periods of dry weather.

It is an obvious economy to grow as many plants as possible from seed and hardy herbaceous perennials are usually both easy and profitable to treat in this manner. And you don't have to wait any longer to get results than if you had bought rooted cuttings. Seed sown one year will produce flowering plants in the following season, provided they have been sown early enough.

If you have delayed somewhat in sowing the seeds, you may have to wait an extra season, but that will be the only delay. There are, too, some plants – such as paeony or flag iris – that take longer to arrive at a flowering size, but even these will generally give you some flowers the year after sowing. What's more, the plants will grow larger in each succeeding year, so they are what might be termed a 'growth investment'.

Here we advise you on plants that can be sown outdoors in mid to late summer (June to July), but there is nothing to stop you sowing the seeds earlier – from late spring (April) onwards, if it is more convenient: and you will end up with

Above left: Anthemis tinctoria, *a daisy-like perennial that requires well-drained soil and a sunny spot in the border*
Above: Achillea taygetea Moonshine *flowers in late summer*

larger plants if you do.

How to sow

Sow the seed outdoors as thinly as possible in rows in the seedbed. As soon as the seedlings are large enough to handle, either thin the rows out or transplant them so that they are farther apart. Alternatively, you can sow the seeds in a pot of seed compost and then either prick the seedlings out directly into the open ground or first prick them out 5cm (2 in) apart into trays containing J.I. No 1 or a soilless mix, and then line them out (transplant them) when they are more established. This second method obviously entails more work but you can look after the seedlings more easily at their most delicate stage. Moreover, even if you sow the seeds in the open ground, you have to be sure that they are kept free of weeds – and this at a time when there is often a lot of other work going on in the garden.

Special cases

Plants with very small seed, such as campanula, are certainly best started in pots and the same would apply to plants that are hard to transplant when large, such as *Lathyrus latifolius*, the everlasting sweet pea (although this can perfectly well be sown where it is to grow). There are a few plants, such as hellebore and gentian, which take a long time to germinate, and for these pots are certainly necessary.

In the case of lupins, either the Russell hybrids or the tree lupins – both of which have nice large seeds – it is probably best to put the seeds singly or in pairs where you want the plants to flower. It is

possible to move lupins, but they send down a long tap-root, like a thin carrot, and if this is damaged the plant may die, so the less they are disturbed the better. An alternative is to sow the seeds singly in 8cm (3 in) pots and then move them on to their permanent positions. In this case do not use a seed compost but J.I. No 1 or the equivalent soilless compost. If you have plenty of seed, put two together and throw the weaker one away if they both germinate.

Preparing the seedbed

If you do sow directly outdoors, you want to make your seedbed what is termed 'friable'; that means that the soil should be aerated and easily penetrable by the young roots of the seedlings. If your soil is naturally rather heavy, incorporate some peat or coarse sand into the top 15cm (6 in) of it; this will have good results. You should also give it a good soaking about two days before you sow your seeds unless, of course, there has been a heavy rainfall (remember that light showers do not penetrate very deeply into the soil).

Draw out a shallow drill 2–3cm (1 in) deep and sow the seeds as thinly as possible and then cover them with raked earth. Keep the seedbed moist until the roots have had a chance to get fairly well down in the soil, which is usually about a fortnight after germination.

After-care

No garden operation is trouble-free, and in this case you must keep the spaces between the drills well hoed and take precautions against slugs and insects; especially if you see evidence of damage. After three or four weeks the young plants will be ready to be lined out. With most herbaceous plants a distance of 25cm (9 in) between the plants will be adequate. Here again, water the soil well (if it needs it) before you transplant your seedlings and see that they do not dry out during the following ten days. This is sufficient time for the plantlets to take root in the new soil.

Final planting

During mid or late autumn (September or October) or mid or late spring (the end of March or early April), lift the plants and put them wherever you want them to flower.

Some plants to choose

Some of the plants that this kind of outdoor treatment will suit include:

Achillea (yarrow) Makes plants up to 75cm (2½ ft) high with flat heads of minute yellow, white or cerise flowers in late summer and early autumn (July and August).

Above: Anchusa azurea, *a short-lived perennial best treated as a biennial and whose flowers are attractive to bees*
Below: Gaillardia grandiflora *Dazzler is a good border plant but not reliably hardy in wet or cold localities*

Anchusa Rather a short-lived perennial and best, perhaps, treated as a biennial, but not to be confused with the annual varieties. The perennials have bristly leaves and tall spikes of flowers which reach a height of 25–120cm (9 in–4 ft), according to variety. The flowers are a wonderful blue colour and open from mid summer (June) onwards.

Anthemis Somewhat spreading plant up to 60cm (2ft) in height, covered from mid summer (June) onwards with quite sizeable yellow daisies or, in the case of *A. sancti-johannis*, orange ones. They are very useful plants for cut flowers as well as for giving a long display in the garden.

Aquilegia (columbine) Splendid decoration for mid summer (June) when the plant opens its long trumpet-shaped flowers of many colours. It grows 30–90cm (1–3 ft) high.

Aubrietia This delightful creeping plant, about 10cm (4 in) high, is a mass of mauve, pink or purple from mid spring

*Above left: summer-flowering
lupins, easy to grow in moderately
good soil*
Above right: Echinops ritro,
*useful in herbaceous borders or
in a wild garden*
Below: Helleborus niger *benefits from a
top dressing of compost after flowering*

until early summer (late March to May).
The earlier it can be sown, the larger the
plants will be.

Bellis The old-fashioned pink and red
double daisy may have been around a
long time, but that is because it is such an
excellent plant and so easy to raise. It
grows up to 15cm (6 in) high and flowers
from late spring (April) onwards.

Delphinium A main stand-by of the
border, with its spires of blue, mauve,
purple or white flowers. Unfortunately
slugs find the plant irresistible, so take
precautions by scattering slug pellets. It
grows up to 1·5m (5 ft) and flowers from
mid summer (June) onwards.

Dianthus This group includes pinks and
carnations and they all grow readily from
seed. However, you may find many of
them produce single flowers only (instead
of doubles), so it is as well to let them
flower in the drills the first year and then
throw out the unsatisfactory ones. There

Above, top: Kniphofia uvaria *Royal Standard*
Above: Dianthus allwoodii *Doris, a hybrid created by crossing pinks with carnations*
Above right: Linum narbonense *Heavenly Blue likes well-drained soil and full sun*

are also some dwarf pinks such as *Dianthus allwoodii, D. deltoides, D. gratianopolitanus* (the Cheddar pink) and *D. plumarius* that come true from seed: that is, they flower as expected and do not revert to their original single-flowered form. The colour range is generally white, pink or red and the height 10–30cm (4–12 in). They flower from early to late summer (May to July).

Echinops (globe thistle) Grows up to 1·2m (4 ft) with heads of blue globular flowers in late summer and early autumn (July and August).

Eryngium (sea holly) Useful plants with heads of teazle-like blue flowers, but they may take an extra season before they flower. Grow up to 60cm (24 in).

Euphorbia (spurges) Produce green and golden flowers in mid summer (June) as well as having interesting leaves. They grow about 25–90cm (9–36 in) tall and about the same across.

Gaillardia, helenium and rudbeckia The perennial varieties are all useful. North American daisies with a mixture of flower colours in late summer (July) onwards. Height up to 90cm (3 ft).

Hemerocallis (day lily) Grows very rapidly from seed, though most varieties will need an extra season before they flower prolifically. Grows 30–90cm (1–3 ft) with flowers in shades of pink, red, purple or yellow.

Kniphofia (red-hot poker) Usually flowers the year after sowing, though some may take a year longer. It is a very effective plant with a long flowering season from late summer to late autumn (July to October). The tall spires of flowers are normally shades of red or yellow, reaching up to 1·2m (4 ft). It is often listed in catalogues as 'tritoma'.

Liatris Throws up spikes of rose-purple flowers about 30cm (12 in) long, which, rather unusually, open from the top downwards in late summer (July). Grows up to 90cm (3 ft).

Linum (flax) Produces myriads of large yellow or blue flowers on very thin stems, so that they seem to float in the air. They open from mid summer to late autumn (June to October). Reaches between 30–90cm (1–3 ft) in height.

Scabiosa Rather slow from seed, but produces heads of purple flowers from mid summer to late autumn (June to October). Grows 60–90cm (2–3 ft) in height.

Sidalcea Enchanting plant like a miniature hollyhock, with mallow-like flowers of pink or red produced in late summer and early autumn (July and August). Grows up to 1·2m (4 ft).

Veronica Has spikes of brilliant blue flowers from mid summer to early autumn (June to August). Can grow up to 60cm (2 ft) high.

Some Late Bulbs in the Garden

Mid summer is the time to think about growing a few late-flowering plants that will provide welcome splashes of colour in the bulb area of your mixed borders in the latter part of summer and also during the autumn.

You can make your choice from a range of bulbs that includes amaryllis and tiger flower, hardy nerine and acidanthera – and don't forget that there are even species of the popular crocus that will flower in the autumn.

Some bulbs seem to do much better when planted in mid summer (June) than when grown earlier in the year. Here we give a full description of each, and provide detailed instructions about planting times and distances, and cultivation.

Acidanthera

First among these, *Acidanthera bicolor murielae*, you may well find offered as either *A. bicolor* or *A. murielae*. There will be no doubt concerning the 'acidanthera' part, although botanists have now decided that the differences between acidanthera and gladioli are not great enough

Tiger flower

to warrant making a fresh genus, and that the correct name should now be *Gladiolus bicolor* (though the plant is not like the generally-recognized gladioli).

Whatever its name, it produces a very handsome and striking flower, with a spike of large trumpet-shaped blossoms, each with a long tube and expanding at the ends to as much as 6cm (2½ in) across. The flowers are white with a brilliant purple blotch at the mouth and they exhale an intoxicating perfume. They open in early and mid autumn (August and September). The leaves are like those of gladioli. There is also *Acidanthera tubergenii*, very similar, but with a

maroon red blotched centre, that flowers a little earlier.

Planting The only real secret in growing them successfully is to wait until the soil has warmed up before you plant the corms. If you plant them too early (which is easily done since the corms look so much like the ordinary gladioli corms that you may well feel they need the same treatment) you could easily find that they just sit in the soil and rot off before they start growing. But if you wait until mid summer (June), or slightly later where there have been frosts in early summer (May), they start to grow immediately, and get away without any checks.

Their habit is like that of the ordinary tall gladioli; they grow to a height of 60–90cm (2–3 ft), and the corms are best

Nerine

Acidanthera

397

planted about 20cm (8 in) apart, with the tops of the corms approximately 8cm (3 in) below the surface of the soil, provided that it is well-drained. These are best grown in full sun, but they may well succeed in lightly-dappled shade. While they are making their first growth they should not be allowed to dry out for any length of time, but it is the roots that need water, so do not worry if the surface of the soil looks dry, so long as it is still moist below. In late autumn (beginning of October) they should be lifted and treated in the same way as gladioli or else hung up to dry, cleaned off, and stored in a dark frost-proof place.

Tiger flower

Tigridia pavonia (or *ferraria*), known as tiger flower, is not that tall, being from 25–30cm (9–12 in) in height, but it bears wide-open flowers up to 10cm (4 in) across, that are coloured in the most brilliant shades of red, pink, orange and yellow, with the centre of the flower speckled with dots in contrasting colours. Although the flowers rival the most

Amaryllis

gorgeous tropical orchids in their shape and colours, they only last for a single day. Since each flower spike will produce from four to six flowers, this is not as serious as it sounds; in fact, a clump will show attractive flowers for a month or more, therefore the display could not be described as short-lived. They are not expensive, even though spectacular, as they come readily from seed, often flowering the same year as sown, making it simple to increase your stock; more-over, the bulbs will produce offsets.

Planting The bulbs should be planted 15cm (6 in) apart, with the tips 5–8cm (2–3 in) below the surface of the soil. They will flower from early autumn (August) to late autumn (end of September).

It is probably well worth your while to save some seed and raise further plants. You sow the seed in a pot in spring, either in J.I. No 1, or in a soilless growing compost. If you can start the seed in early spring (February), either on a warm windowsill or in a greenhouse, you may well have a few flowers in the autumn and you will in any case have plenty of bulbs for next year.

As you will be leaving the plants in the pot for the whole growing season, you must take great care to sow the seeds thinly, if possible 2–3cm (1 in) apart, so you will only want 12 seeds or so to a 13cm (5 in) pot. If you put in any more, the seedlings will be too crowded and the bulbs won't develop adequately.

Once flowering is over, treat the bulbs like gladioli; lift them in late autumn (October), dry them off and store them somewhere dark and frost-free. You can leave your seedling bulbs in their pots if you so wish, but it may be more convenient to store them in the same way. In this instance, stop giving the bulbs water in late autumn (October) and let them dry off in the pots. This sometimes takes a surprisingly long time with young plants and you may still have green left in the leaves in early winter (November).

Hardy nerine

One of the real joys of the autumn is the hardy nerine, *N. bowdenii*, that produces its clusters of shocking pink, spidery flowers in mid and early winter (September and November). Usually nerines produce their flowers before their leaves, but some plants seem to be practically evergreen. Even so, the best time to move them is in late summer (July), and this is also the best time to buy them in. They are rather expensive for some reason, but they produce offshoots very freely, so it is not long before you can have a good clump from just a few bulbs. Later in the

season, if they have not already done so, they produce a number of slightly floppy, strap-shaped, bright green leaves.

Planting The bulbs are best placed at least 30cm (12 in) apart, with the tip of the bulb only just below the surface. As most nerines are frost-tender, they are usually best placed against walls facing south or west, but this is not completely necessary if the garden is a warm one.

Nerines do not like to be disturbed so, once planted, it is as well to leave them until the clumps become too congested, when they can be lifted and split up. Otherwise they are generally quite trouble-free. If seed is set (and this does not happen every year), it can be sown at once and takes about three years to reach bulbs of flowering size.

Crocus

Amaryllis

Another autumn-flowering bulb, that wants planting in late summer (July), is *Amaryllis belladonna* (sometimes cat-alogued as *Hippeastrum equestre*). In temperate climates like Britain, this needs south-facing wall protection and even then can be shy of producing its umbels (clusters) of pale pink, fragrant, lily-like flowers in mid and late autumn (September and October). The strap-like leaves come after the flowers and last until mid summer (June or July). The amaryllis is no trouble to keep alive, but getting it to flower can be difficult. However, if it is grown against a south-facing wall, and the plants are protected from frost by straw or polythene in winter and early spring, lovely flowers should result.

Planting It has large bulbs and it is probably a wise policy just to purchase one to begin with and see how it fares. The top of the bulb should be about 8cm (3 in) below the surface of the ground. If it does well with you, and you plant more, place the bulbs about 30cm (12 in) apart.

Crocus and colchicum

There are a number of autumn-flowering crocus, but two are most commonly grown. These are *Crocus speciosus*, which produces its long, blue-mauve flowers in mid autumn (end of September), and *C. medius*, which has violet flowers in late autumn and early winter (October and November). *C. speciosus* has very handsome flowers, but a light shower of rain may well flatten them. This is not a problem with *C. medius*. There are some colour forms of *C. speciosus*, including a pale blue and a handsome white, and in some gardens you may well find self-sown seedlings coming up. *C. medius* never sets seed, but produces great clumps of corms, so to increase, just lift and divide them. There are many other attractive species and good mixtures can be easily bought.

Colchicum (meadow saffron), has flowers that look just like a large pink, purple or rosy-purple crocus, but the following year they produce enormous leaves that are rather unsightly, so the best place for them is probably the front of the shrubbery. There are quite a few to choose from, the cheapest being the British *C. autumnale*, but the most handsome is *C. speciosum*. These usually flower in mid autumn (September), although *C. autumnale* can be out by the early autumn (end of August).

Planting You also want to plant autumn crocus and colchicum in late summer (July). Grab them as soon as they appear in the shops or the moment you get your bulb catalogue. The crocus are quite cheap, as they increase fairly readily, but the colchicum, which have very large corms, are normally somewhat more expensive. They do produce side corms, but not very freely, and they take years to reach flowering size from seed.

Colchicum corms should be put 25cm (9 in) apart in the late summer (July) and the top of the corm should be 10cm (4 in) below the surface of the soil. The autumn crocus should be 10–15cm (4–6 in) apart and the tops of the corms should be 5–8cm (2–3 in) below the surface. The crocus need full sun, but the colchicum have no objection to dappled shade. Once planted, both may be left in position for years, although you can split clumps.

Colchicum speciosum *(meadow saffron) adds a touch of colour to the autumn garden*

GENERAL WORK
Mid summer (June)

Spring-flowering bulbs that have been lifted for drying and storing until replanting time in the autumn should now have the old soil and dried leaves removed. The cleaned bulbs are then stored in boxes in an airy, dark place. Any bulbs that are soft or diseased should be burnt.

All tulips, except the species, should be lifted and placed in a trench in a spare part of the garden where they can ripen and remain until replanted in the autumn.

Hardy annual plants that were sown *in situ* should be thinned now. Thin tall-growing plants to 30cm (12 in) and shorter ones to 15–25cm (6–9 in).

Prune early-flowering clematis species by removing shoots that have finished flowering. Well-established plants with a mass of growth are best cut back as necessary to keep them within bounds.

The lawn will benefit from an application of a proprietary lawn fertilizer applied now according to the manufacturer's instructions. Be sure to apply it evenly.

Keep an eye on all plants for attacks by pests and disease; take remedial action with pesticides at the first sign of trouble.

Above: half-hardy Tigridia pavonia (tiger flower), notable for its brilliant-coloured flowers; right: sweet-smelling Acidanthera bicolor murielae; below: Amaryllis belladonna will need the protection of a south-facing wall against cooler climates

Above: Crocus speciosus, *one of a number of crocus that will flower in the autumn. Unfortunately, its handsome flowers can be spoiled by a light shower of rain*
Far left: Colchicum autumnale *(meadow saffron) will grow in dappled shade, unlike the crocus, which needs full sun*
Left: hardy Nerine bowdenii *should be planted against a wall facing south or west unless it is in a warm environment*

PART 4

GARDEN CARE

WAYS AND MEANS
Basic Tools

Forks and spades have either a D- or T-shape handle. Many gardeners claim that a D handle allows for better gripping. Try them out in the shop before you buy.

Forks are usually four-pronged and are useful for winter digging, especially on heavy soils.

Spades vary in blade width, from 16–19cm (6–8 in), and blade length, from 26–29cm (10–12 in). You'll find smaller sizes easier to use on heavier soils because less weight is lifted with each spade-load. Lighter, smaller forks and spades are made for women.

A **Dutch hoe** takes the backache out of weeding, and saves time.

When making seed drills you will find a **draw hoe** invaluable. A hand version, known as an **onion hoe**, has a narrower blade and is ideal for cultivating small patches, raised beds, and plants in pots and tubs.

No gardener can do without a **hand fork** and **trowel**. The forks have long and short blades of varying widths; the long, thin ones are excellent for prizing out long-rooted perennial weeds.

You will need a **rake** for breaking down clods to a workable tilth. They range between 30–40cm (12–16 in) wide; when buying ensure that the metal rake is well fixed to the handle.

Wooden ones are wider and are recommended only for very large gardens.

Stainless steel tools cost about twice as much as others, but they are a worthwhile investment. They last much longer, are quick to clean and don't rust. They also slip easily into soil. The handles are made of polypropylene or wood, the former being much lighter.

Pruning can be done with a **pruning knife** or **secateurs**. Well-versed gardeners recommend a sharp knife for most jobs, but many people prefer to use secateurs for trees, shrubs and roses.

The knives must be made of well-hardened steel; cheap ones or pen knives will tear at plant stems and invite infection.

There are two types of secateurs: parrot-billed (scissors action), and anvil (the single blade cuts against a metal block). They should be well-made with sharp blades; blunt ones will only crush plant tissue and frustrate the pruner.

You will need a **reel** and **line** and a **measuring rod** or **tape** in the vegetable garden and for marking out borders.

Wooden or **plastic labels** are best for marking seed-sowings.

Use **gardening gloves** for heavy work and pruning roses.

Your tool shed will not be complete without a **watering can**. Get a 7–9 litre (1½–2 gallon) size with a rose. It is advisable to have a second can for weedkillers.

A **hose** saves time when watering plants. Invest in a frost-proof one. A **hose reel** will also cut watering time and save wear and tear on the hose.

A **bucket** will serve to carry odds and ends until you acquire a **wheelbarrow**. When you choose a wheelbarrow don't forget to consider its weight when filled and its size in relation to your garden paths.

For hedges, lawns and mixed borders you will require a good pair of **shears**. These and other lawn equipment are described on the facing page.

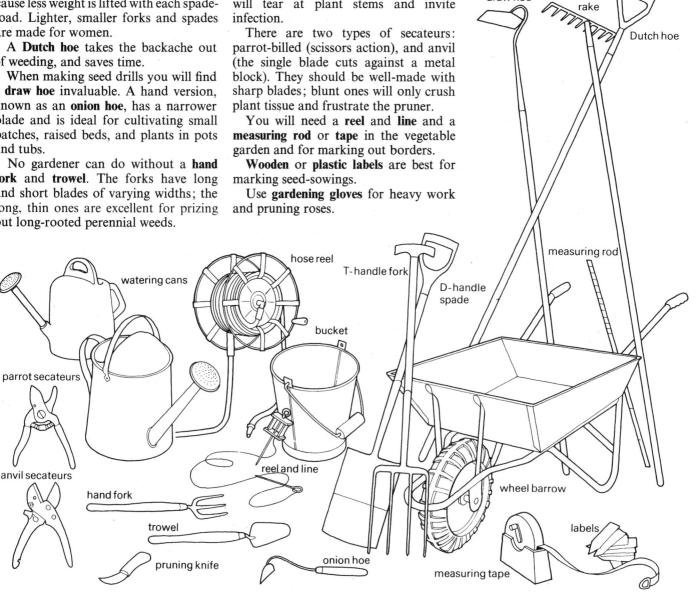

draw hoe | rake | Dutch hoe | measuring rod | hose reel | watering cans | T-handle fork | D-handle spade | bucket | parrot secateurs | anvil secateurs | hand fork | trowel | pruning knife | reel and line | onion hoe | wheel barrow | measuring tape | labels

Lawn equipment

All but the smallest lawns need to be cut with a mower, but before you decide which type to buy compare the various models and list your requirements (this also applies when buying other lawn care equipment). Certain mowers work better on short grass and edges, others on long grass, and all grass boxes are not equally efficient. Choose a lightweight model with adjustable handles if you have steps to negotiate or storage problems.

Hand lawn-mowers

Although it can be tiring to hand mow a large lawn, it is certainly very economical to use a hand machine for small and medium-sized ones. They are also considered to give a better finish than power-operated machines.

Nowadays, due to skilful engineering, cylinder hand mowers are very easy to push and operate. They come in two types: roller and sidewheel and each has its advantages.

Roller types have a small roller in front of the cylinder and a large one behind. The two rollers help to give lawns the striped effect for which many people aim. They also make it easy to cut edges and narrow strips of grass as they simply overhang where necessary. However, these roller types do not operate well if the grass is more than 5cm (2 in) long.

Power lawn-mowers

Power lawn-mowers are precision instruments and often have to stand up to years of rough usage, so you should always buy the best you can afford.

Mains-powered electric mowers are cheap to run and noiseless; but mains-operated types are not suited to large lawns or rough ground. Petrol-driven mowers give more power but can be difficult to start, and require a regular maintenance programme. Apart from the choice between electric and petrol power, the mower may cut by the cylinder or rotary method; the former type cut with a scissor-like action, the latter by beheading the upstanding grass. Cylinder types are good for fine lawns, but not so efficient for grass longer than 5 to 8cm (2 to 3 in) high. The rotary type deal better with long grass and are easier to handle though they do not give a striped lawn effect.

Sidewheel mowers have only the small roller in front of the cutting cylinder and are better for cutting long grass, but they require a balancing act to cut lawn edges, and on soft ground the two side wheels can leave track marks.

Roller mowers cost about twice as much as the sidewheel types and always have the grass box attachment in front. Grass boxes may be fitted to the front or rear of sidewheel models, according to the make. They are usually more efficient when the box is fitted in front of the cutting cylinder.

With cylinder mowers the grass is cut between the cylinder blade and a fixed blade. The effective cutting width, known as the cylinder length, is usually 25 or 30cm (10 or 12 in), although one sidewheel model is available with a 40cm (16 in) cylinder.

The cutting height adjustment and ease of altering it varies according to the model, so compare these facilities before buying. Both power and hand-driven cylinder mowers are available, but rotary ones are always petrol-driven or electrically operated.

Shears for cutting

The first item for your list is a good pair of shears. There are long-handled and short-handled, edging and cutting shears. Blade sizes vary from 15–25cm (6–10 in); handles can be wooden, metal or plastic, and some models are available with rubber buffers to absorb jarring and reduce fatigue when cutting.

The traditional short-handled shears are invaluable for cutting long or short grass. To avoid having to bend, you can get the same blades attached to long handles. There are two basic models in this range, one for edging and the other for general cutting. You can also buy spring-loaded hand shears which allow for one-handed operation; one type comes with an orbital handle so that it can be adjusted to cut at any angle between horizontal and vertical.

The lawn edge trimmer, a modification of edging shears, has spring-loaded blades and you push it along to cut overhanging grass. It has a broad, non-slip rubber roller that guarantees easy guiding and balancing, even on undulating ground.

Brushing and raking

All lawns require brushing and raking to keep them looking well-groomed and pleasant to sit on. A besom, or birch broom, is ideal for sweeping off leaves, but a good stiff broom is required for getting rid of wormcasts.

Steel, spring-tined lawn rakes are essential for removing debris and for scarifying the lawn surface. You can get fixed, or adjustable, tined models, the latter being preferable as they can be used for any job from moss-collecting to leaf-raking.

There is also a lawn comb – a cross between a lawn rake and a garden rake, but it has no particular advantage over other rakes. Wooden lawn rakes are prone to breaking and so are not recommended. The traditional garden rake is best for spreading top dressing on lawns.

Rolling the lawn

It is worth borrowing or hiring a roller each spring to put a new face on your lawn. Winter frosts often lift the turf and rolling will consolidate the surface. It need only be done in spring. It is important to sweep off all wormcasts and debris beforehand and to roll only when the surface is dry and the soil below is damp. Don't roll when the grass is thin or wet and never use a roller weighing over 2 cwt. Bumps should be levelled out properly because rolling will not squash them down.

Tools for aerating

For this you need only use a garden fork. Push it in 7–10cm (3–4 in) deep, at 7–10cm intervals. Easier to use is a fork-like tool fitted with hollow, or solid, tines (sometimes called mechanical spikes), and it gives better results. Wedge-shaped blades can also be attached and are good for compacted areas as they prune the roots and so encourage stronger root growth. For larger areas use an aerator with spiked wheels and interchangeable tines.

Feeding and weeding

Fertilizer-spreaders ensure an even distribution of lawn feeds and lawn sands. Fertilizers and 'feed and weed' mixes come in several forms and should be applied with the spreader in strict accordance with the manufacturers' instructions.

A certain number of weeds eventually die as a result of constant mowing but a few stubborn types will remain and must be dealt with by other methods. Apply spot weedkillers from a small bottle with a squeezy-type top, or dig out stubborn weeds with a hand fork, or a long, narrow trowel.

Tidying up the edges

Finally, to ensure that your lawn never encroaches on the flower borders you should edge-up with a good half-moon edging iron at least twice a year.

Weeds and weed control

There are two basic types of weeds – perennial and annual: the former are far harder to eliminate.

PERENNIAL WEEDS

Most perennial weeds are quick-growing and tenacious, often re-growing from roots or rootstocks. They are, therefore, very difficult to get rid of. Herbaceous types, such as couch grass, bindweed (convolvulus and calystegia species) and ground elder are often notoriously deep-rooted. They store food in their fleshy roots, rhizomes, stolons, tubers or bulbs. It is easy to remove the visible vegetation but difficult to eradicate the roots. With woody plants, such as brambles and ivy, it is harder to get rid of the growth above ground, but comparatively easy to eradicate the roots, which must be burnt.

Manual weeding

Good hand-weeding is still one of the best ways to rid yourself of perennial weeds. Some well-timed work with a trowel will save you much time and trouble later on – providing you don't leave any of the roots in the soil.

If working near decorative or vegetable plants where you don't want to use chemical weedkillers, then manual weeding becomes a necessity. You may need to use a fork, trowel, knife or even a mattock (like a pickaxe). Be careful that you don't just carve them up; this merely helps to propagate them and makes more work in the future. Dig up the weeds, complete with roots, and then burn them or put them in the garbage bin.

When cultivating fresh ground it is essential to remove all the roots and underground storage systems; although hard work, it pays to lift them out by hand. Don't use a rotary cultivator on couch grass or dock-infested land as it will only chop up the weeds and encourage regrowth. Hoeing can have the same effect on a smaller scale unless you take care to remove the root, not just chop off leaves.

Weedkillers

Weedkillers are categorized according to their mode of action, so that you can buy whichever is most suited to your needs.

Total In an area devoid of decorative or culinary plants you can use a 'total' weedkiller, such as aminotriazole, to 'sweep the board'. A total weedkiller will kill all plants with which it comes into contact. You must take great care not to let it drift onto other plants or onto your neighbour's property. There have been many skirmishes over the garden wall as a result of misapplied weedkillers. After using it, remove and burn the debris and plant nothing in the ground for two to three months. If treatment with a total weedkiller is followed by a dose of a residual weedkiller (such as simazine) you will have a weed-free site for several months.

Another total weedkiller is sodium chlorate. It has to be used with great care as it spreads in the soil and can kill plants some distance away from the spot it was applied. Another danger is that, mixed with many other substances, it may be spontaneously inflammable, and it is therefore dangerous to store. It has a residual effect for up to a year.

Total and residual weedkillers are best for clearing paths and driveways.

Above right: the seed clock of the dandelion (Taraxacum officinale), ready to spread a new generation over the garden. Right: daisy (Bellis perrenis)

Residual or pre-emergent These will not kill established weeds but they help to prevent the germination of most weeds for up to three months. There are various degrees of persistence.

Simazine has a long persistence, but it can be harmful to some shrubs (such as deutzia). Propachlor lasts for shorter periods but is less toxic and so is useful for herbaceous borders and shrubberies.

This type remains in a narrow band of the topsoil, so that any weed seeds germinating in this zone take up the chemical and die. It is possible to apply residual weedkiller where bulbs are planted, because their roots are located below the weedkiller band, and they grow quickly through it without suffering any damage. Plants such as runner beans, sweet peas, daffodils and hyacinths will all grow through the weedkiller layer after it has become inactive.

Selective Some weedkillers are termed 'selective' as they kill dicotyledons (broad-leaved plants), but will not damage many monocotyledons – such as grasses. Selective ones like 2,4-D, MCPA, 2,4,5-T or fenoprop (hormone types) kill by causing the plant to overgrow its food reserves so that it literally grows itself to death. Use this kind with great care as the slightest drift will damage crops; tomatoes are especially sensitive to them.

Non-selective The well-known paraquat and diquat weedkillers will only kill perennial weeds while they are still at seedling stage. After a few weeks they become immune and these preparations merely burn off their foliage and allow the roots to re-grow. They are de-activated immediately they meet the soil and are therefore safe to use provided they do not drift. But they must be kept away from children and animals: under no circumstances store them in old lemonade or other misleading bottles.

Methods of application

Always read the maker's instructions on the package and follow them closely; they have been based on years of research. Our recommendations give the chemical name, so when buying proprietary brands check the package label and see that it contains the correct constituents for your purpose. Keep a separate watering can for use with chemical weedkillers, and use a rose fitting or dribble-bar attachment for controlled application.

Specific treatments

Some perennial weeds are particularly stubborn and require special treatment.

Oxalis Remove these plants, which defy all chemical killers, with a sharp knife. Be sure to get up all roots and little bulbs.

Couch grass and perennial oat-grass These persistent grasses, with rhizomes, put up a fight against eradication. The only effective control is dalapon. If they are found in flower or vegetable beds 'spot' apply several doses of dalapon and then dig out the remains.

'Spot treatment' involves applying the weedkiller to the weeds only. It is done most easily by using a bottle with a pourer top or a squeezy-type container.

Docks Repeated action with dichlobenil (not easily obtainable), or spot treatment with 2,4-D, MCPA, fenoprop or mecoprop will keep the plants down. They are difficult to control because the roots, if broken on being dug out, will grow again.

Perennial nettle, bindweed, ground elder and blackberry These tend to grow near hedges or in shrubberies, and once established are likely to remain permanent residents. Apply 2,4,5-T or brushwood killer (usually a mixture of 2,4-D and 2,4,5-T) but avoid spraying onto other plants.

A good way to minimize drift is to make up a solution of this weedkiller in a container and dip the tips of the weeds in it. This will then be taken up through the plant by the sap stream – and kill it. You may need to make several applications over a few days for them to be effective. This method also works on many wild, shrubby plants such as dog rose and ivy (*Hedera helix*).

Thistles These are particularly obstinate weeds that may need pulling out by hand.

Above: bindweed (Convolvulus arvensis)

Above: couch grass (Agropyron repens)
Below: dock (Rumex obtusifolius)

Below: annual nettle (Urtica urens)
Bottom: creeping thistle (Cirsium arvense)

PERENNIAL WEEDS Guide to treatment

PLACE	TYPICAL WEEDS	TREATMENT	OTHER ADVICE
NEW LAND & WASTE LAND	Bindweed; blackberry; couch grass; docks; ivy; ground elder; nettles; oat-grass; thistles	Apply total weedkiller, e.g. aminotriazole; clear away debris and dig carefully, removing all roots, tubers and bulbous roots. Throw away or burn these.	Take care not to let the spray drift on to your own plants or over to other gardens.
LAWNS	Creeping buttercup; daisy; dandelion; plantain; speedwell	Mowing and raking; apply 2,4-D and mecoprop mixtures (ioxynil is needed for speedwell). Lever out old grass and weeds with a sharp trowel or knife.	Do not use 2,4-D or mecoprop on new lawns until the grass is at least six months old; use ioxynil for weeds on young lawns.
	Moss	Lawn sand or mercuric chloride.	Take care not to let children or animals near either of these dangerous poisons.
SHRUBBERIES & MIXED BORDERS	Bindweed; couch grass; docks; ground elder; thistles	Dig out all roots; apply a residual weedkiller to prevent fresh germination; dichlobenil kills many perennial weeds.	Check all instructions to make sure that your borders do not contain plants that are sensitive to some of the residual weedkillers.
ROSE BEDS	Couch grass; many germinating perennials	Treat couch grass with dalapon and remove by hand; simazine will prevent germination and dichlobenil completely kills many of these perennial weeds.	Take care not to let weedkiller get on to roses, especially if in leaf; apply simazine in early spring to last through most of the plant-growing season.
HERBACEOUS & FLOWER BORDERS	Many germinating and established weeds	Propachlor is a good residual weedkiller to check further germination, provided all established weeds are removed by hand or fork first.	Ensure that weather is warm and soil moist before applying propachlor.
FRUIT	Established and germinating perennials (especially couch grass and creeping buttercup in strawberries)	Use diquat or paraquat between rows to kill new weeds; dalapon for couch grass; dichlobenil for established weeds; simazine residual weedkiller around trees, bush and cane fruit.	Dig out weeds from strawberry plants as they are very sensitive to weedkillers, especially when in full leaf.
VEGETABLES	All weeds	Don't let weeds get too large before treatment. Hoe frequently to remove germinating weeds; use propachlor for some crops, but check instructions first to ensure safety of growing plants.	Hoeing is best done on warm days as weeds die from exposure and will not re-root in soil tilth; pull out any large weeds after a shower of rain.
PATHS & DRIVES	All weeds	Apply a total weedkiller, such as aminotriazole, sodium chlorate or simazine.	Avoid contact with cultivated plants in the vicinity.

Above: sow-thistle (Sonchus asper)
Below: chickweed (Stellaria media)

Wait till the ground is slightly moist, and be sure to wear gloves. Repeated doses of 2,4,5-T will help to weaken them.

Lawn weeds

The rosette-forming types (such as daisy, dandelion and plantain) are the most successful on lawns as they tend to escape the lawn-mower blades. To spot-apply weedkillers to lawn weeds use a small dropper bottle.

Dandelion, daisy, creeping buttercup, ribwort and plantain Proprietary lawn weedkillers containing MCPA and 2,4-D with mecoprop or fenoprop usually bring quick death, but must be applied in strict accordance with the makers' instructions.
Speedwell Mecoprop/ioxynil mixture is required to check this weed.
Yarrow Use repeated doses of mecoprop. Feeding the lawn with sulphate of ammonia should hasten the expiry date.
Couch grass and perennial oat-grass Two very difficult grasses to remove from lawns. Close and frequent mowing will go a long way towards finishing them off; otherwise you must dig them out with a knife. Effective weedkillers cannot be used as they would kill the lawn as well.

ANNUAL WEEDS

Annual weeds, by definition, mature, flower, seed and die within one year. 'Seed' is the operative word here, because this is the method by which they reproduce and infest the garden. It is also the key to their control; if you can remove the

seed before it reaches the soil you can stop the next generation of weeds before it starts.

Many species of annual weeds grow quickly and succeed in completing several generations each year. The seeds seem to be able to germinate at any time of the year, even the middle of winter. So never assume that weeds are 'out of season'; although they may grow more slowly in winter they are always lurking.

Some of the most common annual weeds that you are likely to encounter are: chickweed, speedwell, groundsel, knotgrass, shepherd's purse, annual nettle, charlock, sow-thistle, scarlet pimpernel, goose-grass and wild radish.

Weeding by hoeing

One of the most common, and time-honoured, ways of controlling annual weeds is by hoeing. The secret of successful hoeing is to choose a day that is dry, sunny and, preferably, has a steady breeze. All these factors help to dry out the weed seedlings on the soil surface and prevent them re-rooting.

Persicaria (Polygonum lapathifolium)

Don't just decapitate the weeds when you hoe; make sure the roots are removed.

In a way, you make extra work for yourself by hoeing because you constantly bring more weed seeds to the surface where they germinate. Seeds can remain viable in the ground for years, waiting until they come near to the surface before starting to grow. Some seeds are very sensitive to the amount of daylight available and can only spring into life when they are in the topmost layer of soil. Regular hoeing, however, will keep weed seedlings under control.

Controlling with weedkillers

Most annual weeds are more easily controlled by weedkillers than their perennial counterparts. A whole range of annuals succumb to applications of dichlobenil or propachlor. Both these weedkillers are residual, but last only a few months. Diquat and paraquat are

Red deadnettle (Lamium purpureum) also known as bad man's posies

very useful for killing germinating weed seedlings. You can spot apply these anywhere provided you take care not to let them drift onto other plants.

Unlike many perennials, annual weeds germinate within the narrow soil-surface band to which the weedkillers have been applied; therefore they die almost as soon as they start growing. So, on the whole, these weedkillers tend to be more effective against annuals. Always remember where these chemicals have been put down and make sure that no horticultural activities 'break the band' as this will allow the weeds to come through unscathed.

Special treatments

There are a few stubborn annual weeds that do not succumb easily to dichlobenil and propachlor. These usually need an application of another type (or mixture) of weedkiller.

Rayless mayweed (pineapple weed) Treat with mecoprop or mecoprop with ioxynil.
Common persicaria Several doses of propachlor or dichlobenil may be required before you eventually get rid of it.
Red deadnettle Repeated applications of mecoprop will be needed.

Annual lawn weeds

As well as the tough perennial lawn weeds, you are also likely to encounter some troublesome annual ones. One good preventive measure is to use a grass-collecting box on the lawn-mower. This will stop many weeds falling back on the lawn and propagating themselves.

Chickweed Best controlled with mecoprop which is often applied with 2,4-D as a general lawn weedkiller.
Lesser yellow trefoil Several applications of mecoprop may be needed; or use fenoprop.
Lesser common trefoil This weed often flourishes where grass is short of nitrogen. Feed the lawn with sulphate of ammonia in spring to lessen the chance of this weed getting established.

Pests: Prevention and control

The word 'pest' conjures up, for many people, a vision of hordes of greenfly on roses or blackfly on broad beans. The vision is quite justified because both are pests and both tend to infest on an epidemic scale. Agriculturists and horticulturists view any organism that interferes with crops as a pest – whether it be a virus or a predatory animal.

This section leaves aside the viruses (and fungi and bacteria) and the animals like rabbits and moles and concentrates on insects and insect-like pests, including also slugs and snails (molluscs) and eelworms (nematodes).

Insects are the largest group of creatures on earth. In evolutionary terms they are highly successful, and have proved to be man's fiercest competitors. Historically, insects have caused more deaths to mankind than all wars put together.

Insects will attack most plants, whether they live in the garden, the house or the greenhouse. Like all illnesses and disorders, prevention is better than cure and the best way to reduce your losses is to ensure that your plants are healthy when planted and then well cared for. Many physiological disorders of plants (caused, for instance, by too little water or too much nitrogen fertilizer) pave the way for attack by pests. So as soon as you notice any signs of distress or damage—act promptly.

Knowing what to look for

The pest itself may be almost invisible. Eelworms, for instance, are difficult to see under a microscope. But their size bears no relation to the damage they can do. Even visible pests may not always be sitting in full view. You may have to dig underground and study the roots to determine the cause of the trouble, or wait for night to catch such insidious creatures as slugs.

Pests which attack leaves and flowers are the most easily identified because the damage occurs rapidly and is usually quite recognizable. Two main groups of pests attack leaves: those which have biting mouthparts (for example beetles) and those with sucking mouthparts (such as greenfly). They may hide inside or outside the leaves or, like the notorious leaf-miner, burrow between the middle layers of leaf tissue.

Larger pests (like caterpillars) are usually more noticeable but they may attack and run (or fly) away, in which case you should spray, or lay bait, against the next visit.

Fortunately there are many methods of control at your fingertips, providing you diagnose the enemy correctly and act as swiftly as you can.

Understanding the enemy

Knowing something about the life cycles and habits of pests can help you in anticipating and preventing trouble. For instance a major factor in determining how active they are is temperature; the warmer it becomes the busier they get. And up to 35°C (95°F) they breed faster too. Cold winters greatly decrease the numbers tending to spend the entire season in the garden.

Day length also plays a part in controlling the breeding seasons and migration patterns of many insects. This is why they always become scarce in autumn, even before cold weather arrives. Clear away and burn garden refuse every autumn because it provides ideal shelter for overwintering pests. Many overwinter as eggs which can also be destroyed by the use of insecticides.

Use of insecticides

Most pesticides are sold under trade names, partly because the chemical names and formulae are cumbersome and difficult to remember. You can, however, be sure of getting the right product by reading the contents on the label and checking with the chemical, or proper, name given here. Full chemical names are

Left: aphides attack indoor and outdoor plants. Below left: cabbage-root fly larvae is a danger in the vegetable garden. Bottom left: onion fly, enemy of the onion bulb family. Below: cabbage white butterfly, whose caterpillars cause such damage. Below centre: cabbage white caterpillar eating brassica leaves. Bottom: the ubiquitous slug, menace of all gardens. Bottom right: potted palm showing red spider mite damage

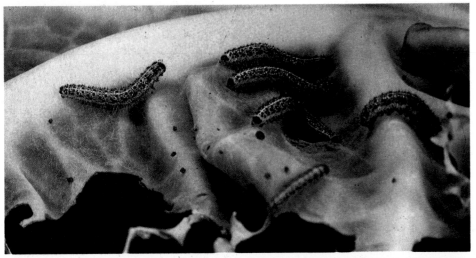

often abbreviated, for instance benzene hexachloride is known as BHC. (It is also sometimes called gamma-BHC.)

Always use protective clothing. Rubber gloves are important and be sure always to wash hands and face thoroughly after using insecticides. Never allow children or animals to be with you when sprays are being applied, and don't let them eat anything that has just been sprayed. Also wash out all spraying equipment after use—but not in the kitchen sink.

In some cases you may be able to use physical methods of combat such as picking caterpillars off plants and burning them. These are always preferable to spraying, because all sprays have some adverse effect on the plant. This is why you must adhere strictly to the manufacturer's recommended rate of application.

How insecticides work

Insecticides kill in two main ways; first as a stomach poison, when the pest either eats it with the leaf or sucks it up with the plant sap. Alternatively, if the pest is sprayed directly, the chemical will poison through the 'skin' or suffocate the pest. The method you choose depends on several factors, such as climate, type of insect and type of plant involved.

Non-systemic ('knock-down') insecticides Many early insecticides killed either by blocking the breathing processes or by poisoning when absorbed through other exterior surfaces. But they did not persist for long and had to be used frequently in order to be effective. However, some are still very useful for certain purposes.

Pyrethrum and derris, for example, are both very effective general insecticides. They are derived from plants and do not persist for long. This means they are safe to use on vegetables—even up to the day before harvesting. Derris, however, is harmful to fish so do not use it near stocked pools.

But DDT, used by gardeners for so many years, has now been withdrawn from the gardening market as other, newer insecticides have proved to be safer and equally (if not more) efficient. Trichlorphon is one good modern substitue for DDT.

Systemic insecticides The systemics are absorbed by the plant and dispersed throughout its entire system; any biting or sucking insect will ingest them while feeding and be killed. These pest-killers remain in the plant for several days (sometimes even weeks) and they act against a wide variety of pests.

But too often spraying can result in the development of pests that are resistant to them. So spray on sighting the enemy rather than 'just in case'.

Dimethoate and formothion are systemic insecticides that control most aphides, red spider mite, scale insect, mealy bug, caterpillars and leaf hoppers. Systemic insecticides are also one of the most successful ways of killing many of the root-feeding insects, such as lettuce root aphid.

PESTS Guide to treatment

PLACE	COMMON PESTS	PLANT AREA	TREATMENT	OTHER ADVICE
GREENHOUSE PLANTS	Aphides Whitefly	Leaves Stems Flowers	Treat as for house plants or fumigate greenhouse with nicotine, dichlorvos or BHC.	Make sure all vents are closed while fumigating. Do not enter until fumes have dispersed.
	Scale insect	Leaves	Wipe off, but if badly infested spray with malathion, nicotine or systemic insecticides.	Scrape insects off where possible.
	Red spider mite	Leaves	Spray malathion, derris or pyrethrum.	Pick off and burn badly-infected leaves.
	Mealy bug	Leaves Stems	Spray with systemic or non-systemic insecticides.	Scrape insects off where possible.
	Leaf hopper	Leaves	Spray with BHC, malathion or nicotine, often available in aerosol or smoke form.	
	Leaf miner	Leaves	Spray with BHC or malathion.	Pick and burn infected leaves.
	Vine weevil	Roots	Remove and destroy grubs found when repotting plants. Drench soil of infected plants with BHC solution.	Incorporate naphthalene or paradichlorbenzene among the crocks when known susceptible plants are repotted.

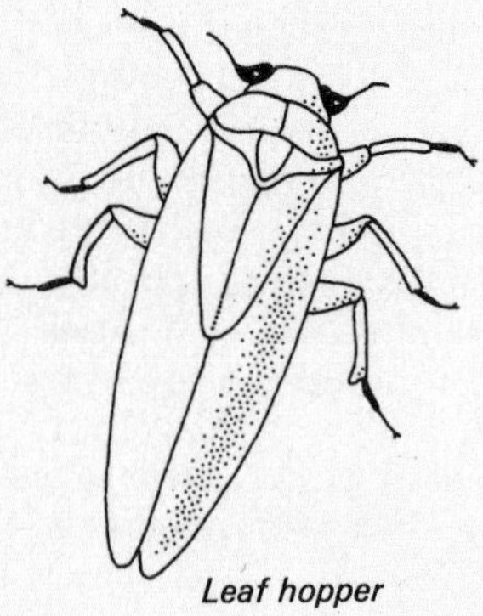

Leaf hopper

PLACE	COMMON PESTS	PLANT AREA	TREATMENT	OTHER ADVICE
HOUSE PLANTS	Aphides Whitefly	Leaves Stems Flowers	Non-systemic sprays: e.g. derris, pyrethrum, are often sufficient. For bad attacks use systemics, e.g. dimethoate.	Check all newly-acquired potted plants and eradicate any pests to prevent them spreading among your existing plants.
	Mealy bug	Leaves Stems	Spray with systemic or non-systemic insecticides, or dab with methylated spirit.	Scrape insects off where possible.
	Scale insect	Leaves	Wipe with a soft cloth dipped in soapy water or methylated spirits, or treat as for aphides and whitefly.	Place your house plants in the greenhouse when you fumigate and do both jobs at once.
	Leaf hopper	Leaves	Spray with BHC, malathion or nicotine (often available in aerosol form).	
	Leaf miner	Leaves	Spray with BHC or malathion.	Pick and burn infected leaves.
	Vine weevil	Roots	See GREENHOUSE PLANTS	

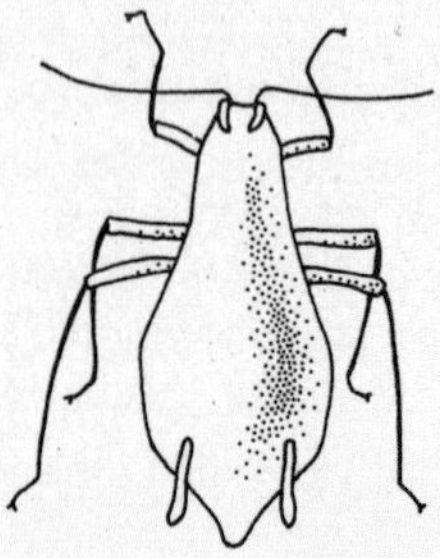

Aphid

PLACE	COMMON PESTS	PLANT AREA	TREATMENT	OTHER ADVICE
FLOWER GARDEN	Aphides Whitefly	Leaves Stems Flowers	Spray with systemic insecticide such as dimethoate or formothion.	Malathion is also effective.
	Scale insect	Leaves Stems	Spray with malathion or systemic insecticide.	Scrape off insects where possible.
	Earwigs	Flowers	Reduce populations by spraying with BHC or trichlorphon prior to flowering.	Place inverted, straw-filled flower pot traps on 1m (3 ft) canes near plants; burn resulting earwig nests.
	Capsid bug	Leaves Stems Flowers	Spray with BHC or malathion as soon as damage appears.	Prompt action is essential.

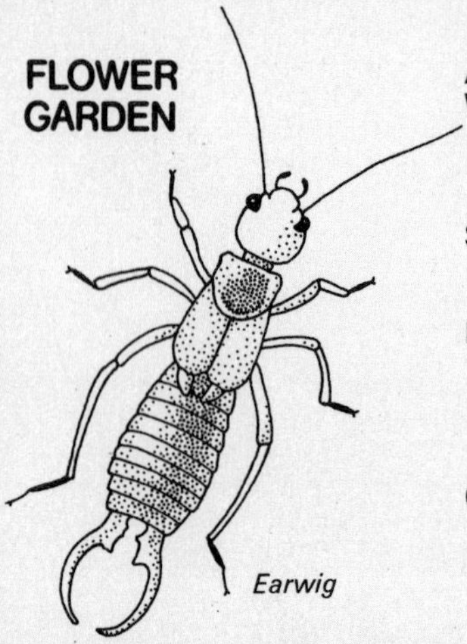

Earwig

PLACE	COMMON PESTS	PLANT AREA	TREATMENT	OTHER ADVICE
VEGETABLE GARDEN 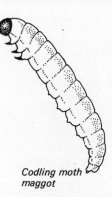 *Thrips*	Caterpillars	Leaves	Spray or dust with BHC, malathion or derris.	Pick caterpillars off where possible.
	Cutworm	Roots Stems	Work BHC dust or bromophos into the soil when planting.	Prevention is better than cure.
	Slugs Snails	Leaves Stems	Spray or apply pellets of metaldehyde or methiocarb.	These pests usually attack at night.
	Pea/bean weevil Grubs Thrips	Leaves Pods Peas	Apply BHC dust or fenitrion.	Apply when first flowers open and again 2 weeks later.
	Flea beetle	Leaves	Apply BHC dust when sowing seeds and at seedling stage.	Keep seedlings covered with dust until true leaves appear.
	Aphides	Leaves Shoots	Spray with systemic insecticides or malathion.	Watch for a reinfestation.
	Whitefly	Leaves	Spray with pyrethrum, dimethoate or BHC.	Malathion is also effective.
	Cabbage-root fly Carrot fly	Roots	Dust or spray BHC.	Keep seedlings covered with dust until true leaves appear.
FRUIT GARDEN *Codling moth maggot*	Caterpillars	Leaves	Spray or dust with BHC, malathion or derris.	Pick caterpillars off where possible.
	Aphides	Leaves Shoots	Spray with a systemic insecticide.	Watch for a reinfestation.
	Woolly aphides	Stems	Spray malathion or a systemic insecticide.	Systemic insecticides can be used, but at least 21 days before harvesting.
	Maggots	Fruits	Spray fenitrothion, BHC or derris.	Spray twice, in mid and late summer, as prevention.
	Gooseberry sawfly	Leaves	Spray thoroughly with derris or malathion.	Attacks usually occur in early summer.
	Capsid bug	Leaves Fruits	Spray with BHC or malathion as soon as damage is noted.	Prompt action is essential.
	Red spider mite	Leaves	Spray malathion, derris or pyrethrum, or a systemic.	Spray systemics 21 days before picking.
FLOWER GARDEN CONTINUED 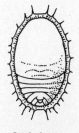 *Scale insect*	Caterpillars	Flowers	Spray with BHC or trichlorphon.	Pick caterpillars off by hand.
	Leaf miner	Leaves	Spray with BHC or malathion or use systemic insecticide.	Pick off and burn badly-infected leaves.
	Frog hopper (Cuckoo spit)	Leaves Stems	Spray with malathion, BHC, derris or pyrethrum.	Can be washed off with spray of soapy water.
	Slugs Snails	Leaves Stems	Spray or apply pellets of metaldehyde or pyrethrum.	These pests are most active at night.
	Thrips	Flowers	Spray pyrethrum.	Prompt action is important.
	Red spider mite	Leaves	Spray malathion, derris or pyrethrum.	Pick off and burn badly-infected leaves.

Fungus diseases: Prevention and control

Fungi, bacteria and viruses are the three main causes of plant disease, and of these the most important to the gardener are the fungi. Unlike insects, they can only live in and with the plant they infect, and they are common in all plants, large or small – from the tiniest seedling affected by 'damping-off' to the tall and sturdy elm tree laid low by Dutch elm disease.

Although it is quite often a simple matter to recognise that a plant is diseased – discoloration, distortion of growth, even a general air of listlessness, are all easily observed symptoms – it is usually much harder to diagnose exactly what is wrong with it. It is important, therefore, to learn to recognize the different kinds of fungal infection, so that the right remedies can be applied where possible and without delay.

Propagation of fungi

Most fungi propagate by spores (which are very similar in kind, although not in appearance, to the seeds of plants), and these can be carried from plant to plant by the wind, rain, soil or plant debris, animals and birds, and other means. Each fungus will produce many spores, and this is one of the reasons why they spread so quickly and potentially dangerously through a bed of plants, a greenhouse, or a whole garden.

Other fungi, and particularly those that attack roots, spread by means of mycelium (a fibrous growth that has much the same function as the roots or stems of plants).

The majority of fungi spread and do most damage in moist, warm conditions. To reduce the likelihood of fungal infection of roots, therefore, it is important to keep the soil well drained; and in the greenhouse adequate ventilation is essential. However, some fungi (of which the powdery mildews are an outstanding example) show a distinct preference for drier conditions.

Fungus infection of seedlings

'Damping off', or seedling blight, is common when seeds are raised under unhygienic conditions. The disease is often due to a complex infection by different species of fungi, some of which are closely related. Pythium species and phytophthora species (sometimes known as watermoulds) thrive under wet conditions, and their spores are present in all soils. This is why it is essential to germinate all seed in sterilized (and therefore fungus-free) soil or compost, and to use clean pots and trays.

On sterilized soil damping-off will rapidly emerge through a batch of newly-emerged seedlings, and it is worthwhile to water with Cheshunt compound before and after germination. If the disease does take hold, watering with Cheshunt compound, captan, thiram or zineb may check it.

Plants that are growing well are less liable to attack, but even sturdy seedlings will still succumb if they are not well-cared for: over-watering and lack of ventilation are the principal cause of infection at this stage. Seedlings that have been too well nourished with excessive nitrogen may show similar symptoms.

Fungal attack of roots

The majority of species of fungus attack the leaves and other aerial parts of the plant, but there are some that spread through the soil.

Bootlace fungus The mycelium grows to look exactly like a black bootlace, but wherever it encounters dead wood it is

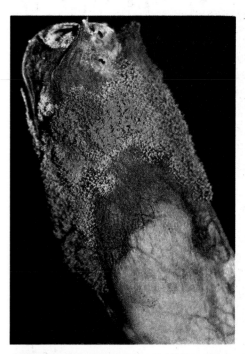

Above right: grey mould (botrytis) attacks many plants, especially in wet weather
Right: damping off (seedling blight) is a fungus infection
Below: bootlace fungus grows from the roots beneath the tree bark

likely to throw up a toadstool, which releases spores into the air. The 'bootlace' grows from the roots beneath the bark of the tree, where it also forms yellowish-white sheets of fungus that have given it the alternative name 'honey fungus'. A tree that is badly affected must be dug up and burnt; and the soil must be sterilized with a mixture of 1 part of formaldehyde to 6 parts of water, applied at a rate of 27 lit per sq m (5 gal per sq yd). Where infection is not too serious, a creosote-like chemical, Armillatox, may be sufficient to control the disease and allow the tree or bush to recover.

Club root Very common and attacks all members of the brassica or cabbage family (and this includes wallflowers). The plants look weak and yellow and the roots are swollen. Liming the soil helps to prevent the disease; so does a crop-rotation system. Calomel dust applied at planting time reduces the likelihood of attack, and dipping the roots in benomyl just before planting has also proved effective.

Crown gall Produces symptoms similar to clubroot, but attacks many different kinds of plant. It is favoured by wet soils: provide adequate drainage, and avoid injury to the roots. Dipping plants in a copper fungicide such as Bordeaux mixture at planting time provides protection.

Brown core Attacks polyanthus and primula roots, and the plants then become weak and sickly. Burn all affected plants and grow no others of the family on that ground for several years.

Above left: conifer gall, a white blight, may affect any conifer tree. Left: club root attacks the brassica family
Below left: roses are susceptible to powdery mildew
Below: downy mildew likes the damp

Violet root rot Affects several plant groups and is easily recognized by the characteristic strands of purple mycelium on the plant roots. Destroy all infected plants and introduce resistant crops. Violet root rot only rarely occurs in land that is in 'good heart' and so attention to drainage and soil fertility is the best means of prevention.

Black root rot Most likely to strike where plants are grown in the same place every year; it also affects pot plants. Drench the soil with captan solution.

Fungal attack of shoots and leaves

Many different fungi attack shoots and leaves, and the following are the most common examples.

Grey mould (botrytis) Prevalent in wet weather, it attacks numerous plants. Remove the infected plants to control spread of the disease, but for really effective control use benomyl, captan, thiram or zineb.

Powdery mildew Found on almost all plants, and there is often a specific species for a particular plant. This is a fungus which favours drier weather for attacks. Plants most commonly infected are roses, gooseberries, apples and Michaelmas daisies. The mildew forms a white powder on the leaves, shoots and flowers. Greenhouse plants also suffer. Cut out infected shoots on trees and shrubs the following autumn, otherwise re-infection can occur. Spray with benomyl, dinocap or thiophanate-methyl. On plants which are not sulphur-shy, sulphur or lime-sulphur sprays may be used. Many varieties of apple are sulphur-shy, for example, so it is important to make sure before using the spray. Generally the container for the mixture lists the plants and varieties for which it is unsuitable.

Downy mildew By contrast with the powdery types, downy mildew thrives in damp, cool conditions. Grey or whitish furry growths appear on leaves and spread very rapidly. Zineb is the best chemical to use.

Potato blight Related to downy mildew, and the treatment is similar. Remove and burn any plants that become very diseased.

White blister Similar to downy mildew, but the spores are liberated from blisters or pustules. The only course is to burn the affected plants, but individual diseased leaves may be removed and burnt if the infection is caught in time.

Silver leaf Affects plums, peaches, cherries and ornamental prunus, turning the leaves silvery. Cut out diseased material and treat all wounds with a protective bituminous paint.

FUNGUS DISEASES OF PLANTS
Non-systemic (knock-down) fungicides

INFECTIONS CONTROLLED	PLANTS COMMONLY INFECTED	CHEMICAL NAME	FORM AVAILABLE
Galls	Azaleas	Bordeaux mixture	Powder
Wilts	Clematis and paeonies		
Peach leaf curl	Many ornamental plants and fruits	Lime-sulphur	Powder or concentrated suspension
Blight	Tomatoes and potatoes		
Cane spot/ spur blight	Raspberries	'Liquid copper'	Concentrated solution
Powdery mildews	Many fruit and ornamental varieties	Sulphur	Powder
Scab	Apples and pears (**Caution**: do not use lime-sulphur or sulphur sprays on sulphur-shy varieties)	Several special formulations of the above are available	
Onion white rot	Onions	Calomel	Powder
Club root	Brassicas and wallflowers		
Moss and turf diseases	Grass/lawns	Other mercury-based mixtures	Mixed with lawn sand
Black spot	Roses	Cheshunt compound	Powder for solution
Leaf spots	Many garden plants	Captan	Wettable powder or dust
Scab	Apples and pears (**Caution**: do not use on fruit to be bottled or used for deep freezing)	Dinocap	Wettable powder dust, liquid or smoke
Soil-borne infections	Many seeds and seedlings		
Grey mould/ downy mildew/ potato blight	Many plants	Thiram	Concentrated solution
Rusts	Many ornamental plants and fruits in the garden	Zineb	Wettable powder
Spur blight	Raspberries	Mancozeb	Wettable powder
		Several formulations and mixtures of the above are available	

Systemic fungicides

INFECTIONS CONTROLLED	PLANTS COMMONLY INFECTED	CHEMICAL NAME	FORM AVAILABLE
Grey mould	Many fruits and vegetables, growing and in storage		
Leaf spots	Many ornamental plants, soft fruit and celery	Benomyl	Wettable powders
Scab	Apples and pears	Thiophanate-methyl	Wettable powders
Powdery mildews	Roses, other ornamentals and fruit		
Black spot	Roses		

Fusarium wilt Often the cause of plants looking sickly, with yellowing leaves which appear to wilt, even in wet weather. This fungus blocks the 'plumbing' system of the plant. The spores lie in the soil for considerable periods; it can be sterilized with formaldehyde, but growing on fresh soil is often the only solution.

Apple scab Common throughout the growing season, attacking ornamental malus species such as crab-apple, pears and culinary apples. It infects leaves, stems and fruits, producing olive-green blotches on the leaves, and brown or black scabs on the fruit. Spray with lime-sulphur when flower buds emerge, but do not use on sulphur-shy varieties (see instructions on the spray container). Benomyl, captan or thiram may be sprayed from bud-burst until late summer (July). Rake up all dead leaves and burn them in the winter to prevent further spread.

Rusts Attack many plants, but hollyhocks are particularly prone. All rusts appear as orange, yellow or brown powdery masses. You can obtain resistant varieties which prevent spores germinating on the leaves. Mancozeb, zineb or maneb fungicides sprayed at fortnightly intervals should cure most rust infections.

Below: apple canker spreads along the bark, killing young shoots, and should be treated without delay
Bottom: the fruiting fungus of silver leaf appears on the bark of affected trees
Below right: rust – a mass of orange, yellow or brown pustules on the leaves
Below, far right: beware apple scab on leaves, stems or fruit in summer

Black spot Attacks roses and is probably one of the most common of fungal diseases. It starts as dark brown spots which grow up to 2cm (1 in) across. Infected leaves fall during mid summer. It also affects stems and will remain on the plant to re-infect the following season. Burn all diseased leaves and stems, and spray with benomyl, captan or zineb at the initial infection stage.

Cane spot and spur blight Affect raspberries and loganberries. Both form purple blotches; spur blight becomes mottled with black, and cane spot as it develops becomes white. Apply a copper fungicide such as Bordeaux mixture at bud-burst and, in the case of cane spot, again when the fruit has set. Thiophanate-methyl or benomyl may be used throughout the blossom period.

Stem cankers Attack many trees and shrubs. The first signs are poor, weak growth and soft patches of bark. These patches later erupt into unsightly reddish-pink pustules that spread along the bark, causing the shoots to die back. There is no chemical control for the disease, and the only solution is to cut off and burn all infected stems at once. Paint the wounds with a protective bituminous paint, such as Arbrex.

Diseases affecting tubers

These diseases can affect the other storage organ type plants as well as tubers.

Basal rot Often occurs on crocuses, narcissi and lilies. It spreads from the base as a brown rot, eventually rotting the whole bulb. It will attack at any time, even when bulbs are in storage. Cut out infected areas, dust with quintozene.

Smoulder and dry rot Attack bulbs, although smoulder is only usual on narcissus. Dry rot has a wider range and can be stopped by dipping healthy bulbs in solutions of benomyl or captan. Smoulder tends to occur in storage and a cool dry storage place helps to prevent it. If you see any signs during the growing season, spray zineb at fortnightly intervals. Other storage rots and some bulb or corm scabs should be treated in a similar manner to dry rot.

White rot and neck rot White rot is very common on spring onions and on main-crop types during the growing season. It persists in the soil and if your crop has been infected grow onions on a new site the following year. Calomel dust in the seed drills reduces the danger.

Parsnip canker Appears as brown patches and cracks on the shoulder of the parsnip, which can then be attacked by pests. The best remedy is to rotate crops or grow resistant varieties.

Fungicides

All fungicides are phytotoxic to some extent—that is, they affect the growth of the plants which they protect. It is essential that only recommended quantities and dilutions are used. Some fungicides based on lime and sulphur are particularly bad at scorching leaves if over-used. The systemic fungicides like benomyl and thiophanate-methyl are often more effective but cost more.

Removal of infected tissue will often stop the spread of a fungus and this is a point that cannot be over-emphasized. Strict garden hygiene is one of the main ways of preventing infection.

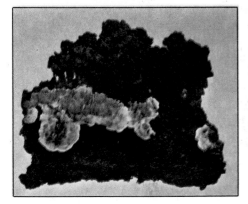

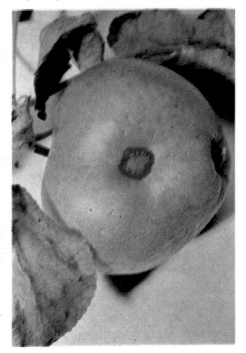

Watering the garden

Plants need water for many reasons. Seeds will not germinate without water and plants can only use the nutrients in the soil if they are in soluble form. Water gives the plant its shape and stiffness; without it the plant becomes limp. If the water loss becomes too great the stomata (holes) in the surface of the 'skin' close and the basic plant processes come to a halt. You must, therefore, ensure that plants always have enough water for all their needs.

During dry weather you must give your plants the water that nature has failed to provide. Too often, however, the mistake is made of watering irregularly and in insufficient quantity. It is essential to give enough water to penetrate the soil down to the layer where the plant roots are growing. If you only sprinkle the surface, the water will simply evaporate in the heat of the sun.

How much water?

Apply sufficient water to penetrate the soil to a depth of at least 15cm (6 in) – preferably more. This means applying at least 2–3cm (1 in) of water, depending on the soil type. The lighter and more sandy the soil, the deeper this amount of water will penetrate. If you are using a sprinkler, you can measure the amount of water being applied by placing a number of tin cans over the area being watered. When there is 2–3cm (1 in) of water on the bottom of the tins you will know it is time to turn off the sprinkler. Eventually you can estimate the time required to cover the area, and the rather tedious business of setting out cans will be unnecessary. If you water with a hosepipe then you will have to dig down into the soil with a hand trowel to see how far the water has penetrated.

Start watering before the soil dries out to any great depth; a good guide is when the top 2–5cm (1–2 in) is becoming dry. In hot, summer weather you may have to water at least once a week.

It is usually best to apply water in the evening, as then none will be evaporated by the sun and it will penetrate the soil to a good depth.

Many people do not realize that wind is a major drying agent (especially in spring and early summer), so watering will be necessary after windy weather.

Sprinklers and hoses

Applying all this water will be very time-consuming if you have to rely on a hosepipe alone. It is therefore a good idea to attach a sprinkler of some kind to the end and let it distribute the water.

There are many types on the market to suit all pockets. The cheapest are those with no moving parts (mini-sprinklers), but which produce a fine circular spray from a static nozzle. Often the base of these is equipped with a spike which you push into the ground to hold the sprinkler firmly.

Rotating sprinklers are slightly more expensive. They have two adjustable nozzles on an arm which is spun round by water pressure, giving a circular pattern. These are probably the most popular for private gardens.

The more sophisticated oscillating sprinklers apply water in a square or rectangular pattern. A tubular bar with a row of nozzles (non-adjustable) moves backwards and forwards, watering a very large area. It is worked by water pressure. Some can be adjusted to water a small or large area.

Sprinkler hoses are perforated plastic hoses of various kinds which are connected to the main hosepipe and produce a gentle spray of water along their complete length. One of these can be laid along rows of crops, or between plants.

You will, of course, want a good reinforced plastic or PVC hosepipe; a 13mm ($\frac{1}{2}$ in) diameter hose is a suitable size for general use. A wide range of sprinklers and hoses is, of course, available to suit individual requirements.

Below: a perforated hose sprinkler, handy for long borders
Above right: use a fine rose for watering cuttings and seedlings

A rotary type sprinkler that waters in a regular circular pattern

Oscillating sprinkler that will deliver an even spray into a corner

Watering vegetables

Most vegetables benefit greatly from regular watering, especially crops like runner, French and broad beans, peas, marrows, lettuce, radish, cucumbers and tomatoes. Vegetables such as cabbages and other greenstuff, and root crops like potatoes and carrots, can get by without regular watering, although their yields will not be so heavy.

All newly-transplanted vegetables must be well watered in if the ground is

dry and then kept moist until established. You can water these individually with a watering can.

Germinating seeds

Seeds must be kept moist to encourage them to germinate. This is especially true of the modern pelleted seeds, which will fail to grow if they lack sufficient moisture.

Fruit trees and bushes

Fruit trees, provided they are well established, will not come to much harm if you do not water during dry spells, but the fruits may be smaller than normal. However, black, red and whitecurrants, raspberries, strawberries, gooseberries, blackberries, loganberries and other hybrid berries really do need watering in dry weather if they are to crop well.

Flowers in beds and containers

It may not be possible to water everything in the garden, especially in a very dry season when there may be restrictions on the use of sprinklers in the garden. If this is the case, the flower garden must take third place – after fruit and vegetables,

which you will be growing to supplement the family budget. However, flowers in containers (such as tubs, troughs, hanging baskets and window boxes) will soon die if not watered regularly. These dry out rapidly in hot weather and may well need watering twice a day – in the morning and again in the evening.

Watering the lawn

Lawns rapidly turn brown in dry weather, although they will green up again once the rains start. To keep a lawn green in the summer you will need to begin watering before it starts to turn brown and continue at weekly intervals, or more frequently, thereafter. Remember also not to cut a lawn too short in dry weather – so raise the mower blades.

Mulching the soil

There is a method of conserving moisture in the soil which will enable you to cut down on watering. It is known as 'mulching' and consists of placing a 5–8cm (2–3 in) layer of organic matter around and between plants – covering the root area. Use garden compost, well-rotted farmyard manure, leaf mould, spent hops, straw, grass mowings or sawdust.

Another method is to use black polythene sheeting. To anchor it to the ground, bury the edges in 'nicks' made with a spade in the soil; then place a few stones or bricks on top. You can buy rolls of special black mulching polythene.

All plants benefit from being mulched, for moisture is conserved and so they do not dry out so rapidly. If you have to limit mulching, however, then concentrate on your vegetables and fruits, rather than on your flowerbeds.

Left and below: mulching trees and shrubs with compost will conserve moisture

Feeding plants

Plants, like people, need a regular supply of food if they are to survive and grow well. The main ways of feeding your plants are by applying fertilizers and bulky organic matter (like manure) to the soil. Manure supplies some nutrients, but its most important function is to improve the soil structure by adding organic material. This turns the soil into a healthy medium in which plants can thrive. Fertilizers provide some, or all, of the basic plant foods (nitrogen, phosphates, potash and trace elements) in concentrated form.

When digging, particularly in late autumn or early winter, it is wise to incorporate in each trench well-rotted farmyard manure, garden compost, seaweed or hop manure. These materials will supply bulky organic matter and a variable amount of plant food. None of them, however, supplies adequate nutrients for the plants to make optimum growth; therefore fertilizers will have to be added at planting time to ensure that the plants are sufficiently provided with the food they require.

The organic matter is digested by bacteria in the soil and turned into humus. This humus is like a sponge; it holds water and prevents rapid drying-out of light soils. It also helps to break up

sticky clay soils by improving drainage. Organic material is, therefore, essential because it greatly improves the soil's structure.

MANURES

Never apply manure at the same time as lime (calcium). This is because the lime can liberate any available nitrogen in the form of ammonia, which may then be lost through evaporation. Also, never grow root crops on ground where fresh manure has been used, for your vegetables may well produce deformed roots.

Seaweed as manure

If your garden is near the coast, use seaweed as a manure. It is excellent for digging – wet or dried – into the soil in the autumn. Seaweed is one of the oldest manures known and contains many plant foods. It is now possible to obtain specially refined seaweed manures from gardening shops. Use these carefully, according to maker's instructions, as they are rather concentrated.

Manure for mulching

Rotted manure or garden compost makes a good mulch for established plants such as trees, shrubs, top and soft fruit, vegetables, roses, dahlias and chrysan-

Above left: Ascophyllum nodosum, 'egg' or knotted wrack, exposed on the rocks at low tide and ready for collection – it can be used wet or dry
Top: fronds of sea belt Laminaria saccharina, left on the beach at low water
Centre: shoddy, or animal hair, laid around the base of a shrub – it is useful as an organic form of plant food
Above: spreading top-dressing of dry fertilizer around the base of the shrub in summer months with a balance of nitrogen, phosphate and potash mixed to suit the particular plant
Right: adding rotted manure to a trench

themums. Place a layer of mulch, 5–8cm (2–3 in) thick, around the plants in spring. It will then provide some food and humus and help prevent evaporation of moisture from the surface soil.

FERTILIZERS

Bulky organic matter is not capable, by itself, of supplying all the foods the plants will require, so fertilizers must also be added to the soil.

As a general rule, dry fertilizers should be applied to moist soil, or else well watered in after application if the ground is dry. Always apply them evenly, and discard or break up any lumps; these can 'burn' roots. Apply all fertilizers carefully and according to maker's instructions. If you exceed the recommended rate of application you may seriously injure your plants.

Before sowing or planting, the usual procedure is to rake in a dry fertilizer which contains the major plants foods (nitrogen, phosphates and potash). There are many of these 'general-purpose' or compound fertilizers on the market. Probably the best known is National Growmore, which is available under numerous brand names. This is suitable for all vegetables, fruit and flowers. You can also apply it as a top dressing in spring or summer by lightly raking it into the soil surface around any of your established plants.

Special dry fertilizers for specific crops (such as roses and tomatoes) are available. These contain the correct balance of nitrogen, phosphates and potash suited to the particular plant.

Lawn fertilizers

There are several proprietary lawn fertilizers which make the lawn 'green up' quickly and grow well due to the high proportion of nitrogen they contain. Feed your lawn once or twice during spring and summer to ensure a lush, deep-green sward. Autumn lawn fertilizer, which is applied in mid autumn (September), contains more potash; this helps to 'ripen' the grass and make it more resistant to hard winter weather.

'Straight' fertilizers

You can also apply 'straight' fertilizers to plants, especially as a supplement to the ready-mixed, general-purpose kinds applied earlier in the growing season; but you must be aware of specific food requirements of individual plants before trying out these fertilizers. Be sure to handle them carefully and accurately.

Sulphate of ammonia and nitro-chalk supply nitrogen which encourages plants to make lush, leafy growth. They are quick-acting fertilizers and should be used very sparingly. They can be used on lawns and also on green vegetables such as cabbage, kale, broccoli and spinach. Apply them in spring and summer only.

Sulphate of potash and muriate of potash both supply the potash (potassium) essential for the production of fruit and flowers. It also helps to ripen the stems, which is necessary for the successful overwintering of all hardy plants. Potash can be applied in summer or early autumn. Wood ashes contain potassium

and, once they have weathered for 3–6 months, can be dug into the soil during autumn digging or raked into the surface.

Superphosphate of lime supplies phosphate (phosphorus). This is also essential for good root production and all-round growth. It is usually applied in spring and summer at the rate of 3g per litre ($\frac{1}{2}$ oz per gal) of water and applied to the soil around plants about once a week. Avoid getting it on the foliage.

Liquid fertilizers
Use liquid fertilizers in conjunction with powdered or granulated fertilizers – not as a substitute. They should be considered as supplementary feeds to boost the growth of plants. They are generally used in the summer when plants are in full growth. Being liquid, they are quickly absorbed by plants and rapidly stimulate growth.

Dilute liquid fertilizers according to maker's instructions, and apply them to moist soil. Use them as frequently as once a week and on all kinds of plants in the

house, greenhouse and garden. You can apply them most easily with a rosed watering can.

There are many brands of liquid fertilizer on the market, some of which are formulated for specific crops.

Foliar feeding
Foliar feeding is a fairly recent technique of applying liquid fertilizers to plants. The fertilizer is sprayed or watered onto the leaves where it is quickly absorbed by the plants and circulated in the sap stream. The nutrients are made im-

mediately available to plants. This makes them particularly useful to transplanted plants before their new roots have become established.

You can buy special foliar feeds from gardening shops. Alternatively you can apply any liquid fertilizer to the foliage and it will be quickly absorbed.

Sulphate of ammonia can be dissolved at the rate of 3g per litre ($\frac{1}{2}$ oz per gal) of water and applied to leaves to promote growth of foliage. Likewise sulphate of potash will encourage fruiting and ripening of growth.

LIME
Lime is another plant food and this is applied on its own, generally in the winter after autumn digging, in the form of dehydrated lime. It is mainly the vegetable plot that will require lime and an application every two or three years will be adequate.

Lime lowers the acidity of the soil, and as many plants (especially vegetables such as brassicas) do not thrive in an acid soil, liming enables you to grow a wider range of plants. But do not lime if you have a naturally alkaline or limy soil with a pH of 7 or above. Hydrated lime is the type generally used.

Above: applying chemical fertilizer by spoon in small measured quantities
Above right: sieving leaf mould into a wheelbarrow for use as compost
Right: fertilizer spreaders give even results
Far right: applying lime by hand

Making a compost heap

Waste not organic materials from the house or garden and want not for compost is a maxim worth following. Compost, when rotted down, will improve and maintain your soil by adding humus-forming matter, plant foods and beneficial bacteria.

Compost is not difficult or time-consuming to make. Certain types of plant and household waste can be used to make it. Suitable plant waste includes grass clippings, flower and vegetable stems that are not too tough, light hedge trimmings, wet peat, wet straw and annual weeds. Leaves can be used, but not in great quantities as they are more valuable for use as leaf mould. A separate bin can be kept in the kitchen for such household waste as tea leaves, vegetable trimmings, hair, egg shells and vacuum cleaner dust. Bonfire ashes, animal manure, and sawdust are also suitable.

Not suitable for the compost heap are coarse plant material such as cabbage stems and tree prunings, diseased plants, pernicious weeds like docks, dandelions, and bindweed roots, any dead plants on which weedkiller has been used, and cooked matter, such as meat or fish.

As a compost heap is not particularly sightly, it is best situated in the working part of the garden and screened from the house. It should be protected from hot sun or cold winds, but not be against a wall or hedge. An ideal site is beneath a tree. The shape of the heap can be

If you lack the space for a compost heap as described, a bin will also give you good results. Below are three main types

circular or rectangular, although most people find a rectangular one easier to cope with. The best size to aim for is about 1m (3 ft) wide, 1½–2m (5–6 ft) long, and 1–1½m (3–5 ft) high when completed.

It pays to construct the site of the heap correctly, rather than tipping the waste straight onto the ground. First dig a shallow pit – about 15cm (6 in) deep. Place the soil on one side as you will need it later. Then put down in the pit an 8cm (3 in) layer of broken bricks or stones mixed with coarse tree prunings, woody cabbage stems, straw and similar tough plant material. These will help essential drainage and allow plenty of air penetration.

When the base is prepared, begin to build up the compost heap. This should be done roughly as follows:
Layer 1: about 15cm (6 in) of organic material.
Layer 2: a sprinkling of a proprietary compost accelerator according to the manufacturer's instructions. This should supply the essential bacteria, nitrogen and chalk necessary to break down the raw matter into usable compost.
Layer 3: a 2–3cm (1 in) layer of soil, taken from the dug-out heap.
These three layers are repeated until the heap reaches the required height.

Follow these rules for successful composting:
1 Always be sure that each layer of organic material is well firmed down (but not too tightly compressed) by treading on it or beating it flat with a spade blade.
2 If using grass clippings in large quantities, mix them with other materials

or they will form a soggy mass in the heap.
3 Check from time to time to make sure that the heap is moist. If it has dried out, either sprinkle water over it or, preferably, hammer stakes into the heap to make holes and then pour water into the holes.
4 To finish off the heap, level the top and put a 2–5cm (1–2 in) thick layer of soil over the top and around the sides to act as a cover.

A properly made compost heap provides material to be used either for digging into the ground or for mulching. Mulch is a top dressing layer on the surface of the soil around the plants. The compost will be ready to be dug in after about 10–14 weeks in summer or 14–18 weeks in winter. When the compost is ready for use the heap will consist of a brownish black, crumbly, pleasant-smelling and easily handled material. If the heap doesn't seem to be rotting down well in the allotted time, something has gone wrong with the construction. If this happens, it is worth the trouble of digging a second shallow pit alongside and rebuilding the first heap into that, turning the top to bottom and sides to middle and following the sandwich layer principle again. In any case, as one heap is finished, a second one should be started so that there is always a supply of essential humus-forming material ready to add to the soil.

The method of compost-making described here is simple and cheap. If, however, you have a very small garden, it may be easier for you to buy a proprietary bin compost unit, which has its own instructions for use.

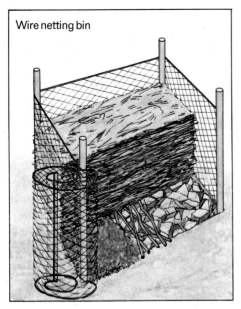
Wire netting bin

Sliding plastic panel bin

Slotted wood bin

Seasonal Workplan

LATE WINTER

Mixed flower borders

There is little work that can be done outside this month, but plan ahead to make sure you are ready for seed sowing and planting later by ordering seeds and plants, seed and cutting composts and other essentials. Also clean all pots and trays to be used for seed sowing and check all equipment.

Helleborus niger, the Christmas rose will still be flowering, also *H. foetidus* should start producing flower buds now.

Trees, shrubs and climbers

Provided weather conditions are suitable for working outdoors and the soil is not too wet, frozen or snow-covered, it is possible to plant new deciduous trees, shrubs and climbers.

Ensure the planting hole is dug large enough to accommodate the roots without cramping them and deep enough so that when finally in position the plant is at the original soil mark on the stem. The planting site is best prepared in advance, but if not, dig in well-rotted manure or compost below root level. Remember to insert stakes for those trees or shrubs requiring them, and trellis or other supports for climbing plants.

If weather conditions are unsuitable for planting, keep the wrapped trees, shrubs and climbers in a cool but frost-free place until the soil is workable. Alternatively, unwrap the plants carefully and put in a shallow trench in a sheltered part of the garden.

To prevent branches being broken by the weight of snow, remove as much snow as possible by hand or with a cane.

Bulbs

Bring forced bulbs in pots and bowls into the house as they reach the correct stage of growth. Narcissi (daffodils) should be about 10cm (4in) tall with the flower bud showing. Hyacinths should also have the leaves about 10cm (4in) high with the flower bud well developed in the centre. Other forced bulbs, such as tulips, snowdrops and crocuses are best left until the flower buds are showing colour, to ensure the flowers open properly and give a good display. All forced bulbs brought into the home

should be kept in a cool, not too sunny position for a week or so. The temperature should not be more than about 10°C (50°F) initially and 16°C (60°F) finally at which time the plants can be placed in full light, but not over a radiator or fire.

Water the bulbs when the fibre or compost needs it, and include liquid fertilizer about once weekly to encourage the formation of plump healthy bulbs for planting in the garden next autumn.

For flowering next month in the home, plant hippeastrum bulbs singly in pots of moist J.I. No 2 or soilless mixture. Keep in a tmperature of about 16°C (60°F) and water occasionally until the leaves and flower stem appear. Then water with added liquid fertilizer regularly.

Lawns
Double dig any area proposed for a lawn to be grown from seed next year. Incorporate well-rotted manure or compost into the lower spit of soil and leave the top layer rough for frosts to condition it.

If soil drainage is likely to be a problem, construct soakaways, or a herringbone drainage system of tile drains, in the second or third spit of soil. Order the grass seeds now. If the weather is very mild, it is possible to create a new lawn from turfs this month, provided the soil has been well-prepared.

Fruit, vegetables and herbs
Order your vegetable seeds, including seed potatoes, and when they arrive keep them in a cool and mouse-free place.

Check all gardening equipment and stock up with soil or soilless composts, seed trays, pots, labels and similar odds and ends.

Where the vegetable garden requires liming, now is a good time to do so. If in doubt, test the soil with a pH kit to get a reading of alkalinity or acidity and calculate how much lime to apply. Further sowings of suitable varieties of peas and broad beans may be made under cloches this month.

Herb plants and seeds should be ordered now for delivery in the spring.

Sow tomato seeds in a heated greenhouse for forcing for early fruiting.

Complete pruning of fruit trees and bushes. Also spray them with tar oil winter wash, according to manufacturer's instructions, to kill any eggs.

General
Keep paths, mowed areas and patios clear of leaves by raking or brushing.

Make a note of any repairs or alterations required to hard surface areas to prevent future puddles or icy patches.

Tread firm any soil round plants that has been raised by frost.

EARLY SPRING
Bulbs
Make sure the forced hyacinths and narcissi still flowering indoors are kept moist. If they are ready, bring the bowls of early tulips indoors but keep them in a cool place for a few days so that they can acclimatize before moving them to the warmer living rooms where they are to flower.

If the weather is mild you can plant healthy, plump lily bulbs where they are to flower. Mulch them with peat or leaves to protect them from frost damage.

Place cloches over iris you plan to use for cut flowers; this will improve the quality of the flowers and hasten the flowering dates.

Trees, shrubs and climbers
Remove any snow that may settle on branches to prevent its weight breaking or damaging them. Tidy up by cutting out all dead, diseased, broken or very twiggy branches and burn them.

Order new trees and shrubs and, if weather is suitably mild and the ground dry, prepare planting sites if this has not already been done. Prepare site for any new hedge.

Lawns
Examine the lawn mower and make sure it is in good working order. If new parts are needed, order them now. Oil and clean it thoroughly, sharpen all the blades; the grass will soon need its first cut. Inspect the lawn surface and if not too wet, use spiker, fork or hollow-tined fork to improve drainage and air penetration. Then brush in a 13mm (½in) layer of a 50/50 mixture of coarse sand and peat.

If you are planning a new lawn from seed, dig over the area, incorporating plenty of well-rotted manure or compost.

Flowerbeds
Make sure you will be ready to sow and plant when the time comes by finishing the ordering of seeds and plants, and seed and cutting composts. If you are starting a new border, plan it carefully

on paper and dig over the area concerned — working in plenty of well-rotted compost or manure, plus some bonemeal.

If the soil is workable, hoe it lightly and work in a general-purpose fertilizer.

Start dahlia tubers into growth in damp peat in a warm place for production of suitable cuttings next month.

Fruit
Continue to prune fruit trees and bushes. Also spray them with tar oil winter wash, according to manufacturer's instructions, to kill any over-wintering eggs.

Dig up and burn all diseased bushes. Fruit trees and bushes can still be planted provided weather conditions are suitable, the soil workable (not waterlogged and frosty) and the planting sites have been well prepared in advance. Stake securely. If the soil is right you can still prepare for mid spring (March) planting.

Check stored fruit and remove any that appear diseased or damaged.

Vegetables
Early spring (February) is the time to finish the sowing plan and planting schedule; make sure that all the seeds have been ordered.

Test the soil and correct the pH by liming the plots dug in the autumn, particularly where brassicas are to be grown. Place cloches in position to warm up the soil.

Bend leaves over winter broccoli heads to protect from damage.

If the soil is warming up, sow the first broad beans, and early peas.

Start chitting potatoes as soon as you get them.

Examine stored vegetables for soundness and remove and that appear diseased or damaged.

Harvest winter crops such as parsnips, leeks and brussels sprouts when required.

Under glass
Clean out the greenhouse thoroughly. Mend any broken glass or gaps in the structure. Examine cloches and frames and treat likewise.

Scrub all seed trays with a disinfectant.

Start tomato and cucumber seeds in peat pots in the propagator for greenhouse crops. Sow sweet peas, three to a peat pot, for early transplanting.

Make a first sowing of leeks in trays of seed compost to go out into a frost-free greenhouse.

General
Inspect all tools and make sure they are in good condition; clean and oil them well. Make sure you have a good supply of nets, stakes, pots, composts, fertilizers and chemicals.

Check dates of any flower shows you may wish to exhibit at, and plan your planting dates accordingly.

WEATHER VARIATIONS
Early spring in the British Isles has the most variable weather of the year. The map shows how spring arrives one to four weeks earlier in the south-west than in central areas, and again up to four weeks later in north-eastern England and most of Scotland

The Gardener's Seasons

early spring	(February)	early autumn	(August)
mid spring	(March)	mid autumn	(September)
late spring	(April)	late autumn	(October)
early summer	(May)	early winter	(November)
mid summer	(June)	mid winter	(December)
late summer	(July)	late winter	(January)

In the North
In this section we will be highlighting any gardening points particularly relevant to the north of England and Scotland due to the colder climate in those regions. At this time of year the ground is still frozen, so be patient. Do all the work that is to be done off the ground, such as planning and ordering, pruning and tidying up.

MID-LATE SPRING
Spring bulbs
Continue to remove dead flower heads from spring flowering blubs in the bulb area and any other areas where they may be growing. If in bare ground, not a grassy area, remove the weeds from around the bulbs.

Mixed flower borders
Plant lily bulbs in the mixed borders and stake to show positions and to provide suppot later. Continue to plant gladiolus corms; if not already put in last month, plant them now. Plant out unsprouted dahlia tubers in the positions they are to flower, and protect with a layer of mulch against frost.

If the mixed flower borders have not already been cleared of winter leaves and debris, do it now. Lightly hoe between all the plants. Remove weeds, hoe in a general fertilizer and put a 2·5 to 5cm (1–2in) layer of mulching material round the perennial plants, trees and shrubs. Sow hardy annuals in their final positions. If the weather is suitably dry and warm, the first of the chrysanthemums should be planted out.

To deter slugs and snails, scatter slug-killing pellets, or water with liquid slug-killer.

Trees, shrubs and climbers
Finish pruning roses if not completed last month. Also prune out dead, diseased, crossing branches from trees and shrubs that have just finished flowering. This includes hedging plants. Cut back evergreen trees and shrubs to near their base if they are overgrown and straggly. Complete planting of trees, shrubs and herbaceous plants. Plant out evergreen hedging plants, water them regularly if the weather is dry, and hoe to control weeds.

Lawns
If moss and wormkiller treatments on lawns were not carried out, or completed, last month, do so now. Prepare new lawn site and sow or turf it. Apply fertilizer to an established lawn after the first mowing.

General
Firmly tread any newly dug ground that may 'heave' (raise up) following late

frost. Spray all decorative plants with a systemic spray to prevent insect attacks.

Fruit, vegetables and herbs
Prepare the soil in the seed bed for continuation sowings of brassicas, brussels sprouts, winter cabbage, purple and green sprouting broccoli, red cabbage and winter cauliflower and leeks. Sow dwarf French beans and runner beans in the greenhouse. Regularly water seedlings and young plants in the greenhouse. Hoe to remove weeds wherever possible, or apply chemical weedkillers. Mulch along rows of raspberry canes and tie in canes to supports.

Thin bulbing onions, lettuces, swedes, turnips and summer cabbage sown outside where they are to mature. Fill gaps in broad bean rows and stake the rows. Protect early potato shoots from frost, and plant maincrops. Spray apple trees and bushes at pink bud stage to control pests.

Now is the time to harden off young plants from the greenhouse for later planting outside. Sow tomato seeds in the greenhouse for planting outdoors. Transplant cucumber seedlings in the greenhouse into their final positions of pots. At the end of this month prepare the ground for, and sow, dwarf French beans in the open or under cloches. Also sow parsnips and parsley. Prepare the 'rings' in the greenhouse for transplanting tomato plants next month, which are to be grown by the ring culture method. Arrange for methods of shading the roof of the greenhouse to prevent too strong sunlight burning the plants.

Give potatoes their first earthing-up to protect stems against buffeting winds. If a pea weevil attacks young peas, dust with derris. Put in supports for pea plants to grow up. Harden off young onions for planting out next month. Finish preparing ground outside where they are to be planted. Transplant lettuce from indoor or outdoor sowings to their final positions, sow further seeds for successional cropping. Also sow short rows of radishes.

EARLY SUMMER
Bulbs
Remove dead flower-heads by cutting off each stem from near the base.

If bulb area is required for summer bedding plants, after all spring bulbs have finished flowering carefully fork them out and put in a trench in spare

part of the garden, where they can ripen, before lifting for planting again in autumn.

Mixed flower borders
Continue to hoe weeds regularly, taking care not to damage shallow roots on stems of cultivated plants.

After hoeing, scatter and rake in general fertilizer such as Growmore and apply mulch layer.

When they have finished flowering, pull up spring bedding plants such as forget-me-nots and wallflowers.

Complete sowing of hardy annuals in the positions in which they are to flower. Towards the end of month, start setting out half-hardy bedding plants where they are to bloom.

Prepare soil in spare corner of garden and sow biennials such as wallflower, sweet William, forget-me-not, canterbury bell, honesty, evening primrose, and hollyhock, for flowering next year.

The taller growing herbaceous perennials should be staked now, and stems tied in as they grow. To help

healthy growth, water with liquid fertilizer from time to time.

Plant out chrysanthemums.

Trees, shrubs and climbers
Evergreen trees and shrubs can be planted at the beginning of the month. After planting, water thoroughly and put mulch over root areas.

Remove rhododendron and azalea flower-heads as they die, taking care not to damage leaves and buds below.

Prune shrubs that complete their flowering period in late spring and early summer. Cut back hard the stems that have carried the flowers, to encourage new shoots to grow for next year's flowering. Also remove dead and spindly growth.

Climbers that finish flowering this month should also have their old flower stems cut out.

Continue to tie in other climbers, and shrubs treated as climbers, to their supports as necessary.

If roses produce too many young shoots, cut out unwanted ones to prevent bushes becoming too entangled with unprolific stems.

Clip hedges, such as privet, from now on as necessary.

Lawns
Mow the lawn at least weekly; cutting to 2–3cm (1–1½in). During drought periods water thoroughly, preferably with a sprinkler.

If necessary, apply weedkiller over whole lawn or as spot treatment.

General
Regularly spray with insecticide against pests, particularly greenfly, blackfly and red spider.

Fruit, vegetables and herbs
Water thoroughly all outdoor vegetables and apply 'booster' feeds in the form of liquid or soluble fertilizers.

Remove cloches from all crops except those susceptible to late frosts. As soon as first flowers appear on greenhouse tomatoes, start liquid feeding and keep soil moist. Cut out sideshoots as they appear. Harvest the first of the shallots. Prepare ground, and sow marrows outdoors where they are to fruit. Make a first sowing of beetroot outdoors. If night frosts appear imminent cover potatoes and dwarf French beans. Thin summer cabbages and cauliflowers; protect against pests. Thin parsnips and tread soil firm. Start transplanting young plants of cabbage and brussels sprouts to final positions. Sow sweet corn in blocks outdoors. Make last outdoor sowing of runner beans against the supports erected earlier. Hoe regularly throughout.

In the greenhouse tie in cucumber shoots to their supports. Remove male flowers as they appear, also tendrils. Apply insecticides to control greenfly, blackfly and whitefly outdoors and in the greenhouse. Sow another row of broad beans. Ventilate the greenhouse according to weather conditions.

MID SUMMER
Bulbs
Lift overcrowded spring-flowering bulbs when leaves have yellowed, put in a box in a dry place and remove old leaves and outer bulb scales when dry.

Dig up tulips and replant them in a trench for ripening, but leave species types *in situ*.

Mixed flower borders
Continue to hoe weeds regularly. Take care not to damage stems or shallow roots of cultivated plants.

If not done already, stake and tie taller-growing plants.

Continue to plant out half-hardy annuals and sow some *in situ*, for flowering later in the season.

Sow biennials in a prepared seedbed if not done last month.

Mulch gladiolus and lilies to conserve moisture in the root area.

Thin out hardy annuals that were sown in the positions in which they were to flower. Thin tall ones to 30cm (12in) apart and smaller ones to 15–25cm (6–9in).

Sow seeds of herbaceous perennials in prepared seedbed or in pots containing J.I. seed sowing compost.

Early-flowering chrysanthemums can still be planted out about 45cm (18in) apart and staked.

Trees, shrubs and climbers
Continue to clip hedges.

For good rose blooms, remove the central flower-buds of each cluster. Dead-head early-flowering roses by

cutting off finished blooms with a 10–15cm (4–6in) length of stem.

Continue to tie in climbers and shrubs trained as climbers to their supports.

Prune early-flowering clematis species by removing shoots that have borne blooms. Well-established plants with a mass of growth can be cut back as necessary.

Prune chaenomeles (quince) by cutting new growths back to 3–4 buds from the main stem.

Lawns

Start mowing twice weekly from now until early autumn (August), cutting the grass to 13–25mm (½–1in) high.

Use a lawn rake before mowing to lift up creeping stems of weeds for cutting with the mower.

Apply weedkiller as overall or spot treatment if required.

Apply general-purpose proprietary lawn fertilizer this month.

General

Regularly spray all plants with appropriate insecticides and fungicides. Water all plants regularly during dry periods, also lawns.

Fruit, vegetables and herbs

Spray potatoes and tomatoes with fungicides to prevent blight fungus.

Protect strawberries from birds, weeds and slugs by netting and laying straw or black polythene around the plants. Destroy runners or use them to increase stock.

Ventilate and damp down the greenhouse daily.

Thin bunches of greenhouse grapes by about one-third.

Picking of tomato fruits under glass commences this month. Keep the plants well-watered and feed with fertilizer weekly.

Plant young tomatoes outdoors, where they are to flower and fruit.

Plant out hardened-off, self-blanching celery and leeks.

Make late successional outdoor sowings of lettuce, summer spinach, radish, carrots, beetroot, early peas and broad beans. Also sow swedes and chocory for winter use.

Start lifting early potatoes.

Plant out from the seedbed brussels sprouts, savoys, autumn and winter cabbage and purple-sprouting broccoli. Water well and regularly, and add fertilizer towards end of month.

Start picking currents; net to protect from birds if necessary.

Plant out thyme and sage sown earlier and make sowings of other herbs in a well-prepared seedbed for transplanting to their permanent positions in the autumn.

Sow alpine strawberry seeds.

If apple fruitlets do not drop naturally, remove the central one from each cluster.

Ensure female marrow flowers are pollinated by removing male flowers and dusting female with pollen.

Support dwarf French beans.

LATE SUMMER

Mixed flower borders

Support annuals with thin sticks. Cut the flowering stems of everlasting annuals as soon as they come into bloom and dry them in a cool airy place.

Many plants, such as delphinium, lupin, paeony and bedding plants, benefit if the flower-heads are removed as they die. This will encourage further flower production.

Gladioli require plenty of moisture, and even if the wet area is mulched, there should be generous watering during drought periods.

Border carnations can be increased by layering non-flowering stems.

Trees, shrubs and climbers

Shrubs that were planted this spring, or have been newly set out from containers, should be watered regularly and mulched to conserve moisture. Overhead spraying is also beneficial. Provided lawn mowings are weed-free, or weedkillers have not been used for at least six weeks, the mowings make useful additional mulching material.

Shrubs that have finished flowering should be pruned to encourage new shoots for next year's blooms. Limit the pruning of shrubs that flower on one-year-old wood, to the removal of unwanted shoots. Hedges should be cut back whenever necessary. Remove dead flower-heads to encourage further blooms.

Bulbs

Finish lifting late-flowering tulips, not forgetting those put in a trench for ripening last month. Clean and store in a dry, dark and cool place.

Commence planting bulbs and corms, such as amaryllis, colchicum, autumn crocus and nerine, for autumn flowering. Start making list of spring-flowering bulbs for autumn planting

and place orders if buying from specialist firms.

Lawns

Continue to mow regularly (about twice weekly), cutting the grass to 1–2·5cm (½–1in) high. 'Spot' treat isolated weeds with weedkiller according to manufacturer's instructions.

Water the lawn thoroughly, preferably with a sprinkler, during dry weather. Keep the edges well trimmed and tidy. If the edges are uneven and crumbling, cut them straight with a turfing iron.

Fruit, vegetable and herbs

Sow endive, fennel, quick-maturing lettuce and carrots, and winter radish in the open ground.

Net ripening raspberries unless grown in a fruit cage, and spray the fruits with derris if you see raspberry beetle or greenfly. If grey mould fungus appears, spray with captan.

After fruits have been picked, prune the plants and tie in new canes to the supports. Hoe and mulch the root area. After cutting cabbage heads, make a cross-cut at the top of the stem to encourage baby cabbages to grow.

Pick vegetables and fruit as they mature – they taste better when young and fresh.

Continue daily to damp down, shade and ventilate the greenhouse, keeping the atmosphere buoyant.

Feed greenhouse tomatoes regularly,

and use sulphate of potash occasionally to encourage fruiting. 'Stop' the plants after the eighth truss has formed. Spray against brown and grey moulds in the greenhouse if necessary. Thin ripening fruits on outdoor peaches to about one per 1000 sq cm (1sq ft). Spray apple trees with BHC and derris if you see tortrix or codling moth caterpillars. Summer prune apple and pear trees.

Lift shallot bulbs and leave sound ones on the ground to ripen, or put them in a sunny, dry spot. Use at once any that are soft and destroy the diseased ones.

Clean the fruited strawberry beds of old leaves and burn straw if used to protect the fruit. Tip propagate blackcurrant stems if new bushes are required. Water and feed runner beans to prevent flower-drop.

General
Remove weeds by hand, hoeing or weedkiller, as necessary. Check all plants and treat them with pesticide at the first sign of attack by insects or fungus.

EARLY AUTUMN
Bulbs
Check bulb catalogues and list bulbs required for planting later in the autumn, to flower next spring.

Mixed flower borders
All herbaceous plants, such as lupin, dephinium and paeony, as well as annual and biennial bedding plants, should have dead flower-heads removed as they fade. This will encourage the plants to produce further flowers.

With chrysanthemums that are required to produce large blooms, remove the weakest stems to leave about eight strong ones for flowering. If single blooms for cutting are wanted, remove all buds except the terminal one from each stem. Tie stems to cane supports as necessary.

Cut back herbaceous perennials that have finished flowering to half their height. Even where plants are muched, water thoroughly and at regular intervals all flowering varieties, especially those herbaceous perennials that flower in the autumn, such as helenium,

chrysanthemum, golden rod, and michaelmas daisy, as well as annual bedding plants. Lilies can be increased by lifting and removing the firm, healthy outer scales from the bulbs and planting them in pots of J.I. No 1 compost. Put a plastic bag over each pot and keep in a frost-proof place over winter.

Trees, shrubs and climbers
Take cuttings of heathers by pulling off young sideshoots with a 'heel'; cut off the tip to make the cutting aout 2—3cm (1in) long, and place in a pot of peaty compost covered with a polythene bag. Keep in a cool frame or greenhouse until next spring.

Dead-head roses as necessary and feed with sulphate of potash at 35g per sq m (1oz per sq yd).

Continue to prune out stems of shrubs, climbers and trees as they finish flowering, and remove any diseased or unwanted wood to encourage new wood for next year's flowering.

Hedges should be cut back as necessary.

Lawns
Continue to mow regularly (about twice weekly), cutting the grass to 1—3cm (½—1in) high.

Water the lawn thoroughly, preferably with a sprinkler, during drought periods. Keep the edges well trimmed and tidy, and apply weedkiller as 'spot' or overall treatment.

General

Remove all weeds by hand, hoeing or weedkiller, and mulch round perennial plants with lawn mowings (provided these have been free of weedkillers for six weeks).

Check all plants and at first sign of insect or disease infestation, apply the appropriate pesticide according to manufacturer's instructions.

Fruit, vegetables and herbs

If broad beans are infested with black-fly, spray with liquid derris on the underside of the leaves.

Use all waste material from the vegetable garden for the compost heap.

Earth-up the stems of brussels sprouts to prevent loosening in wind.

Sow spring cabbage in the seedbed if space for the plants will be available in the spring.

Continue to pick peas and beans regularly, and cut cauliflowers and cabbage heads as they mature. Pull carrots and beetroots as required.

Loosen onion bulbs with a fork to encourage leaves to bend over and help bulbs to ripen; a fortnight later, lift for drying and storing.

The first of the eating and cooking apples should be ready for picking.

Plant out young strawberries raised from runners previously pegged down, and water regularly until growing freely. If necessary, buy in and set out new young plants of strawberries that are of certified stock.

Take out growing-tip of runner beans when the plants reach the top of their supports and remove weeds from the soil between the plants.

Sow winter spinach.

On paper, prepare a vegetable crop-rotation system to benefit the soil and the plants.

In the greenhouse, continue to water and feed tomatoes and cucumbers, damp down each morning and ventilate well on hot, sunny days.

MID AUTUMN

Bulbs

Plant spring-flowering bulbs such as narcissus, daffodil, hyacinth, scilla and muscari in the positions in which they are to bloom. The smaller bulbs should be 5–8cm (2–3in) deep and the larger 10–15cm (4–6in). Tulips are best planted next month.

Plant specially prepared forced bulbs in bowls of moist bulb fibre for early flowering indoors. Place containers in a cool dark place for 6–8 weeks.

Mixed flower borders

Continue to tie in as necessary late-flowering herbaceous perennials.

Cut and dry seed heads for winter indoor flower decoration. Certain trees and plants can have stems of autumn-coloured foliage cut and preserved by placing the bottom few centimetres in one part of glycerine to two parts boiling water. Some evergreens and ferns can be treated similarly.

Continue to dead-head plants as the flowers fade and remove dead stems of perennials.

Start planning and preparing new mixed flower borders now for planting next month. Herbaceous plants that can be put out now include paeony, the various forms of iris, Canterbury bell, and hardy carnations and pinks.

Trees, shrubs and climbers

This is a good month to plant hedges of evergreen shrubs such as conifers (including yew), holly, box and privet. The ground should be well prepared in advance by deep digging and the addition of well-rotted manure or compost.

Mature hedges will benefit from a final trimming towards the end of this month. The aim should be to make them rather wider and thicker at the base than at the top.

Prepare sites for planting decorative trees and shrubs next month by double digging and adding plenty of well-rotted manure or compost to the soil. Dead-head roses to ensure further flowers. Tie in shoots of climbing plants and shrubs treated as climbers to thin supports.

Lawns
The rate of grass growth starts to slow down this month and longer intervals between mowing can occur. The height of the cutting blades should be raised by about 6mm (¼in).

Towards the end of the month rake the lawn to remove old matted growths and trailing weeds. If the lawn is very compacted, aerate it by forking or using a scarifier. If bare patches are visible, sow grass seed, of the same species as the existing lawn, at the rate of 15–30g per sq m (½–1oz per sq yd).

Earthworms may begin to become active at this time and will damage the lawn if not prevented by the application of a proprietary wormkiller.

General
Apply pesticides if any sign of insects or diseases is seen. Water plants and lawn thoroughly during dry periods.

Remove weeds regularly, especially before they start seeding, but take care to hoe shallowly so as not to disturb plant roots.

Fruit, vegetables and herbs
If not already prepared, plan next season's crop rotation of vegetables now to ensure each group of plants benefits from soil conditions, enjoys the most suitable fertilizer level and is in soil free from pests and diseases.

Sow winter spinach where it is to mature. Also sow winter lettuce in the greenhouse or under cloches, spring and Welsh onions in the open, and cauliflowers under glass for next year. Store beetroot, carrots, marrows and maincrop potatoes. Only perserve those roots that are sound and healthy and keep them in a cool, frost-free place.

Also pick and store sound apple fruits.

Remove the pea and bean haulms, and pull up, clean and store thin supports for use again next year.

In the greenhouse, gradually reduce water and feeding and clean the glass to allow maximum light penetration.

Pick green tomato fruits from outdoor plants to ripen indoors.

Where the ground is clear of crops, put a layer of well-rotted manure or compost over it and turn the soil, leaving it rough dug.

Plant out the spring cabbage seedlings.

Prepare the ground thoroughly — order fruit trees and bushes for planting next month.

LATE AUTUMN
General
Sweep or rake up fallen leaves as necessary and either add to the compost heap or make a separate heap for them to rot down and form leaf mould.

Mixed flower borders
Summer-flowering bedding plants should be lifted and put on the compost heap. Lightly fork over the soil and set out spring-flowering bedding plants.

Herbaceous perennials can be cut down to soil level in all but the coldest parts of the country, where they are best left as protection against frost. The cut-off tops can be composted. After cutting, lightly fork over the soil round the plants and remove the weeds.

If herbaceous perennial plants have become overcrowded and formed clumps that are too dense, dig them up and divide them into smaller pieces by pulling them apart, replanting the younger outer portions and discarding the older central sections. If doing this to many plants, label them to ensure replanting in correct positions. Pull up plant supports and store for use next year. Having prepared the ground last month, newly-purchased herbaceous perennials can be set out this month. Lift half-hardy plants used for summer bedding such as pelargoniums, fuchsias and heliotropes, put them in pots and keep them in a cool place over winter, watering only surfficiently to keep the soil slightly moist. Take cuttings of these plants as well, if not already taken.

Trees, shrubs and climbers
If not already done, prepare the ground for the planting of new shrubs, particularly evergreens and roses, that can be set out towards the end of this month or the beginning of next. Deciduous shrubs can also be planted any time during the winter provided the soil is workable and the weather conditons suitable for working outdoors.

Lightly fork over, or hoe, between shrubs to remove weeds and work into the topsoil the mulch applied during the spring.

Cut back hard hedges of deciduous shrubs planted in the spring. This will encourage a bushy base. Roses will probably continue to bloom during this period, but if frost threatens cut the buds and let them open indoors.

Check plant supports of trees, shrubs and climbers to ensure they are sound, and tie in shoots where necessary to prevent damage by winter gales.

Lawns
The last 'tipping' of the grasses will probably take place this month. Bumps and hollows in the lawns can be rectified by cutting back the turf and adding or taking away soil as necessary to get the area level. If worms are still a problem, apply wormkiller.

Bulbs
If not completed last month, continue to plant outdoor spring-flowering bulbs in the positions in which they are to bloom. Planting more bowls of specially-prepared forced bulbs this month will help to give a succession of flowers in the home in late winter and early spring.

Lift half-hardy bulbous plants such as gladioli, ixia, acidanthera and sparaxia. Cut off the leaves close to the storage root organs, dry them quickly and then rub off soil and old roots. If necessary, as with gladioli, also remove the old corm.

Store in boxes in a cool, frost-free place and examine all at regular intervals during the winter for rot or other infestation.

Dahlias and tuberous-rooted begonias should be cut down by the end of this month, be dried, have the old soil rubbed off, then be stored in boxes of peat in a frost-free and cool place.

Fruit, vegetables and herbs
Prepare thoroughly the planned sites for soft fruits such as raspberries, blackberries, loganberries, goose-berries, black, red and whitecurrants, and plant them towards the end of this month. Erect the necessary support for these fruits.

Tie into the supports the canes of existing soft fruits to prevent winter damage.

Check the posts of the supports to ensure soundness. If weak, reinforce or replace.

Thin the winter spinach seedlings from sowings made last month.

Store chicory in a trench in the garden until required for forcing later.

If not already done, lift, cut off tops, rub off soil and store carrot roots in boxes of moist peat.

EARLY WINTER
Lawns
If the weather and soil conditions are suitable, continue to lay turfs, but complete by the end of this month. Any renovation can be done now.

If planning a new lawn from seed next year, double dig the proposed area, incorporating well-rotted manure or compost into the lower spit. If soil drainage is a problem, construct soak-aways or herring-bone drainage system alsoat this time. After replacing the topsoil, leave it rough for winter weather to break it down to a friable tilth.

Apply an autumn fertilizer to an established lawn if not done last month. Apply wormkiller if necessary. Get the lawn-mower overhauled.

Mixed flower borders

Finish forking over the borders, also cutting down herbaceous perennial plants if you plan to do this before cold weather sets in.

Complete planting of newly-purchased herbaceous plants, also spring-flowering subjects, such as wallflowers, forget-me-nots and polyanthus.

Border carnations and pinks can be planted now, perferably in soil that has an alkaline pH of about 6−6·5. Add hydrated lime to the ground if necessary.

Hardy herbaceous perennials raised in the seedbed can be set out in the positions in which they are to flower, provided the soil and weather are suitably mild and not too wet or frosty. In in doubt, leave until mid spring (March).

Trees, shrubs and climbers

Plant roses and evergreens before the end of this month, also deciduous trees and shrubs provided soil and weather conditions are suitable. The ground should have been prepared 3−4 weeks prior to planting. If there is a delay, leave plants wrapped for a few days and

then soak roots in water before planting; or unwrap and set them temporarily in a V-shaped trench in a sheltered spot.

If the soil round plants, especially newly set-out ones, has lifted due to frost, firm it back into position by treading it down carefully.

Young trees and shrubs that are not completely hardy until established, and those mature ones that cannot withstand extremely cold weather, should be given some protection. This can be hessian supported on posts, or sacking and straw covering.

General

Continue to sweep or rake up leaves and add to the compost heap or pile up separately to make leaf mould.

Hoe as necessary to remove weeds, composting annual ones and burning deep-rooted perennial weeds.

Any empty ground should be dug now and left rough for the winter.

Bulbs

The beginning of this month is the last opportunity to plant outside tulip and hyacinth bulbs.

Look at bulbs planted in bowls

earlier in the year. Any showing 2−3cm (1in) or more of tip growth should be moved from darkness to a cool shady position in the home or greenhouse. Water as necessary to prevent the growing medium drying out.

If lily bulbs arrive this month, and the soil is not too cold or wet, plant them in the garden where they are to flower. If the ground is unsuitable, put the bulbs, with the tips just above the surface in slightly damp peat pots or boxes and keep in a cool place until they can be planted out next spring.

Pick flower stems of *Iris unguicularis* as soon as the buds are seen so that the blooms open indoors and do not suffer bird damage.

Fruit, vegetables and herbs

Lightly fork between the rows of spring cabbages, apply sulphate of potash fertilizer, and stake each plant in windy areas.

After clearing the garden of debris, leaves and annual weeds, complete the compost heap with a layer of soil and polythene covering.

Thin winter lettuces sown in mid autumn (September) to 25cm (9in) apart. Protect the plants with cloches. Lift celery roots as required. Make regular sowings of mustard and cress in trays or punnets in the greenhouse.

Make a sowing of broad beans for early picking next year. Protect the plants with cloches in exposed areas.

Plant new rhubarb plants this month when weather and soil conditons allow.

Inspect all stored vegetables and fruit a regular intervals and discard any that are rotting or infected to prevent the problem spreading.

MID WINTER
General
Sweep or rake up leaves from all parts of the garden. Burn diseased ones and compost others.

Any area of ground that has been raised by frost action should be trodden firm.

Look through catalogues to select plants for next year, and prepare planting plans for new areas of the garden.

Mixed flower borders
This is a good month to prepare the soil for new flower borders. The ground should be double-dug if possible and plenty of well-rotted manure and compost added to the lower soil. The topsoil should be left rough-dug to allow the frost to break it down naturally.

Scatter slug pellets around delphiniums and lupins, two herbaceous plants particularly prone to slug attack. Putting a shallow heap of well-weathered cinders or coarse sand around the root area also helps.

To protect leaves and flower-stems of *Helleborus niger* (Christmas rose) from weather damage and to encourage early blooms, put straw or dry peat around the root area and cover the plants with cloches.

Chrysanthemums left in the ground to overwinter should have dry peat lightly forked into the soil above the root area to prevent waterlogging.

Bulbs
Specially forced Christmas-flowering hyacinths and narcissi start blooming this month. Water these pots of bulbs regularly to keep the compost moist. Examine other pot bulbs being forced in darkness and bring them into the light when the stems are a few centimetres (inches) high.

Lily bulbs received or bought now should be plump and firm. If the weather is open and the ground workable they can be planted outdoors where they are to flower. Put shrivelled bulbs in damp peat for 10–14 days before planting. If weather conditions are unsuitable leave the bulbs in the

pots, with their tips just above the surface, and keep in a cool place until ready for planting next spring (February).

Trees, shrubs and climbers
Finish forking over or hoeing between shrubs to remove weeks and work into the ground the mulch applied earlier in the year.

All supports and ties of trees, shrubs and climbers should be examined to ensure they are sound. Renew broken ones to prevent plant damage during winter gales.

If the planting of deciduous trees, shrubs and climbers was delayed by bad weather and soil conditions last month, the plants may still be set out when the weather is suitable.

Lawns
If the edges of the lawn or grass paths are worn and patchy, cut them into longitudinal sections with a sharp spade or turfing iron, lift them by cutting into the root area about 5cm (2in) below the surface, and turn them around so that the inner edge goes to the outside. Fill in any gaps by adding topsoil. Do not

work on a lawn that is waterlogged or frosty.

Fruit, vegetables and herbs
Sow suitable varieties of broad beans and peas outdoors and protect with cloches in very cold or exposed positions.

In the greenhouse, sow cauliflower for early cropping next year. Sow seeds singly in peat pots.

Make regular sowings of mustard and cress in trays or punnets in the greenhouse.

Check all stored vegetables and fruit at regular intervals. Discard any rotten ones to prevent infection spreading.

Prune greenhouse vines and paint with tar oil winter wash.

Prune established and newly-planted fruit trees and bushes, such as apples and pears. Also root-prune any trees that require it.

Remove any rotten fruits and burn them to prevent disease spreading. Spray with tar oil winter wash to kill overwintering insects.

Mulch newly-planted fruit trees and bushes with well-rotted manure or compost.

Generally clear the vegetable garden of leaves and rubbish. Obtain seed and plant catalogues so that orders can be placed in good time for next year.

INDEX

ACKNOWLEDGEMENTS

A-Z Collection, Bernard Alfieri, Alphabet & Image, Heather Angel, Ardea, Barnaby's Picture Library, Ron Broadman, Michael boys, Brecht Einzig Ltd, Pat Brindley, S.T. Buczaki, R.J. Corbin, John. K.B. Cowley, Ernest Crowson, Michael Davies/NHPA, Samuel Dobie & Son, Derek Fell, V. Finnis, Fisons, Monica Fuller, Brian Furner, Michael Gibson, Nancy Mary Goodall, J. Hamilton, Halls Homes & Green-houses, Iris Hardwick Library, A.G.L. Hellyer, Hozelock, G.E. Hyde, ICI, Archivio IGDA, IGDA, Institute of Geological Sciences, Jarrod & Sons Ltd, Leslie Johns, Clay Jones, Michael Leale, Marshall Cavendish, May & Baker, Elsa E. Megson, Tania Midgeley, Ken Muir, Murphy Chemicals, National Vegetable Research Station, Nutting & Thoday, Kenneth I. Oldroyd, Oxford Scientific Films, Pan Brittanica Industries, J. Parkhurst, Picturepoint, Ray Proctor, Kenneth Scowen, Deborah Smith, Donald Smith, Harry Smith Horticultural Photographic Collection, David Stevens, Thompson & Morgan, Brian Tysterman, W.J. Unwin, R. Verey, Michael Warren, Weed Research Organisation, D. Wildridge, Wolf Tools